# ACCOUNTING PRINCIPLES

Weygandt • Kimmel • Keiso

11th Edition/2013

**STRAYER.**
U N I V E R S I T Y

**Wiley Custom Learning Solutions**

ISBN   978-1-118-75175-6
Printed and bound by IPAK..

10 9 8 7 6 5 4 3 2

# Custom Brief Contents

## APPENDICES

## ACCOUNT CLASSIFICATION AND PRESENTATION

| Account Title | Classification | Financial Statement | Normal Balance |
|---|---|---|---|
| **A** | | | |
| Accounts Payable | Current Liability | Balance Sheet | Credit |
| Accounts Receivable | Current Asset | Balance Sheet | Debit |
| Accumulated Depreciation—Buildings | Plant Asset—Contra | Balance Sheet | Credit |
| Accumulated Depreciation—Equipment | Plant Asset—Contra | Balance Sheet | Credit |
| Advertising Expense | Operating Expense | Income Statement | Debit |
| Allowance for Doubtful Accounts | Current Asset—Contra | Balance Sheet | Credit |
| Amortization Expense | Operating Expense | Income Statement | Debit |
| **B** | | | |
| Bad Debt Expense | Operating Expense | Income Statement | Debit |
| Bonds Payable | Long-Term Liability | Balance Sheet | Credit |
| Buildings | Plant Assets | Balance Sheet | Debit |
| **C** | | | |
| Cash | Current Asset | Balance Sheet | Debit |
| Common Stock | Stockholders' Equity | Balance Sheet | Credit |
| Copyrights | Intangible Asset | Balance Sheet | Debit |
| Cost of Goods Sold | Cost of Goods Sold | Income Statement | Debit |
| **D** | | | |
| Debt Investments | Current Asset/Long-Term Investment | Balance Sheet | Debit |
| Depreciation Expense | Operating Expense | Income Statement | Debit |
| Discount on Bonds Payable | Long-Term Liability—Contra | Balance Sheet | Debit |
| Dividends | Temporary account closed to Retained Earnings | Retained Earnings Statement | Debit |
| Dividends Payable | Current Liability | Balance Sheet | Credit |
| **E** | | | |
| Equipment | Plant Asset | Balance Sheet | Debit |
| **F** | | | |
| Freight-Out | Operating Expense | Income Statement | Debit |
| **G** | | | |
| Gain on Disposal of Plant Assets | Other Income | Income Statement | Credit |
| Goodwill | Intangible Asset | Balance Sheet | Debit |
| **I** | | | |
| Income Summary | Temporary account closed to Retained Earnings | Not Applicable | (1) |
| Income Tax Expense | Income Tax Expense | Income Statement | Debit |
| Income Taxes Payable | Current Liability | Balance Sheet | Credit |
| Insurance Expense | Operating Expense | Income Statement | Debit |
| Interest Expense | Other Expense | Income Statement | Debit |
| Interest Payable | Current Liability | Balance Sheet | Credit |
| Interest Receivable | Current Asset | Balance Sheet | Debit |
| Interest Revenue | Other Income | Income Statement | Credit |
| Inventory | Current Asset | Balance Sheet (2) | Debit |

| Account Title | Classification | Financial Statement | Normal Balance |
|---|---|---|---|
| **L** | | | |
| Land | Plant Asset | Balance Sheet | Debit |
| Loss on Disposal of Plant Assets | Other Expense | Income Statement | Debit |
| **M** | | | |
| Maintenance and Repairs Expense | Operating Expense | Income Statement | Debit |
| Mortgage Payable | Long-Term Liability | Balance Sheet | Credit |
| **N** | | | |
| Notes Payable | Current Liability/ Long-Term Liability | Balance Sheet | Credit |
| **O** | | | |
| Owner's Capital | Owner's Equity | Owner's Equity and Balance Sheet | Credit |
| Owner's Drawings | Temporary account closed to Owner's Capital | Owner's Equity | Debit |
| **P** | | | |
| Patents | Intangible Asset | Balance Sheet | Debit |
| Paid-in Capital in Excess of Par— Common Stock | Stockholders' Equity | Balance Sheet | Credit |
| Paid-in Capital in Excess of Par— Preferred Stock | Stockholders' Equity | Balance Sheet | Credit |
| Preferred Stock | Stockholders' Equity | Balance Sheet | Credit |
| Premium on Bonds Payable | Long-Term Liability | Balance Sheet | Credit |
| Prepaid Insurance | Current Asset | Balance Sheet | Debit |
| Prepaid Rent | Current Asset | Balance Sheet | Debit |
| **R** | | | |
| Rent Expense | Operating Expense | Income Statement | Debit |
| Retained Earnings | Stockholders' Equity | Balance Sheet and Retained Earnings Statement | Credit |
| **S** | | | |
| Salaries and Wages Expense | Operating Expense | Income Statement | Debit |
| Salaries and Wages Payable | Current Liability | Balance Sheet | Credit |
| Sales Discounts | Revenue—Contra | Income Statement | Debit |
| Sales Returns and Allowances | Revenue—Contra | Income Statement | Debit |
| Sales Revenue | Revenue | Income Statement | Credit |
| Selling Expenses | Operating Expense | Income Statement | Debit |
| Service Revenue | Revenue | Income Statement | Credit |
| Stock Investments | Current Asset/Long-Term Investment | Balance Sheet | Debit |
| Supplies | Current Asset | Balance Sheet | Debit |
| Supplies Expense | Operating Expense | Income Statement | Debit |
| **T** | | | |
| Treasury Stock | Stockholders' Equity—Contra | Balance Sheet | Debit |
| **U** | | | |
| Unearned Service Revenue | Current Liability | Balance Sheet | Credit |
| Utilities Expense | Operating Expense | Income Statement | Debit |

(1) The normal balance for Income Summary will be credit when there is a net income, debit when there is a net loss. The Income Summary account does not appear on any financial statement.

(2) If a periodic system is used, Inventory also appears on the income statement in the calculation of cost of goods sold.

The following is a sample chart of accounts. It does not represent a comprehensive chart of all the accounts used in this textbook but rather those accounts that are commonly used. This sample chart of accounts is for a company that generates both service revenue as well as sales revenue. It uses the perpetual approach to inventory. If a periodic system was used, the following temporary accounts would be needed to record inventory purchases: Purchases, Freight-In, Purchase Returns and Allowances, and Purchase Discounts.

# CHART OF ACCOUNTS

| Assets | Liabilities | Owner's and Stockholders' Equity | Revenues | Expenses |
|--------|-------------|----------------------------------|----------|----------|
| Cash | Notes Payable | Owner's Capital | Service Revenue | Advertising Expense |
| Accounts Receivable | Accounts Payable | Owner's Drawings | Sales Revenue | Amortization Expense |
| Allowance for Doubtful Accounts | Unearned Service Revenue | Common Stock | Sales Discounts | Bad Debt Expense |
| | Salaries and Wages Payable | Paid-in Capital in Excess of Par— Common Stock | Sales Returns and Allowances | Cost of Goods Sold |
| Interest Receivable | Unearned Rent Revenue | Preferred Stock | Interest Revenue | Depreciation Expense |
| Inventory | Interest Payable | Paid-in Capital in Excess of Par— Preferred Stock | Gain on Disposal of Plant Assets | Freight-Out |
| Supplies | Dividends Payable | | | Income Tax Expense |
| Prepaid Insurance | Income Taxes Payable | Treasury Stock | | Insurance Expense |
| Prepaid Rent | | Retained Earnings | | Interest Expense |
| Land | Bonds Payable | Dividends | | Loss on Disposal of Plant Assets |
| Equipment | Discount on Bonds Payable | Income Summary | | Maintenance and Repairs Expense |
| Accumulated Depreciation— Equipment | Premium on Bonds Payable | | | Rent Expense |
| Buildings | Mortgage Payable | | | Salaries and Wages Expense |
| Accumulated Depreciation— Buildings | | | | Supplies Expense |
| Copyrights | | | | Utilities Expense |
| Goodwill | | | | |
| Patents | | | | |

# ACCOUNTING PRINCIPLES 11e

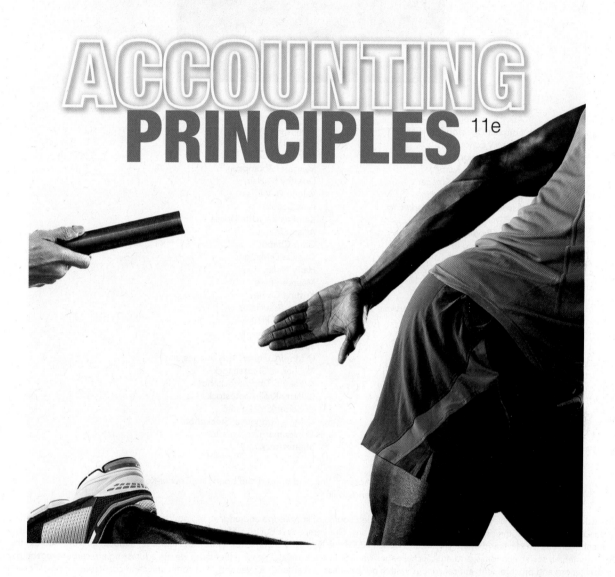

**Jerry J. Weygandt PhD, CPA**
University of Wisconsin—Madison
Madison, Wisconsin

**Paul D. Kimmel PhD, CPA**
University of Wisconsin—Milwaukee
Milwaukee, Wisconsin

**Donald E. Kieso PhD, CPA**
Northern Illinois University
DeKalb, Illinois

**WILEY**

*Dedicated to*
*the **Wiley sales representatives***
*who sell our books and service our*
*adopters in a professional and ethical*
*manner, and to*
*Enid, Merlynn, and Donna*

| | |
|---|---|
| *Vice President & Executive Publisher* | George Hoffman |
| *Associate Publisher* | Christopher DeJohn |
| *Editorial Operations Manager* | Yana Mermel |
| *Content Editor* | Ed Brislin |
| *Senior Development Editor* | Terry Ann Tatro |
| *Development Editor* | Margaret Thompson |
| *Senior Content Manager* | Dorothy Sinclair |
| *Senior Production Editor* | Valerie A. Vargas |
| *Associate Director of Marketing* | Amy Scholz |
| *Marketing Manager* | Karolina Zarychta Honsa |
| *Senior Product Designer* | Allison Morris |
| *Product Designe* | Greg Chaput |
| *Media Specialist* | Daniela DiMaggio |
| *Design Director* | Harry Nolan |
| *Cover Design* | Maureen Eide |
| *Interior Design* | Kristine Carney |
| *Production Management Services* | Ingrao Associates |
| *Senior Photo Editor* | Mary Ann Price |
| *Editorial Assistant* | Jaclyn MacKenzie |
| *Marketing Assistant* | Justine Kay |
| *Cover and title page* | © Moof/Cultura/Getty Images, Inc. |
| *Brief Contents image* | © Cherrus/Shutterstock |
| *Continuing Cookie Chronicle icon* | © Fekete Tibor/iStockphoto |
| *Waterways Problem Set icon* | © Perry Kroll/Photostock |
| *Softbyte icon* | © Cogal/iStockphoto |
| *Pioneer Advertising Agency icon* | © Mike Rodriguez/iStockphoto |
| *Caterpillar icon* | © Filonmar/iStockphoto |
| *All other icons* | Shutterstock |

This book was set in New Aster by Aptara®, Inc. and printed and bound by Courier-Kendallville.
The cover was printed by Courier-Kendallville.

Founded in 1807, John Wiley & Sons, Inc. has been a valued source of knowledge and understanding for more than 200 years, helping people around the world meet their needs and fulfill their aspirations. Our company is built on a foundation of principles that include responsibility to the communities we serve and where we live and work. In 2008, we launched a Corporate Citizenship Initiative, a global effort to address the environmental, social, economic, and ethical challenges we face in our business. Among the issues we are addressing are carbon impact, paper specifications and procurement, ethical conduct within our business and among our vendors, and community and charitable support. For more information, please visit our website: www.wiley.com/go/citizenship.

ISBN-13  978-1-118-13003-2

Binder-Ready Version ISBN  978-1-118-18089-1

Printed in the United States of America

10 9 8 7 6 5 4 3 2 1

# Brief Contents

## APPENDICES

*Available at the book's companion website, **www.wiley.com/college/weygandt**.

# Student success is a team effort.

The Team for Success is focused on helping you get the most out of your accounting courses in the digital age.

## Students
# read it

Access the right amount of information for each course anytime, anywhere, on any device.

## Students
# see it

Illustrations and interactive tutorials bring the content to life and make accounting concepts easier to understand.

## Students
# do it

The **DO IT!** exercises throughout the textbook will help you apply your understanding of accounting. The *WileyPLUS* homework experience imitates a blank sheet of paper experience using type-ahead for account entry, and helps you catch mistakes early by providing feedback at the part level.

## Students
# get it

The powerful combination of quality text, visual approach to learning, and highly intuitive homework experience prepares you for class, exams, and future study.

kieso
weygandt
kimmel
warfield

# www.wileyteamforsuccess.com

# Brief Contents

## APPENDICES

*Available at the book's companion website, **www.wiley.com/college/weygandt**.

# read it!

## REAL-WORLD CONTEXT
Real-world companies and business situations give you glimpses
into how real companies use accounting.

**Feature Stories** introduce chapter topics in
fun ways using real-world companies that are
engaging.

**Issues** that affect
today's business world
are highlighted in the
textbook.

Time Warner completed a spin-off of AOL after years
of trying to integrate the two companies. One

analyst called the failed deal "a nine-year adventure
akin to a marathon through mud."

## Real-World Focus

BYP22-4 The Coca-Cola Company hardly needs an introduction. A line taken from the cover of a recent annual report says it all: If you measured time in servings of Coca-Cola, "a billion Coca-Cola's ago was yesterday morning." On average, every U.S. citizen drinks 363 8-ounce servings of Coca-Cola products each year. Coca-Cola's primary line of business is the making and selling of syrup to bottlers. These bottlers then sell the finished bottles and cans of Coca-Cola to the consumer.

In the annual report of Coca-Cola, the information shown below was provided.

### THE COCA-COLA COMPANY
#### Management Discussion

Our gross margin declined to 61 percent this year from 62 percent in the prior year, primarily due to costs for materials such as sweeteners and packaging.

The increases [in selling expenses] in the last two years were primarily due to higher marketing expenditures in support of our Company's volume growth.

We measure
and (2) uni

### ANATOMY OF A FRAUD

Lawrence Fairbanks, the assistant vice-chancellor of communications at Aesop University, was allowed to make purchases of under $2,500 for his department without external approval. Unfortunately, he also sometimes bought items for himself, such as expensive antiques and other collectibles. How did he do it? He replaced the vendor invoices he received with fake vendor invoices that he created. The fake invoices had descriptions that were more consistent with the communications department's purchases. He submitted these fake invoices to the accounting department as the basis for their journal entries and to the accounts payable department as the basis for payment.

Total take: $475,000

**THE MISSING CONTROL**
***Segregation of duties.*** The university had not properly segregated related purchasing activities. Lawrence was ordering items, receiving the items, and receiving the invoice. By receiving the invoice, he had control over the documents that were used to account for the purchase and thus was able to substitute a fake invoice.

*Source: Adapted from Wells, Fraud Casebook (2007), pp. 3–15.*

## Financial Reporting and Analysis

**Financial Reporting Problem: Apple Inc.**

BYP1-1 The actual financial statements of Apple Inc. for 2011, are presented in Appendix A (at th
bac
ind

**Insight Boxes** frame real-world
company issues through international, ethical, and other perspectives.

### ACCOUNTING ACROSS THE ORGANIZATION

**A Thousand Millionaires!**

Traveling to space or embarking on an expedition to excavate lost Mayan ruins are normally the stuff of adventure novels. But for employees of Facebook, these and other lavish dreams moved closer to reality when the world's No. 1 online social network went public through an initial public offering (IPO) that may have created at least a thousand millionaires. The IPO was the largest in Internet history, valuing Facebook at over $104 billion.

With all these riches to be had, why did Mark Zuckerberg, the founder of Facebook, delay taking his company public? Consider that the main motivation for issuing shares to the public is to raise money so you can grow your business. However, unlike a manufacturer or even an online retailer, Facebook doesn't need major physical resources, it doesn't have inventory, and it doesn't really need much money for marketing. So in the past, the company hasn't had much need for additional cash beyond what it was already generating on its own. Finally, as head of a closely held, nonpublic company, Zuckerberg was subject to far fewer regulations than a public company.

*Source: "Status Update: I'm Rich! Facebook Flotation to Create 1,000 Millionaires Among Rank and File," Daily Mail Reporter (February 1, 2012).*

**?** Why did Mark Zuckerberg, the CEO and founder of Facebook, delay taking his company's shares public through an initial public offering (IPO)? (See page 643.)

### A Look at IFRS

**LEARNING OBJECTIVE 10**

Describe the impact of international accounting standards on U.S. financial reporting.

Most agree that there is a need for one set of international accounting standards. Here is why:

**Multinational corporations.** Today's companies view the entire world as their market. For exam-ple, Coca-Cola, Intel, and McDonald's generate more than 50% of their sales outside the Unit-States, and many foreign companies, such as Toyota, Nestlé, and Sony, find their largest market to be the United States.

**Mergers and acquisitions.** The mergers between Fiat/Chrysler and Vodafone/Mannesmann su-gest that we will see even more such business combinations of companies from different countri-in the future.

**v**

# see it!

**Equation Analysis Illustrations** visually walk you through the steps of journal transactions.

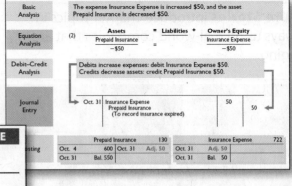

**Cash Flow Analyses** visually summarize the effects of transactions on cash flows.

Retailer receives cash more quickly from credit card issuer

**Infographics** reinforce important textual concepts. All infographics were revised in the Eleventh Edition.

**Illustrations** are clearly identified and often present data in a real-world format.

kieso
weygandt
kimmel
warfield
team for success

**www.wileyteamforsuccess.com**

# do it!

## KNOW THE FUNDAMENTALS

Knowing the fundamentals of accounting will help you understand what is happening in all areas of a business. **DO IT!** exercises throughout the textbook will help you practice your understanding of accounting.

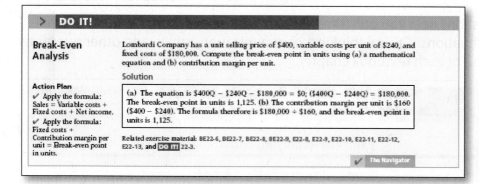

> **DO IT!**

**Break-Even Analysis**

Lombardi Company has a unit selling price of $400, variable costs per unit of $240, and fixed costs of $180,000. Compute the break-even point in units using (a) a mathematical equation and (b) contribution margin per unit.

**Solution**

**Action Plan**
✔ Apply the formula: Sales = Variable costs + Fixed costs + Net income.
✔ Apply the formula: Fixed costs ÷ Contribution margin per unit = Break-even point in units.

(a) The equation is $400Q − $240Q − $180,000 = $0; ($400Q − $240Q) = $180,000. The break-even point in units is 1,125. (b) The contribution margin per unit is $160 ($400 − $240). The formula therefore is $180,000 ÷ $160, and the break-even point in units is 1,125.

Related exercise material: BE22-6, BE22-7, BE22-8, BE22-9, E22-8, E22-9, E22-10, E22-11, E22-12, E22-13, and **DO IT!** 22-3.

✔ The Navigator

Clear **DO IT!** exercises in the textbook narrative provide step-by-step applications of a concept at the precise moment you acquire the knowledge. Each **DO IT!** in the textbook narrative includes a solution, an Action Plan, and a path of related homework exercises.

**Comprehensive DO IT!**'s at the end of each chapter apply the **DO IT!** exercises and address **multiple** topics.

> **Comprehensive DO IT!**

B.T. Hernandez Company, maker of high-quality flashlights, has experienced steady growth over the last 6 years. However, increased competition has led Mr. Hernandez, the president, to believe that an aggressive campaign is needed next year to maintain the company's present growth. The company's accountant has presented Mr. Hernandez with the data on the next page for the current year, 2014, for use in preparing next year's advertising campaign.

> **DO IT! Review**

**DO IT! 22-1** Helena Company reports the following total costs at two levels of production. *Classify types of costs.* (LO 1, 3), C

|  | 5,000 Units | 10,000 Units |
|---|---|---|
| Indirect labor | $ 3,000 | $ 6,000 |
| Property taxes | 7,000 | 7,000 |
| Direct labor | 28,000 | 56,000 |
| Direct materials | 22,000 | 44,000 |
| Depreciation | 4,000 | 4,000 |
| Utilities | 5,000 | 7,000 |
| Maintenance | 9,000 | 11,000 |

Classify each cost as variable, fixed, or mixed.

**DO IT! 22-2** Westerville Company accumulates the following data concerning a mixed cost, using units produced as the activity level. *Compute costs using high-low method and estimate total cost.* (LO 3), AP

|  | Units Produced | Total Cost |
|---|---|---|
| March | 10,000 | $18,000 |
| April | 9,000 | 16,650 |
| May | 10,500 | 18,580 |
| June | 8,800 | 16,200 |
| July | 9,500 | 17,100 |

(a) Compute the variable- and fixed-cost elements using the high-low method.
(b) Estimate the total cost if the company produces 9,200 units.

End-of-Chapter **DO IT!** exercises provide further practice with alternate versions of the in-chapter **DO IT!** exercises.

# get it!

## IMPROVE DECISION-MAKING SKILLS

As an employee, manager, or even a director of your own personal finances, you will make better decisions by learning how to analyze and solve business problems using materials provided at the end of each chapter.

**Broadening Your Perspective** questions help you pull together concepts from a particular chapter and apply them to real-world business situations. Critical thinking, communication, ethics, and other questions are included in this section at the end of each textbook chapter.

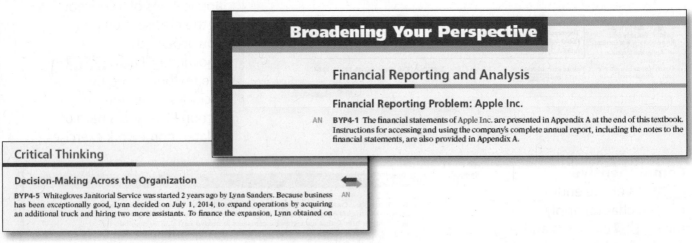

## Broadening Your Perspective

### Financial Reporting and Analysis

#### Financial Reporting Problem: Apple Inc.

AN **BYP4-1** The financial statements of Apple Inc. are presented in Appendix A at the end of this textbook. Instructions for accessing and using the company's complete annual report, including the notes to the financial statements, are also provided in Appendix A.

### Critical Thinking

#### Decision-Making Across the Organization

**BYP4-5** Whitegloves Janitorial Service was started 2 years ago by Lynn Sanders. Because business has been exceptionally good, Lynn decided on July 1, 2014, to expand operations by acquiring an additional truck and hiring two more assistants. To finance the expansion, Lynn obtained on  AN

**Continuing Cookie Chronicle, Waterways Continuing Problem, and Comprehensive Problems** pull together concepts from multiple chapters and provide a macro perspective of accounting in action.

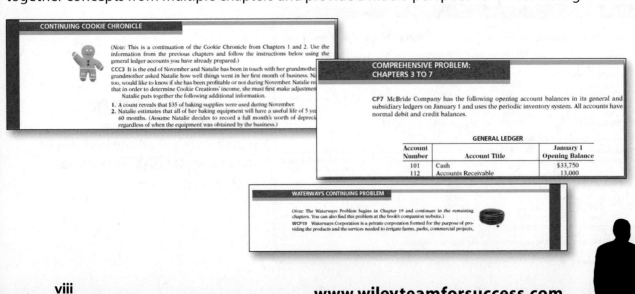

### CONTINUING COOKIE CHRONICLE

(*Note*: This is a continuation of the Cookie Chronicle from Chapters 1 and 2. Use the information from the previous chapters and follow the instructions below using the general ledger accounts you have already prepared.)

**CCC3** It is the end of November and Natalie has been in touch with her grandmother. Her grandmother asked Natalie how well things went in her first month of business. Natalie, too, would like to know if she has been profitable or not during November. Natalie realizes that in order to determine Cookie Creations' income, she must first make adjustments.
Natalie puts together the following additional information.

1. A count reveals that $35 of baking supplies were used during November.
2. Natalie estimates that all of her baking equipment will have a useful life of 5 years or 60 months. (Assume Natalie decides to record a full month's worth of depreciation regardless of when the equipment was obtained by the business.)

### COMPREHENSIVE PROBLEM: CHAPTERS 3 TO 7

**CP7** McBride Company has the following opening account balances in its general and subsidiary ledgers on January 1 and uses the periodic inventory system. All accounts have normal debit and credit balances.

#### GENERAL LEDGER

| Account Number | Account Title | January 1 Opening Balance |
|---|---|---|
| 101 | Cash | $33,750 |
| 112 | Accounts Receivable | 13,000 |

### WATERWAYS CONTINUING PROBLEM

(*Note*: The Waterways Problem begins in Chapter 19 and continues in the remaining chapters. You can also find this problem at the book's companion website.)

**WCP19** Waterways Corporation is a private corporation formed for the purpose of providing the products and the services needed to irrigate farms, parks, commercial projects,

kieso
weygandt
kimmel
warfield

# Contents

# 1 | Accounting in Action

## Feature Story

*The **Feature Story** helps you picture how the chapter topic relates to the real world of accounting and business. You will find references to the story throughout the chapter.*

## Knowing the Numbers

Many students who take this course do not plan to be accountants. If you are in that group, you might be thinking, "If I'm not going to be an accountant, why do I need to know accounting?" Well, consider this quote from Harold Geneen, the former chairman of IT&T: "To be good at your business, you have to know the numbers—cold." In business, accounting and financial statements are the means for communicating the numbers. If you don't know how to read financial statements, you can't really know your business.

Many businesses agree with this view. They see the value of their employees being able to read financial statements and understand how their actions affect the company's financial results. For example, consider Clif Bar & Company. The original Clif Bar® energy bar was created in 1990 after six months of experimentation by Gary Erickson and his mother in her kitchen. Today, the company has almost 300 employees and is considered one of the leading Landor's Breakaway Brands®.

Clif Bar is guided by what it calls its Five Aspirations—Sustaining Our Business, Our Brands, Our People, Our

Community, and the Planet. Its website documents its effor and accomplishments in these five areas. Just a few exampl include the company's use of organic products to protect so water, and biodiversity; the "smart" solar array (the largest North America), which provides nearly all the electrical need for its 115,000-square foot building; and the incentives Clif Bar provides to employees to reduce their personal environ-mental impact, such as $6,500 toward the purchase of an efficient car or $1,000 per year for eco-friendly improvemer toward their homes.

One of the company's proudest moments was the creation an employee stock ownership plan (ESOP) in 2010. This pla gives its employees 20% ownership of the company (Gary and his wife Kit own the other 80%). The ESOP also resulte in Clif Bar enacting an open-book management program, including the commitment to educate all employee-owners about its finances. Armed with this basic financial knowledg employees are more aware of the financial impact of their actions, which leads to better decisions.

Many other companies have adopted this open-book man-agement approach. Even in companies that do not practice

*The **Navigator** is a learning system designed to prompt you to use the learning aids in the chapter and set priorities as you study.*

 **The Navigator**

- ☐ Scan Learning Objectives
- ☐ Read Feature Story
- ☐ Read Preview
- ☐ Read text and answer **DO IT!** p. 11
  - ☐ p. 14 ☐ p. 21 ☐ p. 25
- ☐ Work Comprehensive **DO IT!** p. 26
- ☐ Review Summary of Learning Objectives
- ☐ Answer Self-Test Questions
- ☐ Complete Assignments
- ☐ Go to *WileyPLUS* for practice and tutorials
-  **Read A Look at IFRS** p. 48

*Learning Objectives give you a framework for learning the specific concepts covered in the chapter.*

## Learning Objectives          ✔ The Navigator

*After studying this chapter, you should be able to:*

[1] Explain what accounting is.

[2] Identify the users and uses of accounting.

[3] Understand why ethics is a fundamental business concept.

[4] Explain generally accepted accounting principles.

[5] Explain the monetary unit assumption and the economic entity assumption.

[6] State the accounting equation, and define its components.

[7] Analyze the effects of business transactions on the accounting equation.

[8] Understand the four financial statements and how they are prepared.

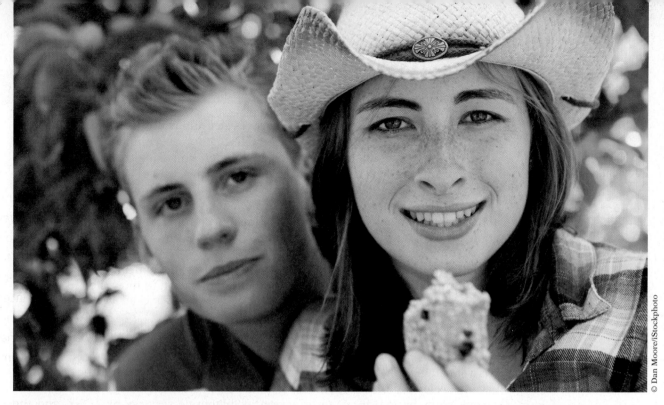

open-book management, employers generally assume that managers in all areas of the company are "financially literate."

Taking this course will go a long way to making you financially literate. In this textbook, you will learn how to read and prepare financial statements, and how to use basic tools to evaluate financial results. Throughout this textbook, we attempt to increase your familiarity with financial reporting by providing numerous references, questions, and exercises that encourage you to explore the financial statements of well-known companies.

# Preview of Chapter 1

✔ The Navigator

The opening story about Clif Bar & Company highlights the importance of having good financial information and knowing how to use it to make effective business decisions. Whatever your pursuits or occupation, the need for financial information is inescapable. You cannot earn a living, spend money, buy on credit, make an investment, or pay taxes without receiving, using, or dispensing financial information. Good decision-making depends on good information.

The purpose of this chapter is to show you that accounting is the system used to provide useful financial information. The content and organization of Chapter 1 are as follows.

*The **Preview** describes and outlines the major topics and subtopics you will see in the chapter.*

## ACCOUNTING IN ACTION

| What Is Accounting? | The Building Blocks of Accounting | The Basic Accounting Equation | Using the Accounting Equation | Financial Statements |
|---|---|---|---|---|
| • Three activities<br>• Who uses accounting data | • Ethics in financial reporting<br>• Generally accepted accounting principles<br>• Measurement principles<br>• Assumptions | • Assets<br>• Liabilities<br>• Owner's equity | • Transaction analysis<br>• Summary of transactions | • Income statement<br>• Owner's equity statement<br>• Balance sheet<br>• Statement of cash flows |

© Dan Moore/iStockphoto

## What Is Accounting?

What consistently ranks as one of the top career opportunities in business? What frequently rates among the most popular majors on campus? What was the undergraduate degree chosen by Nike founder Phil Knight, Home Depot co-founder Arthur Blank, former acting director of the Federal Bureau of Investigation (FBI) Thomas Pickard, and numerous members of Congress? Accounting.[1] Why did these people choose accounting? They wanted to understand what was happening financially to their organizations. Accounting is the financial information system that provides these insights. In short, to understand your organization, you have to know the numbers.

**Accounting** consists of three basic activities—it **identifies**, **records**, and **communicates** the economic events of an organization to interested users. Let's take a closer look at these three activities.

### Three Activities

As a starting point to the accounting process, a company **identifies the economic events relevant to its business**. Examples of economic events are the sale of snack chips by PepsiCo, the provision of telephone services by AT&T, and the payment of wages by Ford Motor Company.

Once a company like PepsiCo identifies economic events, it **records** those events in order to provide a history of its financial activities. Recording consists of keeping a **systematic**, **chronological diary of events**, measured in dollars and cents. In recording, PepsiCo also classifies and summarizes economic events.

Finally, PepsiCo **communicates** the collected information to interested users by means of **accounting reports**. The most common of these reports are called **financial statements**. To make the reported financial information meaningful, PepsiCo reports the recorded data in a standardized way. It accumulates information resulting from similar transactions. For example, PepsiCo accumulates all sales transactions over a certain period of time and reports the data as one amount in the company's financial statements. Such data are said to be reported **in the aggregate**. By presenting the recorded data in the aggregate, the accounting process simplifies a multitude of transactions and makes a series of activities understandable and meaningful.

A vital element in communicating economic events is the accountant's ability to **analyze and interpret** the reported information. Analysis involves use of ratios, percentages, graphs, and charts to highlight significant financial trends and relationships. Interpretation involves **explaining the uses**, **meaning**, **and limitations of reported data**. Appendices A–E show the financial statements of Apple Inc., PepsiCo Inc., The Coca-Cola Company, Amazon.com, Inc., and Wal-Mart Stores, Inc., respectively. (In addition, in the *A Look at IFRS* section at the end of each chapter, the U.K. company Zetar plc is analyzed.) We refer to these statements at various places throughout the textbook. At this point, these financial statements probably strike you as complex and confusing. By the end of this course, you'll be surprised at your ability to understand, analyze, and interpret them.

Illustration 1-1 summarizes the activities of the accounting process.

---

[1]The appendix to this chapter describes job opportunities for accounting majors and explains why accounting is such a popular major.

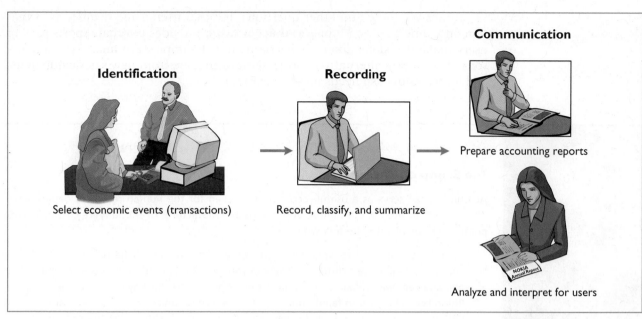

**Identification**

Select economic events (transactions)

**Recording**

Record, classify, and summarize

**Communication**

Prepare accounting reports

Analyze and interpret for users

**Illustration 1-1**
The activities of the accounting process

You should understand that the accounting process **includes** the bookkeeping function. **Bookkeeping** usually involves **only** the recording of economic events. It is therefore just one part of the accounting process. In total, accounting involves **the entire process of identifying, recording, and communicating economic events**.[2]

*Essential terms are printed in blue when they first appear, and are defined in the end-of-chapter glossary.*

**LEARNING OBJECTIVE 2**

Identify the users and uses of accounting.

## Who Uses Accounting Data

The financial information that users need depends upon the kinds of decisions they make. There are two broad groups of users of financial information: internal users and external users.

### INTERNAL USERS

**Internal users** of accounting information are managers who plan, organize, and run the business. These include marketing managers, production supervisors, finance directors, and company officers. In running a business, internal users must answer many important questions, as shown in Illustration 1-2.

### Questions Asked by Internal Users

Snack chips    Beverages

| **Finance** | **Marketing** | **Human Resources** | **Management** |
|---|---|---|---|
| Is cash sufficient to pay dividends to Microsoft stockholders? | What price should Apple charge for an iPod to maximize the company's net income? | Can General Motors afford to give its employees pay raises this year? | Which PepsiCo product line is the most profitable? Should any product lines be eliminated? |

**Illustration 1-2**
Questions that internal users ask

---

[2]The origins of accounting are generally attributed to the work of Luca Pacioli, an Italian Renaissance mathematician. Pacioli was a close friend and tutor to Leonardo da Vinci and a contemporary of Christopher Columbus. In his 1494 text *Summa de Arithmetica, Geometria, Proportione et Proportionalite*, Pacioli described a system to ensure that financial information was recorded efficiently and accurately.

To answer these and other questions, internal users need detailed information on a timely basis. **Managerial accounting** provides internal reports to help users make decisions about their companies. Examples are financial comparisons of operating alternatives, projections of income from new sales campaigns, and forecasts of cash needs for the next year.

## ACCOUNTING ACROSS THE ORGANIZATION

### The Scoop on Accounting

Accounting can serve as a useful recruiting tool even for the human resources department. Rhino Foods, located in Burlington, Vermont, is a manufacturer of specialty ice cream. Its corporate website includes the following:

"Wouldn't it be great to work where you were part of a team? Where your input and hard work made a difference? Where you weren't kept in the dark about what management was thinking? . . . Well—it's not a dream! It's the way we do business . . . Rhino Foods believes in family, honesty and open communication—we really care about and appreciate our employees—and it shows. Operating results are posted and monthly group meetings inform all employees about what's happening in the Company. Employees also share in the Company's profits, in addition to having an excellent comprehensive benefits package."

*Source: www.rhinofoods.com/workforus/workforus.html.*

**?** What are the benefits to the company and to the employees of making the financial statements available to all employees? (See page 47.)

© Agnieszka Pastuszak-Maksim/
iStockphoto

*Accounting Across the Organization boxes demonstrate applications of accounting information in various business functions.*

## EXTERNAL USERS

**External users** are individuals and organizations outside a company who want financial information about the company. The two most common types of external users are investors and creditors. **Investors** (owners) use accounting information to decide whether to buy, hold, or sell ownership shares of a company. **Creditors** (such as suppliers and bankers) use accounting information to evaluate the risks of granting credit or lending money. Illustration 1-3 shows some questions that investors and creditors may ask.

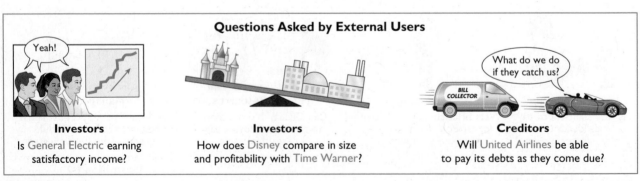

### Questions Asked by External Users

**Investors**
Is General Electric earning satisfactory income?

**Investors**
How does Disney compare in size and profitability with Time Warner?

**Creditors**
Will United Airlines be able to pay its debts as they come due?

**Illustration 1-3**
Questions that external users ask

**Financial accounting** answers these questions. It provides economic and financial information for investors, creditors, and other external users. The information needs of external users vary considerably. **Taxing authorities**, such as the Internal Revenue Service, want to know whether the company complies with tax laws. **Regulatory agencies**, such as the Securities and Exchange Commission or the Federal Trade Commission, want to know whether the company is operating within prescribed rules. **Customers** are interested in whether a company like General Motors will continue to honor product warranties and support its product lines. **Labor unions** such as the Major League Baseball Players Association want to know whether the owners have the ability to pay increased wages and benefits.

## The Building Blocks of Accounting

A doctor follows certain standards in treating a patient's illness. An architect follows certain standards in designing a building. An accountant follows certain standards in reporting financial information. For these standards to work, a fundamental business concept must be at work—ethical behavior.

> **LEARNING OBJECTIVE    3**
>
> Understand why ethics is a fundamental business concept.

### Ethics in Financial Reporting

People won't gamble in a casino if they think it is "rigged." Similarly, people won't play the stock market if they think stock prices are rigged. In recent years, the financial press has been full of articles about financial scandals at Enron, WorldCom, HealthSouth, AIG, and other companies. As the scandals came to light, mistrust of financial reporting in general grew. One article in the *Wall Street Journal* noted that "repeated disclosures about questionable accounting practices have bruised investors' faith in the reliability of earnings reports, which in turn has sent stock prices tumbling." Imagine trying to carry on a business or invest money if you could not depend on the financial statements to be honestly prepared. Information would have no credibility. There is no doubt that a sound, well-functioning economy depends on accurate and dependable financial reporting.

United States regulators and lawmakers were very concerned that the economy would suffer if investors lost confidence in corporate accounting because of unethical financial reporting. In response, Congress passed the **Sarbanes-Oxley Act (SOX)**. Its intent is to reduce unethical corporate behavior and decrease the likelihood of future corporate scandals. As a result of SOX, top management must now certify the accuracy of financial information. In addition, penalties for fraudulent financial activity are much more severe. Also, SOX increased the independence requirements of the outside auditors who review the accuracy of corporate financial statements and increased the oversight role of boards of directors.

The standards of conduct by which actions are judged as right or wrong, honest or dishonest, fair or not fair, are **ethics**. Effective financial reporting depends on sound ethical behavior. To sensitize you to ethical situations in business and to give you practice at solving ethical dilemmas, we address ethics in a number of ways in this textbook:

> ### Ethics Note
>
> Circus-founder P.T. Barnum is alleged to have said, "Trust everyone, but cut the deck." What Sarbanes-Oxley does is to provide measures that (like cutting the deck of playing cards) help ensure that fraud will not occur.

*Ethics Notes help sensitize you to some of the ethical issues in accounting.*

**1.** A number of the *Feature Stories* and other parts of the textbook discuss the central importance of ethical behavior to financial reporting.

2. *Ethics Insight* boxes and marginal *Ethics Notes* highlight ethics situations and issues in actual business settings.

3. Many of the *People, Planet, and Profit Insight* boxes focus on ethical issues that companies face in measuring and reporting social and environmental issues.

4. At the end of the chapter, an *Ethics Case* simulates a business situation and asks you to put yourself in the position of a decision-maker in that case.

When analyzing these various ethics cases, as well as experiences in your own life, it is useful to apply the three steps outlined in Illustration 1-4.

**1. Recognize an ethical situation and the ethical issues involved.**

Use your personal ethics to identify ethical situations and issues. Some businesses and professional organizations provide written codes of ethics for guidance in some business situations.

**2. Identify and analyze the principal elements in the situation.**

Identify the **stakeholders**— persons or groups who may be harmed or benefited. Ask the question: What are the responsibilities and obligations of the parties involved?

**3. Identify the alternatives, and weigh the impact of each alternative on various stakeholders.**

Select the most ethical alternative, considering all the consequences. Sometimes there will be one right answer. Other situations involve more than one right solution; these situations require an evaluation of each and a selection of the best alternative.

**Illustration 1-4**
Steps in analyzing ethics cases and situations

*Insight boxes provide examples of business situations from various perspectives—ethics, investor, international, and corporate social responsibility. Guideline answers are provided near the end of the chapter.*

Gemunu Amarasinghe/AP Photo

## ETHICS INSIGHT

### The Numbers Behind Not-for-Profit Organizations

Accounting plays an important role for a wide range of business organizations worldwide. Just as the integrity of the numbers matters for business, it matters at least as much at not-for-profit organizations. Proper control and reporting help ensure that money is used the way donors intended. Donors are less inclined to give to an organization if they think the organization is subject to waste or theft. The accounting challenges of some large international not-for-profits rival those of the world's largest businesses. For example, after the Haitian earthquake, the Haitian-born musician Wyclef Jean was criticized for the poor accounting controls in a relief fund that he founded. In response, he hired a new accountant and improved the transparency regarding money raised and spent.

 What benefits does a sound accounting system provide to a not-for-profit organization? (See page 47.)

## Generally Accepted Accounting Principles

LEARNING OBJECTIVE 4

Explain generally accepted accounting principles.

The accounting profession has developed standards that are generally accepted and universally practiced. This common set of standards is called **generally accepted accounting principles (GAAP)**. These standards indicate how to report economic events.

The primary accounting standard-setting body in the United States is the **Financial Accounting Standards Board (FASB)**. The **Securities and Exchange Commission (SEC)** is the agency of the U.S. government that oversees U.S. financial markets and accounting standard-setting bodies. The SEC relies on the FASB to develop accounting standards, which public companies must follow. Many countries outside of the United States have adopted the accounting standards issued by the **International Accounting Standards Board (IASB)**. These standards are called **International Financial Reporting Standards (IFRS)**.

As markets become more global, it is often desirable to compare the results of companies from different countries that report using different accounting standards. In order to increase comparability, in recent years the two standard-setting bodies have made efforts to reduce the differences between U.S. GAAP and IFRS. This process is referred to as **convergence**. As a result of these convergence efforts, it is likely that someday there will be a single set of high-quality accounting standards that are used by companies around the world. Because convergence is such an important issue, we highlight any major differences between GAAP and IFRS in *International Notes* (as shown in the margin here) and provide a more in-depth discussion in the *A Look at IRFS* section at the end of each chapter.

> **International Note**
>
> Over 100 countries use International Financial Reporting Standards (called IFRS). For example, all companies in the European Union follow international standards. The differences between U.S. and international standards are not generally significant.

*International Notes highlight differences between U.S. and international accounting standards.*

## Measurement Principles

GAAP generally uses one of two measurement principles, the historical cost principle or the fair value principle. Selection of which principle to follow generally relates to trade-offs between relevance and faithful representation. **Relevance** means that financial information is capable of making a difference in a decision. **Faithful representation** means that the numbers and descriptions match what really existed or happened—they are factual.

**Helpful Hint** *Relevance* and *faithful representation* are two primary qualities that make accounting information useful for decision-making.

*Helpful Hints further clarify concepts being discussed.*

### HISTORICAL COST PRINCIPLE

The **historical cost principle** (or cost principle) dictates that companies record assets at their cost. This is true not only at the time the asset is purchased, but also over the time the asset is held. For example, if Best Buy purchases land for $300,000, the company initially reports it in its accounting records at $300,000. But what does Best Buy do if, by the end of the next year, the fair value of the land has increased to $400,000? Under the historical cost principle, it continues to report the land at $300,000.

### FAIR VALUE PRINCIPLE

The **fair value principle** states that assets and liabilities should be reported at fair value (the price received to sell an asset or settle a liability). Fair value information may be more useful than historical cost for certain types of assets and liabilities. For example, certain investment securities are reported at fair value because market price information is usually readily available for these types of assets. In determining which measurement principle to use, companies weigh the factual nature of cost figures versus the relevance of fair value. In general, most companies choose to use cost. Only in situations where assets are actively traded, such as investment securities, do companies apply the fair value principle extensively.

## INTERNATIONAL INSIGHT

### The Korean Discount

If you think that accounting standards don't matter, consider recent events in South Korea. For many years, international investors complained that the financial reports of South Korean companies were inadequate and inaccurate. Accounting practices there often resulted in huge differences between stated revenues and actual revenues. Because investors did not have faith in the accuracy of the numbers, they were unwilling to pay as much for the shares of these companies relative to shares of comparable companies in different countries. This difference in stock price was often referred to as the "Korean discount."

In response, Korean regulators decided that, beginning in 2011, companies would comply with international accounting standards. This change was motivated by a desire to "make the country's businesses more transparent" in order to build investor confidence and spur economic growth. Many other Asian countries, including China, India, Japan, and Hong Kong, have also decided either to adopt international standards or to create standards that are based on the international standards.

*Source:* Evan Ramstad, "End to 'Korea Discount'?" *Wall Street Journal* (March 16, 2007).

 What is meant by the phrase "make the country's businesses more transparent"? Why would increasing transparency spur economic growth? (See page 48.)

## Assumptions

Assumptions provide a foundation for the accounting process. Two main assumptions are the **monetary unit assumption** and the **economic entity assumption**.

### MONETARY UNIT ASSUMPTION

The **monetary unit assumption** requires that companies include in the accounting records only transaction data that can be expressed in money terms. This assumption enables accounting to quantify (measure) economic events. The monetary unit assumption is vital to applying the historical cost principle.

This assumption prevents the inclusion of some relevant information in the accounting records. For example, the health of a company's owner, the quality of service, and the morale of employees are not included. The reason: Companies cannot quantify this information in money terms. Though this information is important, companies record only events that can be measured in money.

### ECONOMIC ENTITY ASSUMPTION

**An economic entity can be any organization or unit in society.** It may be a company (such as Crocs, Inc.), a governmental unit (the state of Ohio), a municipality (Seattle), a school district (St. Louis District 48), or a church (Southern Baptist). The **economic entity assumption** requires that the activities of the entity be kept separate and distinct from the activities of its owner and all other economic entities. To illustrate, Sally Rider, owner of Sally's Boutique, must keep her personal living costs separate from the expenses of the business. Similarly, McDonald's, Coca-Cola, and Cadbury-Schweppes are segregated into separate economic entities for accounting purposes.

**PROPRIETORSHIP** A business owned by one person is generally a **proprietorship**. The owner is often the manager/operator of the business.

### Ethics Note

The importance of the economic entity assumption is illustrated by scandals involving Adelphia. In this case, senior company employees entered into transactions that blurred the line between the employees' financial interests and those of the company. For example, Adelphia guaranteed over $2 billion of loans to the founding family.

Small service-type businesses (plumbing companies, beauty salons, and auto repair shops), farms, and small retail stores (antique shops, clothing stores, and used-book stores) are often proprietorships. **Usually only a relatively small amount of money (capital) is necessary to start in business as a proprietorship. The owner (proprietor) receives any profits, suffers any losses, and is personally liable for all debts of the business.** There is no legal distinction between the business as an economic unit and the owner, but the accounting records of the business activities are kept separate from the personal records and activities of the owner.

**PARTNERSHIP** A business owned by two or more persons associated as partners is a **partnership**. In most respects a partnership is like a proprietorship except that more than one owner is involved. Typically a partnership agreement (written or oral) sets forth such terms as initial investment, duties of each partner, division of net income (or net loss), and settlement to be made upon death or withdrawal of a partner. Each partner generally has unlimited personal liability for the debts of the partnership. **Like a proprietorship, for accounting purposes the partnership transactions must be kept separate from the personal activities of the partners.** Partnerships are often used to organize retail and service-type businesses, including professional practices (lawyers, doctors, architects, and certified public accountants).

**CORPORATION** A business organized as a separate legal entity under state corporation law and having ownership divided into transferable shares of stock is a **corporation**. The holders of the shares (stockholders) **enjoy limited liability**; that is, they are not personally liable for the debts of the corporate entity. Stockholders **may transfer all or part of their ownership shares to other investors at any time** (i.e., sell their shares). The ease with which ownership can change adds to the attractiveness of investing in a corporation. Because ownership can be transferred without dissolving the corporation, the corporation **enjoys an unlimited life**.

Although the combined number of proprietorships and partnerships in the United States is more than five times the number of corporations, the revenue produced by corporations is eight times greater. Most of the largest companies in the United States—for example, ExxonMobil, Ford, Wal-Mart Stores, Inc., Citigroup, and Apple—are corporations.

*The **DO IT!** exercises ask you to put newly acquired knowledge to work. They outline the Action Plan necessary to complete the exercise, and they show a Solution.*

> **DO IT!**

**Basic Concepts**

Indicate whether each of the five statements presented below is true or false.

1. The three steps in the accounting process are identification, recording, and communication.
2. The two most common types of external users are investors and company officers.
3. Congress passed the Sarbanes-Oxley Act to reduce unethical behavior and decrease the likelihood of future corporate scandals.
4. The primary accounting standard-setting body in the United States is the Financial Accounting Standards Board (FASB).
5. The historical cost principle dictates that companies record assets at their cost. In later periods, however, the fair value of the asset must be used if fair value is higher than its cost.

**Action Plan**

✔ Review the basic concepts learned to date.

✔ Develop an understanding of the key terms used.

**Solution**

1. True   2. False. The two most common types of external users are investors and creditors.   3. True.   4. True.   5. False. The historical cost principle dictates that companies record assets at their cost. Under the historical cost principle, the company must also use cost in later periods.

Related exercise material: **E1-1, E1-2, E1-3, E1-4, and** **DO IT!** **1-1.**

✔ The Navigator

# ACCOUNTING ACROSS THE ORGANIZATION

### Spinning the Career Wheel

How will the study of accounting help you? A working knowledge of accounting is desirable for virtually every field of business. Some examples of how accounting is used in business careers include:

General management:   Managers of Ford Motors, Massachusetts General Hospital, California State University—Fullerton, a McDonald's franchise, and a Trek bike shop all need to understand accounting data in order to make wise business decisions.

Marketing:   A marketing specialist at Procter & Gamble must be sensitive to costs and benefits, which accounting helps them quantify and understand. Making a sale is meaningless unless it is a profitable sale.

Finance:   Do you want to be a banker for Citicorp, an investment analyst for Goldman Sachs, or a stock broker for Merrill Lynch? These fields rely heavily on accounting knowledge to analyze financial statements. In fact, it is difficult to get a good job in a finance function without two or three courses in accounting.

Real estate:   Are you interested in being a real estate broker for Prudential Real Estate? Because a third party—the bank—is almost always involved in financing a real estate transaction, brokers must understand the numbers involved: Can the buyer afford to make the payments to the bank? Does the cash flow from an industrial property justify the purchase price? What are the tax benefits of the purchase?

 How might accounting help you? (See page 48.)

Josef Volavka/iStockphoto

## The Basic Accounting Equation

**State the accounting equation, and define its components.**

The two basic elements of a business are what it owns and what it owes. **Assets** are the resources a business owns. For example, Google has total assets of approximately $40.5 billion. Liabilities and owner's equity are the rights or claims against these resources. Thus, Google has $40.5 billion of claims against its $40.5 billion of assets. Claims of those to whom the company owes money (creditors) are called **liabilities**. Claims of owners are called **owner's equity**. Google has liabilities of $4.5 billion and owners' equity of $36 billion.

We can express the relationship of assets, liabilities, and owner's equity as an equation, as shown in Illustration 1-5.

**Illustration 1-5**
The basic accounting equation

| Assets | = | Liabilities | + | Owner's Equity |

This relationship is the **basic accounting equation**. Assets must equal the sum of liabilities and owner's equity. Liabilities appear before owner's equity in the basic accounting equation because they are paid first if a business is liquidated.

The accounting equation applies to all **economic entities** regardless of size, nature of business, or form of business organization. It applies to a small proprietorship such as a corner grocery store as well as to a giant corporation such as PepsiCo. The equation provides the **underlying framework** for recording and summarizing economic events.

Let's look in more detail at the categories in the basic accounting equation.

## Assets

As noted above, **assets** are resources a business owns. The business uses its assets in carrying out such activities as production and sales. The common characteristic possessed by all assets is **the capacity to provide future services or benefits**. In a business, that service potential or future economic benefit eventually results in cash inflows (receipts). For example, consider Campus Pizza, a local restaurant. It owns a delivery truck that provides economic benefits from delivering pizzas. Other assets of Campus Pizza are tables, chairs, jukebox, cash register, oven, tableware, and, of course, cash.

## Liabilities

**Liabilities** are claims against assets—that is, existing debts and obligations. Businesses of all sizes usually borrow money and purchase merchandise on credit. These economic activities result in payables of various sorts:

- Campus Pizza, for instance, purchases cheese, sausage, flour, and beverages on credit from suppliers. These obligations are called **accounts payable**.
- Campus Pizza also has a **note payable** to First National Bank for the money borrowed to purchase the delivery truck.
- Campus Pizza may also have **salaries and wages payable** to employees and **sales and real estate taxes payable** to the local government.

All of these persons or entities to whom Campus Pizza owes money are its **creditors**.

Creditors may legally force the liquidation of a business that does not pay its debts. In that case, the law requires that creditor claims be paid **before** ownership claims.

## Owner's Equity

The ownership claim on total assets is **owner's equity**. It is equal to total assets minus total liabilities. Here is why: The assets of a business are claimed by either creditors or owners. To find out what belongs to owners, we subtract the creditors' claims (the liabilities) from assets. The remainder is the owner's claim on the assets—the owner's equity. Since the claims of creditors must be paid **before** ownership claims, owner's equity is often referred to as **residual equity**.

### INCREASES IN OWNER'S EQUITY

In a proprietorship, owner's investments and revenues increase owner's equity.

**INVESTMENTS BY OWNER** **Investments by owner** are the assets the owner puts into the business. These investments increase owner's equity. They are recorded in a category called **owner's capital**.

**REVENUES** **Revenues** are the **gross increase in owner's equity resulting from business activities entered into for the purpose of earning income**. Generally, revenues result from selling merchandise, performing services, renting property,

**Helpful Hint** In some places, we use the term "owner's equity" and in others we use "owners' equity." *Owner's* (singular, possessive) refers to one owner (the case with a sole proprietorship). *Owners'* (plural, possessive) refers to multiple owners (the case with partnerships or corporations).

and lending money. Common sources of revenue are sales, fees, services, commissions, interest, dividends, royalties, and rent.

Revenues usually result in an increase in an asset. They may arise from different sources and are called various names depending on the nature of the business. Campus Pizza, for instance, has two categories of sales revenues—pizza sales and beverage sales.

### DECREASES IN OWNER'S EQUITY

In a proprietorship, owner's drawings and expenses decrease owner's equity.

**DRAWINGS** An owner may withdraw cash or other assets for personal use. We use a separate classification called **drawings** to determine the total withdrawals for each accounting period. **Drawings decrease owner's equity.** They are recorded in a category called owner's drawings.

**EXPENSES** **Expenses** are the cost of assets consumed or services used in the process of earning revenue. They are **decreases in owner's equity that result from operating the business**. For example, Campus Pizza recognizes the following expenses: cost of ingredients (meat, flour, cheese, tomato paste, mushrooms, etc.); cost of beverages; salaries and wages expense; utilities expense (electric, gas, and water expense); delivery expense (gasoline, repairs, licenses, etc.); supplies expense (napkins, detergents, aprons, etc.); rent expense; interest expense; and property tax expense.

In summary, owner's equity is increased by an owner's investments and by revenues from business operations. Owner's equity is decreased by an owner's withdrawals of assets and by expenses. Illustration 1-6 expands the basic accounting equation by showing the items that comprise owner's equity. This format is referred to as the **expanded accounting equation**.

**Illustration 1-6**
Expanded accounting equation

| Basic Equation | Assets = Liabilities | + | Owner's Equity | | | |
|---|---|---|---|---|---|---|
| Expanded Equation | Assets = Liabilities | + | Owner's Capital | − Owner's Drawings | + Revenues | − Expenses |

> **DO IT!**

### Owner's Equity Effects

**Action Plan**

✔ Understand the sources of revenue.

✔ Understand what causes expenses.

✔ Review the rules for changes in owner's equity: Investments and revenues increase owner's equity. Expenses and drawings decrease owner's equity.

✔ Recognize that drawings are withdrawals of cash or other assets from the business for personal use.

Classify the following items as investment by owner (I), owner's drawings (D), revenues (R), or expenses (E). Then indicate whether each item increases or decreases owner's equity.

1. Rent Expense
2. Service Revenue
3. Drawings
4. Salaries and Wages Expense

### Solution

1. Rent Expense is an expense (E); it decreases owner's equity. 2. Service Revenue is revenue (R); it increases owner's equity. 3. Drawings is owner's drawings (D); it decreases owner's equity. 4. Salaries and Wages Expense is an expense (E); it decreases owner's equity.

Related exercise material: **BE1-1, BE1-2, BE1-3, BE1-4, BE1-5, E1-5, and** **DO IT!** 1-2.

## Using the Accounting Equation

Transactions (**business transactions**) are a business's economic events recorded by accountants. Transactions may be external or internal. **External transactions** involve economic events between the company and some outside enterprise. For example, Campus Pizza's purchase of cooking equipment from a supplier, payment of monthly rent to the landlord, and sale of pizzas to customers are external transactions. **Internal transactions** are economic events that occur entirely within one company. The use of cooking and cleaning supplies are internal transactions for Campus Pizza.

Companies carry on many activities that do not represent business transactions. Examples are hiring employees, answering the telephone, talking with customers, and placing merchandise orders. Some of these activities may lead to business transactions: Employees will earn wages, and suppliers will deliver ordered merchandise. The company must analyze each event to find out if it affects the components of the accounting equation. If it does, the company will record the transaction. Illustration 1-7 demonstrates the transaction identification process.

> **LEARNING OBJECTIVE    7**
>
> Analyze the effects of business transactions on the accounting equation.

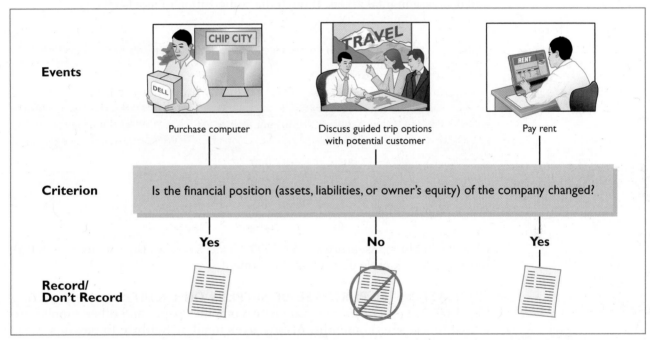

**Events**

Purchase computer

Discuss guided trip options with potential customer

Pay rent

**Criterion**

Is the financial position (assets, liabilities, or owner's equity) of the company changed?

**Yes**      **No**      **Yes**

**Record/ Don't Record**

**Illustration 1-7**
Transaction identification process

Each transaction must have a dual effect on the accounting equation. For example, if an asset is increased, there must be a corresponding (1) decrease in another asset, (2) increase in a specific liability, or (3) increase in owner's equity.

Two or more items could be affected. For example, as one asset is increased $10,000, another asset could decrease $6,000 and a liability could increase $4,000. Any change in a liability or ownership claim is subject to similar analysis.

### Transaction Analysis

To demonstrate how to analyze transactions in terms of the accounting equation, we will review the business activities of Softbyte, a computer programming business. The following business transactions occur during Softbyte's first month of operations.

**TRANSACTION (1). INVESTMENT BY OWNER** Ray Neal decides to open a computer programming service which he names Softbyte. On September 1, 2014, he invests $15,000 cash in the business. This transaction results in an equal increase in assets and owner's equity.

**Helpful Hint** You will want to study these transactions until you are sure you understand them. They are not difficult, but understanding them is important to your success in this course. The ability to analyze transactions in terms of the basic accounting equation is essential in accounting.

| Basic Analysis | The asset Cash increases $15,000, and owner's equity (identified as Owner's Capital) increases $15,000. |
|---|---|

| Equation Analysis | | Assets | = | Liabilities | + | Owner's Equity |
|---|---|---|---|---|---|---|
| | | Cash | = | | | Owner's Capital |
| | (1) | +$15,000 | = | | | +$15,000  Initial investment |

Observe that the equality of the accounting equation has been maintained. Note that the investments by the owner do not represent revenues, and they are excluded in determining net income. Therefore, it is necessary to make clear that the increase is an investment (increasing Owner's Capital) rather than revenue.

**TRANSACTION (2). PURCHASE OF EQUIPMENT FOR CASH** Softbyte purchases computer equipment for $7,000 cash. This transaction results in an equal increase and decrease in total assets, though the composition of assets changes.

| Basic Analysis | The asset Cash decreases $7,000, and the asset Equipment increases $7,000. |
|---|---|

| Equation Analysis | | Assets | | | = | Liabilities | + | Owner's Equity |
|---|---|---|---|---|---|---|---|---|
| | | Cash | + | Equipment | = | | | Owner's Capital |
| | | $15,000 | | | | | | $15,000 |
| | (2) | −7,000 | | +$7,000 | | | | |
| | | $ 8,000 | + | $7,000 | = | | | $15,000 |
| | | | $15,000 | | | | | |

Observe that total assets are still $15,000. Owner's equity also remains at $15,000, the amount of Ray Neal's original investment.

**TRANSACTION (3). PURCHASE OF SUPPLIES ON CREDIT** Softbyte purchases for $1,600 from Acme Supply Company computer paper and other supplies expected to last several months. Acme agrees to allow Softbyte to pay this bill in October. This transaction is a purchase on account (a credit purchase). Assets increase because of the expected future benefits of using the paper and supplies, and liabilities increase by the amount due to Acme Company.

| Basic Analysis | The asset Supplies increases $1,600, and the liability Accounts Payable increases by $1,600. |
|---|---|

| Equation Analysis | | Assets | | | | | = | Liabilities | + | Owner's Equity |
|---|---|---|---|---|---|---|---|---|---|---|
| | | Cash | + | Supplies | + | Equipment | = | Accounts Payable | + | Owner's Capital |
| | | $8,000 | | | | $7,000 | | | | $15,000 |
| | (3) | | | +$1,600 | | | | +$1,600 | | |
| | | $8,000 | + | $1,600 | + | $7,000 | = | $1,600 | + | $15,000 |
| | | | | $16,600 | | | | | $16,600 | |

Total assets are now $16,600. This total is matched by a $1,600 creditor's claim and a $15,000 ownership claim.

**TRANSACTION (4). SERVICES PERFORMED FOR CASH** Softbyte receives $1,200 cash from customers for programming services it has performed. This transaction represents Softbyte's principal revenue-producing activity. Recall that **revenue increases owner's equity**.

| Basic Analysis | The asset Cash increases $1,200, and owner's equity increases $1,200 due to Service Revenue. |
|---|---|

**Equation Analysis**

| | Cash | + Supplies | + Equipment | = Accounts Payable | + Owner's Capital | + Revenues | |
|---|---|---|---|---|---|---|---|
| | $8,000 | $1,600 | $7,000 | $1,600 | $15,000 | | |
| (4) | +1,200 | | | | | +$1,200 | Service Revenue |
| | $9,200 + | $1,600 + | $7,000 | = $1,600 | + $15,000 + | $1,200 | |
| | | $17,800 | | | $17,800 | | |

The two sides of the equation balance at $17,800. Service Revenue is included in determining Softbyte's net income.

Note that we do not have room to give details for each individual revenue and expense account in this illustration. Thus, revenues (and expenses when we get to them) are summarized under one column heading for Revenues and one for Expenses. However, it is important to keep track of the category (account) titles affected (e.g., Service Revenue) as they will be needed when we prepare financial statements later in the chapter.

**TRANSACTION (5). PURCHASE OF ADVERTISING ON CREDIT** Softbyte receives a bill for $250 from the *Daily News* for advertising but postpones payment until a later date. This transaction results in an increase in liabilities and a decrease in owner's equity.

| Basic Analysis | The liability Accounts Payable increases $250, and owner's equity decreases $250 due to Advertising Expense. |
|---|---|

**Equation Analysis**

| | Cash | + Supplies | + Equipment | = Accounts Payable | + Owner's Capital | + Revenues | − Expenses | |
|---|---|---|---|---|---|---|---|---|
| | $9,200 | $1,600 | $7,000 | $1,600 | $15,000 | $1,200 | | |
| (5) | | | | +250 | | | −$250 | Advertising Expense |
| | $9,200 + | $1,600 + | $7,000 | = $1,850 | + $15,000 + | $1,200 | − $250 | |
| | | $17,800 | | | $17,800 | | | |

The two sides of the equation still balance at $17,800. Owner's equity decreases when Softbyte incurs the expense. Expenses are not always paid in cash at the time they are incurred. When Softbyte pays at a later date, the liability Accounts Payable will decrease, and the asset Cash will decrease [see Transaction (8)]. The cost of advertising is an expense (rather than an asset) because the company has **used** the benefits. Advertising Expense is included in determining net income.

**TRANSACTION (6). SERVICES PERFORMED FOR CASH AND CREDIT** Softbyte performs $3,500 of programming services for customers. The company receives cash of $1,500 from customers, and it bills the balance of $2,000 on account. This transaction results in an equal increase in assets and owner's equity.

| Basic Analysis | Three specific items are affected: The asset Cash increases $1,500, the asset Accounts Receivable increases $2,000, and owner's equity increases $3,500 due to Service Revenue. |
| --- | --- |

**Equation Analysis**

| | Assets | | | | = Liabilities + | Owner's Equity | | | |
| --- | --- | --- | --- | --- | --- | --- | --- | --- | --- |
| | Cash | + Accounts Receivable | + Supplies | + Equipment = | Accounts Payable | + Owner's Capital | + Revenues | − Expenses | |
| | $9,200 | | $1,600 | $7,000 | $1,850 | $15,000 | $1,200 | $250 | |
| (6) | +1,500 | +$2,000 | | | | | +3,500 | | Service Revenue |
| | $10,700 + | $2,000 + | $1,600 + | $7,000 = | $1,850 + | $15,000 + | $4,700 − | $250 | |
| | | $21,300 | | | | $21,300 | | | |

Softbyte recognizes $3,500 in revenue when it performs the service. In exchange for this service, it received $1,500 in Cash and Accounts Receivable of $2,000. This Accounts Receivable represents customers' promises to pay $2,000 to Softbyte in the future. When it later receives collections on account, Softbyte will increase Cash and will decrease Accounts Receivable [see Transaction (9)].

**TRANSACTION (7). PAYMENT OF EXPENSES** Softbyte pays the following expenses in cash for September: store rent $600, salaries and wages of employees $900, and utilities $200. These payments result in an equal decrease in assets and owner's equity.

| Basic Analysis | The asset Cash decreases $1,700, and owner's equity decreases $1,700 due to the specific expense categories (Rent Expense, Salaries and Wages Expense, and Utilities Expense). |
| --- | --- |

**Equation Analysis**

| | Assets | | | | = Liabilities + | Owner's Equity | | | |
| --- | --- | --- | --- | --- | --- | --- | --- | --- | --- |
| | Cash | + Accounts Receivable | + Supplies | + Equipment = | Accounts Payable | + Owner's Capital | + Revenues | − Expenses | |
| | $10,700 | $2,000 | $1,600 | $7,000 | $1,850 | $15,000 | $4,700 | $ 250 | |
| (7) | −1,700 | | | | | | | −600 | Rent Expense |
| | | | | | | | | −900 | Sal. and Wages Exp. |
| | | | | | | | | −200 | Utilities Exp. |
| | $9,000 + | $2,000 + | $1,600 + | $7,000 = | $1,850 + | $15,000 + | $4,700 − | $1,950 | |
| | | $19,600 | | | | $19,600 | | | |

The two sides of the equation now balance at $19,600. Three lines in the analysis indicate the different types of expenses that have been incurred.

**TRANSACTION (8). PAYMENT OF ACCOUNTS PAYABLE** Softbyte pays its $250 *Daily News* bill in cash. The company previously [in Transaction (5)] recorded the bill as an increase in Accounts Payable and a decrease in owner's equity.

| Basic Analysis | This cash payment "on account" decreases the asset Cash by $250 and also decreases the liability Accounts Payable by $250. |
|---|---|

Equation Analysis

| | | Assets | | | = Liabilities + | | Owner's Equity | | |
|---|---|---|---|---|---|---|---|---|---|
| Cash | + Accounts Receivable | + Supplies | + Equipment = | Accounts Payable | + Owner's Capital | + Revenues | − Expenses |
| $9,000 | $2,000 | $1,600 | $7,000 | $1,850 | $15,000 | $4,700 | $1,950 |
| (8) −250 | | | | −250 | | | |
| $8,750 + | $2,000 + | $1,600 + | $7,000 = | $1,600 + | $15,000 + | $4,700 − | $1,950 |

$19,350                                                    $19,350

Observe that the payment of a liability related to an expense that has previously been recorded does not affect owner's equity. The company recorded this expense in Transaction (5) and should not record it again.

**TRANSACTION (9). RECEIPT OF CASH ON ACCOUNT** Softbyte receives $600 in cash from customers who had been billed for services [in Transaction (6)]. Transaction (9) does not change total assets, but it changes the composition of those assets.

| Basic Analysis | The asset Cash increases $600, and the asset Accounts Receivable decreases $600. |
|---|---|

Equation Analysis

| | | Assets | | | = Liabilities + | | Owner's Equity | | |
|---|---|---|---|---|---|---|---|---|---|
| Cash | + Accounts Receivable | + Supplies | + Equipment = | Accounts Payable | + Owner's Capital | + Revenues | − Expenses |
| $8,750 | $2,000 | $1,600 | $7,000 | $1,600 | $15,000 | $4,700 | $1,950 |
| (9) +600 | −600 | | | | | | |
| $9,350 + | $1,400 + | $1,600 + | $7,000 = | $1,600 + | $15,000 + | $4,700 − | $1,950 |

$19,350                                                    $19,350

Note that the collection of an account receivable for services previously billed and recorded does not affect owner's equity. Softbyte already recorded this revenue in Transaction (6) and should not record it again.

**TRANSACTION (10). WITHDRAWAL OF CASH BY OWNER** Ray Neal withdraws $1,300 in cash from the business for his personal use. This transaction results in an equal decrease in assets and owner's equity.

| Basic Analysis | The asset Cash decreases $1,300, and owner's equity decreases $1,300 due to owner's withdrawal (Owner's Drawings). |
| --- | --- |

**Equation Analysis**

|  | Assets | | | | = Liabilities + | | Owner's Equity | | | |
| --- | --- | --- | --- | --- | --- | --- | --- | --- | --- | --- |
|  | | Accounts | | | | Accounts | Owner's | Owner's | | | |
|  | Cash + | Receivable + | Supplies + | Equipment = | Payable + | Capital − | Drawings + | Revenues − | Expenses | |
|  | $9,350 | $1,400 | $1,600 | $7,000 | $1,600 | $15,000 | | $4,700 | $1,950 | |
| (10)−1,300 | | | | | | | −$1,300 | | | Drawings |
|  | $8,050 + | $1,400 + | $1,600 + | $7,000 = | $1,600 + | $15,000 − | $1,300 + | $4,700 − | $1,950 | |

$18,050

$18,050

Observe that the effect of a cash withdrawal by the owner is the opposite of the effect of an investment by the owner. **Owner's drawings are not expenses.** Expenses are incurred for the purpose of earning revenue. Drawings do not generate revenue. They are a **disinvestment**. Like owner's investment, the company excludes owner's drawings in determining net income.

## Summary of Transactions

Illustration 1-8 summarizes the September transactions of Softbyte to show their cumulative effect on the basic accounting equation. It also indicates the transaction number and the specific effects of each transaction.

|  | Assets | | | | = Liabilities + | | Owner's Equity | | | |
| --- | --- | --- | --- | --- | --- | --- | --- | --- | --- | --- |
|  | | Accounts | | | | Accounts | Owner's | Owner's | | | |
|  | Cash + | Receivable + | Supplies + | Equipment = | Payable + | Capital − | Drawings + | Rev. − | Exp. | |
| (1) | +$15,000 | | | | | + $15,000 | | | | Initial inv. |
| (2) | −7,000 | | | +$7,000 | | | | | | |
| (3) | | | +$1,600 | | +$1,600 | | | | | |
| (4) | +1,200 | | | | | | | +$1,200 | | Ser. Rev. |
| (5) | | | | | +250 | | | | −$250 | Adv. Exp. |
| (6) | +1,500 | +$2,000 | | | | | | +3,500 | | Ser. Rev. |
| (7) | −600 | | | | | | | | −600 | Rent Exp. |
|  | −900 | | | | | | | | −900 | Sal./Wages Exp. |
|  | −200 | | | | | | | | −200 | Utilities Exp. |
| (8) | −250 | | | | −250 | | | | | |
| (9) | +600 | −600 | | | | | | | | |
| (10) | −1,300 | | | | | | −$1,300 | | | Drawings |
|  | $ 8,050 + | $1,400 + | $1,600 + | $7,000 = | $1,600 + | $15,000 − | $1,300 + | $4,700 − | $1,950 | |

$18,050

$18,050

**Illustration 1-8**
Tabular summary of Softbyte transactions

Illustration 1-8 demonstrates some significant facts:

1. Each transaction is analyzed in terms of its effect on:
   (a) The three components of the basic accounting equation.
   (b) Specific items within each component.
2. The two sides of the equation must always be equal.

There! You made it through your first transaction analysis. If you feel a bit shaky on any of the transactions, it might be a good idea at this point to get up, take a short break, and come back again for a 10- to 15-minute review of the transactions, to make sure you understand them before you go on to the next section.

---

> **DO IT!**

## Tabular Analysis

**Action Plan**

✔ Analyze the effects of each transaction on the accounting equation.

✔ Use appropriate category names (not descriptions).

✔ Keep the accounting equation in balance.

Transactions made by Virmari & Co., a public accounting firm, for the month of August are shown below. Prepare a tabular analysis which shows the effects of these transactions on the expanded accounting equation, similar to that shown in Illustration 1-8.

1. The owner invested $25,000 cash in the business.
2. The company purchased $7,000 of office equipment on credit.
3. The company received $8,000 cash in exchange for services performed.
4. The company paid $850 for this month's rent.
5. The owner withdrew $1,000 cash for personal use.

### Solution

| | Assets | | | = | Liabilities | + | | | Owner's Equity | | | | | |
|---|---|---|---|---|---|---|---|---|---|---|---|---|---|---|
| | Cash | + | Equipment | = | Accounts Payable | + | Owner's Capital | − | Owner's Drawings | + | Revenues | − | Expenses | |
| 1. | +$25,000 | | | | | | +$25,000 | | | | | | | |
| 2. | | | +$7,000 | | +$7,000 | | | | | | | | | |
| 3. | +8,000 | | | | | | | | | | +$8,000 | | | |
| 4. | −850 | | | | | | | | | | | | −$850 | |
| 5. | −1,000 | | | | | | | | −$1,000 | | | | | |
| | $31,150 | + | $7,000 | = | $7,000 | + | $25,000 | − | $1,000 | + | $8,000 | = | $850 | |
| | | $38,150 | | | | | | | $38,150 | | | | | |

Related exercise material: **BE1-6, BE1-7, BE1-8, BE1-9, E1-6, E1-7, E1-8, E1-11, and DO IT! 1-3.**

✔ The Navigator

---

## Financial Statements

Companies prepare four financial statements from the summarized accounting data:

**LEARNING OBJECTIVE** 8

1. An **income statement** presents the revenues and expenses and resulting net income or net loss for a specific period of time.
2. An **owner's equity statement** summarizes the changes in owner's equity for a specific period of time.
3. A **balance sheet** reports the assets, liabilities, and owner's equity at a specific date.
4. A **statement of cash flows** summarizes information about the cash inflows (receipts) and outflows (payments) for a specific period of time.

These statements provide relevant financial data for internal and external users. Illustration 1-9 (page 22) shows the financial statements of Softbyte.

**Understand the four financial statements and how they are prepared.**

### International Note

The primary types of financial statements required by GAAP and IFRS are the same. In practice, some format differences do exist in presentations commonly employed by GAAP companies compared to IFRS companies.

**Illustration 1-9**
Financial statements and their interrelationships

**SOFTBYTE**
**Income Statement**
For the Month Ended September 30, 2014

| | | |
|---|---:|---:|
| Revenues | | |
|   Service revenue | | $ 4,700 |
| Expenses | | |
|   Salaries and wages expense | $900 | |
|   Rent expense | 600 | |
|   Advertising expense | 250 | |
|   Utilities expense | 200 | |
|     Total expenses | | 1,950 |
| Net income | | $ 2,750 |

**Helpful Hint** The heading of each statement identifies the company, the type of statement, and the specific date or time period covered by the statement.

①

**SOFTBYTE**
**Owner's Equity Statement**
For the Month Ended September 30, 2014

| | | |
|---|---:|---:|
| Owner's capital, September 1 | | $ –0– |
| Add: Investments | $15,000 | |
|     Net income | 2,750 | 17,750 |
| | | 17,750 |
| Less: Drawings | | 1,300 |
| Owner's capital, September 30 | | $16,450 |

**Helpful Hint** Note that final sums are double-underlined, and negative amounts (in the statement of cash flows) are presented in parentheses.

**SOFTBYTE**
**Balance Sheet**
September 30, 2014

**Assets**

| | |
|---|---:|
| Cash | $ 8,050 |
| Accounts receivable | 1,400 |
| Supplies | 1,600 |
| Equipment | 7,000 |
|   Total assets | $ 18,050 |

**Liabilities and Owner's Equity**

| | |
|---|---:|
| Liabilities | |
|   Accounts payable | $ 1,600 |
| Owner's equity | |
|   Owner's capital | 16,450 |
|   Total liabilities and owner's equity | $ 18,050 |

②

**SOFTBYTE**
**Statement of Cash Flows**
For the Month Ended September 30, 2014

**Helpful Hint** The arrows in this illustration show the interrelationships of the four financial statements.

③

1. Net income is computed first and is needed to determine the ending balance in owner's equity.
2. The ending balance in owner's equity is needed in preparing the balance sheet.
3. The cash shown on the balance sheet is needed in preparing the statement of cash flows.

| | | |
|---|---:|---:|
| Cash flows from operating activities | | |
|   Cash receipts from revenues | | $ 3,300 |
|   Cash payments for expenses | | (1,950) |
|   Net cash provided by operating activities | | 1,350 |
| Cash flows from investing activities | | |
|   Purchase of equipment | | (7,000) |
| Cash flows from financing activities | | |
|   Investments by owner | $15,000 | |
|   Drawings by owner | (1,300) | 13,700 |
| Net increase in cash | | 8,050 |
| Cash at the beginning of the period | | 0 |
| Cash at the end of the period | | $ 8,050 |

Note that the statements shown in Illustration 1-9 are interrelated:

1. Net income of $2,750 on the **income statement** is added to the beginning balance of owner's capital in the **owner's equity statement**.

2. Owner's capital of $16,450 at the end of the reporting period shown in the **owner's equity statement** is reported on the **balance sheet**.

3. Cash of $8,050 on the **balance sheet** is reported on the **statement of cash flows**.

Also, explanatory notes and supporting schedules are an integral part of every set of financial statements. We illustrate these notes and schedules in later chapters of this textbook.

Be sure to carefully examine the format and content of each statement in Illustration 1-9. We describe the essential features of each in the following sections.

**Helpful Hint** The income statement, owner's equity statement, and statement of cash flows are all for a *period* of time, whereas the balance sheet is for a *point* in time.

## Income Statement

The income statement reports the revenues and expenses for a specific period of time. (In Softbyte's case, this is "For the Month Ended September 30, 2014.") Softbyte's income statement is prepared from the data appearing in the owner's equity columns of Illustration 1-8 (page 20).

The income statement lists revenues first, followed by expenses. Finally the statement shows net income (or net loss). **Net income** results when revenues exceed expenses. A **net loss** occurs when expenses exceed revenues.

Although practice varies, we have chosen in our illustrations and homework solutions to list expenses in order of magnitude. (We will consider alternative formats for the income statement in later chapters.)

Note that the income statement does **not** include investment and withdrawal transactions between the owner and the business in measuring net income. For example, as explained earlier, Ray Neal's withdrawal of cash from Softbyte was not regarded as a business expense.

**Alternative Terminology** The income statement is sometimes referred to as the *statement of operations, earnings statement,* or *profit and loss statement.*

*Alternative Terminology* notes introduce other terms you might hear or read.

## Owner's Equity Statement

The owner's equity statement reports the changes in owner's equity for a specific period of time. The time period is the same as that covered by the income statement. Data for the preparation of the owner's equity statement come from the owner's equity columns of the tabular summary (Illustration 1-8) and from the income statement. The first line of the statement shows the beginning owner's equity amount (which was zero at the start of the business). Then come the owner's investments, net income (or loss), and the owner's drawings. This statement indicates **why** owner's equity has increased or decreased during the period.

What if Softbyte had reported a net loss in its first month? Let's assume that during the month of September 2014, Softbyte lost $10,000. Illustration 1-10 shows the presentation of a net loss in the owner's equity statement.

**SOFTBYTE**
**Owner's Equity Statement**
**For the Month Ended September 30, 2014**

| | | |
|---|---|---|
| Owner's capital, September 1 | | $  –0– |
| Add: Investments | | 15,000 |
| | | 15,000 |
| Less: Drawings | $ 1,300 | |
| Net loss | 10,000 | 11,300 |
| Owner's capital, September 30 | | $ 3,700 |

**Illustration 1-10**
Presentation of net loss

If the owner makes any additional investments, the company reports them in the owner's equity statement as investments.

## Balance Sheet

Softbyte's balance sheet reports the assets, liabilities, and owner's equity at a specific date (in Softbyte's case, September 30, 2014). The company prepares the balance sheet from the column headings of the tabular summary (Illustration 1-8) and the month-end data shown in its last line.

Observe that the balance sheet lists assets at the top, followed by liabilities and owner's equity. Total assets must equal total liabilities and owner's equity. Softbyte reports only one liability—accounts payable—in its balance sheet. In most cases, there will be more than one liability. When two or more liabilities are involved, a customary way of listing is as follows.

**Illustration 1-11**
Presentation of liabilities

| Liabilities | |
|---|---|
| Notes payable | $ 10,000 |
| Accounts payable | 63,000 |
| Salaries and wages payable | 18,000 |
| **Total liabilities** | **$91,000** |

The balance sheet is a snapshot of the company's financial condition at a specific moment in time (usually the month-end or year-end).

## Statement of Cash Flows

The statement of cash flows provides information on the cash receipts and payments for a specific period of time. The statement of cash flows reports (1) the cash effects of a company's operations during a period, (2) its investing activities, (3) its financing activities, (4) the net increase or decrease in cash during the period, and (5) the cash amount at the end of the period.

Reporting the sources, uses, and change in cash is useful because investors, creditors, and others want to know what is happening to a company's most liquid resource. The statement of cash flows provides answers to the following simple but important questions.

1. Where did cash come from during the period?
2. What was cash used for during the period?
3. What was the change in the cash balance during the period?

As shown in Softbyte's statement of cash flows, cash increased $8,050 during the period. Net cash provided by operating activities increased cash $1,350. Cash flow from investing activities decreased cash $7,000. And cash flow from financing activities increased cash $13,700. At this time, you need not be concerned with how these amounts are determined. Chapter 17 will examine the statement of cash flows in detail.

# PEOPLE, PLANET, AND PROFIT INSIGHT

### Beyond Financial Statements

Should we expand our financial statements beyond the income statement, owner's equity statement, balance sheet, and statement of cash flows? Some believe we should take into account ecological and social performance, in addition to financial results, in evaluating a company. The argument is that a company's responsibility lies with anyone who is influenced by its actions. In other words, a company should be interested in benefiting many different parties, instead of only maximizing stockholders' interests.

A socially responsible business does not exploit or endanger any group of individuals. It follows fair trade practices, provides safe environments for workers, and bears responsibility for environmental damage. Granted, measurement of these factors is difficult. How to report this information is also controversial. But many interesting and useful efforts are underway. Throughout this textbook, we provide additional insights into how companies are attempting to meet the challenge of measuring and reporting their contributions to society, as well as their financial results, to stockholders.

**?** Why might a company's stockholders be interested in its environmental and social performance? (See page 48.)

---

## > DO IT!

### Financial Statement Items

Presented below is selected information related to Flanagan Company at December 31, 2014. Flanagan reports financial information monthly.

| | | | |
|---|---|---|---|
| Equipment | $10,000 | Utilities Expense | $ 4,000 |
| Cash | 8,000 | Accounts Receivable | 9,000 |
| Service Revenue | 36,000 | Salaries and Wages Expense | 7,000 |
| Rent Expense | 11,000 | Notes Payable | 16,500 |
| Accounts Payable | 2,000 | Owner's Drawings | 5,000 |

(a) Determine the total assets of Flanagan Company at December 31, 2014.
(b) Determine the net income that Flanagan Company reported for December 2014.
(c) Determine the owner's equity of Flanagan Company at December 31, 2014.

### Solution

**Action Plan**

✔ Remember the basic accounting equation: assets must equal liabilities plus owner's equity.

✔ Review previous financial statements to determine how total assets, net income, and owner's equity are computed.

(a) The total assets are $27,000, comprised of Cash $8,000, Accounts Receivable $9,000, and Equipment $10,000.

(b) Net income is $14,000, computed as follows.

| | | |
|---|---|---|
| Revenues | | |
| Service revenue | | $36,000 |
| Expenses | | |
| Rent expense | $11,000 | |
| Salaries and wages expense | 7,000 | |
| Utilities expense | 4,000 | |
| Total expenses | | 22,000 |
| Net income | | $14,000 |

**(c)** The ending owner's equity of Flanagan Company is $8,500. By rewriting the accounting equation, we can compute owner's equity as assets minus liabilities, as follows.

| | | |
|---|---:|---:|
| Total assets [as computed in (a)] | | $27,000 |
| Less: Liabilities | | |
| Notes payable | $16,500 | |
| Accounts payable | 2,000 | 18,500 |
| Owner's equity | | $ 8,500 |

Note that it is not possible to determine the company's owner's equity in any other way because the beginning total for owner's equity is not provided.

Related exercise material: **BE1-10, BE1-11, E1-9, E1-12, E1-13, E1-14, E1-15, E1-16, and DO IT! 1-4.**

✔ The Navigator

## > Comprehensive DO IT!

*The **Comprehensive DO IT!** is a final review of the chapter. The **Action Plan** gives tips about how to approach the problem, and the **Solution** demonstrates both the form and content of complete answers.*

Joan Robinson opens her own law office on July 1, 2014. During the first month of operations, the following transactions occurred.

1. Joan invested $11,000 in cash in the law practice.
2. Paid $800 for July rent on office space.
3. Purchased office equipment on account $3,000.
4. Performed legal services to clients for cash $1,500.
5. Borrowed $700 cash from a bank on a note payable.
6. Performed legal services for client on account $2,000.
7. Paid monthly expenses: salaries and wages $500, utilities $300, and advertising $100.
8. Joan withdraws $1,000 cash for personal use.

### Instructions
**(a)** Prepare a tabular summary of the transactions.
**(b)** Prepare the income statement, owner's equity statement, and balance sheet at July 31 for Joan Robinson, Attorney.

### Solution to Comprehensive DO IT!

**(a)**

| Trans-action | Cash | + | Accounts Receivable | + | Equipment | = | Notes Payable | + | Accounts Payable | + | Owner's Capital | − | Owner's Drawings | + | Revenues | − | Expenses |
|---|---|---|---|---|---|---|---|---|---|---|---|---|---|---|---|---|---|
| (1) | +$11,000 | | | | | = | | | | | +$11,000 | | | | | | |
| (2) | −800 | | | | | | | | | | | | | | | | −$800 |
| (3) | | | | | +$3,000 | = | | | +$3,000 | | | | | | | | |
| (4) | +1,500 | | | | | | | | | | | | | | +$1,500 | | |
| (5) | +700 | | | | | | +$700 | | | | | | | | | | |
| (6) | | | +$2,000 | | | | | | | | | | | | +2,000 | | |
| (7) | −500 | | | | | | | | | | | | | | | | −500 |
| | −300 | | | | | | | | | | | | | | | | −300 |
| | −100 | | | | | | | | | | | | | | | | −100 |
| (8) | −1,000 | | | | | | | | | | | − | −$1,000 | | | | |
| | $10,500 | + | $2,000 | + | $3,000 | = | $700 | + | $3,000 | + | $11,000 | − | $1,000 | + | $3,500 | − | $1,700 |

Assets = $15,500

Liabilities + Owner's Equity = $15,500

**Action Plan**

✔ Make sure that assets equal liabilities plus owner's equity after each transaction.

✔ Investments and revenues increase owner's equity. Withdrawals and expenses decrease owner's equity.

✔ Prepare the financial statements in the order listed.

✔ The income statement shows revenues and expenses for a period of time.

✔ The owner's equity statement shows the changes in owner's equity for the same period of time as the income statement.

✔ The balance sheet reports assets, liabilities, and owner's equity at a specific date.

### JOAN ROBINSON, ATTORNEY
### Income Statement
### Month Ended July 31, 2014

| | | |
|---|---:|---:|
| Revenues | | |
| Service revenue | | $3,500 |
| Expenses | | |
| Rent expense | $800 | |
| Salaries and wages expense | 500 | |
| Utilities expense | 300 | |
| Advertising expense | 100 | |
| Total expenses | | 1,700 |
| Net income | | $1,800 |

### JOAN ROBINSON, ATTORNEY
### Owner's Equity Statement
### Month Ended July 31, 2014

| | | |
|---|---:|---:|
| Owner's capital, July 1 | | $    0 |
| Add: Investments | $11,000 | |
| Net income | 1,800 | 12,800 |
| | | 12,800 |
| Less: Drawings | | 1,000 |
| Owner's capital, July 31 | | $11,800 |

### JOAN ROBINSON, ATTORNEY
### Balance Sheet
### July 31, 2014

#### Assets

| | |
|---|---:|
| Cash | $10,500 |
| Accounts receivable | 2,000 |
| Equipment | 3,000 |
| Total assets | $15,500 |

#### Liabilities and Owner's Equity

| | | |
|---|---:|---:|
| Liabilities | | |
| Notes payable | | $   700 |
| Accounts payable | | 3,000 |
| Total liabilities | | 3,700 |
| Owner's equity | | |
| Owner's capital | | 11,800 |
| Total liabilities and owner's equity | | $15,500 |

 The Navigator

 The Navigator

# SUMMARY OF LEARNING OBJECTIVES

1 **Explain what accounting is.** Accounting is an information system that identifies, records, and communicates the economic events of an organization to interested users.

2 **Identify the users and uses of accounting.** The major users and uses of accounting are as follows. (a) Management uses accounting information to plan, organize,

and run the business. (b) Investors (owners) decide whether to buy, hold, or sell their financial interests on the basis of accounting data. (c) Creditors (suppliers and bankers) evaluate the risks of granting credit or lending money on the basis of accounting information. Other groups that use accounting information are taxing authorities, regulatory agencies, customers, and labor unions.

3 **Understand why ethics is a fundamental business concept.** Ethics are the standards of conduct by which actions are judged as right or wrong. Effective financial reporting depends on sound ethical behavior.

4 **Explain generally accepted accounting principles.** Generally accepted accounting principles are a common set of standards used by accountants.

5 **Explain the monetary unit assumption and the economic entity assumption.** The monetary unit assumption requires that companies include in the accounting records only transaction data that can be expressed in terms of money. The economic entity assumption requires that the activities of each economic entity be kept separate from the activities of its owner(s) and other economic entities.

6 **State the accounting equation, and define its components.** The basic accounting equation is:

$$\text{Assets} = \text{Liabilities} + \text{Owner's Equity}$$

Assets are resources a business owns. Liabilities are creditorship claims on total assets. Owner's equity is the ownership claim on total assets.

The expanded accounting equation is:

$$\text{Assets} = \text{Liabilities} + \text{Owner's Capital} - \text{Owner's Drawings} + \text{Revenues} - \text{Expenses}$$

Owner's capital is assets the owner puts into the business. Owner's drawings are the assets the owner withdraws for personal use. Revenues are increases in assets resulting from income-earning activities. Expenses are the costs of assets consumed or services used in the process of earning revenue.

7 **Analyze the effects of business transactions on the accounting equation.** Each business transaction must have a dual effect on the accounting equation. For example, if an individual asset increases, there must be a corresponding (1) decrease in another asset, or (2) increase in a specific liability, or (3) increase in owner's equity.

8 **Understand the four financial statements and how they are prepared.** An income statement presents the revenues and expenses, and resulting net income or net loss, for a specific period of time. An owner's equity statement summarizes the changes in owner's equity for a specific period of time. A balance sheet reports the assets, liabilities, and owner's equity at a specific date. A statement of cash flows summarizes information about the cash inflows (receipts) and outflows (payments) for a specific period of time.

## GLOSSARY

**Accounting** The information system that identifies, records, and communicates the economic events of an organization to interested users. (p. 4).

**Assets** Resources a business owns. (p. 13).

**Balance sheet** A financial statement that reports the assets, liabilities, and owner's equity at a specific date. (p. 21).

**Basic accounting equation** Assets = Liabilities + Owner's Equity. (p. 13).

**Bookkeeping** A part of accounting that involves only the recording of economic events. (p. 5).

**Convergence** The process of reducing the differences between U.S. GAAP and IFRS. (p. 9).

**Corporation** A business organized as a separate legal entity under state corporation law, having ownership divided into transferable shares of stock. (p. 11).

**Drawings** Withdrawal of cash or other assets from an unincorporated business for the personal use of the owner(s). (p. 14).

**Economic entity assumption** An assumption that requires that the activities of the entity be kept separate and distinct from the activities of its owner and all other economic entities. (p. 10).

**Ethics** The standards of conduct by which one's actions are judged as right or wrong, honest or dishonest, fair or not fair. (p. 7).

**Expanded accounting equation** Assets = Liabilities + Owner's Capital − Owner's Drawings + Revenues − Expenses. (p. 14).

**Expenses** The cost of assets consumed or services used in the process of earning revenue. (p. 14).

**Fair value principle** An accounting principle stating that assets and liabilities should be reported at fair value (the price received to sell an asset or settle a liability). (p. 9).

**Faithful representation** Numbers and descriptions match what really existed or happened—they are factual. (p. 9).

**Financial accounting** The field of accounting that provides economic and financial information for investors, creditors, and other external users. (p. 6).

**Financial Accounting Standards Board (FASB)** A private organization that establishes generally accepted accounting principles in the United States (GAAP). (p. 9).

**Generally accepted accounting principles (GAAP)** Common standards that indicate how to report economic events. (p. 8).

**Historical cost principle** An accounting principle that states that companies should record assets at their cost. (p. 9).

**Income statement** A financial statement that presents the revenues and expenses and resulting net income or net loss of a company for a specific period of time. (p. 21).

**International Accounting Standards Board (IASB)** An accounting standard-setting body that issues standards adopted by many countries outside of the United States. (p. 9).

**International Financial Reporting Standards (IFRS)** International accounting standards set by the International Accounting Standards Board (IASB). (p. 9).

**Investments by owner** The assets an owner puts into the business. (p. 13).

**Liabilities** Creditor claims against total assets. (p. 13).

**Managerial accounting** The field of accounting that provides internal reports to help users make decisions about their companies. (p. 6).

**Monetary unit assumption** An assumption stating that companies include in the accounting records only transaction data that can be expressed in terms of money. (p. 10).

**Net income** The amount by which revenues exceed expenses. (p. 23).

**Net loss** The amount by which expenses exceed revenues. (p. 23).

**Owner's equity** The ownership claim on total assets. (p. 13).

**Owner's equity statement** A financial statement that summarizes the changes in owner's equity for a specific period of time. (p. 21).

**Partnership** A business owned by two or more persons associated as partners. (p. 11).

**Proprietorship** A business owned by one person. (p. 10).

**Relevance** Financial information that is capable of making a difference in a decision. (p. 9).

**Revenues** The gross increase in owner's equity resulting from business activities entered into for the purpose of earning income. (p. 13).

**Sarbanes-Oxley Act (SOX)** Law passed by Congress intended to reduce unethical corporate behavior. (p. 7).

**Securities and Exchange Commission (SEC)** A governmental agency that oversees U.S. financial markets and accounting standard-setting bodies. (p. 9).

**Statement of cash flows** A financial statement that summarizes information about the cash inflows (receipts) and cash outflows (payments) for a specific period of time. (p. 21).

**Transactions** The economic events of a business that are recorded by accountants. (p. 15).

# APPENDIX 1A    Accounting Career Opportunities

Why is accounting such a popular major and career choice? First, there are a lot of jobs. In many cities in recent years, the demand for accountants exceeded the supply. Not only are there a lot of jobs, but there are a wide array of opportunities. As one accounting organization observed, "accounting is one degree with 360 degrees of opportunity."

> **LEARNING OBJECTIVE  9**
>
> Explain the career opportunities in accounting.

Accounting is also hot because it is obvious that accounting matters. Interest in accounting has increased, ironically, because of the attention caused by the accounting failures of companies such as Enron and WorldCom. These widely publicized scandals revealed the important role that accounting plays in society. Most people want to make a difference, and an accounting career provides many opportunities to contribute to society. Finally, the Sarbanes-Oxley Act (SOX) (see page 7) significantly increased the accounting and internal control requirements for corporations. This dramatically increased demand for professionals with accounting training.

Accountants are in such demand that it is not uncommon for accounting students to have accepted a job offer a year before graduation. As the following discussion reveals, the job options of people with accounting degrees are virtually unlimited.

## Public Accounting

Individuals in **public accounting** offer expert service to the general public, in much the same way that doctors serve patients and lawyers serve clients. A major portion of public accounting involves **auditing**. In auditing, a certified public accountant (CPA) examines company financial statements and provides an opinion as to how accurately the financial statements present the company's results and financial position. Analysts, investors, and creditors rely heavily on these "audit opinions," which CPAs have the exclusive authority to issue.

**Taxation** is another major area of public accounting. The work that tax specialists perform includes tax advice and planning, preparing tax returns, and representing clients before governmental agencies such as the Internal Revenue Service.

A third area in public accounting is **management consulting**. It ranges from installing basic accounting software or highly complex enterprise resource planning systems, to performing support services for major marketing projects and merger and acquisition activities.

Many CPAs are entrepreneurs. They form small- or medium-sized practices that frequently specialize in tax or consulting services.

## Private Accounting

Instead of working in public accounting, you might choose to be an employee of a for-profit company such as Starbucks, Google, or PepsiCo. In **private** (or **managerial**) **accounting**, you would be involved in activities such as cost accounting (finding the cost of producing specific products), budgeting, accounting information system design and support, and tax planning and preparation. You might also be a member of your company's internal audit team. In response to SOX, the internal auditors' job of reviewing the company's operations to ensure compliance with company policies and to increase efficiency has taken on increased importance.

Alternatively, many accountants work for not-for-profit organizations such as the Red Cross or the Bill and Melinda Gates Foundation, or for museums, libraries, or performing arts organizations.

## Governmental Accounting

Another option is to pursue one of the many accounting opportunities in governmental agencies. For example, the Internal Revenue Service (IRS), Federal Bureau of Investigation (FBI), and the Securities and Exchange Commission (SEC) all employ accountants. The FBI has a stated goal that at least 15 percent of its new agents should be CPAs. There is also a very high demand for accounting educators at public colleges and universities and in state and local governments.

## Forensic Accounting

**Forensic accounting** uses accounting, auditing, and investigative skills to conduct investigations into theft and fraud. It is listed among the top 20 career paths of the future. The job of forensic accountants is to catch the perpetrators of the estimated $600 billion per year of theft and fraud occurring at U.S. companies. This includes tracing money-laundering and identity-theft activities as well as tax evasion. Insurance companies hire forensic accountants to detect frauds such as arson, and law offices employ forensic accountants to identify marital assets in divorces. Forensic accountants often have FBI, IRS, or similar government experience.

## "Show Me the Money"

How much can a new accountant make? Take a look at the average salaries for college graduates in public and private accounting. Keep in mind if you also have a CPA license, you'll make 10–15% more when you start out.

**Illustration 1A-1**
Salary estimates for jobs in public and corporate accounting

| Employer | Jr. Level (0–3 yrs.) | Sr. Level (4–6 yrs.) |
|---|---|---|
| Public accounting (large firm) | $48,750–$69,250 | $66,750–$86,000 |
| Public accounting (small firm) | $41,000–$56,000 | $54,000–$69,750 |
| Corporate accounting (large company) | $38,000–$57,250 | $55,750–$73,500 |
| Corporate accounting (small company) | $33,500–$49,000 | $46,500–$58,750 |

Serious earning potential over time gives CPAs great job security. Here are some examples of upper-level salaries for managers in corporate accounting. Note that geographic region, experience, education, CPA certification, and company size each play a role in determining salary.

| Position | Large Company | Small to Medium Company |
|---|---|---|
| Chief financial officer | $183,250–$384,000 | $94,250–$175,750 |
| Corporate controller | $122,000–$180,000 | $80,500–$134,750 |
| Tax manager | $ 92,250–$130,250 | $74,250–$100,250 |

**Illustration 1A-2**
Upper-level management salaries in corporate accounting

For up-to-date salary estimates, as well as a wealth of additional information regarding accounting as a career, check out **www.startheregoplaces.com.**

## SUMMARY OF LEARNING OBJECTIVE FOR APPENDIX 1A

**9 Explain the career opportunities in accounting.** Accounting offers many different jobs in fields such as public and private accounting, governmental, and forensic accounting. Accounting is a popular major because there are many different types of jobs, with unlimited potential for career advancement.

## GLOSSARY FOR APPENDIX 1A

**Auditing** The examination of financial statements by a certified public accountant in order to express an opinion as to the fairness of presentation. (p. 29).

**Forensic accounting** An area of accounting that uses accounting, auditing, and investigative skills to conduct investigations into theft and fraud. (p. 30).

**Management consulting** An area of public accounting ranging from development of accounting and computer systems to support services for marketing projects and merger and acquisition activities. (p. 30).

**Private (or managerial) accounting** An area of accounting within a company that involves such activities

as cost accounting, budgeting, design and support of accounting information systems, and tax planning and preparation. (p. 30).

**Public accounting** An area of accounting in which the accountant offers expert service to the general public. (p. 29).

**Taxation** An area of public accounting involving tax advice, tax planning, preparing tax returns, and representing clients before governmental agencies. (p. 30).

 **Self-Test, Brief Exercises, Exercises, Problem Set A, and many more components are available for practice in *WileyPLUS*.**

**\*Note:** All asterisked Questions, Exercises, and Problems relate to material in the appendix to the chapter.

## SELF-TEST QUESTIONS

*Answers are on page 48.*

(LO 1) **1.** Which of the following is **not** a step in the accounting process?
  (a) Identification.      (c) Recording.
  (b) Verification.        (d) Communication.

(LO 2) **2.** Which of the following statements about users of accounting information is **incorrect**?
  (a) Management is an internal user.
  (b) Taxing authorities are external users.

  (c) Present creditors are external users.
  (d) Regulatory authorities are internal users.

**3.** The historical cost principle states that:  (LO
  (a) assets should be initially recorded at cost and adjusted when the fair value changes.
  (b) activities of an entity are to be kept separate and distinct from its owner.
  (c) assets should be recorded at their cost.

(d) only transaction data capable of being expressed in terms of money be included in the accounting records.

(LO 5) **4.** Which of the following statements about basic assumptions is **correct**?

(a) Basic assumptions are the same as accounting principles.

(b) The economic entity assumption states that there should be a particular unit of accountability.

(c) The monetary unit assumption enables accounting to measure employee morale.

(d) Partnerships are not economic entities.

(LO 5) **5.** The three types of business entities are:

(a) proprietorships, small businesses, and partnerships.

(b) proprietorships, partnerships, and corporations.

(c) proprietorships, partnerships, and large businesses.

(d) financial, manufacturing, and service companies.

(LO 6) **6.** Net income will result during a time period when:

(a) assets exceed liabilities.

(b) assets exceed revenues.

(c) expenses exceed revenues.

(d) revenues exceed expenses.

(LO 6) **7.** As of December 31, 2014, Kent Company has assets of $3,500 and owner's equity of $2,000. What are the liabilities for Kent Company as of December 31, 2014?

(a) $1,500.

(b) $1,000.

(c) $2,500.

(d) $2,000.

(LO 7) **8.** Performing services on account will have the following effects on the components of the basic accounting equation:

(a) increase assets and decrease owner's equity.

(b) increase assets and increase owner's equity.

(c) increase assets and increase liabilities.

(d) increase liabilities and increase owner's equity.

(LO 7) **9.** Which of the following events is **not** recorded in the accounting records?

(a) Equipment is purchased on account.

(b) An employee is terminated.

(c) A cash investment is made into the business.

(d) The owner withdraws cash for personal use.

**10.** During 2014, Bruske Company's assets decreased (LO 7) $50,000 and its liabilities decreased $90,000. Its owner's equity therefore:

(a) increased $40,000.     (c) decreased $40,000.

(b) decreased $140,000.     (d) increased $140,000.

**11.** Payment of an account payable affects the compo- (LO 7) nents of the accounting equation in the following way.

(a) Decreases owner's equity and decreases liabilities.

(b) Increases assets and decreases liabilities.

(c) Decreases assets and increases owner's equity.

(d) Decreases assets and decreases liabilities.

**12.** Which of the following statements is **false**?     (LO 8)

(a) A statement of cash flows summarizes information about the cash inflows (receipts) and outflows (payments) for a specific period of time.

(b) A balance sheet reports the assets, liabilities, and owner's equity at a specific date.

(c) An income statement presents the revenues, expenses, changes in owner's equity, and resulting net income or net loss for a specific period of time.

(d) An owner's equity statement summarizes the changes in owner's equity for a specific period of time.

**13.** On the last day of the period, Alan Cesska Company (LO 8) buys a $900 machine on credit. This transaction will affect the:

(a) income statement only.

(b) balance sheet only.

(c) income statement and owner's equity statement only.

(d) income statement, owner's equity statement, and balance sheet.

**14.** The financial statement that reports assets, liabilities, (LO 8) and owner's equity is the:

(a) income statement.

(b) owner's equity statement.

(c) balance sheet.

(d) statement of cash flows.

***15.** Services performed by a public accountant include:     (LO 9)

(a) auditing, taxation, and management consulting.

(b) auditing, budgeting, and management consulting.

(c) auditing, budgeting, and cost accounting.

(d) internal auditing, budgeting, and management consulting.

Go to the book's companion website, www.wiley.com/college/weygandt, for additional Self-Test Questions.

✔ **The Navigator**

## QUESTIONS

**1.** "Accounting is ingrained in our society and it is vital to our economic system." Do you agree? Explain.

**2.** Identify and describe the steps in the accounting process.

**3.** (a) Who are internal users of accounting data? (b) How does accounting provide relevant data to these users?

**4.** What uses of financial accounting information are made by (a) investors and (b) creditors?

**5.** "Bookkeeping and accounting are the same." Do you agree? Explain.

**6.** Trenton Travel Agency purchased land for $90,000 cash on December 10, 2014. At December 31, 2014, the land's value has increased to $93,000. What amount should be reported for land on Trenton's balance sheet at December 31, 2014? Explain.

7. What is the monetary unit assumption?

8. What is the economic entity assumption?

9. What are the three basic forms of business organizations for profit-oriented enterprises?

10. Rachel Hipp is the owner of a successful printing shop. Recently, her business has been increasing, and Rachel has been thinking about changing the organization of her business from a proprietorship to a corporation. Discuss some of the advantages Rachel would enjoy if she were to incorporate her business.

11. What is the basic accounting equation?

12. **(a)** Define the terms assets, liabilities, and owner's equity.

**(b)** What items affect owner's equity?

13. Which of the following items are liabilities of Siebers Jewelry Stores?

**(a)** Cash.

**(b)** Accounts payable.

**(c)** Owner's drawings.

**(d)** Accounts receivable.

**(e)** Supplies.

**(f)** Equipment.

**(g)** Salaries and wages payable.

**(h)** Service revenue.

**(i)** Rent expense.

14. Can a business enter into a transaction in which only the left side of the basic accounting equation is affected? If so, give an example.

15. Are the following events recorded in the accounting records? Explain your answer in each case.

**(a)** The owner of the company dies.

**(b)** Supplies are purchased on account.

**(c)** An employee is fired.

**(d)** The owner of the business withdraws cash from the business for personal use.

16. Indicate how the following business transactions affect the basic accounting equation.

**(a)** Paid cash for janitorial services.

**(b)** Purchased equipment for cash.

**(c)** Invested cash in the business.

**(d)** Paid accounts payable in full.

17. Listed below are some items found in the financial statements of Tony Gruber Co. Indicate in which financial statement(s) the following items would appear.

**(a)** Service revenue.

**(b)** Equipment.

**(c)** Advertising expense.

**(d)** Accounts receivable.

**(e)** Owner's capital.

**(f)** Salaries and wages payable.

18. In February 2014, Maria Osgood invested an additional $10,000 in her business, Osgood's Pharmacy, which is organized as a proprietorship. Osgood's accountant, Carl Sota, recorded this receipt as an increase in cash and revenues. Is this treatment appropriate? Why or why not?

19. "A company's net income appears directly on the income statement and the owner's equity statement, and it is included indirectly in the company's balance sheet." Do you agree? Explain.

20. Saylor Enterprises had a capital balance of $168,000 at the beginning of the period. At the end of the accounting period, the capital balance was $198,000.

**(a)** Assuming no additional investment or withdrawals during the period, what is the net income for the period?

**(b)** Assuming an additional investment of $13,000 but no withdrawals during the period, what is the net income for the period?

21. Summarized operations for Bayles Co. for the month of July are as follows.

Revenues recognized: for cash $20,000; on account $70,000.

Expenses incurred: for cash $26,000; on account $40,000.

Indicate for Bayles Co. (a) the total revenues, (b) the total expenses, and (c) net income for the month of July.

22. The basic accounting equation is Assets = Liabilities + Owner's Equity. Replacing the words in that equation with dollar amounts, what is Apple's accounting equation at September 24, 2011? (*Hint:* Owner's equity is equivalent to shareholders' equity.)

## BRIEF EXERCISES

**BE1-1** Presented below is the basic accounting equation. Determine the missing amounts.

*Use basic accounting equation.*

(LO 6)

| Assets | = | Liabilities | + | Owner's Equity |
|---|---|---|---|---|
| **(a)** $90,000 | | $50,000 | | ? |
| **(b)** ? | | $40,000 | | $70,000 |
| **(c)** $94,000 | | ? | | $53,000 |

**BE1-2** Given the accounting equation, answer each of the following questions.

*Use basic accounting equation.*

(LO 6)

**(a)** The liabilities of Grieg Company are $120,000 and the owner's equity is $232,000. What is the amount of Grieg Company's total assets?

**(b)** The total assets of Grieg Company are $190,000 and its owner's equity is $91,000. What is the amount of its total liabilities?

**(c)** The total assets of Grieg Company are $800,000 and its liabilities are equal to one-half of its total assets. What is the amount of Grieg Company's owner's equity?

*Use basic accounting equation.*
(LO 6)

**BE1-3** At the beginning of the year, Sielert Company had total assets of $800,000 and total liabilities of $300,000. Answer the following questions.

**(a)** If total assets increased $150,000 during the year and total liabilities decreased $80,000, what is the amount of owner's equity at the end of the year?

**(b)** During the year, total liabilities increased $100,000 and owner's equity decreased $70,000. What is the amount of total assets at the end of the year?

**(c)** If total assets decreased $80,000 and owner's equity increased $120,000 during the year, what is the amount of total liabilities at the end of the year?

*Solve expanded accounting equation.*
(LO 6)

**BE1-4** Use the expanded accounting equation to answer each of the following questions.

**(a)** The liabilities of Roman Company are $90,000. Owner's capital account is $150,000; drawings are $40,000; revenues, $450,000; and expenses, $320,000. What is the amount of Roman Company's total assets?

**(b)** The total assets of Dylan Company are $57,000. Owner's capital account is $25,000; drawings are $7,000; revenues, $52,000; and expenses, $35,000. What is the amount of the company's total liabilities?

**(c)** The total assets of Capp Co. are $600,000 and its liabilities are equal to two-thirds of its total assets. What is the amount of Capp Co.'s owner's equity?

*Identify assets, liabilities, and owner's equity.*
(LO 6)

**BE1-5** Indicate whether each of the following items is an asset (A), liability (L), or part of owner's equity (OE).

_____ **(a)** Accounts receivable        _____ **(d)** Supplies
_____ **(b)** Salaries and wages payable  _____ **(e)** Owner's capital
_____ **(c)** Equipment                   _____ **(f)** Notes payable

*Determine effect of transactions on basic accounting equation.*
(LO 7)

**BE1-6** Presented below are three business transactions. On a sheet of paper, list the letters (a), (b), and (c) with columns for assets, liabilities, and owner's equity. For each column, indicate whether the transactions increased (+), decreased (−), or had no effect (NE) on assets, liabilities, and owner's equity.

**(a)** Purchased supplies on account.
**(b)** Received cash for performing a service.
**(c)** Paid expenses in cash.

*Determine effect of transactions on basic accounting equation.*
(LO 7)

**BE1-7** Follow the same format as in BE1-6. Determine the effect on assets, liabilities, and owner's equity of the following three transactions.

**(a)** Invested cash in the business.
**(b)** Withdrawal of cash by owner.
**(c)** Received cash from a customer who had previously been billed for services performed.

*Classify items affecting owner's equity.*
(LO 7)

**BE1-8** Classify each of the following items as owner's drawings (D), revenue (R), or expense (E).

_____ **(a)** Advertising expense       _____ **(e)** Owner's drawings
_____ **(b)** Service revenue           _____ **(f)** Rent revenue
_____ **(c)** Insurance expense         _____ **(g)** Utilities expense
_____ **(d)** Salaries and wages expense

*Determine effect of transactions on basic owner's equity.*
(LO 7)

**BE1-9** Presented below are three transactions. Mark each transaction as affecting owner's investment (I), owner's drawings (D), revenue (R), expense (E), or not affecting owner's equity (NOE).

_____ **(a)** Received cash for services performed
_____ **(b)** Paid cash to purchase equipment
_____ **(c)** Paid employee salaries

*Prepare a balance sheet.*
(LO 8)

**BE1-10** In alphabetical order below are balance sheet items for Fritz Company at December 31, 2014. Molly Fritz is the owner of Fritz Company. Prepare a balance sheet, following the format of Illustration 1-9.

| | |
|---|---|
| Accounts payable | $90,000 |
| Accounts receivable | $72,500 |
| Cash | $49,000 |
| Owner's capital | $31,500 |

**BE1-11** Indicate whether the following items would appear on the income statement (IS), balance sheet (BS), or owner's equity statement (OE).

_____ **(a)** Notes payable          _____ **(d)** Cash
_____ **(b)** Advertising expense     _____ **(e)** Service revenue
_____ **(c)** Owner's capital

*Determine where items appear on financial statements.*
*(LO 8)*

## > DO IT! Review

**DO IT! 1-1** Indicate whether each of the five statements presented below is true or false.

1. The three steps in the accounting process are identification, recording, and examination.
2. The two most common types of external users are investors and creditors.
3. Congress passed the Sarbanes-Oxley Act to ensure that investors invest only in companies that will be profitable.
4. The primary accounting standard-setting body in the United States is the Securities and Exchange Commission (SEC).
5. The historical cost principle dictates that companies record assets at their cost and continue to report them at their cost over the time the asset is held.

*Review basic concepts.*
*(LO 1, 2, 3, 4)*

**DO IT! 1-2** Classify the following items as investment by owner (I), owner's drawings (D), revenues (R), or expenses (E). Then indicate whether each item increases or decreases owner's equity.

**(1)** Drawings.                    **(3)** Advertising expense.
**(2)** Rent revenue.                **(4)** Owner puts personal assets into the business.

*Evaluate effects of transactions on owner's equity.*
*(LO 6)*

**DO IT! 1-3** Transactions made by J. Depp and Co., a law firm, for the month of March are shown below. Prepare a tabular analysis which shows the effects of these transactions on the expanded accounting equation, similar to that shown in Illustration 1-8.

1. The company performed $20,000 of services for customers, on credit.
2. The company received $20,000 in cash from customers who had been billed for services (in transaction 1).
3. The company received a bill for $2,300 of advertising, but will not pay it until a later date.
4. J. Depp withdrew $3,600 cash from the business for personal use.

*Prepare tabular analysis.*
*(LO 7)*

**DO IT! 1-4** Presented below is selected information related to Howard Company at December 31, 2014. Howard reports financial information monthly.

| | | | |
|---|---|---|---|
| Accounts Payable | $ 3,000 | Salaries and Wages Expense | $16,500 |
| Cash | 4,500 | Notes Payable | 25,000 |
| Advertising Expense | 6,000 | Rent Expense | 10,500 |
| Service Revenue | 51,500 | Accounts Receivable | 13,500 |
| Equipment | 29,000 | Owner's Drawings | 7,500 |

**(a)** Determine the total assets of Howard Company at December 31, 2014.
**(b)** Determine the net income that Howard Company reported for December 2014.
**(c)** Determine the owner's equity of Howard Company at December 31, 2014.

*Calculate effects of transactions on financial statement items.*
*(LO 6, 8)*

## EXERCISES

**E1-1** Zimmerman Company performs the following accounting tasks during the year.

_____Analyzing and interpreting information.
_____Classifying economic events.
_____Explaining uses, meaning, and limitations of data.
_____Keeping a systematic chronological diary of events.
_____Measuring events in dollars and cents.

*Classify the three activities of accounting.*
*(LO 1)*

_____Preparing accounting reports.

_____Reporting information in a standard format.

_____Selecting economic activities relevant to the company.

_____Summarizing economic events.

Accounting is "an information system that **identifies**, **records**, and **communicates** the economic events of an organization to interested users."

**Instructions**

Categorize the accounting tasks performed by Zimmerman as relating to either the identification (I), recording (R), or communication (C) aspects of accounting.

*Identify users of accounting information.*

*(LO 2)*

**E1-2 (a)** The following are users of financial statements.

_____Customers

_____Internal Revenue Service

_____Labor unions

_____Marketing manager

_____Production supervisor

_____Securities and Exchange Commission

_____Store manager

_____Suppliers

_____Vice president of finance

**Instructions**

Identify the users as being either **external users** or **internal users**.

**(b)** The following questions could be asked by an internal user or an external user.

_____Can we afford to give our employees a pay raise?

_____Did the company earn a satisfactory income?

_____Do we need to borrow in the near future?

_____How does the company's profitability compare to other companies?

_____What does it cost us to manufacture each unit produced?

_____Which product should we emphasize?

_____Will the company be able to pay its short-term debts?

**Instructions**

Identify each of the questions as being more likely asked by an **internal user** or an **external user**.

*Discuss ethics and the historical cost principle.*

*(LO 3, 4)*

**E1-3** Jill Motta, president of Motta Company, has instructed Linda Berger, the head of the accounting department for Motta Company, to report the company's land in the company's accounting reports at its fair value of $170,000 instead of its cost of $100,000. Motta says, "Showing the land at $170,000 will make our company look like a better investment when we try to attract new investors next month."

**Instructions**

Explain the ethical situation involved for Linda Berger, identifying the stakeholders and the alternatives.

*Use accounting concepts.*

*(LO 4, 5)*

**E1-4** The following situations involve accounting principles and assumptions.

**1.** Piang Company owns buildings that are worth substantially more than they originally cost. In an effort to provide more relevant information, Piang reports the buildings at fair value in its accounting reports.

**2.** Delta Company includes in its accounting records only transaction data that can be expressed in terms of money.

**3.** Luke Witte, owner of Luke's Photography, records his personal living costs as expenses of the business.

**Instructions**

For each of the three situations, say if the accounting method used is correct or incorrect. If correct, identify which principle or assumption supports the method used. If incorrect, identify which principle or assumption has been violated.

*Classify accounts as assets, liabilities, and owner's equity.*

*(LO 6)*

**E1-5** Tomlin Cleaners has the following balance sheet items.

| | |
|---|---|
| Accounts payable | Accounts receivable |
| Cash | Notes payable |
| Equipment | Salaries and wages payable |
| Supplies | Owner's capital |

**Instructions**

Classify each item as an asset, liability, or owner's equity.

**E1-6** Selected transactions for Tara Lawn Care Company are listed below.

*Analyze the effect of transactions.*

(LO 6, 7)

1. Made cash investment to start business.
2. Paid monthly rent.
3. Purchased equipment on account.
4. Billed customers for services performed.
5. Withdrew cash for owner's personal use.
6. Received cash from customers billed in (4).
7. Incurred advertising expense on account.
8. Purchased additional equipment for cash.
9. Received cash from customers when service was performed.

**Instructions**

List the numbers of the above transactions and describe the effect of each transaction on assets, liabilities, and owner's equity. For example, the first answer is: (1) Increase in assets and increase in owner's equity.

**E1-7** Kam Computer Timeshare Company entered into the following transactions during May 2014.

*Analyze the effect of transactions on assets, liabilities, and owner's equity.*

(LO 6, 7)

1. Purchased computer terminals for $20,000 from Digital Equipment on account.
2. Paid $4,000 cash for May rent on storage space.
3. Received $17,000 cash from customers for contracts billed in April.
4. Performed computer services to Viking Construction Company for $3,000 cash.
5. Paid Tri-State Power Co. $11,000 cash for energy usage in May.
6. Kam invested an additional $29,000 in the business.
7. Paid Digital Equipment for the terminals purchased in (1) above.
8. Incurred advertising expense for May of $1,200 on account.

**Instructions**

Indicate with the appropriate letter whether each of the transactions above results in:

**(a)** An increase in assets and a decrease in assets.
**(b)** An increase in assets and an increase in owner's equity.
**(c)** An increase in assets and an increase in liabilities.
**(d)** A decrease in assets and a decrease in owner's equity.
**(e)** A decrease in assets and a decrease in liabilities.
**(f)** An increase in liabilities and a decrease in owner's equity.
**(g)** An increase in owner's equity and a decrease in liabilities.

**E1-8** An analysis of the transactions made by Liam Agler & Co., a certified public accounting firm, for the month of August is shown below. The expenses were $650 for rent, $4,800 for salaries and wages, and $500 for utilities.

*Analyze transactions and compute net income.*

(LO 7)

|  | Cash | + | Accounts Receivable | + | Supplies | + | Equipment | = | Accounts Payable | + | Owner's Capital | − | Owner's Drawings | + | Revenues | − | Expenses |
|---|---|---|---|---|---|---|---|---|---|---|---|---|---|---|---|---|---|
| 1. | +$15,000 | | | | | | | | | | +$15,000 | | | | | | |
| 2. | −2,000 | | | | | | +$5,000 | | +$3,000 | | | | | | | | |
| 3. | −750 | | | | +$750 | | | | | | | | | | | | |
| 4. | +4,600 | | +$3,900 | | | | | | | | | | | | +$8,500 | | |
| 5. | −1,500 | | | | | | | | −1,500 | | | | | | | | |
| 6. | −2,000 | | | | | | | | | | | | −$2,000 | | | | |
| 7. | −650 | | | | | | | | | | | | | | | | −$650 |
| 8. | +450 | | −450 | | | | | | | | | | | | | | |
| 9. | −4,800 | | | | | | | | | | | | | | | | −4,800 |
| 10. | | | | | | | | | +500 | | | | | | | | −500 |

**Instructions**

**(a)** ▬▬▬ Describe each transaction that occurred for the month.
**(b)** Determine how much owner's equity increased for the month.
**(c)** Compute the amount of net income for the month.

**E1-9** An analysis of transactions for Liam Agler & Co. was presented in E1–8.

*Prepare financial statements.*

(LO 8)

**Instructions**

Prepare an income statement and an owner's equity statement for August and a balance sheet at August 31, 2014. Assume that August is the company's first month of business.

*Determine net income*
*(or loss).*
(LO 6, 8)

**E1-10** Iverson Company had the following assets and liabilities on the dates indicated.

| December 31 | Total Assets | Total Liabilities |
|---|---|---|
| 2013 | $400,000 | $250,000 |
| 2014 | $460,000 | $300,000 |
| 2015 | $590,000 | $400,000 |

Iverson began business on January 1, 2013, with an investment of $100,000.

**Instructions**

From an analysis of the change in owner's equity during the year, compute the net income (or loss) for:

**(a)** 2013, assuming Iverson's drawings were $15,000 for the year.

**(b)** 2014, assuming Iverson made an additional investment of $45,000 and had no drawings in 2014.

**(c)** 2015, assuming Iverson made an additional investment of $15,000 and had drawings of $25,000 in 2015.

*Analyze financial statements items.*
(LO 6, 8)

**E1-11** Two items are omitted from each of the following summaries of balance sheet and income statement data for two proprietorships for the year 2014, Garba's Goods and Zahra Enterprises.

|  | Garba's Goods | Zahra Enterprises |
|---|---|---|
| Beginning of year: |  |  |
| Total assets | $110,000 | $129,000 |
| Total liabilities | 85,000 | (c) |
| Total owner's equity | (a) | 80,000 |
| End of year: |  |  |
| Total assets | 160,000 | 180,000 |
| Total liabilities | 120,000 | 50,000 |
| Total owner's equity | 40,000 | 130,000 |
| Changes during year in owner's equity: |  |  |
| Additional investment | (b) | 25,000 |
| Drawings | 29,000 | (d) |
| Total revenues | 215,000 | 100,000 |
| Total expenses | 175,000 | 60,000 |

**Instructions**

Determine the missing amounts.

*Prepare income statement and owner's equity statement.*
(LO 8)

**E1-12** The following information relates to David Pande Co. for the year 2014.

| | | | |
|---|---|---|---|
| Owner's capital, January 1, 2014 | $48,000 | Advertising expense | $ 1,800 |
| Owner's drawings during 2014 | 6,000 | Rent expense | 10,400 |
| Service revenue | 63,600 | Utilities expense | 3,100 |
| Salaries and wages expense | 29,500 | | |

**Instructions**

After analyzing the data, prepare an income statement and an owner's equity statement for the year ending December 31, 2014.

*Correct an incorrectly prepared balance sheet.*
(LO 8)

**E1-13** Reza Lang is the bookkeeper for Taylor Company. Reza has been trying to get the balance sheet of Taylor Company to balance. Taylor's balance sheet is shown below.

**TAYLOR COMPANY**
Balance Sheet
December 31, 2014

| Assets | | Liabilities | |
|---|---|---|---|
| Cash | $15,000 | Accounts payable | $21,000 |
| Supplies | 8,000 | Accounts receivable | (9,500) |
| Equipment | 46,000 | Owner's capital | 67,500 |
| Owner's drawings | 10,000 | Total liabilities and | |
| Total assets | $79,000 | owner's equity | $79,000 |

*Instructions*
Prepare a correct balance sheet.

**E1-14** Andrew Tym is the sole owner of Deer Park, a public camping ground near the Lake Mead National Recreation Area. Andrew has compiled the following financial information as of December 31, 2014.

*Compute net income and prepare a balance sheet.*

*(LO 8)*

| | | | |
|---|---|---|---|
| Revenues during 2014—camping fees | $140,000 | Fair value of equipment | $140,000 |
| Revenues during 2014—general store | 65,000 | Notes payable | 60,000 |
| Accounts payable | 11,000 | Expenses during 2014 | 150,000 |
| Cash on hand | 23,000 | Accounts receivable | 17,500 |
| Original cost of equipment | 105,500 | | |

*Instructions*
**(a)** Determine Andrew Tym's net income from Deer Park for 2014.
**(b)** Prepare a balance sheet for Deer Park as of December 31, 2014.

**E1-15** Presented below is financial information related to the 2014 operations of Gilligan Cruise Company.

*Prepare an income statement.*

*(LO 8)*

| | |
|---|---|
| Maintenance and repairs expense | $ 95,000 |
| Utilities expense | 10,000 |
| Salaries and wages expense | 142,000 |
| Advertising expense | 24,500 |
| Ticket revenue | 410,000 |

*Instructions*
Prepare the 2014 income statement for Gilligan Cruise Company.

**E1-16** Presented below is information related to the sole proprietorship of Huan Feng attorney.

*Prepare an owner's equity statement.*

*(LO 6, 8)*

| | |
|---|---|
| Legal service revenue—2014 | $335,000 |
| Total expenses—2014 | 211,000 |
| Assets, January 1, 2014 | 96,000 |
| Liabilities, January 1, 2014 | 62,000 |
| Assets, December 31, 2014 | 168,000 |
| Liabilities, December 31, 2014 | 100,000 |
| Drawings—2014 | ? |

*Instructions*
Prepare the 2014 owner's equity statement for Huan Feng's legal practice.

## EXERCISES: SET B AND CHALLENGE EXERCISES

Visit the book's companion website, at **www.wiley.com/college/weygandt**, and choose the Student Companion site to access Exercise Set B and Challenge Exercises.

## PROBLEMS: SET A

**P1-1A** On April 1, Renato Uhrig established Renato's Travel Agency. The following transactions were completed during the month.

*Analyze transactions and compute net income.*

*(LO 6, 7)*

1. Invested $15,000 cash to start the agency.
2. Paid $600 cash for April office rent.
3. Purchased equipment for $3,000 cash.
4. Incurred $700 of advertising costs in the *Chicago Tribune*, on account.
5. Paid $800 cash for office supplies.
6. Performed services worth $10,000: $3,000 cash is received from customers, and the balance of $7,000 is billed to customers on account.
7. Withdrew $500 cash for personal use.

8. Paid *Chicago Tribune* $500 of the amount due in transaction (4).
9. Paid employees' salaries $2,500.
10. Received $4,000 in cash from customers who have previously been billed in transaction (6).

**Instructions**

(a) Total assets $20,900

**(a)** Prepare a tabular analysis of the transactions using the following column headings: Cash, Accounts Receivable, Supplies, Equipment, Accounts Payable, Owner's Capital, Owner's Drawings, Revenues, and Expenses.

(b) Net income $6,200

**(b)** From an analysis of the owner's equity columns, compute the net income or net loss for April.

*Analyze transactions and prepare income statement, owner's equity statement, and balance sheet.*

(LO 6, 7, 8)

**P1-2A** Sue Kojima opened a law office on July 1, 2014. On July 31, the balance sheet showed Cash $5,000, Accounts Receivable $1,500, Supplies $500, Equipment $6,000, Accounts Payable $4,200, and Owner's Capital $8,800. During August, the following transactions occurred.

1. Collected $1,200 of accounts receivable.
2. Paid $2,800 cash on accounts payable.
3. Recognized revenue of $7,500 of which $3,000 is collected in cash and the balance is due in September.
4. Purchased additional equipment for $2,000, paying $400 in cash and the balance on account.
5. Paid salaries $2,500, rent for August $900, and advertising expenses $400.
6. Withdrew $700 in cash for personal use.
7. Received $2,000 from Standard Federal Bank—money borrowed on a note payable.
8. Incurred utility expenses for month on account $270.

**Instructions**

(a) Total assets $16,800

**(a)** Prepare a tabular analysis of the August transactions beginning with July 31 balances. The column headings should be as follows: Cash + Accounts Receivable + Supplies + Equipment = Notes Payable + Accounts Payable + Owner's Capital − Owner's Drawings + Revenues − Expenses.

(b) Net income $3,430
Ending capital $11,530

**(b)** Prepare an income statement for August, an owner's equity statement for August, and a balance sheet at August 31.

*Prepare income statement, owner's equity statement, and balance sheet.*

(LO 8)

**P1-3A** On June 1, Tamara Eder started Crazy Creations Co., a company that provides craft opportunities, by investing $12,000 cash in the business. Following are the assets and liabilities of the company at June 30 and the revenues and expenses for the month of June.

| Cash | $10,150 | Service Revenue | $6,700 |
|---|---|---|---|
| Accounts Receivable | 3,000 | Advertising Expense | 500 |
| Supplies | 2,000 | Rent Expense | 1,600 |
| Equipment | 10,000 | Gasoline Expense | 200 |
| Notes Payable | 9,000 | Utilities Expense | 150 |
| Accounts Payable | 1,200 | | |

Tamara made no additional investment in June but withdrew $1,300 in cash for personal use during the month.

**Instructions**

(a) Net income $4,250
Owner's equity $14,950
Total assets $25,150
(b) Owner's equity $15,700

**(a)** Prepare an income statement and owner's equity statement for the month of June and a balance sheet at June 30, 2014.

**(b)** Prepare an income statement and owner's equity statement for June assuming the following data are not included above: (1) $900 of services were performed and billed but not collected at June 30, and (2) $150 of gasoline expense was incurred but not paid.

*Analyze transactions and prepare financial statements.*

(LO 6, 7, 8)

**P1-4A** Debra Menge started her own consulting firm, Menge Consulting, on May 1, 2014. The following transactions occurred during the month of May.

May 1   Debra invested $7,000 cash in the business.
  2   Paid $900 for office rent for the month.
  3   Purchased $600 of supplies on account.
  5   Paid $125 to advertise in the *County News*.
  9   Received $4,000 cash for services performed.
  12   Withdrew $1,000 cash for personal use.
  15   Performed $5,400 of services on account.

17 Paid $2,500 for employee salaries.
20 Paid for the supplies purchased on account on May 3.
23 Received a cash payment of $4,000 for services performed on account on May 15.
26 Borrowed $5,000 from the bank on a note payable.
29 Purchased equipment for $4,200 on account.
30 Paid $275 for utilities.

**Instructions**

(a) Show the effects of the previous transactions on the accounting equation using the following format.

(a) Total assets $20,800

| | Assets | | | | Liabilities | | Owner's Equity | | | |
|---|---|---|---|---|---|---|---|---|---|---|
| | | Accounts | | | Notes | Accounts | Owner's | Owner's | | |
| Date | Cash + | Receivable + | Supplies + | Equipment = | Payable + | Payable + | Capital − | Drawings + | Revenues − | Expenses |

(b) Prepare an income statement for the month of May.
(c) Prepare a balance sheet at May 31, 2014.

(b) Net income $5,600
(c) Cash $14,600

**P1-5A** Financial statement information about four different companies is as follows.

*Determine financial statement amounts and prepare owner's equity statement.*

*(LO 6, 8)*

| | Farrell Company | Prasad Company | Thao Company | Zinda Company |
|---|---|---|---|---|
| January 1, 2014 | | | | |
| Assets | $ 80,000 | $ 90,000 | (g) | $150,000 |
| Liabilities | 48,000 | (d) | 80,000 | (j) |
| Owner's equity | (a) | 40,000 | 49,000 | 90,000 |
| December 31, 2014 | | | | |
| Assets | (b) | 112,000 | 180,000 | (k) |
| Liabilities | 60,000 | 72,000 | (h) | 100,000 |
| Owner's equity | 50,000 | (e) | 82,000 | 151,000 |
| Owner's equity changes in year | | | | |
| Additional investment | (c) | 8,000 | 10,000 | 15,000 |
| Drawings | 15,000 | (f) | 12,000 | 10,000 |
| Total revenues | 350,000 | 410,000 | (i) | 500,000 |
| Total expenses | 333,000 | 385,000 | 350,000 | (l) |

**Instructions**

(a) Determine the missing amounts. (*Hint:* For example, to solve for (a), Assets − Liabilities = Owner's equity = $32,000.)
(b) Prepare the owner's equity statement for Farrell Company.
(c) ——— Write a memorandum explaining the sequence for preparing financial statements and the interrelationship of the owner's equity statement to the income statement and balance sheet.

## PROBLEMS: SET B

**P1-1B** Solki's Repair Shop was started on May 1 by Solki Lee. A summary of May transactions is presented below.

*Analyze transactions and compute net income.*

*(LO 6, 7)*

1. Invested $10,000 cash to start the repair shop.
2. Purchased equipment for $5,000 cash.
3. Paid $400 cash for May office rent.
4. Paid $500 cash for supplies.
5. Incurred $250 of advertising costs in the *Beacon News* on account.
6. Received $6,100 in cash from customers for repair service.
7. Withdrew $1,000 cash for personal use.
8. Paid part-time employee salaries $2,000.
9. Paid utility bills $170.
10. Performed repair services worth $750 on account.
11. Collected cash of $120 for services billed in transaction (10).

**Instructions**

**(a)** Prepare a tabular analysis of the transactions, using the following column headings: Cash, Accounts Receivable, Supplies, Equipment, Accounts Payable, Owner's Capital, Owner's Drawings, Revenues, and Expenses.

**(b)** From an analysis of the owner's equity columns, compute the net income or net loss for May.

*Analyze transactions and prepare income statement, owner's equity statement, and balance sheet.*

*(LO 6, 7, 8)*

**P1-2B** Peter Nimmer opened a veterinary business in Nashville, Tennessee, on August 1, 2014. On August 31, the balance sheet showed Cash $9,000, Accounts Receivable $1,700, Supplies $600, Equipment $6,000, Accounts Payable $3,600, and Owner's Capital $13,700. During September, the following transactions occurred.

1. Paid $2,900 cash on accounts payable.
2. Collected $1,300 of accounts receivable.
3. Purchased additional equipment for $2,100, paying $800 in cash and the balance on account.
4. Recognized revenue of $7,800, of which $2,500 is received in cash and the balance is due in October.
5. Withdrew $1,100 cash for personal use.
6. Paid salaries $1,700, rent for September $900, and advertising expense $450.
7. Incurred utilities expense for month on account $170.
8. Received $10,000 from Capital Bank (money borrowed on a note payable).

**Instructions**

**(a)** Prepare a tabular analysis of the September transactions beginning with August 31 balances. The column headings should be as follows: Cash + Accounts Receivable + Supplies + Equipment = Notes Payable + Accounts Payable + Owner's Capital − Owner's Drawings + Revenues − Expenses.

**(b)** Prepare an income statement for September, an owner's equity statement for September, and a balance sheet at September 30.

*Prepare income statement, owner's equity statement, and balance sheet.*

*(LO 8)*

**P1-3B** On May 1, R. C. Twining started RC Flying School, a company that provides flying lessons, by investing $40,000 cash in the business. Following are the assets and liabilities of the company on May 31, 2014, and the revenues and expenses for the month of May.

| | | | |
|---|---|---|---|
| Cash | $ 3,400 | Advertising Expense | $ 600 |
| Accounts Receivable | 4,900 | Rent Expense | 1,200 |
| Equipment | 64,000 | Maintenance and Repairs Expense | 400 |
| Notes Payable | 30,000 | Gasoline Expense | 2,500 |
| Accounts Payable | 800 | Utilities Expense | 400 |
| Service Revenue | 8,100 | | |

R. C. Twining made no additional investment in May, but he withdrew $1,500 in cash for personal use.

**Instructions**

**(a)** Prepare an income statement and owner's equity statement for the month of May and a balance sheet at May 31.

**(b)** Prepare an income statement and owner's equity statement for May assuming the following data are not included above: (1) $900 worth of services were performed and billed but not collected at May 31, and (2) $1,500 of gasoline expense was incurred but not paid.

*Analyze transactions and prepare financial statements.*

*(LO 6, 7, 8)*

**P1-4B** Dennis Luljak started his own delivery service, Luljak Deliveries, on June 1, 2014. The following transactions occurred during the month of June.

June 1    Dennis invested $10,000 cash in the business.
     2    Purchased a used van for deliveries for $12,000. Dennis paid $2,000 cash and signed a note payable for the remaining balance.
     3    Paid $500 for office rent for the month.
     5    Performed $4,400 of services on account.
     9    Withdrew $200 cash for personal use.
    12    Purchased supplies for $150 on account.
    15    Received a cash payment of $1,250 for services performed on June 5.
    17    Purchased gasoline for $200 on account.
    20    Received a cash payment of $1,300 for services performed.

23   Made a cash payment of $600 on the note payable.
26   Paid $250 for utilities.
29   Paid for the gasoline purchased on account on June 17.
30   Paid $1,000 for employee salaries.

**Instructions**

**(a)** Show the effects of the previous transactions on the accounting equation using the following format.

(a) Total assets $23,100

| | Assets | | | | Liabilities | | Owner's Equity | | | |
|---|---|---|---|---|---|---|---|---|---|---|
| | | Accounts | | | Notes | Accounts | Owner's | Owner's | | |
| Date | Cash + | Receivable + | Supplies + | Equipment = | Payable + | Payable + | Capital − | Drawings + | Revenues − | Expenses |

**(b)** Prepare an income statement for the month of June.
**(c)** Prepare a balance sheet at June 30, 2014.

(b) Net income $3,750
(c) Cash $7,800

**P1-5B** Financial statement information about four different companies is as follows.

*Determine financial statement amounts and prepare owner's equity statement.*

*(LO 6, 8)*

| | Luo Company | Foster Company | Usher Company | Merritt Company |
|---|---|---|---|---|
| January 1, 2014 | | | | |
| Assets | $ 95,000 | $110,000 | (g) | $170,000 |
| Liabilities | 50,000 | (d) | 75,000 | (j) |
| Owner's equity | (a) | 60,000 | 45,000 | 90,000 |
| December 31, 2014 | | | | |
| Assets | (b) | 141,000 | 200,000 | (k) |
| Liabilities | 55,000 | 75,000 | (h) | 80,000 |
| Owner's equity | 63,000 | (e) | 130,000 | 162,000 |
| Owner's equity changes in year | | | | |
| Additional investment | (c) | 15,000 | 10,000 | 15,000 |
| Drawings | 25,000 | (f) | 14,000 | 20,000 |
| Total revenues | 350,000 | 420,000 | (i) | 520,000 |
| Total expenses | 320,000 | 385,000 | 342,000 | (l) |

**Instructions**

**(a)** Determine the missing amounts. (*Hint:* For example, to solve for (a), Assets − Liabilities = Owner's equity = $45,000.)
**(b)** Prepare the owner's equity statement for Foster Company.
**(c)** ━━━━━ Write a memorandum explaining the sequence for preparing financial statements and the interrelationship of the owner's equity statement to the income statement and balance sheet.

## PROBLEMS: SET C

Visit the book's companion website, at **www.wiley.com/college/weygandt**, and choose the Student Companion site to access Problem Set C.

## CONTINUING COOKIE CHRONICLE

**CCC1** Natalie Koebel spent much of her childhood learning the art of cookie-making from her grandmother. They passed many happy hours mastering every type of cookie imaginable and later creating new recipes that were both healthy and delicious. Now at the start of her second year in college, Natalie is investigating various possibilities for starting her own business as part of the requirements of the entrepreneurship program in which she is enrolled.

*The **Continuing Cookie Chronicle** starts in this chapter and continues in every chapter. **You also can find this problem** at the book's Student Companion site.*

A long-time friend insists that Natalie has to somehow include cookies in her business plan. After a series of brainstorming sessions, Natalie settles on the idea of operating a cookie-making school. She will start on a part-time basis and offer her services in people's homes. Now that she has started thinking about it, the possibilities seem endless. During the fall, she will concentrate on holiday cookies. She will offer individual lessons and group sessions (which will probably be more entertainment than education for the participants). Natalie also decides to include children in her target market.

The first difficult decision is coming up with the perfect name for her business. In the end, she settles on "Cookie Creations" and then moves on to more important issues.

*Instructions*
**(a)** What form of business organization—proprietorship, partnership, or corporation—do you recommend that Natalie use for her business? Discuss the benefits and weaknesses of each form and give the reasons for your choice.
**(b)** Will Natalie need accounting information? If yes, what information will she need and why? How often will she need this information?
**(c)** Identify specific asset, liability, and owner's equity accounts that Cookie Creations will likely use to record its business transactions.
**(d)** Should Natalie open a separate bank account for the business? Why or why not?

# Broadening Your Perspective

## Financial Reporting and Analysis

### Financial Reporting Problem: Apple Inc.

**BYP1-1** The actual financial statements of Apple Inc. for 2011 are presented in Appendix A. Instructions for accessing and using the company's complete annual report, including the notes to the financial statements, are also provided in Appendix A.

*Instructions*
Refer to Apple's financial statements and answer the following questions.

**(a)** What were Apple's total assets at September 24, 2011? At September 25, 2010?
**(b)** How much cash (and cash equivalents) did Apple have on September 24, 2011?
**(c)** What amount of accounts payable did Apple report on September 24, 2011? On September 25, 2010?
**(d)** What were Apple's net sales in 2009? In 2010? In 2011?
**(e)** What is the amount of the change in Apple's net income from 2010 to 2011?

### Comparative Analysis Problem:
### PepsiCo, Inc. vs. The Coca-Cola Company

**BYP1-2** PepsiCo's financial statements are presented in Appendix B. Financial statements of The Coca-Cola Company are presented in Appendix C. Instructions for accessing and using the complete annual reports of PepsiCo and Coca-Cola, including the notes to the financial statements, are also provided in Appendices B and C, respectively.

*Instructions*
**(a)** Based on the information contained in these financial statements, determine the following for each company.
  **(1)** Total assets at December 31, 2011, for PepsiCo and for Coca-Cola at December 31, 2011.
  **(2)** Accounts (notes) receivable, net at December 31, 2011, for PepsiCo and at December 31, 2011, for Coca-Cola.
  **(3)** Net revenues for year ended in 2011.
  **(4)** Net income for year ended in 2011.
**(b)** What conclusions concerning the two companies can be drawn from these data?

## Comparative Analysis Problem:
## Amazon.com, Inc. vs. Wal-Mart Stores, Inc.

**BYP1-3** Amazon.com, Inc.'s financial statements are presented in Appendix D. Financial statements for Wal-Mart Stores, Inc. are presented in Appendix E. Instructions for accessing and using the complete annual reports of Amazon and Wal-Mart, including the notes to the financial statements, are also provided in Appendices D and E, respectively.

*Instructions*
**(a)** Based on the information contained in these financial statements, determine the following for each company.
  **(1)** Total assets at December 31, 2011, for Amazon and for Wal-Mart at January 31, 2012.
  **(2)** Receivables (net) at December 31, 2011, for Amazon and for Wal-Mart at January 31, 2012.
  **(3)** Net sales (product only) for year ended in 2011 (2012 for Wal-Mart).
  **(4)** Net income for the year ended in 2011 (2012 for Wal-Mart).
**(b)** What conclusions concerning these two companies can be drawn from these data?

## Real-World Focus

**BYP1-4** This exercise will familiarize you with skill requirements, job descriptions, and salaries for accounting careers.

*Address:* **www.careers-in-accounting.com**, or go to **www.wiley.com/college/weygandt**

*Instructions*
Go to the site shown above. Answer the following questions.

**(a)** What are the three broad areas of accounting (from "Skills and Talents")?
**(b)** List eight skills required in accounting.
**(c)** How do the three accounting areas differ in terms of these eight required skills?
**(d)** Explain one of the key job options in accounting.
**(e)** What is the overall salary range for a junior staff accountant?

# Critical Thinking

## Decision-Making Across the Organization

**BYP1-5** Kathy and James Mohr, local golf stars, opened the Chip-Shot Driving Range on March 1, 2014, by investing $25,000 of their cash savings in the business. A caddy shack was constructed for cash at a cost of $8,000, and $800 was spent on golf balls and golf clubs. The Mohrs leased five acres of land at a cost of $1,000 per month and paid the first month's rent. During the first month, advertising costs totaled $750, of which $150 was unpaid at March 31, and $400 was paid to members of the high-school golf team for retrieving golf balls. All revenues from customers were deposited in the company's bank account. On March 15, Kathy and James withdrew a total of $1,000 in cash for personal living expenses. A $100 utility bill was received on March 31 but was not paid. On March 31, the balance in the company's bank account was $18,900.

Kathy and James thought they had a pretty good first month of operations. But, their estimates of profitability ranged from a loss of $6,100 to net income of $2,450.

*Instructions*
With the class divided into groups, answer the following.

**(a)** How could the Mohrs have concluded that the business operated at a loss of $6,100? Was this a valid basis on which to determine net income?
**(b)** How could the Mohrs have concluded that the business operated at a net income of $2,450? (*Hint:* Prepare a balance sheet at March 31.) Was this a valid basis on which to determine net income?
**(c)** Without preparing an income statement, determine the actual net income for March.
**(d)** What was the revenue recognized in March?

## Communication Activity

**BYP1-6** Ashley Hirano, the bookkeeper for New York Company, has been trying to get the balance sheet to balance. The company's balance sheet is shown below.

| NEW YORK COMPANY | | | |
|---|---|---|---|
| Balance Sheet | | | |
| For the Month Ended December 31, 2014 | | | |
| **Assets** | | **Liabilities** | |
| Equipment | $25,500 | Owner's capital | $26,000 |
| Cash | 9,000 | Accounts receivable | (6,000) |
| Supplies | 2,000 | Owner's drawings | (2,000) |
| Accounts payable | (8,000) | Notes payable | 10,500 |
| | $28,500 | | $28,500 |

*Instructions*
Explain to Ashley Hirano in a memo why the original balance sheet is incorrect, and what should be done to correct it.

## Ethics Case

**BYP1-7** After numerous campus interviews, Greg Thorpe, a senior at Great Northern College, received two office interview invitations from the Baltimore offices of two large firms. Both firms offered to cover his out-of-pocket expenses (travel, hotel, and meals). He scheduled the interviews for both firms on the same day, one in the morning and one in the afternoon. At the conclusion of each interview, he submitted to both firms his total out-of-pocket expenses for the trip to Baltimore: mileage $112 (280 miles at $0.40), hotel $130, meals $36, and parking and tolls $18, for a total of $296. He believes this approach is appropriate. If he had made two trips, his cost would have been two times $296. He is also certain that neither firm knew he had visited the other on that same trip. Within 10 days, Greg received two checks in the mail, each in the amount of $296.

*Instructions*
**(a)** Who are the stakeholders (affected parties) in this situation?
**(b)** What are the ethical issues in this case?
**(c)** What would you do in this situation?

## All About You

**BYP1-8** Some people are tempted to make their finances look worse to get financial aid. Companies sometimes also manage their financial numbers in order to accomplish certain goals. Earnings management is the planned timing of revenues, expenses, gains, and losses to smooth out bumps in net income. In managing earnings, companies' actions vary from being within the range of ethical activity, to being both unethical and illegal attempts to mislead investors and creditors.

*Instructions*
Provide responses for each of the following questions.

**(a)** Discuss whether you think each of the following actions (adapted from **www.finaid.org/fafsa/ maximize.phtml**) to increase the chances of receiving financial aid is ethical.
    **(1)** Spend down the student's assets and income first, before spending parents' assets and income.
    **(2)** Accelerate necessary expenses to reduce available cash. For example, if you need a new car, buy it before applying for financial aid.
    **(3)** State that a truly financially dependent child is independent.
    **(4)** Have a parent take an unpaid leave of absence for long enough to get below the "threshold" level of income.

(b) What are some reasons why a **company** might want to overstate its earnings?

(c) What are some reasons why a **company** might want to understate its earnings?

(d) Under what circumstances might an otherwise ethical person decide to illegally overstate or understate earnings?

## FASB Codification Activity

**BYP1-9** The FASB has developed the Financial Accounting Standards Board Accounting Standards Codification (or more simply "the Codification"). The FASB's primary goal in developing the Codification is to provide in one place all the authoritative literature related to a particular topic. To provide easy access to the Codification, the FASB also developed the Financial Accounting Standards Board Codification Research System (CRS). CRS is an online, real-time database that provides easy access to the Codification. The Codification and the related CRS provide a topically organized structure, subdivided into topic, subtopics, sections, and paragraphs, using a numerical index system.

You may find this system useful in your present and future studies, and so we have provided an opportunity to use this online system as part of the *Broadening Your Perspective* section.

*Instructions*
Academic access to the FASB Codification is available through university subscriptions, obtained from the American Accounting Association (at **http://aaahq.org/FASB/Access.cfm**), for an annual fee of $150. This subscription covers an unlimited number of students within a single institution. Once this access has been obtained by your school, you should log in (at **http://aaahq.org/ascLogin.cfm**) and familiarize yourself with the resources that are accessible at the FASB Codification site.

## Considering People, Planet, and Profit

**BYP1-10** This chapter's Feature Story discusses the fact that although Clif Bar & Company is not a public company, it does share its financial information with its employees as part of its open-book management approach. Further, although it does not publicly share its financial information, it does provide a different form of an annual report to external users. In this report, the company provides information regarding its sustainability efforts.

*Address:* **www.clifbar.com/uploads/default/ClifBar_AA2010.pdf**

*Instructions*
Access the 2010 annual report of Clif Bar & Company at the site shown above and then answer the following questions.

(a) What are the Five Aspirations?

(b) What are the four key goals of the company's sustainability efforts related to the planet? Give one example of a recent initiative, and a measurable outcome for that initiative, that the company has taken related to each goal.

## Answers to Chapter Questions

### Answers to Insight and Accounting Across the Organization Questions

**p. 6 The Scoop on Accounting   Q:** What are the benefits to the company and to the employees of making the financial statements available to all employees? **A:** If employees can read and use financial reports, a company will benefit in the following ways. The **marketing department** will make better decisions about products to offer and prices to charge. The **finance department** will make better decisions about debt and equity financing and how much to distribute in dividends. The **production department** will make better decisions about when to buy new equipment and how much inventory to produce. The **human resources department** will be better able to determine whether employees can be given raises. Finally, **all employees** will be better informed about the basis on which they are evaluated, which will increase employee morale.

**p. 8 The Numbers Behind Not-for-Profit Organizations   Q:** What benefits does a sound accounting system provide to a not-for-profit organization? **A:** Accounting provides at least two benefits to not-for-profit organizations. First, it helps to ensure that money is used in the way that donors intended. Second, it assures donors that their money is not going to waste and thus increases the likelihood of future donations.

**p. 10 The Korean Discount   Q:** What is meant by the phrase "make the country's businesses more transparent"? Why would increasing transparency spur economic growth? **A:** Transparency refers to the extent to which outsiders have knowledge regarding a company's financial performance and financial position. If a company lacks transparency, its financial reports do not adequately inform investors of critical information that is needed to make investment decisions. If corporate transparency is increased, investors would be more willing to supply the financial capital that businesses need in order to grow, which would spur the country's economic growth.

**p. 12 Spinning the Career Wheel   Q:** How might accounting help you? **A:** You will need to understand financial reports in any enterprise with which you are associated. Whether you become a manager, a doctor, a lawyer, a social worker, a teacher, an engineer, an architect, or an entrepreneur, a working knowledge of accounting is relevant.

**p. 25 Beyond Financial Statements   Q:** Why might a company's stockholders be interested in its environmental and social performance? **A:** Many companies now recognize that being a socially responsible organization is not only the right thing to do, but it also is good for business. Many investment professionals understand, for example, that environmental, social, and proper corporate governance of companies affects the performance of their investment portfolios. For example, British Petroleum's oil spill disaster is a classic example of the problems that can occur for a company and its stockholders. BP's stock price was slashed, its dividend reduced, its executives replaced, and its reputation badly damaged. It is interesting that socially responsible investment funds are now gaining momentum in the marketplace such that companies now recognize this segment as an important investment group.

**Answers to Self-Test Questions**

**1.** b   **2.** d   **3.** c   **4.** b   **5.** b   **6.** d   **7.** a ($3,500 − $2,000)   **8.** b   **9.** b   **10.** a ($90,000 − $50,000)   **11.** d   **12.** c   **13.** b   **14.** c   ***15.** a

# A Look at IFRS

LEARNING OBJECTIVE   10

**Describe the impact of international accounting standards on U.S. financial reporting.**

Most agree that there is a need for one set of international accounting standards. Here is why:

**Multinational corporations.** Today's companies view the entire world as their market. For example, Coca-Cola, Intel, and McDonald's generate more than 50% of their sales outside the United States, and many foreign companies, such as Toyota, Nestlé, and Sony, find their largest market to be the United States.

**Mergers and acquisitions.** The mergers between Fiat/Chrysler and Vodafone/Mannesmann suggest that we will see even more such business combinations of companies from different countries in the future.

**Information technology.** As communication barriers continue to topple through advances in technology, companies and individuals in different countries and markets are becoming more comfortable buying and selling goods and services from one another.

**Financial markets.** Financial markets are of international significance today. Whether it is currency, equity securities (stocks), bonds, or derivatives, there are active markets throughout the world trading these types of instruments.

## Key Points

- International standards are referred to as **International Financial Reporting Standards (IFRS)**, developed by the International Accounting Standards Board (IASB).

- Recent events in the global capital markets have underscored the importance of financial disclosure and transparency not only in the United States but in markets around the world. As a result, many are examining which accounting and financial disclosure rules should be followed. As indicated in the graphic on the next page, much of the world has voted for the standards issued by the IASB. Over 115 countries require or permit use of IFRS.

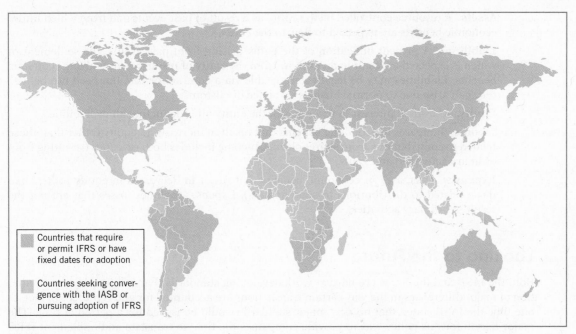

*Source: http://www.pwc.com/us/en/issues/ifrs-reporting/country-adoption/index.jhtml.*

- U.S standards, referred to as generally accepted accounting principles (GAAP), are developed by the Financial Accounting Standards Board (FASB). The fact that there are differences between what is in this textbook (which is based on U.S. standards) and IFRS should not be surprising because the FASB and IASB have responded to different user needs. In some countries, the primary users of financial statements are private investors; in others, the primary users are tax authorities or central government planners. It appears that the United States and the international standard-setting environment are primarily driven by meeting the needs of investors and creditors.

- The internal control standards applicable to Sarbanes-Oxley (SOX) apply only to large public companies listed on U.S. exchanges. There is a continuing debate as to whether non-U.S. companies should have to comply with this extra layer of regulation. Debate about international companies (non-U.S.) adopting SOX-type standards centers on whether the benefits exceed the costs. The concern is that the higher costs of SOX compliance are making the U.S. securities markets less competitive.

- The textbook mentions a number of ethics violations, such as Enron, WorldCom, and AIG. These problems have also occurred internationally, for example, at Satyam Computer Services (India), Parmalat (Italy), and Royal Ahold (the Netherlands).

- IFRS tends to be simpler in its accounting and disclosure requirements; some people say more "principles-based." GAAP is more detailed; some people say it is more "rules-based." This difference in approach has resulted in a debate about the merits of "principles-based" versus "rules-based" standards.

- U.S. regulators have recently eliminated the need for foreign companies that trade shares in U.S. markets to reconcile their accounting with GAAP.

- The three most common forms of business organization, proprietorships, partnerships, and corporations, are also found in countries that use IFRS. Because the choice of business organization is influenced by factors such as legal environment, tax rates and regulations, and degree of entrepreneurism, the relative use of each form will vary across countries.

- The conceptual framework that underlies IFRS is very similar to that used to develop GAAP. The basic definitions provided in this textbook for the key elements of financial statements, that is, assets, liabilities, equity, revenues (**referred to as income**), and expenses, are simplified versions of the official definitions provided by the FASB. The more substantive definitions, using the IASB definitional structure, are as follows.

**Assets.** A resource controlled by the entity as a result of past events and from which future economic benefits are expected to flow to the entity.

**Liabilities.** A present obligation of the entity arising from past events, the settlement of which is expected to result in an outflow from the entity of resources embodying economic benefits. Liabilities may be legally enforceable via a contract or law, but need not be, i.e., they can arise due to normal business practice or customs.

**Equity.** A residual interest in the assets of the entity after deducting all its liabilities.

**Income.** Increases in economic benefits that result in increases in equity (other than those related to contributions from shareholders). Income includes both revenues (resulting from ordinary activities) and gains.

**Expenses.** Decreases in economic benefits that result in decreases in equity (other than those related to distributions to shareholders). Expenses includes losses that are not the result of ordinary activities.

## Looking to the Future

Both the IASB and the FASB are hard at work developing standards that will lead to the elimination of major differences in the way certain transactions are accounted for and reported. In fact, at one time the IASB stated that no new major standards would be issued for a period of time. The major reason for this policy was to provide companies the time to translate and implement IFRS into practice, as much has happened in a very short period of time. Consider, for example, that as a result of a joint project on the conceptual framework, the definitions of the most fundamental elements (assets, liabilities, equity, revenues, and expenses) may actually change. However, whether the IASB adopts internal control provisions similar to those in SOX remains to be seen.

## IFRS Practice

### IFRS Self-Test Questions

1. Which of the following is **not** a reason why a single set of high-quality international accounting standards would be beneficial?
   (a) Mergers and acquisition activity.
   (b) Financial markets.
   (c) Multinational corporations.
   (d) GAAP is widely considered to be a superior reporting system.

2. The Sarbanes-Oxley Act determines:
   (a) international tax regulations.
   (b) internal control standards as enforced by the IASB.
   (c) internal control standards of U.S. publicly traded companies.
   (d) U.S. tax regulations.

3. IFRS is considered to be more:
   (a) principles-based and less rules-based than GAAP.
   (b) rules-based and less principles-based than GAAP.
   (c) detailed than GAAP.
   (d) None of the above.

4. Which of the following statements is **false**?
   (a) IFRS is based on a conceptual framework that is similar to that used to develop GAAP.
   (b) Assets are defined by the IASB as resources controlled by the entity as a result of past events and from which future economic benefits are expected to flow to the entity.
   (c) Non-U.S. companies that trade shares in U.S. markets must reconcile their accounting with GAAP.
   (d) Proprietorships, partnerships, and corporations are also found in countries that use IFRS.

**5.** Which of the following statements is **true**?
  **(a)** Under IFRS, the term income refers to what would be called revenues and gains under GAAP.
  **(b)** The term income is not used under IFRS.
  **(c)** The term income refers only to gains on investments.
  **(d)** Under IFRS, expenses include distributions to owners.

## IFRS Exercises

**IFRS1-1** Who are the two key international players in the development of international accounting standards? Explain their role.

**IFRS1-2** What might explain the fact that different accounting standard-setters have developed accounting standards that are sometimes quite different in nature?

**IFRS1-3** What is the benefit of a single set of high-quality accounting standards?

**IFRS1-4** Discuss the potential advantages and disadvantages that countries outside the United States should consider before adopting regulations, such as those in the Sarbanes-Oxley Act, that increase corporate internal control requirements.

## International Financial Reporting Problem: Zetar plc

**IFRS1-5** The financial statements of Zetar plc are presented in Appendix F. Instructions for accessing and using the company's complete annual report, including the notes to its financial statements, are also provided in Appendix F.

### Instructions
Visit Zetar's corporate website and answer the following questions from Zetar's 2011 annual report.
  **(a)** What accounting firm performed the audit of Zetar's financial statements?
  **(b)** What is the address of the company's corporate headquarters?
  **(c)** What is the company's reporting currency?
  **(d)** What two segments does the company operate in, and what were the sales for each segment in the year ended April 30, 2011?

**Answers to IFRS Self-Test Questions**
**1.** d   **2.** c   **3.** a   **4.** c   **5.** a

# 2 | The Recording Process

## Feature Story

### Accidents Happen

How organized are you financially? Take a short quiz. Answer yes or no to each question:

- Does your wallet contain so many cash machine receipts that you've been declared a walking fire hazard?

- Do you wait until you debit card is denied before checking the status of your funds?

- Was Aaron Rodgers (the quarterback for the Green Bay Packers) playing high school football the last time you verified the accuracy of your bank account?

If you think it is hard to keep track of the many transactions that make up your life, imagine how difficult it is for a big corporation to do so. Not only that, but now consider how important it is for a large company to have good accounting records, especially if it has control of your life savings. MF Global Holdings Ltd is such a company. As a big investment broker, it held billions of dollars of investments for clients. If you had your life savings invested at MF Global, you might be slightly displeased if you heard this from one of its representatives: "You know, I kind of remember an account

for someone with a name like yours—now what did we d with that?"

Unfortunately, that is almost exactly what happened to MF Global's clients shortly before it recently filed for bankrupto During the days immediately following the bankruptcy filin regulators and auditors struggled to piece things together. the words of one regulator, "Their books are a disaster . . we're trying to figure out what numbers are real numbers. One company that considered buying an interest in MF Global walked away from the deal because it "couldn't ge sense of what was on the balance sheet." That company s the information that should have been instantly available instead took days to produce.

It now appears that MF Global did not properly segregate customer accounts from company accounts. And, because its sloppy recordkeeping, customers were not protected when the company had financial troubles. Total customer losses were approximately $1 billion. As you can see, accounting matters!

*Source:* S. Patterson and A. Lucchetti, "Inside the Hunt for MF Global Ca *Wall Street Journal Online* (November 11, 2011).

---

## Learning Objectives   ✔ The Navigator

*After studying this chapter, you should be able to:*

[1] Explain what an account is and how it helps in the recording process.

[2] Define debits and credits and explain their use in recording business transactions.

[3] Identify the basic steps in the recording process.

[4] Explain what a journal is and how it helps in the recording process.

[5] Explain what a ledger is and how it helps in the recording process.

[6] Explain what posting is and how it helps in the recording process.

[7] Prepare a trial balance and explain its purposes.

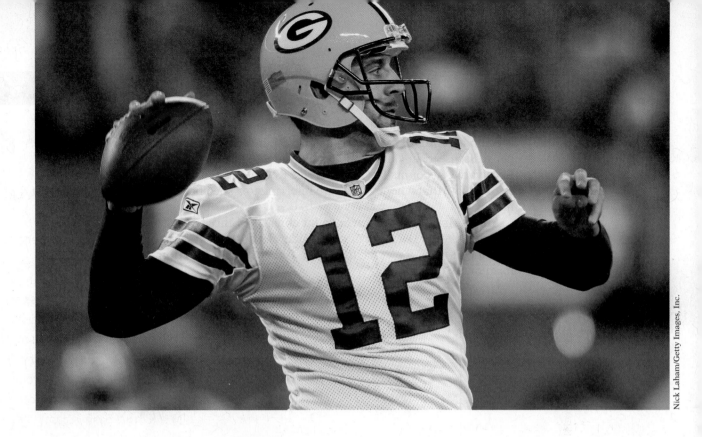

Nick Laham/Getty Images, Inc.

# Preview of Chapter 2

✔ The Navigator

In Chapter 1, we analyzed business transactions in terms of the accounting equation, and we presented the cumulative effects of these transactions in tabular form. Imagine a company like MF Global (as in the Feature Story) using the same tabular format as Softbyte to keep track of its transactions. In a single day, MF Global engaged in thousands of business transactions. To record each transaction this way would be impractical, expensive, and unnecessary. Instead, companies use a set of procedures and records to keep track of transaction data more easily. This chapter introduces and illustrates these basic procedures and records.

The content and organization of Chapter 2 are as follows.

| THE RECORDING PROCESS | | |
|---|---|---|
| **The Account** | **Steps in the Recording Process** | **The Trial Balance** |
| • Debits and credits<br>• Owner's equity relationships<br>• Summary of debit/credit rules | • Journal<br>• Ledger<br>• Posting<br>• Chart of accounts<br>• The recording process illustrated | • Limitations of a trial balance<br>• Locating errors<br>• Use of dollar signs |

# The Account

LEARNING OBJECTIVE **1**

Explain what an account is and how it helps in the recording process.

An **account** is an individual accounting record of increases and decreases in a specific asset, liability, or owner's equity item. For example, Softbyte (the company discussed in Chapter 1) would have separate accounts for Cash, Accounts Receivable, Accounts Payable, Service Revenue, Salaries and Wages Expense, and so on. (Note that whenever we are referring to a specific account, we capitalize the name.)

In its simplest form, an account consists of three parts: (1) a title, (2) a left or debit side, and (3) a right or credit side. Because the format of an account resembles the letter T, we refer to it as a **T-account**. Illustration 2-1 shows the basic form of an account.

**Illustration 2-1**
Basic form of account

We use this form often throughout this book to explain basic accounting relationships.

## Debits and Credits

LEARNING OBJECTIVE **2**

Define debits and credits and explain their use in recording business transactions.

The term **debit** indicates the left side of an account, and **credit** indicates the right side. They are commonly abbreviated as **Dr.** for debit and **Cr.** for credit. They **do not** mean increase or decrease, as is commonly thought. We use the terms **debit** and **credit** repeatedly in the recording process to describe **where** entries are made in accounts. For example, the act of entering an amount on the left side of an account is called **debiting** the account. Making an entry on the right side is **crediting** the account.

When comparing the totals of the two sides, an account shows a **debit balance** if the total of the debit amounts exceeds the credits. An account shows a **credit balance** if the credit amounts exceed the debits. Note the position of the debit side and credit side in Illustration 2-1.

The procedure of recording debits and credits in an account is shown in Illustration 2-2 for the transactions affecting the Cash account of Softbyte. The data are taken from the Cash column of the tabular summary in Illustration 1-8 (page 20).

**Illustration 2-2**
Tabular summary and account form for Softbyte's Cash account

| Tabular Summary | Account Form |
|---|---|

**Cash**

| Cash | |
|---|---|
| $15,000 | |
| −7,000 | |
| 1,200 | |
| 1,500 | |
| −1,700 | |
| −250 | |
| 600 | |
| −1,300 | |
| $ 8,050 | |

**Cash**

| (Debits) | | (Credits) | |
|---|---|---|---|
| | 15,000 | | 7,000 |
| | 1,200 | | 1,700 |
| | 1,500 | | 250 |
| | 600 | | 1,300 |
| Balance | 8,050 | | |
| (Debit) | | | |

Every positive item in the tabular summary represents a receipt of cash. Every negative amount represents a payment of cash. **Notice that in the account form, we record the increases in cash as debits and the decreases in cash as credits.** For example, the $15,000 receipt of cash (in red) is debited to Cash, and the −$7,000 payment of cash (in blue) is credited to Cash.

Having increases on one side and decreases on the other reduces recording errors and helps in determining the totals of each side of the account as well as the account balance. The balance is determined by netting the two sides (subtracting one amount from the other). The account balance, a debit of $8,050, indicates that Softbyte had $8,050 more increases than decreases in cash. That is, since it started with a balance of zero, it has $8,050 in its Cash account.

## DEBIT AND CREDIT PROCEDURE

In Chapter 1, you learned the effect of a transaction on the basic accounting equation. Remember that each transaction must affect two or more accounts to keep the basic accounting equation in balance. In other words, for each transaction, debits must equal credits. The equality of debits and credits provides the basis for the **double-entry system** of recording transactions.

Under the double-entry system, the dual (two-sided) effect of each transaction is recorded in appropriate accounts. This system provides a logical method for recording transactions. As discussed in the Feature Story about MF Global, the double-entry system also helps ensure the accuracy of the recorded amounts as well as the detection of errors. If every transaction is recorded with equal debits and credits, the sum of all the debits to the accounts must equal the sum of all the credits.

The double-entry system for determining the equality of the accounting equation is much more efficient than the plus/minus procedure used in Chapter 1. The following discussion illustrates debit and credit procedures in the double-entry system.

> ### International Note
> Rules for accounting for specific events sometimes differ across countries. For example, European companies rely less on historical cost and more on fair value than U.S. companies. Despite the differences, the double-entry accounting system is the basis of accounting systems worldwide.

## DR./CR. PROCEDURES FOR ASSETS AND LIABILITIES

In Illustration 2-2 for Softbyte, increases in Cash—an asset—were entered on the left side, and decreases in Cash were entered on the right side. We know that both sides of the basic equation (Assets = Liabilities + Owner's Equity) must be equal. It therefore follows that increases and decreases in liabilities will have to be recorded **opposite from** increases and decreases in assets. Thus, increases in liabilities must be entered on the right or credit side, and decreases in liabilities must be entered on the left or debit side. The effects that debits and credits have on assets and liabilities are summarized in Illustration 2-3.

| Debits | Credits |
|---|---|
| Increase assets | Decrease assets |
| Decrease liabilities | Increase liabilities |

**Illustration 2-3**
Debit and credit effects—assets and liabilities

**Asset accounts normally show debit balances.** That is, debits to a specific asset account should exceed credits to that account. Likewise, **liability accounts normally show credit balances**. That is, credits to a liability account should exceed debits to that account. The **normal balance** of an account is on the side where an increase in the account is recorded. Illustration 2-4 (page 56) shows the normal balances for assets and liabilities.

**Illustration 2-4**
Normal balances—assets
and liabilities

Knowing the normal balance in an account may help you trace errors. For example, a credit balance in an asset account such as Land or a debit balance in a liability account such as Salaries and Wages Payable usually indicates an error. Occasionally, though, an abnormal balance may be correct. The Cash account, for example, will have a credit balance when a company has overdrawn its bank balance (i.e., written a check that "bounced").

### DR./CR. PROCEDURES FOR OWNER'S EQUITY

As Chapter 1 indicated, owner's investments and revenues increase owner's equity. Owner's drawings and expenses decrease owner's equity. Companies keep accounts for each of these types of transactions.

**OWNER'S CAPITAL**  Investments by owners are credited to the Owner's Capital account. Credits increase this account, and debits decrease it. When an owner invests cash in the business, the company debits (increases) Cash and credits (increases) Owner's Capital. When the owner's investment in the business is reduced, Owner's Capital is debited (decreased).

Illustration 2-5 shows the rules of debit and credit for the Owner's Capital account.

**Illustration 2-5**
Debit and credit effects—
Owner's Capital

| Debits | Credits |
| --- | --- |
| Decrease Owner's Capital | Increase Owner's Capital |

We can diagram the normal balance in Owner's Capital as follows.

**Illustration 2-6**
Normal balance—Owner's
Capital

**OWNER'S DRAWINGS**  An owner may withdraw cash or other assets for personal use. Withdrawals could be debited directly to Owner's Capital to indicate a decrease in owner's equity. However, it is preferable to use a separate account, called Owner's Drawings. This separate account makes it easier to determine total withdrawals for each accounting period. Owner's Drawings is increased by debits and decreased by credits. Normally, the drawings account will have a debit balance.

Illustration 2-7 shows the rules of debit and credit for the drawings account.

**Illustration 2-7**
Debit and credit effects—
Owner's Drawings

| Debits | Credits |
| --- | --- |
| Increase Owner's Drawings | Decrease Owner's Drawings |

We can diagram the normal balance as shown in Illustration 2-8.

**Owner's Drawings**

| Debit for increase | Credit for decrease |
|---|---|
| **Normal balance** | |

**Illustration 2-8**
Normal balance—Owner's Drawings

**The Owner's Drawings account decreases owner's equity. It is not an income statement account like revenues and expenses.**

---

## INVESTOR INSIGHT

### Keeping Score

The Chicago Cubs baseball team probably has these major revenue and expense accounts:

| Revenues | Expenses |
|---|---|
| Admissions (ticket sales) | Players' salaries |
| Concessions | Administrative salaries |
| Television and radio | Travel |
| Advertising | Ballpark maintenance |

 Do you think that the Chicago Bears football team would be likely to have the same major revenue and expense accounts as the Cubs? (See page 95.)

Jonathan Daniel/Getty Images, Inc.

---

**REVENUES AND EXPENSES** The purpose of earning revenues is to benefit the owner(s) of the business. When a company earns revenues, owner's equity increases. Therefore, **the effect of debits and credits on revenue accounts is the same as their effect on Owner's Capital**. That is, revenue accounts are increased by credits and decreased by debits.

Expenses have the opposite effect. Expenses decrease owner's equity. Since expenses decrease net income and revenues increase it, it is logical that the increase and decrease sides of expense accounts should be the opposite of revenue accounts. Thus, expense accounts are increased by debits and decreased by credits. Illustration 2-9 shows the rules of debits and credits for revenues and expenses.

**Helpful Hint** Because revenues increase owner's equity, a revenue account has the same debit/credit rules as the Owner's Capital account. Expenses have the opposite effect.

**Illustration 2-9**
Debit and credit effects—revenues and expenses

| Debits | Credits |
|---|---|
| Decrease revenues | Increase revenues |
| Increase expenses | Decrease expenses |

Credits to revenue accounts should exceed debits. Debits to expense accounts should exceed credits. Thus, revenue accounts normally show credit balances, and expense accounts normally show debit balances. We can diagram the normal balances as follows.

**Illustration 2-10**
Normal balances—revenues and expenses

**Revenues**

| Debit for decrease | Credit for increase |
|---|---|
| | **Normal balance** |

**Expenses**

| Debit for increase | Credit for decrease |
|---|---|
| **Normal balance** | |

You may
kmark
Illustration 2-11. You
probably will refer to
it often.

## Summary of Debit/Credit Rules

Illustration 2-11 shows a summary of the debit/credit rules and effects on each type of account. Study this diagram carefully. It will help you understand the fundamentals of the double-entry system.

**Illustration 2-11**
Summary of debit/credit rules

---

> **DO IT!**

## Normal Balances

### Action Plan

✔ Determine the types of accounts needed. Kate will need asset accounts for each different type of asset she invests in the business and liability accounts for any debts she incurs.

✔ Understand the types of owner's equity accounts. Only Owner's Capital will be needed when Kate begins the business. Other owner's equity accounts will be needed later.

Kate Browne has just rented space in a shopping mall. In this space, she will open a hair salon to be called "Hair It Is." A friend has advised Kate to set up a double-entry set of accounting records in which to record all of her business transactions.

Identify the balance sheet accounts that Kate will likely need to record the transactions needed to open her business. Indicate whether the normal balance of each account is a debit or a credit.

### Solution

Kate would likely need the following accounts in which to record the transactions necessary to ready her hair salon for opening day:

Cash (debit balance)

Equipment (debit balance)

Supplies (debit balance)

Accounts Payable (credit balance)

If she borrows money: Notes Payable (credit balance)

Owner's Capital (credit balance)

Related exercise material: **BE2-1, BE2-2, BE2-5, E2-1, E2-2, E2-4, and DO IT! 2-1.**

✔ The Navigator

---

## Steps in the Recording Process

**LEARNING OBJECTIVE** 3

**Identify the basic steps in the recording process.**

Although it is possible to enter transaction information directly into the accounts without using a journal, few businesses do so. Practically every business uses three basic steps in the recording process:

1. Analyze each transaction for its effects on the accounts.
2. Enter the transaction information in a **journal**.
3. Transfer the journal information to the appropriate accounts in the **ledger**.

The recording process begins with the transaction. **Business documents**, such as a sales slip, a check, a bill, or a cash register tape, provide evidence of the transaction. The company analyzes this evidence to determine the transaction's effects on specific accounts. The company then enters the transaction in the journal. Finally, it transfers the journal entry to the designated accounts in the ledger. Illustration 2-12 shows the recording process.

The steps in the recording process occur repeatedly. In Chapter 1, we illustrated the first step, the analysis of transactions, and will give further examples in this and later chapters. The other two steps in the recording process are explained in the next sections.

**Ethics Note**

Business documents provide evidence that transactions actually occurred. International Outsourcing Services, LLC was accused of submitting fraudulent documents (store coupons) to companies such as Kraft Foods and PepsiCo for reimbursement of as much as $250 million. Ensuring that all recorded transactions are backed up by proper business documents reduces the likelihood of fraudulent activity.

**The Recording Process**

Analyze each transaction          Enter transaction in a journal          Transfer journal information to ledger accounts

**Illustration 2-12**
The recording process

## The Journal

Companies initially record transactions in chronological order (the order in which they occur). Thus, the **journal** is referred to as the book of original entry. For each transaction, the journal shows the debit and credit effects on specific accounts.

Companies may use various kinds of journals, but every company has the most basic form of journal, a **general journal**. Typically, a general journal has spaces for dates, account titles and explanations, references, and two amount columns. See the format of the journal in Illustration 2-13 (page 60). *Whenever we use the term "journal" in this textbook, we mean the general journal unless we specify otherwise.*

The journal makes several significant contributions to the recording process:

**LEARNING OBJECTIVE   4**

Explain what a journal is and how it helps in the recording process.

1. It discloses in one place the **complete effects of a transaction**.

2. It provides a **chronological record** of transactions.

3. It helps to **prevent or locate errors** because the debit and credit amounts for each entry can be easily compared.

### JOURNALIZING

Entering transaction data in the journal is known as **journalizing**. Companies make separate journal entries for each transaction. A complete entry consists of (1) the date of the transaction, (2) the accounts and amounts to be debited and credited, and (3) a brief explanation of the transaction.

Illustration 2-13 shows the technique of journalizing, using the first two transactions of Softbyte. Recall that on September 1, Ray Neal invested $15,000 cash in the business, and Softbyte purchased computer equipment for $7,000 cash. The number J1 indicates that these two entries are recorded on the first page of the journal. Illustration 2-13 shows the standard form of journal entries for these two transactions. (The boxed numbers correspond to explanations in the list below the illustration.)

**Illustration 2-13**
Technique of journalizing

| GENERAL JOURNAL | | | | | J1 |
|---|---|---|---|---|---|
| **Date** | **Account Titles and Explanation** | | **Ref.** | **Debit** | **Credit** |
| 2014 | | | 5 | | |
| Sept. 1 2 | Cash | | | 15,000 | |
| 1 3 | Owner's Capital | | | | 15,000 |
| 4 | (Owner's investment of cash in business) | | | | |
| 1 | Equipment | | | 7,000 | |
| | Cash | | | | 7,000 |
| | (Purchase of equipment for cash) | | | | |

1 The date of the transaction is entered in the Date column.

2 The debit account title (that is, the account to be debited) is entered first at the extreme left margin of the column headed "Account Titles and Explanation," and the amount of the debit is recorded in the Debit column.

3 The credit account title (that is, the account to be credited) is indented and entered on the next line in the column headed "Account Titles and Explanation," and the amount of the credit is recorded in the Credit column.

4 A brief explanation of the transaction appears on the line below the credit account title. A space is left between journal entries. The blank space separates individual journal entries and makes the entire journal easier to read.

5 The column titled Ref. (which stands for Reference) is left blank when the journal entry is made. This column is used later when the journal entries are transferred to the ledger accounts.

**It is important to use correct and specific account titles in journalizing.** Erroneous account titles lead to incorrect financial statements. However, some flexibility exists initially in selecting account titles. The main criterion is that each title must appropriately describe the content of the account. Once a company chooses the specific title to use, it should record under that account title all later transactions involving the account.[1]

### SIMPLE AND COMPOUND ENTRIES

Some entries involve only two accounts, one debit and one credit. (See, for example, the entries in Illustration 2-13.) An entry like these is considered a **simple entry**. Some transactions, however, require more than two accounts in journalizing. An entry that requires three or more accounts is a **compound entry**. To illustrate, assume that on July 1, Butler Company purchases a delivery truck costing $14,000.

---

[1]*In homework problems, you should use specific account titles when they are given.* When account titles are not given, you may select account titles that identify the nature and content of each account. The account titles used in journalizing should not contain explanations such as Cash Paid or Cash Received.

It pays $8,000 cash now and agrees to pay the remaining $6,000 on account (to be paid later). The compound entry is as follows.

| GENERAL JOURNAL | | | | J1 |
|---|---|---|---|---|
| Date | Account Titles and Explanation | Ref. | Debit | Credit |
| 2014<br>July 1 | Equipment | | 14,000 | |
| | Cash | | | 8,000 |
| | Accounts Payable | | | 6,000 |
| | (Purchased truck for cash with balance<br>on account) | | | |

**Illustration 2-14**
Compound journal entry

In a compound entry, the standard format requires that all debits be listed before the credits.

## ACCOUNTING ACROSS THE ORGANIZATION

### Boosting Microsoft's Profits

At one time, Microsoft's Home and Entertainment Division lost over $4 billion, mostly due to losses on the original Xbox videogame console. With the Xbox 360 videogame console, the division's head of finance, Bryan Lee, hoped the division would become profitable. He set strict goals for sales, revenue, and profit. "A manager seeking to spend more on a feature such as a disk drive has to find allies in the group to cut spending elsewhere, or identify new revenue to offset the increase," he explained.

For example, Microsoft originally designed the Xbox 360 to have 256 megabytes of memory. But the design department said that amount of memory wouldn't support the best special effects. The purchasing department said that adding more memory would cost $30—which was 10% of the estimated selling price of $300. The marketing department, however, "determined that adding the memory would let Microsoft reduce marketing costs and attract more game developers, boosting royalty revenue. It would also extend the life of the console, generating more sales." As a result, Microsoft doubled the memory to 512 megabytes. Today, the division enjoys great success.

*Source:* Robert A. Guth, "New Xbox Aim for Microsoft: Profitability," *Wall Street Journal* (May 24, 2005), p. C1.

 In what ways is this Microsoft division using accounting to assist in its effort to become more profitable? (See page 95.)

## > DO IT!

### Recording Business Activities

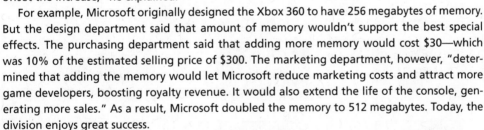

Kate Browne engaged in the following activities in establishing her salon, Hair It Is:

1. Opened a bank account in the name of Hair It Is and deposited $20,000 of her own money in this account as her initial investment.
2. Purchased equipment on account (to be paid in 30 days) for a total cost of $4,800.
3. Interviewed three persons for the position of hair stylist.

In what form (type of record) should Kate record these three activities? Prepare the entries to record the transactions.

## Solution

Each transaction that is recorded is entered in the general journal. The three activities would be recorded as follows.

| | | |
|---|---|---|
| **1.** Cash | 20,000 | |
|     Owner's Capital | | 20,000 |
|       (Owner's investment of cash in business) | | |
| **2.** Equipment | 4,800 | |
|     Accounts Payable | | 4,800 |
|       (Purchase of equipment on account) | | |
| **3.** No entry because no transaction has occurred. | | |

Related exercise material: **BE2-3, BE2-6, E2-3, E2-5, E2-6, E2-7, and** **DO IT!** 2-2.

## The Ledger

The entire group of accounts maintained by a company is the **ledger**. The ledger provides the balance in each of the accounts as well as keeps track of changes in these balances.

Companies may use various kinds of ledgers, but every company has a general ledger. A **general ledger** contains all the asset, liability, and owner's equity accounts, as shown in Illustration 2-15 for J. Lind Company. *Whenever we use the term "ledger" in this textbook, we are referring to the general ledger unless we specify otherwise.*

**Illustration 2-15**
The general ledger, which contains all of a company's accounts

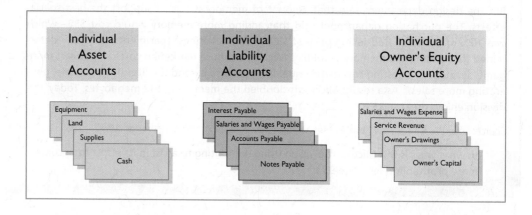

Companies arrange the ledger in the sequence in which they present the accounts in the financial statements, beginning with the balance sheet accounts. First in order are the asset accounts, followed by liability accounts, owner's capital, owner's drawings, revenues, and expenses. Each account is numbered for easier identification.

The ledger provides the balance in each of the accounts. For example, the Cash account shows the amount of cash available to meet current obligations. The Accounts Receivable account shows amounts due from customers. Accounts Payable shows amounts owed to creditors.

## ETHICS INSIGHT

### A Convenient Overstatement

Sometimes a company's investment securities suffer a permanent decline in value below their original cost. When this occurs, the company is supposed to reduce the recorded value of the securities on its balance sheet ("write-them down" in common financial lingo) and record a loss. It appears, however, that during the financial crisis, employees at some financial institutions chose to look the other way as the value of their investments skidded. A number of Wall Street traders that worked for the investment bank Credit Suisse Group were charged with intentionally overstating the value of securities that had suffered declines of approximately $2.85 billion. One reason that they may have been reluctant to record the losses is out of fear that the company's shareholders and clients would panic if they saw the magnitude of the losses. However, personal self-interest might have been equally to blame—the bonuses of the traders were tied to the value of the investment securities.

*Source:* S. Pulliam, J. Eaglesham, and M. Siconolfi, "U.S. Plans Changes on Bond Fraud," *Wall Street Journal Online* (February 1, 2012).

**?** What incentives might employees have had to overstate the value of these investment securities on the company's financial statements? (See page 95.)

## STANDARD FORM OF ACCOUNT

The simple T-account form used in accounting textbooks is often very useful for illustration purposes. However, in practice, the account forms used in ledgers are much more structured. Illustration 2-16 shows a typical form, using assumed data from a cash account.

| CASH | | | | | NO. 101 |
|---|---|---|---|---|---|
| **Date** | **Explanation** | **Ref.** | **Debit** | **Credit** | **Balance** |
| 2014 | | | | | |
| June 1 | | | 25,000 | | 25,000 |
| 2 | | | | 8,000 | 17,000 |
| 3 | | | 4,200 | | 21,200 |
| 9 | | | 7,500 | | 28,700 |
| 17 | | | | 11,700 | 17,000 |
| 20 | | | | 250 | 16,750 |
| 30 | | | | 7,300 | 9,450 |

**Illustration 2-16**
Three-column form of account

This format is called the **three-column form of account**. It has three money columns—debit, credit, and balance. The balance in the account is determined after each transaction. Companies use the explanation space and reference columns to provide special information about the transaction.

## POSTING

Transferring journal entries to the ledger accounts is called **posting**. This phase of the recording process accumulates the effects of journalized transactions into the individual accounts. Posting involves the following steps.

1. In the **ledger**, in the appropriate columns of the account(s) debited, enter the date, journal page, and debit amount shown in the journal.

2. In the reference column of the **journal**, write the account number to which the debit amount was posted.

LEARNING OBJECTIVE 6

Explain what posting is and how it helps in the recording process.

3. In the **ledger**, in the appropriate columns of the account(s) credited, enter the date, journal page, and credit amount shown in the journal.

4. In the reference column of the **journal**, write the account number to which the credit amount was posted.

Illustration 2-17 shows these four steps using Softbyte's first journal entry. The boxed numbers indicate the sequence of the steps.

**Illustration 2-17**

Posting a journal entry

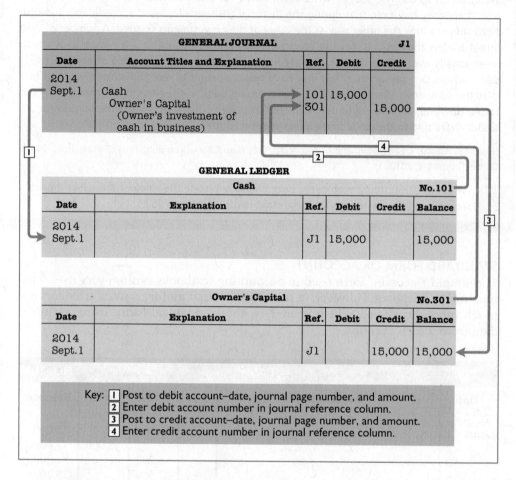

Posting should be performed in chronological order. That is, the company should post all the debits and credits of one journal entry before proceeding to the next journal entry. Postings should be made on a timely basis to ensure that the ledger is up to date.[2]

The reference column of a ledger account indicates the journal page from which the transaction was posted.[3] The explanation space of the ledger account is used infrequently because an explanation already appears in the journal.

## CHART OF ACCOUNTS

The number and type of accounts differ for each company. The number of accounts depends on the amount of detail management desires. For example, the management of one company may want a single account for all types of utility expense. Another may keep separate expense accounts for each type of utility, such as gas, electricity, and water. Similarly, a small company like Softbyte will

---

[2]*In homework problems, you can journalize all transactions before posting any of the journal entries.*
[3]After the last entry has been posted, the accountant should scan the reference column **in the journal**, to confirm that all postings have been made.

have fewer accounts than a corporate giant like Dell. Softbyte may be able to manage and report its activities in 20 to 30 accounts, while Dell may require thousands of accounts to keep track of its worldwide activities.

Most companies have a **chart of accounts**. This chart lists the accounts and the account numbers that identify their location in the ledger. The numbering system that identifies the accounts usually starts with the balance sheet accounts and follows with the income statement accounts.

In this and the next two chapters, we will be explaining the accounting for Pioneer Advertising Agency (a service company). Accounts 101–199 indicate asset accounts; 200–299 indicate liabilities; 301–350 indicate owner's equity accounts; 400–499, revenues; 601–799, expenses; 800–899, other revenues; and 900–999, other expenses. Illustration 2-18 shows Pioneer's chart of accounts. Accounts listed in red are used in this chapter; accounts shown in black are explained in later chapters.

**Helpful Hint** On the textbook's front endpapers, you also will find an expanded chart of accounts.

**Illustration 2-18**
Chart of accounts

### PIONEER ADVERTISING AGENCY
#### Chart of Accounts

| **Assets** | **Owner's Equity** |
|---|---|
| 101 Cash | 301 Owner's Capital |
| 112 Accounts Receivable | 306 Owner's Drawings |
| 126 Supplies | 350 Income Summary |
| 130 Prepaid Insurance | |
| 157 Equipment | **Revenues** |
| 158 Accumulated Depreciation—Equipment | 400 Service Revenue |
| **Liabilities** | **Expenses** |
| 200 Notes Payable | 631 Supplies Expense |
| 201 Accounts Payable | 711 Depreciation Expense |
| 209 Unearned Service Revenue | 722 Insurance Expense |
| 212 Salaries and Wages Payable | 726 Salaries and Wages Expense |
| 230 Interest Payable | 729 Rent Expense |
| | 732 Utilities Expense |
| | 905 Interest Expense |

You will notice that there are gaps in the numbering system of the chart of accounts for Pioneer Advertising. Companies leave gaps to permit the insertion of new accounts as needed during the life of the business.

## The Recording Process Illustrated

Illustrations 2-19 through 2-28 (pages 66–70) show the basic steps in the recording process, using the October transactions of Pioneer Advertising Agency. Pioneer's accounting period is a month. In these illustrations, a basic analysis, an equation analysis, and a debit-credit analysis precede the journal entry and posting of each transaction. For simplicity, we use the T-account form to show the posting instead of the standard account form.

Study these transaction analyses carefully. **The purpose of transaction analysis is first to identify the type of account involved, and then to determine whether to make a debit or a credit to the account.** You should always perform this type of analysis before preparing a journal entry. Doing so will help you understand the journal entries discussed in this chapter as well as more complex journal entries in later chapters.

**Illustration 2-19**
Investment of cash by owner

**Cash Flows**
+10,000

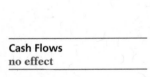

**Helpful Hint** Follow these steps:
1. Determine what type of account is involved.
2. Determine what items increased or decreased and by how much.
3. Translate the increases and decreases into debits and credits.

| | |
|---|---|
| **Transaction** | On October 1, C. R. Byrd invests $10,000 cash in an advertising company called Pioneer Advertising Agency. |
| **Basic Analysis** | The asset Cash increases $10,000, and owner's equity (specifically, Owner's Capital) increases $10,000. |

**Equation Analysis**

$$\underline{\text{Assets}} = \underline{\text{Liabilities}} + \underline{\text{Owner's Equity}}$$

|  Cash  | = | | Owner's Capital |
|---|---|---|---|
| +10,000 | | | +10,000 |

**Debit–Credit Analysis**

Debits increase assets: debit Cash $10,000.
Credits increase owner's equity: credit Owner's Capital $10,000.

**Journal Entry**

| Oct. 1 | Cash | 101 | 10,000 | |
|---|---|---|---|---|
| | Owner's Capital | 301 | | 10,000 |
| | (Owner's investment of cash in business) | | | |

**Posting**

| Cash | | 101 |
|---|---|---|
| Oct. 1 | 10,000 | |

| Owner's Capital | | 301 |
|---|---|---|
| | Oct. 1 | 10,000 |

---

**Illustration 2-20**
Purchase of office equipment

**Cash Flows**
no effect

| | |
|---|---|
| **Transaction** | On October 1, Pioneer purchases office equipment costing $5,000 by signing a 3-month, 12%, $5,000 note payable. |
| **Basic Analysis** | The asset Equipment increases $5,000, and the liability Notes Payable increases $5,000. |

**Equation Analysis**

$$\underline{\text{Assets}} = \underline{\text{Liabilities}} + \underline{\text{Owner's Equity}}$$

| Equipment | = | Notes Payable | |
|---|---|---|---|
| +5,000 | | +5,000 | |

**Debit–Credit Analysis**

Debits increase assets: debit Equipment $5,000.
Credits increase liabilities: credit Notes Payable $5,000.

**Journal Entry**

| Oct. 1 | Equipment | 157 | 5,000 | |
|---|---|---|---|---|
| | Notes Payable | 200 | | 5,000 |
| | (Issued 3-month, 12% note for office equipment) | | | |

**Posting**

| Equipment | | 157 |
|---|---|---|
| Oct. 1 | 5,000 | |

| Notes Payable | | 200 |
|---|---|---|
| | Oct. 1 | 5,000 |

**Transaction**

On October 2, Pioneer receives a $1,200 cash advance from R. Knox, a client, for advertising services that are expected to be completed by December 31.

**Basic Analysis**

The asset Cash increases $1,200; the liability Unearned Service Revenue increases $1,200 because the service has not been performed yet. That is, when Pioneer receives an advance payment, it should record an unearned revenue (a liability) in order to recognize the obligation that exists. Note also that although most liabilities have the word "payable" in their title, unearned revenue is considered a liability even though the word payable is not used.

**Equation Analysis**

| Assets | = | Liabilities | + | Owner's Equity |
|--------|---|-------------|---|----------------|
| | | Unearned Service | | |
| Cash | = | Revenue | | |
| +1,200 | | +1,200 | | |

**Debit–Credit Analysis**

Debits increase assets: debit Cash $1,200.
Credits increase liabilities: credit Unearned Service Revenue $1,200.

**Journal Entry**

| Oct. 2 | Cash | 101 | 1,200 | |
|--------|------|-----|-------|---|
| | Unearned Service Revenue | 209 | | 1,200 |
| | (Received cash from | | | |
| | R. Knox for future service) | | | |

**Posting**

| Cash | | 101 | | Unearned Service Revenue | 209 |
|------|---|-----|---|--------------------------|-----|
| Oct. 1 | 10,000 | | | | Oct. 2 | 1,200 |
| 2 | 1,200 | | | | | |

**Illustration 2-21**
Receipt of cash for future service

**Cash Flows**
+1,200

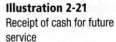

---

**Transaction**

On October 3, Pioneer pays office rent for October in cash, $900.

**Basic Analysis**

The expense account Rent Expense increases $900 because the payment pertains only to the current month; the asset Cash decreases $900.

**Equation Analysis**

| Assets | = | Liabilities | + | Owner's Equity |
|--------|---|-------------|---|----------------|
| | | | | Rent |
| Cash | = | | | Expense |
| -900 | | | | -900 |

**Debit–Credit Analysis**

Debits increase expenses: debit Rent Expense $900.
Credits decrease assets: credit Cash $900.

**Journal Entry**

| Oct. 3 | Rent Expense | 729 | 900 | |
|--------|--------------|-----|-----|---|
| | Cash | 101 | | 900 |
| | (Paid October rent) | | | |

**Posting**

| Cash | | 101 | | | Rent Expense | 729 |
|------|---|-----|---|---|--------------|-----|
| Oct. 1 | 10,000 | Oct. 3 | 900 | | Oct. 3 | 900 | |
| 2 | 1,200 | | | | | | |

**Illustration 2-22**
Payment of monthly rent

**Cash Flows**
−900

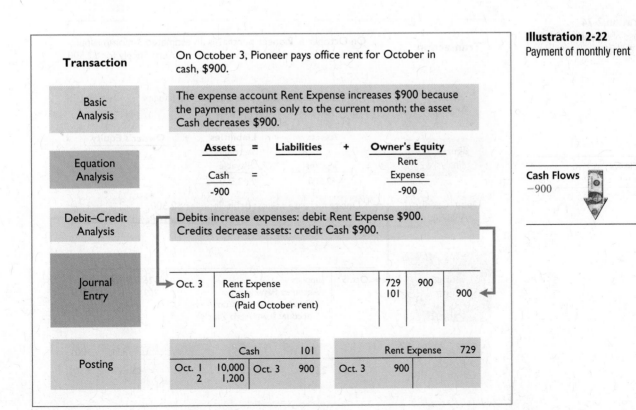

**Illustration 2-23**
Payment for insurance

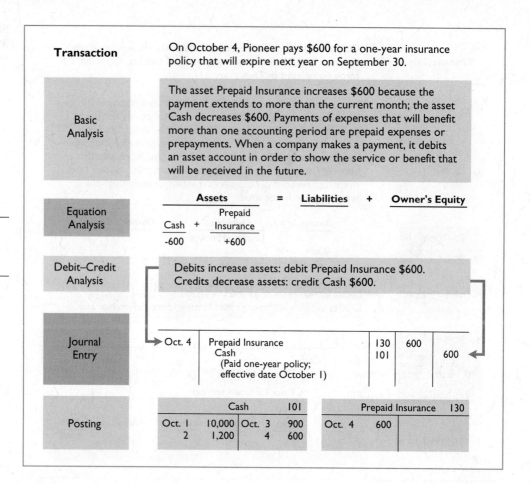

| Transaction | On October 4, Pioneer pays $600 for a one-year insurance policy that will expire next year on September 30. |
|---|---|
| Basic Analysis | The asset Prepaid Insurance increases $600 because the payment extends to more than the current month; the asset Cash decreases $600. Payments of expenses that will benefit more than one accounting period are prepaid expenses or prepayments. When a company makes a payment, it debits an asset account in order to show the service or benefit that will be received in the future. |

**Cash Flows**
−600

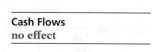

Equation Analysis

|  | Assets | = | Liabilities | + | Owner's Equity |
|---|---|---|---|---|---|
|  | Prepaid |  |  |  |  |
| Cash + | Insurance | = |  |  |  |
| -600 | +600 |  |  |  |  |

Debit–Credit Analysis

Debits increase assets: debit Prepaid Insurance $600.
Credits decrease assets: credit Cash $600.

Journal Entry

| Oct. 4 | Prepaid Insurance | 130 | 600 |  |
|---|---|---|---|---|
|  | Cash | 101 |  | 600 |
|  | (Paid one-year policy; effective date October 1) |  |  |  |

Posting

| Cash | | | 101 | | Prepaid Insurance | | 130 |
|---|---|---|---|---|---|---|---|
| Oct. 1 | 10,000 | Oct. 3 | 900 | Oct. 4 | 600 | | |
| 2 | 1,200 | 4 | 600 | | | | |

**Illustration 2-24**
Purchase of supplies on credit

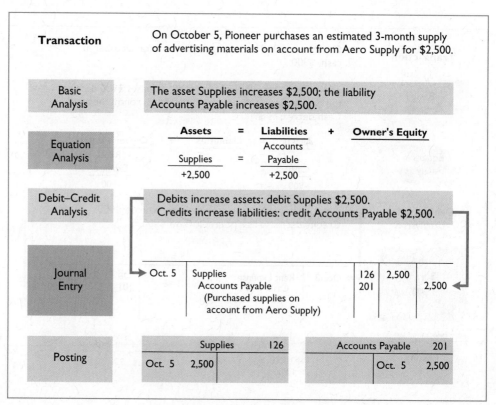

| Transaction | On October 5, Pioneer purchases an estimated 3-month supply of advertising materials on account from Aero Supply for $2,500. |
|---|---|
| Basic Analysis | The asset Supplies increases $2,500; the liability Accounts Payable increases $2,500. |

**Cash Flows**
no effect

Equation Analysis

|  | Assets | = | Liabilities | + | Owner's Equity |
|---|---|---|---|---|---|
|  |  |  | Accounts |  |  |
|  | Supplies | = | Payable |  |  |
|  | +2,500 |  | +2,500 |  |  |

Debit–Credit Analysis

Debits increase assets: debit Supplies $2,500.
Credits increase liabilities: credit Accounts Payable $2,500.

Journal Entry

| Oct. 5 | Supplies | 126 | 2,500 |  |
|---|---|---|---|---|
|  | Accounts Payable | 201 |  | 2,500 |
|  | (Purchased supplies on account from Aero Supply) |  |  |  |

Posting

| Supplies | | 126 | | Accounts Payable | | 201 |
|---|---|---|---|---|---|---|
| Oct. 5 | 2,500 | | | | Oct. 5 | 2,500 |

| Event | On October 9, Pioneer hires four employees to begin work on October 15. Each employee is to receive a weekly salary of $500 for a 5-day work week, payable every 2 weeks—first payment made on October 26. |
|---|---|
| Basic Analysis | A business transaction has not occurred. There is only an agreement between the employer and the employees to enter into a business transaction beginning on October 15. Thus, a debit–credit analysis is not needed because there is no accounting entry. (See transaction of October 26 for first entry.) |

**Illustration 2-25**
Hiring of employees

**Cash Flows**
no effect

---

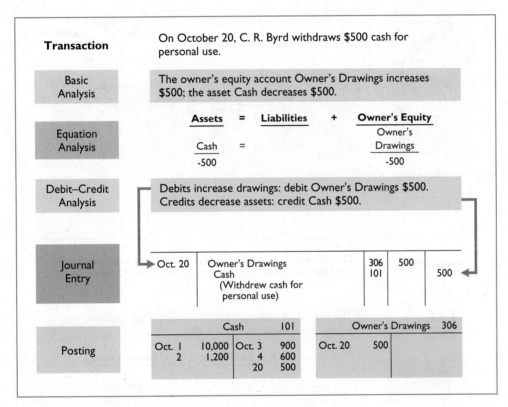

| Transaction | On October 20, C. R. Byrd withdraws $500 cash for personal use. |
|---|---|
| Basic Analysis | The owner's equity account Owner's Drawings increases $500; the asset Cash decreases $500. |

|  | **Assets** | **=** | **Liabilities** | **+** | **Owner's Equity** |
|---|---|---|---|---|---|
| Equation Analysis |  |  |  |  | Owner's |
|  | Cash | = |  |  | Drawings |
|  | -500 |  |  |  | -500 |

| Debit–Credit Analysis | Debits increase drawings: debit Owner's Drawings $500. Credits decrease assets: credit Cash $500. |

| Journal Entry | Oct. 20 | Owner's Drawings | 306 | 500 | |
|---|---|---|---|---|---|
| | | Cash | 101 | | 500 |
| | | (Withdrew cash for personal use) | | | |

Posting

| Cash | | | 101 | | Owner's Drawings | | 306 |
|---|---|---|---|---|---|---|---|
| Oct. 1 | 10,000 | Oct. 3 | 900 | | Oct. 20 | 500 | |
| 2 | 1,200 | 4 | 600 | | | | |
| | | 20 | 500 | | | | |

**Illustration 2-26**
Withdrawal of cash by owner

**Cash Flows**
−500

**Illustration 2-27**
Payment of salaries

**Cash Flows**
−4,000

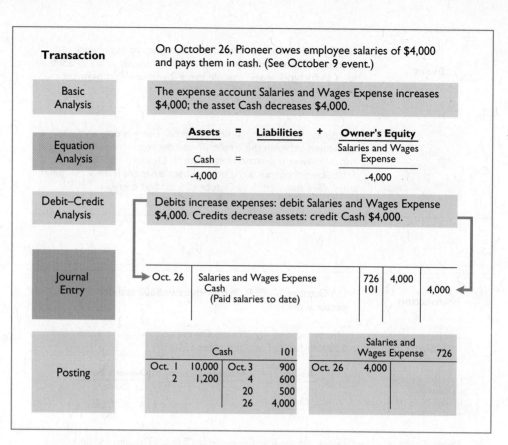

| Transaction | On October 26, Pioneer owes employee salaries of $4,000 and pays them in cash. (See October 9 event.) |
|---|---|
| Basic Analysis | The expense account Salaries and Wages Expense increases $4,000; the asset Cash decreases $4,000. |

Equation Analysis

| Assets | = | Liabilities | + | Owner's Equity |
|---|---|---|---|---|
| | | | | Salaries and Wages Expense |
| Cash | = | | | |
| −4,000 | | | | −4,000 |

Debit–Credit Analysis: Debits increase expenses: debit Salaries and Wages Expense $4,000. Credits decrease assets: credit Cash $4,000.

Journal Entry

| Oct. 26 | Salaries and Wages Expense | 726 | 4,000 | |
|---|---|---|---|---|
| | Cash | 101 | | 4,000 |
| | (Paid salaries to date) | | | |

Posting

| | Cash | | 101 |
|---|---|---|---|
| Oct. 1 | 10,000 | Oct. 3 | 900 |
| 2 | 1,200 | 4 | 600 |
| | | 20 | 500 |
| | | 26 | 4,000 |

| Salaries and Wages Expense | 726 |
|---|---|
| Oct. 26  4,000 | |

**Illustration 2-28**
Receipt of cash for services performed

**Cash Flows**
+10,000

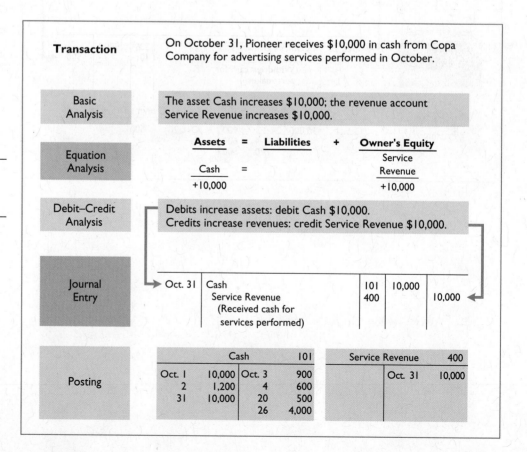

| Transaction | On October 31, Pioneer receives $10,000 in cash from Copa Company for advertising services performed in October. |
|---|---|
| Basic Analysis | The asset Cash increases $10,000; the revenue account Service Revenue increases $10,000. |

Equation Analysis

| Assets | = | Liabilities | + | Owner's Equity |
|---|---|---|---|---|
| | | | | Service Revenue |
| Cash | = | | | |
| +10,000 | | | | +10,000 |

Debit–Credit Analysis: Debits increase assets: debit Cash $10,000. Credits increase revenues: credit Service Revenue $10,000.

Journal Entry

| Oct. 31 | Cash | 101 | 10,000 | |
|---|---|---|---|---|
| | Service Revenue | 400 | | 10,000 |
| | (Received cash for services performed) | | | |

Posting

| | Cash | | 101 |
|---|---|---|---|
| Oct. 1 | 10,000 | Oct. 3 | 900 |
| 2 | 1,200 | 4 | 600 |
| 31 | 10,000 | 20 | 500 |
| | | 26 | 4,000 |

| Service Revenue | 400 |
|---|---|
| | Oct. 31  10,000 |

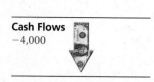

> **DO IT!**

## Posting

Kate Browne recorded the following transactions in a general journal during the month of March.

| | | | | |
|---|---|---|---|---|
| Mar. 4 | Cash | | 2,280 | |
| | Service Revenue | | | 2,280 |
| 15 | Salaries and Wages Expense | | 400 | |
| | Cash | | | 400 |
| 19 | Utilities Expense | | 92 | |
| | Cash | | | 92 |

Post these entries to the Cash account of the general ledger to determine its ending balance. The beginning balance of Cash on March 1 was $600.

### Action Plan

✔ Recall that posting involves transferring the journalized debits and credits to specific accounts in the ledger.

✔ Determine the ending balance by netting the total debits and credits.

### Solution

| Cash | | | |
|---|---|---|---|
| 3/1 | 600 | 3/15 | 400 |
| 3/4 | 2,280 | 3/19 | 92 |
| 3/31 Bal. | 2,388 | | |

Related exercise material: **BE2-7, BE2-8, E2-8, E2-12, and DO IT!** 2-3.

✔ **The Navigator**

## Summary Illustration of Journalizing and Posting

Illustration 2-29 shows the journal for Pioneer Advertising Agency for October.

**Illustration 2-29**
General journal entries

| GENERAL JOURNAL | | | | PAGE J1 |
|---|---|---|---|---|
| **Date** | **Account Titles and Explanation** | **Ref.** | **Debit** | **Credit** |
| 2014 | | | | |
| Oct. 1 | Cash | 101 | 10,000 | |
| | Owner's Capital | 301 | | 10,000 |
| | (Owner's investment of cash in business) | | | |
| 1 | Equipment | 157 | 5,000 | |
| | Notes Payable | 200 | | 5,000 |
| | (Issued 3-month, 12% note for office equipment) | | | |
| 2 | Cash | 101 | 1,200 | |
| | Unearned Service Revenue | 209 | | 1,200 |
| | (Received cash from R. Knox for future service) | | | |
| 3 | Rent Expense | 729 | 900 | |
| | Cash | 101 | | 900 |
| | (Paid October rent) | | | |
| 4 | Prepaid Insurance | 130 | 600 | |
| | Cash | 101 | | 600 |
| | (Paid one-year policy; effective date October 1) | | | |
| 5 | Supplies | 126 | 2,500 | |
| | Accounts Payable | 201 | | 2,500 |
| | (Purchased supplies on account from Aero Supply) | | | |

*(continued)*

**The trial balance proves the mathematical equality of debits and credits after posting.** Under the double-entry system, this equality occurs when the sum of the debit account balances equals the sum of the credit account balances. **A trial balance may also uncover errors in journalizing and posting.** For example, a trial balance may well have detected the error at MF Global discussed in the Feature Story. **In addition, a trial balance is useful in the preparation of financial statements**, as we will explain in the next two chapters.

The steps for preparing a trial balance are:

1. List the account titles and their balances in the appropriate debit or credit column.

2. Total the debit and credit columns.

3. Prove the equality of the two columns.

Illustration 2-31 shows the trial balance prepared from Pioneer Advertising's ledger. Note that the total debits equal the total credits.

**PIONEER ADVERTISING AGENCY**
Trial Balance
October 31, 2014

|  | Debit | Credit |
|---|---|---|
| Cash | $ 15,200 |  |
| Supplies | 2,500 |  |
| Prepaid Insurance | 600 |  |
| Equipment | 5,000 |  |
| Notes Payable |  | $ 5,000 |
| Accounts Payable |  | 2,500 |
| Unearned Service Revenue |  | 1,200 |
| Owner's Capital |  | 10,000 |
| Owner's Drawings | 500 |  |
| Service Revenue |  | 10,000 |
| Salaries and Wages Expense | 4,000 |  |
| Rent Expense | 900 |  |
|  | $28,700 | $28,700 |

A trial balance is a necessary checkpoint for uncovering certain types of errors. For example, if only the debit portion of a journal entry has been posted, the trial balance would bring this error to light.

## Limitations of a Trial Balance

A trial balance does not guarantee freedom from recording errors, however. Numerous errors may exist even though the totals of the trial balance columns agree. For example, the trial balance may balance even when:

1. A transaction is not journalized.

2. A correct journal entry is not posted.

3. A journal entry is posted twice.

4. Incorrect accounts are used in journalizing or posting.

5. Offsetting errors are made in recording the amount of a transaction.

As long as equal debits and credits are posted, even to the wrong account or in the wrong amount, the total debits will equal the total credits. **The trial balance does not prove that the company has recorded all transactions or that the ledger is correct.**

**Ethics Note**

An *error* is the result of an unintentional mistake; it is neither ethical nor unethical. An *irregularity* is an intentional misstatement, which *is* viewed as unethical.

## > DO IT!

**Trial Balance**

The following accounts come from the ledger of SnowGo Company at December 31, 2014.

| | | | | | |
|---|---|---|---|---|---|
| 157 | Equipment | $88,000 | 301 | Owner's Capital | $20,000 |
| 306 | Owner's Drawings | 8,000 | 212 | Salaries and Wages | |
| 201 | Accounts Payable | 22,000 | | Payable | 2,000 |
| 726 | Salaries and Wages | | 200 | Notes Payable | 19,000 |
| | Expense | 42,000 | 732 | Utilities Expense | 3,000 |
| 112 | Accounts Receivable | 4,000 | 130 | Prepaid Insurance | 6,000 |
| 400 | Service Revenue | 95,000 | 101 | Cash | 7,000 |

Prepare a trial balance in good form.

### Solution

**SNOWGO COMPANY**
Trial Balance
December 31, 2014

| | Debit | Credit |
|---|---|---|
| Cash | $ 7,000 | |
| Accounts Receivable | 4,000 | |
| Prepaid Insurance | 6,000 | |
| Equipment | 88,000 | |
| Notes Payable | | $ 19,000 |
| Accounts Payable | | 22,000 |
| Salaries and Wages Payable | | 2,000 |
| Owner's Capital | | 20,000 |
| Owner's Drawings | 8,000 | |
| Service Revenue | | 95,000 |
| Utilities Expense | 3,000 | |
| Salaries and Wages Expense | 42,000 | |
| | $158,000 | $158,000 |

Related exercise material: **BE2-9, BE2-10, E2-9, E2-10, E2-11, E2-13, E2-14, and DO IT! 2-4.**

✔ **The Navigator**

## > Comprehensive DO IT!

Bob Sample opened the Campus Laundromat on September 1, 2014. During the first month of operations, the following transactions occurred.

Sept. 1 Bob invested $20,000 cash in the business.
2 The company paid $1,000 cash for store rent for September.
3 Purchased washers and dryers for $25,000, paying $10,000 in cash and signing a $15,000, 6-month, 12% note payable.
4 Paid $1,200 for a one-year accident insurance policy.
10 Received a bill from the *Daily News* for advertising the opening of the laundromat $200.
20 Bob withdrew $700 cash for personal use.
30 The company determined that cash receipts for laundry services for the month were $6,200.

The chart of accounts for the company is the same as that for Pioneer Advertising Agency plus No. 610 Advertising Expense.

## Instructions

**(a)** Journalize the September transactions. (Use J1 for the journal page number.)

**(b)** Open ledger accounts and post the September transactions.

**(c)** Prepare a trial balance at September 30, 2014.

### Action Plan

✔ Make separate journal entries for each transaction.

✔ In journalizing, make sure debits equal credits.

✔ In journalizing, use specific account titles taken from the chart of accounts.

✔ Provide appropriate description of each journal entry.

✔ Arrange ledger in statement order, beginning with the balance sheet accounts.

✔ Post in chronological order.

✔ Use numbers in the reference column to indicate the amount has been posted.

✔ In the trial balance, list accounts in the order in which they appear in the ledger.

✔ List debit balances in the left column, and credit balances in the right column.

## Solution to Comprehensive DO IT!

**(a)**

| | | GENERAL JOURNAL | | | J1 |
|---|---|---|---|---|---|
| Date | | Account Titles and Explanation | Ref. | Debit | Credit |
| 2014 | | | | | |
| Sept. | 1 | Cash | 101 | 20,000 | |
| | |     Owner's Capital | 301 | | 20,000 |
| | |       (Owner's investment of cash in business) | | | |
| | 2 | Rent Expense | 729 | 1,000 | |
| | |     Cash | 101 | | 1,000 |
| | |       (Paid September rent) | | | |
| | 3 | Equipment | 157 | 25,000 | |
| | |     Cash | 101 | | 10,000 |
| | |     Notes Payable | 200 | | 15,000 |
| | |       (Purchased laundry equipment for cash and 6-month, 12% note payable) | | | |
| | 4 | Prepaid Insurance | 130 | 1,200 | |
| | |     Cash | 101 | | 1,200 |
| | |       (Paid one-year insurance policy) | | | |
| | 10 | Advertising Expense | 610 | 200 | |
| | |     Accounts Payable | 201 | | 200 |
| | |       (Received bill from Daily News for advertising) | | | |
| | 20 | Owner's Drawings | 306 | 700 | |
| | |     Cash | 101 | | 700 |
| | |       (Withdrew cash for personal use) | | | |
| | 30 | Cash | 101 | 6,200 | |
| | |     Service Revenue | 400 | | 6,200 |
| | |       (Received cash for services performed) | | | |

**(b)**

### GENERAL LEDGER

**Cash**      No. 101

| Date | Explanation | Ref. | Debit | Credit | Balance |
|---|---|---|---|---|---|
| 2014 | | | | | |
| Sept. 1 | | J1 | 20,000 | | 20,000 |
| 2 | | J1 | | 1,000 | 19,000 |
| 3 | | J1 | | 10,000 | 9,000 |
| 4 | | J1 | | 1,200 | 7,800 |
| 20 | | J1 | | 700 | 7,100 |
| 30 | | J1 | 6,200 | | 13,300 |

**Prepaid Insurance**      No. 130

| Date | Explanation | Ref. | Debit | Credit | Balance |
|---|---|---|---|---|---|
| 2014 | | | | | |
| Sept. 4 | | J1 | 1,200 | | 1,200 |

**Equipment**      No. 157

| Date | Explanation | Ref. | Debit | Credit | Balance |
|---|---|---|---|---|---|
| 2014 | | | | | |
| Sept. 3 | | J1 | 25,000 | | 25,000 |

**Notes Payable**      No. 200

| Date | Explanation | Ref. | Debit | Credit | Balance |
|---|---|---|---|---|---|
| 2014 | | | | | |
| Sept. 3 | | J1 | | 15,000 | 15,000 |

**Accounts Payable**      No. 201

| Date | Explanation | Ref. | Debit | Credit | Balance |
|---|---|---|---|---|---|
| 2014 | | | | | |
| Sept. 10 | | J1 | | 200 | 200 |

**Owner's Capital**      No. 301

| Date | Explanation | Ref. | Debit | Credit | Balance |
|---|---|---|---|---|---|
| 2014 | | | | | |
| Sept. 1 | | J1 | | 20,000 | 20,000 |

**Owner's Drawings**      No. 306

| Date | Explanation | Ref. | Debit | Credit | Balance |
|---|---|---|---|---|---|
| 2014 | | | | | |
| Sept. 20 | | J1 | 700 | | 700 |

**(b)** **GENERAL LEDGER (*continued*)**

| Service Revenue | | | | | No. 400 |
|---|---|---|---|---|---|
| Date | Explanation | Ref. | Debit | Credit | Balance |
| 2014 Sept. 30 | | J1 | | 6,200 | 6,200 |

| Advertising Expense | | | | | No. 610 |
|---|---|---|---|---|---|
| Date | Explanation | Ref. | Debit | Credit | Balance |
| 2014 Sept. 10 | | J1 | 200 | | 200 |

| Rent Expense | | | | | No. 729 |
|---|---|---|---|---|---|
| Date | Explanation | Ref. | Debit | Credit | Balance |
| 2014 Sept. 2 | | J1 | 1,000 | | 1,000 |

**(c)**

**CAMPUS LAUNDROMAT**
**Trial Balance**
**September 30, 2014**

| | Debit | Credit |
|---|---|---|
| Cash | $13,300 | |
| Prepaid Insurance | 1,200 | |
| Equipment | 25,000 | |
| Notes Payable | | $15,000 |
| Accounts Payable | | 200 |
| Owner's Capital | | 20,000 |
| Owner's Drawings | 700 | |
| Service Revenue | | 6,200 |
| Advertising Expense | 200 | |
| Rent Expense | 1,000 | |
| | $41,400 | $41,400 |

 The Navigator

✔ The Navigator

## SUMMARY OF LEARNING OBJECTIVES

1 **Explain what an account is and how it helps in the recording process.** An account is a record of increases and decreases in specific asset, liability, and owner's equity items.

2 **Define debits and credits and explain their use in recording business transactions.** The terms debit and credit are synonymous with left and right. Assets, drawings, and expenses are increased by debits and decreased by credits. Liabilities, owner's capital, and revenues are increased by credits and decreased by debits.

3 **Identify the basic steps in the recording process.** The basic steps in the recording process are (a) analyze each transaction for its effects on the accounts, (b) enter the transaction information in a journal, (c) transfer the journal information to the appropriate accounts in the ledger.

4 **Explain what a journal is and how it helps in the recording process.** The initial accounting record of a transaction is entered in a journal before the data are entered in the accounts. A journal (a) discloses in one place the complete effects of a transaction, (b) provides a chronological record of transactions, and (c) prevents or locates errors because the debit and credit amounts for each entry can be easily compared.

5 **Explain what a ledger is and how it helps in the recording process.** The ledger is the entire group of accounts maintained by a company. The ledger provides the balance in each of the accounts as well as keeps track of changes in these balances.

6 **Explain what posting is and how it helps in the recording process.** Posting is the transfer of journal entries to the ledger accounts. This phase of the recording process accumulates the effects of journalized transactions in the individual accounts.

7 **Prepare a trial balance and explain its purposes.** A trial balance is a list of accounts and their balances at a given time. Its primary purpose is to prove the equality of debits and credits after posting. A trial balance also uncovers errors in journalizing and posting and is useful in preparing financial statements.

## GLOSSARY

**Account** A record of increases and decreases in specific asset, liability, or owner's equity items. (p. 54).

**Chart of accounts** A list of accounts and the account numbers that identify their location in the ledger. (p. 65).

**Compound entry** A journal entry that involves three or more accounts. (p. 60).

**Credit** The right side of an account. (p. 54).

**Debit** The left side of an account. (p. 54).

**Double-entry system** A system that records in appropriate accounts the dual effect of each transaction. (p. 55).

**General journal** The most basic form of journal. (p. 59).

**General ledger** A ledger that contains all asset, liability, and owner's equity accounts. (p. 62).

**Journal** An accounting record in which transactions are initially recorded in chronological order. (p. 59).

**Journalizing** The entering of transaction data in the journal. (p. 59).

**Ledger** The entire group of accounts maintained by a company. (p. 62).

**Normal balance** An account balance on the side where an increase in the account is recorded. (p. 55).

**Posting** The procedure of transferring journal entries to the ledger accounts. (p. 63).

**Simple entry** A journal entry that involves only two accounts. (p. 60).

**T-account** The basic form of an account. (p. 54).

**Three-column form of account** A form with columns for debit, credit, and balance amounts in an account. (p. 63).

**Trial balance** A list of accounts and their balances at a given time. (p. 72).

 Self-Test, Brief Exercises, Exercises, Problem Set A, and many more components are available for practice in *WileyPLUS*.

## SELF-TEST QUESTIONS

*Answers are on page 96.*

(LO 1) **1.** Which of the following statements about an account is **true**?
  (a) In its simplest form, an account consists of two parts.
  (b) An account is an individual accounting record of increases and decreases in specific asset, liability, and owner's equity items.
  (c) There are separate accounts for specific assets and liabilities but only one account for owner's equity items.
  (d) The left side of an account is the credit or decrease side.

(LO 2) **2.** Debits:
  (a) increase both assets and liabilities.
  (b) decrease both assets and liabilities.
  (c) increase assets and decrease liabilities.
  (d) decrease assets and increase liabilities.

(LO 2) **3.** A revenue account:
  (a) is increased by debits.
  (b) is decreased by credits.
  (c) has a normal balance of a debit.
  (d) is increased by credits.

(LO 2) **4.** Accounts that normally have debit balances are:
  (a) assets, expenses, and revenues.
  (b) assets, expenses, and owner's capital.
  (c) assets, liabilities, and owner's drawings.
  (d) assets, owner's drawings, and expenses.

(LO 2) **5.** The expanded accounting equation is:
  (a) Assets + Liabilities = Owner's Capital + Owner's Drawings + Revenues + Expenses
  (b) Assets = Liabilities + Owner's Capital + Owner's Drawings + Revenues − Expenses

  (c) Assets = Liabilities − Owner's Capital − Owner's Drawings − Revenues − Expenses
  (d) Assets = Liabilities + Owner's Capital − Owner's Drawings + Revenues − Expenses

**6.** Which of the following is **not** part of the recording process?  (LO 3)
  (a) Analyzing transactions.
  (b) Preparing a trial balance.
  (c) Entering transactions in a journal.
  (d) Posting transactions.

**7.** Which of the following statements about a journal is  (LO 4)
**false**?
  (a) It is not a book of original entry.
  (b) It provides a chronological record of transactions.
  (c) It helps to locate errors because the debit and credit amounts for each entry can be readily compared.
  (d) It discloses in one place the complete effect of a transaction.

**8.** The purchase of supplies on account should result in:  (LO 4)
  (a) a debit to Supplies Expense and a credit to Cash.
  (b) a debit to Supplies Expense and a credit to Accounts Payable.
  (c) a debit to Supplies and a credit to Accounts Payable.
  (d) a debit to Supplies and a credit to Accounts Receivable.

**9.** The order of the accounts in the ledger is:  (LO 5)
  (a) assets, revenues, expenses, liabilities, owner's capital, owner's drawings.
  (b) assets, liabilities, owner's capital, owner's drawings, revenues, expenses.
  (c) owner's capital, assets, revenues, expenses, liabilities, owner's drawings.
  (d) revenues, assets, expenses, liabilities, owner's capital, owner's drawings.

(LO 5) **10.** A ledger:
- **(a)** contains only asset and liability accounts.
- **(b)** should show accounts in alphabetical order.
- **(c)** is a collection of the entire group of accounts maintained by a company.
- **(d)** is a book of original entry.

(LO 6) **11.** Posting:
- **(a)** normally occurs before journalizing.
- **(b)** transfers ledger transaction data to the journal.
- **(c)** is an optional step in the recording process.
- **(d)** transfers journal entries to ledger accounts.

(LO 6) **12.** Before posting a payment of $5,000, the Accounts Payable of Senator Company had a normal balance of $16,000. The balance after posting this transaction was:
- **(a)** $21,000.
- **(c)** $11,000.
- **(b)** $5,000.
- **(d)** Cannot be determined.

(LO 7) **13.** A trial balance:
- **(a)** is a list of accounts with their balances at a given time.
- **(b)** proves the mathematical accuracy of journalized transactions.
- **(c)** will not balance if a correct journal entry is posted twice.
- **(d)** proves that all transactions have been recorded.

**14.** A trial balance will not balance if: (LO 7)
- **(a)** a correct journal entry is posted twice.
- **(b)** the purchase of supplies on account is debited to Supplies and credited to Cash.
- **(c)** a $100 cash drawing by the owner is debited to Owner's Drawings for $1,000 and credited to Cash for $100.
- **(d)** a $450 payment on account is debited to Accounts Payable for $45 and credited to Cash for $45.

**15.** The trial balance of Jeong Company had accounts (LO 7) with the following normal balances: Cash $5,000, Service Revenue $85,000, Salaries and Wages Payable $4,000, Salaries and Wages Expense $40,000, Rent Expense $10,000, Owner's Capital $42,000; Owner's Drawings $15,000; Equipment $61,000. In preparing a trial balance, the total in the debit column is:
- **(a)** $131,000.
- **(c)** $91,000.
- **(b)** $216,000.
- **(d)** $116,000.

Go to the book's companion website, www.wiley.com/college/weygandt, for additional Self-Test Questions.

✔ **The Navigator**

## QUESTIONS

1. Describe the parts of a T-account.
2. "The terms debit and credit mean increase and decrease, respectively." Do you agree? Explain.
3. Heath Precourt, a fellow student, contends that the double-entry system means each transaction must be recorded twice. Is Heath correct? Explain.
4. Erica Mendez, a beginning accounting student, believes debit balances are favorable and credit balances are unfavorable. Is Erica correct? Discuss.
5. State the rules of debit and credit as applied to (a) asset accounts, (b) liability accounts, and (c) the owner's equity accounts (revenue, expenses, owner's drawings, and owner's capital).
6. What is the normal balance for each of the following accounts? (a) Accounts Receivable. (b) Cash. (c) Owner's Drawings. (d) Accounts Payable. (e) Service Revenue. (f) Salaries and Wages Expense. (g) Owner's Capital.
7. Indicate whether each of the following accounts is an asset, a liability, or an owner's equity account and whether it has a normal debit or credit balance: (a) Accounts Receivable, (b) Accounts Payable, (c) Equipment, (d) Owner's Drawings, (e) Supplies.
8. For the following transactions, indicate the account debited and the account credited.
   - **(a)** Supplies are purchased on account.
   - **(b)** Cash is received on signing a note payable.
   - **(c)** Employees are paid salaries in cash.
9. Indicate whether the following accounts generally will have (a) debit entries only, (b) credit entries only, or (c) both debit and credit entries.

- **(1)** Cash.
- **(2)** Accounts Receivable.
- **(3)** Owner's Drawings.
- **(4)** Accounts Payable.
- **(5)** Salaries and Wages Expense.
- **(6)** Service Revenue.

10. What are the basic steps in the recording process?
11. What are the advantages of using a journal in the recording process?
12. **(a)** When entering a transaction in the journal, should the debit or credit be written first?
    **(b)** Which should be indented, the debit or credit?
13. Describe a compound entry, and provide an example.
14. **(a)** Should business transaction debits and credits be recorded directly in the ledger accounts?
    **(b)** What are the advantages of first recording transactions in the journal and then posting to the ledger?
15. The account number is entered as the last step in posting the amounts from the journal to the ledger. What is the advantage of this step?
16. Journalize the following business transactions.
    - **(a)** Qing Wei invests $9,000 cash in the business.
    - **(b)** Insurance of $800 is paid for the year.
    - **(c)** Supplies of $2,000 are purchased on account.
    - **(d)** Cash of $7,500 is received for services performed.
17. **(a)** What is a ledger?
    **(b)** What is a chart of accounts and why is it important?
18. What is a trial balance and what are its purposes?
19. Victor Grimm is confused about how accounting information flows through the accounting system. He believes the flow of information is as follows.
    - **(a)** Debits and credits posted to the ledger.
    - **(b)** Business transaction occurs.

**(c)** Information entered in the journal.
**(d)** Financial statements are prepared.
**(e)** Trial balance is prepared.
Is Victor correct? If not, indicate to Victor the proper flow of the information.

20. Two students are discussing the use of a trial balance. They wonder whether the following errors, each considered separately, would prevent the trial balance from balancing.

**(a)** The bookkeeper debited Cash for $600 and credited Salaries and Wages Expense for $600 for payment of wages.

**(b)** Cash collected on account was debited to Cash for $900 and Service Revenue was credited for $90. What would you tell them?

21. What are the normal balances for Apple's Cash, Accounts Payable, and Interest Expense accounts?

## BRIEF EXERCISES

*Indicate debit and credit effects and normal balance.*
*(LO 2)*

**BE2-1** For each of the following accounts, indicate the effects of (a) a debit and (b) a credit on the accounts and (c) the normal balance of the account.

1. Accounts Payable.
2. Advertising Expense.
3. Service Revenue.
4. Accounts Receivable.
5. Owner's Capital.
6. Owner's Drawings.

*Identify accounts to be debited and credited.*
*(LO 2)*

**BE2-2** Transactions for the George Lynch Company for the month of June are presented below. Identify the accounts to be debited and credited for each transaction.

June 1   George Lynch invests $5,000 cash in a small welding business of which he is the sole proprietor.
 2   Purchases equipment on account for $2,100.
 3   $800 cash is paid to landlord for June rent.
 12   Sends a bill to M. Rodero for $300 for welding work performed on account.

*Journalize transactions.*
*(LO 4)*

**BE2-3** Using the data in BE2-2, journalize the transactions. (You may omit explanations.)

*Identify and explain steps in recording process.*
*(LO 3)*

**BE2-4** ──────── Raymond Faust, a fellow student, is unclear about the basic steps in the recording process. Identify and briefly explain the steps in the order in which they occur.

*Indicate basic and debit-credit analysis.*
*(LO 2)*

**BE2-5** H. Xiao has the following transactions during August of the current year. Indicate (a) the effect on the accounting equation and (b) the debit-credit analysis illustrated on pages 66–70 of the text.

Aug. 1   Opens an office as a financial advisor, investing $8,000 in cash.
 4   Pays insurance in advance for 6 months, $1,800 cash.
 16   Receives $3,400 from clients for services performed.
 27   Pays secretary $1,000 salary.

*Journalize transactions.*
*(LO 4)*

**BE2-6** Using the data in BE2-5, journalize the transactions. (You may omit explanations.)

*Post journal entries to T-accounts.*
*(LO 6)*

**BE2-7** Selected transactions for the Joel Berges Company are presented in journal form below. Post the transactions to T-accounts. Make one T-account for each item and determine each account's ending balance.

J1

| Date | Account Titles and Explanation | Ref. | Debit | Credit |
|------|-------------------------------|------|-------|--------|
| May 5 | Accounts Receivable | | 4,100 | |
| | Service Revenue | | | 4,100 |
| | (Billed for services performed) | | | |
| 12 | Cash | | 2,400 | |
| | Accounts Receivable | | | 2,400 |
| | (Received cash in payment of account) | | | |
| 15 | Cash | | 3,000 | |
| | Service Revenue | | | 3,000 |
| | (Received cash for services performed) | | | |

**BE2-8** Selected journal entries for the Joel Berges Company are presented in BE2-7. Post the transactions using the standard form of account.

*Post journal entries to standard form of account.*
*(LO 6)*

**BE2-9** From the ledger balances given below, prepare a trial balance for the Deroche Company at June 30, 2014. List the accounts in the order shown on page 73 of the text. All account balances are normal.

*Prepare a trial balance.*
*(LO 7)*

Accounts Payable $9,000, Cash $5,800, Owner's Capital $15,000, Owner's Drawings $1,200, Equipment $17,000, Service Revenue $10,000, Accounts Receivable $3,000, Salaries and Wages Expense $6,000, and Rent Expense $1,000.

**BE2-10** An inexperienced bookkeeper prepared the following trial balance. Prepare a correct trial balance, assuming all account balances are normal.

*Prepare a correct trial balance.*
*(LO 7)*

**HUEWITT COMPANY**
Trial Balance
December 31, 2014

|  | Debit | Credit |
|---|---|---|
| Cash | $10,800 | |
| Prepaid Insurance | | $ 3,500 |
| Accounts Payable | | 3,000 |
| Unearned Service Revenue | 2,200 | |
| Owner's Capital | | 9,000 |
| Owner's Drawings | | 4,500 |
| Service Revenue | | 25,600 |
| Salaries and Wages Expense | 18,600 | |
| Rent Expense | | 2,400 |
| | $31,600 | $48,000 |

## > DO IT! Review

**DO IT! 2-1** Ivan Klumb has just rented space in a strip mall. In this space, he will open a photography studio, to be called "Picture This!" A friend has advised Ivan to set up a double-entry set of accounting records in which to record all of his business transactions.

Identify the balance sheet accounts that Ivan will likely need to record the transactions needed to open his business. Indicate whether the normal balance of each account is a debit or credit.

*Identify normal balances.*
*(LO 2)*

**DO IT! 2-2** Ivan Klumb engaged in the following activities in establishing his photography studio, Picture This!:

*Record business activities.*
*(LO 4)*

1. Opened a bank account in the name of Picture This! and deposited $6,300 of his own money into this account as his initial investment.

2. Purchased photography supplies at a total cost of $1,100. The business paid $400 in cash and the balance is on account.

3. Obtained estimates on the cost of photography equipment from three different manufacturers.

In what form (type of record) should Ivan record these three activities? Prepare the entries to record the transactions.

**DO IT! 2-3** Ivan Klumb recorded the following transactions during the month of April.

*Post transactions.*
*(LO 6)*

| April 3 | Cash | 3,400 | |
|---|---|---|---|
| | Service Revenue | | 3,400 |
| April 16 | Rent Expense | 700 | |
| | Cash | | 700 |
| April 20 | Salaries and Wages Expense | 300 | |
| | Cash | | 300 |

Post these entries to the Cash T-account of the general ledger to determine the ending balance in cash. The beginning balance in cash on April 1 was $1,600.

*Prepare a trial balance.*
(LO 7)

**DO IT!** **2-4** The following accounts are taken from the ledger of Recha Company at December 31, 2014.

| | | | | | |
|---|---|---|---|---|---|
| 200 | Notes Payable | $20,000 | 101 | Cash | $ 6,000 |
| 301 | Owner's Capital | 28,000 | 126 | Supplies | 6,000 |
| 157 | Equipment | 80,000 | 729 | Rent Expense | 4,000 |
| 306 | Owner's Drawings | 8,000 | 212 | Salaries and Wages Payable | 3,000 |
| 726 | Salaries and Wages Expense | 38,000 | 201 | Accounts Payable | 11,000 |
| 400 | Service Revenue | 88,000 | 112 | Accounts Receivable | 8,000 |

Prepare a trial balance in good form.

# EXERCISES

*Analyze statements about accounting and the recording process.*
(LO 1)

**E2-1** Lixun Zhang has prepared the following list of statements about accounts.

1. An account is an accounting record of either a specific asset or a specific liability.
2. An account shows only increases, not decreases, in the item it relates to.
3. Some items, such as Cash and Accounts Receivable, are combined into one account.
4. An account has a left, or credit side, and a right, or debit side.
5. A simple form of an account consisting of just the account title, the left side, and the right side, is called a T-account.

**Instructions**
Identify each statement as true or false. If false, indicate how to correct the statement.

*Identify debits, credits, and normal balances.*
(LO 2)

**E2-2** Selected transactions for R. Sparks, an interior decorator, in her first month of business, are as follows.

Jan.  2  Invested $10,000 cash in business.
       3  Purchased used car for $4,000 cash for use in business.
       9  Purchased supplies on account for $500.
      11  Billed customers $2,100 for services performed.
      16  Paid $350 cash for advertising.
      20  Received $700 cash from customers billed on January 11.
      23  Paid creditor $300 cash on balance owed.
      28  Withdrew $1,000 cash for personal use by owner.

**Instructions**
For each transaction, indicate the following.

**(a)** The basic type of account debited and credited (asset, liability, owner's equity).
**(b)** The specific account debited and credited (Cash, Rent Expense, Service Revenue, etc.).
**(c)** Whether the specific account is increased or decreased.
**(d)** The normal balance of the specific account.

Use the following format, in which the January 2 transaction is given as an example.

| | Account Debited | | | | Account Credited | | | |
|---|---|---|---|---|---|---|---|---|
| | **(a)** | **(b)** | **(c)** | **(d)** | **(a)** | **(b)** | **(c)** | **(d)** |
| Date | Basic Type | Specific Account | Effect | Normal Balance | Basic Type | Specific Account | Effect | Normal Balance |
| Jan. 2 | Asset | Cash | Increase | Debit | Owner's Equity | Owner's Capital | Increase | Credit |

*Journalize transactions.*
(LO 4)

**E2-3** Data for R. Sparks, interior decorator, are presented in E2-2.

**Instructions**
Journalize the transactions using journal page J1. (You may omit explanations.)

*Analyze transactions and determine their effect on accounts.*
(LO 2)

**E2-4** Presented below is information related to Lachapelle Real Estate Agency.

Oct.  1  Arthur Lachapelle begins business as a real estate agent with a cash investment of $15,000.
       2  Hires an administrative assistant.
       3  Purchases office furniture for $1,900, on account.

6   Sells a house and lot for J. Baxter; bills J. Baxter $3,600 for realty services performed.
27   Pays $1,100 on the balance related to the transaction of October 3.
30   Pays the administrative assistant $2,500 in salary for October.

**Instructions**
Prepare the debit-credit analysis for each transaction as illustrated on pages 66–70.

**E2-5** Transaction data for Lachapelle Real Estate Agency are presented in E2-4.

*Journalize transactions.*
*(LO 4)*

**Instructions**
Journalize the transactions. (You may omit explanations.)

**E2-6** Federlin Industries had the following transactions.

*Analyze transactions and journalize.*
*(LO 2, 3, 4)*

1. Borrowed $5,000 from the bank by signing a note.
2. Paid $3,100 cash for a computer.
3. Purchased $850 of supplies on account.

**Instructions**
(a) Indicate what accounts are increased and decreased by each transaction.
(b) Journalize each transaction. (Omit explanations.)

**E2-7** Kahl Enterprises had the following selected transactions.

*Analyze transactions and journalize.*
*(LO 2, 3, 4)*

1. Jo Kahl invested $4,000 cash in the business.
2. Paid office rent of $950.
3. Performed consulting services and billed a client $5,200.
4. Jo Kahl withdrew $750 cash for personal use.

**Instructions**
(a) Indicate the effect each transaction has on the accounting equation
   (Assets = Liabilities + Owner's Equity), using plus and minus signs.
(b) Journalize each transaction. (Omit explanations.)

**E2-8** Janet Miyoshi has prepared the following list of statements about the general ledger.

*Analyze statements about the ledger.*
*(LO 5)*

1. The general ledger contains all the asset and liability accounts but no owner's equity accounts.
2. The general ledger is sometimes referred to as simply the ledger.
3. The accounts in the general ledger are arranged in alphabetical order.
4. Each account in the general ledger is numbered for easier identification.
5. The general ledger is a book of original entry.

**Instructions**
Identify each statement as true or false. If false, indicate how to correct the statement.

**E2-9** Selected transactions from the journal of Trisha Spoor, investment broker, are presented below.

*Post journal entries and prepare a trial balance.*
*(LO 6, 7)*

| Date | Account Titles and Explanation | Ref. | Debit | Credit |
|------|-------------------------------|------|-------|--------|
| Aug. 1 | Cash | | 5,000 | |
| | Owner's Capital | | | 5,000 |
| | (Owner's investment of cash in business) | | | |
| 10 | Cash | | 2,400 | |
| | Service Revenue | | | 2,400 |
| | (Received cash for services performed) | | | |
| 12 | Equipment | | 5,000 | |
| | Cash | | | 3,000 |
| | Notes Payable | | | 2,000 |
| | (Purchased equipment for cash and notes payable) | | | |
| 25 | Accounts Receivable | | 1,700 | |
| | Service Revenue | | | 1,700 |
| | (Billed clients for services performed) | | | |
| 31 | Cash | | 900 | |
| | Accounts Receivable | | | 900 |
| | (Receipt of cash on account) | | | |

**Instructions**
(a) Post the transactions to T-accounts.
(b) Prepare a trial balance at August 31, 2014.

*Journalize transactions from account data and prepare a trial balance.*
*(LO 4, 7)*

**E2-10** The T-accounts below summarize the ledger of Zimmer Landscaping Company at the end of the first month of operations.

| Cash | | | No. 101 |
|---|---|---|---|
| 4/1 | 12,000 | 4/15 | 1,300 |
| 4/12 | 900 | 4/25 | 1,500 |
| 4/29 | 400 | | |
| 4/30 | 1,000 | | |

| Unearned Service Revenue | | | No. 209 |
|---|---|---|---|
| | | 4/30 | 1,000 |

| Accounts Receivable | | | No. 112 |
|---|---|---|---|
| 4/7 | 3,200 | 4/29 | 400 |

| Owner's Capital | | | No. 301 |
|---|---|---|---|
| | | 4/1 | 12,000 |

| Supplies | | | No. 126 |
|---|---|---|---|
| 4/4 | 1,800 | | |

| Service Revenue | | | No. 400 |
|---|---|---|---|
| | | 4/7 | 3,200 |
| | | 4/12 | 900 |

| Accounts Payable | | | No. 201 |
|---|---|---|---|
| 4/25 | 1,500 | 4/4 | 1,800 |

| Salaries and Wages Expense | | | No. 726 |
|---|---|---|---|
| 4/15 | 1,300 | | |

**Instructions**
(a) Prepare the complete general journal (including explanations) from which the postings to Cash were made.
(b) Prepare a trial balance at April 30, 2014.

*Journalize transactions from account data and prepare a trial balance.*
*(LO 4, 7)*

**E2-11** Presented below is the ledger for Harbach Co.

| Cash | | | No. 101 |
|---|---|---|---|
| 10/1 | 3,000 | 10/4 | 400 |
| 10/10 | 500 | 10/12 | 1,500 |
| 10/10 | 4,000 | 10/15 | 250 |
| 10/20 | 500 | 10/30 | 300 |
| 10/25 | 2,000 | 10/31 | 500 |

| Owner's Capital | | | No. 301 |
|---|---|---|---|
| | | 10/1 | 3,000 |
| | | 10/25 | 2,000 |

| Owner's Drawings | | | No. 306 |
|---|---|---|---|
| 10/30 | 300 | | |

| Accounts Receivable | | | No. 112 |
|---|---|---|---|
| 10/6 | 800 | 10/20 | 500 |
| 10/20 | 940 | | |

| Service Revenue | | | No. 400 |
|---|---|---|---|
| | | 10/6 | 800 |
| | | 10/10 | 500 |
| | | 10/20 | 940 |

| Supplies | | | No. 126 |
|---|---|---|---|
| 10/4 | 400 | | |

| Salaries and Wages Expense | | | No. 726 |
|---|---|---|---|
| 10/31 | 500 | | |

| Equipment | | | No. 157 |
|---|---|---|---|
| 10/3 | 2,000 | | |

| Rent Expense | | | No. 729 |
|---|---|---|---|
| 10/15 | 250 | | |

| Notes Payable | | | No. 200 |
|---|---|---|---|
| | | 10/10 | 4,000 |

| Accounts Payable | | | No. 201 |
|---|---|---|---|
| 10/12 | 1,500 | 10/3 | 2,000 |

**Instructions**
(a) Reproduce the journal entries for the transactions that occurred on October 1, 10, and 20, and provide explanations for each.
(b) Determine the October 31 balance for each of the accounts above, and prepare a trial balance at October 31, 2014.

**E2-12** Selected transactions for Sandra Linke Company during its first month in business are presented below.

*Prepare journal entries and post using standard account form.*
(LO 4, 6)

Sept. 1  Invested $10,000 cash in the business.
    5  Purchased equipment for $12,000 paying $4,000 in cash and the balance on account.
   25  Paid $3,000 cash on balance owed for equipment.
   30  Withdrew $700 cash for personal use.

Linke's chart of accounts shows: No. 101 Cash, No. 157 Equipment, No. 201 Accounts Payable, No. 301 Owner's Capital, and No. 306 Owner's Drawings.

**Instructions**
**(a)** Journalize the transactions on page J1 of the journal. (Omit explanations.)
**(b)** Post the transactions using the standard account form.

**E2-13** The bookkeeper for Jeff Sobol Equipment Repair made a number of errors in journalizing and posting, as described below.

*Analyze errors and their effects on trial balance.*
(LO 7)

1. A credit posting of $525 to Accounts Receivable was omitted.
2. A debit posting of $750 for Prepaid Insurance was debited to Insurance Expense.
3. A collection from a customer of $100 in payment of its account owed was journalized and posted as a debit to Cash $100 and a credit to Service Revenue $100.
4. A credit posting of $415 to Property Taxes Payable was made twice.
5. A cash purchase of supplies for $250 was journalized and posted as a debit to Supplies $25 and a credit to Cash $25.
6. A debit of $475 to Advertising Expense was posted as $457.

**Instructions**
For each error:

**(a)** Indicate whether the trial balance will balance.
**(b)** If the trial balance will not balance, indicate the amount of the difference.
**(c)** Indicate the trial balance column that will have the larger total.

Consider each error separately. Use the following form, in which error (1) is given as an example.

| Error | (a)<br>In Balance | (b)<br>Difference | (c)<br>Larger Column |
|-------|----------|------------|--------------|
| (1) | No | $525 | debit |

**E2-14** The accounts in the ledger of Longoria Delivery Service contain the following balances on July 31, 2014.

*Prepare a trial balance.*
(LO 2, 7)

| | | | |
|---|---|---|---|
| Accounts Receivable | $ 7,642 | Prepaid Insurance | $ 1,968 |
| Accounts Payable | 8,396 | Maintenance and Repairs Expense | 961 |
| Cash | ? | Service Revenue | 10,610 |
| Equipment | 49,360 | Owner's Drawings | 700 |
| Gasoline Expense | 758 | Owner's Capital | 42,000 |
| Utilities Expense | 523 | Salaries and Wages Expense | 4,428 |
| Notes Payable | 17,000 | Salaries and Wages Payable | 815 |

**Instructions**
Prepare a trial balance with the accounts arranged as illustrated in the chapter and fill in the missing amount for Cash.

## EXERCISES: SET B AND CHALLENGE EXERCISES

Visit the book's companion website, at **www.wiley.com/college/weygandt**, and choose the Student Companion site to access Exercise Set B and Challenge Exercises.

*Journalize a series of transactions.*

*(LO 2, 4)*

**P2-1A** McKay Disc Golf Course was opened on March 1 by Evan McKay. The following selected events and transactions occurred during March.

Mar. 1   Invested $20,000 cash in the business.
    3   Purchased Sable's Golf Land for $15,000 cash. The price consists of land $12,000, shed $2,000, and equipment $1,000. (Make one compound entry.)
    5   Paid advertising expenses of $700.
    6   Paid cash $600 for a one-year insurance policy.
    10   Purchased golf discs and other equipment for $1,050 from Taylor Company payable in 30 days.
    18   Received $1,100 in cash for golf fees (McKay records golf fees as service revenue).
    19   Sold 150 coupon books for $10 each. Each book contains 4 coupons that enable the holder to play one round of disc golf.
    25   Withdrew $800 cash for personal use.
    30   Paid salaries of $250.
    30   Paid Taylor Company in full.
    31   Received $2,100 cash for golf fees.

McKay Disc Golf uses the following accounts: Cash, Prepaid Insurance, Land, Buildings, Equipment, Accounts Payable, Unearned Service Revenue, Owner's Capital, Owner's Drawings, Service Revenue, Advertising Expense, and Salaries and Wages Expense.

***Instructions***
Journalize the March transactions.

*Journalize transactions, post, and prepare a trial balance.*

*(LO 2, 4, 6, 7)*

**P2-2A** Bridgette Keyes is a licensed dentist. During the first month of the operation of her business, the following events and transactions occurred.

April 1   Invested $20,000 cash in her business.
    1   Hired a secretary-receptionist at a salary of $700 per week payable monthly.
    2   Paid office rent for the month $1,100.
    3   Purchased dental supplies on account from Smile Company $4,000.
    10   Performed dental services and billed insurance companies $5,100.
    11   Received $1,000 cash advance from Heather Greene for an implant.
    20   Received $2,100 cash for services performed from James Chang.
    30   Paid secretary-receptionist for the month $2,800.
    30   Paid $2,400 to Smile Company for accounts payable due.

Bridgette uses the following chart of accounts: No. 101 Cash, No. 112 Accounts Receivable, No. 126 Supplies, No. 201 Accounts Payable, No. 209 Unearned Service Revenue, No. 301 Owner's Capital, No. 400 Service Revenue, No. 726 Salaries and Wages Expense, and No. 729 Rent Expense.

***Instructions***
**(a)** Journalize the transactions.
**(b)** Post to the ledger accounts.
*(c) Trial balance totals $29,800*   **(c)** Prepare a trial balance on April 30, 2014.

*Journalize transactions, post, and prepare a trial balance.*

*(LO 2, 4, 6, 7)*

**P2-3A** Santa Ana Services was formed on May 1, 2014. The following transactions took place during the first month.

Transactions on May 1:

1. Don Humes invested $40,000 cash in the company, as its sole owner.
2. Hired two employees to work in the warehouse. They will each be paid a salary of $3,050 per month.
3. Signed a 2-year rental agreement on a warehouse; paid $24,000 cash in advance for the first year.
4. Purchased furniture and equipment costing $30,000. A cash payment of $10,000 was made immediately; the remainder will be paid in 6 months.
5. Paid $1,800 cash for a one-year insurance policy on the furniture and equipment.

Transactions during the remainder of the month:

6. Purchased basic office supplies for $500 cash.
7. Purchased more office supplies for $1,500 on account.
8. Total revenues earned were $20,000—$8,000 cash and $12,000 on account.
9. Paid $400 to suppliers for accounts payable due.
10. Received $3,000 from customers in payment of accounts receivable.
11. Received utility bills in the amount of $350, to be paid next month.
12. Paid the monthly salaries of the two employees, totalling $6,100.

**Instructions**
(a) Prepare journal entries to record each of the events listed. (Omit explanations.)
(b) Post the journal entries to T-accounts.
(c) Prepare a trial balance as of May 31, 2014.

*(c) Trial balance totals $81,450*

**P2-4A** The trial balance of Marius Santiago Co. shown below does not balance.

*Prepare a correct trial balance.*

*(LO 7)*

### MARIUS SANTIAGO CO.
### Trial Balance
### June 30, 2014

|  | Debit | Credit |
|---|---|---|
| Cash |  | $ 3,340 |
| Accounts Receivable | $ 2,812 |  |
| Supplies | 1,200 |  |
| Equipment | 2,600 |  |
| Accounts Payable |  | 3,666 |
| Unearned Service Revenue | 1,100 |  |
| Owner's Capital |  | 8,000 |
| Owner's Drawings | 800 |  |
| Service Revenue |  | 2,480 |
| Salaries and Wages Expense | 3,200 |  |
| Utilities Expense | 810 |  |
|  | $12,522 | $17,486 |

Each of the listed accounts has a normal balance per the general ledger. An examination of the ledger and journal reveals the following errors.

1. Cash received from a customer in payment of its account was debited for $580, and Accounts Receivable was credited for the same amount. The actual collection was for $850.
2. The purchase of a computer on account for $710 was recorded as a debit to Supplies for $710 and a credit to Accounts Payable for $710.
3. Services were performed on account for a client for $980. Accounts Receivable was debited for $980, and Service Revenue was credited for $98.
4. A debit posting to Salaries and Wages Expense of $700 was omitted.
5. A payment of a balance due for $306 was credited to Cash for $306 and credited to Accounts Payable for $360.
6. The withdrawal of $600 cash for Santiago's personal use was debited to Salaries and Wages Expense for $600 and credited to Cash for $600.

**Instructions**
Prepare a correct trial balance. (*Hint:* It helps to prepare the correct journal entry for the transaction described and compare it to the mistake made.)

*Trial balance totals $15,462*

**P2-5A** The Lunt Theater, owned by Beth Saxena, will begin operations in March. The Lunt will be unique in that it will show only triple features of sequential theme movies. As of March 1, the ledger of Lunt showed: No. 101 Cash $3,000, No. 140 Land $24,000, No. 145 Buildings (concession stand, projection room, ticket booth, and screen) $10,000, No. 157 Equipment $10,000, No. 201 Accounts Payable $7,000, and No. 301 Owner's Capital $40,000. During the month of March, the following events and transactions occurred.

*Journalize transactions, post, and prepare a trial balance.*

*(LO 2, 4, 6, 7)*

Mar. 2   Rented the three *Indiana Jones* movies to be shown for the first 3 weeks of March. The film rental was $3,500; $1,500 was paid in cash and $2,000 will be paid on March 10.

3   Ordered the *Lord of the Rings* movies to be shown the last 10 days of March. It will cost $200 per night.

    9    Received $4,000 cash from admissions.
    10   Paid balance due on *Indiana Jones* movies rental and $2,100 on March 1
         accounts payable.
    11   Lunt Theater contracted with John Blume to operate the concession stand.
         Blume is to pay 15% of gross concession receipts, payable monthly, for the
         rental of the concession stand.
    12   Paid advertising expenses $800.
    20   Received $5,000 cash from customers for admissions.
    20   Received the *Lord of the Rings* movies and paid the rental fee of $2,000.
    31   Paid salaries of $3,100.
    31   Received statement from John Blume showing gross receipts from concessions of
         $6,000 and the balance due to Lunt Theater of $900 ($6,000 × 15%) for March.
         Blume paid one-half the balance due and will remit the remainder on April 5.
    31   Received $9,000 cash from customers for admissions.

In addition to the accounts identified above, the chart of accounts includes: No. 112 Accounts
Receivable, No. 400 Service Revenue, No. 429 Rent Revenue, No. 610 Advertising Expense,
No. 726 Salaries and Wages Expense, and No. 729 Rent Expense.

### Instructions

**(a)** Enter the beginning balances in the ledger. Insert a check mark (✓) in the reference
column of the ledger for the beginning balance.

**(b)** Journalize the March transactions. Lunt records admission revenue as service revenue,
rental of the concession stand as rent revenue, and film rental expense as rent expense.

**(c)** Post the March journal entries to the ledger. Assume that all entries are posted from
page 1 of the journal.

(d) Trial balance totals $63,800   **(d)** Prepare a trial balance on March 31, 2014.

## PROBLEMS: SET B

*Journalize a series of
transactions.*

(LO 2, 4)

**P2-1B** Frontier Park was started on April 1 by M. Preston. The following selected events
and transactions occurred during April.

Apr.  1   Preston invested $35,000 cash in the business.
      4   Purchased land costing $27,000 for cash.
      8   Incurred advertising expense of $1,800 on account.
      11  Paid salaries to employees $1,500.
      12  Hired park manager at a salary of $4,000 per month, effective May 1.
      13  Paid $1,650 cash for a one-year insurance policy.
      17  Withdrew $1,000 cash for personal use.
      20  Received $6,800 in cash for admission fees.
      25  Sold 100 coupon books for $25 each. Each book contains 10 coupons that
          entitle the holder to one admission to the park.
      30  Received $8,900 in cash admission fees.
      30  Paid $900 on balance owed for advertising incurred on April 8.

Frontier Park uses the following accounts: Cash, Prepaid Insurance, Land, Accounts Payable,
Unearned Service Revenue, Owner's Capital, Owner's Drawings, Service Revenue,
Advertising Expense, and Salaries and Wages Expense.

### Instructions
Journalize the April transactions.

*Journalize transactions, post,
and prepare a trial balance.*

(LO 2, 4, 6, 7)

**P2-2B** Iris Beck is a licensed CPA. During the first month of operations of her business,
the following events and transactions occurred.

May  1   Beck invested $20,000 cash in her business.
     2   Hired a secretary-receptionist at a salary of $2,000 per month.
     3   Purchased $2,500 of supplies on account from Tinio Supply Company.
     7   Paid office rent of $900 cash for the month.
     11  Completed a tax assignment and billed client $3,200 for services performed.
     12  Received $3,500 advance on a management consulting engagement.
     17  Received cash of $1,200 for services performed for Misra Co.
     31  Paid secretary-receptionist $2,000 salary for the month.
     31  Paid 60% of balance due Tinio Supply Company.

Iris uses the following chart of accounts: No. 101 Cash, No. 112 Accounts Receivable, No. 126 Supplies, No. 201 Accounts Payable, No. 209 Unearned Service Revenue, No. 301 Owner's Capital, No. 400 Service Revenue, No. 726 Salaries and Wages Expense, and No. 729 Rent Expense.

**Instructions**
**(a)** Journalize the transactions.
**(b)** Post to the ledger accounts.
**(c)** Prepare a trial balance on May 31, 2014.

(c) Trial balance totals $28,900

**P2-3B** Tony Vian owns and manages a computer repair service, which had the following trial balance on December 31, 2013 (the end of its fiscal year).

*Journalize transactions, post, and prepare a trial balance.*
(LO 2, 4, 6, 7)

**VIAN REPAIR SERVICE**
Trial Balance
December 31, 2013

|  | Debit | Credit |
|---|---|---|
| Cash | $ 8,000 | |
| Accounts Receivable | 15,000 | |
| Supplies | 13,000 | |
| Prepaid Rent | 3,000 | |
| Equipment | 20,000 | |
| Accounts Payable | | $19,000 |
| Owner's Capital | | 40,000 |
| | $59,000 | $59,000 |

Summarized transactions for January 2014 were as follows.

1. Advertising costs, paid in cash, $1,000.
2. Additional supplies acquired on account $4,200.
3. Miscellaneous expenses, paid in cash, $2,000.
4. Cash collected from customers in payment of accounts receivable $14,000.
5. Cash paid to creditors for accounts payable due $15,000.
6. Repair services performed during January: for cash $6,000; on account $9,000.
7. Wages for January, paid in cash, $3,500.
8. Tony's drawings during January were $3,000.

**Instructions**
**(a)** Open T-accounts for each of the accounts listed in the trial balance, and enter the opening balances for 2014.
**(b)** Prepare journal entries to record each of the January transactions. (Omit explanations.)
**(c)** Post the journal entries to the accounts in the ledger. (Add accounts as needed.)
**(d)** Prepare a trial balance as of January 31, 2014.

(d) Trial balance totals $63,200

**P2-4B** The trial balance of the Sean Devine Company shown below does not balance.

*Prepare a correct trial balance.*
(LO 7)

**SEAN DEVINE COMPANY**
Trial Balance
May 31, 2014

|  | Debit | Credit |
|---|---|---|
| Cash | $ 5,850 | |
| Accounts Receivable | | $ 2,750 |
| Prepaid Insurance | 700 | |
| Equipment | 8,000 | |
| Accounts Payable | | 4,500 |
| Unearned Service Revenue | 650 | |
| Owner's Capital | | 11,700 |
| Service Revenue | 6,690 | |
| Salaries and Wages Expense | 4,200 | |
| Advertising Expense | | 1,100 |
| Utilities Expense | 890 | |
| | $26,980 | $20,050 |

Your review of the ledger reveals that each account has a normal balance. You also discover the following errors.

1. The totals of the debit sides of Prepaid Insurance, Accounts Payable, and Utilities Expense were each understated $100.
2. Transposition errors were made in Accounts Receivable and Service Revenue. Based on postings made, the correct balances were $2,570 and $6,960, respectively.
3. A debit posting to Salaries and Wages Expense of $200 was omitted.
4. A $1,000 cash drawing by the owner was debited to Owner's Capital for $1,000 and credited to Cash for $1,000.
5. A $520 purchase of supplies on account was debited to Equipment for $520 and credited to Cash for $520.
6. A cash payment of $540 for advertising was debited to Advertising Expense for $54 and credited to Cash for $54.
7. A collection from a customer for $210 was debited to Cash for $210 and credited to Accounts Payable for $210.

**Instructions**

*Trial balance totals $25,020*

Prepare a correct trial balance. Note that the chart of accounts includes the following: Owner's Drawings and Supplies. (*Hint:* It helps to prepare the correct journal entry for the transaction described and compare it to the mistake made.)

*Journalize transactions, post, and prepare a trial balance.*

*(LO 2, 4, 6, 7)*

**P2-5B** The Classic Theater is owned by Kim Lockerby. All facilities were completed on March 31. At this time, the ledger showed: No. 101 Cash $4,000, No. 140 Land $10,000, No. 145 Buildings (concession stand, projection room, ticket booth, and screen) $8,000, No. 157 Equipment $6,000, No. 201 Accounts Payable $2,000, No. 275 Mortgage Payable $8,000, and No. 301 Owner's Capital $18,000. During April, the following events and transactions occurred.

| | | |
|---|---|---|
| Apr. | 2 | Paid film rental of $1,100 on first movie. |
| | 3 | Ordered two additional films at $1,000 each. |
| | 9 | Received $2,800 cash from admissions. |
| | 10 | Made $2,000 payment on mortgage and $1,000 for accounts payable due. |
| | 11 | Classic Theater contracted with Rhonda Humes to operate the concession stand. Humes is to pay Classic Theater 17% of gross concession receipts, payable monthly, for the rental of the concession stand. |
| | 12 | Paid advertising expenses $500. |
| | 20 | Received one of the films ordered on April 3 and was billed $1,000. The film will be shown in April. |
| | 25 | Received $5,200 cash from admissions. |
| | 29 | Paid salaries $2,000. |
| | 30 | Received statement from Rhonda Humes showing gross concession receipts of $1,000 and the balance due to The Classic Theater of $170 ($1,000 × 17%) for April. Humes paid one-half of the balance due and will remit the remainder on May 5. |
| | 30 | Prepaid $1,200 rental on special film to be run in May. |

In addition to the accounts identified above, the chart of accounts shows: No. 112 Accounts Receivable, No. 136 Prepaid Rent, No. 400 Service Revenue, No. 429 Rent Revenue, No. 610 Advertising Expense, No. 726 Salaries and Wages Expense, and No. 729 Rent Expense.

**Instructions**

**(a)** Enter the beginning balances in the ledger as of April 1. Insert a check mark (✓) in the reference column of the ledger for the beginning balance.

**(b)** Journalize the April transactions. Classic records admission revenue as service revenue, rental of the concession stand as rent revenue, and film rental expense as rent expense.

**(c)** Post the April journal entries to the ledger. Assume that all entries are posted from page 1 of the journal.

*(d) Trial balance totals $34,170*

**(d)** Prepare a trial balance on April 30, 2014.

**PROBLEMS: SET C**

Visit the book's companion website, at **www.wiley.com/college/weygandt**, and choose the Student Companion site to access Problem Set C.

## CONTINUING COOKIE CHRONICLE

(*Note:* This is a continuation of the Cookie Chronicle from Chapter 1.)

**CCC2** After researching the different forms of business organization. Natalie Koebel decides to operate "Cookie Creations" as a proprietorship. She then starts the process of getting the business running. In November 2013, the following activities take place.

Nov. 8 Natalie cashes her U.S. Savings Bonds and receives $520, which she deposits in her personal bank account.

8 She opens a bank account under the name "Cookie Creations" and transfers $500 from her personal account to the new account.

11 Natalie pays $65 for advertising.

13 She buys baking supplies, such as flour, sugar, butter, and chocolate chips, for $125 cash. (*Hint:* Use Supplies account.)

14 Natalie starts to gather some baking equipment to take with her when teaching the cookie classes. She has an excellent top-of-the-line food processor and mixer that originally cost her $750. Natalie decides to start using it only in her new business. She estimates that the equipment is currently worth $300. She invests the equipment in the business.

16 Natalie realizes that her initial cash investment is not enough. Her grandmother lends her $2,000 cash, for which Natalie signs a note payable in the name of the business. Natalie deposits the money in the business bank account. (*Hint:* The note does not have to be repaid for 24 months. As a result, the note payable should be reported in the accounts as the last liability and also on the balance sheet as the last liability.)

17 She buys more baking equipment for $900 cash.

20 She teaches her first class and collects $125 cash.

25 Natalie books a second class for December 4 for $150. She receives $30 cash in advance as a down payment.

30 Natalie pays $1,320 for a one-year insurance policy that will expire on December 1, 2014.

### Instructions
**(a)** Prepare journal entries to record the November transactions.
**(b)** Post the journal entries to general ledger accounts.
**(c)** Prepare a trial balance at November 30.

# Broadening Your Perspective

## Financial Reporting and Analysis

### Financial Reporting Problem: Apple Inc.

**BYP2-1** The financial statements of Apple Inc. are presented in Appendix A. Instructions for accessing and using the company's complete annual report, including the notes to the financial statements, are also provided in Appendix A.

Apple's financial statements contain the following selected accounts, stated in millions of dollars.

Accounts Payable                    Cash and Cash Equivalents
Accounts Receivable                 Research and Development Expense
Property, Plant, and Equipment      Inventories

### Instructions
**(a)** Answer the following questions.
  **(1)** What is the increase and decrease side for each account?
  **(2)** What is the normal balance for each account?

**(b)** Identify the probable other account in the transaction and the effect on that account when:
   **(1)** Accounts Receivable is decreased.
   **(2)** Accounts Payable is decreased.
   **(3)** Inventories are increased.
**(c)** Identify the other account(s) that ordinarily would be involved when:
   **(1)** Research and Development Expense is increased.
   **(2)** Property, Plant, and Equipment is increased.

## Comparative Analysis Problem:
## Amazon.com, Inc. vs. Wal-Mart Stores, Inc.

**BYP2-2** Amazon.com, Inc.'s financial statements are presented in Appendix D. Financial statements for Wal-Mart Stores, Inc. are presented in Appendix E. Instructions for accessing and using the complete annual reports of Amazon and Wal-Mart, including the notes to the financial statements, are also provided in Appendices D and E, respectively.

*Instructions*
**(a)** Based on the information contained in the financial statements, determine the normal balance of the listed accounts for each company.

| Amazon | Wal-Mart |
|---|---|
| **1.** Interest Expense | **1.** Net Sales Revenues |
| **2.** Cash and Cash Equivalents | **2.** Inventories |
| **3.** Accounts Payable | **3.** Cost of Sales |

**(b)** Identify the other account ordinarily involved when:
   **(1)** Accounts Receivable is increased.
   **(2)** Interest Expense is increased.
   **(3)** Salaries and Wages Payable is decreased.
   **(4)** Service Revenue is increased.

## Real-World Focus

**BYP2-3** Much information about specific companies is available on the Internet. Such information includes basic descriptions of the company's location, activities, industry, financial health, and financial performance.

*Address:* **biz.yahoo.com/i**, or go to **www.wiley.com/college/weygandt**

*Steps*
**1.** Type in a company name, or use index to find company name.
**2.** Choose **Profile**. Perform instructions (a)–(c) below.
**3.** Click on the company's specific industry to identify competitors. Perform instructions (d)–(g) below.

*Instructions*
Answer the following questions.
**(a)** What is the company's industry?
**(b)** What is the company's total sales?
**(c)** What is the company's net income?
**(d)** What are the names of four of the company's competitors?
**(e)** Choose one of these competitors.
**(f)** What is this competitor's name? What are its sales? What is its net income?
**(g)** Which of these two companies is larger by size of sales? Which one reported higher net income?

**BYP2-4** The January 27, 2011, edition of the *New York Times* contains an article by Richard Sandomir entitled "N.F.L. Finances, as Seen Through Packers' Records." The article discusses the fact that the Green Bay Packers are the only NFL team that publicly publishes its annual report.

*Instructions*
Read the article and answer the following questions.
**(a)** Why are the Green Bay Packers the only professional football team to publish and distribute an annual report?
**(b)** Why is the football players' labor union particularly interested in the Packers' annual report?

**(c)** In addition to the players' labor union, what other outside party might be interested in the annual report?

**(d)** Even though the Packers' revenue increased in recent years, the company's operating profit fell significantly. How does the article explain this decline?

# Critical Thinking

## Decision-Making Across the Organization

**BYP2-5** Dyanna Craig operates Craig Riding Academy. The academy's primary sources of revenue are riding fees and lesson fees, which are paid on a cash basis. Dyanna also boards horses for owners, who are billed monthly for boarding fees. In a few cases, boarders pay in advance of expected use. For its revenue transactions, the academy maintains the following accounts: Cash, Accounts Receivable, and Service Revenue.

The academy owns 10 horses, a stable, a riding corral, riding equipment, and office equipment. These assets are accounted for in these accounts: Horses, Buildings, and Equipment.

The academy also maintains the following accounts: Supplies, Prepaid Insurance, Accounts Payable, Salaries and Wages Expense, Advertising Expense, Utilities Expense, and Maintenance and Repairs Expense.

Dyanna makes periodic withdrawals of cash for personal living expenses. To record Dyanna's equity in the business and her drawings, two accounts are maintained: Owner's Capital and Owner's Drawings.

During the first month of operations, an inexperienced bookkeeper was employed. Dyanna Craig asks you to review the following eight entries of the 50 entries made during the month. In each case, the explanation for the entry is correct.

| | | | |
|---|---|---|---|
| May 1 | Cash | 18,000 | |
| |     Owner's Capital | | 18,000 |
| |        (Invested $18,000 cash in business) | | |
| 5 | Cash | 250 | |
| |     Service Revenue | | 250 |
| |        (Received $250 cash for lessons provided) | | |
| 7 | Cash | 300 | |
| |     Service Revenue | | 300 |
| |        (Received $300 for boarding of horses beginning June 1) | | |
| 14 | Equipment | 80 | |
| |     Cash | | 800 |
| |        (Purchased desk and other office equipment for $800 cash) | | |
| 15 | Salaries and Wages Expense | 400 | |
| |     Cash | | 400 |
| |        (Issued check to Dyanna Craig for personal use) | | |
| 20 | Cash | 148 | |
| |     Service Revenue | | 184 |
| |        (Received $184 cash for riding fees) | | |
| 30 | Maintenance and Repairs Expense | 75 | |
| |     Accounts Payable | | 75 |
| |        (Received bill of $75 from carpenter for repair services performed) | | |
| 31 | Supplies | 1,700 | |
| |     Cash | | 1,700 |
| |        (Purchased an estimated 2 months' supply of feed and hay for $1,700 on account) | | |

*Instructions*
With the class divided into groups, answer the following.

**(a)** Identify each journal entry that is correct. For each journal entry that is incorrect, prepare the entry that should have been made by the bookkeeper.

**(b)** Which of the incorrect entries would prevent the trial balance from balancing?

**(c)** What was the correct net income for May, assuming the bookkeeper reported net income of $4,500 after posting all 50 entries?

**(d)** What was the correct cash balance at May 31, assuming the bookkeeper reported a balance of $12,475 after posting all 50 entries (and the only errors occurred in the items listed above)?

## Communication Activity

**BYP2-6** Keller's Maid Company offers home-cleaning service. Two recurring transactions for the company are billing customers for services performed and paying employee salaries. For example, on March 15, bills totaling $6,000 were sent to customers and $2,000 was paid in salaries to employees.

*Instructions*

Write a memo to your instructor that explains and illustrates the steps in the recording process for each of the March 15 transactions. Use the format illustrated in the text under the heading, "The Recording Process Illustrated" (p. 65).

## Ethics Cases

**BYP2-7** Meredith Ward is the assistant chief accountant at Frazier Company, a manufacturer of computer chips and cellular phones. The company presently has total sales of $20 million. It is the end of the first quarter. Meredith is hurriedly trying to prepare a trial balance so that quarterly financial statements can be prepared and released to management and the regulatory agencies. The total credits on the trial balance exceed the debits by $1,000. In order to meet the 4 p.m. deadline, Meredith decides to force the debits and credits into balance by adding the amount of the difference to the Equipment account. She chooses Equipment because it is one of the larger account balances; percentage-wise, it will be the least misstated. Meredith "plugs" the difference! She believes that the difference will not affect anyone's decisions. She wishes that she had another few days to find the error but realizes that the financial statements are already late.

*Instructions*

**(a)** Who are the stakeholders in this situation?

**(b)** What are the ethical issues involved in this case?

**(c)** What are Meredith's alternatives?

**BYP2-8** If you haven't already done so, in the not-too-distant future you will prepare a résumé. In some ways, your résumé is like a company's annual report. Its purpose is to enable others to evaluate your past, in an effort to predict your future.

A résumé is your opportunity to create a positive first impression. It is important that it be impressive—but it should also be accurate. In order to increase their job prospects, some people are tempted to "inflate" their résumés by overstating the importance of some past accomplishments or positions. In fact, you might even think that "everybody does it" and that if you don't do it, you will be at a disadvantage.

David Edmondson, the president and CEO of well-known electronics retailer Radio Shack, overstated his accomplishments by claiming that he had earned a bachelor's of science degree, when in fact he had not. Apparently, his employer had not done a background check to ensure the accuracy of his résumé. Should Radio Shack have fired him?

**YES:** Radio Shack is a publicly traded company. Investors, creditors, employees, and others doing business with the company will not trust it if its leader is known to have poor integrity. The "tone at the top" is vital to creating an ethical organization.

**NO:** Mr. Edmondson had been a Radio Shack employee for 11 years. He had served the company in a wide variety of positions, and had earned the position of CEO through exceptional performance. While the fact that he lied 11 years earlier on his résumé was unfortunate, his service since then made this past transgression irrelevant. In addition, the company was in the midst of a massive restructuring, which included closing 700 of its 7,000 stores. It could not afford additional upheaval at this time.

*Instructions*

Write a response indicating your position regarding this situation. Provide support for your view.

## All About You

**BYP2-9** Every company needs to plan in order to move forward. Its top management must consider where it wants the company to be in three to five years. Like a company, you need to think about where you want to be three to five years from now, and you need to start taking steps now in order to get there.

*Instructions*

Provide responses to each of the following items.

**(a)** Where would you like to be working in three to five years? Describe your plan for getting there by identifying between five and 10 specific steps that you need to take.

**(b)** In order to get the job you want, you will need a résumé. Your résumé is the equivalent of a company's annual report. It needs to provide relevant and reliable information about your past accomplishments so that employers can decide whether to "invest" in you. Do a search on the Internet to find a good résumé format. What are the basic elements of a résumé?

**(c)** A company's annual report provides information about a company's accomplishments. In order for investors to use the annual report, the information must be reliable; that is, users must have faith that the information is accurate and believable. How can you provide assurance that the information on your résumé is reliable?

**(d)** Prepare a résumé assuming that you have accomplished the five to 10 specific steps you identified in part (a). Also, provide evidence that would give assurance that the information is reliable.

## Considering People, Planet, and Profit

**BYP2-10** Auditors provide a type of certification of corporate financial statements. Certification is used in many other aspects of business as well. For example, it plays a critical role in the sustainability movement. The February 7, 2012, issue of the *New York Times* contained an article by S. Amanda Caudill entitled "Better Lives in Better Coffee," which discusses the role of certification in the coffee business.

*Address:* **http://scientistatwork.blogs.nytimes.com/2012/02/07/better-lives-in-better-coffee**

*Instructions*

Read the article and answer the following questions.

**(a)** The article mentions three different certification types that coffee growers can obtain from three different certification bodies. Using financial reporting as an example, what potential problems might the existence of multiple certification types present to coffee purchasers?

**(b)** According to the author, which certification is most common among coffee growers? What are the possible reasons for this?

**(c)** What social and environmental benefits are coffee certifications trying to achieve? Are there also potential financial benefits to the parties involved?

## Answers to Chapter Questions

### Answers to Insight and Accounting Across the Organization Questions

**p. 57 Keeping Score Q:** Do you think that the Chicago Bears football team would be likely to have the same major revenue and expense accounts as the Cubs? **A:** Because their businesses are similar—professional sports—many of the revenue and expense accounts for the baseball and football teams might be similar.

**p. 61 Boosting Microsoft's Profits Q:** In what ways is this Microsoft division using accounting to assist in its effort to become more profitable? **A:** The division has used accounting to set very strict sales, revenue, and profit goals. In addition, the managers in this division use accounting to keep a tight rein on product costs. Also, accounting serves as the basis of communication so that the marketing managers and product designers can work with production managers, engineers, and accountants to create an exciting product within specified cost constraints.

**p. 63 A Convenient Overstatement Q:** What incentives might employees have had to overstate the value of these investment securities on the company's financial statements? **A:** One reason that they may have been reluctant to record the losses is out of fear that the company's shareholders and clients would panic if they saw the magnitude of the losses. However, personal self-interest might have been equally to blame—the bonuses of the traders were tied to the value of the investment securities.

**p. 74 Why Accuracy Matters Q:** In order for these companies to prepare and issue financial statements, their accounting equations (debits and credits) must have been in balance at year-end. How could these errors or misstatements have occurred? **A:** A company's accounting equation (its books) can be in balance yet its financial statements have errors or misstatements because of the following: entire transactions were not recorded; transactions were recorded at wrong amounts; transactions were recorded in the wrong accounts; transactions were recorded in the wrong accounting period. Audits of financial statements uncover some but obviously not all errors or misstatements.

**Answers to Self-Test Questions**

**1.** b    **2.** c    **3.** d    **4.** d    **5.** d    **6.** b    **7.** a    **8.** c    **9.** b    **10.** c    **11.** d    **12.** c ($16,000 − $5,000)    **13.** a
**14.** c    **15.** a ($5,000 + $40,000 + $10,000 + $15,000 + $61,000)

# A Look at IFRS

**LEARNING OBJECTIVE    8**

**Compare the procedures for the accounting process under GAAP and IFRS.**

International companies use the same set of procedures and records to keep track of transaction data. Thus, the material in Chapter 2 dealing with the account, general rules of debit and credit, and steps in the recording process—the journal, ledger, and chart of accounts—is the same under both GAAP and IFRS.

## Key Points

- Transaction analysis is the same under IFRS and GAAP but, as you will see in later chapters, different standards sometimes impact how transactions are recorded.

- Rules for accounting for specific events sometimes differ across countries. For example, European companies rely less on historical cost and more on fair value than U.S. companies. Despite the differences, the double-entry accounting system is the basis of accounting systems worldwide.

- Both the IASB and FASB go beyond the basic definitions provided in this textbook for the key elements of financial statements, that is, assets, liabilities, equity, revenues, and expenses. The more substantive definitions, using the IASB definitional structure, are provided in the Chapter 1 *A Look at IFRS* discussion.

- A trial balance under IFRS follows the same format as shown in the textbook.

- As shown in the textbook, dollars signs are typically used only in the trial balance and the financial statements. The same practice is followed under IFRS, using the currency of the country that the reporting company is headquartered.

- In February 2010, the SEC expressed a desire to continue working toward a single set of high-quality standards. In deciding whether the United States should adopt IFRS, some of the issues the SEC said should be considered are:

  ♦ Whether IFRS is sufficiently developed and consistent in application.

  ♦ Whether the IASB is sufficiently independent.

  ♦ Whether IFRS is established for the benefit of investors.

  ♦ The issues involved in educating investors about IFRS.

  ♦ The impact of a switch to IFRS on U.S. laws and regulations.

  ♦ The impact on companies including changes to their accounting systems, contractual arrangements, corporate governance, and litigation.

  ♦ The issues involved in educating accountants, so they can prepare financial statements under IFRS.

## Looking to the Future

The basic recording process shown in this textbook is followed by companies across the globe. It is unlikely to change in the future. The definitional structure of assets, liabilities, equity, revenues, and expenses may change over time as the IASB and FASB evaluate their overall conceptual framework for establishing accounting standards.

# IFRS Practice

## IFRS Self-Test Questions

1. Which statement is **correct** regarding IFRS?
   (a) IFRS reverses the rules of debits and credits, that is, debits are on the right and credits are on the left.
   (b) IFRS uses the same process for recording transactions as GAAP.
   (c) The chart of accounts under IFRS is different because revenues follow assets.
   (d) None of the above statements are correct.

2. The expanded accounting equation under IFRS is as follows:
   (a) Assets = Liabilities + Owner's Capital + Owner's Drawings + Revenues − Expenses.
   (b) Assets + Liabilities = Owner's Capital + Owner's Drawings + Revenues − Expenses.
   (c) Assets = Liabilities + Owner's Capital − Owner's Drawings + Revenues − Expenses.
   (d) Assets = Liabilities + Owner's Capital + Owner's Drawings − Revenues − Expenses.

3. A trial balance:
   (a) is the same under IFRS and GAAP.
   (b) proves that transactions are recorded correctly.
   (c) proves that all transactions have been recorded.
   (d) will not balance if a correct journal entry is posted twice.

4. One difference between IFRS and GAAP is that:
   (a) GAAP uses accrual-accounting concepts and IFRS uses primarily the cash basis of accounting.
   (b) IFRS uses a different posting process than GAAP.
   (c) IFRS uses more fair value measurements than GAAP.
   (d) the limitations of a trial balance are different between IFRS and GAAP.

5. The general policy for using proper currency signs (dollar, yen, pound, etc.) is the same for both IFRS and this textbook. This policy is as follows:
   (a) Currency signs only appear in ledgers and journal entries.
   (b) Currency signs are only shown in the trial balance.
   (c) Currency signs are shown for all compound journal entries.
   (d) Currency signs are shown in trial balances and financial statements.

## IFRS Exercises

**IFRS2-1** Describe some of the issues the SEC must consider in deciding whether the United States should adopt IFRS.

## International Financial Reporting Problem: Zetar plc

**IFRS2-2** The financial statements of Zetar plc are presented in Appendix F. Instructions for accessing and using the company's complete annual report, including the notes to its financial statements, are also provided in Appendix F.

### Instructions
Describe in which statement each of the following items is reported, and the position in the statement (e.g., current asset).

(a) Other administrative expenses.
(b) Cash at bank.
(c) Borrowings and overdrafts.
(d) Finance costs.

### Answers to IFRS Self-Test Questions
**1.** b   **2.** c   **3.** a   **4.** c   **5.** d

 Remember to go back to The Navigator box on the chapter opening page and check off your completed work.

# 3 | Adjusting the Accounts

## Feature Story

### Keeping Track of Groupons

Who doesn't like buying things at a discount? That's why it's not surprising that three years after it started as a company, Groupon was estimated to be worth $16 billion. This translates into an average increase in value of almost $15 million per day.

Now consider that Groupon had previously been estimated to be worth even more than that. What happened? Well, accounting regulators and investors began to question the way that Groupon had accounted for some of its transactions. But if Groupon sells only coupons ("groupons"), you're probably wondering how hard can it be to accurately account for that? It turns out that accounting for coupons is not as easy as you might think.

First, consider what happens when Groupon makes a sale. Suppose it sells a groupon for $30 for Highrise Hamburgers. When it receives the $30 from the customer, it must turn over half of that amount ($15) to Highrise Hamburgers. So should Groupon record revenue for the full $30 or just $15? Until recently, Groupon recorded the full $30. But, in response to an SEC ruling on the issue, Groupon now records revenue of $15 instead.

A second issue is a matter of timing. When should Group● record this $15 revenue? Should it record the revenue w● sells the groupon, or must it wait until the customer uses groupon at Highrise Hamburgers? You can find the answ● this question in the notes to Groupon's financial stateme● It recognizes the revenue once "the number of customer● who purchase the daily deal exceeds the predetermined ● threshold, the Groupon has been electronically delivered ● the purchaser and a listing of Groupons sold has been m● available to the merchant."

The accounting becomes even more complicated when y● consider the company's loyalty programs. Groupon offers ● or discounted groupons to its subscribers for doing thing● such as referring new customers or participating in promo● These groupons are to be used for future purchases, yet t● company must record the expense at the time the custom● receives the groupon. The cost of these programs is huge● Groupon, so the timing of this expense can definitely affe● reported income.

The final kicker is that Groupon, like all other companies● must rely on many estimates in its financial reporting. For example, Groupon reports that "estimates are utilize●

✔ The Navigator

- Scan Learning Objectives
- Read Feature Story
- Read Preview
- Read text and answer **DO IT!** p. 102
    - p. 110　　■ p. 116　　■ p. 121
- Work Comprehensive **DO IT!** p. 122
- Review Summary of Learning Objectives
- Answer Self-Test Questions
- Complete Assignments
- Go to *WileyPLUS* for practice and tutorials

 **Read A Look at IFRS** p. 157

### Learning Objectives
✔ The Navigator

*After studying this chapter, you should be able to:*

[1] Explain the time period assumption.

[2] Explain the accrual basis of accounting.

[3] Explain the reasons for adjusting entries and identify the major types of adjusting entries.

[4] Prepare adjusting entries for deferrals.

[5] Prepare adjusting entries for accruals.

[6] Describe the nature and purpose of an adjusted trial balance.

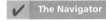
Rudy Archuleta/Redux Pictures

for, but not limited to, stock-based compensation, income taxes, valuation of acquired goodwill and intangible assets, customer refunds, contingent liabilities and the depreciable lives of fixed assets."

It concludes by saying that "actual results could differ materially from those estimates." So, next time you use a coupon, think about what that means for the company's accountants!

# Preview of Chapter 3

✔ The Navigator

In Chapter 1, you learned a neat little formula: Net income = Revenues − Expenses. In Chapter 2, you learned some rules for recording revenue and expense transactions. Guess what? Things are not really that nice and neat. In fact, it is often difficult for companies to determine in what time period they should report some revenues and expenses. In other words, in measuring net income, timing is everything.

The content and organization of Chapter 3 are as follows.

## ADJUSTING THE ACCOUNTS

| Timing Issues | The Basics of Adjusting Entries | The Adjusted Trial Balance and Financial Statements |
|---|---|---|
| • Fiscal and calendar years<br>• Accrual- vs. cash-basis accounting<br>• Recognizing revenues and expenses | • Types of adjusting entries<br>• Adjusting entries for deferrals<br>• Adjusting entries for accruals<br>• Summary of basic relationships | • Preparing the adjusted trial balance<br>• Preparing financial statements |

## Timing Issues

**Time Period Assumption**

Year 1     Year 10

Year 6

**Alternative Terminology**
The time period assumption is also called the *periodicity assumption*.

If we could wait to prepare financial statements until a company ended its operations, no adjustments would be needed. At that point, we could easily determine its final balance sheet and the amount of lifetime income it earned.

However, most companies need immediate feedback about how well they are doing. For example, management usually wants monthly financial statements. The Internal Revenue Service requires all businesses to file annual tax returns. Therefore, **accountants divide the economic life of a business into artificial time periods**. This convenient assumption is referred to as the **time period assumption**.

Many business transactions affect more than one of these arbitrary time periods. For example, the airplanes purchased by Southwest Airlines five years ago are still in use today. We must determine the relevance of each business transaction to specific accounting periods. (How much of the cost of an airplane contributed to operations this year?)

### Fiscal and Calendar Years

Both small and large companies prepare financial statements periodically in order to assess their financial condition and results of operations. **Accounting time periods are generally a month, a quarter, or a year.** Monthly and quarterly time periods are called **interim periods**. Most large companies must prepare both quarterly and annual financial statements.

An accounting time period that is one year in length is a **fiscal year**. A fiscal year usually begins with the first day of a month and ends 12 months later on the last day of a month. Most businesses use the **calendar year** (January 1 to December 31) as their accounting period. Some do not. Companies whose fiscal year differs from the calendar year include Delta Air Lines, June 30, and Walt Disney Productions, September 30. Sometimes a company's year-end will vary from year to year. For example, PepsiCo's fiscal year ends on the Friday closest to December 31, which was December 25 in 2010 and December 30 in 2011.

### Accrual- versus Cash-Basis Accounting

What you will learn in this chapter is **accrual-basis accounting**. Under the accrual basis, companies record transactions that change a company's financial statements **in the periods in which the events occur**. For example, using the accrual basis to determine net income means companies recognize revenues when they perform services (rather than when they receive cash). It also means recognizing expenses when incurred (rather than when paid).

An alternative to the accrual basis is the cash basis. Under **cash-basis accounting**, companies record revenue when they receive cash. They record an expense when they pay out cash. The cash basis seems appealing due to its simplicity, but it often produces misleading financial statements. It fails to record revenue for a company that has performed services but for which it has not received the cash. As a result, it does not match expenses with revenues. **Cash-basis accounting is not in accordance with generally accepted accounting principles (GAAP)**.

Individuals and some small companies do use cash-basis accounting. The cash basis is justified for small businesses because they often have few receivables and payables. Medium and large companies use accrual-basis accounting.

### Recognizing Revenues and Expenses

It can be difficult to determine when to report revenues and expenses. The revenue recognition principle and the expense recognition principle help in this task.

## REVENUE RECOGNITION PRINCIPLE

When a company agrees to perform a service or sell a product to a customer, it has a **performance obligation**. When the company meets this performance obligation, it recognizes revenue. The **revenue recognition principle** therefore requires that companies recognize revenue in the accounting period in which the performance obligation is satisfied.[1] To illustrate, assume that Dave's Dry Cleaning cleans clothing on June 30 but customers do not claim and pay for their clothes until the first week of July. Dave's should record revenue in June when it performed the service (satisfied the performance obligation) rather than in July when it received the cash. At June 30, Dave's would report a receivable on its balance sheet and revenue in its income statement for the service performed.

## EXPENSE RECOGNITION PRINCIPLE

Accountants follow a simple rule in recognizing expenses: "Let the expenses follow the revenues." Thus, expense recognition is tied to revenue recognition. In the dry cleaning example, this means that Dave's should report the salary expense incurred in performing the June 30 cleaning service in the same period in which it recognizes the service revenue. The critical issue in expense recognition is when the expense makes its contribution to revenue. This may or may not be the same period in which the expense is paid. If Dave's does not pay the salary incurred on June 30 until July, it would report salaries payable on its June 30 balance sheet.

This practice of expense recognition is referred to as the **expense recognition principle** (often referred to as the **matching principle**). It dictates that efforts (expenses) be matched with results (revenues). Illustration 3-1 summarizes the revenue and expense recognition principles.

**Revenue Recognition**
Satisfied performance obligation

Customer requests service → Cash received

Revenue is recognized when performance obligation is satisfied.

**Expense Recognition**
Matching Revenues
↑
Delivery
Advertising — Utilities
**Expenses**

**Illustration 3-1**
GAAP relationships in revenue and expense recognition

**Time Period Assumption**

Economic life of business can be divided into artificial time periods.

**Revenue Recognition Principle**

Recognize revenue in the accounting period in which the performance obligation is satisfied.

**Expense Recognition Principle**

Match expenses with revenues in the period when the company makes efforts to generate those revenues.

**Revenue and Expense Recognition**

In accordance with generally accepted accounting principles (GAAP).

---

[1]The definition for the revenue recognition principle is based on the revised exposure draft issued by the FASB.

## ETHICS INSIGHT

### Cooking the Books?

Allegations of abuse of the revenue recognition principle have become all too common in recent years. For example, it was alleged that Krispy Kreme sometimes doubled the number of doughnuts shipped to wholesale customers at the end of a quarter to boost quarterly results. The customers shipped the unsold doughnuts back after the beginning of the next quarter for a refund. Conversely, Computer Associates International was accused of backdating sales—that is, reporting a sale in one period that did not actually occur until the next period in order to achieve the earlier period's sales targets.

**?** What motivates sales executives and finance and accounting executives to participate in activities that result in inaccurate reporting of revenues? (See page 156.)

© Dean Turner/iStockphoto

---

> ## DO IT!

### Timing Concepts

Several timing concepts are discussed on pages 100–101. A list of concepts is provided in the left column below, with a description of the concept in the right column below. There are more descriptions provided than concepts. Match the description of the concept to the concept.

1. ____Accrual-basis accounting.
2. ____Calendar year.
3. ____Time period assumption.
4. ____Expense recognition principle.

**(a)** Monthly and quarterly time periods.
**(b)** Efforts (expenses) should be matched with results (revenues).
**(c)** Accountants divide the economic life of a business into artificial time periods.
**(d)** Companies record revenues when they receive cash and record expenses when they pay out cash.
**(e)** An accounting time period that starts on January 1 and ends on December 31.
**(f)** Companies record transactions in the period in which the events occur.

#### Action Plan
✔ Review the glossary terms identified on page 124.
✔ Study carefully the revenue recognition principle, the expense recognition principle, and the time period assumption.

### Solution

| 1. f   2. e   3. c   4. b |
|---|

Related exercise material: E3-1, E3-2, E3-3, and **DO IT!** 3-1.

✔ **The Navigator**

---

## The Basics of Adjusting Entries

**LEARNING OBJECTIVE** **3**

Explain the reasons for adjusting entries and identify the major types of adjusting entries.

In order for revenues to be recorded in the period in which services are performed and for expenses to be recognized in the period in which they are incurred, companies make adjusting entries. **Adjusting entries ensure that the revenue recognition and expense recognition principles are followed**.

Adjusting entries are necessary because the **trial balance**—the first pulling together of the transaction data—may not contain up-to-date and complete data. This is true for several reasons:

1. Some events are not recorded daily because it is not efficient to do so. Examples are the use of supplies and the earning of wages by employees.

2. Some costs are not recorded during the accounting period because these costs expire with the passage of time rather than as a result of recurring daily transactions. Examples are charges related to the use of buildings and equipment, rent, and insurance.

3. Some items may be unrecorded. An example is a utility service bill that will not be received until the next accounting period.

**Adjusting entries are required every time a company prepares financial statements.** The company analyzes each account in the trial balance to determine whether it is complete and up to date for financial statement purposes. **Every adjusting entry will include one income statement account and one balance sheet account.**

**International Note**

Internal controls are a system of checks and balances designed to detect and prevent fraud and errors. The Sarbanes-Oxley Act requires U.S. companies to enhance their systems of internal control. However, many foreign companies do not have to meet strict internal control requirements. Some U.S. companies believe that this gives foreign firms an unfair advantage because developing and maintaining internal controls can be very expensive.

## Types of Adjusting Entries

Adjusting entries are classified as either **deferrals** or **accruals**. As Illustration 3-2 shows, each of these classes has two subcategories.

**Illustration 3-2**
Categories of adjusting entries

**Deferrals:**

1. Prepaid expenses: Expenses paid in cash before they are used or consumed.

2. Unearned revenues: Cash received before services are performed.

**Accruals:**

1. Accrued revenues: Revenues for services performed but not yet received in cash or recorded.

2. Accrued expenses: Expenses incurred but not yet paid in cash or recorded.

Subsequent sections give examples of each type of adjustment. Each example is based on the October 31 trial balance of Pioneer Advertising Agency from Chapter 2, reproduced in Illustration 3-3.

**Illustration 3-3**
Trial balance

### PIONEER ADVERTISING AGENCY
#### Trial Balance
#### October 31, 2014

|  | Debit | Credit |
|---|---|---|
| Cash | $ 15,200 |  |
| Supplies | 2,500 |  |
| Prepaid Insurance | 600 |  |
| Equipment | 5,000 |  |
| Notes Payable |  | $ 5,000 |
| Accounts Payable |  | 2,500 |
| Unearned Service Revenue |  | 1,200 |
| Owner's Capital |  | 10,000 |
| Owner's Drawings | 500 |  |
| Service Revenue |  | 10,000 |
| Salaries and Wages Expense | 4,000 |  |
| Rent Expense | 900 |  |
|  | $28,700 | $28,700 |

We assume that Pioneer Advertising uses an accounting period of one month. Thus, monthly adjusting entries are made. The entries are dated October 31.

## Adjusting Entries for Deferrals

To defer means to postpone or delay. **Deferrals** are expenses or revenues that are recognized at a date later than the point when cash was originally exchanged. The two types of deferrals are prepaid expenses and unearned revenues.

### PREPAID EXPENSES

When companies record payments of expenses that will benefit more than one accounting period, they record an asset called **prepaid expenses** or **prepayments**. When expenses are prepaid, an asset account is increased (debited) to show the service or benefit that the company will receive in the future. Examples of common prepayments are insurance, supplies, advertising, and rent. In addition, companies make prepayments when they purchase buildings and equipment.

**Prepaid expenses are costs that expire either with the passage of time** (e.g., rent and insurance) **or through use** (e.g., supplies). The expiration of these costs does not require daily entries, which would be impractical and unnecessary. Accordingly, companies postpone the recognition of such cost expirations until they prepare financial statements. At each statement date, they make adjusting entries to record the expenses applicable to the current accounting period and to show the remaining amounts in the asset accounts.

Prior to adjustment, assets are overstated and expenses are understated. Therefore, as shown in Illustration 3-4, **an adjusting entry for prepaid expenses results in an increase (a debit) to an expense account and a decrease (a credit) to an asset account**.

**Illustration 3-4**
Adjusting entries for prepaid expenses

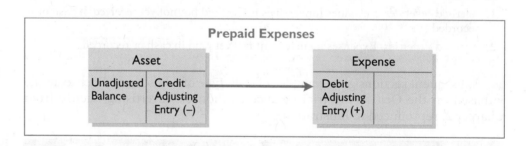

Let's look in more detail at some specific types of prepaid expenses, beginning with supplies.

**SUPPLIES** The purchase of supplies, such as paper and envelopes, results in an increase (a debit) to an asset account. During the accounting period, the company uses supplies. Rather than record supplies expense as the supplies are used, companies recognize supplies expense at the **end** of the accounting period. At the end of the accounting period, the company counts the remaining supplies. As shown in Illustration 3-5, the difference between the unadjusted balance in the Supplies (asset) account and the actual cost of supplies on hand represents the supplies used (an expense) for that period.

Recall from Chapter 2 that Pioneer Advertising Agency purchased supplies costing $2,500 on October 5. Pioneer recorded the purchase by increasing (debiting) the asset Supplies. This account shows a balance of $2,500 in the October 31 trial balance. An inventory count at the close of business on October 31 reveals that $1,000 of supplies are still on hand. Thus, the cost of supplies used is $1,500

($2,500 − $1,000). This use of supplies decreases an asset, Supplies. It also decreases owner's equity by increasing an expense account, Supplies Expense. This is shown in Illustration 3-5.

**Illustration 3-5**
Adjustment for supplies

After adjustment, the asset account Supplies shows a balance of $1,000, which is equal to the cost of supplies on hand at the statement date. In addition, Supplies Expense shows a balance of $1,500, which equals the cost of supplies used in October. **If Pioneer does not make the adjusting entry, October expenses are understated and net income is overstated by $1,500. Moreover, both assets and owner's equity will be overstated by $1,500 on the October 31 balance sheet.**

**INSURANCE** Companies purchase insurance to protect themselves from losses due to fire, theft, and unforeseen events. Insurance must be paid in advance, often for more than one year. The cost of insurance (premiums) paid in advance is recorded as an increase (debit) in the asset account Prepaid Insurance. At the financial statement date, companies increase (debit) Insurance Expense and decrease (credit) Prepaid Insurance for the cost of insurance that has expired during the period.

On October 4, Pioneer Advertising paid $600 for a one-year fire insurance policy. Coverage began on October 1. Pioneer recorded the payment by increasing (debiting) Prepaid Insurance. This account shows a balance of $600 in the October 31 trial balance. Insurance of $50 ($600 ÷ 12) expires each month. The expiration of prepaid insurance decreases an asset, Prepaid Insurance. It also decreases owner's equity by increasing an expense account, Insurance Expense.

As shown in Illustration 3-6 (page 106), the asset Prepaid Insurance shows a balance of $550, which represents the unexpired cost for the remaining 11 months of coverage. At the same time, the balance in Insurance Expense equals the insurance cost that expired in October. **If Pioneer does not make this adjustment, October expenses are understated by $50 and net income is overstated by $50. Moreover, both assets and owner's equity will be overstated by $50 on the October 31 balance sheet.**

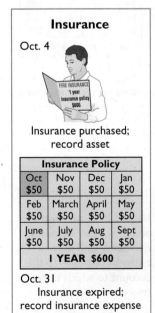

**Insurance**

Oct. 4

Insurance purchased;
record asset

| **Insurance Policy** | | | |
|------|------|------|------|
| Oct | Nov | Dec | Jan |
| $50 | $50 | $50 | $50 |
| Feb | March | April | May |
| $50 | $50 | $50 | $50 |
| June | July | Aug | Sept |
| $50 | $50 | $50 | $50 |
| **1 YEAR  $600** | | | |

Oct. 31
Insurance expired;
record insurance expense

**Illustration 3-6**
Adjustment for insurance

| Basic Analysis | The expense Insurance Expense is increased $50, and the asset Prepaid Insurance is decreased $50. |

| Equation Analysis | (2) | Assets | = | Liabilities | + | Owner's Equity |

Assets — Prepaid Insurance −$50 = Liabilities + Owner's Equity — Insurance Expense −$50

| Debit–Credit Analysis | Debits increase expenses: debit Insurance Expense $50. Credits decrease assets: credit Prepaid Insurance $50. |

| Journal Entry | Oct. 31 | Insurance Expense | 50 |
| | | Prepaid Insurance | | 50 |
| | | (To record insurance expired) | |

Posting

| Prepaid Insurance | | | 130 |
|---|---|---|---|
| Oct. 4 | 600 | Oct. 31 Adj. 50 | |
| Oct. 31 | Bal. 550 | | |

| Insurance Expense | | 722 |
|---|---|---|
| Oct. 31 | Adj. 50 | |
| Oct. 31 | Bal. 50 | |

**DEPRECIATION** A company typically owns a variety of assets that have long lives, such as buildings, equipment, and motor vehicles. The period of service is referred to as the **useful life** of the asset. Because a building is expected to provide service for many years, it is recorded as an asset, rather than an expense, on the date it is acquired. As explained in Chapter 1, companies record such assets **at cost**, as required by the historical cost principle. To follow the expense recognition principle, companies allocate a portion of this cost as an expense during each period of the asset's useful life. **Depreciation** is the process of allocating the cost of an asset to expense over its useful life.

**Need for Adjustment.** The acquisition of long-lived assets is essentially a long-term prepayment for the use of an asset. An adjusting entry for depreciation is needed to recognize the cost that has been used (an expense) during the period and to report the unused cost (an asset) at the end of the period. One very important point to understand: **Depreciation is an allocation concept, not a valuation concept.** That is, depreciation **allocates an asset's cost to the periods in which it is used. Depreciation does not attempt to report the actual change in the value of the asset.**

For Pioneer Advertising, assume that depreciation on the equipment is $480 a year, or $40 per month. As shown in Illustration 3-7, rather than decrease (credit) the asset account directly, Pioneer instead credits Accumulated Depreciation—Equipment. Accumulated Depreciation is called a **contra asset account**. Such an account is offset against an asset account on the balance sheet. Thus, the Accumulated Depreciation—Equipment account offsets the asset Equipment. This account keeps track of the total amount of depreciation expense taken over the life of the asset. To keep the accounting equation in balance, Pioneer decreases owner's equity by increasing an expense account, Depreciation Expense.

The balance in the Accumulated Depreciation—Equipment account will increase $40 each month, and the balance in Equipment remains $5,000.

**Statement Presentation.** As indicated, Accumulated Depreciation—Equipment is a contra asset account. It is offset against Equipment on the balance sheet. The normal balance of a contra asset account is a credit. A theoretical alternative to using a contra asset account would be to decrease (credit) the asset account by the amount of depreciation each period. But using the contra account is preferable for a simple reason: It discloses **both** the original cost of the equipment **and**

**Depreciation**

Oct. 2

Equipment purchased; record asset

| Equipment | | | |
|---|---|---|---|
| Oct $40 | Nov $40 | Dec $40 | Jan $40 |
| Feb $40 | March $40 | April $40 | May $40 |
| June $40 | July $40 | Aug $40 | Sept $40 |
| Depreciation = $480/year | | | |

Oct. 31
Depreciation recognized; record depreciation expense

**Helpful Hint** All contra accounts have increases, decreases, and normal balances opposite to the account to which they relate.

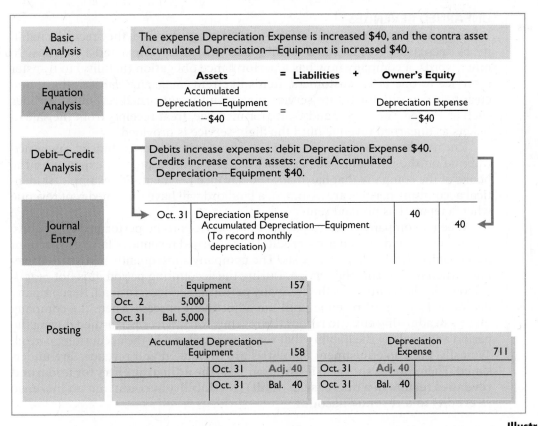

| Basic Analysis | The expense Depreciation Expense is increased $40, and the contra asset Accumulated Depreciation—Equipment is increased $40. |
|---|---|

**Equation Analysis**

| Assets | = | Liabilities | + | Owner's Equity |
|---|---|---|---|---|
| Accumulated Depreciation—Equipment | | | | Depreciation Expense |
| −$40 | = | | | −$40 |

**Debit–Credit Analysis**

Debits increase expenses: debit Depreciation Expense $40.
Credits increase contra assets: credit Accumulated Depreciation—Equipment $40.

**Journal Entry**

| Oct. 31 | Depreciation Expense | 40 | |
| | Accumulated Depreciation—Equipment | | 40 |
| | (To record monthly depreciation) | | |

**Posting**

| Equipment | 157 |
|---|---|
| Oct. 2    5,000 | |
| Oct. 31   Bal. 5,000 | |

| Accumulated Depreciation—Equipment | 158 |
|---|---|
| | Oct. 31   Adj. 40 |
| | Oct. 31   Bal.  40 |

| Depreciation Expense | 711 |
|---|---|
| Oct. 31   Adj. 40 | |
| Oct. 31   Bal.  40 | |

**Illustration 3-7**
Adjustment for depreciation

the total cost that has been expensed to date. Thus, in the balance sheet, Pioneer deducts Accumulated Depreciation—Equipment from the related asset account, as shown in Illustration 3-8.

| Equipment | $ 5,000 |
|---|---|
| Less: Accumulated depreciation—equipment | 40 |
| | **$4,960** |

**Illustration 3-8**
Balance sheet presentation of accumulated depreciation

**Book value** is the difference between the cost of any depreciable asset and its related accumulated depreciation. In Illustration 3-8, the book value of the equipment at the balance sheet date is $4,960. The book value and the fair value of the asset are generally two different values. As noted earlier, **the purpose of depreciation is not valuation but a means of cost allocation**.

*Alternative Terminology*
Book value is also referred to as *carrying value*.

Depreciation expense identifies the portion of an asset's cost that expired during the period (in this case, in October). The accounting equation shows that without this adjusting entry, total assets, total owner's equity, and net income are overstated by $40 and depreciation expense is understated by $40.

Illustration 3-9 summarizes the accounting for prepaid expenses.

**Illustration 3-9**
Accounting for prepaid expenses

| ACCOUNTING FOR PREPAID EXPENSES | | | |
|---|---|---|---|
| **Examples** | **Reason for Adjustment** | **Accounts Before Adjustment** | **Adjusting Entry** |
| Insurance, supplies, advertising, rent, depreciation | Prepaid expenses recorded in asset accounts have been used. | Assets overstated. Expenses understated. | Dr. Expenses Cr. Assets or Contra Assets |

**Unearned Revenues**

Oct. 2

Thank you in advance for your work

I will finish by Dec. 31

$1,200

Cash is received in advance; liability is recorded

Oct. 31

Some service has been performed; some revenue is recorded

## UNEARNED REVENUES

When companies receive cash before services are performed, they record a liability by increasing (crediting) a liability account called **unearned revenues**. In other words, a company now has a performance obligation (liability) to transfer a service to one of its customers. Items like rent, magazine subscriptions, and customer deposits for future service may result in unearned revenues. Airlines such as United, American, and Delta, for instance, treat receipts from the sale of tickets as unearned revenue until the flight service is provided.

Unearned revenues are the opposite of prepaid expenses. Indeed, unearned revenue on the books of one company is likely to be a prepaid expense on the books of the company that has made the advance payment. For example, if identical accounting periods are assumed, a landlord will have unearned rent revenue when a tenant has prepaid rent.

When a company receives payment for services to be performed in a future accounting period, it increases (credits) an unearned revenue (a liability) account to recognize the liability that exists. The company subsequently recognizes revenues when it performs the service. During the accounting period, it is not practical to make daily entries as the company performs services. Instead, the company delays recognition of revenue until the adjustment process. Then, the company makes an adjusting entry to record the revenue for services performed during the period and to show the liability that remains at the end of the accounting period. Typically, prior to adjustment, liabilities are overstated and revenues are understated. Therefore, as shown in Illustration 3-10, **the adjusting entry for unearned revenues results in a decrease (a debit) to a liability account and an increase (a credit) to a revenue account**.

**Illustration 3-10**
Adjusting entries for unearned revenues

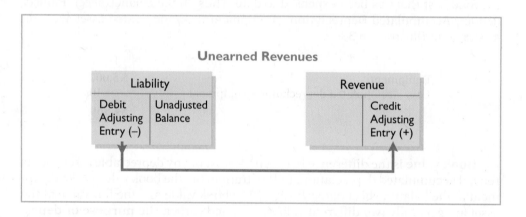

**Unearned Revenues**

| Liability | | Revenue |
|---|---|---|
| Debit Adjusting Entry (−) | Unadjusted Balance | Credit Adjusting Entry (+) |

Pioneer Advertising received $1,200 on October 2 from R. Knox for advertising services expected to be completed by December 31. Pioneer credited the payment to Unearned Service Revenue. This liability account shows a balance of $1,200 in the October 31 trial balance. From an evaluation of the service Pioneer performed for Knox during October, the company determines that it should recognize $400 of revenue in October. The liability (Unearned Service Revenue) is therefore decreased, and owner's equity (Service Revenue) is increased.

As shown in Illustration 3-11, the liability Unearned Service Revenue now shows a balance of $800. That amount represents the remaining advertising services expected to be performed in the future. At the same time, Service Revenue shows total revenue recognized in October of $10,400. **Without this adjustment, revenues and net income are understated by $400 in the income statement. Moreover, liabilities will be overstated and owner's equity will be understated by $400 on the October 31 balance sheet.**

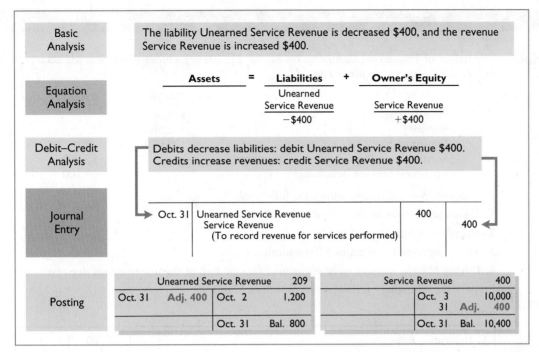

| | |
|---|---|
| Basic Analysis | The liability Unearned Service Revenue is decreased $400, and the revenue Service Revenue is increased $400. |
| Equation Analysis | **Assets** = **Liabilities** + **Owner's Equity**<br>Unearned<br>Service Revenue          Service Revenue<br>−$400                           +$400 |
| Debit–Credit Analysis | Debits decrease liabilities: debit Unearned Service Revenue $400.<br>Credits increase revenues: credit Service Revenue $400. |
| Journal Entry | Oct. 31 \| Unearned Service Revenue                                400<br>          Service Revenue                                                        400<br>          (To record revenue for services performed) |

Posting

| Unearned Service Revenue | | | 209 |
|---|---|---|---|
| Oct. 31 | **Adj. 400** | Oct. 2 | 1,200 |
| | | Oct. 31 | **Bal. 800** |

| Service Revenue | | | 400 |
|---|---|---|---|
| | | Oct. 3 | 10,000 |
| | | 31  **Adj.** | **400** |
| | | Oct. 31 | **Bal. 10,400** |

**Illustration 3-11**
Service revenue accounts after adjustment

Illustration 3-12 summarizes the accounting for unearned revenues.

**Illustration 3-12**
Accounting for unearned revenues

### ACCOUNTING FOR UNEARNED REVENUES

| Examples | Reason for Adjustment | Accounts Before Adjustment | Adjusting Entry |
|---|---|---|---|
| Rent, magazine subscriptions, customer deposits for future service | Unearned revenues recorded in liability accounts are now recognized as revenue for services performed. | Liabilities overstated. Revenues understated. | Dr. Liabilities<br>  Cr. Revenues |

## ACCOUNTING ACROSS THE ORGANIZATION

### Turning Gift Cards into Revenue

Those of you who are marketing majors (and even most of you who are not) know that gift cards are among the hottest marketing tools in merchandising today. Customers purchase gift cards and give them to someone for later use. In a recent year, gift-card sales topped $95 billion.

Although these programs are popular with marketing executives, they create accounting questions. Should revenue be recorded at the time the gift card is sold, or when it is exercised? How should expired gift cards be accounted for? In a recent balance sheet, Best Buy reported unearned revenue related to gift cards of $479 million.

*Source:* Robert Berner, "Gift Cards: No Gift to Investors," *BusinessWeek* (March 14, 2005), p. 86.

 Suppose that Robert Jones purchases a $100 gift card at Best Buy on December 24, 2013, and gives it to his wife, Mary Jones, on December 25, 2013. On January 3, 2014, Mary uses the card to purchase $100 worth of CDs. When do you think Best Buy should recognize revenue and why? (See page 156.)

© Skip ODonnell/iStockphoto

> **DO IT!**

## Adjusting Entries for Deferrals

The ledger of Hammond Company, on March 31, 2014, includes these selected accounts before adjusting entries are prepared.

|  | Debit | Credit |
|---|---|---|
| Prepaid Insurance | $ 3,600 | |
| Supplies | 2,800 | |
| Equipment | 25,000 | |
| Accumulated Depreciation—Equipment | | $5,000 |
| Unearned Service Revenue | | 9,200 |

An analysis of the accounts shows the following.

**1.** Insurance expires at the rate of $100 per month.

**2.** Supplies on hand total $800.

**3.** The equipment depreciates $200 a month.

**4.** During March, services were performed for one-half of the unearned service revenue.

Prepare the adjusting entries for the month of March.

### Solution

**Action Plan**

✔ Make adjusting entries at the end of the period for revenues recognized and expenses incurred in the period.

✔ Don't forget to make adjusting entries for deferrals. Failure to adjust for deferrals leads to overstatement of the asset or liability and understatement of the related expense or revenue.

| | | |
|---|---|---|
| **1.** Insurance Expense | 100 | |
|   Prepaid Insurance | | 100 |
|     (To record insurance expired) | | |
| **2.** Supplies Expense | 2,000 | |
|   Supplies | | 2,000 |
|     (To record supplies used) | | |
| **3.** Depreciation Expense | 200 | |
|   Accumulated Depreciation—Equipment | | 200 |
|     (To record monthly depreciation) | | |
| **4.** Unearned Service Revenue | 4,600 | |
|   Service Revenue | | 4,600 |
|     (To record revenue for services performed) | | |

Related exercise material: **BE3-3, BE3-4, BE3-5, BE3-6, and DO IT! 3-2.**

 ✔ The Navigator

## Adjusting Entries for Accruals

The second category of adjusting entries is **accruals**. Prior to an accrual adjustment, the revenue account (and the related asset account) or the expense account (and the related liability account) are understated. Thus, the adjusting entry for accruals will **increase both a balance sheet and an income statement account**.

### ACCRUED REVENUES

Revenues for services performed but not yet recorded at the statement date are **accrued revenues**. Accrued revenues may accumulate (accrue) with the passing of time, as in the case of interest revenue. These are unrecorded because the earning of interest does not involve daily transactions. Companies do not record interest revenue on a daily basis because it is often impractical to do so. Accrued revenues also may result from services that have been performed but not yet billed nor collected, as in the case of commissions and fees. These may be unrecorded because only a portion of the total service has been performed and the clients will not be billed until the service has been completed.

An adjusting entry records the receivable that exists at the balance sheet date and the revenue for the services performed during the period. Prior to adjustment, both assets and revenues are understated. As shown in Illustration 3-13, **an adjusting entry for accrued revenues results in an increase (a debit) to an asset account and an increase (a credit) to a revenue account**.

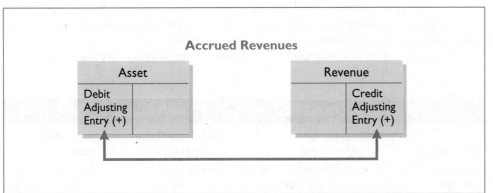

**Illustration 3-13**
Adjusting entries for accrued revenues

In October, Pioneer Advertising performed services worth $200 that were not billed to clients on or before October 31. Because these services are not billed, they are not recorded. The accrual of unrecorded service revenue increases an asset account, Accounts Receivable. It also increases owner's equity by increasing a revenue account, Service Revenue, as shown in Illustration 3-14.

**Illustration 3-14**
Adjustment for accrued revenue

The asset Accounts Receivable shows that clients owe Pioneer $200 at the balance sheet date. The balance of $10,600 in Service Revenue represents the total revenue for services performed by Pioneer during the month ($10,000 + $400 + $200). **Without the adjusting entry, assets and owner's equity on the balance sheet and revenues and net income on the income statement are understated.**

On November 10, Pioneer receives cash of $200 for the services performed in October and makes the following entry.

| A | = | L | + | OE |
|---|---|---|---|---|
| +200 | | | | |
| −200 | | | | |

**Cash Flows**
+200

*Equation analyses summarize the effects of transactions on the three elements of the accounting equation, as well as the effect on cash flows.*

| Nov. 10 | Cash | 200 | |
| | Accounts Receivable | | 200 |
| | (To record cash collected on account) | | |

The company records the collection of the receivables by a debit (increase) to Cash and a credit (decrease) to Accounts Receivable.

Illustration 3-15 summarizes the accounting for accrued revenues.

**Illustration 3-15**
Accounting for accrued revenues

| ACCOUNTING FOR ACCRUED REVENUES | | | |
|---|---|---|---|
| **Examples** | **Reason for Adjustment** | **Accounts Before Adjustment** | **Adjusting Entry** |
| Interest, rent, services | Services performed but not yet received in cash or recorded. | Assets understated. Revenues understated. | Dr. Assets    Cr. Revenues |

### ACCRUED EXPENSES

Expenses incurred but not yet paid or recorded at the statement date are called **accrued expenses**. Interest, taxes, and salaries are common examples of accrued expenses.

Companies make adjustments for accrued expenses to record the obligations that exist at the balance sheet date and to recognize the expenses that apply to the current accounting period. Prior to adjustment, both liabilities and expenses are understated. Therefore, as Illustration 3-16 shows, **an adjusting entry for accrued expenses results in an increase (a debit) to an expense account and an increase (a credit) to a liability account**.

**Illustration 3-16**
Adjusting entries for accrued expenses

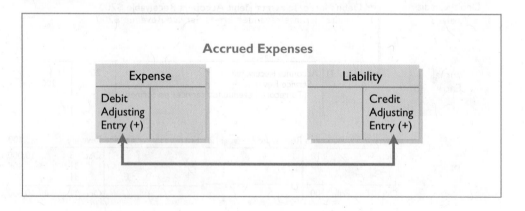

Let's look in more detail at some specific types of accrued expenses, beginning with accrued interest.

**ACCRUED INTEREST** Pioneer Advertising signed a three-month note payable in the amount of $5,000 on October 1. The note requires Pioneer to pay interest at an annual rate of 12%.

The amount of the interest recorded is determined by three factors: (1) the face value of the note; (2) the interest rate, which is always expressed as an annual rate; and (3) the length of time the note is outstanding. For Pioneer, the total interest due on the $5,000 note at its maturity date three months in the future is $150 ($5,000 $\times$ 12% $\times \frac{3}{12}$), or $50 for one month. Illustration 3-17 shows the formula for computing interest and its application to Pioneer for the month of October.

| Face Value of Note | | Annual Interest Rate | | Time in Terms of One Year | | Interest |
|---|---|---|---|---|---|---|
| $5,000 | $\times$ | 12% | $\times$ | $\frac{1}{12}$ | = | $50 |

**Illustration 3-17**
Formula for computing interest

**Helpful Hint**  In computing interest, we express the time period as a fraction of a year.

As Illustration 3-18 shows, the accrual of interest at October 31 increases a liability account, Interest Payable. It also decreases owner's equity by increasing an expense account, Interest Expense.

**Illustration 3-18**
Adjustment for accrued interest

Interest Expense shows the interest charges for the month of October. Interest Payable shows the amount of interest the company owes at the statement date. Pioneer will not pay the interest until the note comes due at the end of three months. Companies use the Interest Payable account, instead of crediting Notes Payable, to disclose the two different types of obligations—interest and principal—in the accounts and statements. **Without this adjusting entry, liabilities and interest expense are understated, and net income and owner's equity are overstated.**

## INTERNATIONAL INSIGHT

### Cashing In on Accrual Accounting

The Chinese government, like most governments, uses cash accounting. A recent report, however, noted that it decided to use accrual accounting versus cash accounting for about $38 billion of expenditures in a recent budget projection. The Chinese government decided to expense the amount in the year in which it was originally allocated rather than when the payments would be made. Why did the Chinese government do this? It enabled the government to keep its projected budget deficit below a 3% threshold. While the Chinese government was able to keep its projected shortfall below 3%, it did suffer some criticism for its inconsistent accounting. Critics charge that this inconsistent treatment reduces the transparency of China's accounting information. That is, it is not easy for outsiders to accurately evaluate what is really going on.

*Source:* Andrew Batson, "China Altered Budget Accounting to Reduce Deficit Figure," *Wall Street Journal Online* (March 15, 2010).

**?** Accrual accounting is often considered superior to cash accounting. Why, then, were some people critical of China's use of accrual accounting in this instance? (See page 157.)

**ACCRUED SALARIES AND WAGES** Companies pay for some types of expenses, such as employee salaries and wages, after the services have been performed. Pioneer paid salaries and wages on October 26 for its employees' first two weeks of work. The next payment of salaries will not occur until November 9. As Illustration 3-19 shows, three working days remain in October (October 29–31).

**Illustration 3-19**
Calendar showing Pioneer's pay periods

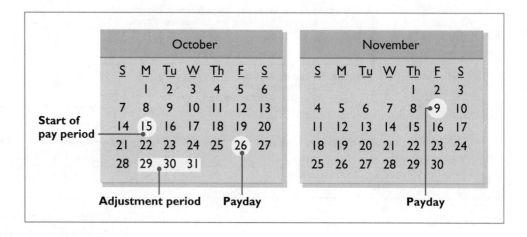

At October 31, the salaries and wages for these three days represent an accrued expense and a related liability to Pioneer. The employees receive total salaries and wages of $2,000 for a five-day work week, or $400 per day. Thus, accrued salaries and wages at October 31 are $1,200 ($400 × 3). This accrual increases a liability, Salaries and Wages Payable. It also decreases owner's equity by increasing an expense account, Salaries and Wages Expense, as shown in Illustration 3-20.

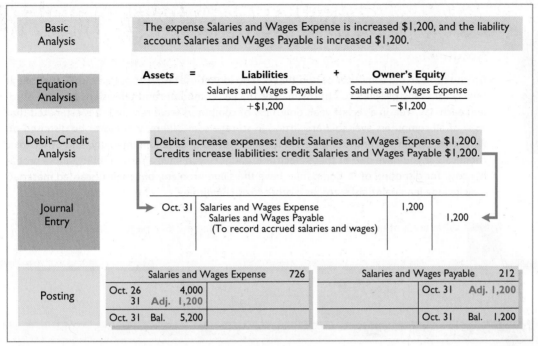

| Basic Analysis | The expense Salaries and Wages Expense is increased $1,200, and the liability account Salaries and Wages Payable is increased $1,200. | | |
|---|---|---|---|

**Equation Analysis**

| Assets | = | Liabilities | + | Owner's Equity |
|---|---|---|---|---|
| | | Salaries and Wages Payable | | Salaries and Wages Expense |
| | | +$1,200 | | −$1,200 |

**Debit–Credit Analysis**

Debits increase expenses: debit Salaries and Wages Expense $1,200.
Credits increase liabilities: credit Salaries and Wages Payable $1,200.

**Journal Entry**

| Oct. 31 | Salaries and Wages Expense | 1,200 | |
|---|---|---|---|
| | Salaries and Wages Payable | | 1,200 |
| | (To record accrued salaries and wages) | | |

**Posting**

| Salaries and Wages Expense | 726 | | | Salaries and Wages Payable | 212 |
|---|---|---|---|---|---|
| Oct. 26 | 4,000 | | | Oct. 31 | Adj. 1,200 |
| 31 Adj. | 1,200 | | | | |
| Oct. 31 Bal. | 5,200 | | | Oct. 31 Bal. | 1,200 |

**Illustration 3-20**
Adjustment for accrued salaries and wages

After this adjustment, the balance in Salaries and Wages Expense of $5,200 (13 days × $400) is the actual salary and wages expense for October. The balance in Salaries and Wages Payable of $1,200 is the amount of the liability for salaries and wages Pioneer owes as of October 31. **Without the $1,200 adjustment for salaries and wages, Pioneer's expenses are understated $1,200 and its liabilities are understated $1,200.**

Pioneer Advertising pays salaries and wages every two weeks. Consequently, the next payday is November 9, when the company will again pay total salaries and wages of $4,000. The payment consists of $1,200 of salaries and wages payable at October 31 plus $2,800 of salaries and wages expense for November (7 working days, as shown in the November calendar × $400). Therefore, Pioneer makes the following entry on November 9.

| Nov. 9 | Salaries and Wages Payable | 1,200 | |
|---|---|---|---|
| | Salaries and Wages Expense | 2,800 | |
| | Cash | | 4,000 |
| | (To record November 9 payroll) | | |

| A | = | L | + | OE |
|---|---|---|---|---|
| | | −1,200 | | |
| | | | | −2,800 |
| −4,000 | | | | |

**Cash Flows**
−4,000

This entry eliminates the liability for Salaries and Wages Payable that Pioneer recorded in the October 31 adjusting entry, and it records the proper amount of Salaries and Wages Expense for the period between November 1 and November 9.

Illustration 3-21 summarizes the accounting for accrued expenses.

**Illustration 3-21**
Accounting for accrued expenses

| ACCOUNTING FOR ACCRUED EXPENSES | | | |
|---|---|---|---|
| **Examples** | **Reason for Adjustment** | **Accounts Before Adjustment** | **Adjusting Entry** |
| Interest, rent, salaries | Expenses have been incurred but not yet paid in cash or recorded. | Expenses understated. Liabilities understated. | Dr. Expenses Cr. Liabilities |

© Nathan Gleave/iStockphoto

## PEOPLE, PLANET, AND PROFIT INSIGHT

### Got Junk?

Do you have an old computer or two that you no longer use? How about an old TV that needs replacing? Many people do. Approximately 163,000 computers and televisions become obsolete **each day**. Yet, in a recent year, only 11% of computers were recycled. It is estimated that 75% of all computers ever sold are sitting in storage somewhere, waiting to be disposed of. Each of these old TVs and computers is loaded with lead, cadmium, mercury, and other toxic chemicals. If you have one of these electronic gadgets, you have a responsibility, and a probable cost, for disposing of it. Companies have the same problem, but their discarded materials may include lead paint, asbestos, and other toxic chemicals.

**?** What accounting issue might this cause for companies? (See page 157.)

---

> **DO IT!**

## Adjusting Entries for Accruals

Micro Computer Services began operations on August 1, 2014. At the end of August 2014, management prepares monthly financial statements. The following information relates to August.

1. At August 31, the company owed its employees $800 in salaries and wages that will be paid on September 1.

2. On August 1, the company borrowed $30,000 from a local bank on a 15-year mortgage. The annual interest rate is 10%.

3. Revenue for services performed but unrecorded for August totaled $1,100.

Prepare the adjusting entries needed at August 31, 2014.

### Solution

**Action Plan**

✔ Make adjusting entries at the end of the period to recognize revenues for services performed and for expenses incurred.

✔ Don't forget to make adjusting entries for accruals. Adjusting entries for accruals will increase both a balance sheet and an income statement account.

| | | |
|---|---|---|
| **1.** Salaries and Wages Expense | 800 | |
|     Salaries and Wages Payable | | 800 |
|       (To record accrued salaries) | | |
| **2.** Interest Expense | 250 | |
|     Interest Payable | | 250 |
|       (To record accrued interest: | | |
|       $30,000 \times 10\% \times \frac{1}{12} = \$250$) | | |
| **3.** Accounts Receivable | 1,100 | |
|     Service Revenue | | 1,100 |
|       (To record revenue for services performed) | | |

Related exercise material: **BE3-2, BE3-7, E3-5, E3-6, E3-7, E3-8, E3-9, and DO IT! 3-3.**

✔ **The Navigator**

## Summary of Basic Relationships

Illustration 3-22 summarizes the four basic types of adjusting entries. Take some time to study and analyze the adjusting entries. Be sure to note that **each adjusting entry affects one balance sheet account and one income statement account.**

| Type of Adjustment | Accounts Before Adjustment | Adjusting Entry |
|---|---|---|
| Prepaid expenses | Assets overstated<br>Expenses understated | Dr. Expenses<br>    Cr. Assets or<br>    Contra Assets |
| Unearned revenues | Liabilities overstated<br>Revenues understated | Dr. Liabilities<br>    Cr. Revenues |
| Accrued revenues | Assets understated<br>Revenues understated | Dr. Assets<br>    Cr. Revenues |
| Accrued expenses | Expenses understated<br>Liabilities understated | Dr. Expenses<br>    Cr. Liabilities |

**Illustration 3-22**
Summary of adjusting entries

Illustrations 3-23 (below) and 3-24 (on page 118) show the journalizing and posting of adjusting entries for Pioneer Advertising Agency on October 31. The ledger identifies all adjustments by the reference J2 because they have been recorded on page 2 of the general journal. The company may insert a center caption "Adjusting Entries" between the last transaction entry and the first adjusting entry in the journal. When you review the general ledger in Illustration 3-24, note that the entries highlighted in color are the adjustments.

| GENERAL JOURNAL | | | | J2 |
|---|---|---|---|---|
| **Date** | **Account Titles and Explanation** | **Ref.** | **Debit** | **Credit** |
| 2014 | Adjusting Entries | | | |
| Oct. 31 | Supplies Expense | 631 | 1,500 | |
| | Supplies | 126 | | 1,500 |
| | (To record supplies used) | | | |
| 31 | Insurance Expense | 722 | 50 | |
| | Prepaid Insurance | 130 | | 50 |
| | (To record insurance expired) | | | |
| 31 | Depreciation Expense | 711 | 40 | |
| | Accumulated Depreciation—Equipment | 158 | | 40 |
| | (To record monthly depreciation) | | | |
| 31 | Unearned Service Revenue | 209 | 400 | |
| | Service Revenue | 400 | | 400 |
| | (To record revenue for services performed) | | | |
| 31 | Accounts Receivable | 112 | 200 | |
| | Service Revenue | 400 | | 200 |
| | (To record revenue for services performed) | | | |
| 31 | Interest Expense | 905 | 50 | |
| | Interest Payable | 230 | | 50 |
| | (To record interest on notes payable) | | | |
| 31 | Salaries and Wages Expense | 726 | 1,200 | |
| | Salaries and Wages Payable | 212 | | 1,200 |
| | (To record accrued salaries and wages) | | | |

**Illustration 3-23**
General journal showing adjusting entries

**Helpful Hint**
(1) Adjusting entries should not involve debits or credits to Cash.
(2) Evaluate whether the adjustment makes sense. For example, an adjustment to recognize supplies used should increase Supplies Expense.
(3) Double-check all computations.
(4) Each adjusting entry affects one balance sheet account and one income statement account.

**Illustration 3-24**
General ledger after adjustment

## GENERAL LEDGER

### Cash      No. 101

| Date | Explanation | Ref. | Debit | Credit | Balance |
|---|---|---|---|---|---|
| 2014 | | | | | |
| Oct. 1 | | J1 | 10,000 | | 10,000 |
| 2 | | J1 | 1,200 | | 11,200 |
| 3 | | J1 | | 900 | 10,300 |
| 4 | | J1 | | 600 | 9,700 |
| 20 | | J1 | | 500 | 9,200 |
| 26 | | J1 | | 4,000 | 5,200 |
| 31 | | J1 | 10,000 | | 15,200 |

### Accounts Receivable      No. 112

| Date | Explanation | Ref. | Debit | Credit | Balance |
|---|---|---|---|---|---|
| 2014 | | | | | |
| Oct. 31 | Adj. entry | J2 | 200 | | 200 |

### Supplies      No. 126

| Date | Explanation | Ref. | Debit | Credit | Balance |
|---|---|---|---|---|---|
| 2014 | | | | | |
| Oct. 5 | | J1 | 2,500 | | 2,500 |
| 31 | Adj. entry | J2 | | 1,500 | 1,000 |

### Prepaid Insurance      No. 130

| Date | Explanation | Ref. | Debit | Credit | Balance |
|---|---|---|---|---|---|
| 2014 | | | | | |
| Oct. 4 | | J1 | 600 | | 600 |
| 31 | Adj. entry | J2 | | 50 | 550 |

### Equipment      No. 157

| Date | Explanation | Ref. | Debit | Credit | Balance |
|---|---|---|---|---|---|
| 2014 | | | | | |
| Oct. 1 | | J1 | 5,000 | | 5,000 |

### Accumulated Depreciation—Equipment      No. 158

| Date | Explanation | Ref. | Debit | Credit | Balance |
|---|---|---|---|---|---|
| 2014 | | | | | |
| Oct. 31 | Adj. entry | J2 | | 40 | 40 |

### Notes Payable      No. 200

| Date | Explanation | Ref. | Debit | Credit | Balance |
|---|---|---|---|---|---|
| 2014 | | | | | |
| Oct. 1 | | J1 | | 5,000 | 5,000 |

### Accounts Payable      No. 201

| Date | Explanation | Ref. | Debit | Credit | Balance |
|---|---|---|---|---|---|
| 2014 | | | | | |
| Oct. 5 | | J1 | | 2,500 | 2,500 |

### Unearned Service Revenue      No. 209

| Date | Explanation | Ref. | Debit | Credit | Balance |
|---|---|---|---|---|---|
| 2014 | | | | | |
| Oct. 2 | | J1 | | 1,200 | 1,200 |
| 31 | Adj. entry | J2 | 400 | | 800 |

### Salaries and Wages Payable      No. 212

| Date | Explanation | Ref. | Debit | Credit | Balance |
|---|---|---|---|---|---|
| 2014 | | | | | |
| Oct. 31 | Adj. entry | J2 | | 1,200 | 1,200 |

### Interest Payable      No. 230

| Date | Explanation | Ref. | Debit | Credit | Balance |
|---|---|---|---|---|---|
| 2014 | | | | | |
| Oct. 31 | Adj. entry | J2 | | 50 | 50 |

### Owner's Capital      No. 301

| Date | Explanation | Ref. | Debit | Credit | Balance |
|---|---|---|---|---|---|
| 2014 | | | | | |
| Oct. 1 | | J1 | | 10,000 | 10,000 |

### Owner's Drawings      No. 306

| Date | Explanation | Ref. | Debit | Credit | Balance |
|---|---|---|---|---|---|
| 2014 | | | | | |
| Oct. 20 | | J1 | 500 | | 500 |

### Service Revenue      No. 400

| Date | Explanation | Ref. | Debit | Credit | Balance |
|---|---|---|---|---|---|
| 2014 | | | | | |
| Oct. 31 | | J1 | | 10,000 | 10,000 |
| 31 | Adj. entry | J2 | | 400 | 10,400 |
| 31 | Adj. entry | J2 | | 200 | 10,600 |

### Supplies Expense      No. 631

| Date | Explanation | Ref. | Debit | Credit | Balance |
|---|---|---|---|---|---|
| 2014 | | | | | |
| Oct. 31 | Adj. entry | J2 | 1,500 | | 1,500 |

### Depreciation Expense      No. 711

| Date | Explanation | Ref. | Debit | Credit | Balance |
|---|---|---|---|---|---|
| 2014 | | | | | |
| Oct. 31 | Adj. entry | J2 | 40 | | 40 |

### Insurance Expense      No. 722

| Date | Explanation | Ref. | Debit | Credit | Balance |
|---|---|---|---|---|---|
| 2014 | | | | | |
| Oct. 31 | Adj. entry | J2 | 50 | | 50 |

### Salaries and Wages Expense      No. 726

| Date | Explanation | Ref. | Debit | Credit | Balance |
|---|---|---|---|---|---|
| 2014 | | | | | |
| Oct. 26 | | J1 | 4,000 | | 4,000 |
| 31 | Adj. entry | J2 | 1,200 | | 5,200 |

### Rent Expense      No. 729

| Date | Explanation | Ref. | Debit | Credit | Balance |
|---|---|---|---|---|---|
| 2014 | | | | | |
| Oct. 3 | | J1 | 900 | | 900 |

### Interest Expense      No. 905

| Date | Explanation | Ref. | Debit | Credit | Balance |
|---|---|---|---|---|---|
| 2014 | | | | | |
| Oct. 31 | Adj. entry | J2 | 50 | | 50 |

## The Adjusted Trial Balance and Financial Statements

After a company has journalized and posted all adjusting entries, it prepares another trial balance from the ledger accounts. This trial balance is called an **adjusted trial balance**. It shows the balances of all accounts, including those adjusted, at the end of the accounting period. The purpose of an adjusted trial balance is to **prove the equality** of the total debit balances and the total credit balances in the ledger after all adjustments. Because the accounts contain all data needed for financial statements, the adjusted trial balance is the **primary basis for the preparation of financial statements**.

LEARNING OBJECTIVE 6

Describe the nature and purpose of an adjusted trial balance.

### Preparing the Adjusted Trial Balance

Illustration 3-25 presents the adjusted trial balance for Pioneer Advertising Agency prepared from the ledger accounts in Illustration 3-24. The amounts affected by the adjusting entries are highlighted in color. Compare these amounts to those in the unadjusted trial balance in Illustration 3-3 on page 103. In this comparison, you will see that there are more accounts in the adjusted trial balance as a result of the adjusting entries made at the end of the month.

**Illustration 3-25**
Adjusted trial balance

### PIONEER ADVERTISING AGENCY
#### Adjusted Trial Balance
#### October 31, 2014

| | Dr. | Cr. |
|---|---|---|
| Cash | $ 15,200 | |
| Accounts Receivable | 200 | |
| Supplies | 1,000 | |
| Prepaid Insurance | 550 | |
| Equipment | 5,000 | |
| Accumulated Depreciation—Equipment | | $ 40 |
| Notes Payable | | 5,000 |
| Accounts Payable | | 2,500 |
| Interest Payable | | 50 |
| Unearned Service Revenue | | 800 |
| Salaries and Wages Payable | | 1,200 |
| Owner's Capital | | 10,000 |
| Owner's Drawings | 500 | |
| Service Revenue | | 10,600 |
| Salaries and Wages Expense | 5,200 | |
| Supplies Expense | 1,500 | |
| Rent Expense | 900 | |
| Insurance Expense | 50 | |
| Interest Expense | 50 | |
| Depreciation Expense | 40 | |
| | $30,190 | $30,190 |

### Preparing Financial Statements

**Companies can prepare financial statements directly from the adjusted trial balance**. Illustrations 3-26 (page 120) and 3-27 (page 121) present the interrelationships of data in the adjusted trial balance and the financial statements.

As Illustration 3-26 shows, companies prepare the income statement from the revenue and expense accounts. Next, they use the owner's capital and drawings accounts and the net income (or net loss) from the income statement to prepare the owner's equity statement.

**Illustration 3-26**
Preparation of the income statement and owner's equity statement from the adjusted trial balance

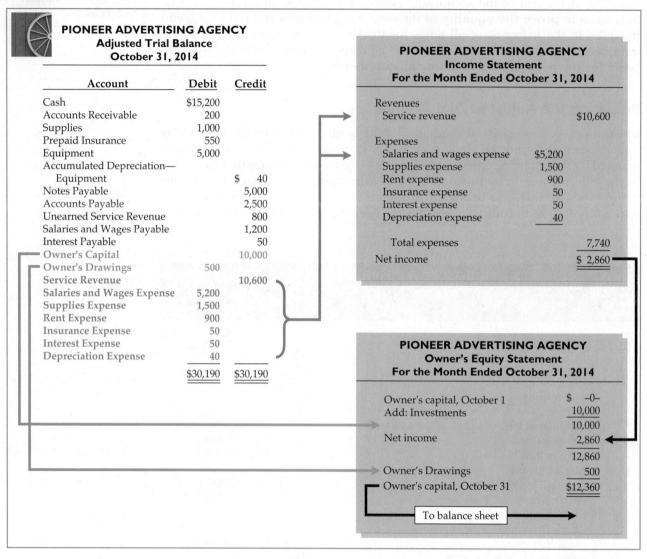

As Illustration 3-27 shows, companies then prepare the balance sheet from the asset and liability accounts and the ending owner's capital balance as reported in the owner's equity statement.

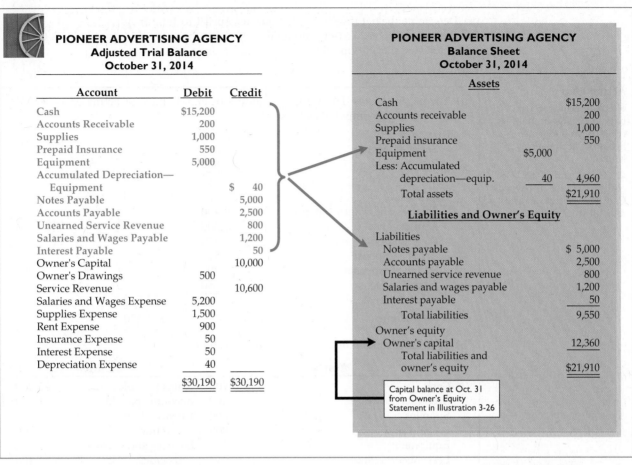

**Illustration 3-27**
Preparation of the balance sheet from the adjusted trial balance

> ## DO IT!

### Trial Balance

Skolnick Co. was organized on April 1, 2014. The company prepares quarterly financial statements. The adjusted trial balance amounts at June 30 are shown below.

| | Debit | | Credit |
|---|---|---|---|
| Cash | $ 6,700 | Accumulated Depreciation— | |
| Accounts Receivable | 600 | Equipment | $    850 |
| Prepaid Rent | 900 | Notes Payable | 5,000 |
| Supplies | 1,000 | Accounts Payable | 1,510 |
| Equipment | 15,000 | Salaries and Wages Payable | 400 |
| Owner's Drawings | 600 | Interest Payable | 50 |
| Salaries and Wages Expense | 9,400 | Unearned Rent Revenue | 500 |
| Rent Expense | 1,500 | Owner's Capital | 14,000 |
| Depreciation Expense | 850 | Service Revenue | 14,200 |
| Supplies Expense | 200 | Rent Revenue | 800 |
| Utilities Expense | 510 | | |
| Interest Expense | 50 | | |
| | $37,310 | | $37,310 |

(a) Determine the net income for the quarter April 1 to June 30.
(b) Determine the total assets and total liabilities at June 30, 2014, for Skolnick Co.
(c) Determine the amount of Owner's Capital at June 30, 2014.

## Solution

**Action Plan**

✔ In an adjusted trial balance, all asset, liability, revenue, and expense accounts are properly stated.

✔ To determine the ending balance in Owner's Capital, add net income and subtract dividends.

(a) The net income is determined by adding revenues and subtracting expenses. The net income is computed as follows.

| | | |
|---|---:|---:|
| Revenues | | |
| Service revenue | $14,200 | |
| Rent revenue | 800 | |
| Total revenues | | $15,000 |
| Expenses | | |
| Salaries and wages expense | 9,400 | |
| Rent expense | 1,500 | |
| Depreciation expense | 850 | |
| Utilities expense | 510 | |
| Supplies expense | 200 | |
| Interest expense | 50 | |
| Total expenses | | 12,510 |
| Net income | | $ 2,490 |

(b) Total assets and liabilities are computed as follows.

| **Assets** | | | **Liabilities** | |
|---|---:|---:|---|---:|
| Cash | | $ 6,700 | Notes payable | $5,000 |
| Accounts receivable | | 600 | Accounts payable | 1,510 |
| Supplies | | 1,000 | Unearned rent | |
| Prepaid rent | | 900 | revenue | 500 |
| Equipment | $15,000 | | Salaries and wages | |
| Less: Accumulated | | | payable | 400 |
| depreciation— | | | Interest payable | 50 |
| equipment | 850 | 14,150 | | |
| Total assets | | $23,350 | Total liabilities | $7,460 |

| | | |
|---|---|---:|
| (c) Owner's capital, April 1 | | $     0 |
| Add: Investments | | 14,000 |
| Net income | | 2,490 |
| Less: Owner's drawings | | 600 |
| Owner's capital, June 30 | | $15,890 |

Related exercise material: **BE3-9, BE3-10, E3-11, E3-12, E3-13, and DO IT! 3-4.**

✔ The Navigator

## > Comprehensive DO IT!

The Green Thumb Lawn Care Company began operations on April 1. At April 30, the trial balance shows the following balances for selected accounts.

| | |
|---|---:|
| Prepaid Insurance | $ 3,600 |
| Equipment | 28,000 |
| Notes Payable | 20,000 |
| Unearned Service Revenue | 4,200 |
| Service Revenue | 1,800 |

Analysis reveals the following additional data.

**1.** Prepaid insurance is the cost of a 2-year insurance policy, effective April 1.

**2.** Depreciation on the equipment is $500 per month.

**3.** The note payable is dated April 1. It is a 6-month, 12% note.

**4.** Seven customers paid for the company's 6-month lawn service package of $600 beginning in April. The company performed services for these customers in April.

**5.** Lawn services performed for other customers but not recorded at April 30 totaled $1,500.

**Instructions**

Prepare the adjusting entries for the month of April. Show computations.

### Solution to Comprehensive DO IT!

**Action Plan**

✔ Note that adjustments are being made for one month.

✔ Make computations carefully.

✔ Select account titles carefully.

✔ Make sure debits are made first and credits are indented.

✔ Check that debits equal credits for each entry.

| GENERAL JOURNAL | | | | J1 |
|---|---|---|---|---|
| **Date** | **Account Titles and Explanation** | **Ref.** | **Debit** | **Credit** |
| | *Adjusting Entries* | | | |
| Apr. 30 | Insurance Expense | | 150 | |
| |     Prepaid Insurance | | | 150 |
| |     (To record insurance expired: $3,600 ÷ 24 = $150 per month) | | | |
| 30 | Depreciation Expense | | 500 | |
| |     Accumulated Depreciation—Equipment | | | 500 |
| |     (To record monthly depreciation) | | | |
| 30 | Interest Expense | | 200 | |
| |     Interest Payable | | | 200 |
| |     (To record interest on notes payable: $20,000 × 12% × 1/12 = $200) | | | |
| 30 | Unearned Service Revenue | | 700 | |
| |     Service Revenue | | | 700 |
| |     (To record revenue for services performed: $600 ÷ 6 = $100; $100 per month × 7 = $700) | | | |
| 30 | Accounts Receivable | | 1,500 | |
| |     Service Revenue | | | 1,500 |
| |     (To record revenue for services performed) | | | |

✔ The Navigator

---

## SUMMARY OF LEARNING OBJECTIVES

✔ The Navigator

**1 Explain the time period assumption.** The time period assumption assumes that the economic life of a business is divided into artificial time periods.

**2 Explain the accrual basis of accounting.** Accrual-basis accounting means that companies record events that change a company's financial statements in the periods in which those events occur, rather than in the periods in which the company receives or pays cash.

**3 Explain the reasons for adjusting entries and identify the major types of adjusting entries.** Companies make adjusting entries at the end of an accounting period. Such entries ensure that companies recognize revenues in the period in which the performance obligation is satisfied and recognize expenses in the period in which they are incurred.

The major types of adjusting entries are deferrals (prepaid expenses and unearned revenues), and accruals (accrued revenues and accrued expenses).

**4 Prepare adjusting entries for deferrals.** Deferrals are either prepaid expenses or unearned revenues. Companies make adjusting entries for deferrals to record the portion of the prepayment that represents the expense incurred or the revenue for services performed in the current accounting period.

**5 Prepare adjusting entries for accruals.** Accruals are either accrued revenues or accrued expenses. Compa-

nies make adjusting entries for accruals to record revenues for services performed and expenses incurred in the current accounting period that have not been recognized through daily entries.

**6 Describe the nature and purpose of an adjusted trial balance.** An adjusted trial balance shows the balances of all accounts, including those that have been adjusted, at the end of an accounting period. Its purpose is to prove the equality of the total debit balances and total credit balances in the ledger after all adjustments.

## GLOSSARY

**Accrual-basis accounting** Accounting basis in which companies record transactions that change a company's financial statements in the periods in which the events occur. (p. 100).

**Accruals** Adjusting entries for either accrued revenues or accrued expenses. (p. 103).

**Accrued expenses** Expenses incurred but not yet paid in cash or recorded. (p. 112).

**Accrued revenues** Revenues for services performed but not yet received in cash or recorded. (p. 110).

**Adjusted trial balance** A list of accounts and their balances after the company has made all adjustments. (p. 119).

**Adjusting entries** Entries made at the end of an accounting period to ensure that companies follow the revenue recognition and expense recognition principles. (p. 102).

**Book value** The difference between the cost of a depreciable asset and its related accumulated depreciation. (p. 107).

**Calendar year** An accounting period that extends from January 1 to December 31. (p. 100).

**Cash-basis accounting** Accounting basis in which companies record revenue when they receive cash and an expense when they pay cash. (p. 100).

**Contra asset account** An account offset against an asset account on the balance sheet. (p. 106).

**Deferrals** Adjusting entries for either prepaid expenses or unearned revenues. (p. 103).

**Depreciation** The process of allocating the cost of an asset to expense over its useful life. (p. 106).

**Expense recognition principle (matching principle)** The principle that companies match efforts (expenses) with accomplishments (revenues). (p. 101).

**Fiscal year** An accounting period that is one year in length. (p. 100).

**Interim periods** Monthly or quarterly accounting time periods. (p. 100).

**Prepaid expenses (prepayments)** Expenses paid in cash before they are used or consumed. (p. 104).

**Revenue recognition principle** The principle that companies recognize revenue in the accounting period in which the performance obligation is satisfied. (p. 101).

**Time period assumption** An assumption that accountants can divide the economic life of a business into artificial time periods. (p. 100).

**Unearned revenues** A liability recorded for cash received before services are performed. (p. 108).

**Useful life** The length of service of a long-lived asset. (p. 106).

## APPENDIX 3A  Alternative Treatment of Prepaid Expenses and Unearned Revenues

**LEARNING OBJECTIVE 7**

Prepare adjusting entries for the alternative treatment of deferrals.

In discussing adjusting entries for prepaid expenses and unearned revenues, we illustrated transactions for which companies made the initial entries to balance sheet accounts. In the case of prepaid expenses, the company debited the prepayment to an asset account. In the case of unearned revenue, the company credited a liability account to record the cash received.

Some companies use an alternative treatment. (1) When a company prepays an expense, it debits that amount to an expense account. (2) When it receives payment for future services, it credits the amount to a revenue account. In this appendix, we describe the circumstances that justify such entries and the different adjusting entries that may be required. This alternative treatment of prepaid expenses and unearned revenues has the same effect on the financial statements as the procedures described in the chapter.

## Prepaid Expenses

Prepaid expenses become expired costs either through the passage of time (e.g., insurance) or through consumption (e.g., advertising supplies). If at the time of purchase the company expects to consume the supplies before the next financial statement date, **it may choose to debit (increase) an expense account rather than an asset account. This alternative treatment is simply more convenient.**

Assume that Pioneer Advertising Agency expects that it will use before the end of the month all of the supplies purchased on October 5. A debit of $2,500 to Supplies Expense (rather than to the asset account Supplies) on October 5 will eliminate the need for an adjusting entry on October 31. At October 31, the Supplies Expense account will show a balance of $2,500, which is the cost of supplies used between October 5 and October 31.

But what if the company does not use all the supplies? For example, what if an inventory of $1,000 of advertising supplies remains on October 31? Obviously, the company would need to make an adjusting entry. Prior to adjustment, the expense account Supplies Expense is overstated $1,000, and the asset account Supplies is understated $1,000. Thus, Pioneer makes the following adjusting entry.

| Oct. 31 | Supplies | 1,000 | |
| | Supplies Expense | | 1,000 |
| | (To record supplies inventory) | | |

A = L + OE
+1,000
　　　　　　　　+1,000 Exp

**Cash Flows**
no effect

After the company posts the adjusting entry, the accounts show:

| Supplies | | Supplies Expense | | | |
|---|---|---|---|---|---|
| 10/31 Adj.  1,000 | | 10/5         2,500 | 10/31 Adj.  1,000 | | |
| | | 10/31 Bal.  1,500 | | | |

**Illustration 3A-1**
Prepaid expenses accounts after adjustment

After adjustment, the asset account Supplies shows a balance of $1,000, which is equal to the cost of supplies on hand at October 31. In addition, Supplies Expense shows a balance of $1,500. This is equal to the cost of supplies used between October 5 and October 31. Without the adjusting entry, expenses are overstated and net income is understated by $1,000 in the October income statement. Also, both assets and owner's equity are understated by $1,000 on the October 31 balance sheet.

Illustration 3A-2 compares the entries and accounts for advertising supplies in the two adjustment approaches.

**Illustration 3A-2**
Adjustment approaches—a comparison

| Prepayment Initially Debited to Asset Account (per chapter) | | | Prepayment Initially Debited to Expense Account (per appendix) | | |
|---|---|---|---|---|---|
| Oct. 5  Supplies | 2,500 | | Oct. 5  Supplies Expense | 2,500 | |
| 　　　　Accounts Payable | | 2,500 | 　　　　Accounts Payable | | 2,500 |
| Oct. 31 Supplies Expense | 1,500 | | Oct. 31 Supplies | 1,000 | |
| 　　　　Supplies | | 1,500 | 　　　　Supplies Expense | | 1,000 |

After Pioneer posts the entries, the accounts appear as follows.

| | (per chapter) Supplies | | | | (per appendix) Supplies | |
|---|---|---|---|---|---|---|
| 10/5 | 2,500 | 10/31 Adj. | 1,500 | 10/31 Adj. | 1,000 | |
| 10/31 Bal. | 1,000 | | | | | |

| | Supplies Expense | | | | Supplies Expense | |
|---|---|---|---|---|---|---|
| 10/31 Adj. | 1,500 | | | 10/5 | 2,500 | 10/31 Adj. | 1,000 |
| | | | | 10/31 Bal. | 1,500 | |

Note that the account balances under each alternative are the same at October 31: Supplies $1,000 and Supplies Expense $1,500.

## Unearned Revenues

Unearned revenues are recognized as revenue at the time services are performed. Similar to the case for prepaid expenses, companies may credit (increase) a revenue account when they receive cash for future services.

To illustrate, assume that Pioneer Advertising received $1,200 for future services on October 2. Pioneer expects to perform the services before October 31.[2] In such a case, the company credits Service Revenue. If Pioneer in fact performs the service before October 31, no adjustment is needed.

However, if at the statement date Pioneer has not performed $800 of the services, it would make an adjusting entry. Without the entry, the revenue account Service Revenue is overstated $800, and the liability account Unearned Service Revenue is understated $800. Thus, Pioneer makes the following adjusting entry.

| A | = | L | + | OE |
|---|---|---|---|---|
| | | | | −800 Rev |
| | | +800 | | |

**Cash Flows**
no effect

| Oct. 31 | Service Revenue | 800 | |
|---|---|---|---|
| | Unearned Service Revenue | | 800 |
| | (To record unearned service revenue) | | |

After Pioneer posts the adjusting entry, the accounts show:

| Unearned Service Revenue | | | Service Revenue | | | |
|---|---|---|---|---|---|---|
| | 10/31 Adj. | 800 | 10/31 Adj. | 800 | 10/2 | 1,200 |
| | | | | | 10/31 Bal. | 400 |

The liability account Unearned Service Revenue shows a balance of $800. This equals the services that will be performed in the future. In addition, the balance in Service Revenue equals the services performed in October. Without the adjusting entry, both revenues and net income are overstated by $800 in the October income statement. Also, liabilities are understated by $800 and owner's equity is overstated by $800 on the October 31 balance sheet.

---

[2]This example focuses only on the alternative treatment of unearned revenues. For simplicity, we have ignored the entries to Service Revenue pertaining to the immediate recognition of revenue ($10,000) and the adjusting entry for accrued revenue ($200).

Illustration 3A-5 compares the entries and accounts for initially recording unearned service revenue in (1) a liability account or (2) a revenue account.

| Unearned Service Revenue Initially Credited to Liability Account (per chapter) | | | Unearned Service Revenue Initially Credited to Revenue Account (per appendix) | | |
|---|---|---|---|---|---|
| Oct. 2  Cash | 1,200 | | Oct. 2  Cash | 1,200 | |
| Unearned Service Revenue | | 1,200 | Service Revenue | | 1,200 |
| Oct. 31 Unearned Service Revenue | 400 | | Oct. 31 Service Revenue | 800 | |
| Service Revenue | | 400 | Unearned Service Revenue | | 800 |

**Illustration 3A-5**
Adjustment approaches—a comparison

After Pioneer posts the entries, the accounts appear as follows.

**Illustration 3A-6**
Comparison of accounts

| (per chapter) Unearned Service Revenue | | | (per appendix) Unearned Service Revenue | | |
|---|---|---|---|---|---|
| 10/31 Adj. | 400 | 10/2     1,200 | | | 10/31 Adj.    800 |
| | | 10/31 Bal.    800 | | | |

| Service Revenue | | | Service Revenue | | |
|---|---|---|---|---|---|
| | | 10/31 Adj.    400 | 10/31 Adj.    800 | | 10/2     1,200 |
| | | | | | 10/31 Bal.    400 |

Note that the balances in the accounts are the same under the two alternatives: Unearned Service Revenue $800 and Service Revenue $400.

## Summary of Additional Adjustment Relationships

Illustration 3A-7 provides a summary of basic relationships for deferrals.

**Illustration 3A-7**
Summary of basic relationships for deferrals

| Type of Adjustment | Reason for Adjustment | Account Balances before Adjustment | Adjusting Entry |
|---|---|---|---|
| 1. Prepaid expenses | (a) Prepaid expenses initially recorded in asset accounts have been used. | Assets overstated Expenses understated | Dr. Expenses Cr. Assets |
| | (b) **Prepaid expenses initially recorded in expense accounts have not been used.** | **Assets understated Expenses overstated** | **Dr. Assets Cr. Expenses** |
| 2. Unearned revenues | (a) Unearned revenues initially recorded in liability accounts are now recognized as revenue. | Liabilities overstated Revenues understated | Dr. Liabilities Cr. Revenues |
| | (b) **Unearned revenues initially recorded in revenue accounts are still unearned.** | **Liabilities understated Revenues overstated** | **Dr. Revenues Cr. Liabilities** |

Alternative adjusting entries **do not apply** to accrued revenues and accrued expenses because **no entries occur before companies make these types of adjusting entries**.

---

## SUMMARY OF LEARNING OBJECTIVE FOR APPENDIX 3A

✔ The Navigator

**7 Prepare adjusting entries for the alternative treatment of deferrals.** Companies may initially debit prepayments to an expense account. Likewise, they may credit unearned revenues to a revenue account. At the end of the period, these accounts may be overstated. The adjusting entries for prepaid expenses are a debit to an asset account and a credit to an expense account. Adjusting entries for unearned revenues are a debit to a revenue account and a credit to a liability account.

---

# APPENDIX 3B    Concepts in Action

**LEARNING OBJECTIVE  8**

Discuss financial reporting concepts.

This appendix provides a summary of the concepts in action used in this textbook. In addition, it provides other useful concepts which accountants use as a basis for recording and reporting financial information.

## Qualities of Useful Information

Recently, the FASB completed the first phase of a project in which it developed a conceptual framework to serve as the basis for future accounting standards. The framework begins by stating that the primary objective of financial reporting is to provide financial information that is **useful** to investors and creditors for making decisions about providing capital. Useful information should possess two fundamental qualities, relevance and faithful representation, as shown in Illustration 3B-1.

**Illustration 3B-1**
Fundamental qualities of useful information

Tell me what I need to know.

BIG SHOT

**Relevance** Accounting information has **relevance** if it would make a difference in a business decision. Information is considered relevant if it provides information that has **predictive value**, that is, helps provide accurate expectations about the future, and has **confirmatory value**, that is, confirms or corrects prior expectations. Materiality is a company-specific aspect of relevance. An item is material when its **size** makes it likely to influence the decision of an investor or creditor.

**Faithful Representation** Faithful representation means that information accurately depicts what really happened. To provide a faithful representation, information must be **complete** (nothing important has been omitted), **neutral** (is not biased toward one position or another), and **free from error**.

### ENHANCING QUALITIES

In addition to the two fundamental qualities, the FASB also describes a number of enhancing qualities of useful information. These include **comparability**, **consistency**, **verifiability**, **timeliness**, and **understandability**. In accounting, comparability results when different companies use the same accounting principles. Another characteristic that enhances comparability is consistency. **Consistency** means that a company uses the same accounting principles and methods from year to year. Information is **verifiable** if independent observers, using the same methods, obtain similar results. For accounting information to have relevance, it must be **timely**. That is, it must be available to decision-makers before it loses its capacity to influence decisions. For example, public companies like Google or Best Buy provide their annual reports to investors within 60 days of their year-end. Information has the quality of **understandability** if it is presented in a clear and concise fashion, so that reasonably informed users of that information can interpret it and comprehend its meaning.

## Assumptions in Financial Reporting

To develop accounting standards, the FASB relies on some key assumptions, as shown in Illustration 3B-2. These include assumptions about the monetary unit, economic entity, time period, and going concern.

**Monetary Unit Assumption** The monetary unit assumption requires that only those things that can be expressed in money are included in the accounting records. This means that certain important information needed by investors, creditors, and managers, such as customer satisfaction, is not reported in the financial statements.

**Economic Entity Assumption** The economic entity assumption states that every economic entity can be separately identified and accounted for. In order to assess a company's performance and financial position accurately, it is important to not blur company transactions with personal transactions (especially those of its managers) or transactions of other companies.

**Time Period Assumption** Notice that the income statement, retained earnings statement, and statement of cash flows all cover periods of one year, and the balance sheet is prepared at the end of each year. The time period assumption states that the life of a business can be divided into artificial time periods and that useful reports covering those periods can be prepared for the business.

**Going Concern Assumption** The going concern assumption states that the business will remain in operation for the foreseeable future. Of course, many businesses do fail, but in general it is reasonable to assume that the business will continue operating.

**Illustration 3B-2**
Key assumptions in financial reporting

## Principles in Financial Reporting

### MEASUREMENT PRINCIPLES

GAAP generally uses one of two measurement principles, the historical cost principle or the fair value principle. Selection of which principle to follow generally relates to trade-offs between relevance and faithful representation.

**HISTORICAL COST PRINCIPLE** The **historical cost principle** (or cost principle, discussed in Chapter 1) dictates that companies record assets at their cost. This is true not only at the time the asset is purchased but also over the time the asset is held. For example, if land that was purchased for $30,000 increases in value to $40,000, it continues to be reported at $30,000.

**FAIR VALUE PRINCIPLE** The **fair value principle** (discussed in Chapter 1) indicates that assets and liabilities should be reported at fair value (the price received to sell an asset or settle a liability). Fair value information may be more useful than historical cost for certain types of assets and liabilities. For example, certain investment securities are reported at fair value because market price information is often readily available for these types of assets. In choosing between cost and fair value, two qualities that make accounting information useful for decision-making are used—relevance and faithful representation. In determining which measurement principle to use, the factual nature of cost figures are weighed versus the relevance of fair value. In general, most assets follow the historical cost principle because fair values may not be representationally faithful. Only in situations where assets are actively traded, such as investment securities, is the fair value principle applied.

### REVENUE RECOGNITION PRINCIPLE

The **revenue recognition principle** requires that companies recognize revenue in the accounting period in which the performance obligation is satisfied. As discussed earlier in the chapter, in a service company, revenue is recognized at the time the service is performed. In a merchandising company, the performance obligation is generally satisfied when the goods transfer from the seller to the buyer (discussed in Chapter 5). At this point, the sales transaction is complete and the sales price established.

### EXPENSE RECOGNITION PRINCIPLE

The **expense recognition principle** (often referred to as the matching principle, discussed earlier in the chapter) dictates that efforts (expenses) be matched with results (revenues). Thus, expenses follow revenues.

### FULL DISCLOSURE PRINCIPLE

The **full disclosure principle** (discussed in Chapter 11) requires that companies disclose all circumstances and events that would make a difference to financial statement users. If an important item cannot reasonably be reported directly in one of the four types of financial statements, then it should be discussed in notes that accompany the statements.

## Cost Constraint

Providing information is costly. In deciding whether companies should be required to provide a certain type of information, accounting standard-setters consider the **cost constraint**. It weighs the cost that companies will incur to provide the information against the benefit that financial statement users will gain from having the information available.

**8  Discuss financial reporting concepts** To be judged useful, information should have the primary characteristics of relevance and faithful representation. In addition, it should be comparable, consistent, verifiable, timely, and understandable.

The **monetary unit assumption** requires that companies include in the accounting records only transaction data that can be expressed in terms of money. The **economic entity assumption** states that economic events can be identified with a particular unit of accountability. The **time period assumption** states that the economic life of a business can be divided into artificial time periods and that meaningful accounting reports can be prepared for each period. The **going concern assumption** states that the company will continue in operation long enough to carry out its existing objectives and commitments.

The **historical cost principle** states that companies should record assets at their cost. The **fair value principle** indicates that assets and liabilities should be reported at fair value. The **revenue recognition principle** requires that companies recognize revenue in the accounting period in which the performance obligation is satisfied. The **expense recognition principle** dictates that efforts (expenses) be matched with results (revenues). The **full disclosure principle** requires that companies disclose circumstances and events that matter to financial statement users.

The **cost constraint** weighs the cost that companies incur to provide a type of information against its benefits to financial statement users.

**Comparability** Ability to compare the accounting information of different companies because they use the same accounting principles. (p. 129).

**Consistency** Use of the same accounting principles and methods from year to year within a company. (p. 129).

**Cost constraint** Constraint that weighs the cost that companies will incur to provide the information against the benefit that financial statement users will gain from having the information available. (p. 130).

**Economic entity assumption** An assumption that every economic entity can be separately identified and accounted for. (p. 129).

**Expense recognition principle** Efforts (expenses) should be matched with results (revenues). (p. 130).

**Fair value principle** Assets and liabilities should be reported at fair value (the price received to sell an asset or settle a liability). (p. 130).

**Faithful representation** Information that accurately depicts what really happened. (p. 128).

**Full disclosure principle** Accounting principle that dictates that companies disclose circumstances and events that make a difference to financial statement users. (p. 130).

**Going concern assumption** The assumption that the company will continue in operation for the foreseeable future. (p. 129).

**Historical cost principle** An accounting principle that states that companies should record assets at their cost. (p. 130).

**Materiality** A company-specific aspect of relevance. An item is material when its size makes it likely to influence the decision of an investor or creditor. (p. 128).

**Monetary unit assumption** An assumption that requires that only those things that can be expressed in money are included in the accounting records. (p. 129).

**Relevance** The quality of information that indicates the information makes a difference in a decision. (p. 128).

**Revenue recognition principle** Companies recognize revenue in the accounting period in which the performance obligation is satisfied. (p. 130).

**Timely** Information that is available to decision-makers before it loses its capacity to influence decisions. (p. 129).

**Time period assumption** An assumption that the life of a business can be divided into artificial time periods and that useful reports covering those periods can be prepared for the business. (p. 129).

**Understandability** Information presented in a clear and concise fashion so that users can interpret it and comprehend its meaning. (p. 129).

**Verifiable** The quality of information that occurs when independent observers, using the same methods, obtain similar results. (p. 129).

**Self-Test, Brief Exercises, Exercises, Problem Set A, and many more components are available for practice in *WileyPLUS*.**

**\*Note:** All asterisked Questions, Exercises, and Problems relate to material in the appendices to the chapter.

## SELF-TEST QUESTIONS

*Answers are on page 157.*

(LO 1)
**1.** The revenue recognition principle states that:
  **(a)** revenue should be recognized in the accounting period in which a performance obligation is satisfied.
  **(b)** expenses should be matched with revenues.
  **(c)** the economic life of a business can be divided into artificial time periods.
  **(d)** the fiscal year should correspond with the calendar year.

(LO 2)
**2.** The time period assumption states that:
  **(a)** companies must wait until the calendar year is completed to prepare financial statements.
  **(b)** companies use the fiscal year to report financial information.
  **(c)** the economic life of a business can be divided into artificial time periods.
  **(d)** companies record information in the time period in which the events occur.

(LO 2)
**3.** Which of the following statements about the accrual basis of accounting is **false**?
  **(a)** Events that change a company's financial statements are recorded in the periods in which the events occur.
  **(b)** Revenue is recognized in the period in which services are performed.
  **(c)** This basis is in accord with generally accepted accounting principles.
  **(d)** Revenue is recorded only when cash is received, and expense is recorded only when cash is paid.

(LO 2)
**4.** The principle or assumption dictating that efforts (expenses) be matched with accomplishments (revenues) is the:
  **(a)** expense recognition principle.
  **(b)** cost assumption.
  **(c)** time period assumption.
  **(d)** revenue recognition principle.

(LO 3)
**5.** Adjusting entries are made to ensure that:
  **(a)** expenses are recognized in the period in which they are incurred.
  **(b)** revenues are recorded in the period in which services are performed.
  **(c)** balance sheet and income statement accounts have correct balances at the end of an accounting period.
  **(d)** All the responses above are correct.

(LO 3)
**6.** Each of the following is a major type (or category) of adjusting entries **except**:
  **(a)** prepaid expenses.
  **(b)** accrued revenues.
  **(c)** accrued expenses.
  **(d)** recognized revenues.

(LO 4)
**7.** The trial balance shows Supplies $1,350 and Supplies Expense $0. If $600 of supplies are on hand at the end of the period, the adjusting entry is:

| | | |
|---|---|---|
| **(a)** Supplies | 600 | |
|     Supplies Expense | | 600 |
| **(b)** Supplies | 750 | |
|     Supplies Expense | | 750 |
| **(c)** Supplies Expense | 750 | |
|     Supplies | | 750 |
| **(d)** Supplies Expense | 600 | |
|     Supplies | | 600 |

(LO 4)
**8.** Adjustments for prepaid expenses:
  **(a)** decrease assets and increase revenues.
  **(b)** decrease expenses and increase assets.
  **(c)** decrease assets and increase expenses.
  **(d)** decrease revenues and increase assets.

(LO 4)
**9.** Accumulated Depreciation is:
  **(a)** a contra asset account.
  **(b)** an expense account.
  **(c)** an owner's equity account.
  **(d)** a liability account.

(LO 4)
**10.** Rivera Company computes depreciation on delivery equipment at $1,000 for the month of June. The adjusting entry to record this depreciation is as follows.

| | | |
|---|---|---|
| **(a)** Depreciation Expense | 1,000 | |
|     Accumulated Depreciation— | | |
|       Rivera Company | | 1,000 |
| **(b)** Depreciation Expense | 1,000 | |
|     Equipment | | 1,000 |
| **(c)** Depreciation Expense | 1,000 | |
|     Accumulated Depreciation— | | |
|       Equipment | | 1,000 |
| **(d)** Equipment Expense | 1,000 | |
|     Accumulated Depreciation— | | |
|       Equipment | | 1,000 |

(LO 4)
**11.** Adjustments for unearned revenues:
  **(a)** decrease liabilities and increase revenues.
  **(b)** have an assets and revenues account relationship.
  **(c)** increase assets and increase revenues.
  **(d)** decrease revenues and decrease assets.

(LO 5)
**12.** Adjustments for accrued revenues:
  **(a)** have a liabilities and revenues account relationship.
  **(b)** have an assets and revenues account relationship.
  **(c)** decrease assets and revenues.
  **(d)** decrease liabilities and increase revenues.

(LO 5)
**13.** Anika Wilson earned a salary of $400 for the last week of September. She will be paid on October 1. The adjusting entry for Anika's employer at September 30 is:
  **(a)** No entry is required.

| | | |
|---|---|---|
| **(b)** Salaries and Wages Expense | 400 | |
|     Salaries and Wages Payable | | 400 |

|   | (c) Salaries and Wages Expense | 400 | |
|---|---|---|---|
|   | Cash | | 400 |
|   | (d) Salaries and Wages Payable | 400 | |
|   | Cash | | 400 |

(LO 6) **14.** Which of the following statements is **incorrect** concerning the adjusted trial balance?

(a) An adjusted trial balance proves the equality of the total debit balances and the total credit balances in the ledger after all adjustments are made.

(b) The adjusted trial balance provides the primary basis for the preparation of financial statements.

(c) The adjusted trial balance lists the account balances segregated by assets and liabilities.

(d) The adjusted trial balance is prepared after the adjusting entries have been journalized and posted.

(LO 7) *__15.__ The trial balance shows Supplies $0 and Supplies Expense $1,500. If $800 of supplies are on hand at the end of the period, the adjusting entry is:

(a) Debit Supplies $800 and credit Supplies Expense $800.

(b) Debit Supplies Expense $800 and credit Supplies $800.

(c) Debit Supplies $700 and credit Supplies Expense $700.

(d) Debit Supplies Expense $700 and credit Supplies $700.

*__16.__ Neutrality is an ingredient of: (LO 8)

|   | **Faithful Representation** | **Relevance** |
|---|---|---|
| (a) | Yes | Yes |
| (b) | No | No |
| (c) | Yes | No |
| (d) | No | Yes |

*__17.__ Which item is a constraint in financial accounting? (LO 8)

(a) Comparability. (c) Cost.

(b) Materiality. (d) Consistency.

Go to the book's companion website, www.wiley.com/college/weygandt, for additional Self-Test Questions.

✔ The Navigator

## QUESTIONS

**1.** (a) How does the time period assumption affect an accountant's analysis of business transactions?

(b) Explain the terms fiscal year, calendar year, and interim periods.

**2.** Define two generally accepted accounting principles that relate to adjusting the accounts.

**3.** Susan Zupan, a lawyer, accepts a legal engagement in March, performs the work in April, and is paid in May. If Zupan's law firm prepares monthly financial statements, when should it recognize revenue from this engagement? Why?

**4.** Why do accrual-basis financial statements provide more useful information than cash-basis statements?

**5.** In completing the engagement in Question 3, Zupan pays no costs in March, $2,000 in April, and $2,500 in May (incurred in April). How much expense should the firm deduct from revenues in the month when it recognizes the revenue? Why?

**6.** "Adjusting entries are required by the historical cost principle of accounting." Do you agree? Explain.

**7.** Why may a trial balance not contain up-to-date and complete financial information?

**8.** Distinguish between the two categories of adjusting entries, and identify the types of adjustments applicable to each category.

**9.** What is the debit/credit effect of a prepaid expense adjusting entry?

**10.** "Depreciation is a valuation process that results in the reporting of the fair value of the asset." Do you agree? Explain.

**11.** Explain the differences between depreciation expense and accumulated depreciation.

**12.** J. Brownlee Company purchased equipment for $18,000. By the current balance sheet date, $6,000 had been depreciated. Indicate the balance sheet presentation of the data.

**13.** What is the debit/credit effect of an unearned revenue adjusting entry?

**14.** A company fails to recognize revenue for services performed but not yet received in cash or recorded. Which of the following accounts are involved in the adjusting entry: (a) asset, (b) liability, (c) revenue, or (d) expense? For the accounts selected, indicate whether they would be debited or credited in the entry.

**15.** A company fails to recognize an expense incurred but not paid. Indicate which of the following accounts is debited and which is credited in the adjusting entry: (a) asset, (b) liability, (c) revenue, or (d) expense.

**16.** A company makes an accrued revenue adjusting entry for $900 and an accrued expense adjusting entry for $700. How much was net income understated prior to these entries? Explain.

**17.** On January 9, a company pays $5,000 for salaries and wages of which $2,000 was reported as Salaries and Wages Payable on December 31. Give the entry to record the payment.

**18.** For each of the following items before adjustment, indicate the type of adjusting entry (prepaid expense, unearned revenue, accrued revenue, or accrued expense) that is needed to correct the misstatement. If an item could result in more than one type of adjusting entry, indicate each of the types.

(a) Assets are understated.

(b) Liabilities are overstated.

(c) Liabilities are understated.

(d) Expenses are understated.

(e) Assets are overstated.

(f) Revenue is understated.

19. One-half of the adjusting entry is given below. Indicate the account title for the other half of the entry.
    (a) Salaries and Wages Expense is debited.
    (b) Depreciation Expense is debited.
    (c) Interest Payable is credited.
    (d) Supplies is credited.
    (e) Accounts Receivable is debited.
    (f) Unearned Service Revenue is debited.
20. "An adjusting entry may affect more than one balance sheet or income statement account." Do you agree? Why or why not?
21. Why is it possible to prepare financial statements directly from an adjusted trial balance?
*22. Dashan Company debits Supplies Expense for all purchases of supplies and credits Rent Revenue for all advanced rentals. For each type of adjustment, give the adjusting entry.
*23. (a) What is the primary objective of financial reporting?
     (b) Identify the characteristics of useful accounting information.

*24. Dan Fineman, the president of King Company, is pleased. King substantially increased its net income in 2014 while keeping its unit inventory relatively the same. Howard Gross, chief accountant, cautions Dan, however. Gross says that since King changed its method of inventory valuation, there is a consistency problem and it is difficult to determine whether King is better off. Is Gross correct? Why or why not?
*25. What is the distinction between comparability and consistency?
*26. Describe the constraint inherent in the presentation of accounting information.
*27. Laurie Belk is president of Better Books. She has no accounting background. Belk cannot understand why fair value is not used as the basis for all accounting measurement and reporting. Discuss.
*28. What is the economic entity assumption? Give an example of its violation.

## BRIEF EXERCISES

*Indicate why adjusting entries are needed.*
(LO 3)

**BE3-1** The ledger of Jung Company includes the following accounts. Explain why each account may require adjustment.
(a) Prepaid Insurance.
(b) Depreciation Expense.
(c) Unearned Service Revenue.
(d) Interest Payable.

*Identify the major types of adjusting entries.*
(LO 3, 4, 5)

**BE3-2** Moteki Company accumulates the following adjustment data at December 31. Indicate (a) the type of adjustment (prepaid expense, accrued revenues and so on), and (b) the status of accounts before adjustment (overstated or understated).
1. Supplies of $100 are on hand.
2. Services provided but not recorded total $900.
3. Interest of $200 has accumulated on a note payable.
4. Rent collected in advance totaling $650 has been earned.

*Prepare adjusting entry for supplies.*
(LO 4)

**BE3-3** Ritter Advertising Company's trial balance at December 31 shows Supplies $6,700 and Supplies Expense $0. On December 31, there are $2,500 of supplies on hand. Prepare the adjusting entry at December 31, and using T-accounts, enter the balances in the accounts, post the adjusting entry, and indicate the adjusted balance in each account.

*Prepare adjusting entry for depreciation.*
(LO 4)

**BE3-4** At the end of its first year, the trial balance of Nygaard Company shows Equipment $30,000 and zero balances in Accumulated Depreciation—Equipment and Depreciation Expense. Depreciation for the year is estimated to be $4,000. Prepare the adjusting entry for depreciation at December 31, post the adjustments to T-accounts, and indicate the balance sheet presentation of the equipment at December 31.

*Prepare adjusting entry for prepaid expense.*
(LO 4)

**BE3-5** On July 1, 2014, Dobbs Co. pays $14,400 to Kalter Insurance Co. for a 3-year insurance contract. Both companies have fiscal years ending December 31. For Dobbs Co., journalize and post the entry on July 1 and the adjusting entry on December 31.

*Prepare adjusting entry for unearned revenue.*
(LO 4)

**BE3-6** Using the data in BE3-5, journalize and post the entry on July 1 and the adjusting entry on December 31 for Kalter Insurance Co. Kalter uses the accounts Unearned Service Revenue and Service Revenue.

*Prepare adjusting entries for accruals.*
(LO 5)

**BE3-7** The bookkeeper for Bradbury Company asks you to prepare the following accrued adjusting entries at December 31.
1. Interest on notes payable of $400 is accrued.
2. Services performed but not recorded total $1,900.
3. Salaries earned by employees of $900 have not been recorded.

Use the following account titles: Service Revenue, Accounts Receivable, Interest Expense, Interest Payable, Salaries and Wages Expense, and Salaries and Wages Payable.

**BE3-8** The trial balance of Yewlett Company includes the following balance sheet accounts, which may require adjustment. For each account that requires adjustment, indicate (a) the type of adjusting entry (prepaid expenses, unearned revenues, accrued revenues, and accrued expenses) and (b) the related account in the adjusting entry.

*Analyze accounts in an unadjusted trial balance.*

*(LO 3, 4, 5)*

    Accounts Receivable                          Interest Payable
    Prepaid Insurance                            Unearned Service Revenue
    Accumulated Depreciation—Equipment

**BE3-9** The adjusted trial balance of Parsons Company at December 31, 2014, includes the following accounts: Owner's Capital $15,600, Owner's Drawings $7,000, Service Revenue $37,000, Salaries and Wages Expense $16,000, Insurance Expense $2,000, Rent Expense $4,000, Supplies Expense $1,500, and Depreciation Expense $1,300. Prepare an income statement for the year.

*Prepare an income statement from an adjusted trial balance.*

*(LO 6)*

**BE3-10** Partial adjusted trial balance data for Parsons Company is presented in BE3-9. The balance in Owner's Capital is the balance as of January 1. Prepare an owner's equity statement for the year assuming net income is $12,200 for the year.

*Prepare an owner's equity statement from an adjusted trial balance.*

*(LO 6)*

**\*BE3-11** Mayes Company records all prepayments in income statement accounts. At April 30, the trial balance shows Supplies Expense $2,800, Service Revenue $9,200, and zero balances in related balance sheet accounts. Prepare the adjusting entries at April 30 assuming (a) $700 of supplies on hand and (b) $3,000 of service revenue should be reported as unearned.

*Prepare adjusting entries under alternative treatment of deferrals.*

*(LO 7)*

**\*BE3-12** The accompanying chart shows the qualitative characteristics of useful accounting information. Fill in the blanks.

*Identify characteristics of useful information.*

*(LO 8)*

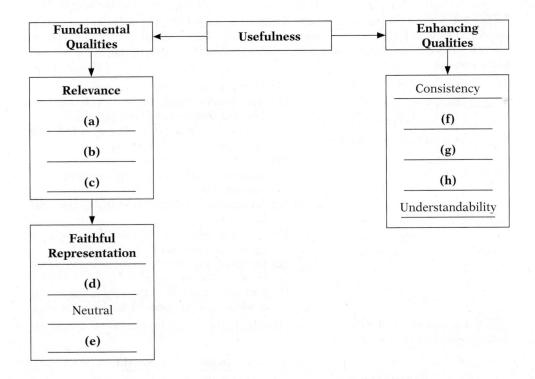

**\*BE3-13** Given the characteristics of useful accounting information, complete each of the following statements.

*Identify characteristics of useful information.*

*(LO 8)*

**(a)** For information to be _____, it should have predictive value, confirmatory value, and be material.

**(b)** _____ is the quality of information that gives assurance that the information accurately depicts what really happened.

**(c)** _____ means using the same accounting principles and methods from year to year within a company.

*Identify characteristics of useful information.*

(LO 8)

**\*BE3-14** Here are some qualitative characteristics of useful accounting information:

**1.** Predictive value      **3.** Verifiable
**2.** Neutral               **4.** Timely

Match each qualitative characteristic to one of the following statements.

_____ **(a)** Accounting information should help provide accurate expectations about future events.
_____ **(b)** Accounting information cannot be selected, prepared, or presented to favor one set of interested users over another.
_____ **(c)** The quality of information that occurs when independent observers, using the same methods, obtain similar results.
_____ **(d)** Accounting information must be available to decision-makers before it loses its capacity to influence their decisions.

*Define full disclosure principle.*

(LO 8)

**\*BE3-15** The full disclosure principle dictates that:

**(a)** financial statements should disclose all assets at their cost.
**(b)** financial statements should disclose only those events that can be measured in currency.
**(c)** financial statements should disclose all events and circumstances that would matter to users of financial statements.
**(d)** financial statements should not be relied on unless an auditor has expressed an unqualified opinion on them.

## > DO IT! Review

*Identify timing concepts.*

(LO 1, 2)

**DO IT! 3-1** Several timing concepts are discussed on pages 100–101. A list of concepts is provided below in the left column, with a description of the concept in the right column. There are more descriptions provided than concepts. Match the description of the concept to the concept.

**1.** ____ Cash-basis accounting.
**2.** ____ Fiscal year.
**3.** ____ Revenue recognition principle.
**4.** ____ Expense recognition principle.

**(a)** Monthly and quarterly time periods.
**(b)** Accountants divide the economic life of a business into artificial time periods.
**(c)** Efforts (expenses) should be matched with accomplishments (revenues).
**(d)** Companies record revenues when they receive cash and record expenses when they pay out cash.
**(e)** An accounting time period that is one year in length.
**(f)** An accounting time period that starts on January 1 and ends on December 31.
**(g)** Companies record transactions in the period in which the events occur.
**(h)** Recognize revenue in the accounting period in which a performance obligation is satisfied.

*Prepare adjusting entries for deferrals.*

(LO 4)

**DO IT! 3-2** The ledger of Herrera, Inc. on March 31, 2014, includes the following selected accounts before adjusting entries.

|                          | Debit  | Credit |
|--------------------------|--------|--------|
| Prepaid Insurance        | 2,400  |        |
| Supplies                 | 2,500  |        |
| Equipment                | 30,000 |        |
| Unearned Service Revenue |        | 9,000  |

An analysis of the accounts shows the following.

**1.** Insurance expires at the rate of $300 per month.
**2.** Supplies on hand total $1,100.

**3.** The equipment depreciates $500 per month.

**4.** During March, services were performed for two-fifths of the unearned service revenue.

Prepare the adjusting entries for the month of March.

**DO IT! 3-3** Javier Computer Services began operations in July 2014. At the end of the month, the company prepares monthly financial statements. It has the following information for the month.

*Prepare adjusting entries for accruals.*
*(LO 5)*

**1.** At July 31, the company owed employees $1,300 in salaries that the company will pay in August.

**2.** On July 1, the company borrowed $20,000 from a local bank on a 10-year note. The annual interest rate is 12%.

**3.** Service revenue unrecorded in July totaled $2,400.

Prepare the adjusting entries needed at July 31, 2014.

**DO IT! 3-4** Lumina Co. was organized on April 1, 2014. The company prepares quarterly financial statements. The adjusted trial balance amounts at June 30 are shown below.

*Calculate amounts from trial balance.*
*(LO 6)*

| | Debit | | Credit |
|---|---|---|---|
| Cash | $ 5,360 | Accumulated Depreciation— | |
| Accounts Receivable | 480 | Equipment | $ 700 |
| Prepaid Rent | 720 | Notes Payable | 4,000 |
| Supplies | 920 | Accounts Payable | 790 |
| Equipment | 12,000 | Salaries and Wages Payable | 300 |
| Owner's Drawings | 500 | Interest Payable | 40 |
| Salaries and Wages Expense | 7,400 | Unearned Rent Revenue | 400 |
| Rent Expense | 1,200 | Owner's Capital | 11,200 |
| Depreciation Expense | 700 | Service Revenue | 11,360 |
| Supplies Expense | 160 | Rent Revenue | 1,100 |
| Utilities Expense | 410 | | $29,890 |
| Interest Expense | 40 | | |
| | $29,890 | | |

**(a)** Determine the net income for the quarter April 1 to June 30.
**(b)** Determine the total assets and total liabilities at June 30, 2014 for Lumina Company.
**(c)** Determine the amount that appears for Owner's Capital at June 30, 2014.

## EXERCISES

**E3-1** Ian Muse has prepared the following list of statements about the time period assumption.

*Explain the time period assumption.*
*(LO 1)*

**1.** Adjusting entries would not be necessary if a company's life were not divided into artificial time periods.
**2.** The IRS requires companies to file annual tax returns.
**3.** Accountants divide the economic life of a business into artificial time periods, but each transaction affects only one of these periods.
**4.** Accounting time periods are generally a month, a quarter, or a year.
**5.** A time period lasting one year is called an interim period.
**6.** All fiscal years are calendar years, but not all calendar years are fiscal years.

*Instructions*
Identify each statement as true or false. If false, indicate how to correct the statement.

**E3-2** On numerous occasions, proposals have surfaced to put the federal government on the accrual basis of accounting. This is no small issue. If this basis were used, it would mean that billions in unrecorded liabilities would have to be booked, and the federal deficit would increase substantially.

*Distinguish between cash and accrual basis of accounting.*
*(LO 2)*

*Instructions* —————

**(a)** What is the difference between accrual-basis accounting and cash-basis accounting?

**(b)** Why would politicians prefer the cash basis over the accrual basis?

**(c)** Write a letter to your senator explaining why the federal government should adopt the accrual basis of accounting.

*Compute cash and accrual accounting income.*

*(LO 2)*

**E3-3** Primo Industries collected $105,000 from customers in 2014. Of the amount collected, $25,000 was for services performed in 2013. In addition, Primo performed services worth $40,000 in 2014, which will not be collected until 2015.

Primo Industries also paid $72,000 for expenses in 2014. Of the amount paid, $30,000 was for expenses incurred on account in 2013. In addition, Primo incurred $42,000 of expenses in 2014, which will not be paid until 2015.

*Instructions*

**(a)** Compute 2014 cash-basis net income.

**(b)** Compute 2014 accrual-basis net income.

*Identify the type of adjusting entry needed.*

*(LO 3, 4, 5)*

**E3-4** Hart Corporation encounters the following situations:

1. Hart collects $1,300 from a customer in 2014 for services to be performed in 2015.
2. Hart incurs utility expense which is not yet paid in cash or recorded.
3. Hart's employees worked 3 days in 2014 but will not be paid until 2015.
4. Hart performs services for customers but has not yet received cash or recorded the transaction.
5. Hart paid $2,400 rent on December 1 for the 4 months starting December 1.
6. Hart received cash for future services and recorded a liability until the service was performed.
7. Hart performed consulting services for a client in December 2014. On December 31, it had not billed the client for services provided of $1,200.
8. Hart paid cash for an expense and recorded an asset until the item was used up.
9. Hart purchased $900 of supplies in 2014; at year-end, $400 of supplies remain unused.
10. Hart purchased equipment on January 1, 2014; the equipment will be used for 5 years.
11. Hart borrowed $10,000 on October 1, 2014, signing an 8% one-year note payable.

*Instructions*

Identify what type of adjusting entry (prepaid expense, unearned revenue, accrued expense, or accrued revenue) is needed in each situation at December 31, 2014.

*Prepare adjusting entries from selected data.*

*(LO 4, 5)*

**E3-5** Verne Cova Company has the following balances in selected accounts on December 31, 2014.

| | |
|---|---|
| Accounts Receivable | $  –0– |
| Accumulated Depreciation—Equipment | –0– |
| Equipment | 7,000 |
| Interest Payable | –0– |
| Notes Payable | 10,000 |
| Prepaid Insurance | 2,100 |
| Salaries and Wages Payable | –0– |
| Supplies | 2,450 |
| Unearned Service Revenue | 30,000 |

All the accounts have normal balances. The information below has been gathered at December 31, 2014.

1. Verne Cova Company borrowed $10,000 by signing a 12%, one-year note on September 1, 2014.
2. A count of supplies on December 31, 2014, indicates that supplies of $900 are on hand.
3. Depreciation on the equipment for 2014 is $1,000.
4. Verne Cova Company paid $2,100 for 12 months of insurance coverage on June 1, 2014.
5. On December 1, 2014, Verne Cova collected $30,000 for consulting services to be performed from December 1, 2014, through March 31, 2015.
6. Verne Cova performed consulting services for a client in December 2014. The client will be billed $4,200.
7. Verne Cova Company pays its employees total salaries of $9,000 every Monday for the preceding 5-day week (Monday through Friday). On Monday, December 29, employees were paid for the week ending December 26. All employees worked the last 3 days of 2014.

*Instructions*
Prepare adjusting entries for the seven items described above.

**E3-6** Lei Company accumulates the following adjustment data at December 31.

1. Services performed but not recorded total $1,000.
2. Supplies of $300 have been used.
3. Utility expenses of $225 are unpaid.
4. Services related to unearned service revenue of $260 were performed.
5. Salaries of $800 are unpaid.
6. Prepaid insurance totaling $350 has expired.

*Instructions*
For each of the above items indicate the following.

**(a)** The type of adjustment (prepaid expense, unearned revenue, accrued revenue, or accrued expense).
**(b)** The status of accounts before adjustment (overstatement or understatement).

*Identify types of adjustments and account relationships.*
*(LO 3, 4, 5)*

**E3-7** The ledger of Perez Rental Agency on March 31 of the current year includes the selected accounts, shown below, before adjusting entries have been prepared.

*Prepare adjusting entries from selected account data.*
*(LO 4, 5)*

|  | Debit | Credit |
|---|---|---|
| Prepaid Insurance | $ 3,600 |  |
| Supplies | 2,800 |  |
| Equipment | 25,000 |  |
| Accumulated Depreciation—Equipment |  | $ 8,400 |
| Notes Payable |  | 20,000 |
| Unearned Rent Revenue |  | 10,200 |
| Rent Revenue |  | 60,000 |
| Interest Expense | –0– |  |
| Salaries and Wages Expense | 14,000 |  |

An analysis of the accounts shows the following.

1. The equipment depreciates $400 per month.
2. One-third of the unearned rent revenue was earned during the quarter.
3. Interest of $500 is accrued on the notes payable.
4. Supplies on hand total $900.
5. Insurance expires at the rate of $200 per month.

*Instructions*
Prepare the adjusting entries at March 31, assuming that adjusting entries are made **quarterly**. Additional accounts are Depreciation Expense, Insurance Expense, Interest Payable, and Supplies Expense.

**E3-8** Robin Shalit, D.D.S., opened a dental practice on January 1, 2014. During the first month of operations, the following transactions occurred.

*Prepare adjusting entries.*
*(LO 4, 5)*

1. Performed services for patients who had dental plan insurance. At January 31, $875 of such services were performed but not yet recorded.
2. Utility expenses incurred but not paid prior to January 31 totaled $650.
3. Purchased dental equipment on January 1 for $80,000, paying $20,000 in cash and signing a $60,000, 3-year note payable. The equipment depreciates $400 per month. Interest is $500 per month.
4. Purchased a one-year malpractice insurance policy on January 1 for $24,000.
5. Purchased $1,600 of dental supplies. On January 31, determined that $400 of supplies were on hand.

*Instructions*
Prepare the adjusting entries on January 31. Account titles are Accumulated Depreciation—Equipment, Depreciation Expense, Service Revenue, Accounts Receivable, Insurance Expense, Interest Expense, Interest Payable, Prepaid Insurance, Supplies, Supplies Expense, Utilities Expense, and Utilities Payable.

**E3-9** The trial balance for Pioneer Advertising Agency is shown in Illustration 3-3 (page 103). Instead of the adjusting entries shown in the text at October 31, assume the following adjustment data.

*Prepare adjusting entries.*
*(LO 4, 5)*

1. Supplies on hand at October 31 total $500.
2. Expired insurance for the month is $100.
3. Depreciation for the month is $50.
4. Services related to unearned service revenue in October worth $600 were performed.
5. Services performed but not recorded at October 31 are $300.
6. Interest accrued at October 31 is $95.
7. Accrued salaries at October 31 are $1,625.

**Instructions**
Prepare the adjusting entries for the items above.

*Prepare correct income statement.*

(LO 2, 4, 5, 6)

**E3-10** The income statement of Gopitkumar Co. for the month of July shows net income of $1,400 based on Service Revenue $5,500, Salaries and Wages Expense $2,300, Supplies Expense $1,200, and Utilities Expense $600. In reviewing the statement, you discover the following.

1. Insurance expired during July of $400 was omitted.
2. Supplies expense includes $250 of supplies that are still on hand at July 31.
3. Depreciation on equipment of $150 was omitted.
4. Accrued but unpaid salaries and wages at July 31 of $300 were not included.
5. Services performed but unrecorded totaled $650.

**Instructions**
Prepare a correct income statement for July 2014.

*Analyze adjusted data.*

(LO 3, 4, 5, 6)

**E3-11** A partial adjusted trial balance of Gehring Company at January 31, 2014, shows the following.

**GEHRING COMPANY**
Adjusted Trial Balance
January 31, 2014

| | **Debit** | **Credit** |
|---|---|---|
| Supplies | $ 850 | |
| Prepaid Insurance | 2,400 | |
| Salaries and Wages Payable | | $ 800 |
| Unearned Service Revenue | | 750 |
| Supplies Expense | 950 | |
| Insurance Expense | 400 | |
| Salaries and Wages Expense | 2,900 | |
| Service Revenue | | 2,000 |

**Instructions**
Answer the following questions, assuming the year begins January 1.

**(a)** If the amount in Supplies Expense is the January 31 adjusting entry, and $1,000 of supplies was purchased in January, what was the balance in Supplies on January 1?
**(b)** If the amount in Insurance Expense is the January 31 adjusting entry, and the original insurance premium was for one year, what was the total premium and when was the policy purchased?
**(c)** If $3,500 of salaries was paid in January, what was the balance in Salaries and Wages Payable at December 31, 2013?

*Journalize basic transactions and adjusting entries.*

(LO 4, 5, 6)

**E3-12** Selected accounts of Koffman Company are shown below and on the next page.

| **Supplies Expense** | |
|---|---|
| 7/31   800 | |

| **Supplies** | | | |
|---|---|---|---|
| 7/1 Bal. | 1,100 | 7/31 | 800 |
| 7/10 | 650 | | |

| **Salaries and Wages Payable** | |
|---|---|
| | 7/31   1,200 |

| Accounts Receivable | | | | Unearned Service Revenue | | |
|---|---|---|---|---|---|---|
| 7/31 | 500 | | | 7/31 | 1,150 | 7/1 Bal.    1,500 |
| | | | | | | 7/20         1,000 |

| Salaries and Wages Expense | | | | Service Revenue | | |
|---|---|---|---|---|---|---|
| 7/15 | 1,200 | | | | | 7/14    2,000 |
| 7/31 | 1,200 | | | | | 7/31    1,150 |
| | | | | | | 7/31      500 |

## Instructions

After analyzing the accounts, journalize **(a)** the July transactions and **(b)** the adjusting entries that were made on July 31. (*Hint:* July transactions were for cash.)

**E3-13** The trial balances before and after adjustment for Frinzi Company at the end of its fiscal year are presented below.

*Prepare adjusting entries from analysis of trial balances.*

*(LO 4, 5, 6)*

### FRINZI COMPANY
### Trial Balance
### August 31, 2014

| | Before Adjustment | | After Adjustment | |
|---|---|---|---|---|
| | Dr. | Cr. | Dr. | Cr. |
| Cash | $10,400 | | $10,400 | |
| Accounts Receivable | 8,800 | | 10,800 | |
| Supplies | 2,300 | | 900 | |
| Prepaid Insurance | 4,000 | | 2,500 | |
| Equipment | 14,000 | | 14,000 | |
| Accumulated Depreciation—Equipment | | $ 3,600 | | $ 4,500 |
| Accounts Payable | | 5,800 | | 5,800 |
| Salaries and Wages Payable | | –0– | | 1,100 |
| Unearned Rent Revenue | | 1,500 | | 600 |
| Owner's Capital | | 15,600 | | 15,600 |
| Service Revenue | | 34,000 | | 36,000 |
| Rent Revenue | | 11,000 | | 11,900 |
| Salaries and Wages Expense | 17,000 | | 18,100 | |
| Supplies Expense | –0– | | 1,400 | |
| Rent Expense | 15,000 | | 15,000 | |
| Insurance Expense | –0– | | 1,500 | |
| Depreciation Expense | –0– | | 900 | |
| | $71,500 | $71,500 | $75,500 | $75,500 |

## Instructions

Prepare the adjusting entries that were made.

**E3-14** The adjusted trial balance for Frinzi Company is given in E3-13.

## Instructions

Prepare the income and owner's equity statements for the year and the balance sheet at August 31.

*Prepare financial statements from adjusted trial balance.*

*(LO 6)*

**E3-15** The following data are taken from the comparative balance sheets of Cascade Billiards Club, which prepares its financial statements using the accrual basis of accounting.

| December 31 | 2014 | 2013 |
|---|---|---|
| Accounts receivable from members | $14,000 | $ 9,000 |
| Unearned service revenue | 17,000 | 25,000 |

*Record transactions on accrual basis; convert revenue to cash receipts.*

*(LO 4, 5)*

Members are billed based upon their use of the club's facilities. Unearned service revenues arise from the sale of gift certificates, which members can apply to their future use of club facilities. The 2014 income statement for the club showed that service revenue of $161,000 was earned during the year.

**Instructions**

(*Hint:* You will probably find it helpful to use T-accounts to analyze these data.)

**(a)** Prepare journal entries for each of the following events that took place during 2014.
  **(1)** Accounts receivable from 2013 were all collected.
  **(2)** Gift certificates outstanding at the end of 2013 were all redeemed.
  **(3)** An additional $38,000 worth of gift certificates were sold during 2014. A portion of these was used by the recipients during the year; the remainder was still outstanding at the end of 2014.
  **(4)** Services performed for members for 2014 were billed to members.
  **(5)** Accounts receivable for 2014 (i.e., those billed in item [4] above) were partially collected.

**(b)** Determine the amount of cash received by the club, with respect to member services, during 2014.

*Journalize adjusting entries.*
*(LO 7)*

**\*E3-16** Aaron Lynch Company has the following balances in selected accounts on December 31, 2014.

| | |
|---|---|
| Service Revenue | $40,000 |
| Insurance Expense | 2,700 |
| Supplies Expense | 2,450 |

All the accounts have normal balances. Aaron Lynch Company debits prepayments to expense accounts when paid, and credits unearned revenues to revenue accounts when received. The following information below has been gathered at December 31, 2014.

**1.** Aaron Lynch Company paid $2,700 for 12 months of insurance coverage on June 1, 2014.
**2.** On December 1, 2014, Aaron Lynch Company collected $40,000 for consulting services to be performed from December 1, 2014, through March 31, 2015.
**3.** A count of supplies on December 31, 2014, indicates that supplies of $900 are on hand.

**Instructions**

Prepare the adjusting entries needed at December 31, 2014.

*Journalize transactions and adjusting entries.*
*(LO 7)*

**\*E3-17** At Cambridge Company, prepayments are debited to expense when paid, and unearned revenues are credited to revenue when cash is received. During January of the current year, the following transactions occurred.

Jan.  2   Paid $1,920 for fire insurance protection for the year.
     10   Paid $1,700 for supplies.
     15   Received $6,100 for services to be performed in the future.

On January 31, it is determined that $2,500 of the services were performed and that there are $650 of supplies on hand.

**Instructions**

**(a)** Journalize and post the January transactions. (Use T-accounts.)
**(b)** Journalize and post the adjusting entries at January 31.
**(c)** Determine the ending balance in each of the accounts.

*Identify accounting assumptions and principles.*
*(LO 8)*

**\*E3-18** Presented below are the assumptions and principles discussed in this chapter.

**1.** Full disclosure principle.          **4.** Time period assumption.
**2.** Going concern assumption.         **5.** Historical cost principle.
**3.** Monetary unit assumption.         **6.** Economic entity assumption.

**Instructions**

Identify by number the accounting assumption or principle that is described below. Do not use a number more than once.

_____ **(a)** Is the rationale for why plant assets are not reported at liquidation value. (*Note:* Do not use the historical cost principle.)
_____ **(b)** Indicates that personal and business record-keeping should be separately maintained.
_____ **(c)** Assumes that the monetary unit is the "measuring stick" used to report on financial performance.
_____ **(d)** Separates financial information into time periods for reporting purposes.

_____ (e) Measurement basis used when a reliable estimate of fair value is not available.

_____ (f) Dictates that companies should disclose all circumstances and events that make a difference to financial statement users.

*E3-19 Rosman Co. had three major business transactions during 2014.

(a) Reported at its fair value of $260,000 merchandise inventory with a cost of $208,000.

(b) The president of Rosman Co., Jay Rosman, purchased a truck for personal use and charged it to his expense account.

(c) Rosman Co. wanted to make its 2014 income look better, so it added 2 more weeks to the year (a 54-week year). Previous years were 52 weeks.

*Identify the assumption or principle that has been violated.*

*(LO 8)*

**Instructions**

In each situation, identify the assumption or principle that has been violated, if any, and discuss what the company should have done.

*E3-20 The following characteristics, assumptions, principles, or constraint guide the FASB when it creates accounting standards.

*Identify financial accounting concepts and principles.*

*(LO 8)*

| | |
|---|---|
| Relevance | Expense recognition principle |
| Faithful representation | Time period assumption |
| Comparability | Going concern assumption |
| Consistency | Historical cost principle |
| Monetary unit assumption | Full disclosure principle |
| Economic entity assumption | Materiality |

Match each item above with a description below.

1. _____ Ability to easily evaluate one company's results relative to another's.
2. _____ Belief that a company will continue to operate for the foreseeable future.
3. _____ The judgment concerning whether an item's size is large enough to matter to decision-makers.
4. _____ The reporting of all information that would make a difference to financial statement users.
5. _____ The practice of preparing financial statements at regular intervals.
6. _____ The quality of information that indicates the information makes a difference in a decision.
7. _____ A belief that items should be reported on the balance sheet at the price that was paid to acquire them.
8. _____ A company's use of the same accounting principles and methods from year to year.
9. _____ Tracing accounting events to particular companies.
10. _____ The desire to minimize bias in financial statements.
11. _____ Reporting only those things that can be measured in monetary units.
12. _____ Dictates that efforts (expenses) be matched with results (revenues).

*E3-21 Net Nanny Software International Inc., headquartered in Vancouver, Canada, specializes in Internet safety and computer security products for both the home and commercial markets. In a recent balance sheet, it reported a deficit of US$5,678,288. It has reported only net losses since its inception. In spite of these losses, Net Nanny's shares of stock have traded anywhere from a high of $3.70 to a low of $0.32 on the Canadian Venture Exchange.

*Comment on the objective and qualitative characteristics of accounting information.*

*(LO 8)*

Net Nanny's financial statements have historically been prepared in Canadian dollars. Recently, the company adopted the U.S. dollar as its reporting currency.

**Instructions**

(a) What is the objective of financial reporting? How does this objective meet or not meet Net Nanny's investors' needs?

(b) Why would investors want to buy Net Nanny's shares if the company has consistently reported losses over the last few years? Include in your answer an assessment of the relevance of the information reported on Net Nanny's financial statements.

(c) Comment on how the change in reporting information from Canadian dollars to U.S. dollars likely affected the readers of Net Nanny's financial statements. Include in your answer an assessment of the comparability of the information.

Comment on the objective
and qualitative characteristics
of financial reporting.
(LO 8)

*E3-22 A friend of yours, Ana Gehrig, recently completed an undergraduate degree in science and has just started working with a biotechnology company. Ana tells you that the owners of the business are trying to secure new sources of financing which are needed in order for the company to proceed with development of a new health-care product. Ana said that her boss told her that the company must put together a report to present to potential investors.

Ana thought that the company should include in this package the detailed scientific findings related to the Phase I clinical trials for this product. She said, "I know that the biotech industry sometimes has only a 10% success rate with new products, but if we report all the scientific findings, everyone will see what a sure success this is going to be! The president was talking about the importance of following some set of accounting principles. Why do we need to look at some accounting rules? What they need to realize is that we have scientific results that are quite encouraging, some of the most talented employees around, and the start of some really great customer relationships. We haven't made any sales yet, but we will. We just need the funds to get through all the clinical testing and get government approval for our product. Then these investors will be quite happy that they bought in to our company early!"

**Instructions**
**(a)** What is accounting information?
**(b)** Comment on how Ana's suggestions for what should be reported to prospective investors conforms to the qualitative characteristics of accounting information. Do you think that the things that Ana wants to include in the information for investors will conform to financial reporting guidelines?

## EXERCISES: SET B AND CHALLENGE EXERCISES

Visit the book's companion website, at **www.wiley.com/college/weygandt**, and choose the Student Companion site to access Exercise Set B and Challenge Exercises.

## PROBLEMS: SET A

Prepare adjusting entries,
post to ledger accounts, and
prepare an adjusted trial
balance.
(LO 4, 5, 6)

**P3-1A** Deanna Nardelli started her own consulting firm, Nardelli Consulting, on May 1, 2014. The trial balance at May 31 is as follows.

**NARDELLI CONSULTING**
Trial Balance
May 31, 2014

| Account Number | | Debit | Credit |
|---|---|---|---|
| 101 | Cash | $ 4,500 | |
| 112 | Accounts Receivable | 6,000 | |
| 126 | Supplies | 1,900 | |
| 130 | Prepaid Insurance | 3,600 | |
| 149 | Equipment | 11,400 | |
| 201 | Accounts Payable | | $ 4,500 |
| 209 | Unearned Service Revenue | | 2,000 |
| 301 | Owner's Capital | | 17,700 |
| 400 | Service Revenue | | 7,500 |
| 726 | Salaries and Wages Expense | 3,400 | |
| 729 | Rent Expense | 900 | |
| | | $31,700 | $31,700 |

In addition to those accounts listed on the trial balance, the chart of accounts for Nardelli Consulting also contains the following accounts and account numbers: No. 150 Accumulated Depreciation—Equipment, No. 212 Salaries and Wages Payable, No. 631 Supplies Expense, No. 717 Depreciation Expense, No. 722 Insurance Expense, and No. 732 Utilities Expense.

Other data:

1. $900 of supplies have been used during the month.
2. Utilities expense incurred but not paid on May 31, 2014, $250.
3. The insurance policy is for 2 years.
4. $400 of the balance in the unearned service revenue account remains unearned at the end of the month.
5. May 31 is a Wednesday, and employees are paid on Fridays. Nardelli Consulting has two employees, who are paid $900 each for a 5-day work week.
6. The office furniture has a 5-year life with no salvage value. It is being depreciated at $190 per month for 60 months.
7. Invoices representing $1,700 of services performed during the month have not been recorded as of May 31.

*Instructions*
(a) Prepare the adjusting entries for the month of May. Use J4 as the page number for your journal.
(b) Post the adjusting entries to the ledger accounts. Enter the totals from the trial balance as beginning account balances and place a check mark in the posting reference column.
(c) Prepare an adjusted trial balance at May 31, 2014.

*(c) Adj. trial balance $34,920*

**P3-2A** The Skyline Motel opened for business on May 1, 2014. Its trial balance before adjustment on May 31 is as follows.

*Prepare adjusting entries, post, and prepare adjusted trial balance and financial statements.*

*(LO 4, 5, 6)*

### SKYLINE MOTEL
### Trial Balance
### May 31, 2014

| Account Number | | Debit | Credit |
|---|---|---|---|
| 101 | Cash | $ 3,500 | |
| 126 | Supplies | 2,080 | |
| 130 | Prepaid Insurance | 2,400 | |
| 140 | Land | 12,000 | |
| 141 | Buildings | 60,000 | |
| 149 | Equipment | 15,000 | |
| 201 | Accounts Payable | | $ 4,800 |
| 208 | Unearned Rent Revenue | | 3,300 |
| 275 | Mortgage Payable | | 40,000 |
| 301 | Owner's Capital | | 41,380 |
| 429 | Rent Revenue | | 10,300 |
| 610 | Advertising Expense | 600 | |
| 726 | Salaries and Wages Expense | 3,300 | |
| 732 | Utilities Expense | 900 | |
| | | $99,780 | $99,780 |

In addition to those accounts listed on the trial balance, the chart of accounts for Skyline Motel also contains the following accounts and account numbers: No. 142 Accumulated Depreciation—Buildings, No. 150 Accumulated Depreciation—Equipment, No. 212 Salaries and Wages Payable, No. 230 Interest Payable, No. 619 Depreciation Expense, No. 631 Supplies Expense, No. 718 Interest Expense, and No. 722 Insurance Expense.

Other data:

1. Prepaid insurance is a 1-year policy starting May 1, 2014.
2. A count of supplies shows $750 of unused supplies on May 31.
3. Annual depreciation is $3,000 on the buildings and $1,500 on equipment.

4. The mortgage interest rate is 12%. (The mortgage was taken out on May 1.)
5. Two-thirds of the unearned rent revenue has been earned.
6. Salaries of $750 are accrued and unpaid at May 31.

*Instructions*
**(a)** Journalize the adjusting entries on May 31.
**(b)** Prepare a ledger using the three-column form of account. Enter the trial balance amounts and post the adjusting entries. (Use J1 as the posting reference.)
**(c)** Prepare an adjusted trial balance on May 31.
**(d)** Prepare an income statement and an owner's equity statement for the month of May and a balance sheet at May 31.

*margin notes:*
(c) Adj. trial balance $101,305
(d) Net income $4,645
Ending capital balance $46,025
Total assets $93,075

*Prepare adjusting entries and financial statements.*
*(LO 4, 5, 6)*

**P3-3A** Everett Co. was organized on July 1, 2014. Quarterly financial statements are prepared. The unadjusted and adjusted trial balances as of September 30 are shown below.

**EVERETT CO.**
Trial Balance
September 30, 2014

|  | Unadjusted | | Adjusted | |
|---|---|---|---|---|
|  | Dr. | Cr. | Dr. | Cr. |
| Cash | $ 8,700 |  | $ 8,700 |  |
| Accounts Receivable | 10,400 |  | 11,500 |  |
| Supplies | 1,500 |  | 650 |  |
| Prepaid Rent | 2,200 |  | 1,200 |  |
| Equipment | 18,000 |  | 18,000 |  |
| Accumulated Depreciation—Equipment |  | $   -0- |  | $    700 |
| Notes Payable |  | 10,000 |  | 10,000 |
| Accounts Payable |  | 2,500 |  | 2,500 |
| Salaries and Wages Payable |  | -0- |  | 725 |
| Interest Payable |  | -0- |  | 100 |
| Unearned Rent Revenue |  | 1,900 |  | 1,050 |
| Owner's Capital |  | 22,000 |  | 22,000 |
| Owner's Drawings | 1,600 |  | 1,600 |  |
| Service Revenue |  | 16,000 |  | 17,100 |
| Rent Revenue |  | 1,410 |  | 2,260 |
| Salaries and Wages Expense | 8,000 |  | 8,725 |  |
| Rent Expense | 1,900 |  | 2,900 |  |
| Depreciation Expense |  |  | 700 |  |
| Supplies Expense |  |  | 850 |  |
| Utilities Expense | 1,510 |  | 1,510 |  |
| Interest Expense |  |  | 100 |  |
|  | $53,810 | $53,810 | $56,435 | $56,435 |

*Instructions*
**(a)** Journalize the adjusting entries that were made.
**(b)** Prepare an income statement and an owner's equity statement for the 3 months ending September 30 and a balance sheet at September 30.
**(c)** If the note bears interest at 12%, how many months has it been outstanding?

*margin notes:*
(b) Net income $4,575
Ending capital $24,975
Total assets $39,350

*Prepare adjusting entries.*
*(LO 4, 5)*
1. Insurance expense $4,890

2. Rent revenue $84,000

**P3-4A** A review of the ledger of Carmel Company at December 31, 2014, produces the following data pertaining to the preparation of annual adjusting entries.

1. Prepaid Insurance $10,440. The company has separate insurance policies on its buildings and its motor vehicles. Policy B4564 on the building was purchased on April 1, 2013, for $7,920. The policy has a term of 3 years. Policy A2958 on the vehicles was purchased on January 1, 2014, for $4,500. This policy has a term of 2 years.
2. Unearned Rent Revenue $429,000. The company began subleasing office space in its new building on November 1. At December 31, the company had the following rental contracts that are paid in full for the entire term of the lease.

| Date | Term (in months) | Monthly Rent | Number of Leases |
|------|------------------|--------------|------------------|
| Nov. 1 | 9 | $5,000 | 5 |
| Dec. 1 | 6 | $8,500 | 4 |

3. Notes Payable $120,000. This balance consists of a note for 9 months at an annual interest rate of 9%, dated November 1.

4. Salaries and Wages Payable $0. There are eight salaried employees. Salaries are paid every Friday for the current week. Five employees receive a salary of $700 each per week, and three employees earn $500 each per week. Assume December 31 is a Tuesday. Employees do not work weekends. All employees worked the last 2 days of December.

*3. Interest expense $1,800*

*4. Salaries and wages expense $2,000*

**Instructions**

Prepare the adjusting entries at December 31, 2014.

**P3-5A** On November 1, 2014, the account balances of Schilling Equipment Repair were as follows.

*Journalize transactions and follow through accounting cycle to preparation of financial statements.*

*(LO 4, 5, 6)*

| No. | | Debit | No. | | Credit |
|-----|---|-------|-----|---|--------|
| 101 | Cash | $ 2,400 | 154 | Accumulated Depreciation—Equipment | $ 2,000 |
| 112 | Accounts Receivable | 4,250 | 201 | Accounts Payable | 2,600 |
| 126 | Supplies | 1,800 | 209 | Unearned Service Revenue | 1,200 |
| 153 | Equipment | 12,000 | 212 | Salaries and Wages Payable | 700 |
| | | | 301 | Owner's Capital | 13,950 |
| | | $20,450 | | | $20,450 |

During November, the following summary transactions were completed.

Nov. 8  Paid $1,700 for salaries due employees, of which $700 is for October salaries.
10  Received $3,420 cash from customers on account.
12  Received $3,100 cash for services performed in November.
15  Purchased equipment on account $2,000.
17  Purchased supplies on account $700.
20  Paid creditors on account $2,700.
22  Paid November rent $400.
25  Paid salaries $1,700.
27  Performed services on account and billed customers for services provided $1,900.
29  Received $600 from customers for future service.

Adjustment data consist of:

1. Supplies on hand $1,400.
2. Accrued salaries payable $350.
3. Depreciation for the month is $200.
4. Services related to unearned service revenue of $1,250 were performed.

**Instructions**

(a) Enter the November 1 balances in the ledger accounts.

(b) Journalize the November transactions.

(c) Post to the ledger accounts. Use J1 for the posting reference. Use the following additional accounts: No. 407 Service Revenue, No. 615 Depreciation Expense, No. 631 Supplies Expense, No. 726 Salaries and Wages Expense, and No. 729 Rent Expense.

(d) Prepare a trial balance at November 30.

(e) Journalize and post adjusting entries.

(f) Prepare an adjusted trial balance.

(g) Prepare an income statement and an owner's equity statement for November and a balance sheet at November 30.

*(d) Trial balance $25,350*

*(f) Adj. trial balance $25,900*

*(g) Net income $1,500; Ending capital $15,450 Total assets $18,950*

*Prepare adjusting entries,*
*adjusted trial balance, and*
*financial statements using*
*appendix.*
(LO 4, 5, 6, 7)

**\*P3-6A** Sommer Graphics Company was organized on January 1, 2014, by Krystal Sommer. At the end of the first 6 months of operations, the trial balance contained the accounts shown below.

|  | Debit |  | Credit |
|---|---|---|---|
|  | **Debit** |  | **Credit** |
| Cash | $   8,600 | Notes Payable | $ 20,000 |
| Accounts Receivable | 14,000 | Accounts Payable | 9,000 |
| Equipment | 45,000 | Owner's Capital | 22,000 |
| Insurance Expense | 2,700 | Sales Revenue | 52,100 |
| Salaries and Wages Expense | 30,000 | Service Revenue | 6,000 |
| Supplies Expense | 3,700 |  |  |
| Advertising Expense | 1,900 |  |  |
| Rent Expense | 1,500 |  |  |
| Utilities Expense | 1,700 |  |  |
|  | $109,100 |  | $109,100 |

Analysis reveals the following additional data.

1. The $3,700 balance in Supplies Expense represents supplies purchased in January. At June 30, $1,500 of supplies are on hand.
2. The note payable was issued on February 1. It is a 9%, 6-month note.
3. The balance in Insurance Expense is the premium on a one-year policy, dated March 1, 2014.
4. Service revenues are credited to revenue when received. At June 30, services revenue of $1,300 are unearned.
5. Revenue for services performed but unrecorded at June 30 totals $2,000.
6. Depreciation is $2,250 per year.

*Instructions*

(b) Adj. trial balance
    $112,975
(c) Net income $18,725
    Ending capital $40,725
    Total assets $71,775

**(a)** Journalize the adjusting entries at June 30. (Assume adjustments are recorded every 6 months.)

**(b)** Prepare an adjusted trial balance.

**(c)** Prepare an income statement and owner's equity statement for the 6 months ended June 30 and a balance sheet at June 30.

## PROBLEMS: SET B

*Prepare adjusting entries,*
*post to ledger accounts, and*
*prepare adjusted trial balance.*
(LO 4, 5, 6)

**P3-1B** Jason Elsner started his own consulting firm, Elsner Company, on June 1, 2014. The trial balance at June 30 is shown below.

**ELSNER COMPANY**
Trial Balance
June 30, 2014

| Account Number |  | Debit | Credit |
|---|---|---|---|
| 101 | Cash | $ 7,150 |  |
| 112 | Accounts Receivable | 6,000 |  |
| 126 | Supplies | 2,000 |  |
| 130 | Prepaid Insurance | 3,000 |  |
| 157 | Equipment | 15,000 |  |
| 201 | Accounts Payable |  | $ 4,500 |
| 209 | Unearned Service Revenue |  | 4,000 |
| 301 | Owner's Capital |  | 21,750 |
| 400 | Service Revenue |  | 7,900 |
| 726 | Salaries and Wages Expense | 4,000 |  |
| 729 | Rent Expense | 1,000 |  |
|  |  | $38,150 | $38,150 |

In addition to those accounts listed on the trial balance, the chart of accounts for Elsner Company also contains the following accounts and account numbers: No. 158 Accumulated Depreciation—Equipment, No. 212 Salaries and Wages Payable, No. 631 Supplies Expense, No. 711 Depreciation Expense, No. 722 Insurance Expense, and No. 732 Utilities Expense.

Other data:

1. Supplies on hand at June 30 are $750.
2. A utility bill for $150 has not been recorded and will not be paid until next month.
3. The insurance policy is for a year.
4. $2,800 of unearned service revenue is recognized for services performed during the month.
5. Salaries of $1,900 are accrued at June 30.
6. The equipment has a 5-year life with no salvage value. It is being depreciated at $250 per month for 60 months.
7. Invoices representing $1,200 of services performed during the month have not been recorded as of June 30.

**Instructions**
(a) Prepare the adjusting entries for the month of June. Use J3 as the page number for your journal.
(b) Post the adjusting entries to the ledger accounts. Enter the totals from the trial balance as beginning account balances and place a check mark in the posting reference column.
(c) Prepare an adjusted trial balance at June 30, 2014.

(c) Adj. trial balance $41,650

**P3-2B** Maquoketa River Resort opened for business on June 1 with eight air-conditioned units. Its trial balance before adjustment on August 31 is as follows.

*Prepare adjusting entries, post, and prepare adjusted trial balance and financial statements.*

(LO 4, 5, 6)

### MAQUOKETA RIVER RESORT
### Trial Balance
### August 31, 2014

| Account Number | | Debit | Credit |
|---|---|---|---|
| 101 | Cash | $ 19,600 | |
| 126 | Supplies | 3,300 | |
| 130 | Prepaid Insurance | 6,000 | |
| 140 | Land | 25,000 | |
| 143 | Buildings | 125,000 | |
| 149 | Equipment | 26,000 | |
| 201 | Accounts Payable | | $ 6,500 |
| 208 | Unearned Rent Revenue | | 7,400 |
| 275 | Mortgage Payable | | 80,000 |
| 301 | Owner's Capital | | 100,000 |
| 306 | Owner's Drawings | 5,000 | |
| 429 | Rent Revenue | | 80,000 |
| 622 | Maintenance and Repairs Expense | 3,600 | |
| 726 | Salaries and Wages Expense | 51,000 | |
| 732 | Utilities Expense | 9,400 | |
| | | $273,900 | $273,900 |

In addition to those accounts listed on the trial balance, the chart of accounts for Maquoketa River Resort also contains the following accounts and account numbers: No. 112 Accounts Receivable, No. 144 Accumulated Depreciation—Buildings, No. 150 Accumulated Depreciation—Equipment, No. 212 Salaries and Wages Payable, No. 230 Interest Payable, No. 620 Depreciation Expense, No. 631 Supplies Expense, No. 718 Interest Expense, and No. 722 Insurance Expense.

Other data:

1. Insurance expires at the rate of $300 per month.
2. A count on August 31 shows $800 of supplies on hand.

3. Annual depreciation is $6,000 on buildings and $2,400 on equipment.
4. Unearned rent revenue of $4,800 was earned prior to August 31.
5. Salaries of $400 were unpaid at August 31.
6. Rentals of $4,000 were due from tenants at August 31. (Use Accounts Receivable.)
7. The mortgage interest rate is 9% per year. (The mortgage was taken out on August 1.)

*Instructions*

(c) Adj. trial balance
$281,000

(d) Net income $18,300
Ending capital balance
$113,300
Total assets $203,400

*Prepare adjusting entries and financial statements.*

(LO 4, 5, 6)

**(a)** Journalize the adjusting entries on August 31 for the 3-month period June 1–August 31.
**(b)** Prepare a ledger using the three-column form of account. Enter the trial balance amounts and post the adjusting entries. (Use J1 as the posting reference.)
**(c)** Prepare an adjusted trial balance on August 31.
**(d)** Prepare an income statement and an owner's equity statement for the 3 months ending August 31 and a balance sheet as of August 31.

**P3-3B** Delgado Advertising Agency was founded by Maria Delgado in January of 2013. Presented below are both the adjusted and unadjusted trial balances as of December 31, 2014.

**DELGADO ADVERTISING AGENCY**
Trial Balance
December 31, 2014

|  | Unadjusted | | Adjusted | |
| --- | --- | --- | --- | --- |
|  | Dr. | Cr. | Dr. | Cr. |
| Cash | $ 11,000 |  | $ 11,000 |  |
| Accounts Receivable | 20,000 |  | 21,500 |  |
| Supplies | 8,600 |  | 4,800 |  |
| Prepaid Insurance | 3,350 |  | 2,500 |  |
| Equipment | 60,000 |  | 60,000 |  |
| Accumulated Depreciation—Equipment |  | $ 28,000 |  | $ 34,000 |
| Accounts Payable |  | 5,000 |  | 5,000 |
| Interest Payable |  | –0– |  | 150 |
| Notes Payable |  | 5,000 |  | 5,000 |
| Unearned Service Revenue |  | 7,200 |  | 5,900 |
| Salaries and Wages Payable |  | –0– |  | 2,100 |
| Owner's Capital |  | 25,500 |  | 25,500 |
| Owner's Drawings | 12,000 |  | 12,000 |  |
| Service Revenue |  | 58,600 |  | 61,400 |
| Salaries and Wages Expense | 10,000 |  | 12,100 |  |
| Insurance Expense |  |  | 850 |  |
| Interest Expense | 350 |  | 500 |  |
| Depreciation Expense |  |  | 6,000 |  |
| Supplies Expense |  |  | 3,800 |  |
| Rent Expense | 4,000 |  | 4,000 |  |
|  | $129,300 | $129,300 | $139,050 | $139,050 |

*Instructions*

(b) Net income $34,150
Ending capital $47,650
Total assets $65,800

(c) (1) 6%
(2) $2,500

**(a)** Journalize the annual adjusting entries that were made.
**(b)** Prepare an income statement and an owner's equity statement for the year ending December 31, 2014, and a balance sheet at December 31.
**(c)** Answer the following questions.
  **(1)** If the note has been outstanding 6 months, what is the annual interest rate on that note?
  **(2)** If the company paid $12,500 in salaries in 2014, what was the balance in Salaries and Wages Payable on December 31, 2013?

*Preparing adjusting entries.*

(LO 4, 5)

1. Salaries and wages
expense $2,640

**P3-4B** A review of the ledger of Almquist Company at December 31, 2014, produces the following data pertaining to the preparation of annual adjusting entries.

1. Salaries and Wages Payable $0. There are eight salaried employees. Salaries are paid every Friday for the current week. Five employees receive a salary of $900 each

per week, and three employees earn $700 each per week. Assume December 31 is a Tuesday. Employees do not work weekends. All employees worked the last 2 days of December.

2. Unearned Rent Revenue $354,000. The company began subleasing office space in its new building on November 1. At December 31, the company had the following rental contracts that are paid in full for the entire term of the lease.

*2. Rent revenue $84,000*

| Date | Term (in months) | Monthly Rent | Number of Leases |
|---|---|---|---|
| Nov. 1 | 6 | $5,000 | 5 |
| Dec. 1 | 6 | $8,500 | 4 |

3. Prepaid Advertising $15,600. This balance consists of payments on two advertising contracts. The contracts provide for monthly advertising in two trade magazines. The terms of the contracts are as follows.

*3. Advertising expense $5,200*

| Contract | Date | Amount | Number of Magazine Issues |
|---|---|---|---|
| A650 | May 1 | $6,000 | 12 |
| B974 | Oct. 1 | 9,600 | 24 |

The first advertisement runs in the month in which the contract is signed.

4. Notes Payable $120,000. This balance consists of a note for one year at an annual interest rate of 9%, dated June 1.

*4. Interest expense $6,300*

**Instructions**
Prepare the adjusting entries at December 31, 2014. (Show all computations.)

**P3-5B** On September 1, 2014, the account balances of Percy Equipment Repair were as follows.

*Journalize transactions and follow through accounting cycle to preparation of financial statements.*

*(LO 4, 5, 6)*

| No. | | Debit | No. | | Credit |
|---|---|---|---|---|---|
| 101 | Cash | $ 4,880 | 154 | Accumulated Depreciation—Equipment | $ 1,500 |
| 112 | Accounts Receivable | 3,520 | 201 | Accounts Payable | 3,400 |
| 126 | Supplies | 2,000 | 209 | Unearned Service Revenue | 1,400 |
| 153 | Equipment | 15,000 | 212 | Salaries and Wages Payable | 500 |
| | | | 301 | Owner's Capital | 18,600 |
| | | $25,400 | | | $25,400 |

During September, the following summary transactions were completed.

Sept. 8    Paid $1,400 for salaries due employees, of which $900 is for September.
    10    Received $1,200 cash from customers on account.
    12    Received $3,400 cash for services performed in September.
    15    Purchased store equipment on account $3,000.
    17    Purchased supplies on account $1,200.
    20    Paid creditors $4,500 on account.
    22    Paid September rent $500.
    25    Paid salaries $1,250.
    27    Performed services on account and billed customers $2,100 for these services.
    29    Received $650 from customers for future service.

Adjustment data consist of:

1. Supplies on hand $1,300.
2. Accrued salaries payable $300.
3. Depreciation is $100 per month.
4. Services related to unearned service revenue of $1,450 were performed.

**Instructions**

**(a)** Enter the September 1 balances in the ledger accounts.

**(b)** Journalize the September transactions.

**(c)** Post to the ledger accounts. Use J1 for the posting reference. Use the following additional accounts: No. 407 Service Revenue, No. 615 Depreciation Expense, No. 631 Supplies Expense, No. 726 Salaries and Wages Expense, and No. 729 Rent Expense.

(d) Trial balance $30,750

**(d)** Prepare a trial balance at September 30.

(f) Adj. trial balance $31,150

**(e)** Journalize and post adjusting entries.

(g) Net income $2,000
Ending capital $20,600
Total assets $24,600

**(f)** Prepare an adjusted trial balance.

**(g)** Prepare an income statement and an owner's equity statement for September and a balance sheet at September 30.

## PROBLEMS: SET C

Visit the book's companion website, at **www.wiley.com/college/weygandt**, and choose the Student Companion site to access Problem Set C.

## CONTINUING COOKIE CHRONICLE

(*Note:* This is a continuation of the Cookie Chronicle from Chapters 1 and 2. Use the information from the previous chapters and follow the instructions below using the general ledger accounts you have already prepared.)

**CCC3** It is the end of November and Natalie has been in touch with her grandmother. Her grandmother asked Natalie how well things went in her first month of business. Natalie, too, would like to know if she has been profitable or not during November. Natalie realizes that in order to determine Cookie Creations' income, she must first make adjustments.

Natalie puts together the following additional information.

1. A count reveals that $35 of baking supplies were used during November.
2. Natalie estimates that all of her baking equipment will have a useful life of 5 years or 60 months. (Assume Natalie decides to record a full month's worth of depreciation, regardless of when the equipment was obtained by the business.)
3. Natalie's grandmother has decided to charge interest of 6% on the note payable extended on November 16. The loan plus interest is to be repaid in 24 months. (Assume that half a month of interest accrued during November.)
4. On November 30, a friend of Natalie's asks her to teach a class at the neighborhood school. Natalie agrees and teaches a group of 35 first-grade students how to make gingerbread cookies. The next day, Natalie prepares an invoice for $300 and leaves it with the school principal. The principal says that he will pass the invoice along to the head office, and it will be paid sometime in December.
5. Natalie receives a utilities bill for $45. The bill is for utilities consumed by Natalie's business during November and is due December 15.

**Instructions**

Using the information that you have gathered through Chapter 2, and based on the new information above, do the following.

**(a)** Prepare and post the adjusting journal entries.

**(b)** Prepare an adjusted trial balance.

**(c)** Using the adjusted trial balance, calculate Cookie Creations' net income or net loss for the month of November. Do not prepare an income statement.

# Broadening Your Perspective

## Financial Reporting and Analysis

### Financial Reporting Problem: Apple Inc.

**BYP3-1** The financial statements of Apple Inc. are presented in Appendix A at the end of this textbook. Instructions for accessing and using the company's complete annual report, including the notes to the financial statements, are also provided in Appendix A.

*Instructions*
**(a)** Using the consolidated financial statements and related information, identify items that may result in adjusting entries for prepayments.
**(b)** Using the consolidated financial statements and related information, identify items that may result in adjusting entries for accruals.
**(c)** What has been the trend since 2009 for net income?

### Comparative Analysis Problem:
### PepsiCo, Inc. vs. The Coca-Cola Company

**BYP3-2** PepsiCo's financial statements are presented in Appendix B. Financial statements for The Coca-Cola Company are presented in Appendix C. Instructions for accessing and using the complete annual reports of PepsiCo and Coca-Cola, including the notes to the financial statements, are also provided in Appendices B and C, respectively.

*Instructions*
Based on information contained in these financial statements, determine the following for each company.

**(a)** Net increase (decrease) in property, plant, and equipment (net) from 2010 to 2011.
**(b)** Increase (decrease) in selling, general, and administrative expenses from 2010 to 2011.
**(c)** Increase (decrease) in long-term debt (obligations) from 2010 to 2011.
**(d)** Increase (decrease) in net income from 2010 to 2011.
**(e)** Increase (decrease) in cash and cash equivalents from 2010 to 2011.

### Comparative Analysis Problem:
### Amazon.com, Inc. vs. Wal-Mart Stores, Inc.

**BYP3-3** Amazon.com, Inc.'s financial statements are presented in Appendix D. Financial statements for Wal-Mart Stores, Inc. are presented in Appendix E. Instructions for accessing and using the complete annual reports of Amazon and Wal-Mart, including the notes to the financial statements, are also provided in Appendices D and E, respectively.

*Instructions*
Based on information contained in these financial statements, determine the following for each company.

**1. (a)** Increase (decrease) in interest expense from 2010 to 2011.
   **(b)** Increase (decrease) in net income from 2010 to 2011.
   **(c)** Increase (decrease) in cash flow from operations from 2010 to 2011.
**2.** Cash flow from operations and net income for each company is different. What are some possible reasons for these differences?

## Real-World Focus

**BYP3-4** No financial decision-maker should ever rely solely on the financial information reported in the annual report to make decisions. It is important to keep abreast of financial news. This activity demonstrates how to search for financial news on the Internet.

*Address:* **http://biz.yahoo.com/i**, or go to **www.wiley.com/college/weygandt**

*Steps:*
1. Type in either Wal-Mart, Target Corp., or Kmart.
2. Choose **News**.
3. Select an article that sounds interesting to you and that would be relevant to an investor in these companies.

*Instructions*
**(a)** What was the source of the article (e.g., Reuters, Businesswire, Prnewswire)?
**(b)** Assume that you are a personal financial planner and that one of your clients owns stock in the company. Write a brief memo to your client summarizing the article and explaining the implications of the article for their investment.

**BYP3-5** The July 6, 2011, edition of the *Wall Street Journal Online* includes an article by Michael Rapoport entitled "U.S. Firms Clash Over Accounting Rules." The article discusses why some U.S. companies favored adoption of International Financial Reporting Standards (IFRS) while other companies opposed it.

*Instructions*
Read the article and answer the following questions.

**(a)** The articles says that the switch to IFRS tends to be favored by "larger companies, big accounting firms, and rule makers." What reasons are given for favoring the switch?
**(b)** What two reasons are given by many smaller companies that oppose the switch?
**(c)** What criticism of IFRS is raised with regard to regulated companies?
**(d)** Explain what is meant by "condorsement."

# Critical Thinking

 ## Decision-Making Across the Organization

**BYP3-6** Happy Camper Park was organized on April 1, 2013, by Barbara Evans. Barbara is a good manager but a poor accountant. From the trial balance prepared by a part-time bookkeeper, Barbara prepared the following income statement for the quarter that ended March 31, 2014.

**HAPPY CAMPER PARK**
Income Statement
For the Quarter Ended March 31, 2014

| | | |
|---|---:|---:|
| Revenues | | |
| Rent revenue | | $90,000 |
| Operating expenses | | |
| Advertising | $ 5,200 | |
| Salaries and wages | 29,800 | |
| Utilities | 900 | |
| Depreciation | 800 | |
| Maintenance and repairs | 4,000 | |
| Total operating expenses | | 40,700 |
| Net income | | $49,300 |

Barbara thought that something was wrong with the statement because net income had never exceeded $20,000 in any one quarter. Knowing that you are an experienced accountant, she asks you to review the income statement and other data.

You first look at the trial balance. In addition to the account balances reported above in the income statement, the ledger contains the following additional selected balances at March 31, 2014.

| | |
|---|---:|
| Supplies | $ 6,200 |
| Prepaid Insurance | 7,200 |
| Notes Payable | 12,000 |

You then make inquiries and discover the following.

1. Rent revenues include advanced rentals for summer occupancy $15,000.
2. There were $1,700 of supplies on hand at March 31.
3. Prepaid insurance resulted from the payment of a one-year policy on January 1, 2014.
4. The mail on April 1, 2014, brought the following bills: advertising for week of March 24, $110; repairs made March 10, $260; and utilities, $180.
5. There are four employees, who receive wages totaling $300 per day. At March 31, 2 days' salaries and wages have been incurred but not paid.
6. The note payable is a 3-month, 10% note dated January 1, 2014.

*Instructions*
With the class divided into groups, answer the following.

**(a)** Prepare a correct income statement for the quarter ended March 31, 2014.
**(b)** Explain to Barbara the generally accepted accounting principles that she did not recognize in preparing her income statement and their effect on her results.

## Communication Activity

**BYP3-7** In reviewing the accounts of Gloria Jean Co. at the end of the year, you discover that adjusting entries have not been made.

*Instructions*
Write a memo to Gloria Jean Hall, the owner of Gloria Jean Co., that explains the following: the nature and purpose of adjusting entries, why adjusting entries are needed, and the types of adjusting entries that may be made.

## Ethics Case

**BYP3-8** Kellner Company is a pesticide manufacturer. Its sales declined greatly this year due to the passage of legislation outlawing the sale of several of Kellner's chemical pesticides. In the coming year, Kellner will have environmentally safe and competitive chemicals to replace these discontinued products. Sales in the next year are expected to greatly exceed any prior year's. The decline in sales and profits appears to be a one-year aberration. But even so, the company president fears a large dip in the current year's profits. He believes that such a dip could cause a significant drop in the market price of Kellner's stock and make the company a takeover target.

To avoid this possibility, the company president calls in Melissa Ray, controller, to discuss this period's year-end adjusting entries. He urges her to accrue every possible revenue and to defer as many expenses as possible. He says to Melissa, "We need the revenues this year, and next year can easily absorb expenses deferred from this year. We can't let our stock price be hammered down!" Melissa didn't get around to recording the adjusting entries until January 17, but she dated the entries December 31 as if they were recorded then. Melissa also made every effort to comply with the president's request.

*Instructions*
**(a)** Who are the stakeholders in this situation?
**(b)** What are the ethical considerations of (1) the president's request and (2) Melissa dating the adjusting entries December 31?
**(c)** Can Melissa accrue revenues and defer expenses and still be ethical?

## All About You

**BYP3-9** Companies must report or disclose in their financial statement information about all liabilities, including potential liabilities related to environmental cleanup. There are many situations in which you will be asked to provide personal financial information about your assets, liabilities, revenue, and expenses. Sometimes you will face difficult decisions regarding what to disclose and how to disclose it.

*Instructions*
Suppose that you are putting together a loan application to purchase a home. Based on your income and assets, you qualify for the mortgage loan, but just barely. How would you address each

of the following situations in reporting your financial position for the loan application? Provide responses for each of the following situations.

**(a)** You signed a guarantee for a bank loan that a friend took out for $20,000. If your friend doesn't pay, you will have to pay. Your friend has made all of the payments so far, and it appears he will be able to pay in the future.

**(b)** You were involved in an auto accident in which you were at fault. There is the possibility that you may have to pay as much as $50,000 as part of a settlement. The issue will not be resolved before the bank processes your mortgage request.

**(c)** The company for which you work isn't doing very well, and it has recently laid off employees. You are still employed, but it is quite possible that you will lose your job in the next few months.

## Considering People, Planet, and Profit

**BYP3-10** Many companies have potential pollution or environmental-disposal problems—not only for electronic gadgets, but also for the lead paint or asbestos they sold. How do we fit these issues into the accounting equation? Are these costs and related liabilities that companies should report?

**YES:** As more states impose laws holding companies responsible, and as more courts levy pollution-related fines, it becomes increasingly likely that companies will have to pay large amounts in the future.

**NO:** The amounts still are too difficult to estimate. Putting inaccurate estimates on the financial statements reduces their usefulness. Instead, why not charge the costs later, when the actual environmental cleanup or disposal occurs, at which time the company knows the actual cost?

*Instructions*
Write a response indicating your position regarding this situation. Provide support for your view.

## FASB Codification Activity

**BYP3-11** If your school has a subscription to the FASB Codification, go to **http://aaahq.org/asclogin.cfm** to log in and prepare responses to the following.

*Instructions*
Access the glossary ("Master Glossary") to answer the following.

**(a)** What is the definition of revenue?
**(b)** What is the definition of compensation?

## Answers to Chapter Questions

### Answers to Insight and Accounting Across the Organization Questions

**p. 102 Cooking the Books?    Q:** What motivates sales executives and finance and accounting executives to participate in activities that result in inaccurate reporting of revenues? **A:** Sales executives typically receive bonuses based on their ability to meet quarterly sales targets. In addition, they often face the possibility of losing their jobs if they miss those targets. Executives in accounting and finance are very aware of the earnings targets of Wall Street analysts and investors. If they fail to meet these targets, the company's stock price will fall. As a result of these pressures, executives sometimes knowingly engage in unethical efforts to misstate revenues. As a result of the Sarbanes-Oxley Act, the penalties for such behavior are now much more severe.

**p. 109 Turning Gift Cards into Revenue    Q:** Suppose that Robert Jones purchases a $100 gift card at Best Buy on December 24, 2013, and gives it to his wife, Mary Jones, on December 25, 2013. On January 3, 2014, Mary uses the card to purchase $100 worth of CDs. When do you think Best Buy should recognize revenue and why? **A:** According to the revenue recognition principle, companies should recognize revenue when the performance obligation is satisfied. In this case, revenue results when Best Buy provides the goods. Thus, when Best Buy receives cash in exchange for the gift card on December 24, 2013, it should recognize a liability, Unearned Sales Revenue, for $100. On January 3, 2014, when Mary Jones exchanges the card for merchandise, Best Buy should recognize revenue and eliminate $100 from the balance in the Unearned Sales Revenue account.

**p. 114 Cashing In on Accrual Accounting   Q:** Accrual accounting is often considered superior to cash accounting. Why, then, were some people critical of China's use of accrual accounting in this instance? **A:** In this case, some people were critical because, in general, China uses cash accounting. By switching to accrual accounting for this transaction, China was not being consistent in its accounting practices. Lack of consistency reduces the transparency and usefulness of accounting information.

**p. 116 Got Junk?   Q:** What accounting issue might this cause for companies? **A:** The balance sheet should provide a fair representation of what a company owns and what it owes. If significant obligations of the company are not reported on the balance sheet, the company's net worth (its equity) will be overstated. While it is true that it is not possible to estimate the **exact** amount of future environmental cleanup costs, it is becoming clear that companies will be held accountable. Therefore, it seems reasonable to accrue for environmental costs. Recognition of these liabilities provides a more accurate picture of the company's financial position. It also has the potential to improve the environment. As companies are forced to report these amounts on their financial statements, they will start to look for more effective and efficient means to reduce toxic waste and therefore reduce their costs.

## Answers to Self-Test Questions

**1.** a  **2.** c  **3.** d  **4.** a  **5.** d  **6.** d  **7.** c  ($1,350 − $600)  **8.** c  **9.** a  **10.** c  **11.** a  **12.** b  **13.** b  **14.** c  *15. a  *16. c  *17. c

# A Look at IFRS

It is often difficult for companies to determine in what time period they should report particular revenues and expenses. Both the IASB and FASB are working on a joint project to develop a common conceptual framework that will enable companies to better use the same principles to record transactions consistently over time.

---

**LEARNING OBJECTIVE    9**

Compare the procedures for adjusting entries under GAAP and IFRS.

---

## Key Points

- In this chapter, you learned accrual-basis accounting applied under GAAP. Companies applying IFRS also use accrual-basis accounting to ensure that they record transactions that change a company's financial statements in the period in which events occur.

- Similar to GAAP, cash-basis accounting is not in accordance with IFRS.

- IFRS also divides the economic life of companies into artificial time periods. Under both GAAP and IFRS, this is referred to as the **time period assumption**.

- IFRS requires that companies present a complete set of financial statements, including comparative information, annually.

- The **general** revenue recognition principle required by GAAP that is used in this textbook is similar to that used under IFRS.

- Revenue recognition fraud is a major issue in U.S. financial reporting. The same situation occurs in other countries, as evidenced by revenue recognition breakdowns at Dutch software company Baan NV, Japanese electronics giant NEC, and Dutch grocer Ahold NV.

- Under IFRS, revaluation (using fair value) of items such as land and buildings is permitted. IFRS allows depreciation based on revaluation of assets, which is not permitted under GAAP.

- The terminology used for revenues and gains, and expenses and losses, differs somewhat between IFRS and GAAP. For example, income under IFRS is defined as:

  Increases in economic benefits during the accounting period in the form of inflows or enhancements of assets or decreases of liabilities that result in increases in equity, other than those relating to contributions from shareholders.

  Income includes both revenues, which arise during the normal course of operating activities, and gains, which arise from activities outside of the normal sales of goods and services. The term income is not used this way under GAAP. Instead, under GAAP income refers to the net difference between revenues and expenses. Expenses under IFRS are defined as:

> Decreases in economic benefits during the accounting period in the form of outflows or depletions of assets or incurrences of liabilities that result in decreases in equity other than those relating to distributions to shareholders.

Note that under IFRS, expenses include both those costs incurred in the normal course of operations as well as losses that are not part of normal operations. This is in contrast to GAAP, which defines each separately.

## Looking to the Future

The IASB and FASB are completing a joint project on revenue recognition. The purpose of this project is to develop comprehensive guidance on when to recognize revenue. It is hoped that this approach will lead to more consistent accounting in this area. For more on this topic, see **www.fasb.org/project/revenue_recognition.shtml**.

## IFRS Practice

### IFRS Self-Test Questions

1. IFRS:
   (a) uses accrual accounting.
   (b) uses cash-basis accounting.
   (c) allows revenue to be recognized when a customer makes an order.
   (d) requires that revenue not be recognized until cash is received.

2. Which of the following statements is **false**?
   (a) IFRS employs the time period assumption.
   (b) IFRS employs accrual accounting.
   (c) IFRS requires that revenues and costs must be capable of being measured reliably.
   (d) IFRS uses the cash basis of accounting.

3. As a result of the revenue recognition project by the FASB and IASB:
   (a) revenue recognition places more emphasis on when the performance obligation is satisfied.
   (b) revenue recognition places more emphasis on when revenue is realized.
   (c) revenue recognition places more emphasis on when expenses are incurred.
   (d) revenue is no longer recorded unless cash has been received.

4. Which of the following is **false**?
   (a) Under IFRS, the term income describes both revenues and gains.
   (b) Under IFRS, the term expenses includes losses.
   (c) Under IFRS, companies do not engage in the adjusting process.
   (d) Under IFRS, revenue recognition fraud is a major issue.

5. Accrual-basis accounting:
   (a) is optional under IFRS.
   (b) results in companies recording transactions that change a company's financial statements in the period in which events occur.
   (c) has been eliminated as a result of the IASB/FASB joint project on revenue recognition.
   (d) is not consistent with the IASB conceptual framework.

### IFRS Exercises

**IFRS3-1** Compare and contrast the rules regarding revenue recognition under IFRS versus GAAP.

**IFRS3-2** Under IFRS, do the definitions of revenues and expenses include gains and losses? Explain.

## International Financial Reporting Problem: Zetar plc

**IFRS3-3** The financial statements of Zetar plc are presented in Appendix F. Instructions for accessing and using the company's complete annual report, including the notes to its financial statements, are also provided in Appendix F.

### Instructions

Visit Zetar's corporate website and answer the following questions from Zetar's 2011 annual report.

**(a)** From the notes to the financial statements, how does the company determine the amount of revenue to record at the time of a sale?

**(b)** From the notes to the financial statements, how does the company determine whether a sale has occurred?

**(c)** Using the consolidated income statement and consolidated statement of financial position, identify items that may result in adjusting entries for deferrals.

**(d)** Using the consolidated income statement, identify two items that may result in adjusting entries for accruals.

### Answers to IFRS Self-Test Questions

**1.** a  **2.** d  **3.** a  **4.** c  **5.** b

✔ The Navigator

# 4 | Completing the Accounting Cycle

## Feature Story

### Everyone Likes to Win

When Ted Castle was a hockey coach at the University of Vermont, his players were self-motivated by their desire to win. Hockey was a game you usually either won or lost. But at Rhino Foods, Inc., a bakery-foods company he founded in Burlington, Vermont, he discovered that manufacturing-line workers were not so self-motivated. Ted thought, what if he turned the food-making business into a game, with rules, strategies, and trophies?

In a game, knowing the score is all-important. Ted felt that only if the employees know the score—know exactly how the business is doing daily, weekly, monthly—could he turn food-making into a game. But Rhino is a closely held, family-owned business, and its financial statements and profits were confidential. Ted wondered, should he open Rhino's books to the employees?

A consultant put Ted's concerns in perspective when he said, "Imagine you're playing touch football. You play for an hour or two, and the whole time I'm sitting there with a book,

keeping score. All of a sudden I blow the whistle, and I s 'OK, that's it. Everybody go home.' I close my book and ' away. How would you feel?" Ted opened his books and revealed the financial statements to his employees.

The next step was to teach employees the rules and stra of how to "win" at making food. The first lesson: "Your opponent at Rhino is expenses. You must cut and contro expenses." Ted and his staff distilled those lessons into d scorecards—production reports and income statements– keep Rhino's employees up-to-date on the game. At noc each day, Ted posts the previous day's results at the entra to the production room. Everyone checks whether they r or lost money on what they produced the day before. Ar not just an academic exercise: There's a bonus check for employee at the end of every four-week "game" that m profitability guidelines.

Rhino has flourished since the first game. Employment h increased from 20 to 130 people, while both revenues ar profits have grown dramatically.

✔ **The Navigator**

- Scan Learning Objectives
- Read Feature Story
- Read Preview
- Read text and answer **DO IT!** p. 167
  - p. 172   ■ p. 181   ■ p. 183
- Work Comprehensive **DO IT!** p. 184
- Review Summary of Learning Objectives
- Answer Self-Test Questions
- Complete Assignments
- Go to *WileyPLUS* for practice and tutorials

 **Read A Look at IFRS** p. 212

## Learning Objectives   ✔ The Navigator

*After studying this chapter, you should be able to:*

[1] Prepare a worksheet.

[2] Explain the process of closing the books.

[3] Describe the content and purpose of a post-closing trial balance.

[4] State the required steps in the accounting cycle.

[5] Explain the approaches to preparing correcting entries.

[6] Identify the sections of a classified balance sheet.

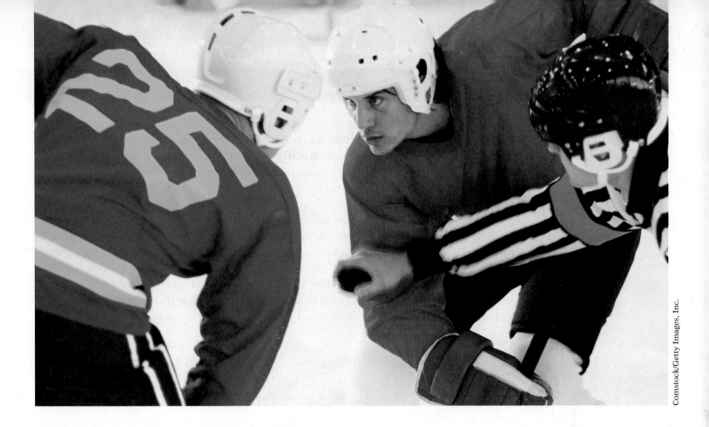

# Preview of Chapter 4

✔ The Navigator

At Rhino Foods, Inc., financial statements help employees understand what is happening in the business. In Chapter 3, we prepared financial statements directly from the adjusted trial balance. However, with so many details involved in the end-of-period accounting procedures, it is easy to make errors. One way to minimize errors in the records and to simplify the end-of-period procedures is to use a worksheet.

In this chapter, we will explain the role of the worksheet in accounting. We also will study the remaining steps in the accounting cycle, especially the closing process, again using Pioneer Advertising Agency as an example. Then we will consider correcting entries and classified balance sheets. The content and organization of Chapter 4 are as follows.

## COMPLETING THE ACCOUNTING CYCLE

| Using a Worksheet | Closing the Books | Summary of the Accounting Cycle | Classified Balance Sheet |
|---|---|---|---|
| • Steps in preparation<br>• Preparing financial statements<br>• Preparing adjusting entries | • Preparing closing entries<br>• Posting closing entries<br>• Preparing a post-closing trial balance | • Reversing entries—An optional step<br>• Correcting entries—An avoidable step | • Current assets<br>• Long-term investments<br>• Property, plant, and equipment<br>• Intangible assets<br>• Current liabilities<br>• Long-term liabilities<br>• Owner's equity |

## Using a Worksheet

A **worksheet** is a multiple-column form used in the adjustment process and in preparing financial statements. As its name suggests, the worksheet is a working tool. **It is not a permanent accounting record.** It is neither a journal nor a part of the general ledger. The worksheet is merely a device used in preparing adjusting entries and the financial statements. Companies generally computerize worksheets using an electronic spreadsheet program such as Excel.

Illustration 4-1 shows the basic form of a worksheet and the five steps for preparing it. Each step is performed in sequence. **The use of a worksheet is optional.** When a company chooses to use one, it prepares financial statements directly from the worksheet. It enters the adjustments in the worksheet columns and then journalizes and posts the adjustments after it has prepared the financial statements. Thus, worksheets make it possible to provide the financial statements to management and other interested parties at an earlier date.

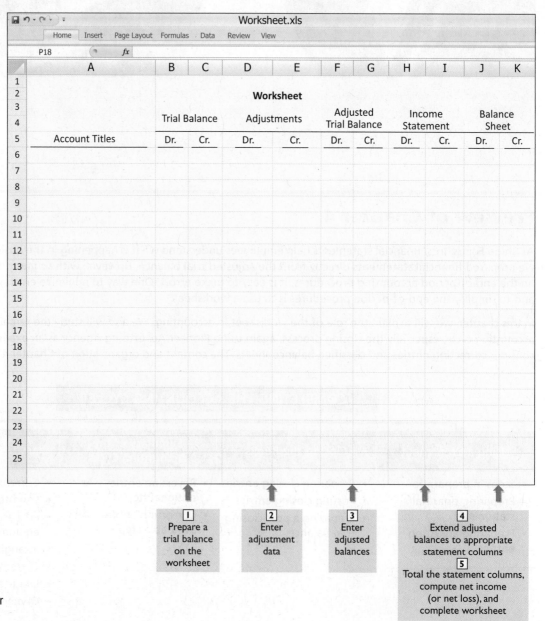

**Illustration 4-1**
Form and procedure for a worksheet

## Steps in Preparing a Worksheet

We will use the October 31 trial balance and adjustment data of Pioneer Advertising Agency from Chapter 3 to illustrate how to prepare a worksheet. We describe each step of the process and demonstrate these steps in Illustration 4-2 (page 164) and transparencies 4-3A, B, C, and D.

### STEP 1. PREPARE A TRIAL BALANCE ON THE WORKSHEET

Enter all ledger accounts with balances in the account titles column. Enter debit and credit amounts from the ledger in the trial balance columns. Illustration 4-2 shows the worksheet trial balance for Pioneer Advertising Agency. This trial balance is the same one that appears in Illustration 2-31 (page 73) and Illustration 3-3 (page 103).

### STEP 2. ENTER THE ADJUSTMENTS IN THE ADJUSTMENTS COLUMNS

**Turn over the first transparency, Illustration 4-3A.** When using a worksheet, enter all adjustments in the adjustments columns. In entering the adjustments, use applicable trial balance accounts. If additional accounts are needed, insert them on the lines immediately below the trial balance totals. A different letter identifies the debit and credit for each adjusting entry. The term used to describe this process is **keying. Companies do not journalize the adjustments until after they complete the worksheet and prepare the financial statements.**

The adjustments for Pioneer Advertising Agency are the same as the adjustments in Illustration 3-23 (page 117). They are keyed in the adjustments columns of the worksheet as follows.

**(a)** Pioneer debits an additional account, Supplies Expense, $1,500 for the cost of supplies used, and credits Supplies $1,500.

**(b)** Pioneer debits an additional account, Insurance Expense, $50 for the insurance that has expired, and credits Prepaid Insurance $50.

**(c)** The company needs two additional depreciation accounts. It debits Depreciation Expense $40 for the month's depreciation, and credits Accumulated Depreciation—Equipment $40.

**(d)** Pioneer debits Unearned Service Revenue $400 for services performed, and credits Service Revenue $400.

**(e)** Pioneer debits an additional account, Accounts Receivable, $200 for services performed but not billed, and credits Service Revenue $200.

**(f)** The company needs two additional accounts relating to interest. It debits Interest Expense $50 for accrued interest, and credits Interest Payable $50.

**(g)** Pioneer debits Salaries and Wages Expense $1,200 for accrued salaries, and credits an additional account, Salaries and Wages Payable, $1,200.

After Pioneer has entered all the adjustments, the adjustments columns are totaled to prove their equality.

### STEP 3. ENTER ADJUSTED BALANCES IN THE ADJUSTED TRIAL BALANCE COLUMNS

**Turn over the second transparency, Illustration 4-3B.** Pioneer determines the adjusted balance of an account by combining the amounts entered in the first four columns of the worksheet for each account. For example, the Prepaid Insurance account in the trial balance columns has a $600 debit balance and a $50 credit in the adjustments columns. The result is a $550 debit balance recorded in the adjusted trial balance columns. **For each account, the amount in the adjusted**

(**Note:** Text continues on page 165, following acetate overlays.)

**Illustration 4-2**
Preparing a trial balance

| | Pioneer Advertising.xls | | | | | | | | | |
|---|---|---|---|---|---|---|---|---|---|---|

Home   Insert   Page Layout   Formulas   Data   Review   View

P18   fx

| | A | B | C | D | E | F | G | H | I | J | K |
|---|---|---|---|---|---|---|---|---|---|---|---|
| 1 | | | | | | | | | | | |
| 2 | | | **PIONEER ADVERTISING AGENCY** | | | | | | | | |
| 3 | | | **Worksheet** | | | | | | | | |
| 4 | | | **For the Month Ended October 31, 2014** | | | | | | | | |
| 5 | | Trial Balance | | Adjustments | | Adjusted Trial Balance | | Income Statement | | Balance Sheet | |
| 6 | | | | | | | | | | | |
| 7 | Account Titles | Dr. | Cr. | Dr. | Cr. | Dr. | Cr. | Dr. | Cr. | Dr. | Cr. |
| 8 | Cash | 15,200 | | | | | | | | | |
| 9 | Supplies | 2,500 | | | | | | | | | |
| 10 | Prepaid Insurance | 600 | | | | | | | | | |
| 11 | Equipment | 5,000 | | | | | | | | | |
| 12 | Notes Payable | | 5,000 | | | | | | | | |
| 13 | Accounts Payable | | 2,500 | | | | | | | | |
| 14 | Unearned Service Revenue | | 1,200 | | | | | | | | |
| 15 | Owner's Capital | | 10,000 | | | | | | | | |
| 16 | Owner's Drawings | 500 | | | | | | | | | |
| 17 | Service Revenue | | 10,000 | | | | | | | | |
| 18 | | | | | | | | | | | |
| 19 | Salaries and Wages Expense | 4,000 | | | | | | | | | |
| 20 | Rent Expense | 900 | | | | | | | | | |
| 21 | Totals | 28,700 | 28,700 | | | | | | | | |
| 22 | | | | | | | | | | | |
| 23 | | | | | | | | | | | |
| 24 | | | | | | | | | | | |
| 25 | | | | | | | | | | | |
| 26 | | | | | | | | | | | |
| 27 | | | | | | | | | | | |
| 28 | | | | | | | | | | | |
| 29 | | | | | | | | | | | |
| 30 | | | | | | | | | | | |
| 31 | | | | | | | | | | | |
| 32 | | | | | | | | | | | |
| 33 | | | | | | | | | | | |
| 34 | | | | | | | | | | | |
| 35 | | | | | | | | | | | |
| 36 | | | | | | | | | | | |

**Include all accounts with balances from ledger.**

**Trial balance amounts come directly from ledger accounts.**

Using a Worksheet    **165**

**Alternative Terminology**
Temporary accounts are sometimes called *nominal accounts*, and permanent accounts are sometimes called *real accounts*.

In contrast, **permanent accounts** relate to one or more future accounting periods. They consist of all balance sheet accounts, including the owner's capital account. **Permanent accounts are not closed from period to period.** Instead, the company carries forward the balances of permanent accounts into the next accounting period. Illustration 4-5 identifies the accounts in each category.

**Illustration 4-5**
Temporary versus permanent accounts

| TEMPORARY | PERMANENT |
| These accounts are closed | These accounts are not closed |

All revenue accounts

All expense accounts

Owner's drawings account

All asset accounts

All liability accounts

Owner's capital account

## Preparing Closing Entries

At the end of the accounting period, the company transfers temporary account balances to the permanent owner's equity account, Owner's Capital, by means of closing entries.[1]

**Closing entries** formally recognize in the ledger the transfer of net income (or net loss) and owner's drawings to owner's capital. The owner's equity statement shows the results of these entries. **Closing entries also produce a zero balance in each temporary account.** The temporary accounts are then ready to accumulate data in the next accounting period separate from the data of prior periods. Permanent accounts are not closed.

**Journalizing and posting closing entries is a required step in the accounting cycle.** (See Illustration 4-12 on page 175.) The company performs this step after it has prepared financial statements. In contrast to the steps in the cycle that you have already studied, companies generally journalize and post closing entries **only at the end of the annual accounting period**. Thus, all temporary accounts will contain data for the entire year.

In preparing closing entries, companies could close each income statement account directly to owner's capital. However, to do so would result in excessive detail in the permanent Owner's Capital account. Instead, companies close the revenue and expense accounts to another temporary account, **Income Summary**, and they transfer the resulting net income or net loss from this account to owner's capital.

Companies **record closing entries in the general journal**. A center caption, Closing Entries, inserted in the journal between the last adjusting entry and the first closing entry, identifies these entries. Then the company posts the closing entries to the ledger accounts.

Companies generally prepare closing entries directly from the adjusted balances in the ledger. They could prepare separate closing entries for each nominal account, but the following four entries accomplish the desired result more efficiently:

1. Debit each revenue account for its balance, and credit Income Summary for total revenues.

2. Debit Income Summary for total expenses, and credit each expense account for its balance.

[1]We explain closing entries for a partnership and for a corporation in Chapters 12 and 13, respectively.

trial balance columns is the balance that will appear in the ledger after journalizing and posting the adjusting entries. The balances in these columns are the same as those in the adjusted trial balance in Illustration 3-25 (page 119).

After Pioneer has entered all account balances in the adjusted trial balance columns, the columns are totaled to prove their equality. If the column totals do not agree, the financial statement columns will not balance and the financial statements will be incorrect.

### STEP 4. EXTEND ADJUSTED TRIAL BALANCE AMOUNTS TO APPROPRIATE FINANCIAL STATEMENT COLUMNS

**Turn over the third transparency, Illustration 4-3C.** The fourth step is to extend adjusted trial balance amounts to the income statement and balance sheet columns of the worksheet. Pioneer enters balance sheet accounts in the appropriate balance sheet debit and credit columns. For instance, it enters Cash in the balance sheet debit column, and Notes Payable in the balance sheet credit column. Pioneer extends Accumulated Depreciation—Equipment to the balance sheet credit column. The reason is that accumulated depreciation is a contra asset account with a credit balance.

**Helpful Hint** Every adjusted trial balance amount must be extended to one of the four statement columns.

Because the worksheet does not have columns for the owner's equity statement, Pioneer extends the balance in owner's capital to the balance sheet credit column. In addition, it extends the balance in owner's drawings to the balance sheet debit column because it is an owner's equity account with a debit balance.

The company enters the expense and revenue accounts such as Salaries and Wages Expense and Service Revenue in the appropriate income statement columns. Illustration 4-3C shows all of these extensions.

### STEP 5. TOTAL THE STATEMENT COLUMNS, COMPUTE THE NET INCOME (OR NET LOSS), AND COMPLETE THE WORKSHEET

**Turn over the fourth transparency, Illustration 4-3D.** The company now must total each of the financial statement columns. The net income or loss for the period is the difference between the totals of the two income statement columns. If total credits exceed total debits, the result is net income. In such a case, as shown in Illustration 4-3D, the company inserts the words "Net Income" in the account titles space. It then enters the amount in the income statement debit column and the balance sheet credit column. **The debit amount balances the income statement columns; the credit amount balances the balance sheet columns.** In addition, the credit in the balance sheet column indicates the increase in owner's equity resulting from net income.

What if total debits in the income statement columns exceed total credits? In that case, the company has a net loss. It enters the amount of the net loss in the income statement credit column and the balance sheet debit column.

After entering the net income or net loss, the company determines new column totals. The totals shown in the debit and credit income statement columns will match. So will the totals shown in the debit and credit balance sheet columns. If either the income statement columns or the balance sheet columns are not equal after the net income or net loss has been entered, there is an error in the worksheet. Illustration 4-3D shows the completed worksheet for Pioneer Advertising Agency.

## Preparing Financial Statements from a Worksheet

After a company has completed a worksheet, it has at hand all the data required for preparation of financial statements. The income statement is prepared from the income statement columns. The balance sheet and owner's equity statement are prepared from the balance sheet columns. Illustration 4-4 (page 166) shows the financial statements prepared from Pioneer's worksheet. At this point, the company

**Illustration 4-4**
Financial statements from a worksheet

### PIONEER ADVERTISING AGENCY
#### Income Statement
#### For the Month Ended October 31, 2014

| | | |
|---|---|---|
| Revenues | | |
| Service revenue | | $10,600 |
| Expenses | | |
| Salaries and wages expense | $5,200 | |
| Supplies expense | 1,500 | |
| Rent expense | 900 | |
| Insurance expense | 50 | |
| Interest expense | 50 | |
| Depreciation expense | 40 | |
| Total expenses | | 7,740 |
| Net income | | $ 2,860 |

### PIONEER ADVERTISING AGENCY
#### Owner's Equity Statement
#### For the Month Ended October 31, 2014

| | | |
|---|---|---|
| Owner's capital, October 1 | | $ –0– |
| Add: Investments | $10,000 | |
| Net income | 2,860 | 12,860 |
| | | 12,860 |
| Less: Drawings | | 500 |
| Owner's capital, October 31 | | $12,360 |

### PIONEER ADVERTISING AGENCY
#### Balance Sheet
#### October 31, 2014

| Assets | | |
|---|---|---|
| Cash | | $15,200 |
| Accounts receivable | | 200 |
| Supplies | | 1,000 |
| Prepaid insurance | | 550 |
| Equipment | $5,000 | |
| Less: Accumulated depreciation—equipment | 40 | 4,960 |
| Total assets | | $21,910 |

| Liabilities and Owner's Equity | | |
|---|---|---|
| Liabilities | | |
| Notes payable | $5,000 | |
| Accounts payable | 2,500 | |
| Interest payable | 50 | |
| Unearned service revenue | 800 | |
| Salaries and wages payable | 1,200 | |
| Total liabilities | | $ 9,550 |
| Owner's equity | | |
| Owner's capital | | 12,360 |
| Total liabilities and owner's equity | | $21,910 |

has not journalized or posted adjusting entries. Therefore, ledger balances for some accounts are not the same as the financial statement amounts.

The amount shown for owner's capital on the worksheet is the account balance **before considering drawings and net income (or loss)**. When the owner has made no additional investments of capital during the period, this worksheet amount for owner's capital is the balance at the beginning of the period.

Using a worksheet, companies can prepare financial statements before they journalize and post adjusting entries. **However, the completed worksheet is not a substitute for formal financial statements.** The format of the data in the financial statement columns of the worksheet is not the same as the format of the financial statements. **A worksheet is essentially a working tool of the accountant**; companies do not distribute it to management and other parties.

### Preparing Adjusting Entries from a Worksheet

**A worksheet is not a journal, and it cannot be used as a basis for posting to ledger accounts.** To adjust the accounts, the company must journalize the adjustments and post them to the ledger. **The adjusting entries are prepared from the adjustments columns of the worksheet.** The reference letters in the adjustments columns and the explanations of the adjustments at the bottom of the worksheet help identify the adjusting entries. The journalizing and posting of adjusting entries **follows** the preparation of financial statements when a worksheet is used. The adjusting entries on October 31 for Pioneer Advertising Agency are the same as those shown in Illustration 3-23 (page 117).

**Helpful Hint** Note that writing the explanation to the adjustment at the bottom of the worksheet is not required.

> **DO IT!**

**Worksheet**

**Action Plan**

✔ Balance sheet: Extend assets to debit column. Extend liabilities to credit column. Extend contra assets to credit column. Extend drawings account to debit column.

✔ Income statement: Extend expenses to debit column. Extend revenues to credit column.

Susan Elbe is preparing a worksheet. Explain to Susan how she should extend the following adjusted trial balance accounts to the financial statement columns of the worksheet.

Cash
Accumulated Depreciation—Equipment
Accounts Payable

Owner's Drawings
Service Revenue
Salaries and Wages Expense

**Solution**

Income statement debit column—Salaries and Wages Expense
Income statement credit column—Service Revenue
Balance sheet debit column—Cash; Owner's Drawings
Balance sheet credit column—Accumulated Depreciation—Equipment; Accounts Payable

Related exercise material: BE4-1, BE4-2, BE4-3, E4-1, E4-2, E4-5, E4-6, and **DO IT!** 4-1.

### Closing the Books

At the end of the accounting period, the company makes the accounts ready for the next period. This is called **closing the books**. In closing the books, the company distinguishes between temporary and permanent accounts.

**Temporary accounts** relate only to a given accounting period. They include all income statement accounts and the owner's drawings account. **The company closes all temporary accounts at the end of the period.**

**trial balance columns is the balance that will appear in the ledger after jour-
nalizing and posting the adjusting entries.** The balances in these columns are
the same as those in the adjusted trial balance in Illustration 3-25 (page 119).

After Pioneer has entered all account balances in the adjusted trial balance
columns, the columns are totaled to prove their equality. If the column totals do
not agree, the financial statement columns will not balance and the financial
statements will be incorrect.

### STEP 4. EXTEND ADJUSTED TRIAL BALANCE AMOUNTS TO APPROPRIATE FINANCIAL STATEMENT COLUMNS

**Turn over the third transparency, Illustration 4-3C.** The fourth step is to
extend adjusted trial balance amounts to the income statement and balance sheet
columns of the worksheet. Pioneer enters balance sheet accounts in the appropriate balance sheet debit and credit columns. For instance, it enters Cash in the
balance sheet debit column, and Notes Payable in the balance sheet credit column.
Pioneer extends Accumulated Depreciation—Equipment to the balance sheet
credit column. The reason is that accumulated depreciation is a contra asset
account with a credit balance.

> **Helpful Hint** Every adjusted trial balance amount must be extended to one of the four statement columns.

Because the worksheet does not have columns for the owner's equity statement, Pioneer extends the balance in owner's capital to the balance sheet credit
column. In addition, it extends the balance in owner's drawings to the balance
sheet debit column because it is an owner's equity account with a debit balance.

The company enters the expense and revenue accounts such as Salaries and
Wages Expense and Service Revenue in the appropriate income statement columns. Illustration 4-3C shows all of these extensions.

### STEP 5. TOTAL THE STATEMENT COLUMNS, COMPUTE THE NET INCOME (OR NET LOSS), AND COMPLETE THE WORKSHEET

**Turn over the fourth transparency, Illustration 4-3D.** The company now must
total each of the financial statement columns. The net income or loss for the
period is the difference between the totals of the two income statement columns.
If total credits exceed total debits, the result is net income. In such a case, as
shown in Illustration 4-3D, the company inserts the words "Net Income" in the
account titles space. It then enters the amount in the income statement debit
column and the balance sheet credit column. **The debit amount balances the
income statement columns; the credit amount balances the balance sheet
columns.** In addition, the credit in the balance sheet column indicates the
increase in owner's equity resulting from net income.

What if total debits in the income statement columns exceed total credits? In
that case, the company has a net loss. It enters the amount of the net loss in the
income statement credit column and the balance sheet debit column.

After entering the net income or net loss, the company determines new column
totals. The totals shown in the debit and credit income statement columns will
match. So will the totals shown in the debit and credit balance sheet columns. If
either the income statement columns or the balance sheet columns are not equal
after the net income or net loss has been entered, there is an error in the worksheet.
Illustration 4-3D shows the completed worksheet for Pioneer Advertising Agency.

## Preparing Financial Statements from a Worksheet

After a company has completed a worksheet, it has at hand all the data required for
preparation of financial statements. The income statement is prepared from the
income statement columns. The balance sheet and owner's equity statement are
prepared from the balance sheet columns. Illustration 4-4 (page 166) shows the
financial statements prepared from Pioneer's worksheet. At this point, the company

**Illustration 4-4**
Financial statements from a
worksheet

### PIONEER ADVERTISING AGENCY
### Income Statement
### For the Month Ended October 31, 2014

| | | |
|---|---|---|
| Revenues | | |
| Service revenue | | $10,600 |
| Expenses | | |
| Salaries and wages expense | $5,200 | |
| Supplies expense | 1,500 | |
| Rent expense | 900 | |
| Insurance expense | 50 | |
| Interest expense | 50 | |
| Depreciation expense | 40 | |
| Total expenses | | 7,740 |
| Net income | | $ 2,860 |

### PIONEER ADVERTISING AGENCY
### Owner's Equity Statement
### For the Month Ended October 31, 2014

| | | |
|---|---|---|
| Owner's capital, October 1 | | $    –0– |
| Add: Investments | $10,000 | |
| Net income | 2,860 | 12,860 |
| | | 12,860 |
| Less: Drawings | | 500 |
| Owner's capital, October 31 | | $12,360 |

### PIONEER ADVERTISING AGENCY
### Balance Sheet
### October 31, 2014

#### Assets

| | | |
|---|---|---|
| Cash | | $15,200 |
| Accounts receivable | | 200 |
| Supplies | | 1,000 |
| Prepaid insurance | | 550 |
| Equipment | $5,000 | |
| Less: Accumulated depreciation—equipment | 40 | 4,960 |
| Total assets | | $21,910 |

#### Liabilities and Owner's Equity

| | | |
|---|---|---|
| Liabilities | | |
| Notes payable | $5,000 | |
| Accounts payable | 2,500 | |
| Interest payable | 50 | |
| Unearned service revenue | 800 | |
| Salaries and wages payable | 1,200 | |
| Total liabilities | | $ 9,550 |
| Owner's equity | | |
| Owner's capital | | 12,360 |
| Total liabilities and owner's equity | | $21,910 |

has not journalized or posted adjusting entries. Therefore, ledger balances for some accounts are not the same as the financial statement amounts.

The amount shown for owner's capital on the worksheet is the account balance **before considering drawings and net income (or loss)**. When the owner has made no additional investments of capital during the period, this worksheet amount for owner's capital is the balance at the beginning of the period.

Using a worksheet, companies can prepare financial statements before they journalize and post adjusting entries. **However, the completed worksheet is not a substitute for formal financial statements.** The format of the data in the financial statement columns of the worksheet is not the same as the format of the financial statements. **A worksheet is essentially a working tool of the accountant**; companies do not distribute it to management and other parties.

## Preparing Adjusting Entries from a Worksheet

**A worksheet is not a journal, and it cannot be used as a basis for posting to ledger accounts.** To adjust the accounts, the company must journalize the adjustments and post them to the ledger. **The adjusting entries are prepared from the adjustments columns of the worksheet.** The reference letters in the adjustments columns and the explanations of the adjustments at the bottom of the worksheet help identify the adjusting entries. The journalizing and posting of adjusting entries **follows** the preparation of financial statements when a worksheet is used. The adjusting entries on October 31 for Pioneer Advertising Agency are the same as those shown in Illustration 3-23 (page 117).

> **Helpful Hint** Note that writing the explanation to the adjustment at the bottom of the worksheet is not required.

---

> **DO IT!**

### Worksheet

Susan Elbe is preparing a worksheet. Explain to Susan how she should extend the following adjusted trial balance accounts to the financial statement columns of the worksheet.

| | |
|---|---|
| Cash | Owner's Drawings |
| Accumulated Depreciation—Equipment | Service Revenue |
| Accounts Payable | Salaries and Wages Expense |

#### Action Plan

✔ Balance sheet: Extend assets to debit column. Extend liabilities to credit column. Extend contra assets to credit column. Extend drawings account to debit column.

✔ Income statement: Extend expenses to debit column. Extend revenues to credit column.

### Solution

Income statement debit column—Salaries and Wages Expense
Income statement credit column—Service Revenue
Balance sheet debit column—Cash; Owner's Drawings
Balance sheet credit column—Accumulated Depreciation—Equipment; Accounts Payable

Related exercise material: **BE4-1, BE4-2, BE4-3, E4-1, E4-2, E4-5, E4-6, and** **DO IT!** **4-1.**

 ✔ **The Navigator**

---

## Closing the Books

At the end of the accounting period, the company makes the accounts ready for the next period. This is called **closing the books**. In closing the books, the company distinguishes between temporary and permanent accounts.

**Temporary accounts** relate only to a given accounting period. They include all income statement accounts and the owner's drawings account. **The company closes all temporary accounts at the end of the period.**

> **LEARNING OBJECTIVE** **2**
>
> Explain the process of closing the books.

**Illustration 4-5**
Temporary versus permanent accounts

In contrast, **permanent accounts** relate to one or more future accounting periods. They consist of all balance sheet accounts, including the owner's capital account. **Permanent accounts are not closed from period to period.** Instead, the company carries forward the balances of permanent accounts into the next accounting period. Illustration 4-5 identifies the accounts in each category.

| TEMPORARY | PERMANENT |
|---|---|
| These accounts are closed | These accounts are not closed |
| All revenue accounts | All asset accounts |
| All expense accounts | All liability accounts |
| Owner's drawings account | Owner's capital account |

## Preparing Closing Entries

At the end of the accounting period, the company transfers temporary account balances to the permanent owner's equity account, Owner's Capital, by means of closing entries.[1]

**Closing entries** formally recognize in the ledger the transfer of net income (or net loss) and owner's drawings to owner's capital. The owner's equity statement shows the results of these entries. **Closing entries also produce a zero balance in each temporary account.** The temporary accounts are then ready to accumulate data in the next accounting period separate from the data of prior periods. Permanent accounts are not closed.

**Journalizing and posting closing entries is a required step in the accounting cycle.** (See Illustration 4-12 on page 175.) The company performs this step after it has prepared financial statements. In contrast to the steps in the cycle that you have already studied, companies generally journalize and post closing entries **only at the end of the annual accounting period**. Thus, all temporary accounts will contain data for the entire year.

In preparing closing entries, companies could close each income statement account directly to owner's capital. However, to do so would result in excessive detail in the permanent Owner's Capital account. Instead, companies close the revenue and expense accounts to another temporary account, **Income Summary**, and they transfer the resulting net income or net loss from this account to owner's capital.

Companies **record closing entries in the general journal**. A center caption, Closing Entries, inserted in the journal between the last adjusting entry and the first closing entry, identifies these entries. Then the company posts the closing entries to the ledger accounts.

Companies generally prepare closing entries directly from the adjusted balances in the ledger. They could prepare separate closing entries for each nominal account, but the following four entries accomplish the desired result more efficiently:

1. Debit each revenue account for its balance, and credit Income Summary for total revenues.

2. Debit Income Summary for total expenses, and credit each expense account for its balance.

---

[1]We explain closing entries for a partnership and for a corporation in Chapters 12 and 13, respectively.

3. Debit Income Summary and credit Owner's Capital for the amount of net income.
4. Debit Owner's Capital for the balance in the Owner's Drawings account, and credit Owner's Drawings for the same amount.

Illustration 4-6 presents a diagram of the closing process. In it, the boxed numbers refer to the four entries required in the closing process.

**Helpful Hint** Owner's Drawings is closed directly to Owner's Capital and not to Income Summary. Owner's Drawings is not an expense.

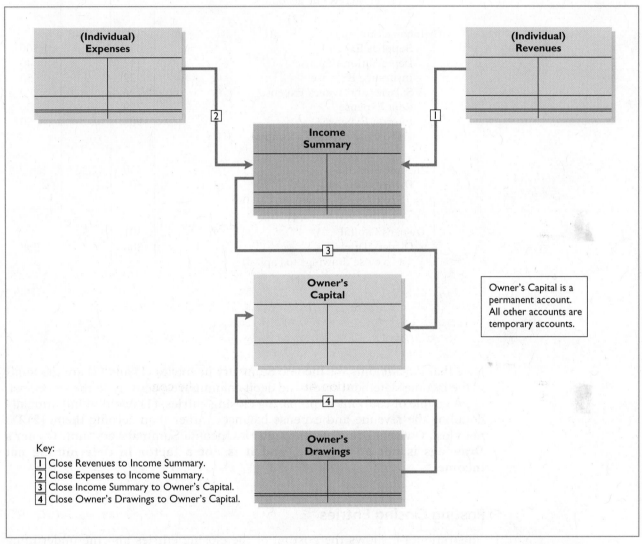

Key:
1 Close Revenues to Income Summary.
2 Close Expenses to Income Summary.
3 Close Income Summary to Owner's Capital.
4 Close Owner's Drawings to Owner's Capital.

Owner's Capital is a permanent account. All other accounts are temporary accounts.

**Illustration 4-6**
Diagram of closing process—proprietorship

If there were a net loss (because expenses exceeded revenues), entry 3 in Illustration 4-6 would be reversed: there would be a credit to Income Summary and a debit to Owner's Capital.

## CLOSING ENTRIES ILLUSTRATED

In practice, companies generally prepare closing entries only at the end of the annual accounting period. However, to illustrate the journalizing and posting of closing entries, we will assume that Pioneer Advertising Agency closes its books monthly. Illustration 4-7 (page 170) shows the closing entries at October 31. (The numbers in parentheses before each entry correspond to the four entries diagrammed in Illustration 4-6.)

**Illustration 4-7**
Closing entries journalized

| | GENERAL JOURNAL | | | J3 |
|---|---|---|---|---|
| **Date** | **Account Titles and Explanation** | **Ref.** | **Debit** | **Credit** |
| | Closing Entries | | | |
| 2014 | (1) | | | |
| Oct. 31 | Service Revenue | 400 | 10,600 | |
| |    Income Summary | 350 | | 10,600 |
| |      (To close revenue account) | | | |
| | (2) | | | |
| 31 | Income Summary | 350 | 7,740 | |
| |    Supplies Expense | 631 | | 1,500 |
| |    Depreciation Expense | 711 | | 40 |
| |    Insurance Expense | 722 | | 50 |
| |    Salaries and Wages Expense | 726 | | 5,200 |
| |    Rent Expense | 729 | | 900 |
| |    Interest Expense | 905 | | 50 |
| |      (To close expense accounts) | | | |
| | (3) | | | |
| 31 | Income Summary | 350 | 2,860 | |
| |    Owner's Capital | 301 | | 2,860 |
| |      (To close net income to capital) | | | |
| | (4) | | | |
| 31 | Owner's Capital | 301 | 500 | |
| |    Owner's Drawings | 306 | | 500 |
| |      (To close drawings to capital) | | | |

Note that the amounts for Income Summary in entries (1) and (2) are the totals of the income statement credit and debit columns, respectively, in the worksheet.

A couple of cautions in preparing closing entries: (1) Avoid unintentionally doubling the revenue and expense balances rather than zeroing them. (2) Do not close Owner's Drawings through the Income Summary account. **Owner's Drawings is not an expense, and it is not a factor in determining net income.**

### Posting Closing Entries

Illustration 4-8 shows the posting of the closing entries and the underlining (ruling) of the accounts. Note that all temporary accounts have zero balances after posting the closing entries. In addition, notice that the balance in owner's capital (Owner's Capital) represents the total equity of the owner at the end of the accounting period. This balance is shown on the balance sheet and is the ending capital reported on the owner's equity statement, as shown in Illustration 4-4 on page 166. Pioneer uses the Income Summary account only in closing. It does not journalize and post entries to this account during the year.

As part of the closing process, Pioneer totals, balances, and double-underlines its temporary accounts—revenues, expenses, and Owner's Drawings, as shown in T-account form in Illustration 4-8. It does not close its permanent accounts—assets, liabilities, and Owner's Capital. Instead, Pioneer draws a single underline beneath the current-period entries for the permanent accounts. The account balance is then entered below the single underline and is carried forward to the next period. (For example, see Owner's Capital.)

**Helpful Hint** The balance in Income Summary before it is closed must equal the net income or net loss for the period.

**Illustration 4-8**
Posting of closing entries

# ACCOUNTING ACROSS THE ORGANIZATION

## Cisco Performs the Virtual Close

Technology has dramatically shortened the closing process. Recent surveys have reported that the average company now takes only six to seven days to close, rather than 20 days. But a few companies do much better. Cisco Systems can perform a "virtual close"—closing within 24 hours on any day in the quarter. The same is true at Lockheed Martin Corp., which improved its closing time by 85% in just the last few years. Not very long ago, it took 14 to 16 days. Managers at these companies emphasize that this increased speed has not reduced the accuracy and completeness of the data.

This is not just showing off. Knowing exactly where you are financially all of the time allows the company to respond faster than competitors. It also means that the hundreds of people who used to spend 10 to 20 days a quarter tracking transactions can now be more usefully employed on things such as mining data for business intelligence to find new business opportunities.

*Source:* "Reporting Practices: Few Do It All," *Financial Executive* (November 2003), p. 11.

**?** Who else benefits from a shorter closing process? (See page 211.)

> **DO IT!**

## Closing Entries

The worksheet for Hancock Company shows the following in the financial statement columns:

Owner's drawings $15,000
Owner's capital $42,000
Net income $18,000

Prepare the closing entries at December 31 that affect owner's capital.

### Solution

**Action Plan**

✔ Close Income Summary to Owner's Capital.

✔ Close Owner's Drawings to Owner's Capital.

| Dec. 31 | Income Summary | 18,000 | |
| | Owner's Capital | | 18,000 |
| | (To close net income to capital) | | |
| 31 | Owner's Capital | 15,000 | |
| | Owner's Drawings | | 15,000 |
| | (To close drawings to capital) | | |

Related exercise material: **BE4-4, BE4-5, BE4-6, E4-4, E4-7, E4-8, E4-11, and DO IT! 4-2.**

✔ The Navigator

## Preparing a Post-Closing Trial Balance

**LEARNING OBJECTIVE    3**

Describe the content and purpose of a post-closing trial balance.

After Pioneer has journalized and posted all closing entries, it prepares another trial balance, called a **post-closing trial balance**, from the ledger. The post-closing trial balance lists permanent accounts and their balances after the journalizing and posting of closing entries. The purpose of the post-closing trial balance is **to prove the equality of the permanent account balances carried forward into the next accounting period**. Since all temporary accounts will have zero balances, **the post-closing trial balance will contain only permanent—balance sheet—accounts**.

Illustration 4-9 shows the post-closing trial balance for Pioneer Advertising Agency.

**Illustration 4-9**
Post-closing trial balance

### PIONEER ADVERTISING AGENCY
#### Post-Closing Trial Balance
#### October 31, 2014

| | Debit | Credit |
|---|---|---|
| Cash | $ 15,200 | |
| Accounts Receivable | 200 | |
| Supplies | 1,000 | |
| Prepaid Insurance | 550 | |
| Equipment | 5,000 | |
| Accumulated Depreciation—Equipment | | $       40 |
| Notes Payable | | 5,000 |
| Accounts Payable | | 2,500 |
| Unearned Service Revenue | | 800 |
| Salaries and Wages Payable | | 1,200 |
| Interest Payable | | 50 |
| Owner's Capital | | 12,360 |
| | $21,950 | $21,950 |

Pioneer prepares the post-closing trial balance from the permanent accounts in the ledger. Illustration 4-10 shows the permanent accounts in Pioneer's general ledger.

**Illustration 4-10**
General ledger, permanent accounts

**(Permanent Accounts Only)**

## GENERAL LEDGER

### Cash                                        No. 101

| Date | Explanation | Ref. | Debit | Credit | Balance |
|------|-------------|------|-------|--------|---------|
| 2014 | | | | | |
| Oct. 1 | | J1 | 10,000 | | 10,000 |
| 2 | | J1 | 1,200 | | 11,200 |
| 3 | | J1 | | 900 | 10,300 |
| 4 | | J1 | | 600 | 9,700 |
| 20 | | J1 | | 500 | 9,200 |
| 26 | | J1 | | 4,000 | 5,200 |
| 31 | | J1 | 10,000 | | 15,200 |

### Accounts Payable                            No. 201

| Date | Explanation | Ref. | Debit | Credit | Balance |
|------|-------------|------|-------|--------|---------|
| 2014 | | | | | |
| Oct. 5 | | J1 | | 2,500 | 2,500 |

### Unearned Service Revenue                    No. 209

| Date | Explanation | Ref. | Debit | Credit | Balance |
|------|-------------|------|-------|--------|---------|
| 2014 | | | | | |
| Oct. 2 | | J1 | | 1,200 | 1,200 |
| 31 | Adj. entry | J2 | 400 | | 800 |

### Accounts Receivable                         No. 112

| Date | Explanation | Ref. | Debit | Credit | Balance |
|------|-------------|------|-------|--------|---------|
| 2014 | | | | | |
| Oct. 31 | Adj. entry | J2 | 200 | | 200 |

### Salaries and Wages Payable                  No. 212

| Date | Explanation | Ref. | Debit | Credit | Balance |
|------|-------------|------|-------|--------|---------|
| 2014 | | | | | |
| Oct. 31 | Adj. entry | J2 | | 1,200 | 1,200 |

### Supplies                                    No. 126

| Date | Explanation | Ref. | Debit | Credit | Balance |
|------|-------------|------|-------|--------|---------|
| 2014 | | | | | |
| Oct. 5 | | J1 | 2,500 | | 2,500 |
| 31 | Adj. entry | J2 | | 1,500 | 1,000 |

### Interest Payable                            No. 230

| Date | Explanation | Ref. | Debit | Credit | Balance |
|------|-------------|------|-------|--------|---------|
| 2014 | | | | | |
| Oct. 31 | Adj. entry | J2 | | 50 | 50 |

### Prepaid Insurance                           No. 130

| Date | Explanation | Ref. | Debit | Credit | Balance |
|------|-------------|------|-------|--------|---------|
| 2014 | | | | | |
| Oct. 4 | | J1 | 600 | | 600 |
| 31 | Adj. entry | J2 | | 50 | 550 |

### Owner's Capital                             No. 301

| Date | Explanation | Ref. | Debit | Credit | Balance |
|------|-------------|------|-------|--------|---------|
| 2014 | | | | | |
| Oct. 1 | | J1 | | 10,000 | 10,000 |
| 31 | Closing entry | J3 | | 2,860 | 12,860 |
| 31 | Closing entry | J3 | 500 | | 12,360 |

### Equipment                                   No. 157

| Date | Explanation | Ref. | Debit | Credit | Balance |
|------|-------------|------|-------|--------|---------|
| 2014 | | | | | |
| Oct. 1 | | J1 | 5,000 | | 5,000 |

*Note:* The permanent accounts for Pioneer Advertising Agency are shown here. Illustration 4-11 (page 174) shows the temporary accounts. Both permanent and temporary accounts are part of the general ledger. They are segregated here to aid in learning.

### Accumulated Depreciation—Equipment         No. 158

| Date | Explanation | Ref. | Debit | Credit | Balance |
|------|-------------|------|-------|--------|---------|
| 2014 | | | | | |
| Oct. 31 | Adj. entry | J2 | | 40 | 40 |

### Notes Payable                              No. 200

| Date | Explanation | Ref. | Debit | Credit | Balance |
|------|-------------|------|-------|--------|---------|
| 2014 | | | | | |
| Oct. 1 | | J1 | | 5,000 | 5,000 |

A post-closing trial balance provides evidence that the company has properly journalized and posted the closing entries. It also shows that the accounting equation is in balance at the end of the accounting period. However, like the trial balance, it does not prove that Pioneer has recorded all transactions or that the ledger is correct. For example, the post-closing trial balance still will balance even if a transaction is not journalized and posted or if a transaction is journalized and posted twice.

The remaining accounts in the general ledger are temporary accounts, shown in Illustration 4-11. After Pioneer correctly posts the closing entries, each temporary account has a zero balance. These accounts are double-underlined to finalize the closing process.

**Illustration 4-11**
General ledger, temporary accounts

(Temporary Accounts Only)

## GENERAL LEDGER

### Owner's Drawings — No. 306

| Date | Explanation | Ref. | Debit | Credit | Balance |
|---|---|---|---|---|---|
| 2014 | | | | | |
| Oct. 20 | | J1 | 500 | | 500 |
| 31 | Closing entry | J3 | | 500 | –0– |

### Income Summary — No. 350

| Date | Explanation | Ref. | Debit | Credit | Balance |
|---|---|---|---|---|---|
| 2014 | | | | | |
| Oct.31 | Closing entry | J3 | | 10,600 | 10,600 |
| 31 | Closing entry | J3 | 7,740 | | 2,860 |
| 31 | Closing entry | J3 | 2,860 | | –0– |

### Service Revenue — No. 400

| Date | Explanation | Ref. | Debit | Credit | Balance |
|---|---|---|---|---|---|
| 2014 | | | | | |
| Oct. 31 | | J1 | | 10,000 | 10,000 |
| 31 | Adj. entry | J2 | | 400 | 10,400 |
| 31 | Adj. entry | J2 | | 200 | 10,600 |
| 31 | Closing entry | J3 | 10,600 | | –0– |

### Supplies Expense — No. 631

| Date | Explanation | Ref. | Debit | Credit | Balance |
|---|---|---|---|---|---|
| 2014 | | | | | |
| Oct. 31 | Adj. entry | J2 | 1,500 | | 1,500 |
| 31 | Closing entry | J3 | | 1,500 | –0– |

### Depreciation Expense — No. 711

| Date | Explanation | Ref. | Debit | Credit | Balance |
|---|---|---|---|---|---|
| 2014 | | | | | |
| Oct. 31 | Adj. entry | J2 | 40 | | 40 |
| 31 | Closing entry | J3 | | 40 | –0– |

### Insurance Expense — No. 722

| Date | Explanation | Ref. | Debit | Credit | Balance |
|---|---|---|---|---|---|
| 2014 | | | | | |
| Oct. 31 | Adj. entry | J2 | 50 | | 50 |
| 31 | Closing entry | J3 | | 50 | –0– |

### Salaries and Wages Expense — No. 726

| Date | Explanation | Ref. | Debit | Credit | Balance |
|---|---|---|---|---|---|
| 2014 | | | | | |
| Oct. 26 | | J1 | 4,000 | | 4,000 |
| 31 | Adj. entry | J2 | 1,200 | | 5,200 |
| 31 | Closing entry | J3 | | 5,200 | –0– |

### Rent Expense — No. 729

| Date | Explanation | Ref. | Debit | Credit | Balance |
|---|---|---|---|---|---|
| 2014 | | | | | |
| Oct. 3 | | J1 | 900 | | 900 |
| 31 | Closing entry | J3 | | 900 | –0– |

### Interest Expense — No. 905

| Date | Explanation | Ref. | Debit | Credit | Balance |
|---|---|---|---|---|---|
| 2014 | | | | | |
| Oct. 31 | Adj. entry | J2 | 50 | | 50 |
| 31 | Closing entry | J3 | | 50 | –0– |

> *Note:* The temporary accounts for Pioneer Advertising Agency are shown here. Illustration 4-10 (page 173) shows the permanent accounts. Both permanent and temporary accounts are part of the general ledger. They are segregated here to aid in learning.

## Summary of the Accounting Cycle

Illustration 4-12 summarizes the steps in the accounting cycle. You can see that the cycle begins with the analysis of business transactions and ends with the preparation of a post-closing trial balance.

**Illustration 4-12**
Steps in the accounting cycle

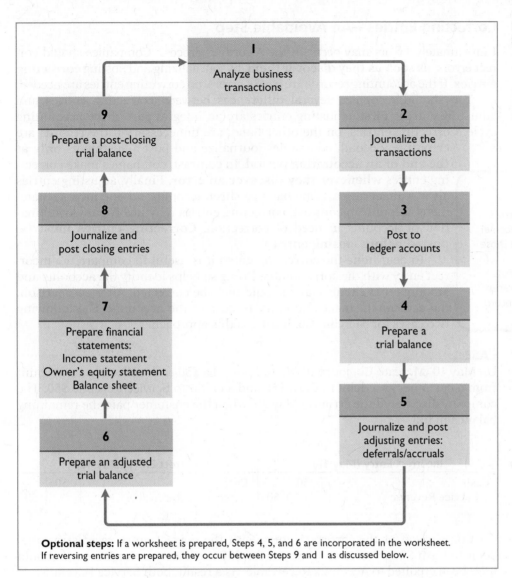

**Optional steps:** If a worksheet is prepared, Steps 4, 5, and 6 are incorporated in the worksheet. If reversing entries are prepared, they occur between Steps 9 and 1 as discussed below.

Steps 1–3 may occur daily during the accounting period. Companies perform Steps 4–7 on a periodic basis, such as monthly, quarterly, or annually. Steps 8 and 9—closing entries and a post-closing trial balance—usually take place only at the end of a company's **annual** accounting period.

There are also two **optional steps** in the accounting cycle. As you have seen, companies may use a worksheet in preparing adjusting entries and financial statements. In addition, they may use reversing entries, as explained below.

## Reversing Entries—An Optional Step

Some accountants prefer to reverse certain adjusting entries by making a **reversing entry** at the beginning of the next accounting period. A reversing entry is the exact opposite of the adjusting entry made in the previous period. **Use of reversing entries is an optional bookkeeping procedure; it is not a required step in the accounting cycle.** Accordingly, we have chosen to cover this topic in an appendix at the end of the chapter.

## Correcting Entries—An Avoidable Step

**LEARNING OBJECTIVE** 5

Explain the approaches to preparing correcting entries.

Unfortunately, errors may occur in the recording process. Companies should correct errors, **as soon as they discover them**, by journalizing and posting **correcting entries**. If the accounting records are free of errors, no correcting entries are needed.

You should recognize several differences between correcting entries and adjusting entries. First, adjusting entries are an integral part of the accounting cycle. Correcting entries, on the other hand, are unnecessary if the records are error-free. Second, companies journalize and post adjustments **only at the end of an accounting period**. In contrast, companies make correcting entries **whenever they discover an error**. Finally, adjusting entries always affect at least one balance sheet account and one income statement account. In contrast, correcting entries may involve any combination of accounts in need of correction. **Correcting entries must be posted before closing entries.**

### Ethics Note

When companies find errors in previously released income statements, they restate those numbers. Perhaps because of the increased scrutiny caused by Sarbanes-Oxley, in a recent year companies filed a record 1,195 restatements.

To determine the correcting entry, it is useful to compare the incorrect entry with the correct entry. Doing so helps identify the accounts and amounts that should—and should not—be corrected. After comparison, the accountant makes an entry to correct the accounts. The following two cases for Mercato Co. illustrate this approach.

### CASE 1

On May 10, Mercato Co. journalized and posted a $50 cash collection on account from a customer as a debit to Cash $50 and a credit to Service Revenue $50. The company discovered the error on May 20, when the customer paid the remaining balance in full.

**Illustration 4-13**
Comparison of entries

| Incorrect Entry (May 10) | | | Correct Entry (May 10) | | |
|---|---|---|---|---|---|
| Cash | 50 | | Cash | 50 | |
|    Service Revenue | | 50 |    Accounts Receivable | | 50 |

Comparison of the incorrect entry with the correct entry reveals that the debit to Cash $50 is correct. However, the $50 credit to Service Revenue should have been credited to Accounts Receivable. As a result, both Service Revenue and Accounts Receivable are overstated in the ledger. Mercato makes the following correcting entry.

**Illustration 4-14**
Correcting entry

A = L + OE
               −50 Rev
−50

**Cash Flows**
no effect

| | Correcting Entry | | |
|---|---|---|---|
| May 20 | Service Revenue | 50 | |
| |    Accounts Receivable | | 50 |
| |    (To correct entry of May 10) | | |

### CASE 2

On May 18, Mercato purchased on account equipment costing $450. The transaction was journalized and posted as a debit to Equipment $45 and a credit to Accounts Payable $45. The error was discovered on June 3, when Mercato received the monthly statement for May from the creditor.

**Illustration 4-15**
Comparison of entries

| Incorrect Entry (May 18) | | | Correct Entry (May 18) | | |
|---|---|---|---|---|---|
| Equipment | 45 | | Equipment | 450 | |
|    Accounts Payable | | 45 |    Accounts Payable | | 450 |

Comparison of the two entries shows that two accounts are incorrect. Equipment is understated $405, and Accounts Payable is understated $405. Mercato makes the following correcting entry.

| | **Correcting Entry** | | |
|---|---|---|---|
| June 3 | Equipment | 405 | |
| | Accounts Payable | | 405 |
| | (To correct entry of May 18) | | |

| A | = | L | + | OE |
|---|---|---|---|---|
| +405 | | | | |
| | | +405 | | |

**Cash Flows**
no effect

**Illustration 4-16**
Correcting entry

Instead of preparing a correcting entry, **it is possible to reverse the incorrect entry and then prepare the correct entry**. This approach will result in more entries and postings than a correcting entry, but it will accomplish the desired result.

## ACCOUNTING ACROSS THE ORGANIZATION

### Yale Express Loses Some Transportation Bills

Yale Express, a short-haul trucking firm, turned over much of its cargo to local truckers to complete deliveries. Yale collected the entire delivery charge. When billed by the local trucker, Yale sent payment for the final phase to the local trucker. Yale used a cutoff period of 20 days into the next accounting period in making its adjusting entries for accrued liabilities. That is, it waited 20 days to receive the local truckers' bills to determine the amount of the unpaid but incurred delivery charges as of the balance sheet date.

On the other hand, Republic Carloading, a nationwide, long-distance freight forwarder, frequently did not receive transportation bills from truckers to whom it passed on cargo until months after the year-end. In making its year-end adjusting entries, Republic waited for months in order to include all of these outstanding transportation bills.

When Yale Express merged with Republic Carloading, Yale's vice president employed the 20-day cutoff procedure for both firms. As a result, millions of dollars of Republic's accrued transportation bills went unrecorded. When the company detected the error and made correcting entries, these and other errors changed a reported profit of $1.14 million into a loss of $1.88 million!

 What might Yale Express's vice president have done to produce more accurate financial statements without waiting months for Republic's outstanding transportation bills? (See page 211.)

© Christian Lagerek/iStockphoto

## The Classified Balance Sheet

The balance sheet presents a snapshot of a company's financial position at a point in time. To improve users' understanding of a company's financial position, companies often use a classified balance sheet. A **classified balance sheet** groups together similar assets and similar liabilities, using a number of standard classifications and sections. This is useful because items within a group have similar economic characteristics. A classified balance sheet generally contains the standard classifications listed in Illustration 4-17.

**LEARNING OBJECTIVE    6**

Identify the sections of a classified balance sheet.

**Illustration 4-17**
Standard balance sheet classifications

| Assets | Liabilities and Owner's Equity |
|---|---|
| Current assets | Current liabilities |
| Long-term investments | Long-term liabilities |
| Property, plant, and equipment | Owner's (Stockholders') equity |
| Intangible assets | |

These groupings help financial statement readers determine such things as (1) whether the company has enough assets to pay its debts as they come due, and (2) the claims of short- and long-term creditors on the company's total assets. Many of these groupings can be seen in the balance sheet of Franklin Company shown in Illustration 4-18 below. In the sections that follow, we explain each of these groupings.

**Illustration 4-18**
Classified balance sheet

| FRANKLIN COMPANY | | | |
|---|---|---|---|
| Balance Sheet | | | |
| October 31, 2014 | | | |
| **Assets** | | | |
| **Current assets** | | | |
| Cash | | $ 6,600 | |
| Debt investments | | 2,000 | |
| Accounts receivable | | 7,000 | |
| Notes receivable | | 1,000 | |
| Inventory | | 3,000 | |
| Supplies | | 2,100 | |
| Prepaid insurance | | 400 | |
| Total current assets | | | $22,100 |
| **Long-term investments** | | | |
| Stock investments | | 5,200 | |
| Investment in real estate | | 2,000 | 7,200 |
| **Property, plant, and equipment** | | | |
| Land | | 10,000 | |
| Equipment | $24,000 | | |
| Less: Accumulated depreciation— | | | |
| equipment | 5,000 | 19,000 | 29,000 |
| **Intangible assets** | | | |
| Patents | | | 3,100 |
| Total assets | | | $61,400 |
| **Liabilities and Owner's Equity** | | | |
| **Current liabilities** | | | |
| Notes payable | | $11,000 | |
| Accounts payable | | 2,100 | |
| Unearned service revenue | | 900 | |
| Salaries and wages payable | | 1,600 | |
| Interest payable | | 450 | |
| Total current liabilities | | | $16,050 |
| **Long-term liabilities** | | | |
| Mortgage payable | | 10,000 | |
| Notes payable | | 1,300 | |
| Total long-term liabilities | | | 11,300 |
| Total liabilities | | | 27,350 |
| **Owner's equity** | | | |
| Owner's capital | | | 34,050 |
| Total liabilities and owner's equity | | | $61,400 |

**Helpful Hint** Recall that the basic accounting equation is Assets = Liabilities + Owner's Equity.

## Current Assets

**Current assets** are assets that a company expects to convert to cash or use up within one year or its operating cycle, whichever is longer. In Illustration 4-18, Franklin Company had current assets of $22,100. For most businesses the cutoff for classification as current assets is one year from the balance sheet date. For example, accounts receivable are current assets because the company will collect them and convert them to cash within one year. Supplies is a current asset because the company expects to use them up in operations within one year.

Some companies use a period longer than one year to classify assets and liabilities as current because they have an operating cycle longer than one year. The **operating cycle** of a company is the average time that it takes to purchase inventory, sell it on account, and then collect cash from customers. For most businesses this cycle takes less than a year, so they use a one-year cutoff. But, for some businesses, such as vineyards or airplane manufacturers, this period may be longer than a year. **Except where noted, we will assume that companies use one year to determine whether an asset or liability is current or long-term.**

Common types of current assets are (1) cash, (2) investments (such as short-term U.S. government securities), (3) receivables (notes receivable, accounts receivable, and interest receivable), (4) inventories, and (5) prepaid expenses (supplies and insurance). **On the balance sheet, companies usually list these items in the order in which they expect to convert them into cash.**

Illustration 4-19 presents the current assets of Southwest Airlines Co.

| Real World | SOUTHWEST AIRLINES CO. Balance Sheet (partial) (in millions) | |
|---|---|---|
| **Current assets** | | |
| Cash and cash equivalents | | $1,390 |
| Short-term investments | | 369 |
| Accounts receivable | | 241 |
| Inventories | | 181 |
| Prepaid expenses and other current assets | | 420 |
| Total current assets | | $2,601 |

**Illustration 4-19**
Current assets section

As explained later in the chapter, a company's current assets are important in assessing its short-term debt-paying ability.

## Long-Term Investments

**Long-term investments** are generally (1) investments in stocks and bonds of other companies that are normally held for many years, (2) long-term assets such as land or buildings that a company is not currently using in its operating activities, and (3) long-term notes receivable. In Illustration 4-18, Franklin Company reported total long-term investments of $7,200 on its balance sheet.

Yahoo! Inc. reported long-term investments in its balance sheet as shown in Illustration 4-20.

**Alternative Terminology**
Long-term investments are often referred to simply as *investments.*

| Real World | YAHOO! INC. Balance Sheet (partial) (in thousands) | |
|---|---|---|
| **Long-term investments** | | |
| Investments in securities | | $90,266 |

**Illustration 4-20**
Long-term investments section

**Alternative Terminology**
Property, plant, and equipment is sometimes called *fixed assets* or *plant assets*.

# Property, Plant, and Equipment

**Property, plant, and equipment** are assets with relatively long useful lives that a company is currently using in operating the business. This category includes land, buildings, machinery and equipment, delivery equipment, and furniture. In Illustration 4-18, Franklin Company reported property, plant, and equipment of $29,000.

**International Note**

Recently, China adopted International Financial Reporting Standards (IFRS). This was done in an effort to reduce fraud and increase investor confidence in financial reports. Under these standards, many items, such as property, plant, and equipment, may be reported at current fair values rather than historical cost.

**Depreciation** is the practice of allocating the cost of assets to a number of years. Companies do this by systematically assigning a portion of an asset's cost as an expense each year (rather than expensing the full purchase price in the year of purchase). The assets that the company depreciates are reported on the balance sheet at cost less accumulated depreciation. The **accumulated depreciation** account shows the total amount of depreciation that the company has expensed thus far in the asset's life. In Illustration 4-18, Franklin Company reported accumulated depreciation of $5,000.

Illustration 4-21 presents the property, plant, and equipment of Cooper Tire & Rubber Company.

**Illustration 4-21**
Property, plant, and equipment section

| COOPER TIRE & RUBBER COMPANY | | |
|---|---:|---:|
| Real World  Balance Sheet (partial) (in thousands) | | |
| **Property, plant, and equipment** | | |
| Land and land improvements | $   41,553 | |
| Buildings | 298,706 | |
| Machinery and equipment | 1,636,091 | |
| Molds, cores, and rings | 268,158 | $2,244,508 |
| Less: Accumulated depreciation | | 1,252,692 |
| | | $  991,816 |

# Intangible Assets

**Helpful Hint** Sometimes intangible assets are reported under a broader heading called "*Other assets.*"

Many companies have long-lived assets that do not have physical substance yet often are very valuable. We call these assets **intangible assets**. One significant intangible asset is goodwill. Others include patents, copyrights, and trademarks or trade names that give the company **exclusive right** of use for a specified period of time. In Illustration 4-18, Franklin Company reported intangible assets of $3,100.

Illustration 4-22 shows the intangible assets of media giant Time Warner, Inc.

**Illustration 4-22**
Intangible assets section

| TIME WARNER, INC. | |
|---|---:|
| Real World  Balance Sheet (partial) (in millions) | |
| **Intangible assets** | |
| Goodwill | $40,953 |
| Film library | 2,690 |
| Customer lists | 2,540 |
| Cable television franchises | 38,048 |
| Sports franchises | 262 |
| Brands, trademarks, and other intangible assets | 8,313 |
| | $92,806 |

## PEOPLE, PLANET, AND PROFIT INSIGHT

### Regaining Goodwill

After falling to unforeseen lows amidst scandals, recalls, and economic crises, the American public's positive perception of the reputation of corporate America is on the rise. Overall corporate reputation is experiencing rehabilitation as the American public gives high marks overall to corporate America, specific industries, and the largest number of individual companies in a dozen years. This is according to the findings of the *2011 Harris Interactive RQ Study*, which measures the reputations of the 60 most visible companies in the United States.

The survey focuses on six reputational dimensions that influence reputation and consumer behavior. Four of these dimensions, along with the five corporations that ranked highest within each, are as follows.

- **Social Responsibility**: (1) Whole Foods Market, (2) Johnson & Johnson, (3) Google, (4) The Walt Disney Company, (5) Procter & Gamble Co.

- **Emotional Appeal**: (1) Johnson & Johnson, (2) Amazon.com, (3) UPS, (4) General Mills, (5) Kraft Foods

- **Financial Performance**: (1) Google, (2) Berkshire Hathaway, (3) Apple, (4) Intel, (5) The Walt Disney Company

- **Products and Services**: (1) Intel Corporation, (2) 3M Company, (3) Johnson & Johnson, (4) Google, (5) Procter & Gamble Co.

*Source: www.harrisinteractive.com.*

 Name two industries today which are probably rated low on the reputational characteristics of "being trusted" and "having high ethical standards." (See page 212.)

---

## > DO IT!

### Assets Section of Classified Balance Sheet

Baxter Hoffman recently received the following information related to Hoffman Company's December 31, 2014, balance sheet.

| | | | |
|---|---|---|---|
| Prepaid insurance | $ 2,300 | Inventory | $3,400 |
| Cash | 800 | Accumulated depreciation— | |
| Equipment | 10,700 | equipment | 2,700 |
| | | Accounts receivable | 1,100 |

Prepare the assets section of Hoffman Company's classified balance sheet.

### Solution

#### Action Plan

✔ Present current assets first. Current assets are cash and other resources that the company expects to convert to cash or use up within one year.

✔ Present current assets in the order in which the company expects to convert them into cash.

✔ Subtract accumulated depreciation—equipment from equipment to determine the book value of equipment.

| Assets | | |
|---|---|---|
| Current assets | | |
| Cash | $ 800 | |
| Accounts receivable | 1,100 | |
| Inventory | 3,400 | |
| Prepaid insurance | 2,300 | |
| Total current assets | | $ 7,600 |
| Property, plant, and equipment | | |
| Equipment | 10,700 | |
| Less: Accumulated depreciation—equipment | 2,700 | 8,000 |
| Total assets | | $15,600 |

Related exercise material: **BE4-10 and DO IT! 4-3.**

 ✔ The Navigator

## Current Liabilities

In the liabilities and owner's equity section of the balance sheet, the first grouping is current liabilities. **Current liabilities** are obligations that the company is to pay within the coming year or its operating cycle, whichever is longer. Common examples are accounts payable, salaries and wages payable, notes payable, interest payable, and income taxes payable. Also included as current liabilities are current maturities of long-term obligations—payments to be made within the next year on long-term obligations. In Illustration 4-18, Franklin Company reported five different types of current liabilities, for a total of $16,050.

Illustration 4-23 shows the current liabilities section adapted from the balance sheet of Marcus Corporation.

**Illustration 4-23**
Current liabilities section

| MARCUS CORPORATION Balance Sheet (partial) (in thousands) | |
|---|---|
| **Current liabilities** | |
| Notes payable | $ 239 |
| Accounts payable | 24,242 |
| Current maturities of long-term debt | 57,250 |
| Other current liabilities | 27,477 |
| Income taxes payable | 11,215 |
| Salaries and wages payable | 6,720 |
| Total current liabilities | $127,143 |

Liquidity

Illiquidity

Users of financial statements look closely at the relationship between current assets and current liabilities. This relationship is important in evaluating a company's **liquidity**—its ability to pay obligations expected to be due within the next year. When current assets exceed current liabilities, the likelihood for paying the liabilities is favorable. When the reverse is true, short-term creditors may not be paid, and the company may ultimately be forced into bankruptcy.

## ACCOUNTING ACROSS THE ORGANIZATION

### Can a Company Be Too Liquid?

There actually is a point where a company can be too liquid—that is, it can have too much working capital (current assets less current liabilities). While it is important to be liquid enough to be able to pay short-term bills as they come due, a company does not want to tie up its cash in extra inventory or receivables that are not earning the company money.

By one estimate from the REL Consultancy Group, the thousand largest U.S. companies have on their books cumulative excess working capital of $764 billion. Based on this figure, companies could have reduced debt by 36% or increased net income by 9%. Given that managers throughout a company are interested in improving profitability, it is clear that they should have an eye toward managing working capital. They need to aim for a "Goldilocks solution"—not too much, not too little, but just right.

*Source:* K. Richardson, "Companies Fall Behind in Cash Management," *Wall Street Journal* (June 19, 2007).

 What can various company managers do to ensure that working capital is managed efficiently to maximize net income? (See page 212.)

## Long-Term Liabilities

**Long-term liabilities** are obligations that a company expects to pay **after** one year. Liabilities in this category include bonds payable, mortgages payable, long-term notes payable, lease liabilities, and pension liabilities. Many companies report long-term debt maturing after one year as a single amount in the balance sheet and show the details of the debt in notes that accompany the financial statements. Others list the various types of long-term liabilities. In Illustration 4-18, Franklin Company reported long-term liabilities of $11,300.

Illustration 4-24 shows the long-term liabilities that The Procter & Gamble Company reported in its balance sheet.

**Illustration 4-24**
Long-term liabilities section

| THE PROCTER & GAMBLE COMPANY Balance Sheet (partial) (in millions) | |
| --- | --- |
| **Long-term liabilities** | |
| Long-term debt | $23,375 |
| Deferred income taxes | 12,015 |
| Other noncurrent liabilities | 5,147 |
| Total long-term liabilities | $40,537 |

## Owner's Equity

The content of the owner's equity section varies with the form of business organization. In a proprietorship, there is one capital account. In a partnership, there is a capital account for each partner. Corporations divide owners' equity into two accounts—Common Stock (sometimes referred to as Capital Stock) and Retained Earnings. Corporations record stockholders' investments in the company by debiting an asset account and crediting the Common Stock account. They record in the Retained Earnings account income retained for use in the business. Corporations combine the Common Stock and Retained Earnings accounts and report them on the balance sheet as **stockholders' equity**. (We'll learn more about these corporation accounts in later chapters.) Nordstrom, Inc. recently reported its stockholders' equity section as follows.

**Alternative Terminology**
Common stock is sometimes called *capital stock*.

**Illustration 4-25**
Stockholders' equity section

| NORDSTROM, INC. Balance Sheet (partial) ($ in thousands) | |
| --- | --- |
| **Stockholders' equity** | |
| Common stock, 271,331 shares | $ 685,934 |
| Retained earnings | 1,406,747 |
| Total stockholders' equity | $2,092,681 |

> **DO IT!**

**Balance Sheet Classifications**

The following accounts were taken from the financial statements of Callahan Company.

_____ Salaries and wages payable
_____ Service revenue
_____ Interest payable
_____ Goodwill
_____ Debt investments (short-term)
_____ Mortgage payable (due in 3 years)

_____ Stock investments (long-term)
_____ Equipment
_____ Accumulated depreciation—equipment
_____ Depreciation expense
_____ Owner's capital
_____ Unearned service revenue

Match each of the following to its proper balance sheet classification, shown below. If the item would not appear on a balance sheet, use "NA."

Current assets (CA)
Long-term investments (LTI)
Property, plant, and equipment (PPE)
Intangible assets (IA)

Current liabilities (CL)
Long-term liabilities (LTL)
Owner's equity (OE)

### Solution

**Action Plan**

✔ Analyze whether each financial statement item is an asset, liability, or owner's equity.

✔ Determine if asset and liability items are short-term or long-term.

| | | | |
|---|---|---|---|
| _CL_ | Salaries and wages payable | _LTI_ | Stock investments (long-term) |
| _NA_ | Service revenue | _PPE_ | Equipment |
| _CL_ | Interest payable | _PPE_ | Accumulated depreciation— |
| _IA_ | Goodwill | | equipment |
| _CA_ | Debt investments (short-term) | _NA_ | Depreciation expense |
| _LTL_ | Mortgage payable (due | _OE_ | Owner's capital |
| | in 3 years) | _CL_ | Unearned service revenue |

Related exercise material: **BE4-11, E4-14, E4-15, E4-16, E4-17, and DO IT! 4-4.**

✔ The Navigator

## > Comprehensive DO IT!

At the end of its first month of operations, Watson Answering Service has the following unadjusted trial balance.

**Action Plan**

✔ In completing the worksheet, be sure to (a) key the adjustments; (b) start at the top of the adjusted trial balance columns and extend adjusted balances to the correct statement columns; and (c) enter net income (or net loss) in the proper columns.

✔ In preparing a classified balance sheet, know the contents of each of the sections.

✔ In journalizing closing entries, remember that there are only four entries and that Owner's Drawings is closed to Owner's Capital.

**WATSON ANSWERING SERVICE**
August 31, 2014
Trial Balance

| | Debit | Credit |
|---|---|---|
| Cash | $ 5,400 | |
| Accounts Receivable | 2,800 | |
| Supplies | 1,300 | |
| Prepaid Insurance | 2,400 | |
| Equipment | 60,000 | |
| Notes Payable | | $40,000 |
| Accounts Payable | | 2,400 |
| Owner's Capital | | 30,000 |
| Owner's Drawings | 1,000 | |
| Service Revenue | | 4,900 |
| Salaries and Wages Expense | 3,200 | |
| Utilities Expense | 800 | |
| Advertising Expense | 400 | |
| | $77,300 | $77,300 |

Other data:

1. Insurance expires at the rate of $200 per month.
2. $1,000 of supplies are on hand at August 31.
3. Monthly depreciation on the equipment is $900.
4. Interest of $500 on the notes payable has accrued during August.

**Instructions**
**(a)** Prepare a worksheet.
**(b)** Prepare a classified balance sheet assuming $35,000 of the notes payable are long-term.
**(c)** Journalize the closing entries.

**Solution to Comprehensive DO IT!**

**(a)**

**WATSON ANSWERING SERVICE**
Worksheet for the Month Ended August 31, 2014

| Account Titles | Trial Balance Dr. | Trial Balance Cr. | Adjustments Dr. | Adjustments Cr. | Adjusted Trial Balance Dr. | Adjusted Trial Balance Cr. | Income Statement Dr. | Income Statement Cr. | Balance Sheet Dr. | Balance Sheet Cr. |
|---|---|---|---|---|---|---|---|---|---|---|
| Cash | 5,400 | | | | 5,400 | | | | 5,400 | |
| Accounts Receivable | 2,800 | | | | 2,800 | | | | 2,800 | |
| Supplies | 1,300 | | | (b) 300 | 1,000 | | | | 1,000 | |
| Prepaid Insurance | 2,400 | | | (a) 200 | 2,200 | | | | 2,200 | |
| Equipment | 60,000 | | | | 60,000 | | | | 60,000 | |
| Notes Payable | | 40,000 | | | | 40,000 | | | | 40,000 |
| Accounts Payable | | 2,400 | | | | 2,400 | | | | 2,400 |
| Owner's Capital | | 30,000 | | | | 30,000 | | | | 30,000 |
| Owner's Drawings | 1,000 | | | | 1,000 | | | | 1,000 | |
| Service Revenue | | 4,900 | | | | 4,900 | | 4,900 | | |
| Salaries and Wages Expense | 3,200 | | | | 3,200 | | 3,200 | | | |
| Utilities Expense | 800 | | | | 800 | | 800 | | | |
| Advertising Expense | 400 | | | | 400 | | 400 | | | |
| Totals | 77,300 | 77,300 | | | | | | | | |
| | | | | | | | | | | |
| Insurance Expense | | | (a) 200 | | 200 | | 200 | | | |
| Supplies Expense | | | (b) 300 | | 300 | | 300 | | | |
| Depreciation Expense | | | (c) 900 | | 900 | | 900 | | | |
| Accumulated Depreciation—Equipment | | | | (c) 900 | | 900 | | | | 900 |
| Interest Expense | | | (d) 500 | | 500 | | 500 | | | |
| Interest Payable | | | | (d) 500 | | 500 | | | | 500 |
| Totals | | | 1,900 | 1,900 | 78,700 | 78,700 | 6,300 | 4,900 | 72,400 | 73,800 |
| Net Loss | | | | | | | | 1,400 | 1,400 | |
| Totals | | | | | | | 6,300 | 6,300 | 73,800 | 73,800 |

Explanation: (a) insurance expired, (b) supplies used, (c) depreciation expensed, (d) interest accrued.

**(b)**

| WATSON ANSWERING SERVICE |
| :---: |
| Balance Sheet |
| August 31, 2014 |

### Assets

| | | |
| --- | ---: | ---: |
| Current assets | | |
| Cash | $ 5,400 | |
| Accounts receivable | 2,800 | |
| Supplies | 1,000 | |
| Prepaid insurance | 2,200 | |
| Total current assets | | $11,400 |
| Property, plant, and equipment | | |
| Equipment | 60,000 | |
| Less: Accumulated depreciation—equipment | 900 | 59,100 |
| Total assets | | $70,500 |

### Liabilities and Owner's Equity

| | | |
| --- | ---: | ---: |
| Current liabilities | | |
| Notes payable | $ 5,000 | |
| Accounts payable | 2,400 | |
| Interest payable | 500 | |
| Total current liabilities | | $ 7,900 |
| Long-term liabilities | | |
| Notes payable | | 35,000 |
| Total liabilities | | 42,900 |
| Owner's equity | | |
| Owner's capital | | 27,600* |
| Total liabilities and owner's equity | | $70,500 |

*Owner's capital, $30,000 less drawings $1,000 and net loss $1,400.

**(c)**

| | | | |
| --- | --- | ---: | ---: |
| Aug. 31 | Service Revenue | 4,900 | |
| | Income Summary | | 4,900 |
| | (To close revenue account) | | |
| 31 | Income Summary | 6,300 | |
| | Salaries and Wages Expense | | 3,200 |
| | Depreciation Expense | | 900 |
| | Utilities Expense | | 800 |
| | Interest Expense | | 500 |
| | Advertising Expense | | 400 |
| | Supplies Expense | | 300 |
| | Insurance Expense | | 200 |
| | (To close expense accounts) | | |
| 31 | Owner's Capital | 1,400 | |
| | Income Summary | | 1,400 |
| | (To close net loss to capital) | | |
| 31 | Owner's Capital | 1,000 | |
| | Owner's Drawings | | 1,000 |
| | (To close drawings to capital) | | |

✔  The Navigator

## SUMMARY OF LEARNING OBJECTIVES

1 **Prepare a worksheet.** The steps in preparing a worksheet are as follows. (a) Prepare a trial balance on the worksheet. (b) Enter the adjustments in the adjustments columns. (c) Enter adjusted balances in the adjusted trial balance columns. (d) Extend adjusted trial balance amounts to appropriate financial statement columns. (e) Total the statement columns, compute net income (or net loss), and complete the worksheet.

2 **Explain the process of closing the books.** Closing the books occurs at the end of an accounting period. The process is to journalize and post closing entries and then underline and balance all accounts. In closing the books, companies make separate entries to close revenues and expenses to Income Summary, Income Summary to Owner's Capital, and Owner's Drawings to Owner's Capital. Only temporary accounts are closed.

3 **Describe the content and purpose of a post-closing trial balance.** A post-closing trial balance contains the balances in permanent accounts that are carried forward to the next accounting period. The purpose of this trial balance is to prove the equality of these balances.

4 **State the required steps in the accounting cycle.** The required steps in the accounting cycle are (1) analyze business transactions, (2) journalize the transactions, (3) post to ledger accounts, (4) prepare a trial balance, (5) journalize and post adjusting entries, (6) prepare an adjusted trial balance, (7) prepare financial statements, (8) journalize and post closing entries, and (9) prepare a post-closing trial balance.

5 **Explain the approaches to preparing correcting entries.** One way to determine the correcting entry is to compare the incorrect entry with the correct entry. After comparison, the company makes a correcting entry to correct the accounts. An alternative to a correcting entry is to reverse the incorrect entry and then prepare the correct entry.

6 **Identify the sections of a classified balance sheet.** A classified balance sheet categorizes assets as current assets; long-term investments; property, plant, and equipment; and intangibles. Liabilities are classified as either current or long-term. There is also an owner's (owners') equity section, which varies with the form of business organization.

## GLOSSARY

**Classified balance sheet** A balance sheet that contains standard classifications or sections. (p. 177).

**Closing entries** Entries made at the end of an accounting period to transfer the balances of temporary accounts to a permanent owner's equity account, Owner's Capital. (p. 168).

**Correcting entries** Entries to correct errors made in recording transactions. (p. 176).

**Current assets** Assets that a company expects to convert to cash or use up within one year. (p. 178).

**Current liabilities** Obligations that a company expects to pay within the coming year or its operating cycle, whichever is longer. (p. 182).

**Income Summary** A temporary account used in closing revenue and expense accounts. (p. 168).

**Intangible assets** Noncurrent assets that do not have physical substance. (p. 180).

**Liquidity** The ability of a company to pay obligations expected to be due within the next year. (p. 182).

**Long-term investments** Generally, (1) investments in stocks and bonds of other companies that companies normally hold for many years, and (2) long-term assets, such as land and buildings, not currently being used in operations. (p. 179).

**Long-term liabilities** Obligations that a company expects to pay after one year. (p. 183).

**Operating cycle** The average time that it takes to purchase inventory, sell it on account, and then collect cash from customers. (p. 179).

**Permanent (real) accounts** Accounts that relate to one or more future accounting periods. Consist of all balance sheet accounts. Balances are carried forward to next accounting period. (p. 168).

**Post-closing trial balance** A list of permanent accounts and their balances after a company has journalized and posted closing entries. (p. 172).

**Property, plant, and equipment** Assets with relatively long useful lives and currently being used in operations. (p. 180).

**Reversing entry** An entry, made at the beginning of the next accounting period, that is the exact opposite of the adjusting entry made in the previous period. (p. 175).

**Stockholders' equity** The ownership claim of shareholders on total assets. It is to a corporation what owner's equity is to a proprietorship. (p. 183).

**Temporary (nominal) accounts** Accounts that relate only to a given accounting period. Consist of all income statement accounts and owner's drawings account. All temporary accounts are closed at end of the accounting period. (p. 167).

**Worksheet** A multiple-column form that may be used in making adjusting entries and in preparing financial statements. (p. 162).

# APPENDIX 4A   Reversing Entries

After preparing the financial statements and closing the books, it is often helpful to reverse some of the adjusting entries before recording the regular transactions of the next period. Such entries are **reversing entries**. Companies make **a reversing entry at the beginning of the next accounting period**. Each reversing entry **is the exact opposite of the adjusting entry made in the previous period**. The recording of reversing entries is an **optional step** in the accounting cycle.

The purpose of reversing entries is to simplify the recording of a subsequent transaction related to an adjusting entry. For example, in Chapter 3 (page 115), the payment of salaries after an adjusting entry resulted in two debits: one to Salaries and Wages Payable and the other to Salaries and Wages Expense. With reversing entries, the company can debit the entire subsequent payment to Salaries and Wages Expense. **The use of reversing entries does not change the amounts reported in the financial statements.** What it does is simplify the recording of subsequent transactions.

## Reversing Entries Example

Companies most often use reversing entries to reverse two types of adjusting entries: accrued revenues and accrued expenses. To illustrate the optional use of reversing entries for accrued expenses, we will use the salaries expense transactions for Pioneer Advertising Agency as illustrated in Chapters 2, 3, and 4. The transaction and adjustment data are as follows.

1. October 26 (initial salary entry): Pioneer pays $4,000 of salaries and wages earned between October 15 and October 26.

2. October 31 (adjusting entry): Salaries and wages earned between October 29 and October 31 are $1,200. The company will pay these in the November 9 payroll.

3. November 9 (subsequent salary entry): Salaries and wages paid are $4,000. Of this amount, $1,200 applied to accrued salaries and wages payable and $2,800 was earned between November 1 and November 9.

Illustration 4A-1 shows the entries with and without reversing entries.

The first three entries are the same whether or not Pioneer uses reversing entries. The last two entries are different. The November 1 **reversing entry** eliminates the $1,200 balance in Salaries and Wages Payable created by the October 31 adjusting entry. The reversing entry also creates a $1,200 credit balance in the Salaries and Wages Expense account. As you know, it is unusual for an expense account to have a credit balance. The balance is correct in this instance, though, because it anticipates that the entire amount of the first salaries and wages payment in the new accounting period will be debited to Salaries and Wages Expense. This debit will eliminate the credit balance. The resulting debit balance in the expense account will equal the salaries and wages expense incurred in the new accounting period ($2,800 in this example).

If Pioneer makes reversing entries, it can debit all cash payments of expenses to the expense account. This means that on November 9 (and every payday) Pioneer can debit Salaries and Wages Expense for the amount paid, without regard to any accrued salaries and wages payable. Being able to make the **same entry each time** simplifies the recording process. The company can record subsequent transactions as if the related adjusting entry had never been made.

| Without Reversing Entries (per chapter) | | | | With Reversing Entries (per appendix) | | |
|---|---|---|---|---|---|---|
| **Initial Salary Entry** | | | | **Initial Salary Entry** | | |
| Oct. 26 | Salaries and Wages Expense | 4,000 | | Oct. 26 | (Same entry) | |
| | Cash | | 4,000 | | | |
| **Adjusting Entry** | | | | **Adjusting Entry** | | |
| Oct. 31 | Salaries and Wages Expense | 1,200 | | Oct. 31 | (Same entry) | |
| | Salaries and Wages Payable | | 1,200 | | | |
| **Closing Entry** | | | | **Closing Entry** | | |
| Oct. 31 | Income Summary | 5,200 | | Oct. 31 | (Same entry) | |
| | Salaries and Wages Expense | | 5,200 | | | |
| **Reversing Entry** | | | | **Reversing Entry** | | |
| Nov. 1 | No reversing entry is made. | | | Nov. 1 | Salaries and Wages Payable | 1,200 |
| | | | | | Salaries and Wages Expense | | 1,200 |
| **Subsequent Salary Entry** | | | | **Subsequent Salary Entry** | | |
| Nov. 9 | Salaries and Wages Payable | 1,200 | | Nov. 9 | Salaries and Wages Expense | 4,000 |
| | Salaries and Wages Expense | 2,800 | | | Cash | | 4,000 |
| | Cash | | 4,000 | | | |

**Illustration 4A-1**
Comparative entries—not reversing vs. reversing

Illustration 4A-2 shows the posting of the entries with reversing entries.

| **Salaries and Wages Expense** | | | | **Salaries and Wages Payable** | | | |
|---|---|---|---|---|---|---|---|
| 10/26 Paid | 4,000 | 10/31 Closing | 5,200 | 11/1 Reversing | 1,200 | 10/31 Adjusting | 1,200 |
| 31 Adjusting | 1,200 | | | | | | |
| | 5,200 | | 5,200 | | | | |
| 11/9 Paid | 4,000 | 11/1 Reversing | 1,200 | | | | |

**Illustration 4A-2**
Postings with reversing entries

A company can also use reversing entries for accrued revenue adjusting entries. For Pioneer Advertising Agency, the adjusting entry was Accounts Receivable (Dr.) $200 and Service Revenue (Cr.) $200. Thus, the reversing entry on November 1 is:

| Nov. 1 | Service Revenue | 200 | |
|---|---|---|---|
| | Accounts Receivable | | 200 |
| | (To reverse October 31 adjusting entry) | | |

| A | = | L | + | OE |
|---|---|---|---|---|
| | | | | −200 Rev |
| −200 | | | | |

**Cash Flows**
no effect

When Pioneer collects the accrued service revenue, it debits Cash and credits Service Revenue.

## SUMMARY OF LEARNING OBJECTIVE FOR APPENDIX 4A

**7 Prepare reversing entries.** Reversing entries are the opposite of the adjusting entries made in the preceding period. Some companies choose to make reversing entries at the beginning of a new accounting period to simplify the recording of later transactions related to the adjusting entries. In most cases, only accrued adjusting entries are reversed.

**Self-Test, Brief Exercises, Exercises, Problem Set A, and many more components are available for practice in *WileyPLUS*.**

***Note:*** All asterisked Questions, Exercises, and Problems relate to material in the appendix to the chapter.

## SELF-TEST QUESTIONS

*Answers are on page 212.*

(LO 1) **1.** Which of the following statements is **incorrect** concerning the worksheet?
  **(a)** The worksheet is essentially a working tool of the accountant.
  **(b)** The worksheet is distributed to management and other interested parties.
  **(c)** The worksheet cannot be used as a basis for posting to ledger accounts.
  **(d)** Financial statements can be prepared directly from the worksheet before journalizing and posting the adjusting entries.

(LO 1) **2.** In a worksheet, net income is entered in the following columns:
  **(a)** income statement (Dr) and balance sheet (Dr).
  **(b)** income statement (Cr) and balance sheet (Dr).
  **(c)** income statement (Dr) and balance sheet (Cr).
  **(d)** income statement (Cr) and balance sheet (Cr).

(LO 1) **3.** In the unadjusted trial balance of its worksheet for the year ended December 31, 2014, Knox Company reported Equipment of $120,000. The year-end adjusting entries require an adjustment of $15,000 for depreciation expense for the equipment. After adjustment, the following adjusted amount should be reported:
  **(a)** a debit of $105,000 for Equipment in the balance sheet column.
  **(b)** a credit of $15,000 for Depreciation Expense—Equipment in the income statement column.
  **(c)** a debit of $120,000 for Equipment in the balance sheet column.
  **(d)** a debit of $15,000 for Accumulated Depreciation—Equipment in the balance sheet column.

(LO 2) **4.** An account that will have a zero balance after closing entries have been journalized and posted is:
  **(a)** Service Revenue.
  **(b)** Supplies.
  **(c)** Prepaid Insurance.
  **(d)** Accumulated Depreciation—Equipment.

(LO 2) **5.** When a net loss has occurred, Income Summary is:
  **(a)** debited and Owner's Capital is credited.
  **(b)** credited and Owner's Capital is debited.
  **(c)** debited and Owner's Drawings is credited.
  **(d)** credited and Owner's Drawings is debited.

(LO 2) **6.** The closing process involves separate entries to close (1) expenses, (2) drawings, (3) revenues, and (4) income summary. The correct sequencing of the entries is:
  **(a)** (4), (3), (2), (1)      **(c)** (3), (1), (4), (2)
  **(b)** (1), (2), (3), (4)      **(d)** (3), (2), (1), (4)

(LO 3) **7.** Which types of accounts will appear in the post-closing trial balance?

  **(a)** Permanent (real) accounts.
  **(b)** Temporary (nominal) accounts.
  **(c)** Accounts shown in the income statement columns of a worksheet.
  **(d)** None of the above.

(LO 4) **8.** All of the following are required steps in the accounting cycle **except**:
  **(a)** journalizing and posting closing entries.
  **(b)** preparing financial statements.
  **(c)** journalizing the transactions.
  **(d)** preparing a worksheet.

(LO 4) **9.** The proper order of the following steps in the accounting cycle is:
  **(a)** prepare unadjusted trial balance, journalize transactions, post to ledger accounts, journalize and post adjusting entries.
  **(b)** journalize transactions, prepare unadjusted trial balance, post to ledger accounts, journalize and post adjusting entries.
  **(c)** journalize transactions, post to ledger accounts, prepare unadjusted trial balance, journalize and post adjusting entries.
  **(d)** prepare unadjusted trial balance, journalize and post adjusting entries, journalize transactions, post to ledger accounts.

(LO 5) **10.** When Ramirez Company purchased supplies worth $500, it incorrectly recorded a credit to Supplies for $5,000 and a debit to Cash for $5,000. Before correcting this error:
  **(a)** Cash is overstated and Supplies is overstated.
  **(b)** Cash is understated and Supplies is understated.
  **(c)** Cash is understated and Supplies is overstated.
  **(d)** Cash is overstated and Supplies is understated.

(LO 5) **11.** Cash of $100 received at the time the service was performed was journalized and posted as a debit to Cash $100 and a credit to Accounts Receivable $100. Assuming the incorrect entry is not reversed, the correcting entry is:
  **(a)** debit Service Revenue $100 and credit Accounts Receivable $100.
  **(b)** debit Accounts Receivable $100 and credit Service Revenue $100.
  **(c)** debit Cash $100 and credit Service Revenue $100.
  **(d)** debit Accounts Receivable $100 and credit Cash $100.

(LO 6) **12.** The correct order of presentation in a classified balance sheet for the following current assets is:
  **(a)** accounts receivable, cash, prepaid insurance, inventory.
  **(b)** cash, inventory, accounts receivable, prepaid insurance.

(c) cash, accounts receivable, inventory, prepaid insurance.

(d) inventory, cash, accounts receivable, prepaid insurance.

(LO 6) **13.** A company has purchased a tract of land. It expects to build a production plant on the land in approximately 5 years. During the 5 years before construction, the land will be idle. The land should be reported as:

(a) property, plant, and equipment.

(b) land expense.

(c) a long-term investment.

(d) an intangible asset.

(LO 6) **14.** In a classified balance sheet, assets are usually classified using the following categories:

(a) current assets; long-term assets; property, plant, and equipment; and intangible assets.

(b) current assets; long-term investments; property, plant, and equipment; and tangible assets.

(c) current assets; long-term investments; tangible assets; and intangible assets.

(d) current assets; long-term investments; property, plant, and equipment; and intangible assets.

**15.** Current assets are listed:  (LO 6)

(a) by expected conversion to cash.

(b) by importance.

(c) by longevity.

(d) alphabetically.

*16. On December 31, Kevin Hartman Company correctly (LO 7) made an adjusting entry to recognize $2,000 of accrued salaries payable. On January 8 of the next year, total salaries of $3,400 were paid. Assuming the correct reversing entry was made on January 1, the entry on January 8 will result in a credit to Cash $3,400 and the following debit(s):

(a) Salaries and Wages Payable $1,400 and Salaries and Wages Expense $2,000.

(b) Salaries and Wages Payable $2,000 and Salaries and Wages Expense $1,400.

(c) Salaries and Wages Expense $3,400.

(d) Salaries and Wages Payable $3,400.

Go to the book's companion website, www.wiley.com/college/weygandt, for additional Self-Test Questions.

✔ The Navigator

## QUESTIONS

1. "A worksheet is a permanent accounting record and its use is required in the accounting cycle." Do you agree? Explain.

2. Explain the purpose of the worksheet.

3. What is the relationship, if any, between the amount shown in the adjusted trial balance column for an account and that account's ledger balance?

4. If a company's revenues are $125,000 and its expenses are $113,000, in which financial statement columns of the worksheet will the net income of $12,000 appear? When expenses exceed revenues, in which columns will the difference appear?

5. Why is it necessary to prepare formal financial statements if all of the data are in the statement columns of the worksheet?

6. Identify the account(s) debited and credited in each of the four closing entries, assuming the company has net income for the year.

7. Describe the nature of the Income Summary account and identify the types of summary data that may be posted to this account.

8. What are the content and purpose of a post-closing trial balance?

9. Which of the following accounts would not appear in the post-closing trial balance? Interest Payable; Equipment; Depreciation Expense; Owner's Drawings; Unearned Service Revenue; Accumulated Depreciation—Equipment; and Service Revenue.

10. Distinguish between a reversing entry and an adjusting entry. Are reversing entries required?

11. Indicate, in the sequence in which they are made, the three required steps in the accounting cycle that involve journalizing.

12. Identify, in the sequence in which they are prepared, the three trial balances that are often used to report financial information about a company.

13. How do correcting entries differ from adjusting entries?

14. What standard classifications are used in preparing a classified balance sheet?

15. What is meant by the term "operating cycle?"

16. Define current assets. What basis is used for arranging individual items within the current assets section?

17. Distinguish between long-term investments and property, plant, and equipment.

18. (a) What is the term used to describe the owner's equity section of a corporation? (b) Identify the two owners' equity accounts in a corporation and indicate the purpose of each.

19. Using Apple's annual report, determine its current liabilities at September 25, 2010, and September 24, 2011. Were current liabilities higher or lower than current assets in these two years?

*20. Cigale Company prepares reversing entries. If the adjusting entry for interest payable is reversed, what type of an account balance, if any, will there be in Interest Payable and Interest Expense after the reversing entry is posted?

*21. At December 31, accrued salaries payable totaled $3,500. On January 10, total salaries of $8,000 are paid. (a) Assume that reversing entries are made at January 1. Give the January 10 entry, and indicate the Salaries and Wages Expense account balance after the entry is posted. (b) Repeat part (a) assuming reversing entries are not made.

## BRIEF EXERCISES

*List the steps in preparing a worksheet.*

(LO 1)

**BE4-1** The steps in using a worksheet are presented in random order below. List the steps in the proper order by placing numbers 1–5 in the blank spaces.

**(a)** _____ Prepare a trial balance on the worksheet.
**(b)** _____ Enter adjusted balances.
**(c)** _____ Extend adjusted balances to appropriate statement columns.
**(d)** _____ Total the statement columns, compute net income (loss), and complete the worksheet.
**(e)** _____ Enter adjustment data.

*Prepare partial worksheet.*

(LO 1)

**BE4-2** The ledger of Clayton Company includes the following unadjusted balances: Prepaid Insurance $3,000, Service Revenue $58,000, and Salaries and Wages Expense $25,000. Adjusting entries are required for (a) expired insurance $1,800; (b) services performed $1,100, but unbilled and uncollected; and (c) accrued salaries payable $800. Enter the unadjusted balances and adjustments into a worksheet and complete the worksheet for all accounts. (*Note:* You will need to add the following accounts: Accounts Receivable, Salaries and Wages Payable, and Insurance Expense.)

*Identify worksheet columns for selected accounts.*

(LO 1)

**BE4-3** The following selected accounts appear in the adjusted trial balance columns of the worksheet for Goulet Company: Accumulated Depreciation; Depreciation Expense; Owner's Capital; Owner's Drawings; Service Revenue; Supplies; and Accounts Payable. Indicate the financial statement column (income statement Dr., balance sheet Cr., etc.) to which each balance should be extended.

*Prepare closing entries from ledger balances.*

(LO 2)

**BE4-4** The ledger of Rios Company contains the following balances: Owner's Capital $30,000; Owner's Drawings $2,000; Service Revenue $50,000; Salaries and Wages Expense $27,000; and Supplies Expense $7,000. Prepare the closing entries at December 31.

*Post closing entries; underline and balance T-accounts.*

(LO 2)

**BE4-5** Using the data in BE4-4, enter the balances in T-accounts, post the closing entries, and underline and balance the accounts.

*Journalize and post closing entries using the three-column form of account.*

(LO 2)

**BE4-6** The income statement for Weeping Willow Golf Club for the month ending July 31 shows Service Revenue $16,400, Salaries and Wages Expense $8,200, Maintenance and Repairs Expense $2,500, and Net Income $5,700. Prepare the entries to close the revenue and expense accounts. Post the entries to the revenue and expense accounts, and complete the closing process for these accounts using the three-column form of account.

*Identify post-closing trial balance accounts.*

(LO 3)

**BE4-7** Using the data in BE4-3, identify the accounts that would be included in a post-closing trial balance.

*List the required steps in the accounting cycle in sequence.*

(LO 4)

**BE4-8** The steps in the accounting cycle are listed in random order below. List the steps in proper sequence, assuming no worksheet is prepared, by placing numbers 1–9 in the blank spaces.

**(a)** _____ Prepare a trial balance.
**(b)** _____ Journalize the transactions.
**(c)** _____ Journalize and post closing entries.
**(d)** _____ Prepare financial statements.
**(e)** _____ Journalize and post adjusting entries.
**(f)** _____ Post to ledger accounts.
**(g)** _____ Prepare a post-closing trial balance.
**(h)** _____ Prepare an adjusted trial balance.
**(i)** _____ Analyze business transactions.

*Prepare correcting entries.*

(LO 5)

**BE4-9** At Creighton Company, the following errors were discovered after the transactions had been journalized and posted. Prepare the correcting entries.

**1.** A collection on account from a customer for $870 was recorded as a debit to Cash $870 and a credit to Service Revenue $870.

**2.** The purchase of store supplies on account for $1,570 was recorded as a debit to Supplies $1,750 and a credit to Accounts Payable $1,750.

*Prepare the current assets section of a balance sheet.*

(LO 6)

**BE4-10** The balance sheet debit column of the worksheet for Hamidi Company includes the following accounts: Accounts Receivable $12,500; Prepaid Insurance $3,600; Cash $4,100; Supplies $5,200; and Debt Investments (short-term) $6,700. Prepare the current assets section of the balance sheet, listing the accounts in proper sequence.

**BE4-11** The following are the major balance sheet classifications:

Current assets (CA)
Long-term investments (LTI)
Property, plant, and equipment (PPE)
Intangible assets (IA)

Current liabilities (CL)
Long-term liabilities (LTL)
Owner's equity (OE)

*Classify accounts on balance sheet.*
*(LO 6)*

Match each of the following accounts to its proper balance sheet classification.

_____ Accounts payable
_____ Accounts receivable
_____ Accumulated depreciation—buildings
_____ Buildings
_____ Cash
_____ Copyrights

_____ Income taxes payable
_____ Debt investments (long-term)
_____ Land
_____ Inventory
_____ Patents
_____ Supplies

***BE4-12** At October 31, Burgess Company made an accrued expense adjusting entry of $2,100 for salaries. Prepare the reversing entry on November 1, and indicate the balances in Salaries and Wages Payable and Salaries and Wages Expense after posting the reversing entry.

*Prepare reversing entries.*
*(LO 7)*

## > DO IT! Review

**DO IT! 4-1** Bradley Decker is preparing a worksheet. Explain to Bradley how he should extend the following adjusted trial balance accounts to the financial statement columns of the worksheet.

*Prepare a worksheet.*
*(LO 1)*

Service Revenue            Accounts Receivable
Notes Payable              Accumulated Depreciation
Owner's Capital            Utilities Expense

**DO IT! 4-2** The worksheet for Tsai Company shows the following in the financial statement columns.

*Prepare closing entries.*
*(LO 2)*

Owner's drawings    $22,000
Owner's capital       70,000
Net income            41,000

Prepare the closing entries at December 31 that affect owner's capital.

**DO IT! 4-3** Ryan Newton recently received the following information related to Ryan Company's December 31, 2014, balance sheet.

*Prepare assets section of the balance sheet.*
*(LO 6)*

Inventory                        $ 2,900   Debt investments (short-term)   $1,200
Cash                               4,300   Accumulated depreciation          5,700
Equipment                         21,700   Accounts receivable               4,300
Stock investments (long-term)      6,500

Prepare the assets section of Ryan Company's classified balance sheet.

**DO IT! 4-4** The following accounts were taken from the financial statements of Lee Company.

*Match accounts to balance sheet classifications.*
*(LO 6)*

_____ Interest revenue
_____ Utilities payable
_____ Accounts payable
_____ Supplies
_____ Bonds payable
_____ Goodwill

_____ Owner's capital
_____ Accumulated depreciation—equipment
_____ Equipment
_____ Salaries and wages expense
_____ Debt investments (long-term)
_____ Unearned rent revenue

Match each of the accounts to its proper balance sheet classification, as shown below. If the item would not appear on a balance sheet, use "NA."

Current assets (CA)
Long-term investments (LTI)
Property, plant, and equipment (PPE)
Intangible assets (IA)

Current liabilities (CL)
Long-term liabilities (LTL)
Owner's equity (OE)

**EXERCISES**

*Complete the worksheet.*
(LO 1)

**E4-1** The trial balance columns of the worksheet for Nanduri Company at June 30, 2014, are as follows.

### NANDURI COMPANY
### Worksheet
### For the Month Ended June 30, 2014

| Account Titles | Trial Balance Dr. | Trial Balance Cr. |
|---|---|---|
| Cash | 2,320 | |
| Accounts Receivable | 2,440 | |
| Supplies | 1,880 | |
| Accounts Payable | | 1,120 |
| Unearned Service Revenue | | 240 |
| Owner's Capital | | 3,600 |
| Service Revenue | | 2,400 |
| Salaries and Wages Expense | 560 | |
| Miscellaneous Expense | 160 | |
| | 7,360 | 7,360 |

Other data:

1. A physical count reveals $500 of supplies on hand.
2. $100 of the unearned revenue is still unearned at month-end.
3. Accrued salaries are $210.

*Instructions*
Enter the trial balance on a worksheet and complete the worksheet.

*Complete the worksheet.*
(LO 1)

**E4-2** The adjusted trial balance columns of the worksheet for DeSousa Company are as follows.

### DESOUSA COMPANY
### Worksheet (partial)
### For the Month Ended April 30, 2014

| Account Titles | Adjusted Trial Balance Dr. | Adjusted Trial Balance Cr. | Income Statement Dr. | Income Statement Cr. | Balance Sheet Dr. | Balance Sheet Cr. |
|---|---|---|---|---|---|---|
| Cash | 10,000 | | | | | |
| Accounts Receivable | 7,840 | | | | | |
| Prepaid Rent | 2,280 | | | | | |
| Equipment | 23,050 | | | | | |
| Accumulated Depreciation—Equip. | | 4,921 | | | | |
| Notes Payable | | 5,700 | | | | |
| Accounts Payable | | 4,920 | | | | |
| Owner's Capital | | 27,960 | | | | |
| Owner's Drawings | 3,650 | | | | | |
| Service Revenue | | 15,590 | | | | |
| Salaries and Wages Expense | 10,840 | | | | | |
| Rent Expense | 760 | | | | | |
| Depreciation Expense | 671 | | | | | |
| Interest Expense | 57 | | | | | |
| Interest Payable | | 57 | | | | |
| Totals | 59,148 | 59,148 | | | | |

*Instructions*
Complete the worksheet.

**E4-3** Worksheet data for DeSousa Company are presented in E4-2. The owner did not make any additional investments in the business in April.

*Prepare financial statements from worksheet.*
*(LO 1, 6)*

**Instructions**
Prepare an income statement, an owner's equity statement, and a classified balance sheet.

**E4-4** Worksheet data for DeSousa Company are presented in E4-2.

*Journalize and post closing entries and prepare a post-closing trial balance.*
*(LO 2, 3)*

**Instructions**
**(a)** Journalize the closing entries at April 30.
**(b)** Post the closing entries to Income Summary and Owner's Capital. Use T-accounts.
**(c)** Prepare a post-closing trial balance at April 30.

**E4-5** The adjustments columns of the worksheet for Misra Company are shown below.

*Prepare adjusting entries from a worksheet, and extend balances to worksheet columns.*
*(LO 1)*

| | Adjustments | |
|---|---|---|
| **Account Titles** | **Debit** | **Credit** |
| Accounts Receivable | 1,100 | |
| Prepaid Insurance | | 300 |
| Accumulated Depreciation—Equipment | | 900 |
| Salaries and Wages Payable | | 500 |
| Service Revenue | | 1,100 |
| Salaries and Wages Expense | 500 | |
| Insurance Expense | 300 | |
| Depreciation Expense | 900 | |
| | 2,800 | 2,800 |

**Instructions**
**(a)** Prepare the adjusting entries.
**(b)** Assuming the adjusted trial balance amount for each account is normal, indicate the financial statement column to which each balance should be extended.

**E4-6** Selected worksheet data for Elsayed Company are presented below.

*Derive adjusting entries from worksheet data.*
*(LO 1)*

| | Trial Balance | | Adjusted Trial Balance | |
|---|---|---|---|---|
| **Account Titles** | **Dr.** | **Cr.** | **Dr.** | **Cr.** |
| Accounts Receivable | ? | | 34,000 | |
| Prepaid Insurance | 26,000 | | 20,000 | |
| Supplies | 7,000 | | ? | |
| Accumulated Depreciation—Equipment | | 12,000 | | ? |
| Salaries and Wages Payable | | ? | | 5,600 |
| Service Revenue | | 88,000 | | 97,000 |
| Insurance Expense | | | ? | |
| Depreciation Expense | | | 10,000 | |
| Supplies Expense | | | 4,500 | |
| Salaries and Wages Expense | ? | | 49,000 | |

**Instructions**
**(a)** Fill in the missing amounts.
**(b)** Prepare the adjusting entries that were made.

**E4-7** Kay Magill Company had the following adjusted trial balance.

*Prepare closing entries, and prepare a post-closing trial balance.*
*(LO 2, 3)*

**KAY MAGILL COMPANY**
Adjusted Trial Balance
For the Month Ended June 30, 2014

| | Adjusted Trial Balance | |
|---|---|---|
| **Account Titles** | **Debit** | **Credit** |
| Cash | $ 3,712 | |
| Accounts Receivable | 3,904 | |
| Supplies | 480 | |
| Accounts Payable | | $ 1,556 |
| Unearned Service Revenue | | 160 |
| Owner's Capital | | 5,760 |
| Owner's Drawings | 628 | |
| Service Revenue | | 4,300 |
| Salaries and Wages Expense | 1,344 | |
| Miscellaneous Expense | 256 | |
| Supplies Expense | 1,900 | |
| Salaries and Wages Payable | | 448 |
| | $12,224 | $12,224 |

**Instructions**
**(a)** Prepare closing entries at June 30, 2014.
**(b)** Prepare a post-closing trial balance.

*Journalize and post closing entries, and prepare a post-closing trial balance.*
*(LO 2, 3)*

**E4-8** Plevin Company ended its fiscal year on July 31, 2014. The company's adjusted trial balance as of the end of its fiscal year is shown below.

**PLEVIN COMPANY**
Adjusted Trial Balance
July 31, 2014

| No. | Account Titles | Debit | Credit |
|---|---|---|---|
| 101 | Cash | $ 9,840 | |
| 112 | Accounts Receivable | 8,780 | |
| 157 | Equipment | 15,900 | |
| 158 | Accumulated Depreciation—Equip. | | $ 7,400 |
| 201 | Accounts Payable | | 4,220 |
| 208 | Unearned Rent Revenue | | 1,800 |
| 301 | Owner's Capital | | 45,200 |
| 306 | Owner's Drawings | 16,000 | |
| 400 | Service Revenue | | 64,000 |
| 429 | Rent Revenue | | 6,500 |
| 711 | Depreciation Expense | 8,000 | |
| 726 | Salaries and Wages Expense | 55,700 | |
| 732 | Utilities Expense | 14,900 | |
| | | $129,120 | $129,120 |

**Instructions**
**(a)** Prepare the closing entries using page J15.
**(b)** Post to Owner's Capital and No. 350 Income Summary accounts. (Use the three-column form.)
**(c)** Prepare a post-closing trial balance at July 31.

*Prepare financial statements.*
*(LO 6)*

**E4-9** The adjusted trial balance for Plevin Company is presented in E4-8.

**Instructions**
**(a)** Prepare an income statement and an owner's equity statement for the year. Plevin did not make any capital investments during the year.
**(b)** Prepare a classified balance sheet at July 31.

**E4-10** Janis Engle has prepared the following list of statements about the accounting cycle.

*Answer questions related to the accounting cycle.*
(LO 4)

1. "Journalize the transactions" is the first step in the accounting cycle.
2. Reversing entries are a required step in the accounting cycle.
3. Correcting entries do not have to be part of the accounting cycle.
4. If a worksheet is prepared, some steps of the accounting cycle are incorporated into the worksheet.
5. The accounting cycle begins with the analysis of business transactions and ends with the preparation of a post-closing trial balance.
6. All steps of the accounting cycle occur daily during the accounting period.
7. The step of "post to the ledger accounts" occurs before the step of "journalize the transactions."
8. Closing entries must be prepared before financial statements can be prepared.

**Instructions**
Identify each statement as true or false. If false, indicate how to correct the statement.

**E4-11** Selected accounts for Heather's Salon are presented below. All June 30 postings are from closing entries.

*Prepare closing entries.*
(LO 2)

**Salaries and Wages Expense**

| 6/10 | 3,200 | 6/30 | 8,800 |
| 6/28 | 5,600 | | |

**Service Revenue**

| 6/30 | 18,100 | 6/15 | 9,700 |
| | | 6/24 | 8,400 |

**Owner's Capital**

| 6/30 | 2,500 | 6/1 | 12,000 |
| | | 6/30 | 5,000 |
| | | Bal. | 14,500 |

**Supplies Expense**

| 6/12 | 600 | 6/30 | 1,300 |
| 6/24 | 700 | | |

**Rent Expense**

| 6/1 | 3,000 | 6/30 | 3,000 |

**Owner's Drawings**

| 6/13 | 1,000 | 6/30 | 2,500 |
| 6/25 | 1,500 | | |

**Instructions**
(a) Prepare the closing entries that were made.
(b) Post the closing entries to Income Summary.

**E4-12** Andrew Clark Company discovered the following errors made in January 2014.

*Prepare correcting entries.*
(LO 5)

1. A payment of Salaries and Wages Expense of $700 was debited to Equipment and credited to Cash, both for $700.
2. A collection of $1,000 from a client on account was debited to Cash $100 and credited to Service Revenue $100.
3. The purchase of equipment on account for $760 was debited to Equipment $670 and credited to Accounts Payable $670.

**Instructions**
(a) Correct the errors by reversing the incorrect entry and preparing the correct entry.
(b) Correct the errors without reversing the incorrect entry.

**E4-13** Keenan Company has an inexperienced accountant. During the first 2 weeks on the job, the accountant made the following errors in journalizing transactions. All entries were posted as made.

*Prepare correcting entries.*
(LO 5)

1. A payment on account of $840 to a creditor was debited to Accounts Payable $480 and credited to Cash $480.
2. The purchase of supplies on account for $560 was debited to Equipment $56 and credited to Accounts Payable $56.
3. A $500 withdrawal of cash for P. Keenan's personal use was debited to Salaries and Wages Expense $500 and credited to Cash $500.

**Instructions**
Prepare the correcting entries.

**E4-14** The adjusted trial balance for Martell Bowling Alley at December 31, 2014, contains the accounts shown on page 198.

*Prepare a classified balance sheet.*
(LO 6)

| | Debit | | Credit |
|---|---|---|---|
| Buildings | $128,800 | Owner's Capital | $115,000 |
| Accounts Receivable | 14,520 | Accumulated Depreciation—Buildings | 42,600 |
| Prepaid Insurance | 4,680 | Accounts Payable | 12,300 |
| Cash | 18,040 | Notes Payable | 97,780 |
| Equipment | 62,400 | Accumulated Depreciation—Equipment | 18,720 |
| Land | 67,000 | Interest Payable | 2,600 |
| Insurance Expense | 780 | Service Revenue | 17,180 |
| Depreciation Expense | 7,360 | | $306,180 |
| Interest Expense | 2,600 | | |
| | $306,180 | | |

**Instructions**

**(a)** Prepare a classified balance sheet; assume that $22,000 of the note payable will be paid in 2015.

**(b)** ━━━ Comment on the liquidity of the company.

*Classify accounts on balance sheet.*

*(LO 6)*

**E4-15** The following are the major balance sheet classifications.

Current assets (CA)
Long-term investments (LTI)
Property, plant, and equipment (PPE)
Intangible assets (IA)

Current liabilities (CL)
Long-term liabilities (LTL)
Owner's equity (OE)

**Instructions**

Classify each of the following accounts taken from Raman Company's balance sheet.

_____ Accounts payable
_____ Accounts receivable
_____ Cash
_____ Owner's capital
_____ Patents
_____ Salaries and wages payable
_____ Inventory
_____ Stock investments
          (to be sold in 7 months)

_____ Accumulated depreciation—equipment
_____ Buildings
_____ Land (in use)
_____ Notes payable (due in 2 years)
_____ Supplies
_____ Equipment
_____ Prepaid expenses

*Prepare a classified balance sheet.*

*(LO 6)*

**E4-16** The following items were taken from the financial statements of D. Gygi Company. (All amounts are in thousands.)

| | | | |
|---|---|---|---|
| Long-term debt | $ 1,000 | Accumulated depreciation—equipment | $ 5,655 |
| Prepaid insurance | 880 | Accounts payable | 1,444 |
| Equipment | 11,500 | Notes payable (due after 2015) | 400 |
| Stock investments (long-term) | 264 | Owner's capital | 12,955 |
| Debt investments (short-term) | 3,690 | Accounts receivable | 1,696 |
| Notes payable (due in 2015) | 500 | Inventory | 1,256 |
| Cash | 2,668 | | |

**Instructions**

Prepare a classified balance sheet in good form as of December 31, 2014.

*Prepare financial statements.*

*(LO 6)*

**E4-17** These financial statement items are for Norsted Company at year-end, July 31, 2014.

| | | | |
|---|---|---|---|
| Salaries and wages payable | $ 2,080 | Notes payable (long-term) | $ 1,800 |
| Salaries and wages expense | 51,700 | Cash | 14,200 |
| Utilities expense | 22,600 | Accounts receivable | 9,780 |
| Equipment | 30,400 | Accumulated depreciation—equipment | 6,000 |
| Accounts payable | 4,100 | Owner's drawings | 3,000 |
| Service revenue | 62,000 | Depreciation expense | 4,000 |
| Rent revenue | 8,500 | Owner's capital (beginning of the year) | 51,200 |

**Instructions**

**(a)** Prepare an income statement and an owner's equity statement for the year. The owner did not make any new investments during the year.

**(b)** Prepare a classified balance sheet at July 31.

*E4-18 Reblin Company pays salaries of $12,000 every Monday for the preceding 5-day week (Monday through Friday). Assume December 31 falls on a Tuesday, so Reblin's employees have worked 2 days without being paid.

*Use reversing entries.*
*(LO 7)*

**Instructions**

(a) Assume the company does not use reversing entries. Prepare the December 31 adjusting entry and the entry on Monday, January 6, when Reblin pays the payroll.

(b) Assume the company does use reversing entries. Prepare the December 31 adjusting entry, the January 1 reversing entry, and the entry on Monday, January 6, when Reblin pays the payroll.

*E4-19 On December 31, the adjusted trial balance of Cisneros Employment Agency shows the following selected data.

*Prepare closing and reversing entries.*
*(LO 2, 4, 7)*

| | | | |
|---|---|---|---|
| Accounts Receivable | $24,500 | Service Revenue | $92,500 |
| Interest Expense | 8,300 | Interest Payable | 2,000 |

Analysis shows that adjusting entries were made to (1) accrue $5,000 of service revenue and (2) accrue $2,000 interest expense.

**Instructions**

(a) Prepare the closing entries for the temporary accounts shown above at December 31.

(b) Prepare the reversing entries on January 1.

(c) Post the entries in (a) and (b). Underline and balance the accounts. (Use T-accounts.)

(d) Prepare the entries to record (1) the collection of the accrued revenue on January 10 and (2) the payment of all interest due ($3,000) on January 15.

(e) Post the entries in (d) to the temporary accounts.

# EXERCISES: SET B AND CHALLENGE EXERCISES

Visit the book's companion website, at **www.wiley.com/college/weygandt**, and choose the Student Companion site to access Exercise Set B and Challenge Exercises.

# PROBLEMS: SET A

**P4-1A** The trial balance columns of the worksheet for Lampert Roofing at March 31, 2014, are as follows.

*Prepare a worksheet, financial statements, and adjusting and closing entries.*
*(LO 1, 2, 3, 6)*

**LAMPERT ROOFING**
Worksheet
For the Month Ended March 31, 2014

| Account Titles | Trial Balance | |
|---|---|---|
| | Dr. | Cr. |
| Cash | 4,500 | |
| Accounts Receivable | 3,200 | |
| Supplies | 2,000 | |
| Equipment | 11,000 | |
| Accumulated Depreciation—Equipment | | 1,250 |
| Accounts Payable | | 2,500 |
| Unearned Service Revenue | | 550 |
| Owner's Capital | | 12,900 |
| Owner's Drawings | 1,100 | |
| Service Revenue | | 6,300 |
| Salaries and Wages Expense | 1,300 | |
| Miscellaneous Expense | 400 | |
| | 23,500 | 23,500 |

Other data:

**1.** A physical count reveals only $550 of roofing supplies on hand.
**2.** Depreciation for March is $250.
**3.** Unearned revenue amounted to $210 at March 31.
**4.** Accrued salaries are $700.

*Instructions*

(a) Adjusted trial balance $24,450

(b) Net income $2,540
Total assets $17,750

**(a)** Enter the trial balance on a worksheet and complete the worksheet.
**(b)** Prepare an income statement and owner's equity statement for the month of March and a classified balance sheet at March 31. C. Lampert made an additional investment in the business of $10,000 in March.
**(c)** Journalize the adjusting entries from the adjustments columns of the worksheet.
**(d)** Journalize the closing entries from the financial statement columns of the worksheet.

*Complete worksheet; prepare financial statements, closing entries, and post-closing trial balance.*

(LO 1, 2, 3, 6)

**P4-2A** The adjusted trial balance columns of the worksheet for Alshwer Company, owned by M. Alshwer, are as follows.

### ALSHWER COMPANY
#### Worksheet
#### For the Year Ended December 31, 2014

| Account No. | Account Titles | Adjusted Trial Balance Dr. | Adjusted Trial Balance Cr. |
|---|---|---|---|
| 101 | Cash | 5,300 | |
| 112 | Accounts Receivable | 10,800 | |
| 126 | Supplies | 1,500 | |
| 130 | Prepaid Insurance | 2,000 | |
| 157 | Equipment | 27,000 | |
| 158 | Accumulated Depreciation—Equipment | | 5,600 |
| 200 | Notes Payable | | 15,000 |
| 201 | Accounts Payable | | 6,100 |
| 212 | Salaries and Wages Payable | | 2,400 |
| 230 | Interest Payable | | 600 |
| 301 | Owner's Capital | | 13,000 |
| 306 | Owner's Drawings | 7,000 | |
| 400 | Service Revenue | | 61,000 |
| 610 | Advertising Expense | 8,400 | |
| 631 | Supplies Expense | 4,000 | |
| 711 | Depreciation Expense | 5,600 | |
| 722 | Insurance Expense | 3,500 | |
| 726 | Salaries and Wages Expense | 28,000 | |
| 905 | Interest Expense | 600 | |
| | Totals | 103,700 | 103,700 |

*Instructions*

(a) Net income $10,900

(b) Current assets $19,600
Current liabilities $14,100

(e) Post-closing trial balance $46,600

**(a)** Complete the worksheet by extending the balances to the financial statement columns.
**(b)** Prepare an income statement, owner's equity statement, and a classified balance sheet. (*Note:* $5,000 of the notes payable become due in 2015.) M. Alshwer did not make any additional investments in the business during the year.
**(c)** Prepare the closing entries. Use J14 for the journal page.
**(d)** Post the closing entries. Use the three-column form of account. Income Summary is No. 350.
**(e)** Prepare a post-closing trial balance.

*Prepare financial statements, closing entries, and post-closing trial balance.*

(LO 1, 2, 3, 6)

**P4-3A** The completed financial statement columns of the worksheet for Fleming Company are shown on the next page.

**FLEMING COMPANY**
Worksheet
For the Year Ended December 31, 2014

| Account No. | Account Titles | Income Statement Dr. | Income Statement Cr. | Balance Sheet Dr. | Balance Sheet Cr. |
|---|---|---|---|---|---|
| 101 | Cash | | | 8,900 | |
| 112 | Accounts Receivable | | | 10,800 | |
| 130 | Prepaid Insurance | | | 2,800 | |
| 157 | Equipment | | | 24,000 | |
| 158 | Accumulated Depreciation—Equip. | | | | 4,500 |
| 201 | Accounts Payable | | | | 9,000 |
| 212 | Salaries and Wages Payable | | | | 2,400 |
| 301 | Owner's Capital | | | | 19,500 |
| 306 | Owner's Drawings | | | 11,000 | |
| 400 | Service Revenue | | 60,000 | | |
| 622 | Maintenance and Repairs Expense | 1,600 | | | |
| 711 | Depreciation Expense | 3,100 | | | |
| 722 | Insurance Expense | 1,800 | | | |
| 726 | Salaries and Wages Expense | 30,000 | | | |
| 732 | Utilities Expense | 1,400 | | | |
| | Totals | 37,900 | 60,000 | 57,500 | 35,400 |
| | Net Income | 22,100 | | | 22,100 |
| | | 60,000 | 60,000 | 57,500 | 57,500 |

**Instructions**

**(a)** Prepare an income statement, an owner's equity statement, and a classified balance sheet.

**(b)** Prepare the closing entries. J. Fleming did not make any additional investments during the year.

**(c)** Post the closing entries and underline and balance the accounts. (Use T-accounts.) Income Summary is account No. 350.

**(d)** Prepare a post-closing trial balance.

(a) Ending capital $30,600
Total current assets
$22,500

(d) Post-closing trial balance
$46,500

**P4-4A** Jarmuz Management Services began business on January 1, 2014, with a capital investment of $120,000. The company manages condominiums for owners (Service Revenue) and rents space in its own office building (Rent Revenue). The trial balance and adjusted trial balance columns of the worksheet at the end of the first year are as follows.

*Complete worksheet; prepare classified balance sheet, entries, and post-closing trial balance.*

(LO 1, 2, 3, 6)

**JARMUZ MANAGEMENT SERVICES**
Worksheet
For the Year Ended December 31, 2014

| Account Titles | Trial Balance Dr. | Trial Balance Cr. | Adjusted Trial Balance Dr. | Adjusted Trial Balance Cr. |
|---|---|---|---|---|
| Cash | 13,800 | | 13,800 | |
| Accounts Receivable | 28,300 | | 28,300 | |
| Prepaid Insurance | 3,600 | | 2,400 | |
| Land | 67,000 | | 67,000 | |
| Buildings | 127,000 | | 127,000 | |
| Equipment | 59,000 | | 59,000 | |
| Accounts Payable | | 12,500 | | 12,500 |
| Unearned Rent Revenue | | 6,000 | | 1,500 |
| Mortgage Payable | | 120,000 | | 120,000 |
| Owner's Capital | | 144,000 | | 144,000 |
| Owner's Drawings | 22,000 | | 22,000 | |
| Service Revenue | | 90,700 | | 90,700 |
| Rent Revenue | | 29,000 | | 33,500 |
| Salaries and Wages Expense | 42,000 | | 42,000 | |
| Advertising Expense | 20,500 | | 20,500 | |
| Utilities Expense | 19,000 | | 19,000 | |
| Totals | 402,200 | 402,200 | | |

| Account Titles | Trial Balance | | Adjusted Trial Balance | |
|---|---|---|---|---|
| | Dr. | Cr. | Dr. | Cr. |
| Insurance Expense | | | 1,200 | |
| Depreciation Expense | | | 6,600 | |
| Accumulated Depreciation—Buildings | | | | 3,000 |
| Accumulated Depreciation—Equipment | | | | 3,600 |
| Interest Expense | | | 10,000 | |
| Interest Payable | | | | 10,000 |
| Totals | | | 418,800 | 418,800 |

**Instructions**

(a) Net income $24,900

(b) Total current assets
$44,500

(e) Post-closing trial balance
$297,500

(a) Prepare a complete worksheet.
(b) Prepare a classified balance sheet. (*Note*: $30,000 of the mortgage note payable is due for payment next year.)
(c) Journalize the adjusting entries.
(d) Journalize the closing entries.
(e) Prepare a post-closing trial balance.

*Complete all steps in accounting cycle.*

(LO 1, 2, 3, 4, 6)

**P4-5A** Heidi Jara opened Jara's Cleaning Service on July 1, 2014. During July, the following transactions were completed.

| | | |
|---|---|---|
| July | 1 | Jara invested $20,000 cash in the business. |
| | 1 | Purchased used truck for $9,000, paying $4,000 cash and the balance on account. |
| | 3 | Purchased cleaning supplies for $2,100 on account. |
| | 5 | Paid $1,800 cash on a 1-year insurance policy effective July 1. |
| | 12 | Billed customers $4,500 for cleaning services. |
| | 18 | Paid $1,500 cash on amount owed on truck and $1,400 on amount owed on cleaning supplies. |
| | 20 | Paid $2,500 cash for employee salaries. |
| | 21 | Collected $3,400 cash from customers billed on July 12. |
| | 25 | Billed customers $6,000 for cleaning services. |
| | 31 | Paid $350 for the monthly gasoline bill for the truck. |
| | 31 | Withdraw $5,600 cash for personal use. |

The chart of accounts for Jara's Cleaning Service contains the following accounts: No. 101 Cash, No. 112 Accounts Receivable, No. 126 Supplies, No. 130 Prepaid Insurance, No. 157 Equipment, No. 158 Accumulated Depreciation—Equipment, No. 201 Accounts Payable, No. 212 Salaries and Wages Payable, No. 301 Owner's Capital, No. 306 Owner's Drawings, No. 350 Income Summary, No. 400 Service Revenue, No. 631 Supplies Expense, No. 633 Gasoline Expense, No. 711 Depreciation Expense, No. 722 Insurance Expense, and No. 726 Salaries and Wages Expense.

**Instructions**

(a) Journalize and post the July transactions. Use page J1 for the journal and the three-column form of account.

(b) Trial balance $34,700

(c) Adjusted trial balance
$38,900

(b) Prepare a trial balance at July 31 on a worksheet.
(c) Enter the following adjustments on the worksheet and complete the worksheet.
　(1) Unbilled and uncollected revenue for services performed at July 31 were $2,700.
　(2) Depreciation on equipment for the month was $500.
　(3) One-twelfth of the insurance expired.
　(4) An inventory count shows $600 of cleaning supplies on hand at July 31.
　(5) Accrued but unpaid employee salaries were $1,000.

(d) Net income $7,200
Total assets $26,800

(d) Prepare the income statement and owner's equity statement for July and a classified balance sheet at July 31.
(e) Journalize and post adjusting entries. Use page J2 for the journal.
(f) Journalize and post closing entries and complete the closing process. Use page J3 for the journal.

(g) Post-closing trial balance
$27,300

(g) Prepare a post-closing trial balance at July 31.

**P4-6A** Dao Vang, CPA, was retained by Universal Cable to prepare financial statements for April 2014. Vang accumulated all the ledger balances per Universal's records and found the following.

*Analyze errors and prepare correcting entries and trial balance.*

*(LO 5)*

### UNIVERSAL CABLE
### Trial Balance
### April 30, 2014

| | Debit | Credit |
|---|---|---|
| Cash | $ 4,100 | |
| Accounts Receivable | 3,200 | |
| Supplies | 800 | |
| Equipment | 10,600 | |
| Accumulated Depreciation—Equip. | | $ 1,350 |
| Accounts Payable | | 2,100 |
| Salaries and Wages Payable | | 700 |
| Unearned Service Revenue | | 890 |
| Owner's Capital | | 12,900 |
| Service Revenue | | 5,450 |
| Salaries and Wages Expense | 3,300 | |
| Advertising Expense | 600 | |
| Miscellaneous Expense | 290 | |
| Depreciation Expense | 500 | |
| | $23,390 | $23,390 |

Dao Vang reviewed the records and found the following errors.

1. Cash received from a customer on account was recorded as $950 instead of $590.
2. A payment of $75 for advertising expense was entered as a debit to Miscellaneous Expense $75 and a credit to Cash $75.
3. The first salary payment this month was for $1,900, which included $700 of salaries payable on March 31. The payment was recorded as a debit to Salaries and Wages Expense $1,900 and a credit to Cash $1,900. (No reversing entries were made on April 1.)
4. The purchase on account of a printer costing $310 was recorded as a debit to Supplies and a credit to Accounts Payable for $310.
5. A cash payment of repair expense on equipment for $96 was recorded as a debit to Equipment $69 and a credit to Cash $69.

**Instructions**
**(a)** Prepare an analysis of each error showing (1) the incorrect entry, (2) the correct entry, and (3) the correcting entry. Items 4 and 5 occurred on April 30, 2014.
**(b)** Prepare a correct trial balance.

*(b) Trial balance $22,690*

## PROBLEMS: SET B

**P4-1B** Michael Pevnick began operations as a private investigator on January 1, 2014. The trial balance columns of the worksheet for Michael Pevnick, P.I., at March 31 are as follows.

*Prepare worksheet, financial statements, and adjusting and closing entries.*

*(LO 1, 2, 3, 6)*

### MICHAEL PEVNICK, P.I.
### Worksheet
### For the Quarter Ended March 31, 2014

| | Trial Balance | |
|---|---|---|
| **Account Titles** | **Dr.** | **Cr.** |
| Cash | 11,400 | |
| Accounts Receivable | 5,620 | |
| Supplies | 1,050 | |
| Prepaid Insurance | 2,400 | |
| Equipment | 30,000 | |

|  | Trial Balance | |
| Account Titles | Dr. | Cr. |
| --- | --- | --- |
| Notes Payable | | 10,000 |
| Accounts Payable | | 12,350 |
| Owner's Capital | | 20,000 |
| Owner's Drawings | 600 | |
| Service Revenue | | 13,620 |
| Salaries and Wages Expense | 2,200 | |
| Travel Expense | 1,300 | |
| Rent Expense | 1,200 | |
| Miscellaneous Expense | 200 | |
| | 55,970 | 55,970 |

Other data:

1. Supplies on hand total $480.
2. Depreciation is $800 per quarter.
3. Interest accrued on 6-month note payable, issued January 1, $300.
4. Insurance expires at the rate of $200 per month.
5. Services performed but unbilled at March 31 total $1,030.

*Instructions*

(a) Adjusted trial balance $58,100

(b) Net income $7,480
Total assets $49,530

(a) Enter the trial balance on a worksheet and complete the worksheet.
(b) Prepare an income statement and owner's equity statement for the quarter and a classified balance sheet at March 31. M. Pevnick did not make any additional investments in the business during the quarter ended March 31, 2014.
(c) Journalize the adjusting entries from the adjustments columns of the worksheet.
(d) Journalize the closing entries from the financial statement columns of the worksheet.

*Complete worksheet; prepare financial statements, closing entries, and post-closing trial balance.*

(LO 1, 2, 3, 6)

**P4-2B** The adjusted trial balance columns of the worksheet for Greenwood Company are as follows.

**GREENWOOD COMPANY**
Worksheet
For the Year Ended December 31, 2014

| Account No. | Account Titles | Adjusted Trial Balance | |
| --- | --- | --- | --- |
| | | Dr. | Cr. |
| 101 | Cash | 18,800 | |
| 112 | Accounts Receivable | 16,200 | |
| 126 | Supplies | 2,300 | |
| 130 | Prepaid Insurance | 4,400 | |
| 157 | Equipment | 46,000 | |
| 158 | Accumulated Depreciation—Equipment | | 20,000 |
| 200 | Notes Payable | | 20,000 |
| 201 | Accounts Payable | | 8,000 |
| 212 | Salaries and Wages Payable | | 2,600 |
| 230 | Interest Payable | | 1,000 |
| 301 | Owner's Capital | | 26,000 |
| 306 | Owner's Drawings | 12,000 | |
| 400 | Service Revenue | | 87,800 |
| 610 | Advertising Expense | 10,000 | |
| 631 | Supplies Expense | 3,700 | |
| 711 | Depreciation Expense | 8,000 | |
| 722 | Insurance Expense | 4,000 | |
| 726 | Salaries and Wages Expense | 39,000 | |
| 905 | Interest Expense | 1,000 | |
| | Totals | 165,400 | 165,400 |

## Instructions

**(a)** Complete the worksheet by extending the balances to the financial statement columns.

**(b)** Prepare an income statement, owner's equity statement, and a classified balance sheet. (*Note:* $5,000 of the notes payable become due in 2015.) T. Greenwood did not make any additional investments in the business during 2014.

**(c)** Prepare the closing entries. Use J14 for the journal page.

**(d)** Post the closing entries. Use the three-column form of account. Income Summary is account No. 350.

**(e)** Prepare a post-closing trial balance.

(a) Net income $22,100

(b) Current assets $41,700
Current liabilities $16,600

(e) Post-closing trial balance
$87,700

**P4-3B** The completed financial statement columns of the worksheet for Niho Company are shown below.

*Prepare financial statements, closing entries, and post-closing trial balance.*

(LO 1, 2, 3, 6)

### NIHO COMPANY
### Worksheet
### For the Year Ended December 31, 2014

| Account No. | Account Titles | Income Statement Dr. | Income Statement Cr. | Balance Sheet Dr. | Balance Sheet Cr. |
|---|---|---|---|---|---|
| 101 | Cash | | | 6,200 | |
| 112 | Accounts Receivable | | | 7,500 | |
| 130 | Prepaid Insurance | | | 1,800 | |
| 157 | Equipment | | | 33,000 | |
| 158 | Accumulated Depreciation—Equip. | | | | 8,600 |
| 201 | Accounts Payable | | | | 11,700 |
| 212 | Salaries and Wages Payable | | | | 3,000 |
| 301 | Owner's Capital | | | | 34,000 |
| 306 | Owner's Drawings | | | 7,200 | |
| 400 | Service Revenue | | 46,000 | | |
| 622 | Maintenance and Repairs Expense | 4,400 | | | |
| 711 | Depreciation Expense | 2,800 | | | |
| 722 | Insurance Expense | 1,200 | | | |
| 726 | Salaries and Wages Expense | 35,200 | | | |
| 732 | Utilities Expense | 4,000 | | | |
| | Totals | 47,600 | 46,000 | 55,700 | 57,300 |
| | Net Loss | | 1,600 | 1,600 | |
| | | 47,600 | 47,600 | 57,300 | 57,300 |

## Instructions

**(a)** Prepare an income statement, owner's equity statement, and a classified balance sheet. S. Niho made an additional investment in the business of $4,000 during 2014.

**(b)** Prepare the closing entries.

**(c)** Post the closing entries and underline and balance the accounts. (Use T-accounts.) Income Summary is account No. 350.

**(d)** Prepare a post-closing trial balance.

(a) Net loss $1,600
Ending capital $25,200
Total assets $39,900

(d) Post-closing trial balance
$48,500

**P4-4B** Avalon Amusement Park has a fiscal year ending on September 30. Selected data from the September 30 worksheet are presented below.

*Complete worksheet; prepare classified balance sheet, entries, and post-closing trial balance.*

(LO 1, 2, 3, 6)

### AVALON AMUSEMENT PARK
### Worksheet
### For the Year Ended September 30, 2014

| | Trial Balance Dr. | Trial Balance Cr. | Adjusted Trial Balance Dr. | Adjusted Trial Balance Cr. |
|---|---|---|---|---|
| Cash | 41,400 | | 41,400 | |
| Supplies | 18,600 | | 2,200 | |
| Prepaid Insurance | 31,900 | | 10,900 | |
| Land | 80,000 | | 80,000 | |
| Equipment | 120,000 | | 120,000 | |

| | Trial Balance | | Adjusted Trial Balance | |
|---|---|---|---|---|
| | Dr. | Cr. | Dr. | Cr. |
| Accumulated Depreciation—Equip. | | 36,200 | | 42,200 |
| Accounts Payable | | 14,600 | | 14,600 |
| Unearned Ticket Revenue | | 3,700 | | 1,000 |
| Mortgage Payable | | 50,000 | | 50,000 |
| Owner's Capital | | 109,700 | | 109,700 |
| Owner's Drawings | 14,000 | | 14,000 | |
| Ticket Revenue | | 277,500 | | 280,200 |
| Salaries and Wages Expense | 105,000 | | 105,000 | |
| Maintenance and Repairs Expense | 30,500 | | 30,500 | |
| Advertising Expense | 9,400 | | 9,400 | |
| Utilities Expense | 16,900 | | 16,900 | |
| Property Tax Expense | 18,000 | | 21,000 | |
| Interest Expense | 6,000 | | 10,000 | |
| Totals | 491,700 | 491,700 | | |
| Insurance Expense | | | 21,000 | |
| Supplies Expense | | | 16,400 | |
| Interest Payable | | | | 4,000 |
| Depreciation Expense | | | 6,000 | |
| Property Taxes Payable | | | | 3,000 |
| Totals | | | 504,700 | 504,700 |

### Instructions

(a) Net income $44,000

(b) Total current assets $54,500

(e) Post-closing trial balance $254,500

(a) Prepare a complete worksheet.

(b) Prepare a classified balance sheet. (*Note:* $15,000 of the mortgage note payable is due for payment in the next fiscal year.)

(c) Journalize the adjusting entries using the worksheet as a basis.

(d) Journalize the closing entries using the worksheet as a basis.

(e) Prepare a post-closing trial balance.

*Complete all steps in accounting cycle.*

(LO 1, 2, 3, 4, 6)

**P4-5B** Gillian Shaw opened Shaw's Carpet Cleaners on March 1. During March, the following transactions were completed.

Mar. 1  Invested $10,000 cash in the business.
  1  Purchased used truck for $6,000, paying $3,000 cash and the balance on account.
  3  Purchased cleaning supplies for $1,200 on account.
  5  Paid $1,200 cash on a 1-year insurance policy effective March 1.
  14  Billed customers $4,800 for cleaning services.
  18  Paid $1,500 cash on amount owed on truck and $500 on amount owed on cleaning supplies.
  20  Paid $1,800 cash for employee salaries.
  21  Collected $1,400 cash from customers billed on March 14.
  28  Billed customers $2,500 for cleaning services.
  31  Paid $200 for the monthly gasoline bill for the truck.
  31  Withdrew $700 cash for personal use.

The chart of accounts for Shaw's Carpet Cleaners contains the following accounts: No. 101 Cash, No. 112 Accounts Receivable, No. 126 Supplies, No. 130 Prepaid Insurance, No. 157 Equipment, No. 158 Accumulated Depreciation—Equipment, No. 201 Accounts Payable, No. 212 Salaries and Wages Payable, No. 301 Owner's Capital, No. 306 Owner's Drawings, No. 350 Income Summary, No. 400 Service Revenue, No. 631 Supplies Expense, No. 633 Gasoline Expense, No. 711 Depreciation Expense, No. 722 Insurance Expense, and No. 726 Salaries and Wages Expense.

### Instructions

(a) Journalize and post the March transactions. Use page J1 for the journal and the three-column form of account.

(b) Trial balance $19,500

(c) Adjusted trial balance $20,850

(b) Prepare a trial balance at March 31 on a worksheet.

(c) Enter the following adjustments on the worksheet and complete the worksheet.
  (1) Unbilled revenue for services performed at March 31 was $500.
  (2) Depreciation on equipment for the month was $300.

(3)  One-twelfth of the insurance expired.

(4)  An inventory count shows $250 of cleaning supplies on hand at March 31.

(5)  Accrued but unpaid employee salaries were $550.

(d) Prepare the income statement and owner's equity statement for March and a classified balance sheet at March 31.

(e) Journalize and post adjusting entries. Use page J2 for the journal.

(f) Journalize and post closing entries and complete the closing process. Use page J3 for the journal.

(g) Prepare a post-closing trial balance at March 31.

(d) Net income $3,900
Total assets $15,950

(g) Post-closing trial balance
$16,250

## PROBLEMS: SET C

Visit the book's companion website, at **www.wiley.com/college/weygandt**, and choose the Student Companion site to access Problem Set C.

## COMPREHENSIVE PROBLEM: CHAPTERS 2 TO 4

**CP4**  Kristin Malone opened Kristin's Maids Cleaning Service on July 1, 2014. During July, the company completed the following transactions.

July  1   Invested $14,000 cash in the business.
     1   Purchased a used truck for $10,000, paying $3,000 cash and the balance on account.
     3   Purchased cleaning supplies for $800 on account.
     5   Paid $1,800 on a 1-year insurance policy, effective July 1.
     12  Billed customers $3,800 for cleaning services.
     18  Paid $1,000 of amount owed on truck, and $400 of amount owed on cleaning supplies.
     20  Paid $1,600 for employee salaries.
     21  Collected $1,400 from customers billed on July 12.
     25  Billed customers $1,500 for cleaning services.
     31  Paid gasoline for the month on the truck, $400.
     31  Withdrew $600 cash for personal use.

The chart of accounts for Kristin's Maids Cleaning Service contains the following accounts: No. 101 Cash, No. 112 Accounts Receivable, No. 126 Supplies, No. 130 Prepaid Insurance, No. 157 Equipment, No. 158 Accumulated Depreciation—Equipment, No. 201 Accounts Payable, No. 212 Salaries and Wages Payable, No. 301 Owner's Capital, No. 306 Owner's Drawings, No. 350 Income Summary, No. 400 Service Revenue, No. 631 Supplies Expense, No. 633 Gasoline Expense, No. 711 Depreciation Expense, No. 722 Insurance Expense, and No. 726 Salaries and Wages Expense.

### Instructions

(a) Journalize and post the July transactions. Use page J1 for the journal.

(b) Prepare a trial balance at July 31 on a worksheet.

(c) Enter the following adjustments on the worksheet, and complete the worksheet.

(1)  Unbilled fees for services performed at July 31 were $1,300.

(2)  Depreciation on equipment for the month was $200.

(3)  One-twelfth of the insurance expired.

(4)  An inventory count shows $100 of cleaning supplies on hand at July 31.

(5)  Accrued but unpaid employee salaries were $500.

(d) Prepare the income statement and owner's equity statement for July, and a classified balance sheet at July 31, 2014.

(e) Journalize and post the adjusting entries. Use page J2 for the journal.

(f) Journalize and post the closing entries, and complete the closing process. Use page J3 for the journal.

(g) Prepare a post-closing trial balance at July 31.

(b) Trial balance totals
$25,700

(d) Net income $3,050
Total assets $23,350

(g) Trial balance totals
$23,550

## CONTINUING COOKIE CHRONICLE

(*Note:* This is a continuation of the Cookie Chronicle from Chapters 1 through 3.)

**CCC4** Natalie had a very busy December. At the end of the month, after journalizing and posting the December transactions and adjusting entries, Natalie prepared the following adjusted trial balance.

**COOKIE CREATIONS**
Adjusted Trial Balance
December 31, 2013

|  | Debit | Credit |
|---|---|---|
| Cash | $1,180 | |
| Accounts Receivable | 875 | |
| Supplies | 350 | |
| Prepaid Insurance | 1,210 | |
| Equipment | 1,200 | |
| Accumulated Depreciation—Equipment | | $    40 |
| Accounts Payable | | 75 |
| Salaries and Wages Payable | | 56 |
| Interest Payable | | 15 |
| Unearned Service Revenue | | 300 |
| Notes Payable | | 2,000 |
| Owner's Capital | | 800 |
| Owner's Drawings | 500 | |
| Service Revenue | | 4,515 |
| Salaries and Wages Expense | 1,006 | |
| Utilities Expense | 125 | |
| Advertising Expense | 165 | |
| Supplies Expense | 1,025 | |
| Depreciation Expense | 40 | |
| Insurance Expense | 110 | |
| Interest Expense | 15 | |
|  | $7,801 | $7,801 |

*Instructions*

Using the information in the adjusted trial balance, do the following.

**(a)** Prepare an income statement and an owner's equity statement for the 2 months ended December 31, 2013, and a classified balance sheet at December 31, 2013. The note payable has a stated interest rate of 6%, and the principal and interest are due on November 16, 2015.

**(b)** Natalie has decided that her year-end will be December 31, 2013. Prepare and post closing entries as of December 31, 2013.

**(c)** Prepare a post-closing trial balance.

# Broadening Your Perspective

## Financial Reporting and Analysis

### Financial Reporting Problem: Apple Inc.

**BYP4-1** The financial statements of Apple Inc. are presented in Appendix A at the end of this textbook. Instructions for accessing and using the company's complete annual report, including the notes to the financial statements, are also provided in Appendix A.

*Instructions*

Answer the questions below using Apple's Consolidated Balance Sheets.

**(a)** What were Apple's total current assets at September 24, 2011, and September 25, 2010?
**(b)** Are assets that Apple included under current assets listed in proper order? Explain.
**(c)** How are Apple's assets classified?
**(d)** What was Apple's "Cash and cash equivalents" at September 24, 2011?
**(e)** What were Apple's total current liabilities at September 24, 2011, and September 25, 2010?

## Comparative Analysis Problem:
## PepsiCo, Inc. vs. The Coca-Cola Company

**BYP4-2** PepsiCo's financial statements are presented in Appendix B. Financial statements for The Coca-Cola Company are presented in Appendix C. Instructions for accessing and using the complete annual reports of PepsiCo and Coca-Cola, including the notes to the financial statements, are also provided in Appendices B and C, respectively.

*Instructions*

**(a)** Based on the information contained in these financial statements, determine each of the following for PepsiCo at December 31, 2011, and for Coca-Cola at December 31, 2011.
  **(1)** Total current assets.
  **(2)** Net amount of property, plant, and equipment (land, buildings, and equipment).
  **(3)** Total current liabilities.
  **(4)** Total equity.
**(b)** What conclusions concerning the companies' respective financial positions can be drawn?

## Comparative Analysis Problem:
## Amazon.com, Inc. vs. Wal-Mart Stores, Inc.

**BYP4-3** Amazon.com, Inc.'s financial statements are presented in Appendix D. Financial statements for Wal-Mart Stores, Inc. are presented in Appendix E. Instructions for accessing and using the complete annual reports of Amazon and Wal-Mart, including the notes to the financial statements, are also provided in Appendices D and E, respectively.

*Instructions*

**(a)** Based on the information contained in these financial statements, determine the following for Amazon at December 31, 2011, and Wal-Mart at January 31, 2012.
  **(1)** Total current assets.
  **(2)** Net amount of property and equipment (fixed assets), net.
  **(3)** Total current liabilities.
  **(4)** Total equity.
**(b)** What conclusions concerning these two companies can be drawn from these data?

## Real-World Focus

**BYP4-4** Numerous companies have established home pages on the Internet, e.g., Capt'n Eli Root Beer Company (**www.captneli.com/rootbeer.php**) and Kodak (**www.kodak.com**).

*Instructions*

Examine the home pages of any two companies and answer the following questions.

**(a)** What type of information is available?
**(b)** Is any accounting-related information presented?
**(c)** Would you describe the home page as informative, promotional, or both? Why?

# Critical Thinking

## Decision-Making Across the Organization

**BYP4-5** Whitegloves Janitorial Service was started 2 years ago by Lynn Sanders. Because business has been exceptionally good, Lynn decided on July 1, 2014, to expand operations by acquiring an additional truck and hiring two more assistants. To finance the expansion, Lynn obtained on

July 1, 2014, a $25,000, 10% bank loan, payable $10,000 on July 1, 2015, and the balance on July 1, 2016. The terms of the loan require the borrower to have $10,000 more current assets than current liabilities at December 31, 2014. If these terms are not met, the bank loan will be refinanced at 15% interest. At December 31, 2014, the accountant for Whitegloves Janitorial Service Inc. prepared the balance sheet shown below.

Lynn presented the balance sheet to the bank's loan officer on January 2, 2015, confident that the company had met the terms of the loan. The loan officer was not impressed. She said, "We need financial statements audited by a CPA." A CPA was hired and immediately realized that the balance sheet had been prepared from a trial balance and not from an adjusted trial balance. The adjustment data at the balance sheet date consisted of the following.

1. Unbilled janitorial services performed were $3,700.
2. Janitorial supplies on hand were $2,500.
3. Prepaid insurance was a 3-year policy dated January 1, 2014.
4. December expenses incurred but unpaid at December 31, $500.
5. Interest on the bank loan was not recorded.
6. The amounts for property, plant, and equipment presented in the balance sheet were reported net of accumulated depreciation (cost less accumulated depreciation). These amounts were $4,000 for cleaning equipment and $5,000 for delivery trucks as of January 1, 2014. Depreciation for 2014 was $2,000 for cleaning equipment and $5,000 for delivery trucks.

**WHITEGLOVES JANITORIAL SERVICE**
Balance Sheet
December 31, 2014

| Assets | | Liabilities and Owner's Equity | |
|---|---:|---|---:|
| Current assets | | Current liabilities | |
| Cash | $ 6,500 | Notes payable | $10,000 |
| Accounts receivable | 9,000 | Accounts payable | 2,500 |
| Supplies | 5,200 | Total current liabilities | 12,500 |
| Prepaid insurance | 4,800 | Long-term liability | |
| Total current assets | 25,500 | Notes payable | 15,000 |
| Property, plant, and equipment | | Total liabilities | 27,500 |
| Equipment (net) | 22,000 | Owner's equity | |
| Delivery trucks (net) | 34,000 | Owner's capital | 54,000 |
| Total property, plant, and equipment | 56,000 | | |
| Total assets | $81,500 | Total liabilities and owner's equity | $81,500 |

*Instructions*
With the class divided into groups, answer the following.

**(a)** Prepare a correct balance sheet.
**(b)** Were the terms of the bank loan met? Explain.

## Communication Activity

**BYP4-6** The accounting cycle is important in understanding the accounting process.

*Instructions*
Write a memo to your instructor that lists the steps of the accounting cycle in the order they should be completed. End with a paragraph that explains the optional steps in the cycle.

## Ethics Case

**BYP4-7** As the controller of Take No Prisoners Perfume Company, you discover a misstatement that overstated net income in the prior year's financial statements. The misleading financial statements appear in the company's annual report which was issued to banks and other creditors less than a month ago. After much thought about the consequences of telling the president, Jeb Wilde, about this misstatement, you gather your courage to inform him. Jeb says, "Hey! What they don't know won't hurt them. But, just so we set the record straight, we'll adjust this year's financial

statements for last year's misstatement. We can absorb that misstatement better in this year than in last year anyway! Just don't make such a mistake again."

**Instructions**
**(a)** Who are the stakeholders in this situation?
**(b)** What are the ethical issues in this situation?
**(c)** What would you do as a controller in this situation?

## All About You

**BYP4-8** Companies prepare balance sheets in order to know their financial position at a specific point in time. This enables them to make a comparison to their position at previous points in time, and gives them a basis for planning for the future. In order to evaluate your financial position, you need to prepare a personal balance sheet. Assume that you have compiled the following information regarding your finances. (*Hint:* Some of the items might not be used in your personal balance sheet.)

| | |
|---|---:|
| Amount owed on student loan balance (long-term) | $ 5,000 |
| Balance in checking account | 1,200 |
| Certificate of deposit (6-month) | 3,000 |
| Annual earnings from part-time job | 11,300 |
| Automobile | 7,000 |
| Balance on automobile loan (current portion) | 1,500 |
| Balance on automobile loan (long-term portion) | 4,000 |
| Home computer | 800 |
| Amount owed to you by younger brother | 300 |
| Balance in money market account | 1,800 |
| Annual tuition | 6,400 |
| Video and stereo equipment | 1,250 |
| Balance owed on credit card (current portion) | 150 |
| Balance owed on credit card (long-term portion) | 1,650 |

**Instructions**
Prepare a personal balance sheet using the format you have learned for a classified balance sheet for a company. For the capital account, use Owner's Capital.

## FASB Codification Activity

**BYP4-9** If your school has a subscription to the FASB Codification, go to **http://aaahq.org/ ascLogin.cfm** to log in and prepare responses to the following.

**Instructions**
**(a)** Access the glossary ("Master Glossary") at the FASB Codification website to answer the following.
    **(1)** What is the definition of current assets?
    **(2)** What is the definition of current liabilities?
**(b)** A company wants to offset its accounts payable against its cash account and show a cash amount net of accounts payable on its balance sheet. Identify the criteria (found in the FASB Codification) under which a company has the right of set off. Does the company have the right to offset accounts payable against the cash account?

## Answers to Chapter Questions

### Answers to Insight and Accounting Across the Organization Questions

**p. 171 Cisco Performs the Virtual Close    Q:** Who else benefits from a shorter closing process? **A:** Investors benefit from a shorter closing process. The shorter the closing, the sooner the company can report its financial results. This means that the financial information is more timely and therefore more relevant to investors.

**p. 177 Yale Express Loses Some Transportation Bills    Q:** What might Yale Express's vice president have done to produce more accurate financial statements without waiting months for

Republic's outstanding transportation bills? **A:** Yale's vice president could have engaged his accountants and auditors to prepare an adjusting entry based on an estimate of the outstanding transportation bills. (The estimate could have been made using past experience and the current volume of business.)

**p. 181 Regaining Goodwill   Q:** Name two industries today which are probably rated low on the reputational characteristics of "being trusted" and "having high ethical standards." **A:** Two possible industries are financial companies (Goldman Sachs or AIG) or oil companies (BP).

**p. 182 Can a Company Be Too Liquid?   Q:** What can various company managers do to ensure that working capital is managed efficiently to maximize net income? **A:** Marketing and sales managers must understand that by extending generous repayment terms, they are expanding the company's receivables balance and slowing the company's cash flow. Production managers must strive to minimize the amount of excess inventory on hand. Managers must coordinate efforts to speed up the collection of receivables, while also ensuring that the company pays its payables on time but never too early.

**Answers to Self-Test Questions**

1. b  2. c  3. c  4. a  5. b  6. c  7. a  8. d  9. c  10. d  11. b  12. c  13. c  14. d
15. a  *16. c

# A Look at IFRS

**LEARNING OBJECTIVE    8**

**Compare the procedures for the closing process under GAAP and IFRS.**

The classified balance sheet, although generally required internationally, contains certain variations in format when reporting under IFRS.

## Key Points

- The procedures of the closing process are applicable to all companies, whether they are using IFRS or GAAP.

- IFRS recommends but does not require the use of the title "statement of financial position" rather than balance sheet.

- The format of statement of financial position information is often presented differently under IFRS. Although no specific format is required, most companies that follow IFRS present statement of financial position information in this order:

  ◆ Noncurrent assets

  ◆ Current assets

  ◆ Equity

  ◆ Noncurrent liabilities

  ◆ Current liabilities

- IFRS requires a classified statement of financial position except in very limited situations. IFRS follows the same guidelines as this textbook for distinguishing between current and noncurrent assets and liabilities.

- Under IFRS, current assets are usually listed in the reverse order of liquidity. For example, under GAAP cash is listed first, but under IFRS it is listed last.

- Some companies report the subtotal **net assets**, which equals total assets minus total liabilities. See, for example, the statement of financial position of Zetar plc in Appendix F.

- IFRS has many differences in terminology from what are shown in your textbook. For example, in the sample statement of financial position illustrated on the next page, notice in the investment category that stock is called shares.

**FRANKLIN COMPANY**
Statement of Financial Position
October 31, 2014

### Assets

| | | | |
|---|---|---|---|
| **Intangible assets** | | | |
| Patents | | | $ 3,100 |
| **Property, plant, and equipment** | | | |
| Land | | $10,000 | |
| Equipment | $24,000 | | |
| Less: Accumulated depreciation | 5,000 | 19,000 | 29,000 |
| **Long-term investments** | | | |
| Share investments | | 5,200 | |
| Investment in real estate | | 2,000 | 7,200 |
| **Current assets** | | | |
| Prepaid insurance | | 400 | |
| Supplies | | 2,100 | |
| Inventory | | 3,000 | |
| Notes receivable | | 1,000 | |
| Accounts receivable | | 7,000 | |
| Debt investments | | 2,000 | |
| Cash | | 6,600 | 22,100 |
| Total assets | | | $61,400 |

### Equity and Liabilities

| | | | |
|---|---|---|---|
| **Equity** | | | |
| Owner's capital | | | $34,050 |
| **Non-current liabilities** | | | |
| Mortgage payable | | $10,000 | |
| Notes payable | | 1,300 | 11,300 |
| **Current liabilities** | | | |
| Notes payable | | 11,000 | |
| Accounts payable | | 2,100 | |
| Salaries and wages payable | | 1,600 | |
| Unearned service revenue | | 900 | |
| Interest payable | | 450 | 16,050 |
| Total equity and liabilities | | | $61,400 |

- Both IFRS and GAAP require disclosures about (1) accounting policies followed, (2) judgments that management has made in the process of applying the entity's accounting policies, and (3) the key assumptions and estimation uncertainty that could result in a material adjustment to the carrying amounts of assets and liabilities within the next financial year.

- Comparative prior-period information must be presented and financial statements must be prepared annually.

- Both GAAP and IFRS are increasing the use of fair value to report assets. However, at this point IFRS has adopted it more broadly. As examples, under IFRS companies can apply fair value to property, plant, and equipment; natural resources; and in some cases intangible assets.

## Looking to the Future

The IASB and the FASB are working on a project to converge their standards related to financial statement presentation. A key feature of the proposed framework is that each of the statements will be organized in the same format, to separate an entity's financing activities from its operating and investing activities and, further, to separate financing activities into transactions with owners and creditors. Thus, the same classifications used in the statement of financial position would also be used in the income statement and the statement of cash flows. The project has three phases. You can follow the joint financial presentation project at the following link: **http://www.fasb.org/project/financial_statement_presentation.shtml**.

The IASB and the FASB face a difficult task in attempting to update, modify, and complete a converged conceptual framework. For example, how do companies choose between information that is highly relevant but difficult to verify versus information that is less relevant but easy to verify? How do companies define control when developing a definition of an asset? Is a liability the future sacrifice itself or the obligation to make the sacrifice? Should a single measurement method, such as historical cost or fair value, be used, or does it depend on whether it is an asset or liability that is being measured? It appears that the new document will be a significant improvement over its predecessors and will lead to principles-based standards, which will help financial statement users make better decisions.

# IFRS Practice

## IFRS Self-Test Questions

1. Which of the following statements is **false**?
   (a) Assets equals liabilities plus equity.
   (b) Under IFRS, companies sometimes net liabilities against assets to report "net assets."
   (c) The FASB and IASB are working on a joint conceptual framework project.
   (d) Under IFRS, the statement of financial position is usually referred to as the statement of assets and equity.

2. A company has purchased a tract of land and expects to build a production plant on the land in approximately 5 years. During the 5 years before construction, the land will be idle. Under IFRS, the land should be reported as:
   (a) land expense.
   (b) property, plant, and equipment.
   (c) an intangible asset.
   (d) a long-term investment.

3. Current assets under IFRS are listed generally:
   (a) by importance.
   (b) in the reverse order of their expected conversion to cash.
   (c) by longevity.
   (d) alphabetically.

4. Companies that use IFRS:
   (a) may report all their assets on the statement of financial position at fair value.
   (b) may offset assets against liabilities and show net assets and net liabilities on their statement of financial positions, rather than the underlying detailed line items.
   (c) may report noncurrent assets before current assets on the statement of financial position.
   (d) do not have any guidelines as to what should be reported on the statement of financial position.

5. Companies that follow IFRS to prepare a statement of financial position generally use the following order of classification:
   (a) current assets, current liabilities, noncurrent assets, noncurrent liabilities, equity.
   (b) noncurrent assets, noncurrent liabilities, current assets, current liabilities, equity.
   (c) noncurrent assets, current assets, equity, noncurrent liabilities, current liabilities.
   (d) equity, noncurrent assets, current assets, noncurrent liabilities, current liabilities.

## IFRS Exercises

**IFRS4-1** In what ways does the format of a statement of financial of position under IFRS often differ from a balance sheet presented under GAAP?

**IFRS4-2** What term is commonly used under IFRS in reference to the balance sheet?

**IFRS4-3** The statement of financial position for Sundell Company includes the following accounts (in British pounds): Accounts Receivable £12,500; Prepaid Insurance £3,600; Cash £15,400; Supplies £5,200; and Debt Investments (short-term) £6,700. Prepare the current assets section of the statement of financial position, listing the accounts in proper sequence.

**IFRS4-4** Glarus Company recently received the following information related to the company's December 31, 2014, statement of financial position (in Swiss francs).

| | | | |
|---|---|---|---|
| Inventory | CHF 2,900 | Debt investments (short-term) | CHF 120 |
| Cash | 13,400 | Accumulated depreciation— | |
| Equipment | 21,700 | equipment | 5,700 |
| Share investments | | Accounts receivable | 4,300 |
| (long-term) | 6,500 | | |

Prepare the assets section of the company's classified statement of financial position.

**IFRS4-5** The following information is available for Lessila Bowling Alley at December 31, 2014.

| | | | |
|---|---|---|---|
| Buildings | $128,800 | Owner's Capital | $115,000 |
| Accounts Receivable | 14,520 | Accumulated Depreciation—Buildings | 42,600 |
| Prepaid Insurance | 4,680 | Accounts Payable | 12,300 |
| Cash | 18,040 | Notes Payable | 97,780 |
| Equipment | 62,400 | Accumulated Depreciation—Equipment | 18,720 |
| Land | 64,000 | Interest Payable | 2,600 |
| Insurance Expense | 780 | Bowling Revenues | 14,180 |
| Depreciation Expense | 7,360 | | |
| Interest Expense | 2,600 | | |

Prepare a classified statement of financial position. Assume that $13,900 of the notes payable will be paid in 2015.

**IFRS4-6** Nate Roche is interested in comparing the liquidity and solvency of a U.S. software company with a Chinese competitor. Is this possible if the two companies report using different currencies?

## International Comparative Analysis Problem:
## Apple vs. Zetar plc

**IFRS4-7** The financial statements of Zetar plc are presented in Appendix F. Instructions for accessing and using the company's complete annual report, including the notes to its financial statements, are also provided in Appendix F.

*Instructions*
Identify five differences in the format of the statement of financial position used by Zetar plc compared to a company, such as Apple, that follows GAAP. (Apple's financial statements are available in Appendix A.)

**Answers to IFRS Self-Test Questions**
1. d   2. d   3. b   4. c   5. c

✔   The Navigator

# 5 | Accounting for Merchandising Operations

## Feature Story

### Buy Now, Vote Later

Have you ever shopped for outdoor gear at an REI (Recreational Equipment Incorporated) store? If so, you might have been surprised if a salesclerk asked if you were a member. A member? What do you mean a member? You soon realize that REI might not be your typical store. In fact, there's a lot about REI that makes it different.

REI is a consumer cooperative, or "co-op" for short. To figure out what that means, consider this quote from the company's annual report:

> As a cooperative, the Company is owned by its members. Each member is entitled to one vote in the election of the Company's Board of Directors. Since January 1, 2008, the nonrefundable, nontransferable, one-time membership fee has been $20 dollars. As of December 31, 2010, there were approximately 10.8 million members.

Voting rights? Now that's something you don't get from shopping at Wal-Mart. REI members get other benefits as well, including sharing in the company's profits through a dividend at the end of the year, which can be used for purchases at REI stores during the next two years. The m you spend, the bigger your dividend.

Since REI is a co-op, you might wonder whether manage ment's incentives might be a little different. For example, management still concerned about making a profit? The answer is yes, as it ensures the long-term viability of the company. At the same time, REI's members want the com pany to be run efficiently, so that prices remain low. In or for its members to evaluate just how well management is doing, REI publishes an audited annual report, just like publicly traded companies do. So, while profit maximizat might not be the ultimate goal for REI, the accounting ar reporting issues are similar to those of a typical corporati

How well is this business model working for REI? Well, it consistently been rated as one of the best places to work the United States. It was ranked 8th on *Fortune*'s 2012 li Also, REI had sustainable business practices long before s responsibility became popular at other companies. The C Stewardship Report states "we reduced the absolute amo of energy we use despite opening four new stores and growing our business; we grew the amount of FSC-certif

## The Navigator

- Scan Learning Objectives
- Read Feature Story
- Read Preview
- Read text and answer **DO IT!** p. 225
    - p. 229    p. 232    p. 237
- Work Comprehensive **DO IT!** p. 238
- Review Summary of Learning Objectives
- Answer Self-Test Questions
- Complete Assignments
- Go to *WileyPLUS* for practice and tutorials
-  **Read A Look at IFRS** p. 271

## Learning Objectives    ✔ The Navigator

*After studying this chapter, you should be able to:*

[1] Identify the differences between service and merchandising companies.

[2] Explain the recording of purchases under a perpetual inventory system.

[3] Explain the recording of sales revenues under a perpetual inventory system.

[4] Explain the steps in the accounting cycle for a merchandising company.

[5] Distinguish between a multiple-step and a single-step income statement.

paper we use to 58.4 percent of our total paper footprint—including our cash register receipt paper; we facilitated 2.2 million volunteer hours and we provided $3.7 million to more than 330 conservation and recreation nonprofits."

So, while REI, like other retailers, closely monitors its financial results, it also strives to succeed in other areas. And, with over 10 million votes at stake, REI's management knows that it has to deliver.

# Preview of Chapter 5

✔ The Navigator

Merchandising is one of the largest and most influential industries in the United States. It is likely that a number of you will work for a merchandiser. Therefore, understanding the financial statements of merchandising companies is important. In this chapter, you will learn the basics about reporting merchandising transactions. In addition, you will learn how to prepare and analyze a commonly used form of the income statement—the multiple-step income statement. The content and organization of the chapter are as follows.

## ACCOUNTING FOR MERCHANDISING OPERATIONS

| Merchandising Operations | Recording Purchases of Merchandise | Recording Sales of Merchandise | Completing the Accounting Cycle | Forms of Financial Statements |
|---|---|---|---|---|
| • Operating cycles <br> • Flow of costs— perpetual and periodic inventory systems <br> • Advantages of the perpetual system | • Freight costs <br> • Purchase returns and allowances <br> • Purchase discounts <br> • Summary of purchasing transactions | • Sales returns and allowances <br> • Sales discounts | • Adjusting entries <br> • Closing entries <br> • Summary of merchandising entries | • Multiple-step income statement <br> • Single-step income statement <br> • Classified balance sheet |

## Merchandising Operations

LEARNING OBJECTIVE   1

Identify the differences between service and merchandising companies.

REI, Wal-Mart, and Amazon.com are called merchandising companies because they buy and sell merchandise rather than perform services as their primary source of revenue. Merchandising companies that purchase and sell directly to consumers are called **retailers**. Merchandising companies that sell to retailers are known as **wholesalers**. For example, retailer Walgreens might buy goods from wholesaler McKesson. Retailer Office Depot might buy office supplies from wholesaler United Stationers. The primary source of revenues for merchandising companies is the sale of merchandise, often referred to simply as **sales revenue** or **sales**. A merchandising company has two categories of expenses: cost of goods sold and operating expenses.

**Cost of goods sold** is the total cost of merchandise sold during the period. This expense is directly related to the revenue recognized from the sale of goods. Illustration 5-1 shows the income measurement process for a merchandising company. The items in the two blue boxes are unique to a merchandising company; they are not used by a service company.

**Illustration 5-1**

Income measurement process for a merchandising company

## Operating Cycles

The operating cycle of a merchandising company ordinarily is longer than that of a service company. The purchase of merchandise inventory and its eventual sale lengthen the cycle. Illustration 5-2 shows the operating cycle of a service company.

**Illustration 5-2**

Operating cycle for a service company

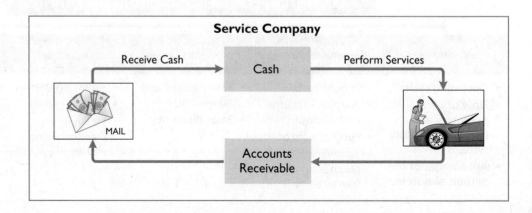

Illustration 5-3 shows the operating cycle of a merchandising company.

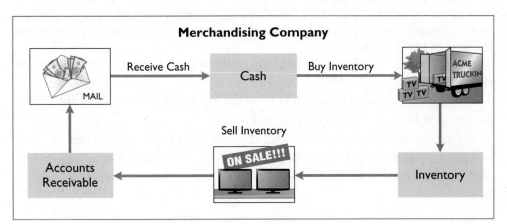

**Illustration 5-3**
Operating cycle for a merchandising company

Note that the added asset account for a merchandising company is the Inventory account. Companies report inventory as a current asset on the balance sheet.

## Flow of Costs

The flow of costs for a merchandising company is as follows. Beginning inventory plus the cost of goods purchased is the cost of goods available for sale. As goods are sold, they are assigned to cost of goods sold. Those goods that are not sold by the end of the accounting period represent ending inventory. Illustration 5-4 describes these relationships. Companies use one of two systems to account for inventory: a **perpetual inventory system** or a **periodic inventory system**.

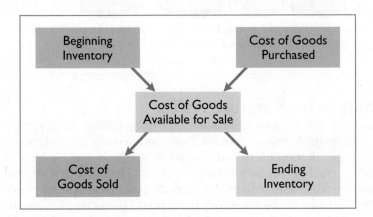

**Illustration 5-4**
Flow of costs

### PERPETUAL SYSTEM

In a **perpetual inventory system**, companies keep detailed records of the cost of each inventory purchase and sale. These records continuously—perpetually— show the inventory that should be on hand for every item. For example, a Ford dealership has separate inventory records for each automobile, truck, and van on its lot and showroom floor. Similarly, a Kroger grocery store uses bar codes and optical scanners to keep a daily running record of every box of cereal and every jar of jelly that it buys and sells. Under a perpetual inventory system, a company determines the cost of goods sold **each time a sale occurs**.

**Helpful Hint** For control purposes, companies take a physical inventory count under the perpetual system, even though it is not needed to determine cost of goods sold.

## PERIODIC SYSTEM

In a **periodic inventory system**, companies do not keep detailed inventory records of the goods on hand throughout the period. Instead, they determine the cost of goods sold **only at the end of the accounting period**—that is, periodically. At that point, the company takes a physical inventory count to determine the cost of goods on hand.

To determine the cost of goods sold under a periodic inventory system, the following steps are necessary:

1. Determine the cost of goods on hand at the beginning of the accounting period.

2. Add to it the cost of goods purchased.

3. Subtract the cost of goods on hand at the end of the accounting period.

Illustration 5-5 graphically compares the sequence of activities and the timing of the cost of goods sold computation under the two inventory systems.

**Illustration 5-5**

Comparing perpetual and periodic inventory systems

## ADVANTAGES OF THE PERPETUAL SYSTEM

Companies that sell merchandise with high unit values, such as automobiles, furniture, and major home appliances, have traditionally used perpetual systems. The growing use of computers and electronic scanners has enabled many more companies to install perpetual inventory systems. The perpetual inventory system is so named because the accounting records continuously—perpetually—show the quantity and cost of the inventory that should be on hand at any time.

A perpetual inventory system provides better control over inventories than a periodic system. Since the inventory records show the quantities that should be on hand, the company can count the goods at any time to see whether the amount of goods actually on hand agrees with the inventory records. If shortages are uncovered, the company can investigate immediately. Although a perpetual inventory system requires additional clerical work and additional cost to maintain the subsidiary records, a computerized system can minimize this cost. Much of Amazon.com's success is attributed to its sophisticated inventory system.

Some businesses find it either unnecessary or uneconomical to invest in a sophisticated, computerized perpetual inventory system such as Amazon's. Many small merchandising businesses find that basic computerized accounting packages provide some of the essential benefits of a perpetual inventory system. Also, managers of some small businesses still find that they can control their merchandise and manage day-to-day operations using a periodic inventory system.

**Because of the widespread use of the perpetual inventory system, we illustrate it in this chapter.** Appendix 5B describes the journal entries for the periodic system.

---

## INVESTOR INSIGHT

### Morrow Snowboards Improves Its Stock Appeal

Investors are often eager to invest in a company that has a hot new product. However, when snowboard-maker Morrow Snowboards, Inc. issued shares of stock to the public for the first time, some investors expressed reluctance to invest in Morrow because of a number of accounting control problems. To reduce investor concerns, Morrow implemented a perpetual inventory system to improve its control over inventory. In addition, it stated that it would perform a physical inventory count every quarter until it felt that the perpetual inventory system was reliable.

 If a perpetual system keeps track of inventory on a daily basis, why do companies ever need to do a physical count? (See page 270.)

© Ben Blankenburg/iStockphoto

---

## Recording Purchases of Merchandise

Companies purchase inventory using cash or credit (on account). They normally record purchases when they receive the goods from the seller. Every purchase should be supported by business documents that provide written evidence of the transaction. Each cash purchase should be supported by a canceled check or a cash register receipt indicating the items purchased and amounts paid. Companies record cash purchases by an increase in Inventory and a decrease in Cash.

A **purchase invoice** should support each credit purchase. This invoice indicates the total purchase price and other relevant information. However, the purchaser does not prepare a separate purchase invoice. Instead, the purchaser uses as a purchase invoice a copy of the sales invoice sent by the seller. In Illustration 5-6 (page 222), for example, Sauk Stereo (the buyer) uses as a purchase invoice the sales invoice prepared by PW Audio Supply (the seller).

Sauk Stereo makes the following journal entry to record its purchase from PW Audio Supply. The entry increases (debits) Inventory and increases (credits) Accounts Payable.

| LEARNING OBJECTIVE | 2 |
|---|---|

**Explain the recording of purchases under a perpetual inventory system.**

| May 4 | Inventory | 3,800 | |
|---|---|---|---|
| | Accounts Payable | | 3,800 |
| | (To record goods purchased on account from PW Audio Supply) | | |

| A | = | L | + | OE |
|---|---|---|---|---|
| +3,800 | | | | |
| | | +3,800 | | |

**Cash Flows**
no effect

**Illustration 5-6**
Sales invoice used as purchase invoice by Sauk Stereo

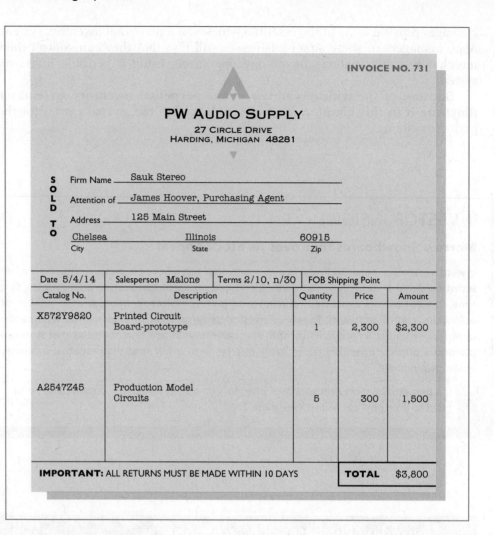

**Helpful Hint** To better understand the contents of this invoice, identify these items:
1. Seller
2. Invoice date
3. Purchaser
4. Salesperson
5. Credit terms
6. Freight terms
7. Goods sold: catalog number, description, quantity, price per unit
8. Total invoice amount

Under the perpetual inventory system, companies record purchases of merchandise for sale in the Inventory account. Thus, REI would increase (debit) Inventory for clothing, sporting goods, and anything else purchased for resale to customers.

Not all purchases are debited to Inventory, however. Companies record purchases of assets acquired for use and not for resale, such as supplies, equipment, and similar items, as increases to specific asset accounts rather than to Inventory. For example, to record the purchase of materials used to make shelf signs or for cash register receipt paper, REI would increase (debit) Supplies.

### Freight Costs

The sales agreement should indicate who—the seller or the buyer—is to pay for transporting the goods to the buyer's place of business. When a common carrier such as a railroad, trucking company, or airline transports the goods, the carrier prepares a freight bill in accord with the sales agreement.

Freight terms are expressed as either FOB shipping point or FOB destination. The letters FOB mean **free on board**. Thus, **FOB shipping point** means that the seller places the goods free on board the carrier, and the buyer pays the freight costs. Conversely, **FOB destination** means that the seller places the goods free on board to the buyer's place of business, and the seller pays the freight. For example, the sales invoice in Illustration 5-6 indicates FOB shipping point. Thus, the buyer (Sauk Stereo) pays the freight charges. Illustration 5-7 (on the next page) illustrates these shipping terms.

Illustration 5-7
Shipping terms

## FREIGHT COSTS INCURRED BY THE BUYER

When the buyer incurs the transportation costs, these costs are considered part of the cost of purchasing inventory. Therefore, the buyer debits (increases) the Inventory account. For example, if Sauk Stereo (the buyer) pays Public Carrier Co. $150 for freight charges on May 6, the entry on Sauk Stereo's books is:

| May 6 | Inventory | 150 | |
|---|---|---|---|
| | Cash | | 150 |
| | (To record payment of freight on goods purchased) | | |

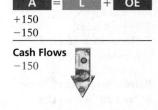

Thus, any freight costs incurred by the buyer are part of the cost of merchandise purchased. The reason: Inventory cost should include all costs to acquire the inventory, including freight necessary to deliver the goods to the buyer. Companies recognize these costs as cost of goods sold when inventory is sold.

## FREIGHT COSTS INCURRED BY THE SELLER

In contrast, **freight costs incurred by the seller on outgoing merchandise are an operating expense to the seller**. These costs increase an expense account titled Freight-Out (sometimes called Delivery Expense). For example, if the freight terms on the invoice in Illustration 5-6 had required PW Audio Supply (the seller) to pay the freight charges, the entry by PW Audio Supply would be:

| May 4 | Freight-Out (or Delivery Expense) | 150 | |
|---|---|---|---|
| | Cash | | 150 |
| | (To record payment of freight on goods sold) | | |

When the seller pays the freight charges, the seller will usually establish a higher invoice price for the goods to cover the shipping expense.

## Purchase Returns and Allowances

A purchaser may be dissatisfied with the merchandise received because the goods are damaged or defective, of inferior quality, or do not meet the purchaser's specifications. In such cases, the purchaser may return the goods to the seller for credit if the sale was made on credit, or for a cash refund if the purchase was for cash. This transaction is known as a **purchase return**. Alternatively, the purchaser may choose to keep the merchandise if the seller is willing to grant an allowance (deduction) from the purchase price. This transaction is known as a **purchase allowance**.

Assume that Sauk Stereo returned goods costing $300 to PW Audio Supply on May 8. The following entry by Sauk Stereo for the returned merchandise decreases (debits) Accounts Payable and decreases (credits) Inventory.

**Cash Flows**
no effect

| May 8 | Accounts Payable | 300 | |
|---|---|---|---|
| | Inventory | | 300 |
| | (To record return of goods purchased from PW Audio Supply) | | |

Because Sauk Stereo increased Inventory when the goods were received, Inventory is decreased when Sauk Stereo returns the goods.

Suppose instead that Sauk Stereo chose to keep the goods after being granted a $50 allowance (reduction in price). It would reduce (debit) Accounts Payable and reduce (credit) Inventory for $50.

## Purchase Discounts

The credit terms of a purchase on account may permit the buyer to claim a cash discount for prompt payment. The buyer calls this cash discount a **purchase discount**. This incentive offers advantages to both parties. The purchaser saves money, and the seller is able to shorten the operating cycle by converting the accounts receivable into cash.

**Helpful Hint** The term *net* in "net 30" means the remaining amount due after subtracting any sales returns and allowances and partial payments.

**Credit terms** specify the amount of the cash discount and time period in which it is offered. They also indicate the time period in which the purchaser is expected to pay the full invoice price. In the sales invoice in Illustration 5-6 (page 222), credit terms are 2/10, n/30, which is read "two-ten, net thirty." This means that the buyer may take a 2% cash discount on the invoice price, less ("net of") any returns or allowances, if payment is made within 10 days of the invoice date (the **discount period**). Otherwise, the invoice price, less any returns or allowances, is due 30 days from the invoice date.

Alternatively, the discount period may extend to a specified number of days following the month in which the sale occurs. For example, 1/10 EOM (end of month) means that a 1% discount is available if the invoice is paid within the first 10 days of the next month.

When the seller elects not to offer a cash discount for prompt payment, credit terms will specify only the maximum time period for paying the balance due. For example, the invoice may state the time period as n/30, n/60, or n/10 EOM. This means, respectively, that the buyer must pay the net amount in 30 days, 60 days, or within the first 10 days of the next month.

When the buyer pays an invoice within the discount period, the amount of the discount decreases Inventory. Why? Because companies record inventory at cost and, by paying within the discount period, the buyer has reduced its cost. To illustrate, assume Sauk Stereo pays the balance due of $3,500 (gross invoice price of $3,800 less purchase returns and allowances of $300) on May 14, the last day of the discount period. The cash discount is $70 ($3,500 × 2%), and Sauk Stereo pays $3,430 ($3,500 − $70). The entry Sauk Stereo makes to record its May 14 payment decreases (debits) Accounts Payable by the amount of the gross invoice price, reduces (credits) Inventory by the $70 discount, and reduces (credits) Cash by the net amount owed.

**Cash Flows**
−3,430

| May 14 | Accounts Payable | 3,500 | |
|---|---|---|---|
| | Cash | | 3,430 |
| | Inventory | | 70 |
| | (To record payment within discount period) | | |

If Sauk Stereo failed to take the discount, and instead made full payment of $3,500 on June 3, it would debit Accounts Payable and credit Cash for $3,500 each.

| June 3 | Accounts Payable | 3,500 | |
| | Cash | | 3,500 |
| | (To record payment with no discount taken) | | |

A merchandising company usually should take all available discounts. Passing up the discount may be viewed as **paying interest** for use of the money. For example, passing up the discount offered by PW Audio Supply would be comparable to Sauk Stereo paying an interest rate of 2% for the use of $3,500 for 20 days. This is the equivalent of an annual interest rate of approximately 36.5% (2% × 365/20). Obviously, it would be better for Sauk Stereo to borrow at prevailing bank interest rates of 6% to 10% than to lose the discount.

## Summary of Purchasing Transactions

The following T-account (with transaction descriptions in red) provides a summary of the effect of the previous transactions on Inventory. Sauk Stereo originally purchased $3,800 worth of inventory for resale. It then returned $300 of goods. It paid $150 in freight charges, and finally, it received a $70 discount off the balance owed because it paid within the discount period. This results in a balance in Inventory of $3,580.

| | | Inventory | | | |
|---|---|---|---|---|---|
| Purchase | May 4 | 3,800 | May 8 | 300 | Purchase return |
| Freight-in | 6 | 150 | 14 | 70 | Purchase discount |
| Balance | | 3,580 | | | |

---

> ## DO IT!

**Purchase Transactions**

On September 5, De La Hoya Company buys merchandise on account from Junot Diaz Company. The selling price of the goods is $1,500, and the cost to Diaz Company was $800. On September 8, De La Hoya returns defective goods with a selling price of $200. Record the transactions on the books of De La Hoya Company.

**Solution**

**Action Plan**

✔ Purchaser records goods at cost.

✔ When goods are returned, purchaser reduces Inventory.

| Sept. 5 | Inventory | 1,500 | |
| | Accounts Payable | | 1,500 |
| | (To record goods purchased on account) | | |
| 8 | Accounts Payable | 200 | |
| | Inventory | | 200 |
| | (To record return of defective goods) | | |

Related exercise material: **BE5-2, BE5-4, E5-2, E5-3, E5-4, and DO IT! 5-1.**

✔ The Navigator

## Recording Sales of Merchandise

**LEARNING OBJECTIVE**    **3**

Explain the recording of sales revenues under a perpetual inventory system.

In accordance with the revenue recognition principle, companies record sales revenue when the performance obligation is satisfied. Typically, the performance obligation is satisfied when the goods transfer from the seller to the buyer. At this point, the sales transaction is complete and the sales price established.

Sales may be made on credit or for cash. A **business document** should support every sales transaction, to provide written evidence of the sale. **Cash register documents** provide evidence of cash sales. A **sales invoice**, like the one shown in Illustration 5-6 (page 222), provides support for a credit sale. The original copy of the invoice goes to the customer, and the seller keeps a copy for use in recording the sale. The invoice shows the date of sale, customer name, total sales price, and other relevant information.

The seller makes two entries for each sale. **The first entry records the sale**: The seller increases (debits) Cash (or Accounts Receivable, if a credit sale) and also increases (credits) Sales Revenue. **The second entry records the cost of the merchandise sold**: The seller increases (debits) Cost of Goods Sold and also decreases (credits) Inventory for the cost of those goods. As a result, the Inventory account will show at all times the amount of inventory that should be on hand.

To illustrate a credit sales transaction, PW Audio Supply records its May 4 sale of $3,800 to Sauk Stereo (see Illustration 5-6) as follows (assume the merchandise cost PW Audio Supply $2,400).

| May 4 | Accounts Receivable | 3,800 | |
| | Sales Revenue | | 3,800 |
| | (To record credit sale to Sauk Stereo per invoice #731) | | |
| | | | |
| 4 | Cost of Goods Sold | 2,400 | |
| | Inventory | | 2,400 |
| | (To record cost of merchandise sold on invoice #731 to Sauk Stereo) | | |

A = L + OE
+3,800
     +3,800 Rev
**Cash Flows**
no effect

A = L + OE
          −2,400 Exp
−2,400
**Cash Flows**
no effect

For internal decision-making purposes, merchandising companies may use more than one sales account. For example, PW Audio Supply may decide to keep separate sales accounts for its sales of TV sets, DVD recorders, and microwave ovens. REI might use separate accounts for camping gear, children's clothing, and ski equipment—or it might have even more narrowly defined accounts. By using separate sales accounts for major product lines, rather than a single combined sales account, company management can more closely monitor sales trends and respond more strategically to changes in sales patterns. For example, if TV sales are increasing while microwave oven sales are decreasing, PW Audio Supply might reevaluate both its advertising and pricing policies on these items to ensure they are optimal.

On its income statement presented to outside investors, a merchandising company normally would provide only a single sales figure—the sum of all of its individual sales accounts. This is done for two reasons. First, providing detail on all of its individual sales accounts would add considerable length to its income statement. Second, companies do not want their competitors to know the details of their operating results. However, Microsoft recently expanded its disclosure of revenue from three to five types. The reason: The additional categories enabled financial statement users to better evaluate the growth of the company's consumer and Internet businesses.

### Ethics Note

Many companies are trying to improve the quality of their financial reporting. For example, General Electric now provides more detail on its revenues and operating profits.

### ANATOMY OF A FRAUD[1]

Holly Harmon was a cashier at a national superstore for only a short while when she began stealing merchandise using three methods. Under the first method, her husband or friends took UPC labels from cheaper items and put them on more expensive items. Holly then scanned the goods at the register. Using the second method Holly scanned an item at the register but then voided the sale and left the merchandise in the shopping cart. A third approach was to put goods into large plastic containers. She scanned the plastic containers but not the goods within them. One day, Holly did not call in sick or show up for work. In such instances, the company reviews past surveillance tapes to look for suspicious activity by employees. This enabled the store to observe the thefts and to identify the participants.

Total take: $12,000

**THE MISSING CONTROLS**

*Human resource controls.* A background check would have revealed Holly's previous criminal record. She would not have been hired as a cashier.

*Physical controls.* Software can flag high numbers of voided transactions or a high number of sales of low-priced goods. Random comparisons of video records with cash register records can ensure that the goods reported as sold on the register are the same goods that are shown being purchased on the video recording. Finally, employees should be aware that they are being monitored.

*Source:* Adapted from Wells, *Fraud Casebook* (2007), pp. 251–259.

## Sales Returns and Allowances

We now look at the "flip side" of purchase returns and allowances, which the seller records as **sales returns and allowances**. These are transactions where the seller either accepts goods back from the buyer (a return) or grants a reduction in the purchase price (an allowance) so the buyer will keep the goods. PW Audio Supply's entries to record credit for returned goods involve (1) an increase (debit) in Sales Returns and Allowances (a contra account to Sales Revenue) and a decrease (credit) in Accounts Receivable at the $300 selling price, and (2) an increase (debit) in Inventory (assume a $140 cost) and a decrease (credit) in Cost of Goods Sold, as shown below (assuming that the goods were not defective).

| May 8 | Sales Returns and Allowances | 300 | |
| | Accounts Receivable | | 300 |
| | (To record credit granted to Sauk Stereo for returned goods) | | |
| 8 | Inventory | 140 | |
| | Cost of Goods Sold | | 140 |
| | (To record cost of goods returned) | | |

A = L + OE
−300              −300 Rev
**Cash Flows**
no effect

A = L + OE
+140
                  +140 Exp
**Cash Flows**
no effect

If Sauk Stereo returns goods because they are damaged or defective, then PW Audio Supply's entry to Inventory and Cost of Goods Sold should be for the fair value of the returned goods, rather than their cost. For example, if the returned

---

[1]The "Anatomy of a Fraud" stories in this textbook are adapted from *Fraud Casebook: Lessons from the Bad Side of Business,* edited by Joseph T. Wells (Hoboken, NJ: John Wiley & Sons, Inc., 2007). Used by permission. The names of some of the people and organizations in the stories are fictitious, but the facts in the stories are true.

goods were defective and had a fair value of $50, PW Audio Supply would debit Inventory for $50 and credit Cost of Goods Sold for $50.

What happens if the goods are not returned but the seller grants the buyer an allowance by reducing the purchase price? In this case, the seller debits Sales Returns and Allowances and credits Accounts Receivable for the amount of the allowance. An allowance has no impact on Inventory or Cost of Goods Sold.

As mentioned above, Sales Returns and Allowances is a **contra revenue account** to Sales Revenue. This means that it is offset against a revenue account on the income statement. The normal balance of Sales Returns and Allowances is a debit. Companies use a contra account, instead of debiting Sales Revenue, to disclose in the accounts and in the income statement the amount of sales returns and allowances. Disclosure of this information is important to management. Excessive returns and allowances may suggest problems—inferior merchandise, inefficiencies in filling orders, errors in billing customers, or delivery or shipment mistakes. Moreover, a decrease (debit) recorded directly to Sales Revenue would obscure the relative importance of sales returns and allowances as a percentage of sales. It also could distort comparisons between total sales in different accounting periods.

## ACCOUNTING ACROSS THE ORGANIZATION

### Should Costco Change Its Return Policy?

In most industries, sales returns are relatively minor. But returns of consumer electronics can really take a bite out of profits. Recently, the marketing executives at Costco Wholesale Corp. faced a difficult decision. Costco has always prided itself on its generous return policy. Most goods have had an unlimited grace period for returns. A new policy will require that certain electronics must be returned within 90 days of their purchase. The reason? The cost of returned products such as high-definition TVs, computers, and iPods cut an estimated 8¢ per share off Costco's earnings per share, which was $2.30.

*Source:* Kris Hudson, "Costco Tightens Policy on Returning Electronics," *Wall Street Journal* (February 27, 2007), p. B4.

© Jacob Wackerhausen/iStockphoto

 If a company expects significant returns, what are the implications for revenue recognition? (See page 270.)

## Sales Discounts

As mentioned in our discussion of purchase transactions, the seller may offer the customer a cash discount—called by the seller a **sales discount**—for the prompt payment of the balance due. Like a purchase discount, a sales discount is based on the invoice price less returns and allowances, if any. The seller increases (debits) the Sales Discounts account for discounts that are taken. For example, PW Audio Supply makes the following entry to record the cash receipt on May 14 from Sauk Stereo within the discount period.

| A | = | L | + | OE |
|---|---|---|---|---|
| +3,430 | | | | |
| | | | | −70 Rev |
| −3,500 | | | | |

**Cash Flows**
+3,430

| May 14 | Cash | 3,430 | |
|---|---|---|---|
| | Sales Discounts | 70 | |
| |    Accounts Receivable | | 3,500 |
| |      (To record collection within 2/10, n/30 | | |
| |      discount period from Sauk Stereo) | | |

Like Sales Returns and Allowances, Sales Discounts is a **contra revenue account** to Sales Revenue. Its normal balance is a debit. PW Audio Supply uses this account, instead of debiting Sales Revenue, to disclose the amount of cash discounts taken by customers. If Sauk Stereo does not take the discount, PW

Audio Supply increases (debits) Cash for $3,500 and decreases (credits) Accounts Receivable for the same amount at the date of collection.

The following T-accounts summarize the three sales-related transactions and show their combined effect on net sales.

| Sales Revenue | Sales Returns and Allowances | Sales Discounts |
|---|---|---|
| 3,800 | 300 | 70 |

Net Sales
$3,430

---

## PEOPLE, PLANET, AND PROFIT INSIGHT

### Selling Green

Here is a question an executive of PepsiCo was asked: Should PepsiCo market green? The executive indicated that the company should, as he believes it's the No. 1 thing consumers all over the world care about. Here are some of his thoughts on this issue:

"Sun Chips are part of the food business I run. It's a 'healthy snack.' We decided that Sun Chips, if it's a healthy snack, should be made in facilities that have a net-zero footprint. In other words, I want off the electric grid everywhere we make Sun Chips. We did that. Sun Chips should be made in a facility that puts back more water than it uses. It does that. And we partnered with our suppliers and came out with the world's first compostable chip package.

Now, there was an issue with this package: It was louder than the New York subway, louder than jet engines taking off. What would a company that's committed to green do: walk away or stay committed? If your people are passionate, they're going to fix it for you as long as you stay committed. Six months later, the compostable bag has half the noise of our current package.

So the view today is: we should market green, we should be proud to do it . . . it has to be a 360-degree process, both internal and external. And if you do that, you can monetize environmental sustainability for the shareholders."

*Source:* "Four Problems—and Solutions," *Wall Street Journal* (March 7, 2011), p. R2.

 What is meant by "monetize environmental sustainability" for shareholders? (See page 270.)

---

## > DO IT!

### Sales Transactions

**Action Plan**

✔ Seller records both the sale and the cost of goods sold at the time of the sale.

✔ When goods are returned, the seller records the return in a contra account, Sales Returns and Allowances, and reduces Accounts Receivable.

On September 5, De La Hoya Company buys merchandise on account from Junot Diaz Company. The selling price of the goods is $1,500, and the cost to Diaz Company was $800. On September 8, De La Hoya returns defective goods with a selling price of $200 and a fair value of $30. Record the transactions on the books of Junot Diaz Company.

**Solution**

| | | | |
|---|---|---|---|
| Sept. 5 | Accounts Receivable | 1,500 | |
| |    Sales Revenue | | 1,500 |
| |      (To record credit sale) | | |
| 5 | Cost of Goods Sold | 800 | |
| |    Inventory | | 800 |
| |      (To record cost of goods sold on account) | | |

230    **5** Accounting for Merchandising Operations

**Action Plan (cont'd)**

✔ Any goods returned increase Inventory and reduce Cost of Goods Sold. Defective or damaged inventory is recorded at fair value (scrap value).

| | | | | |
|---|---|---|---|---|
| 8 | Sales Returns and Allowances | | 200 | |
| | Accounts Receivable | | | 200 |
| | (To record credit granted for receipt of returned goods) | | | |
| 8 | Inventory | | 30 | |
| | Cost of Goods Sold | | | 30 |
| | (To record fair value of goods returned) | | | |

Related exercise material: **BE5-2, BE5-3, E5-3, E5-4, E5-5, and DO IT! 5-2.**

✔ **The Navigator**

## Completing the Accounting Cycle

**LEARNING OBJECTIVE** 4

**Explain the steps in the accounting cycle for a merchandising company.**

Up to this point, we have illustrated the basic entries for transactions relating to purchases and sales in a perpetual inventory system. Now we consider the remaining steps in the accounting cycle for a merchandising company. Each of the required steps described in Chapter 4 for service companies apply to merchandising companies. Appendix 5A to this chapter shows use of a worksheet by a merchandiser (an optional step).

### Adjusting Entries

A merchandising company generally has the same types of adjusting entries as a service company. However, a merchandiser using a perpetual system will require one additional adjustment to make the records agree with the actual inventory on hand. Here's why: At the end of each period, for control purposes, a merchandising company that uses a perpetual system will take a physical count of its goods on hand. The company's unadjusted balance in Inventory usually does not agree with the actual amount of inventory on hand. The perpetual inventory records may be incorrect due to recording errors, theft, or waste. Thus, the company needs to adjust the perpetual records to make the recorded inventory amount agree with the inventory on hand. **This involves adjusting Inventory and Cost of Goods Sold.**

For example, suppose that PW Audio Supply has an unadjusted balance of $40,500 in Inventory. Through a physical count, PW Audio Supply determines that its actual merchandise inventory at year-end is $40,000. The company would make an adjusting entry as follows.

A = L + OE
−500
       −500 Exp

**Cash Flows**
no effect

| | | | |
|---|---|---|---|
| Cost of Goods Sold | | 500 | |
| Inventory | | | 500 |
| (To adjust inventory to physical count) | | | |

### Closing Entries

A merchandising company, like a service company, closes to Income Summary all accounts that affect net income. In journalizing, the company credits all temporary accounts with debit balances, and debits all temporary accounts with credit balances, as shown below for PW Audio Supply. Note that PW Audio Supply closes Cost of Goods Sold to Income Summary.

**Helpful Hint** The easiest way to prepare the first two closing entries is to identify the temporary accounts by their balances and then prepare one entry for the credits and one entry for the debits.

| | | | | |
|---|---|---|---|---|
| Dec. 31 | Sales Revenue | | 480,000 | |
| | Income Summary | | | 480,000 |
| | (To close income statement accounts with credit balances) | | | |

| | | | |
|---|---|---|---|
| 31 | Income Summary | 450,000 | |
| | Sales Returns and Allowances | | 12,000 |
| | Sales Discounts | | 8,000 |
| | Cost of Goods Sold | | 316,000 |
| | Salaries and Wages Expense | | 64,000 |
| | Freight-Out | | 7,000 |
| | Advertising Expense | | 16,000 |
| | Utilities Expense | | 17,000 |
| | Depreciation Expense | | 8,000 |
| | Insurance Expense | | 2,000 |
| | (To close income statement accounts with debit balances) | | |
| 31 | Income Summary | 30,000 | |
| | Owner's Capital | | 30,000 |
| | (To close net income to capital) | | |
| 31 | Owner's Capital | 15,000 | |
| | Owner's Drawings | | 15,000 |
| | (To close drawings to capital) | | |

After PW Audio Supply has posted the closing entries, all temporary accounts have zero balances. Also, Owner's Capital has a balance that is carried over to the next period.

## Summary of Merchandising Entries

Illustration 5-8 summarizes the entries for the merchandising accounts using a perpetual inventory system.

**Illustration 5-8**
Daily recurring and adjusting and closing entries

| | Transactions | Daily Recurring Entries | Dr. | Cr. |
|---|---|---|---|---|
| **Sales Transactions** | Selling merchandise to customers. | Cash or Accounts Receivable | XX | |
| | | Sales Revenue | | XX |
| | | Cost of Goods Sold | XX | |
| | | Inventory | | XX |
| | Granting sales returns or allowances to customers. | Sales Returns and Allowances | XX | |
| | | Cash or Accounts Receivable | | XX |
| | | Inventory | XX | |
| | | Cost of Goods Sold | | XX |
| | Paying freight costs on sales; FOB destination. | Freight-Out | XX | |
| | | Cash | | XX |
| | Receiving payment from customers within discount period. | Cash | XX | |
| | | Sales Discounts | XX | |
| | | Accounts Receivable | | XX |
| **Purchase Transactions** | Purchasing merchandise for resale. | Inventory | XX | |
| | | Cash or Accounts Payable | | XX |
| | Paying freight costs on merchandise purchased; FOB shipping point. | Inventory | XX | |
| | | Cash | | XX |
| | Receiving purchase returns or allowances from suppliers. | Cash or Accounts Payable | XX | |
| | | Inventory | | XX |
| | Paying suppliers within discount period. | Accounts Payable | XX | |
| | | Inventory | | XX |
| | | Cash | | XX |

| Events | Adjusting and Closing Entries | | |
|---|---|---|---|
| Adjust because book amount is higher than the inventory amount determined to be on hand. | Cost of Goods Sold<br>    Inventory | XX | XX |
| Closing temporary accounts with credit balances. | Sales Revenue<br>    Income Summary | XX | XX |
| Closing temporary accounts with debit balances. | Income Summary<br>    Sales Returns and Allowances<br>    Sales Discounts<br>    Cost of Goods Sold<br>    Freight-Out<br>    Expenses | XX | XX<br>XX<br>XX<br>XX<br>XX |

**Illustration 5-8**
(*continued*)

> **DO IT!**

### Closing Entries

The trial balance of Celine's Sports Wear Shop at December 31 shows Inventory $25,000, Sales Revenue $162,400, Sales Returns and Allowances $4,800, Sales Discounts $3,600, Cost of Goods Sold $110,000, Rent Revenue $6,000, Freight-Out $1,800, Rent Expense $8,800, and Salaries and Wages Expense $22,000. Prepare the closing entries for the above accounts.

**Solution**

**Action Plan**

✔ Close all temporary accounts with credit balances to Income Summary by debiting these accounts.

✔ Close all temporary accounts with debit balances, except drawings, to Income Summary by crediting these accounts.

| The two closing entries are: | | | |
|---|---|---|---|
| Dec. 31 | Sales Revenue | 162,400 | |
| | Rent Revenue | 6,000 | |
| |    Income Summary | | 168,400 |
| |      (To close accounts with credit balances) | | |
| 31 | Income Summary | 151,000 | |
| |    Cost of Goods Sold | | 110,000 |
| |    Sales Returns and Allowances | | 4,800 |
| |    Sales Discounts | | 3,600 |
| |    Freight-Out | | 1,800 |
| |    Rent Expense | | 8,800 |
| |    Salaries and Wages Expense | | 22,000 |
| |      (To close accounts with debit balances) | | |

Related exercise material: **BE5-5, BE5-6, E5-6, E5-7, E5-8, and DO IT! 5-3.**

✔ **The Navigator**

## Forms of Financial Statements

LEARNING OBJECTIVE    **5**

Distinguish between a multiple-step and a single-step income statement.

Merchandising companies widely use the classified balance sheet introduced in Chapter 4 and one of two forms for the income statement. This section explains the use of these financial statements by merchandisers.

### Multiple-Step Income Statement

The **multiple-step income statement** is so named because it shows several steps in determining net income. Two of these steps relate to the company's principal operating activities. A multiple-step statement also distinguishes between

**operating** and **nonoperating activities**. Finally, the statement also highlights intermediate components of income and shows subgroupings of expenses.

## INCOME STATEMENT PRESENTATION OF SALES

The multiple-step income statement begins by presenting **sales revenue**. It then deducts contra revenue accounts—sales returns and allowances, and sales discounts—from sales revenue to arrive at **net sales**. Illustration 5-9 presents the sales revenues section for PW Audio Supply, using assumed data.

**Illustration 5-9**
Computation of net sales

| PW AUDIO SUPPLY | | |
|---|---|---|
| Income Statement (partial) | | |
| **Sales revenues** | | |
| Sales revenue | | $ 480,000 |
| Less: Sales returns and allowances | $12,000 | |
| Sales discounts | 8,000 | 20,000 |
| **Net sales** | | **$460,000** |

## GROSS PROFIT

From Illustration 5-1, you learned that companies deduct cost of goods sold from sales revenue to determine **gross profit**. For this computation, companies use **net sales** (which takes into consideration Sales Returns and Allowances and Sales Discounts) as the amount of sales revenue. On the basis of the sales data in Illustration 5-9 (net sales of $460,000) and cost of goods sold under the perpetual inventory system (assume $316,000), PW Audio Supply's gross profit is $144,000, computed as follows.

**Alternative Terminology**
Gross profit is sometimes referred to as *gross margin.*

**Illustration 5-10**
Computation of gross profit

| Net sales | $ 460,000 |
|---|---|
| Cost of goods sold | 316,000 |
| **Gross profit** | **$144,000** |

We also can express a company's gross profit as a percentage, called the **gross profit rate**. To do so, we divide the amount of gross profit by net sales. For PW Audio Supply, the **gross profit rate** is 31.3%, computed as follows.

**Illustration 5-11**
Gross profit rate formula and computation

| Gross Profit | ÷ | Net Sales | = | Gross Profit Rate |
|---|---|---|---|---|
| $144,000 | ÷ | $460,000 | = | 31.3% |

Analysts generally consider the gross profit **rate** to be more useful than the gross profit **amount**. The rate expresses a more meaningful (qualitative) relationship between net sales and gross profit. For example, a gross profit of $1,000,000 may sound impressive. But if it is the result of a gross profit rate of only 7%, it is not so impressive. The gross profit rate tells how many cents of each sales dollar go to gross profit.

Gross profit represents the **merchandising profit** of a company. It is not a measure of the overall profitability because operating expenses are not yet deducted. But managers and other interested parties closely watch the amount and trend of gross profit. They compare current gross profit with amounts reported in past periods. They also compare the company's gross profit rate with rates of competitors and with industry averages. Such comparisons provide information about the effectiveness of a company's purchasing function and the soundness of its pricing policies.

### OPERATING EXPENSES AND NET INCOME

**Operating expenses** are the next component in measuring net income for a merchandising company. They are the expenses incurred in the process of earning sales revenue. These expenses are similar in merchandising and service companies. At PW Audio Supply, operating expenses were $114,000. The company determines its net income by subtracting operating expenses from gross profit. Thus, net income is $30,000, as shown below.

**Illustration 5-12**
Operating expenses in computing net income

| | |
|---|---|
| Gross profit | $144,000 |
| **Operating expenses** | **114,000** |
| Net income | $ 30,000 |

The net income amount is the so-called "bottom line" of a company's income statement.

### NONOPERATING ACTIVITIES

**Nonoperating activities** consist of various revenues and expenses and gains and losses that are unrelated to the company's main line of operations. When nonoperating items are included, the label "**Income from operations**" (or "Operating income") precedes them. This label clearly identifies the results of the company's normal operations, an amount determined by subtracting cost of goods sold and operating expenses from net sales. The results of nonoperating activities are shown in the categories "**Other revenues and gains**" and "**Other expenses and losses**." Illustration 5-13 lists examples of each.

**Illustration 5-13**
Other items of nonoperating activities

| **Other Revenues and Gains** |
|---|
| **Interest revenue** from notes receivable and marketable securities. |
| **Dividend revenue** from investments in common stock. |
| **Rent revenue** from subleasing a portion of the store. |
| **Gain** from the sale of property, plant, and equipment. |

| **Other Expenses and Losses** |
|---|
| **Interest expense** on notes and loans payable. |
| **Casualty losses** from recurring causes, such as vandalism and accidents. |
| **Loss** from the sale or abandonment of property, plant, and equipment. |
| **Loss** from strikes by employees and suppliers. |

 **Ethics Note**

Companies manage earnings in various ways. ConAgra Foods recorded a non-recurring gain for $186 million from the sale of Pilgrim's Pride stock to help meet an earnings projection for the quarter.

Merchandising companies report the nonoperating activities in the income statement immediately after the company's operating activities. Illustration 5-14 shows these sections for PW Audio Supply, using assumed data.

The distinction between operating and nonoperating activities is crucial to many external users of financial data. These users view operating income as sustainable and many nonoperating activities as nonrecurring. Therefore, when forecasting next year's income, analysts put the most weight on this year's operating income, and less weight on this year's nonoperating activities.

**Illustration 5-14**
Multiple-step income statement

| **PW AUDIO SUPPLY** |
| --- |
| Income Statement |
| For the Year Ended December 31, 2014 |

| | | | |
| --- | --- | --- | --- |
| **Sales** | | | |
| Sales revenue | | | $480,000 |
| Less: Sales returns and allowances | $12,000 | | |
| Sales discounts | 8,000 | | 20,000 |
| Net sales | | | 460,000 |
| **Cost of goods sold** | | | 316,000 |
| **Gross profit** | | | 144,000 |
| **Operating expenses** | | | |
| Salaries and wages expense | 64,000 | | |
| Utilities expense | 17,000 | | |
| Advertising expense | 16,000 | | |
| Depreciation expense | 8,000 | | |
| Freight-out | 7,000 | | |
| Insurance expense | 2,000 | | |
| Total operating expenses | | | 114,000 |
| **Income from operations** | | | 30,000 |
| **Other revenues and gains** | | | |
| Interest revenue | 3,000 | | |
| Gain on disposal of plant assets | 600 | | 3,600 |
| **Other expenses and losses** | | | |
| Interest expense | 1,800 | | |
| Casualty loss from vandalism | 200 | | 2,000 |
| **Net income** | | | $ 31,600 |

Left-margin bracket labels:
- Calculation of gross profit
- Calculation of income from operations
- Results of nonoperating activities

## ETHICS INSIGHT

### Disclosing More Details

After Enron, increased investor criticism and regulator scrutiny forced many companies to improve the clarity of their financial disclosures. For example, IBM began providing more detail regarding its "Other gains and losses." It had previously included these items in its selling, general, and administrative expenses, with little disclosure.

Disclosing other gains and losses in a separate line item on the income statement will not have any effect on bottom-line income. However, analysts complained that burying these details in the selling, general, and administrative expense line reduced their ability to fully understand how well IBM was performing. For example, previously if IBM sold off one of its buildings at a gain, it would include this gain in the selling, general and administrative expense line item, thus reducing that expense. This made it appear that the company had done a better job of controlling operating expenses than it actually had.

As another example, when eBay recently sold the remainder of its investment in Skype to Microsoft, it reported a gain in "Other revenues and gains" of $1.7 billion. Since eBay's total income from operations was $2.4 billion, it was very important that the gain from the Skype sale not be buried in operating income.

ImageRite/Getty Images, Inc.

**?** Why have investors and analysts demanded more accuracy in isolating "Other gains and losses" from operating items? (See page 270.)

## Single-Step Income Statement

Another income statement format is the **single-step income statement**. The statement is so named because only one step—subtracting total expenses from total revenues—is required in determining net income.

In a single-step statement, all data are classified into two categories: (1) **revenues**, which include both operating revenues and other revenues and gains; and (2) **expenses**, which include cost of goods sold, operating expenses, and other expenses and losses. Illustration 5-15 shows a single-step statement for PW Audio Supply.

**Illustration 5-15**
Single-step income statement

| PW AUDIO SUPPLY | | |
|---|---|---|
| Income Statement | | |
| For the Year Ended December 31, 2014 | | |
| **Revenues** | | |
| Net sales | | $460,000 |
| Interest revenue | | 3,000 |
| Gain on disposal of plant assets | | 600 |
|    Total revenues | | 463,600 |
| **Expenses** | | |
| Cost of goods sold | $316,000 | |
| Operating expenses | 114,000 | |
| Interest expense | 1,800 | |
| Casualty loss from vandalism | 200 | |
|    Total expenses | | 432,000 |
| **Net income** | | $ 31,600 |

There are two primary reasons for using the single-step format. (1) A company does not realize any type of profit or income until total revenues exceed total expenses, so it makes sense to divide the statement into these two categories. (2) The format is simpler and easier to read. *For homework problems, however, you should use the single-step format only when specifically instructed to do so.*

## Classified Balance Sheet

In the balance sheet, merchandising companies report inventory as a current asset immediately below accounts receivable. Recall from Chapter 4 that companies generally list current asset items in the order of their closeness to cash (liquidity). Inventory is less close to cash than accounts receivable because the goods must first be sold and then collection made from the customer. Illustration 5-16 presents the assets section of a classified balance sheet for PW Audio Supply.

**Illustration 5-16**
Assets section of a classified balance sheet

**Helpful Hint** The $40,000 is the cost of the inventory on hand, not its expected selling price.

| PW AUDIO SUPPLY | | |
|---|---|---|
| Balance Sheet (Partial) | | |
| December 31, 2014 | | |
| **Assets** | | |
| Current assets | | |
| Cash | | $ 9,500 |
| Accounts receivable | | 16,100 |
| **Inventory** | | 40,000 |
| Prepaid insurance | | 1,800 |
|    Total current assets | | 67,400 |
| Property, plant, and equipment | | |
| Equipment | $80,000 | |
| Less: Accumulated depreciation—equipment | 24,000 | 56,000 |
|    Total assets | | $123,400 |

# > DO IT!

## Financial Statement Classifications

You are presented with the following list of accounts from the adjusted trial balance for merchandiser Gorman Company. Indicate in which financial statement and under what classification each of the following would be reported.

Accounts Payable
Accounts Receivable
Accumulated Depreciation—Buildings
Accumulated Depreciation—Equipment
Advertising Expense
Buildings
Cash
Depreciation Expense
Equipment
Freight-Out
Gain on Disposal of Plant Assets
Insurance Expense
Interest Expense

Interest Payable
Inventory
Land
Notes Payable (due in 3 years)
Owner's Capital (beginning balance)
Owner's Drawings
Property Taxes Payable
Salaries and Wages Expense
Salaries and Wages Payable
Sales Returns and Allowances
Sales Revenue
Utilities Expense

### Action Plan

✔ Review the major sections of the income statement: sales revenues, cost of goods sold, operating expenses, other revenues and gains, and other expenses and losses.

✔ Add net income and investments to beginning capital and deduct drawings to arrive at ending capital in the owner's equity statement.

✔ Review the major sections of the balance sheet, income statement, and owner's equity statement.

### Solution

| Account | Financial Statement | Classification |
| --- | --- | --- |
| Accounts Payable | Balance sheet | Current liabilities |
| Accounts Receivable | Balance sheet | Current assets |
| Accumulated Depreciation—Buildings | Balance sheet | Property, plant, and equipment |
| Accumulated Depreciation—Equipment | Balance sheet | Property, plant, and equipment |
| Advertising Expense | Income statement | Operating expenses |
| Buildings | Balance sheet | Property, plant, and equipment |
| Cash | Balance sheet | Current assets |
| Depreciation Expense | Income statement | Operating expenses |
| Equipment | Balance sheet | Property, plant, and equipment |
| Freight-Out | Income statement | Operating expenses |
| Gain on Disposal of Plant Assets | Income statement | Other revenues and gains |
| Insurance Expense | Income statement | Operating expenses |
| Interest Expense | Income statement | Other expenses and losses |
| Interest Payable | Balance sheet | Current liabilities |
| Inventory | Balance sheet | Current assets |
| Land | Balance sheet | Property, plant, and equipment |
| Notes Payable (due in 3 years) | Balance sheet | Long-term liabilities |
| Owner's Capital | Owner's equity statement | Beginning balance |
| Owner's Drawings | Owner's equity statement | Deduction section |
| Property Taxes Payable | Balance sheet | Current liabilities |
| Salaries and Wages Expense | Income statement | Operating expenses |
| Salaries and Wages Payable | Balance sheet | Current liabilities |
| Sales Returns and Allowances | Income statement | Sales revenues |
| Sales Revenue | Income statement | Sales revenues |
| Utilities Expense | Income statement | Operating expenses |

Related exercise material: **BE5-7, BE5-8, BE5-9, E5-9, E5-10, E5-12, E5-13, E5-14, and DO IT! 5-4.**

 ✔ The Navigator

## > Comprehensive DO IT!

The adjusted trial balance columns of Falcetto Company's worksheet for the year ended December 31, 2014, are as follows.

| | Debit | | Credit |
|---|---|---|---|
| Cash | 14,500 | Accumulated Depreciation— | |
| Accounts Receivable | 11,100 | Equipment | 18,000 |
| Inventory | 29,000 | Notes Payable | 25,000 |
| Prepaid Insurance | 2,500 | Accounts Payable | 10,600 |
| Equipment | 95,000 | Owner's Capital | 81,000 |
| Owner's Drawings | 12,000 | Sales Revenue | 536,800 |
| Sales Returns and Allowances | 6,700 | Interest Revenue | 2,500 |
| Sales Discounts | 5,000 | | 673,900 |
| Cost of Goods Sold | 363,400 | | |
| Freight-Out | 7,600 | | |
| Advertising Expense | 12,000 | | |
| Salaries and Wages Expense | 56,000 | | |
| Utilities Expense | 18,000 | | |
| Rent Expense | 24,000 | | |
| Depreciation Expense | 9,000 | | |
| Insurance Expense | 4,500 | | |
| Interest Expense | 3,600 | | |
| | 673,900 | | |

### Instructions

Prepare a multiple-step income statement for Falcetto Company.

### Solution to Comprehensive DO IT!

**Action Plan**

✔ Remember that the key components of the income statement are net sales, cost of goods sold, gross profit, total operating expenses, and net income (loss). Report these components in the right-hand column of the income statement.

✔ Put nonoperating items after income from operations.

**FALCETTO COMPANY**
**Income Statement**
**For the Year Ended December 31, 2014**

| | | |
|---|---|---|
| Sales revenues | | |
| Sales revenue | | $536,800 |
| Less: Sales returns and allowances | $ 6,700 | |
| Sales discounts | 5,000 | 11,700 |
| Net sales | | 525,100 |
| Cost of goods sold | | 363,400 |
| Gross profit | | 161,700 |
| Operating expenses | | |
| Salaries and wages expense | 56,000 | |
| Rent expense | 24,000 | |
| Utilities expense | 18,000 | |
| Advertising expense | 12,000 | |
| Depreciation expense | 9,000 | |
| Freight-out | 7,600 | |
| Insurance expense | 4,500 | |
| Total operating expenses | | 131,100 |
| Income from operations | | 30,600 |
| Other revenues and gains | | |
| Interest revenue | 2,500 | |
| Other expenses and losses | | |
| Interest expense | 3,600 | 1,100 |
| Net income | | $ 29,500 |

## SUMMARY OF LEARNING OBJECTIVES

The Navigator

1 **Identify the differences between service and merchandising companies.** Because of inventory, a merchandising company has sales revenue, cost of goods sold, and gross profit. To account for inventory, a merchandising company must choose between a perpetual and a periodic inventory system.

2 **Explain the recording of purchases under a perpetual inventory system.** The company debits the Inventory account for all purchases of merchandise and freight-in, and credits it for purchase discounts and purchase returns and allowances.

3 **Explain the recording of sales revenues under a perpetual inventory system.** When a merchandising company sells inventory, it debits Accounts Receivable (or Cash) and credits Sales Revenue for the **selling price** of the merchandise. At the same time, it debits Cost of Goods Sold and credits Inventory for the **cost** of the inventory items sold. Sales Returns and Allowances and Sales Discounts are debited and are contra revenue accounts.

4 **Explain the steps in the accounting cycle for a merchandising company.** Each of the required steps in the accounting cycle for a service company applies to a merchandising company. A worksheet is again an optional step. Under a perpetual inventory system, the company must adjust the Inventory account to agree with the physical count.

5 **Distinguish between a multiple-step and a single-step income statement.** A multiple-step income statement shows numerous steps in determining net income, including nonoperating activities sections. A single-step income statement classifies all data under two categories, revenues or expenses, and determines net income in one step.

## GLOSSARY

**Contra revenue account** An account that is offset against a revenue account on the income statement. (p. 228).

**Cost of goods sold** The total cost of merchandise sold during the period. (p. 218).

**FOB destination** Freight terms indicating that the seller places the goods free on board to the buyer's place of business, and the seller pays the freight. (p. 222).

**FOB shipping point** Freight terms indicating that the seller places goods free on board the carrier, and the buyer pays the freight costs. (p. 222).

**Gross profit** The excess of net sales over the cost of goods sold. (p. 233).

**Gross profit rate** Gross profit expressed as a percentage, by dividing the amount of gross profit by net sales. (p. 233).

**Income from operations** Income from a company's principal operating activity; determined by subtracting cost of goods sold and operating expenses from net sales. (p. 234).

**Multiple-step income statement** An income statement that shows several steps in determining net income. (p. 232).

**Net sales** Sales revenue less sales returns and allowances and less sales discounts. (p. 233).

**Nonoperating activities** Various revenues, expenses, gains, and losses that are unrelated to a company's main line of operations. (p. 234).

**Operating expenses** Expenses incurred in the process of earning sales revenue. (p. 234).

**Other expenses and losses** A nonoperating-activities section of the income statement that shows expenses and losses unrelated to the company's main line of operations. (p. 234).

**Other revenues and gains** A nonoperating-activities section of the income statement that shows revenues and gains unrelated to the company's main line of operations. (p. 234).

**Periodic inventory system** An inventory system under which the company does not keep detailed inventory records throughout the accounting period but determines the cost of goods sold only at the end of an accounting period. (p. 220).

**Perpetual inventory system** An inventory system under which the company keeps detailed records of the cost of each inventory purchase and sale, and the records continuously show the inventory that should be on hand. (p. 219).

**Purchase allowance** A deduction made to the selling price of merchandise, granted by the seller so that the buyer will keep the merchandise. (p. 223).

**Purchase discount** A cash discount claimed by a buyer for prompt payment of a balance due. (p. 224).

**Purchase invoice** A document that supports each credit purchase. (p. 221).

**Purchase return** A return of goods from the buyer to the seller for a cash or credit refund. (p. 223).

**Sales discount** A reduction given by a seller for prompt payment of a credit sale. (p. 228).

**Sales invoice** A document that supports each credit sale. (p. 226).

**Sales returns and allowances** Purchase returns and allowances from the seller's perspective. See *Purchase return* and *Purchase allowance*, above. (p. 227).

**Sales revenue (Sales)** The primary source of revenue in a merchandising company. (p. 218).

**Single-step income statement** An income statement that shows only one step in determining net income. (p. 236).

# APPENDIX 5A    Worksheet for a Merchandising Company—Perpetual Inventory

## Using a Worksheet

LEARNING OBJECTIVE    **6**

**Prepare a worksheet for a merchandising company.**

As indicated in Chapter 4, a worksheet enables companies to prepare financial statements before they journalize and post adjusting entries. The steps in preparing a worksheet for a merchandising company are the same as for a service company (see pages 163–165). Illustration 5A-1 shows the worksheet for PW Audio Supply (excluding nonoperating items). The unique accounts for a merchandiser using a **perpetual inventory system** are in red.

| | | PW Audio Supply.xls | | | | | | | | |
|---|---|---|---|---|---|---|---|---|---|---|
| Home | Insert | Page Layout | Formulas | Data | Review | View | | | | |

P18    fx

**PW AUDIO SUPPLY**
**Worksheet**
**For the Year Ended December 31, 2014**

| | Trial Balance | | Adjustments | | Adjusted Trial Balance | | Income Statement | | Balance Sheet | |
|---|---|---|---|---|---|---|---|---|---|---|
| Accounts | Dr. | Cr. | Dr. | Cr. | Dr. | Cr. | Dr. | Cr. | Dr. | Cr. |
| Cash | 9,500 | | | | 9,500 | | | | 9,500 | |
| Accounts Receivable | 16,100 | | | | 16,100 | | | | 16,100 | |
| Inventory | 40,500 | | | (a) 500 | 40,000 | | | | 40,000 | |
| Prepaid Insurance | 3,800 | | | (b) 2,000 | 1,800 | | | | 1,800 | |
| Equipment | 80,000 | | | | 80,000 | | | | 80,000 | |
| Accumulated Depreciation—Equipment | | 16,000 | | (c) 8,000 | | 24,000 | | | | 24,000 |
| Accounts Payable | | 20,400 | | | | 20,400 | | | | 20,400 |
| Owner's Capital | | 83,000 | | | | 83,000 | | | | 83,000 |
| Owner's Drawings | 15,000 | | | | 15,000 | | | | 15,000 | |
| Sales Revenue | | 480,000 | | | | 480,000 | | 480,000 | | |
| Sales Returns and Allowances | 12,000 | | | | 12,000 | | 12,000 | | | |
| Sales Discounts | 8,000 | | | | 8,000 | | 8,000 | | | |
| Cost of Goods Sold | 315,500 | | (a) 500 | | 316,000 | | 316,000 | | | |
| Freight-Out | 7,000 | | | | 7,000 | | 7,000 | | | |
| Advertising Expense | 16,000 | | | | 16,000 | | 16,000 | | | |
| Salaries and Wages Expense | 59,000 | | (d) 5,000 | | 64,000 | | 64,000 | | | |
| Utilities Expense | 17,000 | | | | 17,000 | | 17,000 | | | |
| Totals | 599,400 | 599,400 | | | | | | | | |
| Insurance Expense | | | (b) 2,000 | | 2,000 | | 2,000 | | | |
| Depreciation Expense | | | (c) 8,000 | | 8,000 | | 8,000 | | | |
| Salaries and Wages Payable | | | | (d) 5,000 | | 5,000 | | | | 5,000 |
| Totals | | | 15,500 | 15,500 | 612,400 | 612,400 | 450,000 | 480,000 | 162,400 | 132,400 |
| Net Income | | | | | | | 30,000 | | | 30,000 |
| Totals | | | | | | | 480,000 | 480,000 | 162,400 | 162,400 |

Key: (a) Adjustment to inventory on hand. (b) Insurance expired. (c) Depreciation expense. (d) Salaries accrued.

**Illustration 5A-1**
Worksheet for merchandising company—perpetual inventory system

## TRIAL BALANCE COLUMNS

Data for the trial balance come from the ledger balances of PW Audio Supply at December 31. The amount shown for Inventory, $40,500, is the year-end inventory amount from the perpetual inventory system.

## ADJUSTMENTS COLUMNS

A merchandising company generally has the same types of adjustments as a service company. As you see in the worksheet, adjustments (b), (c), and (d) are for insurance, depreciation, and salaries. Pioneer Advertising Agency, as illustrated in Chapters 3 and 4, also had these adjustments. Adjustment (a) was required to adjust the perpetual inventory carrying amount to the actual count.

After PW Audio Supply enters all adjustments data on the worksheet, it establishes the equality of the adjustments column totals. It then extends the balances in all accounts to the adjusted trial balance columns.

## ADJUSTED TRIAL BALANCE

The adjusted trial balance shows the balance of all accounts after adjustment at the end of the accounting period.

## INCOME STATEMENT COLUMNS

Next, the merchandising company transfers the accounts and balances that affect the income statement from the adjusted trial balance columns to the income statement columns. PW Audio Supply shows Sales Revenue of $480,000 in the credit column. It shows the contra revenue accounts Sales Returns and Allowances $12,000 and Sales Discounts $8,000 in the debit column. The difference of $460,000 is the net sales shown on the income statement (Illustration 5-14, page 235).

Finally, the company totals all the credits in the income statement column and compares those totals to the total of the debits in the income statement column. If the credits exceed the debits, the company has net income. PW Audio Supply has net income of $30,000. If the debits exceed the credits, the company would report a net loss.

## BALANCE SHEET COLUMNS

The major difference between the balance sheets of a service company and a merchandiser is inventory. PW Audio Supply shows the ending inventory amount of $40,000 in the balance sheet debit column. The information to prepare the owner's equity statement is also found in these columns. That is, the Owner's Capital account is $83,000. Owner's Drawings are $15,000. Net income results when the total of the debit column exceeds the total of the credit column in the balance sheet columns. A net loss results when the total of the credits exceeds the total of the debit balances.

---

## SUMMARY OF LEARNING OBJECTIVE FOR APPENDIX 5A                          ✔ The Navigator

**6  Prepare a worksheet for a merchandising company.** The steps in preparing a worksheet for a merchandising company are the same as for a service company. The unique accounts for a merchandiser are Inventory, Sales Revenue, Sales Returns and Allowances, Sales Discounts, and Cost of Goods Sold.

---

# APPENDIX 5B    Periodic Inventory System

As described in this chapter, companies may use one of two basic systems of accounting for inventories: (1) the perpetual inventory system or (2) the periodic inventory system. In the chapter, we focused on the characteristics of the perpetual inventory system. In this appendix, we discuss and illustrate the **periodic**

LEARNING OBJECTIVE    7

Explain the recording of purchases and sales of inventory under a periodic inventory system.

**inventory system**. One key difference between the two systems is the point at which the company computes cost of goods sold. For a visual reminder of this difference, refer back to Illustration 5-5 (on page 220).

## Determining Cost of Goods Sold Under a Periodic System

Determining cost of goods sold is different when a periodic inventory system is used rather than a perpetual system. As you have seen, a company using a **perpetual system** makes an entry to record cost of goods sold and to reduce inventory each time a sale is made. A company using a **periodic system** does not determine cost of goods sold until the end of the period. At the end of the period, the company performs a count to determine the ending balance of inventory. It then **calculates cost of goods sold by subtracting ending inventory from the goods available for sale**. Goods available for sale is the sum of beginning inventory plus purchases, as shown in Illustration 5B-1.

**Illustration 5B-1**
Basic formula for cost of goods sold using the periodic system

$$
\begin{array}{l}
\text{Beginning Inventory} \\
+ \ \underline{\text{Cost of Goods Purchased}} \\
\text{Cost of Goods Available for Sale} \\
- \ \underline{\text{Ending Inventory}} \\
\textbf{Cost of Goods Sold}
\end{array}
$$

Another difference between the two approaches is that the perpetual system directly adjusts the Inventory account for any transaction that affects inventory (such as freight costs, returns, and discounts). The periodic system does not do this. Instead, it creates different accounts for purchases, freight costs, returns, and discounts. These various accounts are shown in Illustration 5B-2, which presents the calculation of cost of goods sold for PW Audio Supply using the periodic approach.

**Illustration 5B-2**
Cost of goods sold for a merchandiser using a periodic inventory system

**Helpful Hint** The far right column identifies the primary items that make up cost of goods sold of $316,000. The middle column explains cost of goods purchased of $320,000. The left column reports contra purchase items of $17,200.

| PW AUDIO SUPPLY<br>Cost of Goods Sold<br>For the Year Ended December 31, 2014 | | | |
|---|---:|---:|---:|
| Cost of goods sold | | | |
| **Inventory, January 1** | | | $ 36,000 |
| Purchases | | $325,000 | |
| Less: Purchase returns and | | | |
| allowances | $10,400 | | |
| Purchase discounts | 6,800 | 17,200 | |
| Net purchases | | 307,800 | |
| Add: Freight-in | | 12,200 | |
| **Cost of goods purchased** | | | 320,000 |
| Cost of goods available for sale | | | 356,000 |
| **Inventory, December 31** | | | 40,000 |
| **Cost of goods sold** | | | $316,000 |

Note that the basic elements from Illustration 5B-1 are highlighted in Illustration 5B-2. You will learn more in Chapter 6 about how to determine cost of goods sold using the periodic system.

The use of the periodic inventory system does not affect the form of presentation in the balance sheet. As under the perpetual system, a company reports inventory in the current assets section.

## Recording Merchandise Transactions

In a **periodic inventory system**, companies record revenues from the sale of merchandise when sales are made, just as in a perpetual system. Unlike the perpetual system, however, companies **do not attempt on the date of sale to record the cost of the merchandise sold**. Instead, they take a physical inventory count at the **end of the period** to determine (1) the cost of the merchandise then on hand and (2) the cost of the goods sold during the period. And, **under a periodic system, companies record purchases of merchandise in the Purchases account rather than the Inventory account**. Also, in a periodic system, purchase returns and allowances, purchase discounts, and freight costs on purchases are recorded in separate accounts.

To illustrate the recording of merchandise transactions under a periodic inventory system, we will use purchase/sale transactions between PW Audio Supply and Sauk Stereo, as illustrated for the perpetual inventory system in this chapter.

## Recording Purchases of Merchandise

On the basis of the sales invoice (Illustration 5-6, shown on page 222) and receipt of the merchandise ordered from PW Audio Supply, Sauk Stereo records the $3,800 purchase as follows.

**Helpful Hint** Be careful not to debit purchases of equipment or supplies to a Purchases account.

| May 4 | Purchases | 3,800 | |
|---|---|---|---|
| | Accounts Payable | | 3,800 |
| | (To record goods purchased on account from PW Audio Supply) | | |

Purchases is a temporary account whose normal balance is a debit.

### FREIGHT COSTS

When the purchaser directly incurs the freight costs, it debits the account Freight-In (or Transportation-In). For example, if Sauk Stereo pays Public Carrier Co. $150 for freight charges on its purchase from PW Audio Supply on May 6, the entry on Sauk Stereo's books is:

**Alternative Terminology** Freight-In is also called *Transportation-In.*

| May 6 | Freight-In (Transportation-In) | 150 | |
|---|---|---|---|
| | Cash | | 150 |
| | (To record payment of freight on goods purchased) | | |

Like Purchases, Freight-In is a temporary account whose normal balance is a debit. **Freight-In is part of cost of goods purchased.** The reason is that cost of goods purchased should include any freight charges necessary to bring the goods to the purchaser. Freight costs are not subject to a purchase discount. Purchase discounts apply only to the invoice cost of the merchandise.

### PURCHASE RETURNS AND ALLOWANCES

Sauk Stereo returns $300 of goods to PW Audio Supply and prepares the following entry to recognize the return.

| May 8 | Accounts Payable | 300 | |
| | Purchase Returns and Allowances | | 300 |
| | (To record return of goods purchased | | |
| | from PW Audio Supply) | | |

Purchase Returns and Allowances is a temporary account whose normal balance is a credit.

## PURCHASE DISCOUNTS

On May 14, Sauk Stereo pays the balance due on account to PW Audio Supply, taking the 2% cash discount allowed by PW Audio Supply for payment within 10 days. Sauk Stereo records the payment and discount as follows.

| May 14 | Accounts Payable ($3,800 − $300) | 3,500 | |
| | Purchase Discounts ($3,500 × .02) | | 70 |
| | Cash | | 3,430 |
| | (To record payment within the | | |
| | discount period) | | |

Purchase Discounts is a temporary account whose normal balance is a credit.

## Recording Sales of Merchandise

The seller, PW Audio Supply, records the sale of $3,800 of merchandise to Sauk Stereo on May 4 (sales invoice No. 731, Illustration 5-6, page 222) as follows.

| May 4 | Accounts Receivable | 3,800 | |
| | Sales Revenue | | 3,800 |
| | (To record credit sales per invoice #731 | | |
| | to Sauk Stereo) | | |

### SALES RETURNS AND ALLOWANCES

To record the returned goods received from Sauk Stereo on May 8, PW Audio Supply records the $300 sales return as follows.

| May 8 | Sales Returns and Allowances | 300 | |
| | Accounts Receivable | | 300 |
| | (To record credit granted to Sauk Stereo | | |
| | for returned goods) | | |

### SALES DISCOUNTS

On May 14, PW Audio Supply receives payment of $3,430 on account from Sauk Stereo. PW Audio Supply honors the 2% cash discount and records the payment of Sauk Stereo's account receivable in full as follows.

| May 14 | Cash | 3,430 | |
| | Sales Discounts ($3,500 × .02) | 70 | |
| | Accounts Receivable ($3,800 − $300) | | 3,500 |
| | (To record collection within 2/10, n/30 | | |
| | discount period from Sauk Stereo) | | |

### COMPARISON OF ENTRIES—PERPETUAL VS. PERIODIC

Illustration 5B-3 summarizes the periodic inventory entries shown in this appendix and compares them to the perpetual-system entries from the chapter. Entries that differ in the two systems are shown in color.

| ENTRIES ON SAUK STEREO'S BOOKS | | | | |
|---|---|---|---|---|
| **Transaction** | **Perpetual Inventory System** | | **Periodic Inventory System** | |
| May  4  Purchase of merchandise on credit. | **Inventory**      Accounts Payable | 3,800        3,800 | **Purchases**      Accounts Payable | 3,800        3,800 |
| 6  Freight costs on purchases. | **Inventory**      Cash | 150        150 | **Freight-In**      Cash | 150        150 |
| 8  Purchase returns and allowances. | Accounts Payable      **Inventory** | 300        300 | Accounts Payable      **Purchase Returns and Allowances** | 300         300 |
| 14  Payment on account with a discount. | Accounts Payable      Cash      **Inventory** | 3,500        3,430        70 | Accounts Payable      Cash      **Purchase Discounts** | 3,500        3,430        70 |

| ENTRIES ON PW AUDIO SUPPLY'S BOOKS | | | | |
|---|---|---|---|---|
| **Transaction** | **Perpetual Inventory System** | | **Periodic Inventory System** | |
| May  4  Sale of merchandise on credit. | Accounts Receivable      Sales Revenue | 3,800        3,800 | Accounts Receivable      Sales Revenue | 3,800        3,800 |
|  | **Cost of Goods Sold**      **Inventory** | 2,400        2,400 | **No entry for cost of goods sold** | |
| 8  Return of merchandise sold. | Sales Returns and Allowances      Accounts Receivable | 300        300 | Sales Returns and Allowances      Accounts Receivable | 300        300 |
|  | **Inventory**      **Cost of Goods Sold** | 140        140 | **No entry** | |
| 14  Cash received on account with a discount. | Cash      Sales Discounts      Accounts Receivable | 3,430        70        3,500 | Cash      Sales Discounts      Accounts Receivable | 3,430        70        3,500 |

**Illustration 5B-3**

Comparison of entries for perpetual and periodic inventory systems

## Journalizing and Posting Closing Entries

For a merchandising company, like a service company, all accounts that affect the determination of net income are closed to Income Summary. Data for the preparation of closing entries may be obtained from the income statement columns of the worksheet. In journalizing, all debit column amounts are credited, and all credit columns amounts are debited. To close the merchandise inventory in a periodic inventory system:

1. The beginning inventory balance is debited to Income Summary and credited to Inventory.

2. The ending inventory balance is debited to Inventory and credited to Income Summary.

The two entries for PW Audio Supply are:

(1)

| | | | |
|---|---|---|---|
| Dec. 31 | Income Summary | 36,000 | |
| |    Inventory | | 36,000 |
| |     (To close beginning inventory) | | |

(2)

| | | | |
|---|---|---|---|
| 31 | Inventory | 40,000 | |
| |    Income Summary | | 40,000 |
| |     (To record ending inventory) | | |

After posting, the Inventory and Income Summary accounts will show the following.

**Illustration 5B-4**
Posting closing entries for merchandise inventory

| Inventory | | | Income Summary | |
|---|---|---|---|---|
| 1/1　Bal.　36,000 | 12/31 Close **36,000** | | 12/31 Close **36,000** | 12/31 Close **40,000** |
| 12/31 Close **40,000** | | | | |
| 12/31 Bal.　40,000 | | | | |

Often, the closing of inventory is included with other closing entries, as shown below for PW Audio Supply.

**Helpful Hint** Except for merchandise inventory, the easiest way to prepare the first two closing entries is to identify the temporary accounts by their balances and then prepare one entry for the credits and one for the debits.

**Helpful Hint** Close inventory with other accounts in homework problems unless stated otherwise.

| | | | |
|---|---|---|---|
| Dec. 31 | **Inventory (Dec. 31)** | **40,000** | |
| | Sales Revenue | 480,000 | |
| | Purchase Returns and Allowances | 10,400 | |
| | Purchase Discounts | 6,800 | |
| | 　Income Summary | | 537,200 |
| | 　　(To record ending inventory and close | | |
| | 　　accounts with credit balances) | | |
| 31 | Income Summary | 507,200 | |
| | 　**Inventory (Jan. 1)** | | **36,000** |
| | 　Sales Returns and Allowances | | 12,000 |
| | 　Sales Discounts | | 8,000 |
| | 　Purchases | | 325,000 |
| | 　Freight-In | | 12,200 |
| | 　Salaries and Wages Expense | | 64,000 |
| | 　Freight-Out | | 7,000 |
| | 　Advertising Expense | | 16,000 |
| | 　Utilities Expense | | 17,000 |
| | 　Depreciation Expense | | 8,000 |
| | 　Insurance Expense | | 2,000 |
| | 　　(To close beginning inventory and | | |
| | 　　other income statement accounts with | | |
| | 　　debit balances) | | |
| 31 | Income Summary | 30,000 | |
| | 　Owner's Capital | | 30,000 |
| | 　　(To transfer net income to capital) | | |
| 31 | Owner's Capital | 15,000 | |
| | 　Owner's Drawings | | 15,000 |
| | 　　(To close drawings to capital) | | |

After the closing entries are posted, all temporary accounts have zero balances. In addition, Owner's Capital has a credit balance of $98,000: beginning balance + net income − drawings ($83,000 + $30,000 − $15,000).

## Using a Worksheet

As indicated in Chapter 4, a worksheet enables companies to prepare financial statements before journalizing and posting adjusting entries. The steps in preparing a worksheet for a merchandising company are the same as they are for a service company (see pages 163–165).

### TRIAL BALANCE COLUMNS
Data for the trial balance come from the ledger balances of PW Audio Supply at December 31. The amount shown for Inventory, $36,000, is the beginning inventory amount from the periodic inventory system.

## ADJUSTMENTS COLUMNS

A merchandising company generally has the same types of adjustments as a service company. As you see in the worksheet in Illustration 5B-5, adjustments (a), (b), and (c) are for insurance, depreciation, and salaries and wages. These adjustments were also required for Pioneer Advertising Agency, as illustrated in Chapters 3 and 4. The unique accounts for a merchandiser using a **periodic inventory system** are shown in capital red letters. Note, however, that the worksheet excludes nonoperating items.

After all adjustment data are entered on the worksheet, the equality of the adjustment column totals is established. The balances in all accounts are then extended to the adjusted trial balance columns.

**Illustration 5B-5**
Worksheet for merchandising company—periodic inventory system

PW Audio Supply.xls

Home    Insert    Page Layout    Formulas    Data    Review    View

P18        fx

PW AUDIO SUPPLY
Worksheet
For the Year Ended December 31, 2014

| Accounts | Trial Balance Dr. | Trial Balance Cr. | Adjustments Dr. | Adjustments Cr. | Adjusted Trial Balance Dr. | Adjusted Trial Balance Cr. | Income Statement Dr. | Income Statement Cr. | Balance Sheet Dr. | Balance Sheet Cr. |
|---|---|---|---|---|---|---|---|---|---|---|
| Cash | 9,500 | | | | 9,500 | | | | 9,500 | |
| Accounts Receivable | 16,100 | | | | 16,100 | | | | 16,100 | |
| INVENTORY | 36,000 | | | | 36,000 | | 36,000 | 40,000 | 40,000 | |
| Prepaid Insurance | 3,800 | | | (a) 2,000 | 1,800 | | | | 1,800 | |
| Equipment | 80,000 | | | | 80,000 | | | | 80,000 | |
| Accumulated Depreciation— Equipment | | 16,000 | | (b) 8,000 | | 24,000 | | | | 24,000 |
| Accounts Payable | | 20,400 | | | | 20,400 | | | | 20,400 |
| Owner's Capital | | 83,000 | | | | 83,000 | | | | 83,000 |
| Owner's Drawings | 15,000 | | | | 15,000 | | | | 15,000 | |
| SALES REVENUE | | 480,000 | | | | 480,000 | | 480,000 | | |
| SALES RETURNS AND ALLOWANCES | 12,000 | | | | 12,000 | | 12,000 | | | |
| SALES DISCOUNTS | 8,000 | | | | 8,000 | | 8,000 | | | |
| PURCHASES | 325,000 | | | | 325,000 | | 325,000 | | | |
| PURCHASE RETURNS AND ALLOWANCES | | 10,400 | | | | 10,400 | | 10,400 | | |
| PURCHASE DISCOUNTS | | 6,800 | | | | 6,800 | | 6,800 | | |
| FREIGHT-IN | 12,200 | | | | 12,200 | | 12,200 | | | |
| Freight-Out | 7,000 | | | | 7,000 | | 7,000 | | | |
| Advertising Expense | 16,000 | | | | 16,000 | | 16,000 | | | |
| Salaries and Wages Expense | 59,000 | | (c) 5,000 | | 64,000 | | 64,000 | | | |
| Utilities Expense | 17,000 | | | | 17,000 | | 17,000 | | | |
| Totals | 616,600 | 616,600 | | | | | | | | |
| Insurance Expense | | | (a) 2,000 | | 2,000 | | 2,000 | | | |
| Depreciation Expense | | | (b) 8,000 | | 8,000 | | 8,000 | | | |
| Salaries and Wages Payable | | | | (c) 5,000 | | 5,000 | | | | 5,000 |
| Totals | | | 15,000 | 15,000 | 629,600 | 629,600 | 507,200 | 537,200 | 162,400 | 132,400 |
| Net Income | | | | | | | 30,000 | | | 30,000 |
| Totals | | | | | | | 537,200 | 537,200 | 162,400 | 162,400 |

Key: (a) Insurance expired. (b) Depreciation expense. (c) Salaries and wages accrued.

## INCOME STATEMENT COLUMNS

Next, PW Audio Supply transfers the accounts and balances that affect the income statement from the adjusted trial balance columns to the income statements columns. The company shows Sales Revenue of $480,000 in the credit column. It shows the contra revenue accounts, Sales Returns and Allowances of $12,000 and Sales Discounts of $8,000 in the debit column. The difference of $460,000 is the net sales shown on the income statement (Illustration 5-9, page 233). Similarly, Purchases of $325,000 and Freight-In of $12,200 are extended to the debit column. The contra purchase accounts, Purchase Returns and Allowances of $10,400 and Purchase Discounts of $6,800, are extended to the credit columns.

The worksheet procedures for the Inventory account merit specific comment. The procedures are:

1. The beginning balance, $36,000, is extended from the adjusted trial balance column to the **income statement debit column**. From there it can be added in reporting cost of goods available for sale in the income statement.

2. The ending inventory, $40,000, is added to the worksheet by an **income statement credit and a balance sheet debit**. The credit makes it possible to deduct ending inventory from the cost of goods available for sale in the income statement to determine cost of goods sold. The debit means the ending inventory can be reported as an asset on the balance sheet.

These two procedures are specifically illustrated below:

**Illustration 5B-6**
Worksheet procedures for inventories

|  | Income Statement | | Balance Sheet | |
|---|---|---|---|---|
|  | Dr. | Cr. | Dr. | Cr. |
| Inventory | (1)  36,000 | 40,000 ← (2) → 40,000 | | |

The computation for cost of goods sold, taken from the income statement column in Illustration 5B-5, is as follows.

**Illustration 5B-7**
Computation of cost of goods sold from worksheet columns

**Helpful Hint** In a periodic system, cost of goods sold is a computation—it is not a separate account with a balance.

| Debit Column | | Credit Column | |
|---|---|---|---|
| Beginning inventory | $  36,000 | Ending inventory | $40,000 |
| Purchases | 325,000 | Purchase returns and allowances | 10,400 |
| Freight-in | 12,200 | Purchase discounts | 6,800 |
| Total debits | 373,200 | Total credits | $57,200 |
| Less: Total credits | 57,200 | | |
| **Cost of goods sold** | **$316,000** | | |

Finally, PW Audio Supply totals all the credits in the income statement column and compares these totals to the total of the debits in the income statement column. If the credits exceed the debits, the company has net income. PW Audio Supply has net income of $30,000. If the debits exceed the credits, the company would report a net loss.

## BALANCE SHEET COLUMNS

The major difference between the balance sheets of a service company and a merchandising company is inventory. PW Audio Supply shows ending inventory of $40,000 in the balance sheet debit column. The information to prepare the owner's equity statement is also found in these columns. That is, the Owner's Capital account is $83,000. Owner's Drawings are $15,000. Net income results when the total of the debit column exceeds the total of the credit column in the balance sheet columns. A net loss results when the total of the credits exceeds the total of the debit balances.

## SUMMARY OF LEARNING OBJECTIVE FOR APPENDIX 5B

**7** **Explain the recording of purchases and sales of inventory under a periodic inventory system.** In recording purchases under a periodic system, companies must make entries for (a) cash and credit purchases, (b) purchase returns and allowances, (c) purchase discounts, and (d) freight costs. In recording sales, companies must make entries for (a) cash and credit sales, (b) sales returns and allowances, and (c) sales discounts.

**Self-Test, Brief Exercises, Exercises, Problem Set A, and many more components are available for practice in *WileyPLUS.***

***Note:** All asterisked Questions, Exercises, and Problems relate to material in the appendices to the chapter.

## SELF-TEST QUESTIONS

*Answers are on page 271.*

(LO 1) **1.** Gross profit will result if:
   **(a)** operating expenses are less than net income.
   **(b)** sales revenues are greater than operating expenses.
   **(c)** sales revenues are greater than cost of goods sold.
   **(d)** operating expenses are greater than cost of goods sold.

(LO 2) **2.** Under a perpetual inventory system, when goods are purchased for resale by a company:
   **(a)** purchases on account are debited to Inventory.
   **(b)** purchases on account are debited to Purchases.
   **(c)** purchase returns are debited to Purchase Returns and Allowances.
   **(d)** freight costs are debited to Freight-Out.

(LO 3) **3.** The sales accounts that normally have a debit balance are:
   **(a)** Sales Discounts.
   **(b)** Sales Returns and Allowances.
   **(c)** Both (a) and (b).
   **(d)** Neither (a) nor (b).

(LO 3) **4.** A credit sale of $750 is made on June 13, terms 2/10, net/30. A return of $50 is granted on June 16. The amount received as payment in full on June 23 is:
   **(a)** $700.          **(c)** $685.
   **(b)** $686.          **(d)** $650.

(LO 2) **5.** Which of the following accounts will normally appear in the ledger of a merchandising company that uses a perpetual inventory system?
   **(a)** Purchases.          **(c)** Cost of Goods Sold.
   **(b)** Freight-In.          **(d)** Purchase Discounts.

(LO 3) **6.** To record the sale of goods for cash in a perpetual inventory system:
   **(a)** only one journal entry is necessary to record cost of goods sold and reduction of inventory.
   **(b)** only one journal entry is necessary to record the receipt of cash and the sales revenue.
   **(c)** two journal entries are necessary: one to record the receipt of cash and sales revenue, and one to record the cost of goods sold and reduction of inventory.

   **(d)** two journal entries are necessary: one to record the receipt of cash and reduction of inventory, and one to record the cost of goods sold and sales revenue.

(LO 4) **7.** The steps in the accounting cycle for a merchandising company are the same as those in a service company **except**:
   **(a)** an additional adjusting journal entry for inventory may be needed in a merchandising company.
   **(b)** closing journal entries are not required for a merchandising company.
   **(c)** a post-closing trial balance is not required for a merchandising company.
   **(d)** a multiple-step income statement is required for a merchandising company.

(LO 5) **8.** The multiple-step income statement for a merchandising company shows each of the following features **except**:
   **(a)** gross profit.
   **(b)** cost of goods sold.
   **(c)** a sales revenue section.
   **(d)** an investing activities section.

(LO 5) **9.** If sales revenues are $400,000, cost of goods sold is $310,000, and operating expenses are $60,000, the gross profit is:
   **(a)** $30,000.          **(c)** $340,000.
   **(b)** $90,000.          **(d)** $400,000.

(LO 5) **10.** A single-step income statement:
   **(a)** reports gross profit.
   **(b)** does not report cost of goods sold.
   **(c)** reports sales revenues and "Other revenues and gains" in the revenues section of the income statement.
   **(d)** reports operating income separately.

(LO 5) **11.** Which of the following appears on both a single-step and a multiple-step income statement?
   **(a)** Inventory.
   **(b)** Gross profit.
   **(c)** Income from operations.
   **(d)** Cost of goods sold.

LO 6) *12. In a worksheet using a perpetual inventory system, Inventory is shown in the following columns:
  (a) adjusted trial balance debit and balance sheet debit.
  (b) income statement debit and balance sheet debit.
  (c) income statement credit and balance sheet debit.
  (d) income statement credit and adjusted trial balance debit.

LO 7) *13. In determining cost of goods sold in a periodic system:
  (a) purchase discounts are deducted from net purchases.
  (b) freight-out is added to net purchases.
  (c) purchase returns and allowances are deducted from net purchases.
  (d) freight-in is added to net purchases.

*14. If beginning inventory is $60,000, cost of goods purchased is $380,000, and ending inventory is $50,000, cost of goods sold is: (LO 7)
  (a) $390,000.        (c) $330,000.
  (b) $370,000.        (d) $420,000.

*15. When goods are purchased for resale by a company using a periodic inventory system: (LO 7)
  (a) purchases on account are debited to Inventory.
  (b) purchases on account are debited to Purchases.
  (c) purchase returns are debited to Purchase Returns and Allowances.
  (d) freight costs are debited to Purchases.

Go to the book's companion website, www.wiley.com/college/weygandt, for additional Self-Test Questions.

 The Navigator

## QUESTIONS

1. (a) "The steps in the accounting cycle for a merchandising company are different from the accounting cycle for a service company." Do you agree or disagree? (b) Is the measurement of net income for a merchandising company conceptually the same as for a service company? Explain.

2. Why is the normal operating cycle for a merchandising company likely to be longer than for a service company?

3. (a) How do the components of revenues and expenses differ between merchandising and service companies? (b) Explain the income measurement process in a merchandising company.

4. How does income measurement differ between a merchandising and a service company?

5. When is cost of goods sold determined in a perpetual inventory system?

6. Distinguish between FOB shipping point and FOB destination. Identify the freight terms that will result in a debit to Inventory by the buyer and a debit to Freight-Out by the seller.

7. Explain the meaning of the credit terms 2/10, n/30.

8. Goods costing $2,000 are purchased on account on July 15 with credit terms of 2/10, n/30. On July 18, a $200 credit memo is received from the supplier for damaged goods. Give the journal entry on July 24 to record payment of the balance due within the discount period using a perpetual inventory system.

9. Ming Xu believes revenues from credit sales may be recorded before they are collected in cash. Do you agree? Explain.

10. (a) What is the primary source document for recording (1) cash sales, (2) credit sales. (b) Using XXs for amounts, give the journal entry for each of the transactions in part (a).

11. A credit sale is made on July 10 for $900, terms 2/10, n/30. On July 12, $100 of goods are returned for credit. Give the journal entry on July 19 to record the receipt of the balance due within the discount period.

12. Explain why the Inventory account will usually require adjustment at year-end.

13. Prepare the closing entries for the Sales Revenue account, assuming a balance of $200,000 and the Cost of Goods Sold account with a $145,000 balance.

14. What merchandising account(s) will appear in the post-closing trial balance?

15. Minnick Co. has sales revenue of $105,000, cost of goods sold of $70,000, and operating expenses of $20,000. What is its gross profit and its gross profit rate?

16. Paul Scott Company reports net sales of $800,000, gross profit of $370,000, and net income of $240,000. What are its operating expenses?

17. Identify the distinguishing features of an income statement for a merchandising company.

18. Identify the sections of a multiple-step income statement that relate to (a) operating activities, and (b) nonoperating activities.

19. How does the single-step form of income statement differ from the multiple-step form?

20. Determine Apple's gross profit rate for 2011 and 2010. Indicate whether it increased or decreased from 2010 to 2011.

*21. Indicate the columns of the worksheet in a perpetual system in which (a) inventory and (b) cost of goods sold will be shown.

*22. Identify the accounts that are added to or deducted from Purchases in a periodic system to determine the cost of goods purchased. For each account, indicate whether it is added or deducted.

*23. Goods costing $3,000 are purchased on account on July 15 with credit terms of 2/10, n/30. On July 18, a $200 credit was received from the supplier for damaged goods. Give the journal entry on July 24 to record payment of the balance due within the discount period, assuming a periodic inventory system.

## BRIEF EXERCISES

**BE5-1** Presented below are the components in Gates Company's income statement. Determine the missing amounts.

| | Sales Revenue | Cost of Goods Sold | Gross Profit | Operating Expenses | Net Income |
|---|---|---|---|---|---|
| (a) | $75,000 | ? | $30,000 | ? | $10,800 |
| (b) | $108,000 | $70,000 | ? | ? | $29,500 |
| (c) | ? | $83,900 | $79,600 | $39,500 | ? |

*Compute missing amounts in determining net income.*
*(LO 1)*

**BE5-2** Radomir Company buys merchandise on account from Lemke Company. The selling price of the goods is $780, and the cost of the goods is $470. Both companies use perpetual inventory systems. Journalize the transaction on the books of both companies.

*Journalize perpetual inventory entries.*
*(LO 2, 3)*

**BE5-3** Prepare the journal entries to record the following transactions on Kwang Company's books using a perpetual inventory system.

*Journalize sales transactions.*
*(LO 3)*

**(a)** On March 2, Kwang Company sold $900,000 of merchandise to Sensat Company, terms 2/10, n/30. The cost of the merchandise sold was $620,000.

**(b)** On March 6, Sensat Company returned $90,000 of the merchandise purchased on March 2. The cost of the returned merchandise was $62,000.

**(c)** On March 12, Kwang Company received the balance due from Sensat Company.

**BE5-4** From the information in BE5-3, prepare the journal entries to record these transactions on Sensat Company's books under a perpetual inventory system.

*Journalize purchase transactions.*
*(LO 2)*

**BE5-5** At year-end, the perpetual inventory records of Litwin Company showed merchandise inventory of $98,000. The company determined, however, that its actual inventory on hand was $95,700. Record the necessary adjusting entry.

*Prepare adjusting entry for inventory.*
*(LO 4)*

**BE5-6** Hudson Company has the following account balances: Sales Revenue $195,000, Sales Discounts $2,000, Cost of Goods Sold $117,000, and Inventory $40,000. Prepare the entries to record the closing of these items to Income Summary.

*Prepare closing entries for accounts.*
*(LO 4)*

**BE5-7** Arndt Company provides the following information for the month ended October 31, 2014: sales on credit $280,000, cash sales $100,000, sales discounts $5,000, and sales returns and allowances $11,000. Prepare the sales revenues section of the income statement based on this information.

*Prepare sales revenues section of income statement.*
*(LO 5)*

**BE5-8** ⸺⸺ Explain where each of the following items would appear on (1) a multiple-step income statement, and on (2) a single-step income statement: (a) gain on sale of equipment, (b) interest expense, (c) casualty loss from vandalism, and (d) cost of goods sold.

*Contrast presentation in multiple-step and single-step income statements.*
*(LO 5)*

**BE5-9** Assume Kader Company has the following reported amounts: Sales revenue $510,000, Sales returns and allowances $15,000, Cost of goods sold $330,000, and Operating expenses $110,000. Compute the following: (a) net sales, (b) gross profit, (c) income from operations, and (d) gross profit rate. (Round to one decimal place.)

*Compute net sales, gross profit, income from operations, and gross profit rate.*
*(LO 5)*

**\*BE5-10** Presented below is the format of the worksheet using the perpetual inventory system presented in Appendix 5A.

*Identify worksheet columns for selected accounts.*
*(LO 6)*

| Trial Balance | | Adjustments | | Adjusted Trial Balance | | Income Statement | | Balance Sheet | |
|---|---|---|---|---|---|---|---|---|---|
| Dr. | Cr. | Dr. | Cr. | Dr. | Cr. | Dr. | Cr. | Dr. | Cr. |

Indicate where the following items will appear on the worksheet: (a) Cash, (b) Inventory, (c) Sales revenue, and (d) Cost of goods sold.

*Example:*
Cash: Trial balance debit column; Adjusted trial balance debit column; and Balance sheet debit column.

*Compute net purchases and cost of goods purchased.*

(LO 7)

**\*BE5-11** Assume that Gallant Company uses a periodic inventory system and has these account balances: Purchases $450,000; Purchase Returns and Allowances $13,000; Purchase Discounts $8,000; and Freight-In $16,000. Determine net purchases and cost of goods purchased.

*Compute cost of goods sold and gross profit.*

(LO 7)

**\*BE5-12** Assume the same information as in BE5-11 and also that Gallant Company has beginning inventory of $60,000, ending inventory of $90,000, and net sales of $730,000. Determine the amounts to be reported for cost of goods sold and gross profit.

*Journalize purchase transactions.*

(LO 7)

**\*BE5-13** Prepare the journal entries to record these transactions on Nimmer Company's books using a periodic inventory system.

**(a)** On March 2, Nimmer Company purchased $900,000 of merchandise from Sen Company, terms 2/10, n/30.

**(b)** On March 6, Nimmer Company returned $130,000 of the merchandise purchased on March 2.

**(c)** On March 12, Nimmer Company paid the balance due to Sen Company.

*Prepare closing entries for merchandise accounts.*

(LO 7)

**\*BE5-14** A. Hall Company has the following merchandise account balances: Sales Revenue $180,000, Sales Discounts $2,000, Purchases $120,000, and Purchases Returns and Allowances $30,000. In addition, it has a beginning inventory of $40,000 and an ending inventory of $30,000. Prepare the entries to record the closing of these items to Income Summary using the periodic inventory system.

*Identify worksheet columns for selected accounts*

(LO 7)

**\*BE5-15** Presented below is the format of the worksheet using the periodic inventory system presented in Appendix 5B.

| Trial Balance | | Adjustments | | Adjusted Trial Balance | | Income Statement | | Balance Sheet | |
|---|---|---|---|---|---|---|---|---|---|
| Dr. | Cr. | Dr. | Cr. | Dr. | Cr. | Dr. | Cr. | Dr. | Cr. |

Indicate where the following items will appear on the worksheet: (a) cash, (b) beginning inventory, (c) accounts payable, (d) ending inventory.

*Example*

Cash: Trial balance debit column; Adjustment trial balance debit column; and Balance sheet debit column.

## > DO IT! Review

*Record transactions of purchasing company.*

(LO 2)

**DO IT! 5-1** On October 5, Loomis Company buys merchandise on account from Brooke Company. The selling price of the goods is $5,000, and the cost to Brooke Company is $3,100. On October 8, Loomis returns defective goods with a selling price of $650 and a fair value of $100. Record the transactions on the books of Loomis Company.

*Record transactions of selling company.*

(LO 3)

**DO IT! 5-2** Assume information similar to that in **DO IT!** 5-1: On October 5, Loomis Company buys merchandise on account from Brooke Company. The selling price of the goods is $5,000, and the cost to Brooke Company is $3,100. On October 8, Loomis returns defective goods with a selling price of $650 and a fair value of $100. Record the transactions on the books of Brooke Company.

*Prepare closing entries for a merchandising company.*

(LO 4)

**DO IT! 5-3** The trial balance of Optique Boutique at December 31 shows Inventory $21,000, Sales Revenue $156,000, Sales Returns and Allowances $4,000, Sales Discounts $3,000, Cost of Goods Sold $92,400, Interest Revenue $5,000, Freight-Out $1,500, Utilities Expense $7,400, and Salaries and Wages Expense $19,500. Prepare the closing entries for Optique.

*Classify financial statement accounts.*

(LO 5)

**DO IT! 5-4** Estes Company is preparing its multiple-step income statement, owner's equity statement, and classified balance sheet. Using the column heads **Account, Financial Statement, and Classification**, indicate in which financial statement and under what classification each of the following would be reported.

| Account | Financial Statement | Classification |
|---|---|---|
| Accounts Payable | | |
| Accounts Receivable | | |
| Accumulated Depreciation—Buildings | | |
| Cash | | |
| Casualty Loss from Vandalism | | |
| Cost of Goods Sold | | |
| Depreciation Expense | | |
| Equipment | | |
| Freight-Out | | |
| Insurance Expense | | |
| Interest Payable | | |
| Inventory | | |
| Land | | |
| Notes Payable (due in 5 years) | | |
| Owner's Capital (beginning balance) | | |
| Owner's Drawings | | |
| Property Taxes Payable | | |
| Salaries and Wages Expense | | |
| Salaries and Wages Payable | | |
| Sales Returns and Allowances | | |
| Sales Revenue | | |
| Unearned Rent Revenue | | |
| Utilities Expense | | |

# EXERCISES

**E5-1** Mr. Etemadi has prepared the following list of statements about service companies and merchandisers.

*Answer general questions about merchandisers.*

(LO 1)

1. Measuring net income for a merchandiser is conceptually the same as for a service company.
2. For a merchandiser, sales less operating expenses is called gross profit.
3. For a merchandiser, the primary source of revenues is the sale of inventory.
4. Sales salaries and wages is an example of an operating expense.
5. The operating cycle of a merchandiser is the same as that of a service company.
6. In a perpetual inventory system, no detailed inventory records of goods on hand are maintained.
7. In a periodic inventory system, the cost of goods sold is determined only at the end of the accounting period.
8. A periodic inventory system provides better control over inventories than a perpetual system.

**Instructions**

Identify each statement as true or false. If false, indicate how to correct the statement.

**E5-2** Information related to Harwick Co. is presented below.

*Journalize purchase transactions.*

(LO 2)

1. On April 5, purchased merchandise from Botham Company for $23,000, terms 2/10, net/30, FOB shipping point.
2. On April 6, paid freight costs of $900 on merchandise purchased from Botham.
3. On April 7, purchased equipment on account for $26,000.
4. On April 8, returned damaged merchandise to Botham Company and was granted a $3,000 credit for returned merchandise.
5. On April 15, paid the amount due to Botham Company in full.

**Instructions**

(a) Prepare the journal entries to record these transactions on the books of Harwick Co. under a perpetual inventory system.
(b) Assume that Harwick Co. paid the balance due to Botham Company on May 4 instead of April 15. Prepare the journal entry to record this payment.

*Journalize perpetual inventory entries.*
(LO 2, 3)

**E5-3**  On September 1, Boylan Office Supply had an inventory of 30 calculators at a cost of $18 each. The company uses a perpetual inventory system. During September, the following transactions occurred.

Sept.  6   Purchased with cash 80 calculators at $20 each from Guthrie.
        9   Paid freight of $80 on calculators purchased from Guthrie Co.
       10   Returned 3 calculators to Guthrie Co. for $63 credit (including freight) because they did not meet specifications.
       12   Sold 26 calculators costing $21 (including freight) for $31 each to Lee Book Store, terms n/30.
       14   Granted credit of $31 to Lee Book Store for the return of one calculator that was not ordered.
       20   Sold 30 calculators costing $21 for $32 each to Orr's Card Shop, terms n/30.

**Instructions**
Journalize the September transactions.

*Prepare purchase and sale entries.*
(LO 2, 3)

**E5-4**  On June 10, Tuzun Company purchased $8,000 of merchandise from Epps Company, FOB shipping point, terms 2/10, n/30. Tuzun pays the freight costs of $400 on June 11. Damaged goods totaling $300 are returned to Epps for credit on June 12. The fair value of these goods is $70. On June 19, Tuzun pays Epps Company in full, less the purchase discount. Both companies use a perpetual inventory system.

**Instructions**
(a) Prepare separate entries for each transaction on the books of Tuzun Company.
(b) Prepare separate entries for each transaction for Epps Company. The merchandise purchased by Tuzun on June 10 had cost Epps $4,800.

*Journalize sales transactions.*
(LO 3)

**E5-5**  Presented below are transactions related to Bogner Company.

1. On December 3, Bogner Company sold $570,000 of merchandise to Maris Co., terms 2/10, n/30, FOB shipping point. The cost of the merchandise sold was $350,000.
2. On December 8, Maris Co. was granted an allowance of $20,000 for merchandise purchased on December 3.
3. On December 13, Bogner Company received the balance due from Maris Co.

**Instructions**
(a) Prepare the journal entries to record these transactions on the books of Bogner Company using a perpetual inventory system.
(b) Assume that Bogner Company received the balance due from Maris Co. on January 2 of the following year instead of December 13. Prepare the journal entry to record the receipt of payment on January 2.

*Prepare sales revenues section and closing entries.*
(LO 4, 5)

**E5-6**  The adjusted trial balance of Tsai Company shows the following data pertaining to sales at the end of its fiscal year October 31, 2014: Sales Revenue $820,000, Freight-Out $16,000, Sales Returns and Allowances $25,000, and Sales Discounts $13,000.

**Instructions**
(a) Prepare the sales revenues section of the income statement.
(b) Prepare separate closing entries for (1) sales revenue, and (2) the contra accounts to sales revenue.

*Prepare adjusting and closing entries.*
(LO 4)

**E5-7**  Juan Morales Company had the following account balances at year-end: Cost of Goods Sold $60,000; Inventory $15,000; Operating Expenses $29,000; Sales Revenue $115,000; Sales Discounts $1,200; and Sales Returns and Allowances $1,700. A physical count of inventory determines that merchandise inventory on hand is $13,900.

**Instructions**
(a) Prepare the adjusting entry necessary as a result of the physical count.
(b) Prepare closing entries.

*Prepare adjusting and closing entries.*
(LO 4)

**E5-8**  Presented below is information related to Garland Co. for the month of January 2014.

| | | | |
|---|---|---|---|
| Ending inventory per perpetual records | $ 21,600 | Insurance expense | $ 12,000 |
| | | Rent expense | 20,000 |
| Ending inventory actually on hand | 21,000 | Salaries and wages expense | 55,000 |
| | | Sales discounts | 10,000 |
| Cost of goods sold | 218,000 | Sales returns and allowances | 13,000 |
| Freight-out | 7,000 | Sales revenue | 380,000 |

**Instructions**
**(a)** Prepare the necessary adjusting entry for inventory.
**(b)** Prepare the necessary closing entries.

**E5-9** Presented below is information for Furlow Company for the month of March 2014.

*Prepare multiple-step income statement.*

*(LO 5)*

| | | | |
|---|---|---|---|
| Cost of goods sold | $212,000 | Rent expense | $ 32,000 |
| Freight-out | 7,000 | Sales discounts | 8,000 |
| Insurance expense | 6,000 | Sales returns and allowances | 13,000 |
| Salaries and wages expense | 58,000 | Sales revenue | 380,000 |

**Instructions**
**(a)** Prepare a multiple-step income statement.
**(b)** Compute the gross profit rate.

**E5-10** In its income statement for the year ended December 31, 2014, Lemere Company reported the following condensed data.

*Prepare multiple-step and single-step income statements.*

*(LO 5)*

| | | | |
|---|---|---|---|
| Operating expenses | $ 725,000 | Interest revenue | $ 28,000 |
| Cost of goods sold | 1,289,000 | Loss on disposal of plant assets | 17,000 |
| Interest expense | 70,000 | Net sales | 2,200,000 |

**Instructions**
**(a)** Prepare a multiple-step income statement.
**(b)** Prepare a single-step income statement.

**E5-11** An inexperienced accountant for Huang Company made the following errors in recording merchandising transactions.

*Prepare correcting entries for sales and purchases.*

*(LO 2, 3)*

1. A $195 refund to a customer for faulty merchandise was debited to Sales Revenue $195 and credited to Cash $195.
2. A $180 credit purchase of supplies was debited to Inventory $180 and credited to Cash $180.
3. A $215 sales discount was debited to Sales Revenue.
4. A cash payment of $20 for freight on merchandise purchases was debited to Freight-Out $200 and credited to Cash $200.

**Instructions**
Prepare separate correcting entries for each error, assuming that the incorrect entry is not reversed. (Omit explanations.)

**E5-12** In 2014, Matt Cruz Company had net sales of $900,000 and cost of goods sold of $522,000. Operating expenses were $225,000, and interest expense was $11,000. Cruz prepares a multiple-step income statement.

*Compute various income measures.*

*(LO 5)*

**Instructions**
**(a)** Compute Cruz's gross profit.
**(b)** Compute the gross profit rate. Why is this rate computed by financial statement users?
**(c)** What is Cruz's income from operations and net income?
**(d)** If Cruz prepared a single-step income statement, what amount would it report for net income?
**(e)** In what section of its classified balance sheet should Cruz report merchandise inventory?

**E5-13** Presented below is financial information for two different companies.

*Compute missing amounts and compute gross profit rate.*

*(LO 5)*

| | May Company | Reed Company |
|---|---|---|
| Sales revenue | $90,000 | (d) |
| Sales returns | (a) | $ 5,000 |
| Net sales | 87,000 | 102,000 |
| Cost of goods sold | 56,000 | (e) |
| Gross profit | (b) | 41,500 |
| Operating expenses | 15,000 | (f) |
| Net income | (c) | 15,000 |

**Instructions**
**(a)** Determine the missing amounts.
**(b)** Determine the gross profit rates. (Round to one decimal place.)

*Compute missing amounts.*
(LO 5)

**E5-14** Financial information is presented below for three different companies.

|  | Allen Cosmetics | Bast Grocery | Corr Wholesalers |
|---|---|---|---|
| Sales revenue | $90,000 | $ (e) | $122,000 |
| Sales returns and allowances | (a) | 5,000 | 12,000 |
| Net sales | 86,000 | 95,000 | (i) |
| Cost of goods sold | 56,000 | (f) | (j) |
| Gross profit | (b) | 38,000 | 24,000 |
| Operating expenses | 15,000 | (g) | 18,000 |
| Income from operations | (c) | (h) | (k) |
| Other expenses and losses | 4,000 | 7,000 | (l) |
| Net income | (d) | 11,000 | 5,000 |

*Instructions*
Determine the missing amounts.

*Complete worksheet using a perpetual inventory system.*
(LO 6)

**\*E5-15** Presented below are selected accounts for Salazar Company as reported in the worksheet using a perpetual inventory system at the end of May 2014.

| Accounts | Adjusted Trial Balance | | Income Statement | | Balance Sheet | |
|---|---|---|---|---|---|---|
|  | Dr. | Cr. | Dr. | Cr. | Dr. | Cr. |
| Cash | 11,000 | | | | | |
| Inventory | 76,000 | | | | | |
| Sales Revenue | | 480,000 | | | | |
| Sales Returns and Allowances | 10,000 | | | | | |
| Sales Discounts | 9,000 | | | | | |
| Cost of Goods Sold | 300,000 | | | | | |

*Instructions*
Complete the worksheet by extending amounts reported in the adjusted trial balance to the appropriate columns in the worksheet. Do not total individual columns.

*Prepare a worksheet using a perpetual inventory system.*
(LO 6)

**\*E5-16** The trial balance columns of the worksheet using a perpetual inventory system for Marquez Company at June 30, 2014, are as follows.

**MARQUEZ COMPANY**
Worksheet
For the Month Ended June 30, 2014

| Account Titles | Trial Balance | |
|---|---|---|
|  | Debit | Credit |
| Cash | 1,920 | |
| Accounts Receivable | 2,440 | |
| Inventory | 11,640 | |
| Accounts Payable | | 1,120 |
| Owner's Capital | | 3,500 |
| Sales Revenue | | 42,500 |
| Cost of Goods Sold | 20,560 | |
| Operating Expenses | 10,560 | |
|  | 47,120 | 47,120 |

Other data:
Operating expenses incurred on account, but not yet recorded, total $1,500.

*Instructions*
Enter the trial balance on a worksheet and complete the worksheet.

*E5-17 The trial balance of D. Savage Company at the end of its fiscal year, August 31, 2014, includes these accounts: Inventory $17,200; Purchases $149,000; Sales Revenue $190,000; Freight-In $5,000; Sales Returns and Allowances $3,000; Freight-Out $1,000; and Purchase Returns and Allowances $2,000. The ending merchandise inventory is $23,000.

*Prepare cost of goods sold section.*

*(LO 7)*

**Instructions**
Prepare a cost of goods sold section for the year ending August 31 (periodic inventory).

*E5-18 On January 1, 2014, Christel Madan Corporation had inventory of $50,000. At December 31, 2014, Christel Madan had the following account balances.

*Compute various income statement items.*

*(LO 7)*

| | |
|---|---:|
| Freight-in | $   4,000 |
| Purchases | 509,000 |
| Purchase discounts | 6,000 |
| Purchase returns and allowances | 2,000 |
| Sales revenue | 840,000 |
| Sales discounts | 5,000 |
| Sales returns and allowances | 10,000 |

At December 31, 2014, Christel Madan determines that its ending inventory is $60,000.

**Instructions**
(a) Compute Christel Madan's 2014 gross profit.
(b) Compute Christel Madan's 2014 operating expenses if net income is $130,000 and there are no nonoperating activities.

*E5-19 Below is a series of cost of goods sold sections for companies B, F, L, and R.

*Prepare cost of goods sold section.*

*(LO 7)*

| | B | F | L | R |
|---|---:|---:|---:|---:|
| Beginning inventory | $   150 | $   70 | $1,000 | $   (j) |
| Purchases | 1,620 | 1,060 | (g) | 43,590 |
| Purchase returns and allowances | 40 | (d) | 290 | (k) |
| Net purchases | (a) | 1,030 | 6,210 | 41,090 |
| Freight-in | 110 | (e) | (h) | 2,240 |
| Cost of goods purchased | (b) | 1,280 | 7,940 | (l) |
| Cost of goods available for sale | 1,840 | 1,350 | (i) | 49,530 |
| Ending inventory | 310 | (f) | 1,450 | 6,230 |
| Cost of goods sold | (c) | 1,230 | 7,490 | 43,300 |

**Instruction**
Fill in the lettered blanks to complete the cost of goods sold sections.

*E5-20 This information relates to Rana Co.

*Journalize purchase transactions.*

*(LO 7)*

1. On April 5, purchased merchandise from Craig Company for $25,000, terms 2/10, net/30, FOB shipping point.
2. On April 6, paid freight costs of $900 on merchandise purchased from Craig Company.
3. On April 7, purchased equipment on account for $30,000.
4. On April 8, returned some of April 5 merchandise, which cost $2,800, to Craig Company.
5. On April 15, paid the amount due to Craig Company in full.

**Instructions**
(a) Prepare the journal entries to record these transactions on the books of Rana Co. using a periodic inventory system.
(b) Assume that Rana Co. paid the balance due to Craig Company on May 4 instead of April 15. Prepare the journal entry to record this payment.

*E5-21 Presented below is information related to Lor Co.

*Journalize purchase transactions.*

*(LO 7)*

1. On April 5, purchased merchandise from Garcia Company for $19,000, terms 2/10, net/30, FOB shipping point.
2. On April 6, paid freight costs of $800 on merchandise purchased from Garcia.
3. On April 7, purchased equipment on account from Holifield Mfg. Co. for $23,000.
4. On April 8, returned merchandise, which cost $4,000, to Garcia Company.
5. On April 15, paid the amount due to Garcia Company in full.

*Instructions*
**(a)** Prepare the journal entries to record these transactions on the books of Lor Co. using a periodic inventory system.
**(b)** Assume that Lor Co. paid the balance due to Garcia Company on May 4 instead of April 15. Prepare the journal entry to record this payment.

*Complete worksheet.*
(LO 7)

**\*E5-22** Presented below are selected accounts for B. Midler Company as reported in the worksheet at the end of May 2014. Ending inventory is $75,000.

| Accounts | Adjusted Trial Balance | | Income Statement | | Balance Sheet | |
|---|---|---|---|---|---|---|
| | Dr. | Cr. | Dr. | Cr. | Dr. | Cr. |
| Cash | 9,000 | | | | | |
| Inventory | 80,000 | | | | | |
| Purchases | 240,000 | | | | | |
| Purchase Returns and Allowances | | 30,000 | | | | |
| Sales Revenue | | 450,000 | | | | |
| Sales Returns and Allowances | 10,000 | | | | | |
| Sales Discounts | 5,000 | | | | | |
| Rent Expense | 42,000 | | | | | |

*Instructions*
Complete the worksheet by extending amounts reported in the adjustment trial balance to the appropriate columns in the worksheet. The company uses the periodic inventory system.

## EXERCISES: SET B AND CHALLENGE EXERCISES

Visit the book's companion website, at **www.wiley.com/college/weygandt**, and choose the Student Companion site to access Exercise Set B and Challenge Exercises.

## PROBLEMS: SET A

*Journalize purchase and sales transactions under a perpetual inventory system.*
(LO 2, 3)

**P5-1A** Powell's Book Warehouse distributes hardcover books to retail stores and extends credit terms of 2/10, n/30 to all of its customers. At the end of May, Powell's inventory consisted of books purchased for $1,800. During June, the following merchandising transactions occurred.

June  1   Purchased books on account for $1,600 from Kline Publishers, FOB destination, terms 2/10, n/30. The appropriate party also made a cash payment of $50 for the freight on this date.
      3   Sold books on account to Reading Rainbow for $2,500. The cost of the books sold was $1,440.
      6   Received $100 credit for books returned to Kline Publishers.
      9   Paid Kline Publishers in full, less discount.
      15  Received payment in full from Reading Rainbow.
      17  Sold books on account to Blanco Books for $1,800. The cost of the books sold was $1,080.

20    Purchased books on account for $1,500 from Dietz Publishers, FOB destination, terms 2/15, n/30. The appropriate party also made a cash payment of $50 for the freight on this date.

24    Received payment in full from Blanco Books.

26    Paid Dietz Publishers in full, less discount.

28    Sold books on account to Reddy Bookstore for $1,400. The cost of the books sold was $850.

30    Granted Reddy Bookstore $120 credit for books returned costing $72.

Powell's Book Warehouse's chart of accounts includes the following: No. 101 Cash, No. 112 Accounts Receivable, No. 120 Inventory, No. 201 Accounts Payable, No. 401 Sales Revenue, No. 412 Sales Returns and Allowances, No. 414 Sales Discounts, and No. 505 Cost of Goods Sold.

**Instructions**
Journalize the transactions for the month of June for Powell's Book Warehouse using a perpetual inventory system.

**P5-2A** Latona Hardware Store completed the following merchandising transactions in the month of May. At the beginning of May, the ledger of Latona showed Cash of $5,000 and Owner's Capital of $5,000.

*Journalize, post, and prepare a partial income statement.*
*(LO 2, 3, 5)*

May   1    Purchased merchandise on account from Gray's Wholesale Supply $4,200, terms 2/10, n/30.

2    Sold merchandise on account $2,100, terms 1/10, n/30. The cost of the merchandise sold was $1,300.

5    Received credit from Gray's Wholesale Supply for merchandise returned $300.

9    Received collections in full, less discounts, from customers billed on sales of $2,100 on May 2.

10   Paid Gray's Wholesale Supply in full, less discount.

11   Purchased supplies for cash $400.

12   Purchased merchandise for cash $1,400.

15   Received refund for poor quality merchandise from supplier on cash purchase $150.

17   Purchased merchandise from Amland Distributors $1,300, FOB shipping point, terms 2/10, n/30.

19   Paid freight on May 17 purchase $130.

24   Sold merchandise for cash $3,200. The merchandise sold had a cost of $2,000.

25   Purchased merchandise from Horvath, Inc. $620, FOB destination, terms 2/10, n/30.

27   Paid Amland Distributors in full, less discount.

29   Made refunds to cash customers for defective merchandise $70. The returned merchandise had a fair value of $30.

31   Sold merchandise on account $1,000 terms n/30. The cost of the merchandise sold was $560.

Latona Hardware's chart of accounts includes the following: No. 101 Cash, No. 112 Accounts Receivable, No. 120 Inventory, No. 126 Supplies, No. 201 Accounts Payable, No. 301 Owner's Capital, No. 401 Sales Revenue, No. 412 Sales Returns and Allowances, No. 414 Sales Discounts, and No. 505 Cost of Goods Sold.

**Instructions**
**(a)** Journalize the transactions using a perpetual inventory system.
**(b)** Enter the beginning cash and capital balances and post the transactions. (Use J1 for the journal reference.)
**(c)** Prepare an income statement through gross profit for the month of May 2014.

*(c) Gross profit $2,379*

**P5-3A** The Deluxe Store is located in midtown Madison. During the past several years, net income has been declining because of suburban shopping centers. At the end of the company's fiscal year on November 30, 2014, the following accounts appeared in two of its trial balances.

*Prepare financial statements and adjusting and closing entries.*
*(LO 4, 5)*

| | Unadjusted | Adjusted | | Unadjusted | Adjusted |
|---|---|---|---|---|---|
| Accounts Payable | $ 25,200 | $ 25,200 | Notes Payable | $ 37,000 | $ 37,000 |
| Accounts Receivable | 30,500 | 30,500 | Owner's Capital | 101,700 | 101,700 |
| Accumulated Depr.—Equip. | 34,000 | 45,000 | Owner's Drawings | 10,000 | 10,000 |
| Cash | 26,000 | 26,000 | Prepaid Insurance | 10,500 | 3,500 |
| Cost of Goods Sold | 507,000 | 507,000 | Property Tax Expense | | 2,500 |
| Freight-Out | 6,500 | 6,500 | Property Taxes Payable | | 2,500 |
| Equipment | 146,000 | 146,000 | Rent Expense | 15,000 | 15,000 |
| Depreciation Expense | | 11,000 | Salaries and Wages Expense | 96,000 | 96,000 |
| Insurance Expense | | 7,000 | Sales Revenue | 700,000 | 700,000 |
| Interest Expense | 6,400 | 6,400 | Sales Commissions Expense | 6,500 | 11,000 |
| Interest Revenue | 8,000 | 8,000 | Sales Commissions Payable | | 4,500 |
| Inventory | 29,000 | 29,000 | Sales Returns and Allowances | 8,000 | 8,000 |
| | | | Utilities Expense | 8,500 | 8,500 |

**Instructions**

(a) Net income $29,100
   Owner's capital $120,800
   Total assets $190,000

**(a)** Prepare a multiple-step income statement, an owner's equity statement, and a classified balance sheet. Notes payable are due in 2017.

**(b)** Journalize the adjusting entries that were made.

**(c)** Journalize the closing entries that are necessary.

*Journalize, post, and prepare a trial balance.*

(LO 2, 3, 4)

**P5-4A** Adam Nichols, a former disc golf star, operates Adam's Discorama. At the beginning of the current season on April 1, the ledger of Adam's Discorama showed Cash $1,800, Inventory $2,500, and Owner's Capital $4,300. The following transactions were completed during April.

Apr.   5   Purchased golf discs, bags, and other inventory on account from Rayford Co. $1,200, FOB shipping point, terms 2/10, n/60.
7   Paid freight on the Rayford purchase $50.
9   Received credit from Rayford Co. for merchandise returned $100.
10   Sold merchandise on account for $900, terms n/30. The merchandise sold had a cost of $540.
12   Purchased disc golf shirts and other accessories on account from Galaxy Sportswear $670, terms 1/10, n/30.
14   Paid Rayford Co. in full, less discount.
17   Received credit from Galaxy Sportswear for merchandise returned $70.
20   Made sales on account for $610, terms n/30. The cost of the merchandise sold was $370.
21   Paid Galaxy Sportswear in full, less discount.
27   Granted an allowance to customers for clothing that was flawed $20.
30   Received payments on account from customers $900.

The chart of accounts for the store includes the following: No. 101 Cash, No. 112 Accounts Receivable, No. 120 Inventory, No. 201 Accounts Payable, No. 301 Owner's Capital, No. 401 Sales Revenue, No. 412 Sales Returns and Allowances, and No. 505 Cost of Goods Sold.

**Instructions**

**(a)** Journalize the April transactions using a perpetual inventory system.

**(b)** Enter the beginning balances in the ledger accounts and post the April transactions. (Use J1 for the journal reference.)

(c) Total debits $5,810

**(c)** Prepare a trial balance on April 30, 2014.

*Complete accounting cycle beginning with a worksheet.*

(LO 4, 5, 6)

**\*P5-5A** The trial balance of Valdez Fashion Center contained the following accounts at November 30, the end of the company's fiscal year.

**VALDEZ FASHION CENTER**
Trial Balance
November 30, 2014

|  | Debit | Credit |
|---|---:|---:|
| Cash | $ 8,700 | |
| Accounts Receivable | 30,700 | |
| Inventory | 44,700 | |
| Supplies | 6,200 | |
| Equipment | 133,000 | |
| Accumulated Depreciation—Equipment | | $ 28,000 |
| Notes Payable | | 51,000 |
| Accounts Payable | | 48,500 |
| Owner's Capital | | 90,000 |
| Owner's Drawings | 12,000 | |
| Sales Revenue | | 755,200 |
| Sales Returns and Allowances | 8,800 | |
| Cost of Goods Sold | 497,400 | |
| Salaries and Wages Expense | 140,000 | |
| Advertising Expense | 24,400 | |
| Utilities Expense | 14,000 | |
| Maintenance and Repairs Expense | 12,100 | |
| Freight-Out | 16,700 | |
| Rent Expense | 24,000 | |
| Totals | $972,700 | $972,700 |

Adjustment data:

1. Supplies on hand totaled $2,000.
2. Depreciation is $11,500 on the equipment.
3. Interest of $4,000 is accrued on notes payable at November 30.
4. Inventory actually on hand is $44,400.

*Instructions*
(a) Enter the trial balance on a worksheet, and complete the worksheet.
(b) Prepare a multiple-step income statement and an owner's equity statement for the year, and a classified balance sheet as of November 30, 2014. Notes payable of $20,000 are due in January 2015.
(c) Journalize the adjusting entries.
(d) Journalize the closing entries.
(e) Prepare a post-closing trial balance.

*(a) Adj. trial balance*
*$988,200*
*Net loss $2,200*
*(b) Gross profit $248,700*
*Total assets $179,300*

**\*P5-6A** At the end of Dayton Department Store's fiscal year on November 30, 2014, these accounts appeared in its adjusted trial balance.

| | |
|---|---:|
| Freight-In | $ 7,500 |
| Inventory | 40,000 |
| Purchases | 585,000 |
| Purchase Discounts | 6,300 |
| Purchase Returns and Allowances | 2,700 |
| Sales Revenue | 1,000,000 |
| Sales Returns and Allowances | 20,000 |

*Determine cost of goods sold and gross profit under periodic approach.*

*(LO 5, 7)*

Additional facts:

1. Merchandise inventory on November 30, 2014, is $52,600.
2. Dayton Department Store uses a periodic system.

*Instructions*
Prepare an income statement through gross profit for the year ended November 30, 2014.

*Gross profit $409,100*

*Calculate missing amounts
and assess profitability.*

(LO 5, 7)

**\*P5-7A** Alana Inc. operates a retail operation that purchases and sells home entertainment products. The company purchases all merchandise inventory on credit and uses a periodic inventory system. The Accounts Payable account is used for recording inventory purchases only; all other current liabilities are accrued in separate accounts. You are provided with the following selected information for the fiscal years 2011 through 2014, inclusive.

|  | 2011 | 2012 | 2013 | 2014 |
|---|---|---|---|---|
| **Income Statement Data** | | | | |
| Sales revenue | | $55,000 | $    (e) | $47,000 |
| Cost of goods sold | | (a) | 13,800 | 14,300 |
| Gross profit | | 38,300 | 35,200 | (i) |
| Operating expenses | | 34,900 | (f) | 28,600 |
| Net income | | $    (b) | $ 2,500 | $    (j) |
| **Balance Sheet Data** | | | | |
| Inventory | $7,200 | $    (c) | $ 8,100 | $    (k) |
| Accounts payable | 3,200 | 3,600 | 2,500 | (l) |
| **Additional Information** | | | | |
| Purchases of merchandise inventory on account | | $14,200 | $    (g) | $13,200 |
| Cash payments to suppliers | | (d) | (h) | 13,600 |

(c) $4,700
(g) $17,200
(i) $32,700

**Instructions**
(a) Calculate the missing amounts.
(b) Sales declined over the 3-year fiscal period, 2012–2014. Does that mean that profitability necessarily also declined? Explain, computing the gross profit rate and the profit margin for each fiscal year to help support your answer. (Round to one decimal place.)

*Journalize, post, and prepare
trial balance and partial
income statement using
periodic approach.*

(LO 7)

**\*P5-8A** At the beginning of the current season on April 1, the ledger of Kokott Pro Shop showed Cash $3,000; Inventory $4,000; and Owner's Capital $7,000. These transactions occurred during April 2014.

| Apr. | 5 | Purchased golf bags, clubs, and balls on account from Hogan Co. $1,200, FOB shipping point, terms 2/10, n/60. |
|---|---|---|
| | 7 | Paid freight on Hogan Co. purchases $50. |
| | 9 | Received credit from Hogan Co. for merchandise returned $100. |
| | 10 | Sold merchandise on account to customers $600, terms n/30. |
| | 12 | Purchased golf shoes, sweaters, and other accessories on account from Duffer Sportswear $450, terms 1/10, n/30. |
| | 14 | Paid Hogan Co. in full. |
| | 17 | Received credit from Duffer Sportswear for merchandise returned $50. |
| | 20 | Made sales on account to customers $600, terms n/30. |
| | 21 | Paid Duffer Sportswear in full. |
| | 27 | Granted credit to customers for clothing that had flaws $35. |
| | 30 | Received payments on account from customers $600. |

The chart of accounts for the pro shop includes Cash, Accounts Receivable, Inventory, Accounts Payable, Owner's Capital, Sales Revenue, Sales Returns and Allowances, Purchases, Purchase Returns and Allowances, Purchase Discounts, and Freight-In.

**Instructions**
(a) Journalize the April transactions using a periodic inventory system.
(b) Using T-accounts, enter the beginning balances in the ledger accounts and post the April transactions.

(c) Tot. trial balance $8,376
Gross profit $465

(c) Prepare a trial balance on April 30, 2014.
(d) Prepare an income statement through gross profit, assuming merchandise inventory on hand at April 30 is $4,824.

## PROBLEMS: SET B

**P5-1B** Urdan Co. distributes suitcases to retail stores and extends credit terms of 1/10, n/30 to all of its customers. At the end of June, Urdan's inventory consisted of suitcases costing $1,200. During the month of July, the following merchandising transactions occurred.

*Journalize purchase and sales transactions under a perpetual inventory system.*

(LO 2, 3)

| July | 1 | Purchased suitcases on account for $1,800 from Hostad Manufacturers, FOB destination, terms 2/10, n/30. The appropriate party also made a cash payment of $100 for freight on this date. |
|---|---|---|
| | 3 | Sold suitcases on account to Kaye Satchels for $2,000. The cost of suitcases sold is $1,200. |
| | 9 | Paid Hostad Manufacturers in full. |
| | 12 | Received payment in full from Kaye Satchels. |
| | 17 | Sold suitcases on account to The Going Concern for $1,800. The cost of the suitcases sold was $1,080. |
| | 18 | Purchased suitcases on account for $1,900 from Nelson Manufacturers, FOB shipping point, terms 1/10, n/30. The appropriate party also made a cash payment of $125 for freight on this date. |
| | 20 | Received $300 credit (including freight) for suitcases returned to Nelson Manufacturers. |
| | 21 | Received payment in full from The Going Concern. |
| | 22 | Sold suitcases on account to Wopat's for $2,250. The cost of suitcases sold was $1,350. |
| | 30 | Paid Nelson Manufacturers in full. |
| | 31 | Granted Wopat's $200 credit for suitcases returned costing $120. |

Urdan's chart of accounts includes the following: No. 101 Cash, No. 112 Accounts Receivable, No. 120 Inventory, No. 201 Accounts Payable, No. 401 Sales Revenue, No. 412 Sales Returns and Allowances, No. 414 Sales Discounts, and No. 505 Cost of Goods Sold.

### Instructions
Journalize the transactions for the month of July for Urdan using a perpetual inventory system.

**P5-2B** Rose Distributing Company completed the following merchandising transactions in the month of April. At the beginning of April, the ledger of Rose showed Cash of $9,000 and Owner's Capital of $9,000.

*Journalize, post, and prepare a partial income statement.*

(LO 2, 3, 5)

| Apr. | 2 | Purchased merchandise on account from Kwon Supply Co. $6,900, terms 1/10, n/30. |
|---|---|---|
| | 4 | Sold merchandise on account $6,500, FOB destination, terms 1/10, n/30. The cost of the merchandise sold was $3,900. |
| | 5 | Paid $240 freight on April 4 sale. |
| | 6 | Received credit from Kwon Supply Co. for merchandise returned $500. |
| | 11 | Paid Kwon Supply Co. in full, less discount. |
| | 13 | Received collections in full, less discounts, from customers billed on April 4. |
| | 14 | Purchased merchandise for cash $3,800. |
| | 16 | Received refund from supplier for returned goods on cash purchase of April 14, $500. |
| | 18 | Purchased merchandise from Davis Distributors $4,500, FOB shipping point, terms 2/10, n/30. |
| | 20 | Paid freight on April 18 purchase $100. |
| | 23 | Sold merchandise for cash $7,400. The merchandise sold had a cost of $4,120. |
| | 26 | Purchased merchandise for cash $2,300. |
| | 27 | Paid Davis Distributors in full, less discount. |
| | 29 | Made refunds to cash customers for defective merchandise $90. The returned merchandise had a fair value of $30. |
| | 30 | Sold merchandise on account $3,700, terms n/30. The cost of the merchandise sold was $2,800. |

Rose Distributing Company's chart of accounts includes the following: No. 101 Cash, No. 112 Accounts Receivable, No. 120 Inventory, No. 201 Accounts Payable, No. 301 Owner's Capital, No. 401 Sales Revenue, No. 412 Sales Returns and Allowances, No. 414 Sales Discounts, No. 505 Cost of Goods Sold, and No. 644 Freight-Out.

***Instructions***
**(a)** Journalize the transactions using a perpetual inventory system.
**(b)** Enter the beginning cash and capital balances, and post the transactions. (Use J1 for the journal reference.)

(c) Gross profit $6,655

**(c)** Prepare the income statement through gross profit for the month of April 2014.

*Prepare financial statements and adjusting and closing entries.*

(LO 4, 5)

**P5-3B** Mackey Department Store is located near the Village Shopping Mall. At the end of the company's calendar year on December 31, 2014, the following accounts appeared in two of its trial balances.

| | Unadjusted | Adjusted | | Unadjusted | Adjusted |
|---|---|---|---|---|---|
| Accounts Payable | $ 79,300 | $ 80,300 | Inventory | $ 75,000 | $ 75,000 |
| Accounts Receivable | 50,300 | 50,300 | Mortgage Payable | 80,000 | 80,000 |
| Accumulated Depr.—Buildings | 42,100 | 52,500 | Owner's Capital | 176,600 | 176,600 |
| Accumulated Depr.—Equipment | 29,600 | 42,900 | Owner's Drawings | 28,000 | 28,000 |
| Buildings | 290,000 | 290,000 | Prepaid Insurance | 9,600 | 2,400 |
| Cash | 23,800 | 23,800 | Property Tax Expense | | 4,800 |
| Cost of Goods Sold | 412,700 | 412,700 | Property Taxes Payable | | 4,800 |
| Depreciation Expense | | 23,700 | Salaries and Wages Expense | 108,000 | 108,000 |
| Equipment | 110,000 | 110,000 | Sales Commissions Expense | 10,200 | 14,500 |
| Insurance Expense | | 7,200 | Sales Commissions Payable | | 4,300 |
| Interest Expense | 3,000 | 12,000 | Sales Returns and Allowances | 8,000 | 8,000 |
| Interest Payable | | 9,000 | Sales Revenue | 728,000 | 728,000 |
| Interest Revenue | 4,000 | 4,000 | Utilities Expense | 11,000 | 12,000 |

***Instructions***

(a) Net income $129,100
    Owner's capital $277,700
    Total assets $456,100

**(a)** Prepare a multiple-step income statement, an owner's equity statement, and a classified balance sheet. $25,000 of the mortgage payable is due for payment next year.
**(b)** Journalize the adjusting entries that were made.
**(c)** Journalize the closing entries that are necessary.

*Journalize, post, and prepare a trial balance.*

(LO 2, 3, 4)

**P5-4B** Alex Diaz, a former professional tennis star, operates Diaz Tennis Shop at the Cedar Lake Resort. At the beginning of the current season, the ledger of Diaz Tennis Shop showed Cash $2,500, Inventory $1,700, and Owner's Capital $4,200. The following transactions were completed during April.

Apr.  4   Purchased racquets and balls from Marx Co. $840, FOB shipping point, terms 2/10, n/30.
      6   Paid freight on purchase from Marx Co. $40.
      8   Sold merchandise to members $1,150, terms n/30. The merchandise sold had a cost of $790.
     10   Received credit of $40 from Marx Co. for a racquet that was returned.
     11   Purchased tennis shoes from Rupp Sports for cash, $420.
     13   Paid Marx Co. in full.
     14   Purchased tennis shirts and shorts from Hayley's Sportswear $900, FOB shipping point, terms 3/10, n/60.
     15   Received cash refund of $50 from Rupp Sports for damaged merchandise that was returned.
     17   Paid freight on Hayley's Sportswear purchase $30.
     18   Sold merchandise to members $900, terms n/30. The cost of the merchandise sold was $540.
     20   Received $600 in cash from customers in settlement of their accounts.
     21   Paid Hayley's Sportswear in full.
     27   Granted an allowance of $40 to members for tennis clothing that did not fit properly.
     30   Received cash payments on account from customers, $710.

The chart of accounts for the tennis shop includes the following: No. 101 Cash, No. 112 Accounts Receivable, No. 120 Inventory, No. 201 Accounts Payable, No. 301 Owner's Capital, No. 401 Sales Revenue, No. 412 Sales Returns and Allowances, and No. 505 Cost of Goods Sold.

*Instructions*
(a) Journalize the April transactions using a perpetual inventory system.
(b) Enter the beginning balances in the ledger accounts and post the April transactions. (Use J1 for the journal reference.)
(c) Prepare a trial balance on April 30, 2014.

*(c) Total debits $6,250*

**\*P5-5B** At the end of Roshek Department Store's fiscal year on December 31, 2014, these accounts appeared in its adjusted trial balance.

*Determine cost of goods sold and gross profit under periodic approach.*

*(LO 5, 7)*

| | |
|---|---:|
| Freight-In | $   5,600 |
| Inventory | 40,500 |
| Purchases | 447,000 |
| Purchase Discounts | 12,000 |
| Purchase Returns and Allowances | 6,400 |
| Sales Revenue | 725,000 |
| Sales Returns and Allowances | 11,000 |

Additional facts:

1. Merchandise inventory on December 31, 2014, is $65,000.
2. Roshek Department Store uses a periodic system.

*Instructions*
Prepare an income statement through gross profit for the year ended December 31, 2014.

*Gross profit $304,300*

**\*P5-6B** Val Knight operates a retail clothing operation. She purchases all merchandise inventory on credit and uses a periodic inventory system. The Accounts Payable account is used for recording inventory purchases only; all other current liabilities are accrued in separate accounts. You are provided with the following selected information for the fiscal years 2011–2014.

*Calculate missing amounts and assess profitability.*

*(LO 5, 7)*

| | 2011 | 2012 | 2013 | 2014 |
|---|---|---|---|---|
| Inventory (ending) | $13,000 | $ 11,300 | $ 14,700 | $ 12,200 |
| Accounts payable (ending) | 20,000 | | | |
| Sales revenue | | 239,000 | 237,000 | 235,000 |
| Purchases of merchandise inventory on account | | 146,000 | 145,000 | 129,000 |
| Cash payments to suppliers | | 135,000 | 161,000 | 127,000 |

*Instructions*
(a) Calculate cost of goods sold for each of the 2012, 2013, and 2014 fiscal years.
(b) Calculate the gross profit for each of the 2012, 2013, and 2014 fiscal years.
(c) Calculate the ending balance of accounts payable for each of the 2012, 2013, and 2014 fiscal years.
(d) Sales declined in fiscal 2014. Does that mean that profitability, as measured by the gross profit rate, necessarily also declined? Explain, calculating the gross profit rate for each fiscal year to help support your answer. (Round to one decimal place.)

*(a) 2013 $141,600*

*(c) 2013 Ending accts payable $15,000*

**\*P5-7B** At the beginning of the current season, the ledger of Everett Tennis Shop showed Cash $2,500; Inventory $1,700; and Owner's Capital $4,200. The following transactions were completed during April.

*Journalize, post, and prepare trial balance and partial income statement using periodic approach.*

*(LO 7)*

Apr.  4  Purchased racquets and balls from Riggs Co. $740, terms 3/10, n/30.
      6  Paid freight on Riggs Co. purchase $60.
      8  Sold merchandise to customers $900, terms n/30.
     10  Received credit of $40 from Riggs Co. for a racquet that was returned.
     11  Purchased tennis shoes from King Sports for cash $300.
     13  Paid Riggs Co. in full.
     14  Purchased tennis shirts and shorts from BJ Sportswear $700, terms 2/10, n/60.
     15  Received cash refund of $50 from King Sports for damaged merchandise that was returned.

17    Paid freight on BJ Sportswear purchase $30.
18    Sold merchandise to customers $1,000, terms n/30.
20    Received $500 in cash from customers in settlement of their accounts.
21    Paid BJ Sportswear in full.
27    Granted an allowance of $25 to customers for tennis clothing that did not fit properly.
30    Received cash payments on account from customers $550.

The chart of accounts for the tennis shop includes Cash, Accounts Receivable, Inventory, Accounts Payable, Owner's Capital, Sales Revenue, Sales Returns and Allowances, Purchases, Purchase Returns and Allowances, Purchase Discounts, and Freight-In.

*Instructions*
**(a)** Journalize the April transactions using a periodic inventory system.
**(b)** Using T-accounts, enter the beginning balances in the ledger accounts and post the April transactions.
**(c)** Prepare a trial balance on April 30, 2014.
**(d)** Prepare an income statement through gross profit, assuming inventory on hand at April 30 is $2,296.

(c) Tot. trial balance $6,225

(d) Gross profit $766

## PROBLEMS: SET C

Visit the book's companion website, at **www.wiley.com/college/weygandt**, and choose the Student Companion site to access Problem Set C.

## COMPREHENSIVE PROBLEM

**CP5** On December 1, 2014, Prosen Distributing Company had the following account balances.

| | Debit | | Credit |
|---|---|---|---|
| Cash | $ 7,200 | Accumulated Depreciation— | |
| Accounts Receivable | 4,600 | Equipment | $ 2,200 |
| Inventory | 12,000 | Accounts Payable | 4,500 |
| Supplies | 1,200 | Salaries and Wages Payable | 1,000 |
| Equipment | 22,000 | Owner's Capital | 39,300 |
| | $47,000 | | $47,000 |

During December, the company completed the following summary transactions.

Dec.  6   Paid $1,600 for salaries and wages due employees, of which $600 is for December and $1,000 is for November salaries and wages payable.
8    Received $1,900 cash from customers in payment of account (no discount allowed).
10   Sold merchandise for cash $6,300. The cost of the merchandise sold was $4,100.
13   Purchased merchandise on account from Maglio Co. $9,000, terms 2/10, n/30.
15   Purchased supplies for cash $2,000.
18   Sold merchandise on account $12,000, terms 3/10, n/30. The cost of the merchandise sold was $8,000.
20   Paid salaries and wages $1,800.
23   Paid Maglio Co. in full, less discount.
27   Received collections in full, less discounts, from customers billed on December 18.

Adjustment data:

**1.** Accrued salaries and wages payable $800.
**2.** Depreciation $200 per month.
**3.** Supplies on hand $1,500.

## Instructions

**(a)** Journalize the December transactions using a perpetual inventory system.
**(b)** Enter the December 1 balances in the ledger T-accounts and post the December transactions. Use Cost of Goods Sold, Depreciation Expense, Salaries and Wages Expense, Sales Revenue, Sales Discounts, and Supplies Expense.
**(c)** Journalize and post adjusting entries.
**(d)** Prepare an adjusted trial balance.
**(e)** Prepare an income statement and an owner's equity statement for December and a classified balance sheet at December 31.

(d) Totals $65,300
(e) Net income $740

## CONTINUING COOKIE CHRONICLE

(*Note:* This is a continuation of the Cookie Chronicle from Chapters 1 through 4.)

**CCC5** Because Natalie has had such a successful first few months, she is considering other opportunities to develop her business. One opportunity is the sale of fine European mixers. The owner of Kzinski Supply Company has approached Natalie to become the exclusive U.S. distributor of these fine mixers in her state. The current cost of a mixer is approximately $525 (U.S.), and Natalie would sell each one for $1,050. Natalie comes to you for advice on how to account for these mixers.

*Go to the book's companion website,* **www.wiley.com/college/weygandt**, *to see the completion of this problem.*

# Broadening Your Perspective

## Financial Reporting and Analysis

### Financial Reporting Problem: Apple Inc.

**BYP5-1** The financial statements of Apple Inc. are presented in Appendix A at the end of this textbook. Instructions for accessing and using the company's complete annual report, including the notes to the financial statements, are also provided in Appendix A.

#### Instructions
Answer the following questions using Apple's Consolidated Statement of Income.

**(a)** What was the percentage change in (1) sales and in (2) net income from 2009 to 2010 and from 2010 to 2011?
**(b)** What was the company's gross profit rate in 2009, 2010, and 2011?
**(c)** What was the company's percentage of net income to net sales in 2009, 2010, and 2011? Comment on any trend in this percentage.

### Comparative Analysis Problem:
### PepsiCo, Inc. vs. The Coca-Cola Company

**BYP5-2** PepsiCo's financial statements are presented in Appendix B. Financial statements of The Coca-Cola Company are presented in Appendix C. Instructions for accessing and using the complete annual reports of PepsiCo and Coca-Cola, including the notes to the financial statements, are also provided in Appendices B and C, respectively.

#### Instructions
**(a)** Based on the information contained in these financial statements, determine each of the following for each company.
**(1)** Gross profit for 2011.
**(2)** Gross profit rate for 2011.

(3) Operating income for 2011.

(4) Percentage change in operating income from 2010 to 2011.

(b) What conclusions concerning the relative profitability of the two companies can you draw from these data?

## Comparative Analysis Problem: Amazon.com, Inc. vs. Wal-Mart Stores, Inc.

**BYP5-3** Amazon.com, Inc.'s financial statements are presented in Appendix D. Financial statements of Wal-Mart Stores, Inc. are presented in Appendix E. (Use Wal-Mart's January 31, 2012, financial statements for comparative purposes.) Instructions for accessing and using the complete annual reports of Amazon and Wal-Mart, including the notes to the financial statements, are also provided in Appendices D and E, respectively.

*Instructions*

(a) Based on the information contained in these financial statements, determine each of the following for each company. Use Amazon's net product sales to compute gross profit information.

(1) Gross profit for 2011.

(2) Gross profit rate for 2011.

(3) Operating income for 2011.

(4) Percentage change in operating income from 2010 to 2011.

(b) What conclusions concerning the relative profitability of the two companies can you draw from these data?

## Real-World Focus

**BYP5-4** No financial decision-maker should ever rely solely on the financial information reported in the annual report to make decisions. It is important to keep abreast of financial news. This activity demonstrates how to search for financial news on the Web.

*Address:* **biz.yahoo.com/i**, or go to **www.wiley.com/college/weygandt**

*Steps:*

1. Type in either PepsiCo or Coca-Cola.

2. Choose **News**.

3. Select an article that sounds interesting to you.

*Instructions*

(a) What was the source of the article (e.g., Reuters, Businesswire, PR Newswire)?

(b) Assume that you are a personal financial planner and that one of your clients owns stock in the company. Write a brief memo to your client, summarizing the article and explaining the implications of the article for his or her investment.

# Critical Thinking

## Decision-Making Across the Organization

**BYP5-5** Three years ago, Dana Mann and her brother-in-law Eric Boldt opened Family Department Store. For the first two years, business was good, but the following condensed income results for 2013 were disappointing.

**FAMILY DEPARTMENT STORE**
Income Statement
For the Year Ended December 31, 2013

| | | |
|---|---:|---:|
| Net sales | | $700,000 |
| Cost of goods sold | | 553,000 |
| Gross profit | | 147,000 |
| Operating expenses | | |
| Selling expenses | $100,000 | |
| Administrative expenses | 20,000 | 120,000 |
| Net income | | $ 27,000 |

Dana believes the problem lies in the relatively low gross profit rate (gross profit divided by net sales) of 21%. Eric believes the problem is that operating expenses are too high.

Dana thinks the gross profit rate can be improved by making both of the following changes. She does not anticipate that these changes will have any effect on operating expenses.

1. Increase average selling prices by 17%. This increase is expected to lower sales volume so that total sales will increase only 6%.
2. Buy merchandise in larger quantities and take all purchase discounts. These changes are expected to increase the gross profit rate by 3 percentage points.

Eric thinks expenses can be cut by making both of the following changes. He feels that these changes will not have any effect on net sales.

1. Cut 2013 sales salaries of $60,000 in half and give sales personnel a commission of 2% of net sales.
2. Reduce store deliveries to one day per week rather than twice a week. This change will reduce 2013 delivery expenses of $30,000 by 40%.

Dana and Eric come to you for help in deciding the best way to improve net income.

*Instructions*
With the class divided into groups, answer the following.

**(a)** Prepare a condensed income statement for 2014, assuming (1) Dana's changes are implemented and (2) Eric's ideas are adopted.
**(b)** What is your recommendation to Dana and Eric?
**(c)** Prepare a condensed income statement for 2014, assuming both sets of proposed changes are made.

## Communication Activity

**BYP5-6** The following situation is in chronological order.

1. Connor decides to buy a surfboard.
2. He calls Surfing USA Co. to inquire about its surfboards.
3. Two days later, he requests Surfing USA Co. to make a surfboard.
4. Three days later, Surfing USA Co. sends him a purchase order to fill out.
5. He sends back the purchase order.
6. Surfing USA Co. receives the completed purchase order.
7. Surfing USA Co. completes the surfboard.
8. Connor picks up the surfboard.
9. Surfing USA Co. bills Connor.
10. Surfing USA Co. receives payment from Connor.

*Instructions*
In a memo to the president of Surfing USA Co., answer the following.

**(a)** When should Surfing USA Co. record the sale?
**(b)** Suppose that with his purchase order, Connor is required to make a down payment. Would that change your answer?

## Ethics Case

**BYP5-7** Jacquie Boynton was just hired as the assistant treasurer of Key West Stores. The company is a specialty chain store with nine retail stores concentrated in one metropolitan area. Among other things, the payment of all invoices is centralized in one of the departments Jacquie will manage. Her primary responsibility is to maintain the company's high credit rating by paying all bills when due and to take advantage of all cash discounts.

Phelan Carter, the former assistant treasurer who has been promoted to treasurer, is training Jacquie in her new duties. He instructs Jacquie that she is to continue the practice of preparing all checks "net of discount" and dating the checks the last day of the discount period. "But," Phelan continues, "we always hold the checks at least 4 days beyond the discount period before mailing them. That way, we get another 4 days of interest on our money. Most of our creditors need our business and don't complain. And, if they scream about our missing the discount period, we blame it on the mail room or the post office. We've only lost one discount out of every hundred we take that way. I think everybody does it. By the way, welcome to our team!"

*Instructions*
**(a)** What are the ethical considerations in this case?
**(b)** Who are the stakeholders that are harmed or benefitted in this situation?
**(c)** Should Jacquie continue the practice started by Phelan? Does she have any choice?

## All About You

**BYP5-8** There are many situations in business where it is difficult to determine the proper period in which to record revenue. Suppose that after graduation with a degree in finance, you take a job as a manager at a consumer electronics store called Impact Electronics. The company has expanded rapidly in order to compete with Best Buy. Impact has also begun selling gift cards for its electronic products. The cards are available in any dollar amount and allow the holder of the card to purchase an item for up to 2 years from the time the card is purchased. If the card is not used during that 2 years, it expires.

*Instructions*
Answer the following questions.

At what point should the revenue from the gift cards be recognized? Should the revenue be recognized at the time the card is sold, or should it be recorded when the card is redeemed? Explain the reasoning to support your answers.

## FASB Codification Activity

**BYP5-9** If your school has a subscription to the FASB Codification, go to **http://aaahq.org/ascLogin.cfm** to log in and prepare responses to the following.

*Instructions*
**(a)** Access the glossary ("Master Glossary") to answer the following:
 **(1)** What is the definition provided for inventory?
 **(2)** What is a customer?
**(b)** What guidance does the Codification provide concerning reporting inventories above cost?

## Answers to Chapter Questions

### Answers to Insight and Accounting Across the Organization Questions

**p. 221 Morrow Snowboards Improves Its Stock Appeal** **Q:** If a perpetual system keeps track of inventory on a daily basis, why do companies ever need to do a physical count? **A:** A perpetual system keeps track of all sales and purchases on a continuous basis. This provides a constant record of the number of units in the inventory. However, if employees make errors in recording sales or purchases, or if there is theft, the inventory value will not be correct. As a consequence, all companies do a physical count of inventory at least once a year.

**p. 228 Should Costco Change Its Return Policy?** **Q:** If a company expects significant returns, what are the implications for revenue recognition? **A:** If a company expects significant returns, it should make an adjusting entry at the end of the year, reducing sales by the estimated amount of sales returns. This is necessary so as not to overstate the amount of revenue recognized in the period.

**p. 229 Selling Green** **Q:** What is meant by "monetize environmental sustainability" for shareholders? **A:** By marketing green, not only does PepsiCo help the environment in the long run, but it also leads to long-term profitability as well. In other words, sound sustainability practices are good business and lead to sound financial results.

**p. 235 Disclosing More Details** **Q:** Why have investors and analysts demanded more accuracy in isolating "Other gains and losses" from operating items? **A:** Greater accuracy in the classification of operating versus nonoperating ("Other gains and losses") items permits investors and analysts to judge the real operating margin, the results of continuing operations, and management's ability to control operating expenses.

# A Look at IFRS

The basic accounting entries for merchandising are the same under both GAAP and IFRS. The income statement is a required statement under both sets of standards. The basic format is similar although some differences do exist.

**LEARNING OBJECTIVE    8**

Compare the accounting procedures for merchandising under GAAP and IFRS.

## Key Points

- Under both GAAP and IFRS, a company can choose to use either a perpetual or a periodic system.

- Inventories are defined by IFRS as held-for-sale in the ordinary course of business, in the process of production for such sale, or in the form of materials or supplies to be consumed in the production process or in the providing of services.

- Under GAAP, companies generally classify income statement items by function. Classification by function leads to descriptions like administration, distribution, and manufacturing. Under IFRS, companies must classify expenses either by nature or by function. Classification by nature leads to descriptions such as the following: salaries, depreciation expense, and utilities expense. If a company uses the functional-expense method on the income statement, disclosure by nature is required in the notes to the financial statements.

- Presentation of the income statement under GAAP follows either a single-step or multiple-step format. IFRS does not mention a single-step or multiple-step approach.

- Under IFRS, revaluation of land, buildings, and intangible assets is permitted. The initial gains and losses resulting from this revaluation are reported as adjustments to equity, often referred to as **other comprehensive income**. The effect of this difference is that the use of IFRS results in more transactions affecting equity (other comprehensive income) but not net income.

- *IAS 1*, "Presentation of Financial Statements," provides general guidelines for the reporting of income statement information. Subsequently, a number of international standards have been issued that provide additional guidance to issues related to income statement presentation.

- Similar to GAAP, comprehensive income under IFRS includes unrealized gains and losses (such as those on so-called "non-trading securities") that are not included in the calculation of net income.

- IFRS requires that two years of income statement information be presented, whereas GAAP requires three years.

## Looking to the Future

The IASB and FASB are working on a project that would rework the structure of financial statements. Specifically, this project will address the issue of how to classify various items in the income statement. A main goal of this new approach is to provide information that better represents how businesses are run. In addition, this approach draws attention away from just one number—net income. It will adopt major groupings similar to those currently used by the statement of cash flows (operating, investing, and financing), so that numbers can be more readily traced across statements. For example, the amount of income that is generated by operations would be traceable to the assets and liabilities used to generate the income. Finally, this approach would also provide detail, beyond that currently seen in most statements (either GAAP or IFRS), by requiring that line items be presented both by function and by nature. The new financial statement format was heavily influenced by suggestions from financial statement analysts.

## IFRS Practice

### IFRS Self-Test Questions

1. Which of the following would **not** be included in the definition of inventory under IFRS?
   (a) Photocopy paper held for sale by an office-supply store.
   (b) Stereo equipment held for sale by an electronics store.
   (c) Used office equipment held for sale by the human relations department of a plastics company.
   (d) All of the above would meet the definition.

2. Which of the following would **not** be a line item of a company reporting costs by nature?
   (a) Depreciation expense.
   (b) Salaries expense.
   (c) Interest expense.
   (d) Manufacturing expense.

3. Which of the following would **not** be a line item of a company reporting costs by function?
   (a) Administration.
   (b) Manufacturing.
   (c) Utilities expense.
   (d) Distribution.

4. Which of the following statements is **false**?
   (a) IFRS specifically requires use of a multiple-step income statement.
   (b) Under IFRS, companies can use either a perpetual or periodic system.
   (c) The proposed new format for financial statements was heavily influenced by the suggestions of financial statement analysts.
   (d) The new income statement format will try to de-emphasize the focus on the "net income" line item.

5. Under the new format for financial statements being proposed under a joint IASB/FASB project:
   (a) all financial statements would adopt headings similar to the current format of the balance sheet.
   (b) financial statements would be presented consistent with the way management usually run companies.
   (c) companies would be required to report income statement line items by function only.
   (d) the amount of detail shown in the income statement would decrease compared to current presentations.

### IFRS Exercises

**IFRS5-1** Explain the difference between the "nature-of-expense" and "function-of-expense" classifications.

**IFRS5-2** For each of the following income statement line items, state whether the item is a "by nature" expense item or a "by function" expense item.

_____ Cost of goods sold
_____ Depreciation expense
_____ Salaries and wages expense
_____ Selling expenses
_____ Utilities expense
_____ Delivery expense
_____ General and administrative expenses

**IFRS5-3** Matilda Company reported the following amounts (in euros) in 2014: Net income, €150,000; Unrealized gain related to revaluation of buildings, €10,000; and Unrealized loss on non-trading securities, €(35,000). Determine Matilda's total comprehensive income for 2014.

## International Financial Reporting Problem: Zetar plc

**IFRS5-4** The financial statements of Zetar plc are presented in Appendix F. Instructions for accessing and using the company's complete annual report, including the notes to its financial statements, are also provided in Appendix F.

### Instructions
Use Zetar's annual report to answer the following questions.

**(a)** Does Zetar use a multiple-step or a single-step income statement format? Explain how you made your determination.

**(b)** Instead of "interest expense," what label does Zetar use for interest costs that it incurs?

**(c)** Using the notes to the company's financial statements, explain what each of the following are:
    **(1)** Adjusted results.
    **(2)** One-off items.

### Answers to IFRS Self-Test Questions
**1.** c    **2.** d    **3.** c    **4.** a    **5.** b

The Navigator

# 6 | Inventories

## "Where Is That Spare Bulldozer Blade?"

Let's talk inventory—big, bulldozer-size inventory. Caterpillar Inc. is the world's largest manufacturer of construction and mining equipment, diesel and natural gas engines, and industrial gas turbines. It sells its products in over 200 countries, making it one of the most successful U.S. exporters. More than 70% of its productive assets are located domestically, and nearly 50% of its sales are foreign.

In the past, Caterpillar's profitability suffered, but today it is very successful. A big part of this turnaround can be attributed to effective management of its inventory. Imagine what it costs Caterpillar to have too many bulldozers sitting around in inventory—a situation the company definitely wants to avoid. Conversely, Caterpillar must make sure it has enough inventory to meet demand.

At one time during a 7-year period, Caterpillar's sales increased by 100%, while its inventory increased by only 50%. To achieve this dramatic reduction in the amount of resourc tied up in inventory, while continuing to meet customers needs, Caterpillar used a two-pronged approach. First, it completed a factory modernization program, which grea increased its production efficiency. The program reduced 60% the amount of inventory the company processed a one time. It also reduced by an incredible 75% the time it takes to manufacture a part.

Second, Caterpillar dramatically improved its parts distrib system. It ships more than 100,000 items daily from its 2 distribution centers strategically located around the worl (10 million square feet of warehouse space—remember, talking bulldozers). The company can virtually guarantee it can get any part to anywhere in the world within 24 h

After these changes, Caterpillar had record exports, prof and revenues. It would seem that things couldn't be bett But industry analysts, as well as the company's managers thought otherwise. In order to maintain Caterpillar's posi as the industry leader, management began another majo

## Learning Objectives ✔ The Navigator

*After studying this chapter, you should be able to:*

**[1]** Determine how to classify inventory and inventory quantities.

**[2]** Explain the accounting for inventories and apply the inventory cost flow methods.

**[3]** Explain the financial effects of the inventory cost flow assumptions.

**[4]** Explain the lower-of-cost-or-market basis of accounting for inventories.

**[5]** Indicate the effects of inventory errors on the financial statements.

**[6]** Compute and interpret the inventory turnover.

overhaul of inventory production and inventory management processes. The goal: to cut the number of repairs in half, increase productivity by 20%, and increase inventory turnover by 40%.

In short, Caterpillar's ability to manage its inventory has been a key reason for its past success, and inventory management will very likely play a huge part in its ability to succeed in the future.

# Preview of Chapter 6

✔ The Navigator

In the previous chapter, we discussed the accounting for merchandise inventory using a perpetual inventory system. In this chapter, we explain the methods used to calculate the cost of inventory on hand at the balance sheet date and the cost of goods sold.

The content and organization of this chapter are as follows.

| INVENTORIES | | | |
|---|---|---|---|
| **Classifying and Determining Inventory** | **Inventory Costing** | **Inventory Errors** | **Statement Presentation and Analysis** |
| • Classifying inventory<br>• Determining inventory quantities | • Specific identification<br>• Cost flow assumptions<br>• Financial statement and tax effects<br>• Consistent use<br>• Lower-of-cost-or-market | • Income statement effects<br>• Balance sheet effects | • Presentation<br>• Analysis |

## Classifying and Determining Inventory

LEARNING OBJECTIVE    1

Determine how to classify inventory and inventory quantities.

Two important steps in the reporting of inventory at the end of the accounting period are the classification of inventory based on its degree of completeness and the determination of inventory amounts.

### Classifying Inventory

How a company classifies its inventory depends on whether the firm is a merchandiser or a manufacturer. In a **merchandising** company, such as those described in Chapter 5, inventory consists of many different items. For example, in a grocery store, canned goods, dairy products, meats, and produce are just a few of the inventory items on hand. These items have two common characteristics: (1) They are owned by the company, and (2) they are in a form ready for sale to customers in the ordinary course of business. Thus, merchandisers need only one inventory classification, **merchandise inventory**, to describe the many different items that make up the total inventory.

In a **manufacturing** company, some inventory may not yet be ready for sale. As a result, manufacturers usually classify inventory into three categories: finished goods, work in process, and raw materials. **Finished goods inventory** is manufactured items that are completed and ready for sale. **Work in process** is that portion of manufactured inventory that has been placed into the production process but is not yet complete. **Raw materials** are the basic goods that will be used in production but have not yet been placed into production.

For example, Caterpillar classifies earth-moving tractors completed and ready for sale as **finished goods**. It classifies the tractors on the assembly line in various stages of production as **work in process**. The steel, glass, tires, and other components that are on hand waiting to be used in the production of tractors are identified as **raw materials**. Illustration 6-1 shows an excerpt from Note 7 of Caterpillar's annual report, which shows the significant increases in each type of Caterpillar's inventory levels as the economy began to recover during this period.

**Helpful Hint** Regardless of the classification, companies report all inventories under Current Assets on the balance sheet.

**Illustration 6-1**
Composition of Caterpillar's inventory

| (millions of dollars) | December 31 | | |
|---|---|---|---|
| | 2011 | 2010 | 2009 |
| Raw materials | $ 3,872 | $2,766 | $1,979 |
| Work-in-process | 2,845 | 1,483 | 656 |
| Finished goods | 7,570 | 5,098 | 3,465 |
| Other | 257 | 240 | 260 |
| **Total inventories** | **$14,544** | **$9,587** | **$6,360** |

**By observing the levels and changes in the levels of these three inventory types, financial statement users can gain insight into management's production plans.** For example, low levels of raw materials and high levels of finished goods suggest that management believes it has enough inventory on hand, and production will be slowing down—perhaps in anticipation of a recession. On the other hand, high levels of raw materials and low levels of finished goods probably signal that management is planning to step up production.

Many companies have significantly lowered inventory levels and costs using **just-in-time (JIT) inventory** methods. Under a just-in-time method, companies manufacture or purchase goods just in time for use. Dell is famous for having developed a system for making computers in response to individual customer requests. Even though it makes each computer to meet each customer's particular specifications, Dell is able to assemble the computer and put it on a truck in less than 48 hours. The success of the JIT system depends on reliable suppliers. By integrating its information systems with those of its suppliers, Dell reduced its inventories to nearly zero. This is a huge advantage in an industry where products become obsolete nearly overnight.

The accounting concepts discussed in this chapter apply to the inventory classifications of both merchandising and manufacturing companies. Our focus here is on merchandise inventory. Additional issues specific to manufacturing companies are discussed later in the managerial section of this textbook (Chapters 19–26).

## ACCOUNTING ACROSS THE ORGANIZATION

### A Big Hiccup

JIT can save a company a lot of money, but it isn't without risk. An unexpected disruption in the supply chain can cost a company a lot of money. Japanese automakers experienced just such a disruption when a 6.8-magnitude earthquake caused major damage to the company that produces 50% of their piston rings. The rings themselves cost only $1.50, but without them you cannot make a car. No other supplier could quickly begin producing sufficient quantities of the rings to match the desired specifications. As a result, the automakers were forced to shut down production for a few days—a loss of tens of thousands of cars.

Similarly, a major snowstorm halted production at Canadian plants of General Motors and Ford. A Ford spokesperson said, "Because the plants run with just-in-time inventory, we don't have large stockpiles of parts sitting around. When you have a somewhat significant disruption, you can pretty quickly run out of parts."

*Source:* Amy Chozick, "A Key Strategy of Japan's Car Makers Backfires," *Wall Street Journal* (July 20, 2007); Kate Linebaugh, "Canada Military Evacuates Motorists Stranded by Snow," *Wall Street Journal* (December 15, 2010).

 What steps might the companies take to avoid such a serious disruption in the future? (See page 324.)

## Determining Inventory Quantities

No matter whether they are using a periodic or perpetual inventory system, all companies need to determine inventory quantities at the end of the accounting period. If using a perpetual system, companies take a physical inventory for the following reasons:

1. To check the accuracy of their perpetual inventory records.
2. To determine the amount of inventory lost due to wasted raw materials, shoplifting, or employee theft.

Companies using a periodic inventory system take a physical inventory for **two different purposes**: to determine the inventory on hand at the balance sheet date, and to determine the cost of goods sold for the period.

Determining inventory quantities involves two steps: (1) taking a physical inventory of goods on hand and (2) determining the ownership of goods.

### TAKING A PHYSICAL INVENTORY

Companies take a physical inventory at the end of the accounting period. Taking a physical inventory involves actually counting, weighing, or measuring each kind of inventory on hand. In many companies, taking an

**Ethics Note**

In a famous fraud, a salad oil company filled its storage tanks mostly with water. The oil rose to the top, so auditors thought the tanks were full of oil. The company also said it had more tanks than it really did: It repainted numbers on the tanks to confuse auditors.

inventory is a formidable task. Retailers such as Target, True Value Hardware, or Home Depot have thousands of different inventory items. An inventory count is generally more accurate when goods are not being sold or received during the counting. Consequently, companies often "take inventory" when the business is closed or when business is slow. Many retailers close early on a chosen day in January—after the holiday sales and returns, when inventories are at their lowest level—to count inventory. Wal-Mart Stores, Inc., for example, has a year-end of January 31.

© Greg Brookes/iStockphoto

## ETHICS INSIGHT

### Falsifying Inventory to Boost Income

Managers at women's apparel maker Leslie Fay were convicted of falsifying inventory records to boost net income—and consequently to boost management bonuses. In another case, executives at Craig Consumer Electronics were accused of defrauding lenders by manipulating inventory records. The indictment said the company classified "defective goods as new or refurbished" and claimed that it owned certain shipments "from overseas suppliers" when, in fact, Craig either did not own the shipments or the shipments did not exist.

**?** What effect does an overstatement of inventory have on a company's financial statements? (See page 324.)

## DETERMINING OWNERSHIP OF GOODS

One challenge in computing inventory quantities is determining what inventory a company owns. To determine ownership of goods, two questions must be answered: Do all of the goods included in the count belong to the company? Does the company own any goods that were not included in the count?

**GOODS IN TRANSIT** A complication in determining ownership is **goods in transit** (on board a truck, train, ship, or plane) at the end of the period. The company may have purchased goods that have not yet been received, or it may have sold goods that have not yet been delivered. To arrive at an accurate count, the company must determine ownership of these goods.

Goods in transit should be included in the inventory of the company that has legal title to the goods. Legal title is determined by the terms of the sale, as shown in Illustration 6-2 and described below.

**Illustration 6-2**
Terms of sale

1. When the terms are **FOB (free on board) shipping point**, ownership of the goods passes to the buyer when the public carrier accepts the goods from the seller.
2. When the terms are **FOB destination**, ownership of the goods remains with the seller until the goods reach the buyer.

If goods in transit at the statement date are ignored, inventory quantities may be seriously miscounted. Assume, for example, that Hargrove Company has 20,000 units of inventory on hand on December 31. It also has the following goods in transit:

1. Sales of 1,500 units shipped December 31 FOB destination.
2. Purchases of 2,500 units shipped FOB shipping point by the seller on December 31.

Hargrove has legal title to both the 1,500 units sold and the 2,500 units purchased. If the company ignores the units in transit, it would understate inventory quantities by 4,000 units (1,500 + 2,500).

As we will see later in the chapter, inaccurate inventory counts affect not only the inventory amount shown on the balance sheet but also the cost of goods sold calculation on the income statement.

**CONSIGNED GOODS** In some lines of business, it is common to hold the goods of other parties and try to sell the goods for them for a fee, but without taking ownership of the goods. These are called **consigned goods**.

For example, you might have a used car that you would like to sell. If you take the item to a dealer, the dealer might be willing to put the car on its lot and charge you a commission if it is sold. Under this agreement, the dealer **would not take ownership** of the car, which would still belong to you. Therefore, if an inventory count were taken, the car would not be included in the dealer's inventory because the dealer does not own it.

Many car, boat, and antique dealers sell goods on consignment to keep their inventory costs down and to avoid the risk of purchasing an item that they will not be able to sell. Today, even some manufacturers are making consignment agreements with their suppliers in order to keep their inventory levels low.

---

### ANATOMY OF A FRAUD

Ted Nickerson, CEO of clock manufacturer Dally Industries, was feared by all of his employees. Ted also had expensive tastes. To support his expensive tastes, Ted took out large loans, which he collateralized with his shares of Dally Industries stock. If the price of Dally's stock fell, he was required to provide the bank with more shares of stock. To achieve target net income figures and thus maintain the stock price, Ted coerced employees in the company to alter inventory figures. Inventory quantities were manipulated by changing the amounts on inventory control tags after the year-end physical inventory count. For example, if a tag said there were 20 units of a particular item, the tag was changed to 220. Similarly, the unit costs that were used to determine the value of ending inventory were increased from, for example, $125 per unit to $1,250. Both of these fraudulent changes had the effect of increasing the amount of reported ending inventory. This reduced cost of goods sold and increased net income.

**Total take: $245,000**

**THE MISSING CONTROL**
***Independent internal verification.*** The company should have spot-checked its inventory records periodically, verifying that the number of units in the records agreed with the amount on hand and that the unit costs agreed with vendor price sheets.

*Source:* Adapted from Wells, *Fraud Casebook* (2007), pp. 502–509.

## > DO IT!

### Rules of Ownership

Hasbeen Company completed its inventory count. It arrived at a total inventory value of $200,000. As a new member of Hasbeen's accounting department, you have been given the information listed below. Discuss how this information affects the reported cost of inventory.

**1.** Hasbeen included in the inventory goods held on consignment for Falls Co., costing $15,000.

**2.** The company did not include in the count purchased goods of $10,000 which were in transit (terms: FOB shipping point).

**3.** The company did not include in the count sold inventory with a cost of $12,000 which was in transit (terms: FOB shipping point).

### Solution

The goods of $15,000 held on consignment should be deducted from the inventory count. The goods of $10,000 purchased FOB shipping point should be added to the inventory count. Sold goods of $12,000 which were in transit FOB shipping point should not be included in the ending inventory. Thus, inventory should be carried at $195,000 ($200,000 − $15,000 + $10,000).

#### Action Plan

✔ Apply the rules of ownership to goods held on consignment.

✔ Apply the rules of ownership to goods in transit.

Related exercise material: **BE6-1, E6-1, E6-2, and DO IT! 6-1.**

✔ The Navigator

---

## Inventory Costing

**LEARNING OBJECTIVE**   **2**

**Explain the accounting for inventories and apply the inventory cost flow methods.**

Inventory is accounted for at cost. Cost includes all expenditures necessary to acquire goods and place them in a condition ready for sale. For example, freight costs incurred to acquire inventory are added to the cost of inventory, but the cost of shipping goods to a customer are a selling expense.

After a company has determined the quantity of units of inventory, it applies unit costs to the quantities to compute the total cost of the inventory and the cost of goods sold. This process can be complicated if a company has purchased inventory items at different times and at different prices.

For example, assume that Crivitz TV Company purchases three identical 50-inch TVs on different dates at costs of $700, $750, and $800. During the year, Crivitz sold two sets at $1,200 each. These facts are summarized in Illustration 6-3.

**Illustration 6-3**
Data for inventory costing example

| Purchases | | | |
|---|---|---|---|
| February 3 | 1 TV | at | $700 |
| March 5 | 1 TV | at | $750 |
| May 22 | 1 TV | at | $800 |
| **Sales** | | | |
| June 1 | 2 TVs | for | $2,400 ($1,200 × 2) |

Cost of goods sold will differ depending on which two TVs the company sold. For example, it might be $1,450 ($700 + $750), or $1,500 ($700 + $800), or $1,550 ($750 + $800). In this section, we discuss alternative costing methods available to Crivitz.

## Specific Identification

If Crivitz can positively identify which particular units it sold and which are still in ending inventory, it can use the **specific identification method** of inventory costing. For example, if Crivitz sold the TVs it purchased on February 3 and May 22, then its cost of goods sold is $1,500 ($700 + $800), and its ending inventory is $750 (see Illustration 6-4). Using this method, companies can accurately determine ending inventory and cost of goods sold.

**Illustration 6-4**
Specific identification method

Specific identification requires that companies keep records of the original cost of each individual inventory item. Historically, specific identification was possible only when a company sold a limited variety of high-unit-cost items that could be identified clearly from the time of purchase through the time of sale. Examples of such products are cars, pianos, or expensive antiques.

Today, bar coding, electronic product codes, and radio frequency identification make it theoretically possible to do specific identification with nearly any type of product. The reality is, however, that this practice is still relatively rare. Instead, rather than keep track of the cost of each particular item sold, most companies make assumptions, called **cost flow assumptions**, about which units were sold.

**Ethics Note**

A major disadvantage of the specific identification method is that management may be able to manipulate net income. For example, it can boost net income by selling units purchased at a low cost, or reduce net income by selling units purchased at a high cost.

## Cost Flow Assumptions

Because specific identification is often impractical, other cost flow methods are permitted. These differ from specific identification in that they **assume** flows of costs that may be unrelated to the physical flow of goods. There are three assumed cost flow methods:

1. First-in, first-out (FIFO)
2. Last-in, first-out (LIFO)
3. Average-cost

**There is no accounting requirement that the cost flow assumption be consistent with the physical movement of the goods.** Company management selects the appropriate cost flow method.

To demonstrate the three cost flow methods, we will use a **periodic** inventory system. We assume a periodic system because **very few companies use** *perpetual* **LIFO, FIFO, or average-cost** to cost their inventory and related cost of goods sold. Instead, companies that use perpetual systems often use an assumed cost (called a standard cost) to record cost of goods sold at the time of sale. Then, at the end of the period when they count their inventory, they **recalculate cost of** goods sold using *periodic* **FIFO, LIFO, or average-cost** as shown in this chapter and adjust cost of goods sold to this recalculated number.[1]

To illustrate the three inventory cost flow methods, we will use the data for Houston Electronics' Astro condensers, shown in Illustration 6-5.

**Illustration 6-5**
Data for Houston Electronics

| \ HOUSTON ELECTRONICS | | | | |
|---|---|---|---|---|
| \ Astro Condensers | | | | |
| **Date** | **Explanation** | **Units** | **Unit Cost** | **Total Cost** |
| Jan.  1 | Beginning inventory | 100 | $10 | $  1,000 |
| Apr. 15 | Purchase | 200 | 11 | 2,200 |
| Aug. 24 | Purchase | 300 | 12 | 3,600 |
| Nov. 27 | Purchase | 400 | 13 | 5,200 |
| | Total units available for sale | 1,000 | | $12,000 |
| | Units in ending inventory | 450 | | |
| | Units sold | 550 | | |

The cost of goods sold formula in a periodic system is:

> **(Beginning Inventory + Purchases) − Ending Inventory = Cost of Goods Sold**

Houston Electronics had a total of 1,000 units available to sell during the period (beginning inventory plus purchases). The total cost of these 1,000 units is $12,000, referred to as **cost of goods available for sale**. A physical inventory taken at December 31 determined that there were 450 units in ending inventory. Therefore, Houston sold 550 units (1,000 − 450) during the period. To determine the cost of the 550 units that were sold (the cost of goods sold), we assign a cost to the ending inventory and subtract that value from the cost of goods available for sale. The value assigned to the ending inventory **will depend on which cost flow method we use**. No matter which cost flow assumption we use, though, the sum of cost of goods sold plus the cost of the ending inventory must equal the cost of goods available for sale—in this case, $12,000.

### FIRST-IN, FIRST-OUT (FIFO)

The **first-in, first-out (FIFO) method** assumes that the **earliest goods** purchased are the first to be sold. FIFO often parallels the actual physical flow of merchandise. That is, it generally is good business practice to sell the oldest units first. Under the FIFO method, therefore, the **costs** of the earliest goods purchased are the first to be recognized in determining cost of goods sold. (This does not necessarily mean that the oldest units **are** sold first, but that the costs of the oldest units are **recognized** first. In a bin of picture hangers at the hardware store, for example, no one really knows, nor would it matter, which hangers are sold first.) Illustration 6-6 shows the allocation of the cost of goods available for sale at Houston Electronics under FIFO.

---

[1]Also, some companies use a perpetual system to keep track of units, but they do not make an entry for perpetual cost of goods sold. In addition, firms that employ LIFO tend to use **dollar-value LIFO**, a method discussed in upper-level courses. FIFO periodic and FIFO perpetual give the same result. Therefore, companies should not incur the additional cost to use FIFO perpetual. Few companies use perpetual average-cost because of the added cost of recordkeeping. Finally, for instructional purposes, we believe it is easier to demonstrate the cost flow assumptions under the periodic system, which makes it more pedagogically appropriate.

**Illustration 6-6**
Allocation of costs—FIFO method

| COST OF GOODS AVAILABLE FOR SALE | | | | |
|---|---|---|---|---|
| **Date** | **Explanation** | **Units** | **Unit Cost** | **Total Cost** |
| Jan.  1 | Beginning inventory | 100 | $10 | $  1,000 |
| Apr. 15 | Purchase | 200 | 11 | 2,200 |
| Aug. 24 | Purchase | 300 | 12 | 3,600 |
| Nov. 27 | Purchase | 400 | 13 | 5,200 |
| | Total | 1,000 | | $12,000 |

**Helpful Hint** Note the sequencing of the allocation: (1) Compute ending inventory, and (2) determine cost of goods sold.

| STEP 1: ENDING INVENTORY | | | | STEP 2: COST OF GOODS SOLD | |
|---|---|---|---|---|---|
| **Date** | **Units** | **Unit Cost** | **Total Cost** | | |
| Nov. 27 | 400 | $13 | $ 5,200 | Cost of goods available for sale | $12,000 |
| Aug. 24 | 50 | 12 | 600 | Less: Ending inventory | 5,800 |
| Total | 450 | | $5,800 | Cost of goods sold | $ 6,200 |

**Helpful Hint** Another way of thinking about the calculation of FIFO ending inventory is the *LISH assumption*—last in still here.

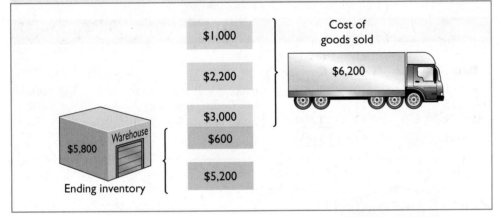

Under FIFO, since it is assumed that the first goods purchased were the first goods sold, ending inventory is based on the prices of the most recent units purchased. That is, **under FIFO, companies obtain the cost of the ending inventory by taking the unit cost of the most recent purchase and working backward until all units of inventory have been costed**. In this example, Houston Electronics prices the 450 units of ending inventory using the **most recent** prices. The last purchase was 400 units at $13 on November 27. The remaining 50 units are priced using the unit cost of the second most recent purchase, $12, on August 24. Next, Houston Electronics calculates cost of goods sold by subtracting the cost of the units **not sold** (ending inventory) from the cost of all goods available for sale.

Illustration 6-7 demonstrates that companies also can calculate cost of goods sold by pricing the 550 units sold using the prices of the first 550 units acquired. Note that of the 300 units purchased on August 24, only 250 units are assumed sold. This agrees with our calculation of the cost of ending inventory, where 50 of these units were assumed unsold and thus included in ending inventory.

| Date | Units | Unit Cost | Total Cost |
|---|---|---|---|
| Jan.  1 | 100 | $10 | $ 1,000 |
| Apr. 15 | 200 | 11 | 2,200 |
| Aug. 24 | 250 | 12 | 3,000 |
| Total | 550 | | $6,200 |

**Illustration 6-7**
Proof of cost of goods sold

## LAST-IN, FIRST-OUT (LIFO)

The **last-in, first-out (LIFO) method** assumes that the **latest goods** purchased are the first to be sold. LIFO seldom coincides with the actual physical flow of inventory. (Exceptions include goods stored in piles, such as coal or hay, where goods are removed from the top of the pile as they are sold.) Under the LIFO method, the **costs** of the latest goods purchased are the first to be recognized in determining cost of goods sold. Illustration 6-8 shows the allocation of the cost of goods available for sale at Houston Electronics under LIFO.

**Illustration 6-8**
Allocation of costs—LIFO method

### COST OF GOODS AVAILABLE FOR SALE

| Date | Explanation | Units | Unit Cost | Total Cost |
|---|---|---|---|---|
| Jan. 1 | Beginning inventory | 100 | $10 | $ 1,000 |
| Apr. 15 | Purchase | 200 | 11 | 2,200 |
| Aug. 24 | Purchase | 300 | 12 | 3,600 |
| Nov. 27 | Purchase | 400 | 13 | 5,200 |
| | Total | 1,000 | | $12,000 |

### STEP 1: ENDING INVENTORY

| Date | Units | Unit Cost | Total Cost |
|---|---|---|---|
| Jan. 1 | 100 | $10 | $ 1,000 |
| Apr. 15 | 200 | 11 | 2,200 |
| Aug. 24 | 150 | 12 | 1,800 |
| Total | 450 | | $5,000 |

### STEP 2: COST OF GOODS SOLD

| | |
|---|---|
| Cost of goods available for sale | $12,000 |
| Less: Ending inventory | 5,000 |
| Cost of goods sold | $ 7,000 |

**Helpful Hint** Another way of thinking about the calculation of LIFO **ending inventory** is the *FISH assumption*—first in still here.

Under LIFO, since it is assumed that the first goods sold were those that were most recently purchased, ending inventory is based on the prices of the oldest units purchased. That is, **under LIFO, companies obtain the cost of the ending inventory by taking the unit cost of the earliest goods available for sale and working forward until all units of inventory have been costed**. In this example, Houston Electronics prices the 450 units of ending inventory using the **earliest** prices. The first purchase was 100 units at $10 in the January 1 beginning inventory. Then, 200 units were purchased at $11. The remaining 150 units needed are priced at $12 per unit (August 24 purchase). Next, Houston Electronics calculates cost of goods sold by subtracting the cost of the units **not sold** (ending inventory) from the cost of all goods available for sale.

Illustration 6-9 demonstrates that companies also can calculate cost of goods sold by pricing the 550 units sold using the prices of the last 550 units acquired. Note that of the 300 units purchased on August 24, only 150 units are assumed sold. This agrees with our calculation of the cost of ending inventory, where 150 of these units were assumed unsold and thus included in ending inventory.

**Illustration 6-9**
Proof of cost of goods sold

| Date | Units | Unit Cost | Total Cost |
|---|---|---|---|
| Nov. 27 | 400 | $13 | $5,200 |
| Aug. 24 | 150 | 12 | 1,800 |
| Total | 550 | | $7,000 |

Under a periodic inventory system, which we are using here, **all goods purchased during the period are assumed to be available for the first sale, regardless of the date of purchase**.

### AVERAGE-COST

The **average-cost method** allocates the cost of goods available for sale on the basis of the **weighted-average unit cost** incurred. The average-cost method assumes that goods are similar in nature. Illustration 6-10 presents the formula and a sample computation of the weighted-average unit cost.

**Illustration 6-10**
Formula for weighted-average unit cost

| Cost of Goods Available for Sale | ÷ | Total Units Available for Sale | = | Weighted-Average Unit Cost |
|---|---|---|---|---|
| $12,000 | ÷ | 1,000 | = | $12 |

The company then applies the weighted-average unit cost to the units on hand to determine the cost of the ending inventory. Illustration 6-11 shows the allocation of the cost of goods available for sale at Houston Electronics using average-cost.

**Illustration 6-11**
Allocation of costs—average-cost method

| COST OF GOODS AVAILABLE FOR SALE | | | | |
|---|---|---|---|---|
| Date | Explanation | Units | Unit Cost | Total Cost |
| Jan. 1 | Beginning inventory | 100 | $10 | $ 1,000 |
| Apr. 15 | Purchase | 200 | 11 | 2,200 |
| Aug. 24 | Purchase | 300 | 12 | 3,600 |
| Nov. 27 | Purchase | 400 | 13 | 5,200 |
| | Total | 1,000 | | $12,000 |

**STEP 1: ENDING INVENTORY**

$12,000 ÷ 1,000 = $12

| Units | Unit Cost | Total Cost |
|---|---|---|
| 450 | $12 | $5,400 |

**STEP 2: COST OF GOODS SOLD**

| | |
|---|---|
| Cost of goods available for sale | $12,000 |
| Less: Ending inventory | 5,400 |
| Cost of goods sold | $ 6,600 |

We can verify the cost of goods sold under this method by multiplying the units sold times the weighted-average unit cost (550 × $12 = $6,600). Note that this method does not use the average of the unit costs. That average is $11.50 ($10 + $11 + $12 + $13 = $46; $46 ÷ 4). The average-cost method instead uses the average **weighted by** the quantities purchased at each unit cost.

---

> **DO IT!**

### Cost Flow Methods

The accounting records of Shumway Ag Implements show the following data.

| | |
|---|---|
| Beginning inventory | 4,000 units at $ 3 |
| Purchases | 6,000 units at $ 4 |
| Sales | 7,000 units at $12 |

Determine the cost of goods sold during the period under a periodic inventory system using (a) the FIFO method, (b) the LIFO method, and (c) the average-cost method.

#### Solution

Cost of goods available for sale = (4,000 × $3) + (6,000 × $4) = $36,000

Ending inventory = 10,000 − 7,000 = 3,000 units

**(a)** FIFO: $36,000 − (3,000 × $4) = $24,000

**(b)** LIFO: $36,000 − (3,000 × $3) = $27,000

**(c)** Average cost per unit: [(4,000 @ $3) + (6,000 @ $4)] ÷ 10,000 = $3.60
   Average-cost: $36,000 − (3,000 × $3.60) = $25,200

Related exercise material: **BE6-3, BE6-4, BE6-5, E6-3, E6-4, E6-5, E6-6, E6-7, E6-8, and DO IT! 6-2.**

#### Action Plan

✔ Understand the periodic inventory system.

✔ Allocate costs between goods sold and goods on hand (ending inventory) for each cost flow method.

✔ Compute cost of goods sold for each method.

✔ **The Navigator**

---

## Financial Statement and Tax Effects of Cost Flow Methods

**LEARNING OBJECTIVE  3**

Explain the financial effects of the inventory cost flow assumptions.

Each of the three assumed cost flow methods is acceptable for use. For example, Reebok International Ltd. and Wendy's International currently use the FIFO method of inventory costing. Campbell Soup Company, Krogers, and Walgreen Drugs use LIFO for part or all of their inventory. Bristol-Myers Squibb, Starbucks, and Motorola use the average-cost method. In fact, a company may also use more than one cost flow method at the same time. Stanley Black & Decker Manufacturing Company, for example, uses LIFO for domestic inventories and FIFO for foreign inventories. Illustration 6-12 (in the margin) shows the use of the three cost flow methods in 500 large U.S. companies.

The reasons companies adopt different inventory cost flow methods are varied, but they usually involve one of three factors: (1) income statement effects, (2) balance sheet effects, or (3) tax effects.

**Illustration 6-12**
Use of cost flow methods in major U.S. companies

### INCOME STATEMENT EFFECTS

To understand why companies might choose a particular cost flow method, let's examine the effects of the different cost flow assumptions on the financial statements of Houston Electronics. The condensed income statements in Illustration 6-13 assume that Houston sold its 550 units for $18,500, had operating expenses of $9,000, and is subject to an income tax rate of 30%.

| HOUSTON ELECTRONICS Condensed Income Statements | | | |
|---|---|---|---|
| | **FIFO** | **LIFO** | **Average-Cost** |
| Sales revenue | $18,500 | $18,500 | $18,500 |
| Beginning inventory | 1,000 | 1,000 | 1,000 |
| Purchases | 11,000 | 11,000 | 11,000 |
| Cost of goods available for sale | 12,000 | 12,000 | 12,000 |
| Ending inventory | 5,800 | 5,000 | 5,400 |
| Cost of goods sold | 6,200 | 7,000 | 6,600 |
| Gross profit | 12,300 | 11,500 | 11,900 |
| Operating expenses | 9,000 | 9,000 | 9,000 |
| Income before income taxes* | 3,300 | 2,500 | 2,900 |
| Income tax expense (30%) | 990 | 750 | 870 |
| Net income | $ 2,310 | $ 1,750 | $ 2,030 |

**Illustration 6-13**
Comparative effects of cost flow methods

*We are assuming that Houston Electronics is a corporation, and corporations are required to pay income taxes.

Note the cost of goods available for sale ($12,000) is the same under each of the three inventory cost flow methods. However, the ending inventories and the costs of goods sold are different. This difference is due to the unit costs that the company allocated to cost of goods sold and to ending inventory. Each dollar of difference in ending inventory results in a corresponding dollar difference in income before income taxes. For Houston, an $800 difference exists between FIFO and LIFO cost of goods sold.

In periods of changing prices, the cost flow assumption can have a significant impact on income and on evaluations based on income. In most instances, prices are rising (inflation). In a period of inflation, FIFO produces a higher net income because the lower unit costs of the first units purchased are matched against revenues. In a period of rising prices (as is the case in the Houston example), FIFO reports the highest net income ($2,310) and LIFO the lowest ($1,750); average-cost falls in the middle ($2,030). If prices are falling, the results from the use of FIFO and LIFO are reversed. FIFO will report the lowest net income and LIFO the highest.

To management, higher net income is an advantage. It causes external users to view the company more favorably. In addition, management bonuses, if based on net income, will be higher. Therefore, when prices are rising (which is usually the case), companies tend to prefer FIFO because it results in higher net income.

Some argue that the use of LIFO in a period of inflation enables the company to avoid reporting **paper** (or **phantom**) **profit** as economic gain. To illustrate, assume that Kralik Company buys 200 units of a product at $20 per unit on January 10 and 200 more on December 31 at $24 each. During the year, Kralik sells 200 units at $30 each. Illustration 6-14 shows the results under FIFO and LIFO.

| | FIFO | LIFO |
|---|---|---|
| Sales revenue (200 × $30) | $6,000 | $6,000 |
| **Cost of goods sold** | 4,000 (200 × $20) | 4,800 (200 × $24) |
| Gross profit | $2,000 | $1,200 |

**Illustration 6-14**
Income statement effects compared

Under LIFO, Kralik Company has recovered the current replacement cost ($4,800) of the units sold. Thus, the gross profit in economic terms is real. However, under FIFO, the company has recovered only the January 10 cost ($4,000). To replace the units sold, it must reinvest $800 (200 × $4) of the gross profit. Thus, $800 of the gross profit is said to be phantom or illusory. As a result, reported net income is also overstated in real terms.

### BALANCE SHEET EFFECTS

A major advantage of the FIFO method is that in a period of inflation, the costs allocated to ending inventory will approximate their current cost. For example, for Houston Electronics, 400 of the 450 units in the ending inventory are costed under FIFO at the higher November 27 unit cost of $13.

Conversely, a major shortcoming of the LIFO method is that in a period of inflation, the costs allocated to ending inventory may be significantly understated in terms of current cost. The understatement becomes greater over prolonged periods of inflation if the inventory includes goods purchased in one or more prior accounting periods. For example, Caterpillar has used LIFO for more than 50 years. Its balance sheet shows ending inventory of $14,544 million. But the inventory's actual current cost if FIFO had been used is $16,966 million.

### TAX EFFECTS

**Helpful Hint** A tax rule, often referred to as the *LIFO conformity rule*, requires that if companies use LIFO for tax purposes they must also use it for financial reporting purposes. This means that if a company chooses the LIFO method to reduce its tax bills, it will also have to report lower net income in its financial statements.

We have seen that both inventory on the balance sheet and net income on the income statement are higher when companies use FIFO in a period of inflation. Yet, many companies have selected LIFO. Why? The reason is that LIFO results in the lowest income taxes (because of lower net income) during times of rising prices. For example, at Houston Electronics, income taxes are $750 under LIFO, compared to $990 under FIFO. The tax savings of $240 makes more cash available for use in the business.

## Using Inventory Cost Flow Methods Consistently

Whatever cost flow method a company chooses, it should use that method consistently from one accounting period to another. This approach is often referred to as the **consistency concept**, which means that a company uses the same accounting principles and methods from year to year. Consistent application enhances the comparability of financial statements over successive time periods. In contrast, using the FIFO method one year and the LIFO method the next year would make it difficult to compare the net incomes of the two years.

Although consistent application is preferred, it does not mean that a company may never change its inventory costing method. When a company adopts a different method, it should disclose in the financial statements the change and its effects on net income. Illustration 6-15 shows a typical disclosure, using information from recent financial statements of Quaker Oats (now a unit of PepsiCo).

**Illustration 6-15**
Disclosure of change in cost flow method

| Real World | QUAKER OATS |
|---|---|
| | Notes to the Financial Statements |

**Note 1:**  Effective July 1, the Company adopted the LIFO cost flow assumption for valuing the majority of U.S. Grocery Products inventories. The Company believes that the use of the LIFO method better matches current costs with current revenues. The effect of this change on the current year was to decrease net income by $16.0 million.

## INTERNATIONAL INSIGHT

### Is LIFO Fair?

ExxonMobil Corporation, like many U.S. companies, uses LIFO to value its inventory for financial reporting and tax purposes. In one recent year, this resulted in a cost of goods sold figure that was $5.6 billion higher than under FIFO. By increasing cost of goods sold, ExxonMobil reduces net income, which reduces taxes. Critics say that LIFO provides an unfair "tax dodge." As Congress looks for more sources of tax revenue, some lawmakers favor the elimination of LIFO. Supporters of LIFO argue that the method is conceptually sound because it matches current costs with current revenues. In addition, they point out that this matching provides protection against inflation.

International accounting standards do not allow the use of LIFO. Because of this, the net income of foreign oil companies such as BP and Royal Dutch Shell are not directly comparable to U.S. companies, which makes analysis difficult.

*Source:* David Reilly, "Big Oil's Accounting Methods Fuel Criticism," *Wall Street Journal* (August 8, 2006), p. C1.

**?** What are the arguments for and against the use of LIFO? (See page 324.)

## Lower-of-Cost-or-Market

The value of inventory for companies selling high-technology or fashion goods can drop very quickly due to changes in technology or fashions. These circumstances sometimes call for inventory valuation methods other than those presented so far. For example, at one time purchasing managers at Ford decided to make a large purchase of palladium, a precious metal used in vehicle emission devices. They made this purchase because they feared a future shortage. The shortage did not materialize, and by the end of the year the price of palladium had plummeted. Ford's inventory was then worth $1 billion less than its original cost. Do you think Ford's inventory should have been stated at cost, in accordance with the historical cost principle, or at its lower replacement cost?

> **LEARNING OBJECTIVE 4**
>
> Explain the lower-of-cost-or-market basis of accounting for inventories.

As you probably reasoned, this situation requires a departure from the cost basis of accounting. This is done by valuing the inventory at the **lower-of-cost-or-market (LCM)** in the period in which the price decline occurs. LCM is a basis whereby inventory is stated at the lower of either its cost or market value as determined by current replacement cost. LCM is an example of the accounting convention of **conservatism**. Conservatism means that the approach adopted among accounting alternatives is the method that is least likely to overstate assets and net income.

> **International Note**
>
> Under U.S. GAAP, companies cannot reverse inventory write-downs if inventory increases in value in subsequent periods. IFRS permits companies to reverse write-downs in some circumstances.

Companies apply LCM to the items in inventory after they have used one of the cost flow methods (specific identification, FIFO, LIFO, or average-cost) to determine cost. Under the LCM basis, market is defined as **current replacement cost**, not selling price. For a merchandising company, current replacement cost is the cost of purchasing the same goods at the present time from the usual suppliers in the usual quantities. Current replacement cost is used because a decline in the replacement cost of an item usually leads to a decline in the selling price of the item.

To illustrate the application of LCM, assume that Ken Tuckie TV has the following lines of merchandise with costs and market values as indicated. LCM produces the results shown in Illustration 6-16 (page 290). Note that the amounts shown in the final column are the lower-of-cost-or-market amounts for each item.

**Illustration 6-16**
Computation of lower-of-cost-or-market

|  | Cost | Market | Lower-of-Cost-or-Market |
|---|---|---|---|
| Flat-screen TVs | $60,000 | $55,000 | $  55,000 |
| Satellite radios | 45,000 | 52,000 | 45,000 |
| DVD recorders | 48,000 | 45,000 | 45,000 |
| DVDs | 15,000 | 14,000 | 14,000 |
| Total inventory |  |  | $159,000 |

## Inventory Errors

**LEARNING OBJECTIVE    5**

**Indicate the effects of inventory errors on the financial statements.**

Unfortunately, errors occasionally occur in accounting for inventory. In some cases, errors are caused by failure to count or price the inventory correctly. In other cases, errors occur because companies do not properly recognize the transfer of legal title to goods that are in transit. When errors occur, they affect both the income statement and the balance sheet.

### Income Statement Effects

Under a periodic inventory system, both the beginning and ending inventories appear in the income statement. The ending inventory of one period automatically becomes the beginning inventory of the next period. Thus, inventory errors affect the computation of cost of goods sold and net income in two periods.

The effects on cost of goods sold can be computed by entering incorrect data in the formula in Illustration 6-17 and then substituting the correct data.

**Illustration 6-17**
Formula for cost of goods sold

| Beginning Inventory | + | Cost of Goods Purchased | − | Ending Inventory | = | Cost of Goods Sold |
|---|---|---|---|---|---|---|

If the error understates **beginning** inventory, cost of goods sold will be understated. If the error understates **ending** inventory, cost of goods sold will be overstated. Illustration 6-18 shows the effects of inventory errors on the current year's income statement.

**Illustration 6-18**
Effects of inventory errors on current year's income statement

| When Inventory Error: | Cost of Goods Sold Is: | Net Income Is: |
|---|---|---|
| Understates beginning inventory | Understated | Overstated |
| Overstates beginning inventory | Overstated | Understated |
| Understates ending inventory | Overstated | Understated |
| Overstates ending inventory | Understated | Overstated |

### Ethics Note

Inventory fraud increases during recessions. Such fraud includes pricing inventory at amounts in excess of its actual value, or claiming to have inventory when no inventory exists. Inventory fraud usually overstates ending inventory, thereby understating cost of goods sold and creating higher income.

So far, the effects of inventory errors are fairly straightforward. Now, though, comes the (at first) surprising part: An error in the ending inventory of the current period will have a **reverse effect on net income of the next accounting period**. Illustration 6-19 shows this effect. As you study the illustration, you will see that the reverse effect comes from the fact that understating ending inventory in 2013 results in understating beginning inventory in 2014 and overstating net income in 2014.

Over the two years, though, total net income is correct because the errors **offset each other**. Notice that total income using incorrect data is $35,000 ($22,000 + $13,000), which is the same as the total income of

## SAMPLE COMPANY
### Condensed Income Statements

| | 2013 Incorrect | 2013 Correct | 2014 Incorrect | 2014 Correct |
|---|---|---|---|---|
| Sales revenue | $80,000 | $80,000 | $90,000 | $90,000 |
| Beginning inventory | $20,000 | $20,000 | $12,000 | $15,000 |
| Cost of goods purchased | 40,000 | 40,000 | 68,000 | 68,000 |
| Cost of goods available for sale | 60,000 | 60,000 | 80,000 | 83,000 |
| Ending inventory | 12,000 | 15,000 | 23,000 | 23,000 |
| Cost of goods sold | 48,000 | 45,000 | 57,000 | 60,000 |
| Gross profit | 32,000 | 35,000 | 33,000 | 30,000 |
| Operating expenses | 10,000 | 10,000 | 20,000 | 20,000 |
| Net income | $22,000 | $25,000 | $13,000 | $10,000 |

$(3,000)
Net income understated

$3,000
Net income overstated

**The errors cancel. Thus the combined total income for the 2-year period is correct.**

**Illustration 6-19**
Effects of inventory errors on two years' income statements

$35,000 ($25,000 + $10,000) using correct data. Also note in this example that an error in the beginning inventory does not result in a corresponding error in the ending inventory for that period. The correctness of the ending inventory depends entirely on the accuracy of taking and costing the inventory at the balance sheet date under the periodic inventory system.

## Balance Sheet Effects

Companies can determine the effect of ending inventory errors on the balance sheet by using the basic accounting equation: Assets = Liabilities + Owner's Equity. Errors in the ending inventory have the effects shown in Illustration 6-20.

**Illustration 6-20**
Effects of ending inventory errors on balance sheet

| Ending Inventory Error | Assets | Liabilities | Owner's Equity |
|---|---|---|---|
| Overstated | Overstated | No effect | Overstated |
| Understated | Understated | No effect | Understated |

The effect of an error in ending inventory on the subsequent period was shown in Illustration 6-19. Recall that if the error is not corrected, the combined total net income for the two periods would be correct. Thus, total owner's equity reported on the balance sheet at the end of 2014 will also be correct.

## > DO IT!

**LCM Basis; Inventory Errors**

(a) Tracy Company sells three different types of home heating stoves (gas, wood, and pellet). The cost and market value of its inventory of stoves are as follows.

| | Cost | Market |
|---|---|---|
| Gas | $ 84,000 | $ 79,000 |
| Wood | 250,000 | 280,000 |
| Pellet | 112,000 | 101,000 |

Determine the value of the company's inventory under the lower-of-cost-or-market approach.

**Solution**

The lowest value for each inventory type is gas $79,000, wood $250,000, and pellet $101,000. The total inventory value is the sum of these amounts, $430,000.

**(b)** Visual Company overstated its 2013 ending inventory by $22,000. Determine the impact this error has on ending inventory, cost of goods sold, and owner's equity in 2013 and 2014.

**Solution**

|  | 2013 | 2014 |
|---|---|---|
| Ending inventory | $22,000 overstated | No effect |
| Cost of goods sold | $22,000 understated | $22,000 overstated |
| Owner's equity | $22,000 overstated | No effect |

Related exercise material: **BE6-7, BE6-8, E6-9, E6-10, E6-11, E6-12, and DO IT! 6-3.**

✔ The Navigator

**Action Plan**

✔ Determine whether cost or market value is lower for each inventory type.

✔ Sum the lowest value of each inventory type to determine the total value of inventory.

**Action Plan**

✔ An ending inventory error in one period will have an equal and opposite effect on cost of goods sold and net income in the next period.

✔ After two years, the errors have offset each other.

# Statement Presentation and Analysis

## Presentation

As indicated in Chapter 5, inventory is classified in the balance sheet as a current asset immediately below receivables. In a multiple-step income statement, cost of goods sold is subtracted from sales. There also should be disclosure of (1) the major inventory classifications, (2) the basis of accounting (cost, or lower-of-cost-or-market), and (3) the cost method (FIFO, LIFO, or average-cost).

Wal-Mart Stores, Inc., for example, in its January 31, 2011, balance sheet reported inventories of $36,318 million under current assets. The accompanying notes to the financial statements, as shown in Illustration 6-21, disclosed the following information.

**Illustration 6-21**
Inventory disclosures by Wal-Mart

**WAL-MART STORES, INC.**
Notes to the Financial Statements

**Note 1. Summary of Significant Accounting Policies**

**Inventories**

The Company values inventories at the lower of cost or market as determined primarily by the retail method of accounting, using the last-in, first-out ("LIFO") method for substantially all of the WalMart U.S. segment's merchandise inventories. The retail method of accounting results in inventory being valued at the lower of cost or market since permanent markdowns are currently taken as a reduction of the retail value of inventory. The Sam's Club segment's merchandise is valued based on the weighted-average cost using the LIFO method. Inventories for the Walmart International operations are primarily valued by the retail method of accounting and are stated using the first-in, first-out ("FIFO") method. At January 31, 2011 and 2010, our inventories valued at LIFO approximate those inventories as if they were valued at FIFO.

As indicated in this note, Wal-Mart values its inventories at the lower-of-cost-or-market using LIFO and FIFO.

## Analysis

The amount of inventory carried by a company has significant economic consequences. And inventory management is a double-edged sword that requires constant attention. On the one hand, management wants to have a great variety and quantity on hand so that customers have a wide selection and items are always in stock. But, such a policy may incur high carrying costs (e.g., investment, storage, insurance, obsolescence, and damage). On the other hand, low inventory levels lead to stock-outs and lost sales. Common ratios used to manage and evaluate inventory levels are inventory turnover and a related measure, days in inventory.

**Inventory turnover** measures the number of times on average the inventory is sold during the period. Its purpose is to measure the liquidity of the inventory. The inventory turnover is computed by dividing cost of goods sold by the average inventory during the period. Unless seasonal factors are significant, average inventory can be computed from the beginning and ending inventory balances. For example, Wal-Mart reported in its 2011 annual report a beginning inventory of $32,713 million, an ending inventory of $36,318 million, and cost of goods sold for the year ended January 31, 2011, of $315,287 million. The inventory turnover formula and computation for Wal-Mart are shown below.

> **LEARNING OBJECTIVE 6**
> Compute and interpret the inventory turnover.

| Cost of Goods Sold | ÷ | Average Inventory | = | Inventory Turnover |
|---|---|---|---|---|
| $315,287 | ÷ | $\dfrac{\$36,318 + \$32,713}{2}$ | = | 9.1 times |

**Illustration 6-22**
Inventory turnover formula and computation for Wal-Mart

A variant of the inventory turnover is **days in inventory**. This measures the average number of days inventory is held. It is calculated as 365 divided by the inventory turnover. For example, Wal-Mart's inventory turnover of 9.1 times divided into 365 is approximately 40.1 days. This is the approximate time that it takes a company to sell the inventory once it arrives at the store.

There are typical levels of inventory in every industry. Companies that are able to keep their inventory at lower levels and higher turnovers and still satisfy customer needs are the most successful.

## ACCOUNTING ACROSS THE ORGANIZATION

### Too Many TVs or Too Few?

Financial analysts closely monitored the inventory management practices of companies during the recent recession. For example, some analysts following Sony expressed concern because the company built up its inventory of televisions in an attempt to sell 25 million liquid crystal display (LCD) TVs—a 60% increase over the prior year. A year earlier, Sony had cut its inventory levels so that its quarterly days in inventory was down to 38 days, compared to 61 days for the same quarter a year before that. But now, as a result of its inventory build-up, days in inventory rose to 59 days. While management was saying that it didn't think that Sony's inventory levels were now too high, analysts were concerned that the company would have to engage in very heavy discounting in order to sell off its inventory. Analysts noted that the losses from discounting can be "punishing."

*Source:* Daisuke Wakabayashi, "Sony Pledges to Corral Inventory," *Wall Street Journal* Online (November 2, 2010).

? For Sony, what are the advantages and disadvantages of having a low days in inventory measure? (See page 324.)

## > DO IT!

### Inventory Turnover

Early in 2014, Westmoreland Company switched to a just-in-time inventory system. Its sales revenue, cost of goods sold, and inventory amounts for 2013 and 2014 are shown below.

|  | 2013 | 2014 |
|---|---|---|
| Sales revenue | $2,000,000 | $1,800,000 |
| Cost of goods sold | 1,000,000 | 910,000 |
| Beginning inventory | 290,000 | 210,000 |
| Ending inventory | 210,000 | 50,000 |

Determine the inventory turnover and days in inventory for 2013 and 2014. Discuss the changes in the amount of inventory, the inventory turnover and days in inventory, and the amount of sales across the two years.

### Solution

#### Action Plan

✔ To find the inventory turnover, divide cost of goods sold by average inventory.

✔ To determine days in inventory, divide 365 days by the inventory turnover.

✔ Just-in-time inventory reduces the amount of inventory on hand, which reduces carrying costs. Reducing inventory levels by too much has potential negative implications for sales.

|  | 2013 | 2014 |
|---|---|---|
| Inventory turnover | $\dfrac{\$1,000,000}{(\$290,000 + \$210,000)/2} = 4$ | $\dfrac{\$910,000}{(\$210,000 + \$50,000)/2} = 7$ |
| Days in inventory | $365 \div 4 = 91.3$ days | $365 \div 7 = 52.1$ days |

The company experienced a very significant decline in its ending inventory as a result of the just-in-time inventory. This decline improved its inventory turnover and its days in inventory. However, its sales declined by 10%. It is possible that this decline was caused by the dramatic reduction in the amount of inventory that was on hand, which increased the likelihood of "stock-outs." To determine the optimal inventory level, management must weigh the benefits of reduced inventory against the potential lost sales caused by stock-outs.

Related exercise material: **BE6-9, E6-13, E6-14, and DO IT!** 6-4.

 **The Navigator**

## > Comprehensive DO IT! 1

Gerald D. Englehart Company has the following inventory, purchases, and sales data for the month of March.

| Inventory: | March 1 | 200 units @ $4.00 | $  800 |
|---|---|---|---|
| Purchases: |  |  |  |
|  | March 10 | 500 units @ $4.50 | 2,250 |
|  | March 20 | 400 units @ $4.75 | 1,900 |
|  | March 30 | 300 units @ $5.00 | 1,500 |
| Sales: |  |  |  |
|  | March 15 | 500 units |  |
|  | March 25 | 400 units |  |

The physical inventory count on March 31 shows 500 units on hand.

**Instructions**

Under a **periodic inventory system**, determine the cost of inventory on hand at March 31 and the cost of goods sold for March under (a) FIFO, (b) LIFO, and (c) average-cost.

## Solution to Comprehensive DO IT! 1

**Action Plan**

✔ Compute the total goods available for sale, in both units and dollars.

✔ Compute the cost of ending inventory under the periodic FIFO method by allocating to the units on hand the **latest costs**.

✔ Compute the cost of ending inventory under the periodic LIFO method by allocating to the units on hand the **earliest costs**.

✔ Compute the cost of ending inventory under the periodic average-cost method by allocating to the units on hand a **weighted-average cost**.

The cost of goods available for sale is $6,450, as follows.

| | | | |
|---|---|---|---|
| Inventory: | | 200 units @ $4.00 | $ 800 |
| Purchases: | | | |
| | March 10 | 500 units @ $4.50 | 2,250 |
| | March 20 | 400 units @ $4.75 | 1,900 |
| | March 30 | 300 units @ $5.00 | 1,500 |
| Total: | | 1,400 | $6,450 |

Under a **periodic inventory system**, the cost of goods sold under each cost flow method is as follows.

### FIFO Method

Ending inventory:

| Date | Units | Unit Cost | Total Cost | |
|---|---|---|---|---|
| March 30 | 300 | $5.00 | $1,500 | |
| March 20 | 200 | 4.75 | 950 | $2,450 |

Cost of goods sold: $6,450 − $2,450 = $4,000

### LIFO Method

Ending inventory:

| Date | Units | Unit Cost | Total Cost | |
|---|---|---|---|---|
| March 1 | 200 | $4.00 | $ 800 | |
| March 10 | 300 | 4.50 | 1,350 | $2,150 |

Cost of goods sold: $6,450 − $2,150 = $4,300

### Average-Cost Method

Average unit cost: $6,450 ÷ 1,400 = $4.607

Ending inventory: 500 × $4.607 = $2,303.50

Cost of goods sold: $6,450 − $2,303.50 = $4,146.50

✔ The Navigator

✔ The Navigator

# SUMMARY OF LEARNING OBJECTIVES

**1 Determine how to classify inventory and inventory quantities.** Merchandisers need only one inventory classification, merchandise inventory, to describe the different items that make up total inventory. Manufacturers, on the other hand, usually classify inventory into three categories: finished goods, work in process, and raw materials. To determine inventory quantities, manufacturers (1) take a physical inventory of goods on hand and (2) determine the ownership of goods in transit or on consignment.

**2 Explain the accounting for inventories and apply the inventory cost flow methods.** The primary basis of accounting for inventories is cost. Cost of goods available for sale includes (a) cost of beginning inventory and (b) cost of goods purchased. The inventory cost flow methods are specific identification and three assumed cost flow methods—FIFO, LIFO, and average-cost.

**3 Explain the financial effects of the inventory cost flow assumptions.** Companies may allocate the cost of goods available for sale to cost of goods sold and ending inventory by specific identification or by a method based on an assumed cost flow. When prices are rising, the first-in, first-out (FIFO) method results in lower cost of goods sold and higher net income than the other methods. The reverse is true when prices are falling. In the balance sheet, FIFO results in an ending inventory that is closest to current value. Inventory under LIFO is the farthest from current value. LIFO results in the lowest income taxes.

**4 Explain the lower-of-cost-or-market basis of accounting for inventories.** Companies use the lower-of-cost-or-market (LCM) basis when the current replacement cost (market) is less than cost. Under LCM, companies recognize the loss in the period in which the price decline occurs.

**5 Indicate the effects of inventory errors on the financial statements.** In the income statement of the current year: (a) An error in beginning inventory will have a reverse effect on net income. (b) An error in ending inventory will have a similar effect on net income. In the following period, its effect on net income for that period is reversed, and total net income for the two years will be correct.

In the balance sheet: Ending inventory errors will have the same effect on total assets and total owner's equity and no effect on liabilities.

**6 Compute and interpret the inventory turnover.** The inventory turnover is cost of goods sold divided by average inventory. To convert it to average days in inventory, divide 365 days by the inventory turnover.

## GLOSSARY

**Average-cost method** Inventory costing method that uses the weighted-average unit cost to allocate to ending inventory and cost of goods sold the cost of goods available for sale. (p. 285).

**Consigned goods** Goods held for sale by one party although ownership of the goods is retained by another party. (p. 279).

**Consistency concept** Dictates that a company use the same accounting principles and methods from year to year. (p. 288).

**Current replacement cost** The current cost to replace an inventory item. (p. 289).

**Days in inventory** Measure of the average number of days inventory is held; calculated as 365 divided by inventory turnover. (p. 293).

**Finished goods inventory** Manufactured items that are completed and ready for sale. (p. 276).

**First-in, first-out (FIFO) method** Inventory costing method that assumes that the costs of the earliest goods purchased are the first to be recognized as cost of goods sold. (p. 282).

**FOB (free on board) destination** Freight terms indicating that ownership of the goods remains with the seller until the goods reach the buyer. (p. 278).

**FOB (free on board) shipping point** Freight terms indicating that ownership of the goods passes to the buyer when the public carrier accepts the goods from the seller. (p. 278).

**Inventory turnover** A ratio that measures the number of times on average the inventory sold during the period; computed by dividing cost of goods sold by the average inventory during the period. (p. 293).

**Just-in-time (JIT) inventory** Inventory system in which companies manufacture or purchase goods just in time for use. (p. 276).

**Last-in, first-out (LIFO) method** Inventory costing method that assumes the costs of the latest units purchased are the first to be allocated to cost of goods sold. (p. 284).

**Lower-of-cost-or-market (LCM)** A basis whereby inventory is stated at the lower of either its cost or its market value as determined by current replacement cost. (p. 289).

**Raw materials** Basic goods that will be used in production but have not yet been placed into production. (p. 276).

**Specific identification method** An actual physical flow costing method in which items still in inventory are specifically costed to arrive at the total cost of the ending inventory. (p. 281).

**Weighted-average unit cost** Average cost that is weighted by the number of units purchased at each unit cost. (p. 285).

**Work in process** That portion of manufactured inventory that has been placed into the production process but is not yet complete. (p. 276).

## APPENDIX 6A   Inventory Cost Flow Methods in Perpetual Inventory Systems

What inventory cost flow methods do companies employ if they use a perpetual inventory system? Simple—they can use any of the inventory cost flow methods described in the chapter. To illustrate the application of the three assumed cost flow methods (FIFO, LIFO, and average-cost), we will use the data shown in Illustration 6A-1 and in this chapter for Houston Electronics' Astro condensers.

**LEARNING OBJECTIVE   7**

Apply the inventory cost flow methods to perpetual inventory records.

**Illustration 6A-1**
Inventoriable units and costs

| HOUSTON ELECTRONICS | | | | | |
| Astro Condensers | | | | | |
| Date | Explanation | Units | Units Cost | Total Cost | Balance in Units |
| --- | --- | --- | --- | --- | --- |
| 1/1 | Beginning inventory | 100 | $10 | $ 1,000 | 100 |
| 4/15 | Purchases | 200 | 11 | 2,200 | 300 |
| 8/24 | Purchases | 300 | 12 | 3,600 | 600 |
| 9/10 | Sale | 550 | | | 50 |
| 11/27 | Purchases | 400 | 13 | 5,200 | 450 |
| | | | | $12,000 | |

### First-In, First-Out (FIFO)

Under perpetual FIFO, the company charges to cost of goods sold the cost of the earliest goods on hand **prior to each sale**. Therefore, the cost of goods sold on September 10 consists of the units on hand January 1 and the units purchased April 15 and August 24. Illustration 6A-2 shows the inventory under a FIFO method perpetual system.

**Illustration 6A-2**
Perpetual system—FIFO

| Date | Purchases | Cost of Goods Sold | Balance (in units and cost) |
| --- | --- | --- | --- |
| January 1 | | | (100 @ $10)   $ 1,000 |
| April 15 | (200 @ $11)   $2,200 | | (100 @ $10) <br> (200 @ $11) } $ 3,200 |
| August 24 | (300 @ $12)   $3,600 | | (100 @ $10) <br> (200 @ $11) } $ 6,800 <br> (300 @ $12) |
| September 10 | | (100 @ $10) <br> (200 @ $11) <br> (250 @ $12) <br> $6,200 | ( 50 @ $12)   $   600 |
| November 27 | (400 @ $13)   $5,200 | | ( 50 @ $12) <br> (400 @ $13) } $5,800 |

**Cost of goods sold**

**Ending inventory**

The ending inventory in this situation is $5,800, and the cost of goods sold is $6,200 [(100 @ $10) + (200 @ $11) + (250 @ $12)].

Compare Illustrations 6-6 (page 283) and 6A-2. You can see that the results under FIFO in a perpetual system are the **same as in a periodic system**. In both cases, the ending inventory is $5,800 and cost of goods sold is $6,200. Regardless of the system, the first costs in are the costs assigned to cost of goods sold.

## Last-In, First-Out (LIFO)

Under the LIFO method using a perpetual system, the company charges to cost of goods sold the cost of the most recent purchase prior to sale. Therefore, the cost of the goods sold on September 10 consists of all the units from the August 24 and April 15 purchases plus 50 of the units in beginning inventory. Illustration 6A-3 shows the computation of the ending inventory under the LIFO method.

**Illustration 6A-3**
Perpetual system—LIFO

| Date | Purchases | | Cost of Goods Sold | Balance (in units and cost) | |
|---|---|---|---|---|---|
| January 1 | | | | (100 @ $10) | $ 1,000 |
| April 15 | (200 @ $11) | $2,200 | | (100 @ $10)<br>(200 @ $11) | $ 3,200 |
| August 24 | (300 @ $12) | $3,600 | | (100 @ $10)<br>(200 @ $11)<br>(300 @ $12) | $ 6,800 |
| September 10 | | | (300 @ $12)<br>(200 @ $11)<br>( 50 @ $10) | (50 @ $10) | $  500 |
| **Cost of goods sold** | | | **$6,300** | | |
| November 27 | (400 @ $13) | $5,200 | | (50 @ $10)<br>(400 @ $13) | $5,700 |
| **Ending inventory** | | | | | |

The use of LIFO in a perpetual system will usually produce cost allocations that differ from those using LIFO in a periodic system. In a perpetual system, the company allocates the latest units purchased **prior to each sale** to cost of goods sold. In contrast, in a periodic system, the latest units purchased **during the period** are allocated to cost of goods sold. Thus, when a purchase is made after the last sale, the LIFO periodic system will apply this purchase to the previous sale. Compare Illustrations 6-8 (page 284) and 6A-3. Illustration 6-8 shows that the 400 units at $13 purchased on November 27 applied to the sale of 550 units on September 10. Under the LIFO perpetual system in Illustration 6A-3, the 400 units at $13 purchased on November 27 are all applied to the ending inventory.

The ending inventory in this LIFO perpetual illustration is $5,700, and cost of goods sold is $6,300, as compared to the LIFO periodic Illustration 6-8 (on page 284) where the ending inventory is $5,000 and cost of goods sold is $7,000.

## Average-Cost

The average-cost method in a perpetual inventory system is called the **moving-average method**. Under this method, the company computes a new average **after each purchase**, by dividing the cost of goods available for sale by the units on hand. The average cost is then applied to (1) the units sold, to determine the cost of goods sold, and (2) the remaining units on hand, to determine the ending inventory amount. Illustration 6A-4 shows the application of the moving-average cost method by Houston Electronics.

**Illustration 6A-4**
Perpetual system—average-cost method

| Date | Purchases | | Cost of Goods Sold | Balance (in units and cost) | |
|---|---|---|---|---|---|
| January 1 | | | | (100 @ $10) | $ 1,000 |
| April 15 | (200 @ $11) | $2,200 | | (300 @ $10.667) | $ 3,200 |
| August 24 | (300 @ $12) | $3,600 | | (600 @ $11.333) | $ 6,800 |
| September 10 | | | (550 @ $11.333) | (50 @ $11.333) | $   567 |
| **Cost of goods sold** | | | **$6,233** | | |
| November 27 | (400 @ $13) | $5,200 | | (450 @ $12.816) | **$5,767** |
| **Ending inventory** | | | | | |

As indicated, Houston Electronics computes **a new average each time it makes a purchase**. On April 15, after it buys 200 units for $2,200, a total of 300 units costing $3,200 ($1,000 + $2,200) are on hand. The average unit cost is $10.667 ($3,200 ÷ 300). On August 24, after Houston Electronics buys 300 units for $3,600, a total of 600 units costing $6,800 ($1,000 + $2,200 + $3,600) are on hand, at an average cost per unit of $11.333 ($6,800 ÷ 600). Houston Electronics uses this unit cost of $11.333 in costing sales until it makes another purchase, when the company computes a new unit cost. Accordingly, the unit cost of the 550 units sold on September 10 is $11.333, and the total cost of goods sold is $6,233. On November 27, following the purchase of 400 units for $5,200, there are 450 units on hand costing $5,767 ($567 + $5,200) with a new average cost of $12.816 ($5,767 ÷ 450).

Compare this moving-average cost under the perpetual inventory system to Illustration 6-11 (on page 285) showing the average-cost method under a periodic inventory system.

## > Comprehensive DO IT! 2

**Comprehensive DO IT!** 1 on page 294 showed cost of goods sold computations under a periodic inventory system. Now let's assume that Gerald D. Englehart Company uses a perpetual inventory system. The company has the same inventory, purchases, and sales data for the month of March as shown earlier:

| | | | |
|---|---|---|---|
| Inventory: | March 1 | 200 units @ $4.00 | $ 800 |
| Purchases: | March 10 | 500 units @ $4.50 | 2,250 |
| | March 20 | 400 units @ $4.75 | 1,900 |
| | March 30 | 300 units @ $5.00 | 1,500 |
| Sales: | March 15 | 500 units | |
| | March 25 | 400 units | |

The physical inventory count on March 31 shows 500 units on hand.

### Instructions

Under a **perpetual inventory system**, determine the cost of inventory on hand at March 31 and the cost of goods sold for March under (a) FIFO, (b) LIFO, and (c) moving-average cost.

**Action Plan**

✔ Compute the cost of goods sold under the perpetual FIFO method by allocating to the goods sold the **earliest** cost of goods purchased.

✔ Compute the cost of goods sold under the perpetual LIFO method by allocating to the goods sold the **latest** cost of goods purchased.

✔ Compute the cost of goods sold under the perpetual average-cost method by allocating to the goods sold a **moving-average** cost.

### Solution to Comprehensive DO IT! 2

The cost of goods available for sale is $6,450, as follows.

| | | | |
|---|---|---|---|
| Inventory: | | 200 units @ $4.00 | $ 800 |
| Purchases: | March 10 | 500 units @ $4.50 | 2,250 |
| | March 20 | 400 units @ $4.75 | 1,900 |
| | March 30 | 300 units @ $5.00 | 1,500 |
| Total: | | 1,400 | $6,450 |

Under a **perpetual inventory system**, the cost of goods sold under each cost flow method is as follows.

**FIFO Method**

| Date | Purchases | Cost of Goods Sold | Balance |
|---|---|---|---|
| March 1 | | | (200 @ $4.00)  $ 800 |
| March 10 | (500 @ $4.50)  $2,250 | | (200 @ $4.00) $3,050 (500 @ $4.50) |

| Date | Purchases | | Cost of Goods Sold | | Balance | |
|---|---|---|---|---|---|---|
| March 15 | | | (200 @ \$4.00) | | | |
| | | | (300 @ \$4.50) | | (200 @ \$4.50) | \$ 900 |
| | | | $2,150 | | | |
| March 20 | (400 @ \$4.75) | \$1,900 | | | (200 @ \$4.50) ⎫ (400 @ \$4.75) ⎬ | \$2,800 |
| March 25 | | | (200 @ \$4.50) | | | |
| | | | (200 @ \$4.75) | | (200 @ \$4.75) | \$ 950 |
| | | | $1,850 | | | |
| March 30 | (300 @ \$5.00) | \$1,500 | | | (200 @ \$4.75) ⎫ (300 @ \$5.00) ⎬ | \$2,450 |
| | Ending inventory \$2,450 | | Cost of goods sold: \$2,150 + \$1,850 = \$4,000 | | | |

### LIFO Method

| Date | Purchases | | Cost of Goods Sold | | Balance | |
|---|---|---|---|---|---|---|
| March 1 | | | | | (200 @ \$4.00) | \$ 800 |
| March 10 | (500 @ \$4.50) | \$2,250 | | | (200 @ \$4.00) ⎫ (500 @ \$4.50) ⎬ | \$3,050 |
| March 15 | | | (500 @ \$4.50) | \$2,250 | (200 @ \$4.00) | \$ 800 |
| March 20 | (400 @ \$4.75) | \$1,900 | | | (200 @ \$4.00) ⎫ (400 @ \$4.75) ⎬ | \$2,700 |
| March 25 | | | (400 @ \$4.75) | \$1,900 | (200 @ \$4.00) | \$ 800 |
| March 30 | (300 @ \$5.00) | \$1,500 | | | (200 @ \$4.00) ⎫ (300 @ \$5.00) ⎬ | \$2,300 |
| | Ending inventory \$2,300 | | Cost of goods sold: \$2,250 + \$1,900 = \$4,150 | | | |

### Moving-Average Cost Method

| Date | Purchases | | Cost of Goods Sold | | Balance | |
|---|---|---|---|---|---|---|
| March 1 | | | | | (200 @ \$ 4.00) | \$ 800 |
| March 10 | (500 @ \$4.50) | \$2,250 | | | (700 @ \$4.357) | \$3,050 |
| March 15 | | | (500 @ \$4.357) | \$2,179 | (200 @ \$4.357) | \$ 871 |
| March 20 | (400 @ \$4.75) | \$1,900 | | | (600 @ \$4.618) | \$2,771 |
| March 25 | | | (400 @ \$4.618) | \$1,847 | (200 @ \$4.618) | \$ 924 |
| March 30 | (300 @ \$5.00) | \$1,500 | | | (500 @ \$4.848) | \$2,424 |
| | Ending inventory \$2,424 | | Cost of goods sold: \$2,179 + \$1,847 = \$4,026 | | | |

✔ The Navigator

## SUMMARY OF LEARNING OBJECTIVE FOR APPENDIX 6A

✔ The Navigator

**7 Apply the inventory cost flow methods to perpetual inventory records.** Under FIFO and a perpetual inventory system, companies charge to cost of goods sold the cost of the earliest goods on hand prior to each sale. Under LIFO and a perpetual system, companies charge to cost of goods sold the cost of the most recent purchase prior to sale. Under the moving-average (average cost) method and a perpetual system, companies compute a new average cost after each purchase.

## APPENDIX 6B  Estimating Inventories

**LEARNING OBJECTIVE 8**

**Describe the two methods of estimating inventories.**

In the chapter, we assumed that a company would be able to physically count its inventory. What if it cannot? What if the inventory were destroyed by fire or flood, for example? In that case, the company would use an estimate.

Two circumstances explain why companies sometimes estimate inventories. First, a casualty such as fire, flood, or earthquake may make it impossible to take a physical inventory. Second, managers may want monthly or quarterly financial statements, but a physical inventory is taken only annually. The need for estimating inventories occurs primarily with a periodic inventory system because of the absence of perpetual inventory records.

There are two widely used methods of estimating inventories: (1) the gross profit method, and (2) the retail inventory method.

## Gross Profit Method

The **gross profit method** estimates the cost of ending inventory by applying a gross profit rate to net sales. This method is relatively simple but effective. Accountants, auditors, and managers frequently use the gross profit method to test the reasonableness of the ending inventory amount. It will detect large errors.

To use this method, a company needs to know its net sales, cost of goods available for sale, and gross profit rate. The company then can estimate its gross profit for the period. Illustration 6B-1 shows the formulas for using the gross profit method.

| | | | | | | |
|---|---|---|---|---|---|---|
| **Step 1:** | **Net Sales** | − | **Estimated Gross Profit** | = | **Estimated Cost of Goods Sold** | |
| **Step 2:** | **Cost of Goods Available for Sale** | − | **Estimated Cost of Goods Sold** | = | **Estimated Cost of Ending Inventory** | |

**Illustration 6B-1**
Gross profit method formulas

To illustrate, assume that Kishwaukee Company wishes to prepare an income statement for the month of January. Its records show net sales of $200,000, beginning inventory $40,000, and cost of goods purchased $120,000. In the preceding year, the company realized a 30% gross profit rate. It expects to earn the same rate this year. Given these facts and assumptions, Kishwaukee can compute the estimated cost of the ending inventory at January 31 under the gross profit method as follows.

**Illustration 6B-2**
Example of gross profit method

**Step 1:**

| | |
|---|---|
| Net sales | $ 200,000 |
| Less: Estimated gross profit (30% × $200,000) | 60,000 |
| **Estimated cost of goods sold** | **$140,000** |

**Step 2:**

| | |
|---|---|
| Beginning inventory | $ 40,000 |
| Cost of goods purchased | 120,000 |
| Cost of goods available for sale | 160,000 |
| Less: Estimated cost of goods sold | 140,000 |
| **Estimated cost of ending inventory** | **$ 20,000** |

The gross profit method is based on the assumption that the gross profit rate will remain constant. But, it may not remain constant, due to a change in merchandising policies or in market conditions. In such cases, the company should adjust the rate to reflect current operating conditions. In some cases, companies can obtain a more accurate estimate by applying this method on a department or product-line basis.

Note that companies should not use the gross profit method to prepare financial statements at the end of the year. These statements should be based on a physical inventory count.

## Retail Inventory Method

A retail store such as Home Depot, Ace Hardware, or Wal-Mart has thousands of different types of merchandise at low unit costs. In such cases, it is difficult and time-consuming to apply unit costs to inventory quantities. An alternative is to use the **retail inventory method** to estimate the cost of inventory. Most retail companies can establish a relationship between cost and sales price. The company then applies the cost-to-retail percentage to the ending inventory at retail prices to determine inventory at cost.

Under the retail inventory method, a company's records must show both the cost and retail value of the goods available for sale. Illustration 6B-3 presents the formulas for using the retail inventory method.

**Illustration 6B-3**
Retail inventory method formulas

| | | | | | | |
|---|---|---|---|---|---|---|
| Step 1: | Goods Available for Sale at Retail | − | Net Sales | = | Ending Inventory at Retail | |
| Step 2: | Goods Available for Sale at Cost | ÷ | Goods Available for Sale at Retail | = | Cost-to-Retail Ratio | |
| Step 3: | Ending Inventory at Retail | × | Cost-to-Retail Ratio | = | Estimated Cost of Ending Inventory | |

We can demonstrate the logic of the retail method by using unit-cost data. Assume that Ortiz Inc. has marked 10 units purchased at $7 to sell for $10 per unit. Thus, the cost-to-retail ratio is 70% ($70 ÷ $100). If four units remain unsold, their retail value is $40 (4 × $10), and their cost is $28 ($40 × 70%). This amount agrees with the total cost of goods on hand on a per unit basis (4 × $7).

Illustration 6B-4 shows application of the retail method for Valley West. Note that it is not necessary to take a physical inventory to determine the estimated cost of goods on hand at any given time.

**Illustration 6B-4**
Application of retail inventory method

| | At Cost | At Retail |
|---|---|---|
| Beginning inventory | $14,000 | $ 21,500 |
| Goods purchased | 61,000 | 78,500 |
| Goods available for sale | $75,000 | 100,000 |
| Less: Net sales | | 70,000 |
| Step (1) Ending inventory at retail = | | $ 30,000 |

Step (2) Cost-to-retail ratio = $75,000 ÷ $100,000 = 75%
Step (3) Estimated cost of ending inventory = $30,000 × 75% = **$22,500**

**Helpful Hint** In determining inventory at retail, companies use selling prices of the units.

The retail inventory method also facilitates taking a physical inventory at the end of the year. Valley West can value the goods on hand at the prices marked on the merchandise, and then apply the cost-to-retail ratio to the goods on hand at retail to determine the ending inventory at cost.

The major disadvantage of the retail method is that it is an averaging technique. Thus, it may produce an incorrect inventory valuation if the mix of the ending inventory is not representative of the mix in the goods available for sale. Assume, for example, that the cost-to-retail ratio of 75% for Valley West consists of equal proportions of inventory items that have cost-to-retail ratios of 70%, 75%, and 80%. If the ending inventory contains only items with a 70% ratio, an incorrect inventory cost will result. Companies can minimize this problem by applying the retail method on a department or product-line basis.

## SUMMARY OF LEARNING OBJECTIVE FOR APPENDIX 6B

**8 Describe the two methods of estimating inventories.** The two methods of estimating inventories are the gross profit method and the retail inventory method. Under the gross profit method, companies apply a gross profit rate to net sales to determine estimated cost of goods sold. They then subtract estimated cost of goods sold from cost of goods available for sale to determine the estimated cost of the ending inventory.

Under the retail inventory method, companies compute a cost-to-retail ratio by dividing the cost of goods available for sale by the retail value of the goods available for sale. They then apply this ratio to the ending inventory at retail to determine the estimated cost of the ending inventory.

## GLOSSARY FOR APPENDIX 6B

**Gross profit method** A method for estimating the cost of the ending inventory by applying a gross profit rate to net sales and subtracting estimated cost of goods sold from cost of goods available for sale. (p. 301).

**Retail inventory method** A method for estimating the cost of the ending inventory by applying a cost-to-retail ratio to the ending inventory at retail. (p. 302).

 **Self-Test, Brief Exercises, Exercises, Problem Set A, and many more components are available for practice in *WileyPLUS*.**

*Note:** All asterisked Questions, Exercises, and Problems relate to material in the appendices to the chapter.

## SELF-TEST QUESTIONS

*Answers are on page 324.*

(LO 1)  **1.** Which of the following should **not** be included in the physical inventory of a company?
  **(a)** Goods held on consignment from another company.
  **(b)** Goods shipped on consignment to another company.
  **(c)** Goods in transit from another company shipped FOB shipping point.
  **(d)** None of the above.

(LO 1)  **2.** As a result of a thorough physical inventory, Railway Company determined that it had inventory worth $180,000 at December 31, 2014. This count did not take into consideration the following facts: Rogers Consignment store currently has goods worth $35,000 on its sales floor that belong to Railway but are being sold on consignment by Rogers. The selling price of these goods is $50,000. Railway purchased $13,000 of goods that were shipped on December 27, FOB destination, that will be received by Railway on January 3. Determine the correct amount of inventory that Railway should report.
  **(a)** $230,000.          **(c)** $228,000.
  **(b)** $215,000.          **(d)** $193,000.

**3.** Cost of goods available for sale consists of two elements: beginning inventory and (LO 2)
  **(a)** ending inventory.
  **(b)** cost of goods purchased.
  **(c)** cost of goods sold.
  **(d)** All of the above.

(LO 2)  **4.** Poppins Company has the following:

|  | Units | Unit Cost |
|---|---|---|
| Inventory, Jan. 1 | 8,000 | $11 |
| Purchase, June 19 | 13,000 | 12 |
| Purchase, Nov. 8 | 5,000 | 13 |

If Poppins has 9,000 units on hand at December 31, the cost of the ending inventory under FIFO is:

**(a)** $99,000.  **(c)** $113,000.
**(b)** $108,000.  **(d)** $117,000.

(LO 2)  **5.** Using the data in Question 4 above, the cost of the ending inventory under LIFO is:

**(a)** $113,000.  **(c)** $99,000.
**(b)** $108,000.  **(d)** $100,000.

(LO 2)  **6.** Hansel Electronics has the following:

|  | Units | Unit Cost |
|---|---|---|
| Inventory, Jan. 1 | 5,000 | $ 8 |
| Purchase, April 2 | 15,000 | $10 |
| Purchase, Aug. 28 | 20,000 | $12 |

If Hansel has 7,000 units on hand at December 31, the cost of ending inventory under the average-cost method is:

**(a)** $84,000.  **(c)** $56,000.
**(b)** $70,000.  **(d)** $75,250.

(LO 3)  **7.** In periods of rising prices, LIFO will produce:

**(a)** higher net income than FIFO.
**(b)** the same net income as FIFO.
**(c)** lower net income than FIFO.
**(d)** higher net income than average-cost.

(LO 3)  **8.** Factors that affect the selection of an inventory costing method do **not** include:

**(a)** tax effects.
**(b)** balance sheet effects.
**(c)** income statement effects.
**(d)** perpetual vs. periodic inventory system.

(LO 4)  **9.** Norton Company purchased 1,000 widgets and has 200 widgets in its ending inventory at a cost of $91 each and a current replacement cost of $80 each. The ending inventory under lower-of-cost-or-market is:

**(a)** $91,000.  **(c)** $18,200.
**(b)** $80,000.  **(d)** $16,000.

(LO 5)  **10.** Falk Company's ending inventory is understated $4,000. The effects of this error on the current year's cost of goods sold and net income, respectively, are:

**(a)** understated, overstated.
**(b)** overstated, understated.
**(c)** overstated, overstated.
**(d)** understated, understated.

**11.** Pauline Company overstated its inventory by $15,000 (LO 4) at December 31, 2013. It did not correct the error in 2013 or 2014. As a result, Pauline's owner's equity was:

**(a)** overstated at December 31, 2013, and understated at December 31, 2014.
**(b)** overstated at December 31, 2013, and properly stated at December 31, 2014.
**(c)** understated at December 31, 2013, and understated at December 31, 2014.
**(d)** overstated at December 31, 2013, and overstated at December 31, 2014.

**12.** Santana Company had beginning inventory of (LO 5) $80,000, ending inventory of $110,000, cost of goods sold of $285,000, and sales of $475,000. Santana's days in inventory is:

**(a)** 73 days.  **(c)** 102.5 days.
**(b)** 121.7 days.  **(d)** 84.5 days.

**13.** Which of these would cause the inventory turnover to (LO 6) increase the most?

**(a)** Increasing the amount of inventory on hand.
**(b)** Keeping the amount of inventory on hand constant but increasing sales.
**(c)** Keeping the amount of inventory on hand constant but decreasing sales.
**(d)** Decreasing the amount of inventory on hand and increasing sales.

*14. In a perpetual inventory system:  (LO 7)

**(a)** LIFO cost of goods sold will be the same as in a periodic inventory system.
**(b)** average costs are a simple average of unit costs incurred.
**(c)** a new average is computed under the average-cost method after each sale.
**(d)** FIFO cost of goods sold will be the same as in a periodic inventory system.

*15. King Company has sales of $150,000 and cost of goods (LO 8) available for sale of $135,000. If the gross profit rate is 30%, the estimated cost of the ending inventory under the gross profit method is:

**(a)** $15,000.  **(c)** $45,000.
**(b)** $30,000.  **(d)** $75,000.

Go to the book's companion website, www.wiley.com/college/weygandt, for additional Self-Test Questions.

✔ The Navigator

## QUESTIONS

**1.** "The key to successful business operations is effective inventory management." Do you agree? Explain.

**2.** An item must possess two characteristics to be classified as inventory by a merchandiser. What are these two characteristics?

**3.** Your friend Theo Dolan has been hired to help take the physical inventory in Silker Hardware Store. Explain to Theo Dolan what this job will entail.

**4. (a)** Rochelle Company ships merchandise to Jay Company on December 30. The merchandise reaches the buyer on January 6. Indicate the terms of sale that will result in the goods being included in (1) Rochelle's December 31 inventory, and (2) Jay's December 31 inventory.

(b) Under what circumstances should Rochelle Company include consigned goods in its inventory?

5. Katz Hat Shop received a shipment of hats for which it paid the wholesaler $2,970. The price of the hats was $3,000 but Katz was given a $30 cash discount and required to pay freight charges of $50. In addition, Katz paid $130 to cover the travel expenses of an employee who negotiated the purchase of the hats. What amount will Katz record for inventory? Why?

6. Explain the difference between the terms FOB shipping point and FOB destination.

7. Kyle Ebert believes that the allocation of inventoriable costs should be based on the actual physical flow of the goods. Explain to Kyle why this may be both impractical and inappropriate.

8. What is a major advantage and a major disadvantage of the specific identification method of inventory costing?

9. "The selection of an inventory cost flow method is a decision made by accountants." Do you agree? Explain. Once a method has been selected, what accounting requirement applies?

10. Which assumed inventory cost flow method:
    (a) usually parallels the actual physical flow of merchandise?
    (b) assumes that goods available for sale during an accounting period are identical?
    (c) assumes that the latest units purchased are the first to be sold?

11. In a period of rising prices, the inventory reported in Gumby Company's balance sheet is close to the current cost of the inventory. Pokey Company's inventory is considerably below its current cost. Identify the inventory cost flow method being used by each company. Which company has probably been reporting the higher gross profit?

12. Davey Company has been using the FIFO cost flow method during a prolonged period of rising prices. During the same time period, Davey has been paying out all of its net income as dividends. What adverse effects may result from this policy?

13. Josh Kuchin is studying for the next accounting midterm examination. What should Josh know about (a) departing from the cost basis of accounting for inventories and (b) the meaning of "market" in the lower-of-cost-or-market method?

14. Taylor Music Center has 5 CD players on hand at the balance sheet date. Each cost $400. The current replacement cost is $380 per unit. Under the lower-of-cost-or-market basis of accounting for inventories, what value should be reported for the CD players on the balance sheet? Why?

15. Bonnie Stores has 20 toasters on hand at the balance sheet date. Each costs $27. The current replacement cost is $30 per unit. Under the lower-of-cost-or-market basis of accounting for inventories, what value should Bonnie report for the toasters on the balance sheet? Why?

16. Kuzu Company discovers in 2014 that its ending inventory at December 31, 2013, was $7,000 understated. What effect will this error have on (a) 2013 net income, (b) 2014 net income, and (c) the combined net income for the 2 years?

17. Ryder Company's balance sheet shows Inventory $162,800. What additional disclosures should be made?

18. Under what circumstances might inventory turnover be too high? That is, what possible negative consequences might occur?

19. What inventory cost flow does Apple use for its inventories? (*Hint:* You will need to examine the notes for Apple's financial statements.)

*20. "When perpetual inventory records are kept, the results under the FIFO and LIFO methods are the same as they would be in a periodic inventory system." Do you agree? Explain.

*21. How does the average-cost method of inventory costing differ between a perpetual inventory system and a periodic inventory system?

*22. When is it necessary to estimate inventories?

*23. Both the gross profit method and the retail inventory method are based on averages. For each method, indicate the average used, how it is determined, and how it is applied.

*24. Wiggins Company has net sales of $400,000 and cost of goods available for sale of $300,000. If the gross profit rate is 35%, what is the estimated cost of the ending inventory? Show computations.

*25. Emporia Shoe Shop had goods available for sale in 2014 with a retail price of $120,000. The cost of these goods was $84,000. If sales during the period were $80,000, what is the ending inventory at cost using the retail inventory method?

## BRIEF EXERCISES

**BE6-1** Farley Company identifies the following items for possible inclusion in the taking of a physical inventory. Indicate whether each item should be included or excluded from the inventory taking.

*Identify items to be included in taking a physical inventory.*
(LO 1)

(a) Goods shipped on consignment by Farley to another company.
(b) Goods in transit from a supplier shipped FOB destination.

**(c)** Goods sold but being held for customer pickup.
**(d)** Goods held on consignment from another company.

*Identify the components of goods available for sale.*
*(LO 2)*

**BE6-2** Wilbur Company has the following items: (a) Freight-In, (b) Purchase Returns and Allowances, (c) Purchases, (d) Sales Discounts, and (e) Purchase Discounts. Identify which items are included in goods available for sale.

*Compute ending inventory using FIFO and LIFO.*
*(LO 2)*

**BE6-3** In its first month of operations, Bethke Company made three purchases of merchandise in the following sequence: (1) 300 units at $6, (2) 400 units at $7, and (3) 200 units at $8. Assuming there are 360 units on hand, compute the cost of the ending inventory under the (a) FIFO method and (b) LIFO method. Bethke uses a periodic inventory system.

*Compute the ending inventory using average-cost.*
*(LO 2)*

**BE6-4** Data for Bethke Company are presented in BE6-3. Compute the cost of the ending inventory under the average-cost method, assuming there are 360 units on hand.

*Explain the financial statement effect of inventory cost flow assumptions.*
*(LO 3)*

**BE6-5** The management of Svetlana Corp. is considering the effects of inventory-costing methods on its financial statements and its income tax expense. Assuming that the price the company pays for inventory is increasing, which method will:

**(a)** Provide the highest net income?
**(b)** Provide the highest ending inventory?
**(c)** Result in the lowest income tax expense?
**(d)** Result in the most stable earnings over a number of years?

*Explain the financial statement effect of inventory cost flow assumptions.*
*(LO 3)*

**BE6-6** In its first month of operation, Franklin Company purchased 120 units of inventory for $6, then 200 units for $7, and finally 140 units for $8. At the end of the month, 180 units remained. Compute the amount of phantom profit that would result if the company used FIFO rather than LIFO. Explain why this amount is referred to as **phantom profit**. The company uses the periodic method.

*Determine the LCM valuation using inventory categories.*
*(LO 4)*

**BE6-7** Central Appliance Center accumulates the following cost and market data at December 31.

| Inventory Categories | Cost Data | Market Data |
|---|---|---|
| Cameras | $12,000 | $12,100 |
| Camcorders | 9,500 | 9,700 |
| DVD players | 14,000 | 12,800 |

Compute the lower-of-cost-or-market valuation for the company's total inventory.

*Determine correct income statement amounts.*
*(LO 5)*

**BE6-8** Pettit Company reports net income of $90,000 in 2014. However, ending inventory was understated $7,000. What is the correct net income for 2014? What effect, if any, will this error have on total assets as reported in the balance sheet at December 31, 2014?

*Compute inventory turnover and days in inventory.*
*(LO 6)*

**BE6-9** At December 31, 2014, the following information was available for A. Kamble Company: ending inventory $40,000, beginning inventory $60,000, cost of goods sold $270,000, and sales revenue $380,000. Calculate inventory turnover and days in inventory for A. Kamble Company.

*Apply cost flow methods to perpetual inventory records.*
*(LO 7)*

*BE6-10** Gregory Department Store uses a perpetual inventory system. Data for product E2-D2 include the following purchases.

| Date | Number of Units | Unit Price |
|---|---|---|
| May 7 | 50 | $10 |
| July 28 | 30 | 13 |

On June 1, Gregory sold 26 units, and on August 27, 40 more units. Prepare the perpetual inventory schedule for the above transactions using (a) FIFO, (b) LIFO, and (c) moving-average cost.

*Apply the gross profit method.*
*(LO 8)*

*BE6-11** At May 31, Suarez Company has net sales of $330,000 and cost of goods available for sale of $230,000. Compute the estimated cost of the ending inventory, assuming the gross profit rate is 35%.

*Apply the retail inventory method.*
*(LO 8)*

*BE6-12** On June 30, Calico Fabrics has the following data pertaining to the retail inventory method. Goods available for sale: at cost $38,000; at retail $50,000; net sales $40,000; and ending inventory at retail $10,000. Compute the estimated cost of the ending inventory using the retail inventory method.

> ## DO IT! Review

**DO IT! 6-1** Gomez Company just took its physical inventory. The count of inventory items on hand at the company's business locations resulted in a total inventory cost of $300,000. In reviewing the details of the count and related inventory transactions, you have discovered the following.

*Apply rules of ownership to determine inventory cost.*

*(LO 1)*

1. Gomez has sent inventory costing $26,000 on consignment to Kako Company. All of this inventory was at Kako's showrooms on December 31.

2. The company did not include in the count inventory (cost, $20,000) that was sold on December 28, terms FOB shipping point. The goods were in transit on December 31.

3. The company did not include in the count inventory (cost, $17,000) that was purchased with terms of FOB shipping point. The goods were in transit on December 31.

Compute the correct December 31 inventory.

**DO IT! 6-2** The accounting records of Old Towne Electronics show the following data.

*Compute cost of goods sold under different cost flow methods.*

*(LO 2)*

| | |
|---|---|
| Beginning inventory | 3,000 units at $5 |
| Purchases | 8,000 units at $7 |
| Sales | 9,400 units at $10 |

Determine cost of goods sold during the period under a periodic inventory system using (a) the FIFO method, (b) the LIFO method, and (c) the average-cost method. (Round unit cost to nearest tenth of a cent.)

**DO IT! 6-3** (a) Moberg Company sells three different categories of tools (small, medium, and large). The cost and market value of its inventory of tools are as follows.

*Compute inventory value under LCM.*

*(LO 4)*

| | Cost | Market Value |
|---|---|---|
| Small | $ 64,000 | $ 73,000 |
| Medium | 290,000 | 260,000 |
| Large | 152,000 | 171,000 |

Determine the value of the company's inventory under the lower-of-cost-or-market approach.

(b) Janus Company understated its 2013 ending inventory by $31,000. Determine the impact this error has on ending inventory, cost of goods sold, and owner's equity in 2013 and 2014.

**DO IT! 6-4** Early in 2014, Chien Company switched to a just-in-time inventory system. Its sales, cost of goods sold, and inventory amounts for 2013 and 2014 are shown below.

*Compute inventory turnover and assess inventory level.*

*(LO 6)*

| | 2013 | 2014 |
|---|---|---|
| Sales | $3,120,000 | $3,713,000 |
| Cost of goods sold | 1,200,000 | 1,425,000 |
| Beginning inventory | 180,000 | 220,000 |
| Ending inventory | 220,000 | 100,000 |

Determine the inventory turnover and days in inventory for 2013 and 2014. Discuss the changes in the amount of inventory, the inventory turnover and days in inventory, and the amount of sales across the two years.

## EXERCISES

**E6-1** Tri-State Bank and Trust is considering giving Josef Company a loan. Before doing so, management decides that further discussions with Josef's accountant may be desirable. One area of particular concern is the inventory account, which has a year-end balance of $297,000. Discussions with the accountant reveal the following.

*Determine the correct inventory amount.*

*(LO 1)*

1. Josef sold goods costing $38,000 to Sorci Company, FOB shipping point, on December 28. The goods are not expected to arrive at Sorci until January 12. The goods were not included in the physical inventory because they were not in the warehouse.

2. The physical count of the inventory did not include goods costing $95,000 that were shipped to Josef FOB destination on December 27 and were still in transit at year-end.

3. Josef received goods costing $22,000 on January 2. The goods were shipped FOB shipping point on December 26 by Solita Co. The goods were not included in the physical count.

4. Josef sold goods costing $35,000 to Natali Co., FOB destination, on December 30. The goods were received at Natali on January 8. They were not included in Josef's physical inventory.

5. Josef received goods costing $44,000 on January 2 that were shipped FOB destination on December 29. The shipment was a rush order that was supposed to arrive December 31. This purchase was included in the ending inventory of $297,000.

**Instructions**

Determine the correct inventory amount on December 31.

*Determine the correct inventory amount.*

(LO 1)

**E6-2** Rachel Warren, an auditor with Laplante CPAs, is performing a review of Schuda Company's inventory account. Schuda did not have a good year, and top management is under pressure to boost reported income. According to its records, the inventory balance at year-end was $740,000. However, the following information was not considered when determining that amount.

1. Included in the company's count were goods with a cost of $250,000 that the company is holding on consignment. The goods belong to Harmon Corporation.

2. The physical count did not include goods purchased by Schuda with a cost of $40,000 that were shipped FOB destination on December 28 and did not arrive at Schuda warehouse until January 3.

3. Included in the inventory account was $14,000 of office supplies that were stored in the warehouse and were to be used by the company's supervisors and managers during the coming year.

4. The company received an order on December 29 that was boxed and sitting on the loading dock awaiting pick-up on December 31. The shipper picked up the goods on January 1 and delivered them on January 6. The shipping terms were FOB shipping point. The goods had a selling price of $40,000 and a cost of $28,000. The goods were not included in the count because they were sitting on the dock.

5. On December 29, Schuda shipped goods with a selling price of $80,000 and a cost of $60,000 to Reza Sales Corporation FOB shipping point. The goods arrived on January 3. Reza Sales had only ordered goods with a selling price of $10,000 and a cost of $8,000. However, a sales manager at Schuda had authorized the shipment and said that if Reza wanted to ship the goods back next week, it could.

6. Included in the count was $40,000 of goods that were parts for a machine that the company no longer made. Given the high-tech nature of Schuda's products, it was unlikely that these obsolete parts had any other use. However, management would prefer to keep them on the books at cost, "since that is what we paid for them, after all."

**Instructions**

Prepare a schedule to determine the correct inventory amount. Provide explanations for each item above, saying why you did or did not make an adjustment for each item.

*Calculate cost of goods sold using specific identification and FIFO.*

(LO 2, 3)

**E6-3** On December 1, Marzion Electronics Ltd. has three DVD players left in stock. All are identical, all are priced to sell at $150. One of the three DVD players left in stock, with serial #1012, was purchased on June 1 at a cost of $100. Another, with serial #1045, was purchased on November 1 for $90. The last player, serial #1056, was purchased on November 30 for $80.

**Instructions**

(a) Calculate the cost of goods sold using the FIFO periodic inventory method assuming that two of the three players were sold by the end of December, Marzion Electronics' year-end.

(b) If Marzion Electronics used the specific identification method instead of the FIFO method, how might it alter its earnings by "selectively choosing" which particular players to sell to the two customers? What would Marzion's cost of goods sold be if the company wished to minimize earnings? Maximize earnings?

(c) Which of the two inventory methods do you recommend that Marzion use? Explain why.

**E6-4** Linda's Boards sells a snowboard, Xpert, that is popular with snowboard enthusiasts. Information relating to Linda's purchases of Xpert snowboards during September is shown below. During the same month, 121 Xpert snowboards were sold. Linda's uses a periodic inventory system.

*Compute inventory and cost of goods sold using FIFO and LIFO.*

(LO 2)

| Date | Explanation | Units | Unit Cost | Total Cost |
|---|---|---|---|---|
| Sept. 1 | Inventory | 26 | $ 97 | $ 2,522 |
| Sept. 12 | Purchases | 45 | 102 | 4,590 |
| Sept. 19 | Purchases | 20 | 104 | 2,080 |
| Sept. 26 | Purchases | 50 | 105 | 5,250 |
| | Totals | 141 | | $14,442 |

*Instructions*
**(a)** Compute the ending inventory at September 30 and cost of goods sold using the FIFO and LIFO methods. Prove the amount allocated to cost of goods sold under each method.
**(b)** For both FIFO and LIFO, calculate the sum of ending inventory and cost of goods sold. What do you notice about the answers you found for each method?

**E6-5** Xiong Co. uses a periodic inventory system. Its records show the following for the month of May, in which 65 units were sold.

*Compute inventory and cost of goods sold using FIFO and LIFO.*

(LO 2)

| | | Units | Unit Cost | Total Cost |
|---|---|---|---|---|
| May 1 | Inventory | 30 | $ 8 | $240 |
| 15 | Purchases | 25 | 11 | 275 |
| 24 | Purchases | 35 | 12 | 420 |
| | Totals | 90 | | $935 |

*Instructions*
Compute the ending inventory at May 31 and cost of goods sold using the FIFO and LIFO methods. Prove the amount allocated to cost of goods sold under each method.

**E6-6** Kaleta Company reports the following for the month of June.

*Compute inventory and cost of goods sold using FIFO and LIFO.*

(LO 2, 3)

| | | Units | Unit Cost | Total Cost |
|---|---|---|---|---|
| June 1 | Inventory | 200 | $5 | $1,000 |
| 12 | Purchase | 400 | 6 | 2,400 |
| 23 | Purchase | 300 | 7 | 2,100 |
| 30 | Inventory | 100 | | |

*Instructions*
**(a)** Compute the cost of the ending inventory and the cost of goods sold under (1) FIFO and (2) LIFO.
**(b)** Which costing method gives the higher ending inventory? Why?
**(c)** Which method results in the higher cost of goods sold? Why?

**E6-7** Lisa Company had 100 units in beginning inventory at a total cost of $10,000. The company purchased 200 units at a total cost of $26,000. At the end of the year, Lisa had 80 units in ending inventory.

*Compute inventory under FIFO, LIFO, and average-cost.*

(LO 2, 3)

*Instructions*
**(a)** Compute the cost of the ending inventory and the cost of goods sold under (1) FIFO, (2) LIFO, and (3) average-cost.
**(b)** Which cost flow method would result in the highest net income?
**(c)** Which cost flow method would result in inventories approximating current cost in the balance sheet?
**(d)** Which cost flow method would result in Lisa paying the least taxes in the first year?

**E6-8** Inventory data for Kaleta Company are presented in E6-6.

*Compute inventory and cost of goods sold using average-cost.*

(LO 2, 3)

*Instructions*
**(a)** Compute the cost of the ending inventory and the cost of goods sold using the average-cost method.
**(b)** Will the results in (a) be higher or lower than the results under (1) FIFO and (2) LIFO?
**(c)** Why is the average unit cost not $6?

Determine ending inventory under LCM.

(LO 4)

**E6-9** Optix Camera Shop uses the lower-of-cost-or-market basis for its inventory. The following data are available at December 31.

| Item | Units | Unit Cost | Market |
|------|-------|-----------|--------|
| Cameras: | | | |
| Minolta | 5 | $170 | $156 |
| Canon | 6 | 150 | 152 |
| Light meters: | | | |
| Vivitar | 12 | 125 | 115 |
| Kodak | 14 | 120 | 135 |

**Instructions**

Determine the amount of the ending inventory by applying the lower-of-cost-or-market basis.

Compute lower-of-cost-or-market.

(LO 4)

**E6-10** Serebin Company applied FIFO to its inventory and got the following results for its ending inventory.

| | |
|---|---|
| Cameras | 100 units at a cost per unit of $65 |
| DVD players | 150 units at a cost per unit of $75 |
| iPods | 125 units at a cost per unit of $80 |

The cost of purchasing units at year-end was cameras $71, DVD players $67, and iPods $78.

**Instructions**

Determine the amount of ending inventory at lower-of-cost-or-market.

Determine effects of inventory errors.

(LO 5)

**E6-11** Hamid's Hardware reported cost of goods sold as follows.

| | **2013** | **2014** |
|---|---|---|
| Beginning inventory | $ 20,000 | $ 30,000 |
| Cost of goods purchased | 150,000 | 175,000 |
| Cost of goods available for sale | 170,000 | 205,000 |
| Ending inventory | 30,000 | 35,000 |
| Cost of goods sold | $140,000 | $170,000 |

Hamid's made two errors: (1) 2013 ending inventory was overstated $3,000, and (2) 2014 ending inventory was understated $6,000.

**Instructions**

Compute the correct cost of goods sold for each year.

Prepare correct income statements.

(LO 5)

**E6-12** Rulix Watch Company reported the following income statement data for a 2-year period.

| | **2013** | **2014** |
|---|---|---|
| Sales revenue | $220,000 | $250,000 |
| Cost of goods sold | | |
| Beginning inventory | 32,000 | 44,000 |
| Cost of goods purchased | 173,000 | 202,000 |
| Cost of goods available for sale | 205,000 | 246,000 |
| Ending inventory | 44,000 | 52,000 |
| Cost of goods sold | 161,000 | 194,000 |
| Gross profit | $ 59,000 | $ 56,000 |

Rulix uses a periodic inventory system. The inventories at January 1, 2013, and December 31, 2014, are correct. However, the ending inventory at December 31, 2013, was overstated $6,000.

**Instructions**

**(a)** Prepare correct income statement data for the 2 years.
**(b)** What is the cumulative effect of the inventory error on total gross profit for the 2 years?
**(c)** ━━━ Explain in a letter to the president of Rulix Watch Company what has happened, i.e., the nature of the error and its effect on the financial statements.

**E6-13** This information is available for Quick's Photo Corporation for 2012, 2013, and 2014.

*Compute inventory turnover, days in inventory, and gross profit rate.*

(LO 6)

|  | **2012** | **2013** | **2014** |
|---|---|---|---|
| Beginning inventory | $ 100,000 | $ 300,000 | $ 400,000 |
| Ending inventory | 300,000 | 400,000 | 480,000 |
| Cost of goods sold | 900,000 | 1,120,000 | 1,300,000 |
| Sales revenue | 1,200,000 | 1,600,000 | 1,900,000 |

**Instructions**

Calculate inventory turnover, days in inventory, and gross profit rate (from Chapter 5) for Quick's Photo Corporation for 2012, 2013, and 2014. Comment on any trends.

**E6-14** The cost of goods sold computations for Alpha Company and Omega Company are shown below.

*Compute inventory turnover and days in inventory.*

(LO 6)

|  | **Alpha Company** | **Omega Company** |
|---|---|---|
| Beginning inventory | $ 45,000 | $ 71,000 |
| Cost of goods purchased | 200,000 | 290,000 |
| Cost of goods available for sale | 245,000 | 361,000 |
| Ending inventory | 55,000 | 69,000 |
| Cost of goods sold | $190,000 | $292,000 |

**Instructions**

(a) Compute inventory turnover and days in inventory for each company.

(b) Which company moves its inventory more quickly?

**\*E6-15** Bufford Appliance uses a perpetual inventory system. For its flat-screen television sets, the January 1 inventory was 3 sets at $600 each. On January 10, Bufford purchased 6 units at $660 each. The company sold 2 units on January 8 and 4 units on January 15.

*Apply cost flow methods to perpetual records.*

(LO 7)

**Instructions**

Compute the ending inventory under (1) FIFO, (2) LIFO, and (3) moving-average cost.

**\*E6-16** Kaleta Company reports the following for the month of June.

*Calculate inventory and cost of goods sold using three cost flow methods in a perpetual inventory system.*

(LO 7)

| Date | Explanation | Units | Unit Cost | Total Cost |
|---|---|---|---|---|
| June 1 | Inventory | 200 | $5 | $1,000 |
| 12 | Purchase | 400 | 6 | 2,400 |
| 23 | Purchase | 300 | 7 | 2,100 |
| 30 | Inventory | 100 | | |

**Instructions**

(a) Calculate the cost of the ending inventory and the cost of goods sold for each cost flow assumption, using a perpetual inventory system. Assume a sale of 440 units occurred on June 15 for a selling price of $8 and a sale of 360 units on June 27 for $9.

(b) How do the results differ from E6-6 and E6-8?

(c) Why is the average unit cost not $6 [($5 + $6 + $7) ÷ 3 = $6]?

**\*E6-17** Information about Linda's Boards is presented in E6-4. Additional data regarding Linda's sales of Xpert snowboards are provided below. Assume that Linda's uses a perpetual inventory system.

*Apply cost flow methods to perpetual records.*

(LO 7)

| Date | | Units | Unit Price | Total Revenue |
|---|---|---|---|---|
| Sept. 5 | Sale | 12 | $199 | $ 2,388 |
| Sept. 16 | Sale | 50 | 199 | 9,950 |
| Sept. 29 | Sale | 59 | 209 | 12,331 |
| | Totals | 121 | | $24,669 |

**Instructions**

(a) Compute ending inventory at September 30 using FIFO, LIFO, and moving-average cost.

(b) Compare ending inventory using a perpetual inventory system to ending inventory using a periodic inventory system (from E6-4).

(c) Which inventory cost flow method (FIFO, LIFO) gives the same ending inventory value under both periodic and perpetual? Which method gives different ending inventory values?

*Use the gross profit method to estimate inventory.*

*(LO 8)*

**\*E6-18** Brenda Company reported the following information for November and December 2014.

|  | November | December |
|---|---|---|
| Cost of goods purchased | $536,000 | $ 610,000 |
| Inventory, beginning-of-month | 130,000 | 120,000 |
| Inventory, end-of-month | 120,000 | ? |
| Sales revenue | 840,000 | 1,000,000 |

Brenda's ending inventory at December 31 was destroyed in a fire.

**Instructions**

**(a)** Compute the gross profit rate for November.

**(b)** Using the gross profit rate for November, determine the estimated cost of inventory lost in the fire.

*Determine merchandise lost using the gross profit method of estimating inventory.*

*(LO 8)*

**\*E6-19** The inventory of Hauser Company was destroyed by fire on March 1. From an examination of the accounting records, the following data for the first 2 months of the year are obtained: Sales Revenue $51,000, Sales Returns and Allowances $1,000, Purchases $31,200, Freight-In $1,200, and Purchase Returns and Allowances $1,400.

**Instructions**

Determine the merchandise lost by fire, assuming:

**(a)** A beginning inventory of $20,000 and a gross profit rate of 40% on net sales.

**(b)** A beginning inventory of $30,000 and a gross profit rate of 30% on net sales.

*Determine ending inventory at cost using retail method.*

*(LO 8)*

**\*E6-20** Gepetto Shoe Store uses the retail inventory method for its two departments, Women's Shoes and Men's Shoes. The following information for each department is obtained.

| Item | Women's Shoes | Men's Shoes |
|---|---|---|
| Beginning inventory at cost | $ 25,000 | $ 45,000 |
| Cost of goods purchased at cost | 110,000 | 136,300 |
| Net sales | 178,000 | 185,000 |
| Beginning inventory at retail | 46,000 | 60,000 |
| Cost of goods purchased at retail | 179,000 | 185,000 |

**Instructions**

Compute the estimated cost of the ending inventory for each department under the retail inventory method.

# EXERCISES: SET B AND CHALLENGE EXERCISES

Visit the book's companion website, at **www.wiley.com/college/weygandt**, and choose the Student Companion site to access Exercise Set B and Challenge Exercises.

# PROBLEMS: SET A

*Determine items and amounts to be recorded in inventory.*

*(LO 1)*

**P6-1A** Austin Limited is trying to determine the value of its ending inventory as of February 28, 2014, the company's year-end. The following transactions occurred, and the accountant asked your help in determining whether they should be recorded or not.

**(a)** On February 26, Austin shipped goods costing $800 to a customer and charged the customer $1,000. The goods were shipped with terms FOB shipping point and the receiving report indicates that the customer received the goods on March 2.

**(b)** On February 26, Louis Inc. shipped goods to Austin under terms FOB shipping point. The invoice price was $450 plus $30 for freight. The receiving report indicates that the goods were received by Austin on March 2.

**(c)** Austin had $650 of inventory isolated in the warehouse. The inventory is designated for a customer who has requested that the goods be shipped on March 10.

**(d)** Also included in Austin's warehouse is $700 of inventory that Ryhn Producers shipped to Austin on consignment.

**(e)** On February 26, Austin issued a purchase order to acquire goods costing $900. The goods were shipped with terms FOB destination on February 27. Austin received the goods on March 2.

**(f)** On February 26, Austin shipped goods to a customer under terms FOB destination. The invoice price was $350; the cost of the items was $200. The receiving report indicates that the goods were received by the customer on March 2.

*Instructions*

For each of the above transactions, specify whether the item in question should be included in ending inventory, and if so, at what amount.

**P6-2A** Express Distribution markets CDs of the performing artist Fishe. At the beginning of October, Express had in beginning inventory 2,000 of Fishe's CDs with a unit cost of $7. During October, Express made the following purchases of Fishe's CDs.

| | | | |
|---|---|---|---|
| Oct. 3 | 2,500 @ $8 | Oct. 19 | 3,000 @ $10 |
| Oct. 9 | 3,500 @ $9 | Oct. 25 | 4,000 @ $11 |

During October, 10,900 units were sold. Express uses a periodic inventory system.

*Instructions*

**(a)** Determine the cost of goods available for sale.

**(b)** Determine (1) the ending inventory and (2) the cost of goods sold under each of the assumed cost flow methods (FIFO, LIFO, and average-cost). Prove the accuracy of the cost of goods sold under the FIFO and LIFO methods.

**(c)** Which cost flow method results in (1) the highest inventory amount for the balance sheet and (2) the highest cost of goods sold for the income statement?

*Determine cost of goods sold and ending inventory using FIFO, LIFO, and average-cost with analysis.*

*(LO 2, 3)*

(b)(2) Cost of goods sold:
FIFO          $ 94,500
LIFO          $108,700
Average    $101,370

**P6-3A** Ziad Company had a beginning inventory on January 1 of 150 units of Product 4-18-15 at a cost of $20 per unit. During the year, the following purchases were made.

| | | | |
|---|---|---|---|
| Mar. 15 | 400 units at $23 | Sept. 4 | 350 units at $26 |
| July 20 | 250 units at $24 | Dec. 2 | 100 units at $29 |

1,000 units were sold. Ziad Company uses a periodic inventory system.

*Instructions*

**(a)** Determine the cost of goods available for sale.

**(b)** Determine (1) the ending inventory, and (2) the cost of goods sold under each of the assumed cost flow methods (FIFO, LIFO, and average-cost). Prove the accuracy of the cost of goods sold under the FIFO and LIFO methods.

**(c)** Which cost flow method results in (1) the highest inventory amount for the balance sheet, and (2) the highest cost of goods sold for the income statement?

*Determine cost of goods sold and ending inventory, using FIFO, LIFO, and average-cost with analysis.*

*(LO 2, 3)*

(b)(2) Cost of goods sold:
FIFO          $23,400
LIFO          $24,900
Average    $24,160

**P6-4A** The management of Felipe Inc. is reevaluating the appropriateness of using its present inventory cost flow method, which is average-cost. The company requests your help in determining the results of operations for 2014 if either the FIFO or the LIFO method had been used. For 2014, the accounting records show these data:

*Compute ending inventory, prepare income statements, and answer questions using FIFO and LIFO.*

*(LO 2, 3)*

| Inventories | | Purchases and Sales | |
|---|---|---|---|
| Beginning (7,000 units) | $14,000 | Total net sales (180,000 units) | $747,000 |
| Ending (17,000 units) | | Total cost of goods purchased | |
| | | (190,000 units) | 466,000 |

Purchases were made quarterly as follows.

| Quarter | Units | Unit Cost | Total Cost |
|---|---|---|---|
| 1 | 50,000 | $2.20 | $110,000 |
| 2 | 40,000 | 2.35 | 94,000 |
| 3 | 40,000 | 2.50 | 100,000 |
| 4 | 60,000 | 2.70 | 162,000 |
| | 190,000 | | $466,000 |

Operating expenses were $130,000, and the company's income tax rate is 40%.

*Instructions*

**(a)** Prepare comparative condensed income statements for 2014 under FIFO and LIFO. (Show computations of ending inventory.)

(a) Gross profit:
FIFO    $312,900
LIFO    $303,000

**(b)** ⊶ Answer the following questions for management.
**(1)** Which cost flow method (FIFO or LIFO) produces the more meaningful inventory amount for the balance sheet? Why?
**(2)** Which cost flow method (FIFO or LIFO) produces the more meaningful net income? Why?
**(3)** Which cost flow method (FIFO or LIFO) is more likely to approximate the actual physical flow of goods? Why?
**(4)** How much more cash will be available for management under LIFO than under FIFO? Why?
**(5)** Will gross profit under the average-cost method be higher or lower than FIFO? Than LIFO? (*Note:* It is not necessary to quantify your answer.)

*Calculate ending inventory, cost of goods sold, gross profit, and gross profit rate under periodic method; compare results.*

*(LO 2, 3)*

**P6-5A** You are provided with the following information for Najera Inc. for the month ended June 30, 2014. Najera uses the periodic method for inventory.

| Date | Description | Quantity | Unit Cost or Selling Price |
|---|---|---|---|
| June 1 | Beginning inventory | 40 | $40 |
| June 4 | Purchase | 135 | 44 |
| June 10 | Sale | 110 | 70 |
| June 11 | Sale return | 15 | 70 |
| June 18 | Purchase | 55 | 46 |
| June 18 | Purchase return | 10 | 46 |
| June 25 | Sale | 65 | 75 |
| June 28 | Purchase | 30 | 50 |

*(a) (iii) Gross profit:*
*LIFO    $4,215*
*FIFO    $4,645*
*Average  $4,414.60*

**Instructions**
**(a)** Calculate (i) ending inventory, (ii) cost of goods sold, (iii) gross profit, and (iv) gross profit rate under each of the following methods.
**(1)** LIFO.    **(2)** FIFO.    **(3)** Average-cost.
**(b)** Compare results for the three cost flow assumptions.

*Compare specific identification, FIFO, and LIFO under periodic method; use cost flow assumption to justify price increase.*

*(LO 2, 3)*

**P6-6A** You are provided with the following information for Barton Inc. Barton Inc. uses the periodic method of accounting for its inventory transactions.

March  1  Beginning inventory 2,000 liters at a cost of 60¢ per liter.
March  3  Purchased 2,500 liters at a cost of 65¢ per liter.
March  5  Sold 2,300 liters for $1.05 per liter.
March 10  Purchased 4,000 liters at a cost of 72¢ per liter.
March 20  Purchased 2,500 liters at a cost of 80¢ per liter.
March 30  Sold 5,200 liters for $1.25 per liter.

**Instructions**
**(a)** Prepare partial income statements through gross profit, and calculate the value of ending inventory that would be reported on the balance sheet, under each of the following cost flow assumptions. (Round ending inventory and cost of goods sold to the nearest dollar.)
**(1)** Specific identification method assuming:
**(i)** The March 5 sale consisted of 1,000 liters from the March 1 beginning inventory and 1,300 liters from the March 3 purchase; and
**(ii)** The March 30 sale consisted of the following number of units sold from beginning inventory and each purchase: 450 liters from March 1; 550 liters from March 3; 2,900 liters from March 10; 1,300 liters from March 20.
**(2)** FIFO.
**(3)** LIFO.
**(b)** How can companies use a cost flow method to justify price increases? Which cost flow method would best support an argument to increase prices?

*(a) Gross profit:*
*(1) Specific identification $3,715*

*(2) FIFO    $3,930*
*(3) LIFO    $3,385*

*Compute ending inventory, prepare income statements, and answer questions using FIFO and LIFO.*

*(LO 2, 3)*

**P6-7A** The management of Sherlynn Co. asks your help in determining the comparative effects of the FIFO and LIFO inventory cost flow methods. For 2014, the accounting records provide the following data.

| Inventory, January 1 (10,000 units) | $ 45,000 |
|---|---|
| Cost of 100,000 units purchased | 532,000 |
| Selling price of 80,000 units sold | 700,000 |
| Operating expenses | 140,000 |

Units purchased consisted of 35,000 units at $5.10 on May 10; 35,000 units at $5.30 on August 15; and 30,000 units at $5.60 on November 20. Income taxes are 30%.

*Instructions*
**(a)** Prepare comparative condensed income statements for 2014 under FIFO and LIFO. (Show computations of ending inventory.)

**(b)** ━━━ Answer the following questions for management.

  **(1)** Which inventory cost flow method produces the most meaningful inventory amount for the balance sheet? Why?

  **(2)** Which inventory cost flow method produces the most meaningful net income? Why?

  **(3)** Which inventory cost flow method is most likely to approximate actual physical flow of the goods? Why?

  **(4)** How much additional cash will be available for management under LIFO than under FIFO? Why?

  **(5)** How much of the gross profit under FIFO is illusory in comparison with the gross profit under LIFO?

*(a) Net income*
*FIFO  $105,700*
*LIFO  $91,000*

**\*P6-8A** Mercer Inc. is a retailer operating in British Columbia. Mercer uses the perpetual inventory method. All sales returns from customers result in the goods being returned to inventory; the inventory is not damaged. Assume that there are no credit transactions; all amounts are settled in cash. You are provided with the following information for Mercer Inc. for the month of January 2014.

*Calculate cost of goods sold and ending inventory under LIFO, FIFO, and moving-average cost under the perpetual system; compare gross profit under each assumption.*

*(LO 7)*

| Date | Description | Quantity | Unit Cost or Selling Price |
|---|---|---|---|
| January 1 | Beginning inventory | 100 | $15 |
| January 5 | Purchase | 140 | 18 |
| January 8 | Sale | 110 | 28 |
| January 10 | Sale return | 10 | 28 |
| January 15 | Purchase | 55 | 20 |
| January 16 | Purchase return | 5 | 20 |
| January 20 | Sale | 90 | 32 |
| January 25 | Purchase | 20 | 22 |

*Instructions*
**(a)** For each of the following cost flow assumptions, calculate (i) cost of goods sold, (ii) ending inventory, and (iii) gross profit.

  **(1)** LIFO.      **(2)** FIFO.      **(3)** Moving-average cost.

**(b)** Compare results for the three cost flow assumptions.

*(a)(iii) Gross profit:*
*LIFO       $2,160*
*FIFO       $2,560*
*Average    $2,421*

**\*P6-9A** Terando Co. began operations on July 1. It uses a perpetual inventory system. During July, the company had the following purchases and sales.

*Determine ending inventory under a perpetual inventory system.*

*(LO 7)*

| | Purchases | | |
|---|---|---|---|
| Date | Units | Unit Cost | Sales Units |
| July 1 | 5 | $120 | |
| July 6 | | | 4 |
| July 11 | 7 | $136 | |
| July 14 | | | 3 |
| July 21 | 8 | $147 | |
| July 27 | | | 6 |

*Instructions*
**(a)** Determine the ending inventory under a perpetual inventory system using (1) FIFO, (2) moving-average cost, and (3) LIFO.

**(b)** Which costing method produces the highest ending inventory valuation?

*(a) Ending inventory*
*FIFO  $1,029*
*Avg.  $994*
*LIFO  $958*

*Compute gross profit rate and inventory loss using gross profit method.*

(LO 8)

XLS

**\*P6-10A** Suzuki Company lost all of its inventory in a fire on December 26, 2014. The accounting records showed the following gross profit data for November and December.

|  | November | December (to 12/26) |
|---|---|---|
| Net sales | $600,000 | $700,000 |
| Beginning inventory | 32,000 | 36,000 |
| Purchases | 389,000 | 420,000 |
| Purchase returns and allowances | 13,300 | 14,900 |
| Purchase discounts | 8,500 | 9,500 |
| Freight-in | 8,800 | 9,900 |
| Ending inventory | 36,000 | ? |

Suzuki is fully insured for fire losses but must prepare a report for the insurance company.

**Instructions**

(a) Gross profit rate 38%

**(a)** Compute the gross profit rate for November.

**(b)** Using the gross profit rate for November, determine the estimated cost of the inventory lost in the fire.

*Compute ending inventory using retail method.*

(LO 8)

**\*P6-11A** Dixon Books uses the retail inventory method to estimate its monthly ending inventories. The following information is available for two of its departments at October 31, 2014.

|  | Hardcovers | | Paperbacks | |
|---|---|---|---|---|
|  | Cost | Retail | Cost | Retail |
| Beginning inventory | $ 420,000 | $ 700,000 | $ 280,000 | $ 360,000 |
| Purchases | 2,135,000 | 3,200,000 | 1,155,000 | 1,540,000 |
| Freight-in | 24,000 |  | 12,000 |  |
| Purchase discounts | 44,000 |  | 22,000 |  |
| Net sales |  | 3,100,000 |  | 1,570,000 |

At December 31, Dixon Books takes a physical inventory at retail. The actual retail values of the inventories in each department are Hardcovers $790,000 and Paperbacks $335,000.

**Instructions**

(a) Hardcovers: End. Inv. $520,000

**(a)** Determine the estimated cost of the ending inventory for each department at **October 31**, 2014, using the retail inventory method.

**(b)** Compute the ending inventory at cost for each department at **December 31**, assuming the cost-to-retail ratios for the year are 65% for Hardcovers and 75% for Paperbacks.

# PROBLEMS: SET B

*Determine items and amounts to be recorded in inventory.*

(LO 1)

**P6-1B** Weber Limited is trying to determine the value of its ending inventory at February 28, 2014, the company's year-end. The accountant counted everything that was in the warehouse as of February 28, which resulted in an ending inventory valuation of $48,000. However, she didn't know how to treat the following transactions so she didn't record them.

**(a)** On February 26, Weber shipped to a customer goods costing $800. The goods were shipped FOB shipping point, and the receiving report indicates that the customer received the goods on March 2.

**(b)** On February 26, Gretel Inc. shipped goods to Weber FOB destination. The invoice price was $350. The receiving report indicates that the goods were received by Weber on March 2.

**(c)** Weber had $500 of inventory at a customer's warehouse "on approval." The customer was going to let Weber know whether it wanted the merchandise by the end of the week, March 4.

**(d)** Weber also had $400 of inventory on consignment at a Roslyn craft shop.

**(e)** On February 26, Weber ordered goods costing $750. The goods were shipped FOB shipping point on February 27. Weber received the goods on March 1.

**(f)** On February 28, Weber packaged goods and had them ready for shipping to a customer FOB destination. The invoice price was $350; the cost of the items was $250. The receiving report indicates that the goods were received by the customer on March 2.

**(g)** Weber had damaged goods set aside in the warehouse because they are no longer saleable. These goods cost $400 and Weber originally expected to sell these items for $600.

*Instructions*

For each of the above transactions, specify whether the item in question should be included in ending inventory and, if so, at what amount. For each item that is not included in ending inventory, indicate who owns it and in what account, if any, it should have been recorded.

**P6-2B** Xinxin Distribution markets CDs of the performing artist Carly. At the beginning of March, Xinxin had in beginning inventory 1,500 Carly CDs with a unit cost of $7. During March Xinxin made the following purchases of Carly CDs.

*Determine cost of goods sold and ending inventory using FIFO, LIFO, and average-cost with analysis.*

*(LO 2, 3)*

| March 5 | 3,000 @ $8 | March 21 | 4,000 @ $10 |
| March 13 | 4,500 @ $9 | March 26 | 2,500 @ $11 |

During March, 12,000 units were sold. Xinxin uses a periodic inventory system.

*Instructions*

**(a)** Determine the cost of goods available for sale.

**(b)** Determine (1) the ending inventory and (2) the cost of goods sold under each of the assumed cost flow methods (FIFO, LIFO, and average-cost). Prove the accuracy of the cost of goods sold under the FIFO and LIFO methods.

**(c)** Which cost flow method results in (1) the highest inventory amount for the balance sheet and (2) the highest cost of goods sold for the income statement?

(b)(2) Cost of goods sold:
FIFO        $105,000
LIFO        $116,000
Average   $110,321

**P6-3B** Walz Company had a beginning inventory of 400 units of Product Ribo at a cost of $8 per unit. During the year, purchases were:

*Determine cost of goods sold and ending inventory using FIFO, LIFO, and average-cost with analysis.*

*(LO 2, 3)*

| Feb. 20 | 600 units at $9 | Aug. 12 | 300 units at $11 |
| May 5 | 500 units at $10 | Dec. 8 | 200 units at $12 |

Walz Company uses a periodic inventory system. Sales totaled 1,500 units.

*Instructions*

**(a)** Determine the cost of goods available for sale.

**(b)** Determine (1) the ending inventory and (2) the cost of goods sold under each of the assumed cost flow methods (FIFO, LIFO, and average-cost). Prove the accuracy of the cost of goods sold under the FIFO and LIFO methods.

**(c)** Which cost flow method results in (1) the lowest inventory amount for the balance sheet, and (2) the lowest cost of goods sold for the income statement?

(b) Cost of goods sold:
FIFO        $13,600
LIFO        $15,200
Average   $14,475

**P6-4B** The management of Patel Co. is reevaluating the appropriateness of using its present inventory cost flow method, which is average-cost. They request your help in determining the results of operations for 2014 if either the FIFO method or the LIFO method had been used. For 2014, the accounting records show the following data.

*Compute ending inventory, prepare income statements, and answer questions using FIFO and LIFO.*

*(LO 2, 3)*

| Inventories | | Purchases and Sales | |
|---|---|---|---|
| Beginning (15,000 units) | $32,000 | Total net sales (217,000 units) | $865,000 |
| Ending (28,000 units) | | Total cost of goods purchased | |
| | | (230,000 units) | 600,000 |

Purchases were made quarterly as follows.

| Quarter | Units | Unit Cost | Total Cost |
|---|---|---|---|
| 1 | 60,000 | $2.40 | $144,000 |
| 2 | 50,000 | 2.50 | 125,000 |
| 3 | 50,000 | 2.70 | 135,000 |
| 4 | 70,000 | 2.80 | 196,000 |
| | 230,000 | | $600,000 |

Operating expenses were $147,000, and the company's income tax rate is 34%.

### Instructions

**(a)** Prepare comparative condensed income statements for 2014 under FIFO and LIFO. (Show computations of ending inventory.)

**(b)** ◆━━━ Answer the following questions for management.

  **(1)** Which cost flow method (FIFO or LIFO) produces the more meaningful inventory amount for the balance sheet? Why?

  **(2)** Which cost flow method (FIFO or LIFO) produces the more meaningful net income? Why?

  **(3)** Which cost flow method (FIFO or LIFO) is more likely to approximate actual physical flow of the goods? Why?

  **(4)** How much additional cash will be available for management under LIFO than under FIFO? Why?

  **(5)** Will gross profit under the average-cost method be higher or lower than (i) FIFO and (ii) LIFO? (*Note:* It is not necessary to quantify your answer.)

**P6-5B** You are provided with the following information for Perkins Inc. for the month ended October 31, 2014. Perkins uses a periodic method for inventory.

| Date | Description | Units | Unit Cost or Selling Price |
|---|---|---|---|
| October 1 | Beginning inventory | 60 | $25 |
| October 9 | Purchase | 120 | 26 |
| October 11 | Sale | 100 | 35 |
| October 17 | Purchase | 70 | 27 |
| October 22 | Sale | 60 | 40 |
| October 25 | Purchase | 80 | 28 |
| October 29 | Sale | 110 | 40 |

### Instructions

**(a)** Calculate (i) ending inventory, (ii) cost of goods sold, (iii) gross profit, and (iv) gross profit rate under each of the following methods.

  **(1)** LIFO.
  **(2)** FIFO.
  **(3)** Average-cost.

**(b)** Compare results for the three cost flow assumptions.

**P6-6B** You have the following information for Princess Diamonds. Princess Diamonds uses the periodic method of accounting for its inventory transactions. Princess only carries one brand and size of diamonds—all are identical. Each batch of diamonds purchased is carefully coded and marked with its purchase cost.

| | |
|---|---|
| March 1 | Beginning inventory 150 diamonds at a cost of $300 per diamond. |
| March 3 | Purchased 200 diamonds at a cost of $360 each. |
| March 5 | Sold 180 diamonds for $600 each. |
| March 10 | Purchased 350 diamonds at a cost of $380 each. |
| March 25 | Sold 400 diamonds for $650 each. |

### Instructions

**(a)** Assume that Princess Diamonds uses the specific identification cost flow method.

  **(1)** Demonstrate how Princess Diamonds could maximize its gross profit for the month by specifically selecting which diamonds to sell on March 5 and March 25.

  **(2)** Demonstrate how Princess Diamonds could minimize its gross profit for the month by selecting which diamonds to sell on March 5 and March 25.

**(b)** Assume that Princess Diamonds uses the FIFO cost flow assumption. Calculate cost of goods sold. How much gross profit would Princess Diamonds report under this cost flow assumption?

**(c)** Assume that Princess Diamonds uses the LIFO cost flow assumption. Calculate cost of goods sold. How much gross profit would the company report under this cost flow assumption?

**(d)** Which cost flow method should Princess Diamonds select? Explain.

**P6-7B** The management of Chelsea Inc. asks your help in determining the comparative effects of the FIFO and LIFO inventory cost flow methods. For 2014, the accounting records provide the following data.

| Inventory, January 1 (10,000 units) | $ 35,000 |
|---|---|
| Cost of 120,000 units purchased | 504,500 |
| Selling price of 100,000 units sold | 665,000 |
| Operating expenses | 130,000 |

Units purchased consisted of 35,000 units at $4.00 on May 10; 60,000 units at $4.20 on August 15; and 25,000 units at $4.50 on November 20. Income taxes are 28%.

**Instructions**

**(a)** Prepare comparative condensed income statements for 2014 under FIFO and LIFO. (Show computations of ending inventory.)

**(b)** ━━━ Answer the following questions for management in the form of a business letter.

**(1)** Which inventory cost flow method produces the most meaningful inventory amount for the balance sheet? Why?

**(2)** Which inventory cost flow method produces the most meaningful net income? Why?

**(3)** Which inventory cost flow method is most likely to approximate the actual physical flow of the goods? Why?

**(4)** How much more cash will be available for management under LIFO than under FIFO? Why?

**(5)** How much of the gross profit under FIFO is illusionary in comparison with the gross profit under LIFO?

*(a) Gross profit:*
*FIFO  $259,000*
*LIFO  $240,500*

**\*P6-8B** Minsoo Ltd. is a retailer operating in Edmonton, Alberta. Minsoo uses the perpetual inventory method. All sales returns from customers result in the goods being returned to inventory; the inventory is not damaged. Assume that there are no credit transactions; all amounts are settled in cash. You are provided with the following information for Minsoo Ltd. for the month of January 2014.

*Calculate cost of goods sold and ending inventory for FIFO, moving-average cost, and LIFO under the perpetual system; compare gross profit under each assumption.*
*(LO 7)*

| Date | Description | Quantity | Unit Cost or Selling Price |
|---|---|---|---|
| December 31 | Ending inventory | 160 | $17 |
| January 2 | Purchase | 100 | 21 |
| January 6 | Sale | 150 | 40 |
| January 9 | Sale return | 10 | 40 |
| January 9 | Purchase | 80 | 24 |
| January 10 | Purchase return | 10 | 24 |
| January 10 | Sale | 60 | 45 |
| January 23 | Purchase | 100 | 28 |
| January 30 | Sale | 110 | 50 |

**Instructions**

**(a)** For each of the following cost flow assumptions, calculate (i) cost of goods sold, (ii) ending inventory, and (iii) gross profit.

**(1)** LIFO.    **(2)** FIFO.    **(3)** Moving-average cost.

**(b)** Compare results for the three cost flow assumptions.

*(a)(iii) Gross profit:*
*LIFO   $6,540*
*FIFO   $7,780*
*Average  $7,354*

**\*P6-9B** Buffet Appliance Mart began operations on May 1. It uses a perpetual inventory system. During May, the company had the following purchases and sales for its Model 25 Sureshot camera.

*Determine ending inventory under a perpetual inventory system.*
*(LO 7)*

| Date | Units | Unit Cost | Sales Units |
|---|---|---|---|
| | | **Purchases** | |
| May 1 | 7 | $150 | |
| 4 | | | 4 |
| 8 | 8 | $170 | |
| 12 | | | 5 |
| 15 | 6 | $185 | |
| 20 | | | 3 |
| 25 | | | 4 |

**Instructions**

**(a)** Determine the ending inventory under a perpetual inventory system using (1) FIFO, (2) moving-average cost, and (3) LIFO.

**(b)** Which costing method produces (1) the highest ending inventory valuation and (2) the lowest ending inventory valuation?

*(a) FIFO   $925*
*Average  $874*
*LIFO    $790*

*Estimate inventory loss using gross profit method.*
(LO 8)

XLS

**\*P6-10B** Liis Company lost 70% of its inventory in a fire on March 25, 2014. The accounting records showed the following gross profit data for February and March.

|  | February | March (to 3/25) |
|---|---|---|
| Net sales | $300,000 | $250,000 |
| Net purchases | 176,800 | 139,000 |
| Freight-in | 3,900 | 3,000 |
| Beginning inventory | 4,500 | 20,200 |
| Ending inventory | 20,200 | ? |

Liis Company is fully insured for fire losses but must prepare a report for the insurance company.

**Instructions**

*(a) Gross profit rate 45%*

**(a)** Compute the gross profit rate for the month of February.

**(b)** Using the gross profit rate for February, determine both the estimated total inventory and inventory lost in the fire in March.

*Compute ending inventory using retail method.*
(LO 8)

**\*P6-11B** Belden Department Store uses the retail inventory method to estimate its monthly ending inventories. The following information is available for two of its departments at August 31, 2014.

|  | Sporting Goods Cost | Sporting Goods Retail | Jewelry and Cosmetics Cost | Jewelry and Cosmetics Retail |
|---|---|---|---|---|
| Net sales |  | $1,000,000 |  | $1,160,000 |
| Purchases | $675,000 | 1,066,000 | $741,000 | 1,158,000 |
| Purchase returns | (26,000) | (40,000) | (12,000) | (20,000) |
| Purchase discounts | (12,360) | — | (2,440) | — |
| Freight-in | 9,000 | — | 14,000 | — |
| Beginning inventory | 47,360 | 74,000 | 39,440 | 62,000 |

At December 31, Belden Department Store takes a physical inventory at retail. The actual retail values of the inventories in each department are Sporting Goods $95,000 and Jewelry and Cosmetics $44,000.

**Instructions**

*(b) Sporting Goods: End. Inv. $63,000*

**(a)** Determine the estimated cost of the ending inventory for each department on **August 31**, 2014, using the retail inventory method.

**(b)** Compute the ending inventory at cost for each department at **December 31**, assuming the cost-to-retail ratios are 60% for Sporting Goods and 64% for Jewelry and Cosmetics.

## PROBLEMS: SET C

Visit the book's companion website, at **www.wiley.com/college/weygandt**, and choose the Student Companion site to access Problem Set C.

## COMPREHENSIVE PROBLEM

**CP6** On December 1, 2014, Matthias Company had the account balances shown below.

| Debit |  | Credit |  |
|---|---|---|---|
| Cash | $ 4,800 | Accumulated Depreciation—Equipment | $ 1,500 |
| Accounts Receivable | 3,900 | Accounts Payable | 3,000 |
| Inventory | 1,800* | Owner's Capital | 27,000 |
| Equipment | 21,000 |  | $31,500 |
|  | $31,500 |  |  |

*(3,000 × $0.60)

The following transactions occurred during December.

Dec.  3   Purchased 4,000 units of inventory on account at a cost of $0.72 per unit.
      5   Sold 4,400 units of inventory on account for $0.90 per unit. (It sold 3,000 of
          the $0.60 units and 1,400 of the $0.72.)
      7   Granted the December 5 customer $180 credit for 200 units of inventory
          returned costing $120. These units were returned to inventory.
     17   Purchased 2,200 units of inventory for cash at $0.80 each.
     22   Sold 2,000 units of inventory on account for $0.95 per unit. (It sold 2,000 of
          the $0.72 units.)

**Adjustment data:**

1. Accrued salaries payable $400.
2. Depreciation $200 per month.

*Instructions*

(a) Journalize the December transactions and adjusting entries, assuming Matthias uses
    the perpetual inventory method.
(b) Enter the December 1 balances in the ledger T-accounts and post the December trans-
    actions. In addition to the accounts mentioned above, use the following additional
    accounts: Cost of Goods Sold, Depreciation Expense, Salaries and Wages Expense,
    Salaries and Wages Payable, Sales Revenue, and Sales Returns and Allowances.
(c) Prepare an adjusted trial balance as of December 31, 2014.
(d) Prepare an income statement for December 2014 and a classified balance sheet at
    December 31, 2014.
(e) Compute ending inventory and cost of goods sold under FIFO, assuming Matthias
    Company uses the periodic inventory system.
(f) Compute ending inventory and cost of goods sold under LIFO, assuming Matthias
    Company uses the periodic inventory system.

## CONTINUING COOKIE CHRONICLE

(*Note:* This is a continuation of the Cookie Chronicle from Chapters 1 through 5.)

**CCC6** Natalie is busy establishing both divisions of her business (cookie classes and mixer
sales) and completing her business degree. Her goals for the next 11 months are to sell one
mixer per month and to give two to three classes per week.

The cost of the fine European mixers is expected to increase. Natalie has just negotiated new terms with Kzinski that include shipping costs in the negotiated purchase price
(mixers will be shipped FOB destination). Natalie must choose a cost flow assumption for
her mixer inventory.

*Go to the book's companion website,* **www.wiley.com/college/weygandt,** *to see the completion
of this problem.*

# Broadening Your Perspective

# Financial Reporting and Analysis

## Financial Reporting Problem: Apple Inc.

**BYP6-1** The notes that accompany a company's financial statements provide informative details that
would clutter the amounts and descriptions presented in the statements. Refer to the financial statements
of Apple Inc. in Appendix A as well as its annual report. Instructions for accessing and using the company's
complete annual report, including the notes to the financial statements, are also provided in Appendix A.

*Instructions*

Answer the following questions. Complete the requirements in millions of dollars, as shown in
Apple's annual report.

(a) What did Apple report for the amount of inventories in its consolidated balance sheet at
    September 25, 2010? At September 24, 2011?

**(b)** Compute the dollar amount of change and the percentage change in inventories between 2010 and 2011. Compute inventory as a percentage of current assets at September 24, 2011.

**(c)** How does Apple value its inventories? Which inventory cost flow method does Apple use? (See Notes to the Financial Statements.)

**(d)** What is the cost of sales (cost of goods sold) reported by Apple for 2011, 2010, and 2009? Compute the percentage of cost of sales to net sales in 2011.

## Comparative Analysis Problem: PepsiCo, Inc. vs. The Coca-Cola Company

**BYP6-2** PepsiCo's financial statements are presented in Appendix B. Financial statements of The Coca-Cola Company are presented in Appendix C. Instructions for accessing and using the complete annual reports of PepsiCo and Coca-Cola, including the notes to the financial statements, are also provided in Appendices B and C, respectively.

*Instructions*

**(a)** Based on the information contained in these financial statements, compute the following 2011 ratios for each company.
  **(1)** Inventory turnover.
  **(2)** Days in inventory.

**(b)** What conclusions concerning the management of the inventory can you draw from these data?

## Comparative Analysis Problem: Amazon.com, Inc. vs. Wal-Mart Stores, Inc.

**BYP6-3** Amazon.com, Inc.'s financial statements are presented in Appendix D. Financial statements of Wal-Mart Stores, Inc. are presented in Appendix E. Instructions for accessing and using the complete annual reports of Amazon and Wal-Mart, including the notes to the financial statements, are also provided in Appendices D and E, respectively.

*Instructions*

**(a)** Based on the information contained in these financial statements, compute the following 2011 ratios for each company.
  **(1)** Inventory turnover.
  **(2)** Days in inventory.

**(b)** What conclusions concerning the management of the inventory can you draw from these data?

## Real-World Focus

**BYP6-4** A company's annual report usually will identify the inventory method used. Knowing that, you can analyze the effects of the inventory method on the income statement and balance sheet.

*Address:* **www.cisco.com**, or go to **www.wiley.com/college/weygandt**

*Instructions*

Answer the following questions based on the current year's annual report on Cisco's website.

**(a)** At Cisco's fiscal year-end, what was the inventory on the balance sheet?
**(b)** How has this changed from the previous fiscal year-end?
**(c)** How much of the inventory was finished goods?
**(d)** What inventory method does Cisco use?

# Critical Thinking

 ## Decision-Making Across the Organization

**BYP6-5** On April 10, 2014, fire damaged the office and warehouse of Corvet Company. Most of the accounting records were destroyed, but the following account balances were determined as of March 31, 2014: Inventory (January 1, 2014), $80,000; Sales Revenue (January 1–March 31, 2014), $180,000; Purchases (January 1–March 31, 2014), $94,000.

The company's fiscal year ends on December 31. It uses a periodic inventory system.

From an analysis of the April bank statement, you discover cancelled checks of $4,200 for cash purchases during the period April 1–10. Deposits during the same period totaled $18,500. Of that amount, 60% were collections on accounts receivable, and the balance was cash sales.

Correspondence with the company's principal suppliers revealed $12,400 of purchases on account from April 1 to April 10. Of that amount, $1,600 was for merchandise in transit on April 10 that was shipped FOB destination.

Correspondence with the company's principal customers produced acknowledgments of credit sales totaling $37,000 from April 1 to April 10. It was estimated that $5,600 of credit sales will never be acknowledged or recovered from customers.

Corvet Company reached an agreement with the insurance company that its fire-loss claim should be based on the average of the gross profit rates for the preceding 2 years. The financial statements for 2012 and 2013 showed the following data.

|  | 2013 | 2012 |
| --- | --- | --- |
| Net sales | $600,000 | $480,000 |
| Cost of goods purchased | 404,000 | 356,000 |
| Beginning inventory | 60,000 | 40,000 |
| Ending inventory | 80,000 | 60,000 |

Inventory with a cost of $17,000 was salvaged from the fire.

### Instructions

With the class divided into groups, answer the following.

**(a)** Determine the balances in (1) Sales Revenue and (2) Purchases at April 10.

*__(b)__ Determine the average gross profit rate for the years 2012 and 2013. (*Hint:* Find the gross profit rate for each year and divide the sum by 2.)

*__(c)__ Determine the inventory loss as a result of the fire, using the gross profit method.

## Communication Activity

**BYP6-6** You are the controller of Small Toys Inc. Marta Johns, the president, recently mentioned to you that she found an error in the 2013 financial statements which she believes has corrected itself. She determined, in discussions with the Purchasing Department, that 2013 ending inventory was overstated by $1 million. Marta says that the 2014 ending inventory is correct. Thus, she assumes that 2014 income is correct. Marta says to you, "What happened has happened—there's no point in worrying about it anymore."

### Instructions

You conclude that Marta is incorrect. Write a brief, tactful memo to Marta, clarifying the situation.

## Ethics Case

**BYP6-7** R. J. Graziano Wholesale Corp. uses the LIFO method of inventory costing. In the current year, profit at R. J. Graziano is running unusually high. The corporate tax rate is also high this year, but it is scheduled to decline significantly next year. In an effort to lower the current year's net income and to take advantage of the changing income tax rate, the president of R. J. Graziano Wholesale instructs the plant accountant to recommend to the purchasing department a large purchase of inventory for delivery 3 days before the end of the year. The price of the inventory to be purchased has doubled during the year, and the purchase will represent a major portion of the ending inventory value.

### Instructions

**(a)** What is the effect of this transaction on this year's and next year's income statement and income tax expense? Why?

**(b)** If R. J. Graziano Wholesale had been using the FIFO method of inventory costing, would the president give the same directive?

**(c)** Should the plant accountant order the inventory purchase to lower income? What are the ethical implications of this order?

## All About You

**BYP6-8** Some of the largest business frauds ever perpetrated have involved the misstatement of inventory. Two classics were at Leslie Fay and McKesson Corporation.

### Instructions

There is considerable information regarding inventory frauds available on the Internet. Search for information about one of the two cases mentioned above, or inventory fraud at any other company, and prepare a short explanation of the nature of the inventory fraud.

## FASB Codification Activity

**BYP6-9** If your school has a subscription to the FASB Codification, go to **http://aaahq.org/ ascLogin.cfm** to log in and prepare responses to the following.

*Instructions*

**(a)** The primary basis for accounting for inventories is cost. How is cost defined in the Codification?

**(b)** What does the Codification state regarding the use of consistency in the selection or employment of a basis for inventory?

**(c)** What does the Codification indicate is a justification for the use of the lower-of-cost-or-market for inventory valuation?

## Answers to Chapter Questions

### Answers to Insight and Accounting Across the Organization Questions

**p. 277 A Big Hiccup    Q:** What steps might the companies take to avoid such a serious disruption in the future? **A:** The manufacturer of the piston rings should spread its manufacturing facilities across a few locations that are far enough apart that they would not all be at risk at once. In addition, the automakers might consider becoming less dependent on a single supplier as well as having weather contingency plans.

**p. 278 Falsifying Inventory to Boost Income    Q:** What effect does an overstatement of inventory have on a company's financial statements? **A:** The balance sheet looks stronger because inventory and retained earnings are overstated. The income statement looks better because cost of goods sold is understated and income is overstated.

**p. 289 Is LIFO Fair?    Q:** What are the arguments for and against the use of LIFO? **A:** Proponents of LIFO argue that it is conceptually superior because it matches the most recent cost with the most recent selling price. Critics contend that it artificially understates the company's net income and consequently reduces tax payments. Also, because most foreign companies are not allowed to use LIFO, its use by U.S. companies reduces the ability of investors to compare U.S. companies with foreign companies.

**p. 293 Too Many TVs or Too Few?    Q:** For Sony, what are the advantages and disadvantages of having a low days in inventory measure? **A:** If Sony has a low days in inventory, it reduces the amount of cash it has tied up in inventory. It also minimizes the risk it will be stuck with excess inventory that could force it to provide big discounts, resulting in punishing losses. Sony also faces the risk that the TVs will become obsolete before they are sold. However, Sony increases the risk that it will encounter "stock-outs," that is, it will not have adequate inventory to meet customer demand.

### Answers to Self-Test Questions

**1.** a   **2.** b ($180,000 + $35,000)   **3.** b   **4.** c [(5,000 × $13) + (4,000 × $12)]   **5.** d [(8,000 × $11) + (1,000 × $12)]   **6.** d ((5,000 × $8) + (15,000 × $10) + (20,000 × $12)) ÷ 40,000 = $10.75; $10.75 × 7,000   **7.** c   **8.** d   **9.** d (200 × $80)   **10.** b   **11.** b   **12.** b $285,000 ÷ [($80,000 + $110,000) ÷ 2] = 3; 365 ÷ 3   **13.** d   **\*14.** d   **\*15.** b [$150,000 − (30% × $150,000)] = $105,000; $135,000 − $105,000

# A Look at IFRS

LEARNING OBJECTIVE    9

Compare the accounting procedures for inventories under GAAP and IFRS.

The major IFRS requirements related to accounting and reporting for inventories are the same as GAAP. The major differences are that IFRS prohibits the use of the LIFO cost flow assumption and determines market in the lower-of-cost-or-market inventory valuation differently.

## Key Points

- The requirements for accounting for and reporting inventories are more principles-based under IFRS. That is, GAAP provides more detailed guidelines in inventory accounting.

- The definitions for inventory are essentially similar under IFRS and GAAP. Both define inventory as assets held-for-sale in the ordinary course of business, in the process of production for sale (work in process), or to be consumed in the production of goods or services (e.g., raw materials).

- Who owns the goods—goods in transit or consigned goods—as well as the costs to include in inventory, are accounted for the same under IFRS and GAAP.

- Both GAAP and IFRS permit specific identification where appropriate. IFRS actually requires that the specific identification method be used where the inventory items are not interchangeable (i.e., can be specifically identified). If the inventory items are not specifically identifiable, a cost flow assumption is used. GAAP does not specify situations in which specific identification must be used.

- A major difference between IFRS and GAAP relates to the LIFO cost flow assumption. GAAP permits the use of LIFO for inventory valuation. IFRS prohibits its use. FIFO and average-cost are the only two acceptable cost flow assumptions permitted under IFRS.

- IFRS requires companies to use the same cost flow assumption for all goods of a similar nature. GAAP has no specific requirement in this area.

- In the lower-of-cost-or-market test for inventory valuation, IFRS defines market as net realizable value. Net realizable value is the estimated selling price in the ordinary course of business, less the estimated costs of completion and estimated selling expenses. In other words, net realizable value is the best estimate of the net amounts that inventories are expected to realize. GAAP, on the other hand, defines market as essentially replacement cost.

- Under GAAP, if inventory is written down under the lower-of-cost-or-market valuation, the new basis is now considered its cost. As a result, the inventory may not be written back up to its original cost in a subsequent period. Under IFRS, the write-down may be reversed in a subsequent period up to the amount of the previous write-down. Both the write-down and any subsequent reversal should be reported on the income statement as an expense. An item-by-item approach is generally followed under IFRS.

- An example of the use of lower-of-cost-or-net realizable value (LCNRV) under IFRS follows.

---

Mendel Company has the following four items in its ending inventory as of December 31, 2014. The company uses the lower-of-cost-or-net realizable value approach for inventory valuation following IFRS.

| Item No. | Cost | Net Realizable Value |
|---|---|---|
| 1320 | $3,600 | $3,400 |
| 1333 | 4,000 | 4,100 |
| 1428 | 2,800 | 2,100 |
| 1510 | 5,000 | 4,700 |

The computation of the ending inventory value to be reported in the financial statements at December 31, 2014, is as follows.

| Item No. | Cost | Net Realizable Value | LCNRV |
|---|---|---|---|
| 1320 | $ 3,600 | $ 3,400 | $ 3,400 |
| 1333 | 4,000 | 4,100 | 4,000 |
| 1428 | 2,800 | 2,100 | 2,100 |
| 1510 | 5,000 | 4,700 | 4,700 |
| Total | $15,400 | $14,300 | $14,200 |

---

- Unlike property, plant, and equipment, IFRS does not permit the option of valuing inventories at fair value. As indicated above, IFRS requires inventory to be written down, but inventory cannot be written up above its original cost.

- Similar to GAAP, certain agricultural products and mineral products can be reported at net realizable value using IFRS.

- IFRS allows companies to report inventory at standard cost if it does not differ significantly from actual cost. Standard cost is addressed in managerial accounting courses.

## Looking to the Future

One convergence issue that will be difficult to resolve relates to the use of the LIFO cost flow assumption. As indicated, IFRS specifically prohibits its use. Conversely, the LIFO cost flow assumption is widely used in the United States because of its favorable tax advantages. In addition, many argue that LIFO from a financial reporting point of view provides a better matching of current costs against revenue and, therefore, enables companies to compute a more realistic income.

## IFRS Practice

### IFRS Self-Test Questions

1. Which of the following should **not** be included in the inventory of a company using IFRS?
   (a) Goods held on consignment from another company.
   (b) Goods shipped on consignment to another company.
   (c) Goods in transit from another company shipped FOB shipping point.
   (d) None of the above.

2. Which method of inventory costing is prohibited under IFRS?
   (a) Specific identification.      (c) FIFO.
   (b) LIFO.                          (d) Average-cost.

3. Yang Company purchased 2,000 widgets and has 400 widgets in its ending inventory at a cost of $90 each and a current replacement cost of $80 each. The net realizable value of each unit in the ending inventory is $70. The ending inventory under lower-of-cost-or-net realizable value is:
   (a) $36,000.                       (c) $28,000.
   (b) $32,000.                       (d) None of the above.

4. Specific identification:
   (a) must be used under IFRS if the inventory items are not interchangeable.
   (b) cannot be used under IFRS.
   (c) cannot be used under GAAP.
   (d) must be used under IFRS if it would result in the most conservative net income.

5. IFRS requires the following:
   (a) Ending inventory is written up and down to net realizable value each reporting period.
   (b) Ending inventory is written down to net realizable value but cannot be written up.
   (c) Ending inventory is written down to net realizable value and may be written up in future periods to its net realizable value but not above its original cost.
   (d) Ending inventory is written down to net realizable value and may be written up in future periods to its net realizable value.

### IFRS Exercises

**IFRS6-1** Briefly describe some of the similarities and differences between GAAP and IFRS with respect to the accounting for inventories.

**IFRS6-2** LaTour Inc. is based in France and prepares its financial statements (in euros) in accordance with IFRS. In 2014, it reported cost of goods sold of €578 million and average inventory of €154 million. Briefly discuss how analysis of LaTour's inventory turnover (and comparisons to a company using GAAP) might be affected by differences in inventory accounting between IFRS and GAAP.

**IFRS6-3** Franklin Company has the following four items in its ending inventory as of December 31, 2014. The company uses the lower-of-cost-or-net realizable value approach for inventory valuation following IFRS.

| Item No. | Cost | Net Realizable Value |
|---|---|---|
| AB | $1,700 | $1,400 |
| TRX | 2,200 | 2,300 |
| NWA | 7,800 | 7,100 |
| SGH | 3,000 | 3,700 |

Compute the lower-of-cost-or-net realizable value.

## International Financial Reporting Problem: Zetar plc

**IFRS6-4** The financial statements of Zetar plc are presented in Appendix F. Instructions for accessing and using the company's complete annual report, including the notes to its financial statements, are also provided in Appendix F.

### Instructions

Using the notes to the company's financial statements, answer the following questions.

**(a)** What cost flow assumption does the company use to value inventory?

**(b)** What was the amount of expense that the company reported for inventory write-downs during 2011?

**(c)** What amount of raw materials, work in process, and finished goods inventory did the company report at April 30, 2011?

**Answers to IFRS Self-Test Questions**
**1.** a  **2.** b  **3.** c  **4.** a  **5.** c

The Navigator

## Feature Story

### QuickBooks® Helps This Retailer Sell Guitars

Starting a small business requires many decisions. For example, you have to decide where to locate, how much space you need, how much inventory to have, how many employees to hire, and where to advertise. Small business owners are typically so concerned about the product and sales side of their business that they often do not give enough thought to something that is critical to their success—how to keep track of financial results.

Small business owners today can choose either manual or computerized accounting systems. For example, Paul and Laura West are the owners of the first independent dealership of Carvin guitars and professional audio equipment. When they founded their company, in Sacramento, California, they decided to purchase a computerized accounting system that would integrate many aspects of their retail operations. They wanted to use their accounting software to manage their inventory of guitars and amplifiers, enter sales, record and report financial data, and process credit card and debit card

transactions. They evaluated a number of options and ch QuickBooks® by Intuit Inc.

QuickBooks®, like most other popular software packages programs designed for the needs of a specific business, v in this case is retailing. This QuickBooks® retailing packag automatically collects sales information from its point-of-scanning devices. It also keeps track of inventory levels a automatically generates purchase orders for popular iten when re-order points are reached. It even supports sales efforts by compiling a customer database from which the Wests send out targeted direct mailings to potential custo The computerized system enables data files to be emaile the company's accountant. This keeps costs down and makes it easier and more efficient to generate financial reports as needed. The Wests believe that the investmen the computerized system has saved them time and mone and allowed them to spend more time on other aspects their business.

*Source:* Intuit Inc., "QuickBooks® and ProAdvisor® Help Make Guitar Stor Hit," *Journal of Accountancy* (May 2006), p. 101.

✔ The Navigator

- Scan Learning Objectives
- Read Feature Story
- Read Preview
- Read text and answer **DO IT!** p. 335
  - p. 348
- Work Comprehensive **DO IT!** p. 349
- Review Summary of Learning Objectives
- Answer Self-Test Questions
- Complete Assignments
- Go to *WileyPLUS* for practice and tutorials
-  **Read A Look at IFRS** p. 371

### Learning Objectives  ✔ The Navigator

*After studying this chapter, you should be able to:*

[1] Identify the basic concepts of an accounting information system.

[2] Describe the nature and purpose of a subsidiary ledger.

[3] Explain how companies use special journals in journalizing.

Terra Images/Age Fotostock America, Inc.

# Preview of Chapter 7

✔ The Navigator

As you see from the Feature Story, a reliable information system is a necessity for any company. Whether companies use pen, pencil, or computers in maintaining accounting records, certain principles and procedures apply. The purpose of this chapter is to explain and illustrate these features.

The content and organization of Chapter 7 are as follows.

| ACCOUNTING INFORMATION SYSTEMS | | |
| --- | --- | --- |
| **Basic Concepts of Accounting Information Systems** | **Subsidiary Ledgers** | **Special Journals** |
| • Computerized accounting systems<br>• Manual accounting systems | • Example<br>• Advantages | • Sales journal<br>• Cash receipts journal<br>• Purchases journal<br>• Cash payments journal<br>• Effects of special journals on general journal |

## Basic Concepts of Accounting Information Systems

The **accounting information system** collects and processes transaction data and communicates financial information to decision-makers. It includes each of the steps in the accounting cycle that you studied in earlier chapters. It also includes the documents that provide evidence of the transactions, and the records, trial balances, worksheets, and financial statements that result. An **accounting system** may be either manual or computerized. Most businesses these days use some sort of computerized accounting system, whether it is an off-the-shelf system for small businesses, like QuickBooks or Peachtree, or a more complex custom-made system.

Efficient and effective accounting information systems are based on certain basic principles. These principles, as described in Illustration 7-1, are (1) cost-effectiveness, (2) usefulness, and (3) flexibility. If the accounting system is cost-effective, provides useful output, and has the flexibility to meet future needs, it can contribute to both individual and organizational goals.

**Illustration 7-1**
Principles of an efficient and effective accounting information system

**Cost-Effectiveness**
The accounting system must be cost-effective. Benefits of information must outweigh the cost of providing it.

**Useful Output**
To be useful, information must be understandable, relevant, reliable, timely, and accurate. Designers of accounting systems must consider the needs and knowledge of various users.

**Flexibility**
The accounting system should accommodate a variety of users and changing information needs. The system should be sufficiently flexible to meet the resulting changes in the demands made upon it.

## Computerized Accounting Systems

Many small businesses eventually replace their manual accounting system with a computerized general ledger accounting system. **General ledger accounting systems** are software programs that integrate the various accounting functions related to sales, purchases, receivables, payables, cash receipts and disbursements, and payroll. They also generate financial statements. Computerized systems have a number of advantages over manual systems. First, the company typically enters data only once in a computerized system. Second, because the computer does most steps automatically, it eliminates many errors resulting from human intervention in a manual system, such as errors in posting or preparation of financial statements. Computerized systems also provide information up-to-the-minute. More timely information results in better business decisions. Many different general ledger software packages are available.

## CHOOSING A SOFTWARE PACKAGE

To identify the right software for your business, you must understand your company's operations. For example, consider its needs with regard to inventory, billing, payroll, and cash management. In addition, the company might have specific needs that are not supported by all software systems. For example, you might want to track employees' hours on individual jobs or to extract information for determining sales commissions. Choosing the right system is critical because installation of even a basic system is time-consuming, and learning a new system will require many hours of employee time.

## ENTRY-LEVEL SOFTWARE

Software publishers tend to classify businesses into groups based on revenue and the number of employees. Companies with revenues of less than $5 million and up to 20 employees generally use **entry-level programs**. The two leading entry-level programs are Intuit's QuickBooks and The Sage Group's Sage 50. These programs control more than 90% of the market. Each of these entry-level programs comes in many different industry-specific versions. For example, some are designed for very specific industry applications such as restaurants, retailing, construction, manufacturing, or nonprofit.

Quality entry-level packages typically involve more than recording transactions and preparing financial statements. Here are some common features and benefits:

- **Easy data access and report preparation.** Users can easily access information related to specific customers or suppliers. For example, you can view all transactions, invoices, payments, as well as contact information for a specific client.
- **Audit trail.** As a result of the Sarbanes-Oxley Act, companies are now far more concerned that their accounting system minimizes opportunities for fraud. Many programs provide an "audit trail" that enables the tracking of all transactions.
- **Internal controls.** Some systems have an internal accounting review that identifies suspicious transactions or likely mistakes such as wrong account numbers or duplicate transactions.
- **Customization.** This feature enables the company to create data fields specific to the needs of its business.
- **Network-compatibility.** Multiple users in the company can access the system at the same time.

**Ethics Note**

Entire books and movies have used computer-system tampering as a major theme. Most programmers would agree that tamper-proofing and debugging programs are the most difficult and time-consuming phases of their jobs.

## ENTERPRISE RESOURCE PLANNING SYSTEMS

**Enterprise resource planning (ERP) systems** are typically used by manufacturing companies with more than 500 employees and $500 million in sales. The best-known of these systems are SAP AG's SAP ERP (the most widely used) and Oracle's ERP. ERP systems go far beyond the functions of an entry-level general ledger package. They integrate all aspects of the organization, including accounting, sales, human resource management, and manufacturing. Because of the complexity of an ERP system, implementation can take three years and cost five times as much as the purchase price of the system. Purchase and implementation of ERP systems can cost from $250,000 to as much as $50 million for the largest multi-national corporations.

## ETHICS INSIGHT

### Curbing Fraudulent Activity with Software

The Sarbanes-Oxley Act (SOX) requires that companies demonstrate that they have adequate controls in place to detect significant fraudulent behavior by employees. Recently, about 15% of publicly traded companies reported at least one material weakness in their controls that needed to be remedied.

The SOX requirements have created a huge market for software that can monitor and trace every recorded transaction and adjusting entry. This enables companies to pinpoint who used the accounting system and when they used it. These systems also require "electronic signatures" by employees for all significant transactions. Such signatures verify that employees have followed all required procedures, and that all actions are properly authorized. SOX-related technology spending was estimated to be approximately $2 billion at one time. One firm that specializes in compliance software had 10 clients prior to SOX and 250 after SOX.

*Source:* W. M. Bulkeley and C. Forelle, "Anti-Crime Program: How Corporate Scandals Gave Tech Firms a New Business Line," *Wall Street Journal* (December 9, 2005), p. A1.

 Why might this software help reduce fraudulent activity by employees? (See page 371.)

## Manual Accounting Systems

**Manual accounting systems** perform each of the steps in the accounting cycle by hand. For example, someone manually enters each accounting transaction in the journal and manually posts each to the ledger. Other manual computations must be made to obtain ledger account balances and to prepare a trial balance and financial statements. In the remainder of this chapter, we illustrate the use of a manual system.

You might be wondering, "Why cover manual accounting systems if the real world uses computerized systems?" First, small businesses still abound. Most of them begin operations with manual accounting systems and convert to computerized systems as the business grows. You may work in a small business or start your own someday, so it is useful to know how a manual system works. Second, to understand what computerized accounting systems do, you also need to understand manual accounting systems.

The manual accounting system represented in the first six chapters of this textbook is satisfactory in a company with a low volume of transactions. However, in most companies, it is necessary to add additional ledgers and journals to the accounting system to record transaction data efficiently.

## Subsidiary Ledgers

**LEARNING OBJECTIVE 2**

Describe the nature and purpose of a subsidiary ledger.

Imagine a business that has several thousand charge (credit) customers and shows the transactions with these customers in only one general ledger account—Accounts Receivable. It would be nearly impossible to determine the balance owed by an individual customer at any specific time. Similarly, the amount payable to one creditor would be difficult to locate quickly from a single Accounts Payable account in the general ledger.

Instead, companies use subsidiary ledgers to keep track of individual balances. A **subsidiary ledger** is a group of accounts with a common characteristic (for example, all accounts receivable). It is an addition to and an expansion of the general ledger. The subsidiary ledger frees the general ledger from the details of individual balances.

Two common subsidiary ledgers are:

1. The **accounts receivable** (or **customers') subsidiary ledger**, which collects transaction data of individual customers.

2. The **accounts payable** (or **creditors') subsidiary ledger**, which collects transaction data of individual creditors.

In each of these subsidiary ledgers, companies usually arrange individual accounts in alphabetical order.

A general ledger account summarizes the detailed data from a subsidiary ledger. For example, the detailed data from the accounts receivable subsidiary ledger are summarized in Accounts Receivable in the general ledger. The general ledger account that summarizes subsidiary ledger data is called a **control account**. Illustration 7-2 presents an overview of the relationship of subsidiary ledgers to the general ledger. There, the general ledger control accounts and subsidiary ledger accounts are in green. Note that Cash and Owner's Capital in this illustration are not control accounts because there are no subsidiary ledger accounts related to these accounts.

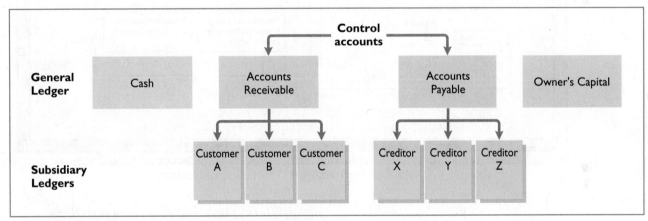

**Illustration 7-2**
Relationship of general ledger and subsidiary ledgers

**At the end of an accounting period, each general ledger control account balance must equal the composite balance of the individual accounts in the related subsidiary ledger.** For example, the balance in Accounts Payable in Illustration 7-2 must equal the total of the subsidiary balances of Creditors X + Y + Z.

## Subsidiary Ledger Example

Illustration 7-3 lists credit sales and collections on account for Pujols Company.

**Illustration 7-3**
Sales and collection transactions

| Credit Sales | | | Collections on Account | | |
|---|---|---|---|---|---|
| Jan. 10 | Aaron Co. | $ 6,000 | Jan. 19 | Aaron Co. | $4,000 |
| 12 | Branden Inc. | 3,000 | 21 | Branden Inc. | 3,000 |
| 20 | Caron Co. | 3,000 | 29 | Caron Co. | 1,000 |
| | | $12,000 | | | $8,000 |

Illustration 7-4 provides an example of a control account and subsidiary ledger for Pujols Company. (Due to space considerations, the explanation column in these accounts is not shown in this and subsequent illustrations.) Illustration 7-4 is based on the transactions listed in Illustration 7-3.

**Illustration 7-4**

Relationship between general and subsidiary ledgers

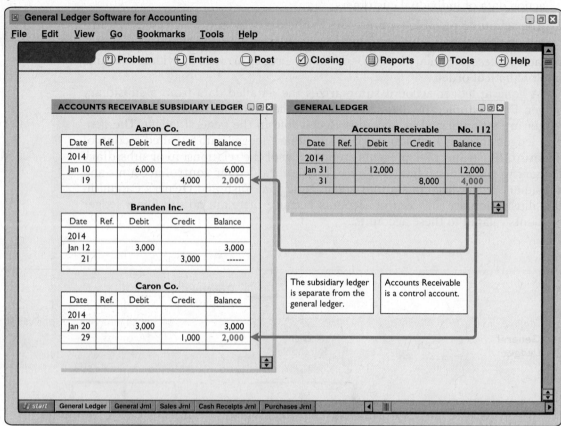

Pujols can reconcile the total debits ($12,000) and credits ($8,000) in Accounts Receivable in the general ledger to the detailed debits and credits in the subsidiary accounts. Also, the balance of $4,000 in the control account agrees with the total of the balances in the individual accounts (Aaron Co. $2,000 + Branden Inc. $0 + Caron Co. $2,000) in the subsidiary ledger.

As Illustration 7-4 shows, companies make monthly postings to the control accounts in the general ledger. This practice allows them to prepare monthly financial statements. Companies post to the individual accounts in the subsidiary ledger daily. Daily posting ensures that account information is current. This enables the company to monitor credit limits, bill customers, and answer inquiries from customers about their account balances.

## Advantages of Subsidiary Ledgers

Subsidiary ledgers have several advantages:

1. **They show in a single account transactions affecting one customer or one creditor**, thus providing up-to-date information on specific account balances.

2. **They free the general ledger of excessive details.** As a result, a trial balance of the general ledger does not contain vast numbers of individual account balances.

3. **They help locate errors in individual accounts** by reducing the number of accounts in one ledger and by using control accounts.

4. **They make possible a division of labor** in posting. One employee can post to the general ledger while someone else posts to the subsidiary ledgers.

---

## ACCOUNTING ACROSS THE ORGANIZATION

### "I'm John Smith, a.k.a. 13695071642"

Rather than relying on customer or creditor names in a subsidiary ledger, a computerized system expands the account number of the control account in a pre-specified manner. For example, if Accounts Receivable was numbered 10010, the first account in the accounts receivable subsidiary ledger might be numbered 10010–0001. Most systems allow inquiries about specific accounts in the subsidiary ledger (by account number) or about the control account. With the latter, the system would automatically total all the subsidiary accounts whenever an inquiry to the control account was made.

© Niels Laan/iStockphoto

**?** Why use numbers to identify names in a computerized system? (See page 371.)

---

## > DO IT!

### Subsidiary Ledgers

Presented below is information related to Sims Company for its first month of operations. Determine the balances that appear in the accounts payable subsidiary ledger. What Accounts Payable balance appears in the general ledger at the end of January?

| Credit Purchases | | | Cash Paid | | |
|---|---|---|---|---|---|
| Jan. 5 | Devon Co. | $11,000 | Jan. 9 | Devon Co. | $7,000 |
| 11 | Shelby Co. | 7,000 | 14 | Shelby Co. | 2,000 |
| 22 | Taylor Co. | 14,000 | 27 | Taylor Co. | 9,000 |

### Action Plan

✔ Subtract cash paid from credit purchases to determine the balances in the accounts payable subsidiary ledger.

✔ Sum the individual balances to determine the Accounts Payable balance.

**Solution**

Subsidiary ledger balances:

Devon Co.  $4,000 ($11,000 − $7,000)

Shelby Co. $5,000 ($7,000 − $2,000)

Taylor Co.  $5,000 ($14,000 − $9,000)

General ledger Accounts Payable balance: $14,000 ($4,000 + $5,000 + $5,000)

Related exercise material: **BE7-4, BE7-5, E7-1, E7-2, E7-4, E7-5, and DO IT! 7-1.**

✔ The Navigator

---

## Special Journals

So far you have learned to journalize transactions in a two-column general journal and post each entry to the general ledger. This procedure is satisfactory in only very small companies. To expedite journalizing and posting, most companies use special journals **in addition to the general journal**.

**LEARNING OBJECTIVE    3**

Explain how companies use special journals in journalizing.

Companies use **special journals** to record similar types of transactions. Examples are all sales of merchandise on account or all cash receipts. The types of transactions that occur frequently in a company determine what special journals the company uses. Most merchandising companies record daily transactions using the journals shown in Illustration 7-5.

**Illustration 7-5**
Use of special journals and the general journal

| **Sales Journal** | **Cash Receipts Journal** | **Purchases Journal** | **Cash Payments Journal** | **General Journal** |
|---|---|---|---|---|
| Used for:<br>All sales of merchandise on account | Used for:<br>All cash received (including cash sales) | Used for:<br>All purchases of merchandise on account | Used for:<br>All cash paid (including cash purchases) | Used for:<br>Transactions that cannot be entered in a special journal, including correcting, adjusting, and closing entries |

**If a transaction cannot be recorded in a special journal, the company records it in the general journal.** For example, if a company had special journals for only the four types of transactions listed above, it would record purchase returns and allowances in the general journal. Similarly, **correcting, adjusting, and closing entries are recorded in the general journal**. In some situations, companies might use special journals other than those listed above. For example, when sales returns and allowances are frequent, a company might use a special journal to record these transactions.

Special journals **permit greater division of labor** because several people can record entries in different journals at the same time. For example, one employee may journalize all cash receipts, and another may journalize all credit sales. Also, the use of special journals **reduces the time needed to complete the posting process**. With special journals, companies may post some accounts monthly, instead of daily, as we will illustrate later in the chapter. On the following pages, we discuss the four special journals shown in Illustration 7-5.

## Sales Journal

In the **sales journal**, companies record **sales of merchandise on account**. Cash sales of merchandise go in the cash receipts journal. Credit sales of assets other than merchandise go in the general journal.

### JOURNALIZING CREDIT SALES

**Helpful Hint** Postings are also made daily to individual ledger accounts in the inventory subsidiary ledger to maintain a perpetual inventory.

To demonstrate use of a sales journal, we will use data for Karns Wholesale Supply, which uses a **perpetual inventory system**. Under this system, each entry in the sales journal results in one entry **at selling price** and another entry **at cost**. The entry at selling price is a debit to Accounts Receivable (a control account) and a credit of equal amount to Sales Revenue. The entry at cost is a debit to Cost of Goods Sold and a credit of equal amount to Inventory (a control account). Using a sales journal with two amount columns, the company can show on only one line a sales transaction at both selling price and cost. Illustration 7-6 shows this two-column sales journal of Karns Wholesale Supply, using assumed credit sales transactions (for sales invoices 101–107).

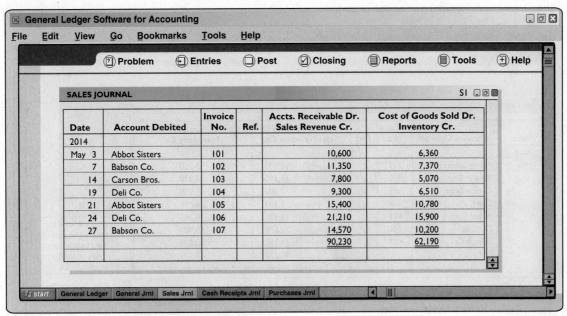

Illustration 7-6
Journalizing the sales journal—perpetual inventory system

Note that, unlike the general journal, an explanation is not required for each entry in a special journal. Also, note that use of prenumbered invoices ensures that all invoices are journalized and no invoices are duplicated. Finally, note that the reference (Ref.) column is not used in journalizing. It is used in posting the sales journal, as explained in the next section.

## POSTING THE SALES JOURNAL

Companies make daily postings from the sales journal **to the individual accounts receivable** in the subsidiary ledger. Posting **to the general ledger** is done **monthly**. Illustration 7-7 (page 338) shows both the daily and monthly postings.

A check mark (✓) is inserted in the reference column to indicate that the daily posting to the customer's account has been made. If the subsidiary ledger accounts were numbered, the account number would be entered in place of the check mark. At the end of the month, Karns posts the column totals of the sales journal to the general ledger. Here, the column totals are as follows. From the selling-price column, a debit of $90,230 to Accounts Receivable (account No. 112), and a credit of $90,230 to Sales Revenue (account No. 401). From the cost column, a debit of $62,190 to Cost of Goods Sold (account No. 505), and a credit of $62,190 to Inventory (account No. 120). Karns inserts the account numbers below the column totals to indicate that the postings have been made. In both the general ledger and subsidiary ledger accounts, the reference **S1** indicates that the posting came from page 1 of the sales journal.

## PROVING THE LEDGERS

The next step is to "prove" the ledgers. To do so, Karns must determine two things: (1) The total of the general ledger debit balances must equal the total of the general ledger credit balances. (2) The sum of the subsidiary ledger balances must equal the balance in the control account. Illustration 7-8 (page 339) shows the proof of the postings from the sales journal to the general and subsidiary ledgers.

## ADVANTAGES OF THE SALES JOURNAL

The use of a special journal to record sales on account has a number of advantages. First, the one-line entry for each sales transaction saves time. In the sales journal, it is not necessary to write out the four account titles for each transaction.

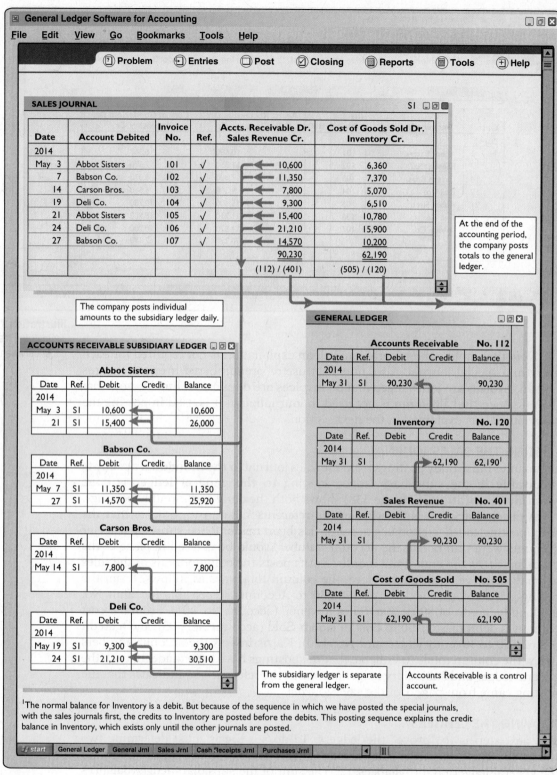

**Illustration 7-7**
Posting the sales journal

Second, only totals, rather than individual entries, are posted to the general ledger. This saves posting time and reduces the possibilities of errors in posting. Finally, a division of labor results because one individual can take responsibility for the sales journal.

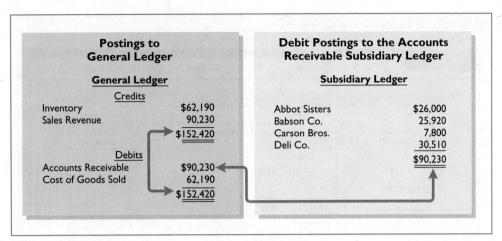

**Illustration 7-8**
Proving the equality of the
postings from the sales journal

## Cash Receipts Journal

In the **cash receipts journal**, companies record all receipts of cash. The most
common types of cash receipts are cash sales of merchandise and collections of
accounts receivable. Many other possibilities exist, such as receipt of money from
bank loans and cash proceeds from disposal of equipment. A one- or two-column
cash receipts journal would not have space enough for all possible cash receipt
transactions. Therefore, companies use a multiple-column cash receipts journal.

Generally, a cash receipts journal includes the following columns: debit columns for Cash and Sales Discounts, and credit columns for Accounts Receivable, Sales Revenue, and "Other Accounts." Companies use the "Other Accounts"
category when the cash receipt does not involve a cash sale or a collection of
accounts receivable. Under a perpetual inventory system, each sales entry also is
accompanied by an entry that debits Cost of Goods Sold and credits Inventory for
the cost of the merchandise sold. Illustration 7-9 (page 340) shows a six-column
cash receipts journal.

Companies may use additional credit columns if these columns significantly
reduce postings to a specific account. For example, a loan company such as
Household International receives thousands of cash collections from customers.
Using separate credit columns for Loans Receivable and Interest Revenue, rather
than the Other Accounts credit column, would reduce postings.

### JOURNALIZING CASH RECEIPTS TRANSACTIONS

To illustrate the journalizing of cash receipts transactions, we will continue
with the May transactions of Karns Wholesale Supply. Collections from customers relate to the entries recorded in the sales journal in Illustration 7-6. The
entries in the cash receipts journal are based on the following cash receipts.

May  1   D. A. Karns makes an investment of $5,000 in the business.
     7   Cash sales of merchandise total $1,900 (cost, $1,240).
    10   Received a check for $10,388 from Abbot Sisters in payment of invoice No. 101
         for $10,600 less a 2% discount.
    12   Cash sales of merchandise total $2,600 (cost, $1,690).
    17   Received a check for $11,123 from Babson Co. in payment of invoice No. 102
         for $11,350 less a 2% discount.
    22   Received cash by signing a note for $6,000.
    23   Received a check for $7,644 from Carson Bros. in full for invoice No. 103 for
         $7,800 less a 2% discount.
    28   Received a check for $9,114 from Deli Co. in full for invoice No. 104 for
         $9,300 less a 2% discount.

Further information about the columns in the cash receipts journal is listed on
page 341.

**Illustration 7-9**
Journalizing and posting the cash receipts journal

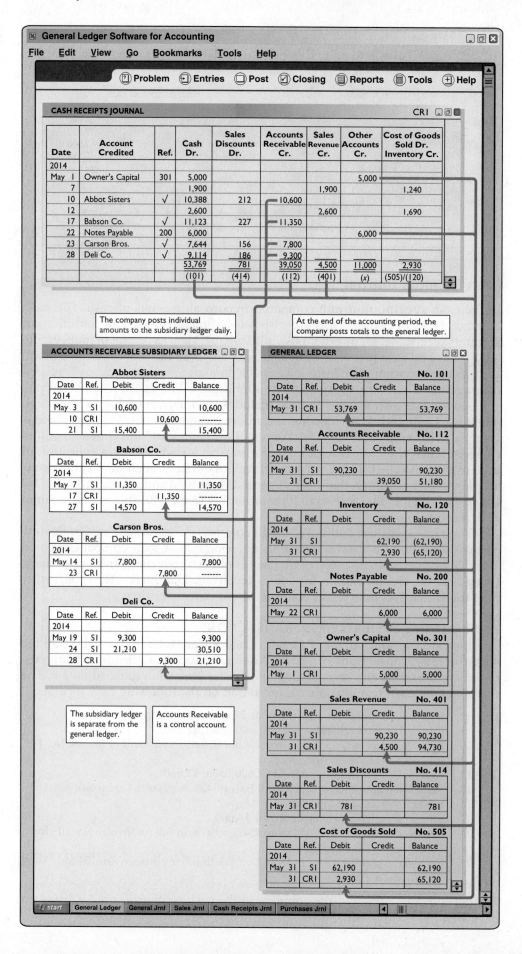

## Debit Columns:

1. **Cash.** Karns enters in this column the amount of cash actually received in each transaction. The column total indicates the total cash receipts for the month.

2. **Sales Discounts.** Karns includes a Sales Discounts column in its cash receipts journal. By doing so, it does not need to enter sales discount items in the general journal. As a result, the cash receipts journal shows on one line the collection of an account receivable within the discount period.

## Credit Columns:

3. **Accounts Receivable.** Karns uses the Accounts Receivable column to record cash collections on account. The amount entered here is the amount to be credited to the individual customer's account.

4. **Sales Revenue.** The Sales Revenue column records all cash sales of merchandise. Cash sales of other assets (plant assets, for example) are not reported in this column.

5. **Other Accounts.** Karns uses the Other Accounts column whenever the credit is other than to Accounts Receivable or Sales Revenue. For example, in the first entry, Karns enters $5,000 as a credit to Owner's Capital. This column is often referred to as the sundry accounts column.

**Helpful Hint** When is an account title entered in the "Account Credited" column of the cash receipts journal? Answer: A *subsidiary ledger* account is entered when the entry involves a collection of accounts receivable. A *general ledger* account is entered when the account is not shown in a special column (and an amount must be entered in the Other Accounts column). Otherwise, no account is shown in the "Account Credited" column.

## Debit and Credit Column:

6. **Cost of Goods Sold and Inventory.** This column records debits to Cost of Goods Sold and credits to Inventory.

In a multi-column journal, generally only one line is needed for each entry. Debit and credit amounts for each line must be equal. When Karns journalizes the collection from Abbot Sisters on May 10, for example, three amounts are indicated. Note also that the Account Credited column identifies both general ledger and subsidiary ledger account titles. General ledger accounts are illustrated in the May 1 and May 22 entries. A subsidiary account is illustrated in the May 10 entry for the collection from Abbot Sisters.

When Karns has finished journalizing a multi-column journal, it totals the amount columns and compares the totals to prove the equality of debits and credits. Illustration 7-10 shows the proof of the equality of Karns's cash receipts journal.

**Illustration 7-10**
Proving the equality of the cash receipts journal

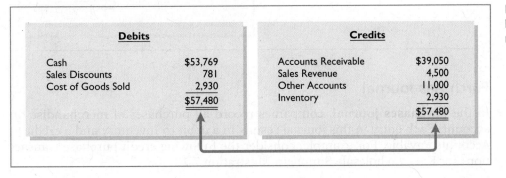

| Debits | | Credits | |
|---|---|---|---|
| Cash | $53,769 | Accounts Receivable | $39,050 |
| Sales Discounts | 781 | Sales Revenue | 4,500 |
| Cost of Goods Sold | 2,930 | Other Accounts | 11,000 |
| | $57,480 | Inventory | 2,930 |
| | | | $57,480 |

Totaling the columns of a journal and proving the equality of the totals is called **footing** and **cross-footing** a journal.

## POSTING THE CASH RECEIPTS JOURNAL

Posting a multi-column journal (Illustration 7-9, page 340) involves the following steps.

1. **At the end of the month**, the company posts all column totals, except for the Other Accounts total, to the account title(s) specified in the column heading

(such as Cash or Accounts Receivable). The company then enters account numbers below the column totals to show that they have been posted. For example, Karns has posted Cash to account No. 101, Accounts Receivable to account No. 112, Inventory to account No. 120, Sales Revenue to account No. 401, Sales Discounts to account No. 414, and Cost of Goods Sold to account No.505.

2. The company **separately posts the individual amounts comprising the Other Accounts total** to the general ledger accounts specified in the Account Credited column. See, for example, the credit posting to Owner's Capital. The total amount of this column has not been posted. The symbol (X) is inserted below the total to this column to indicate that the amount has not been posted.

3. The individual amounts in a column, posted in total to a control account (Accounts Receivable, in this case), are posted **daily to the subsidiary ledger** account specified in the Account Credited column. See, for example, the credit posting of $10,600 to Abbot Sisters.

The symbol **CR**, used in both the subsidiary and general ledgers, identifies postings from the cash receipts journal.

### PROVING THE LEDGERS

After posting of the cash receipts journal is completed, Karns proves the ledgers. As shown in Illustration 7-11, the general ledger totals agree. Also, the sum of the subsidiary ledger balances equals the control account balance.

**Illustration 7-11**

Proving the ledgers after posting the sales and the cash receipts journals

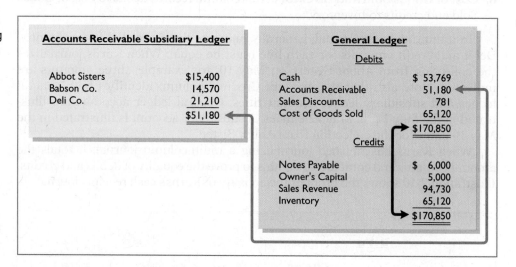

### Purchases Journal

In the **purchases journal**, companies record all purchases of merchandise on account. Each entry in this journal results in a debit to Inventory and a credit to Accounts Payable. For example, consider the following credit purchase transactions for Karns Wholesale Supply in Illustration 7-12.

**Illustration 7-12**

Credit purchase transactions

| Date | Supplier | Amount |
|---|---|---|
| 5/6 | Jasper Manufacturing Inc. | $11,000 |
| 5/10 | Eaton and Howe Inc. | 7,200 |
| 5/14 | Fabor and Son | 6,900 |
| 5/19 | Jasper Manufacturing Inc. | 17,500 |
| 5/26 | Fabor and Son | 8,700 |
| 5/29 | Eaton and Howe Inc. | 12,600 |

Illustration 7-13 shows the purchases journal for Karns Wholesale Supply. When using a one-column purchases journal (as in Illustration 7-13), a company cannot journalize other types of purchases on account or cash purchases in it. For example, in the purchases journal in Illustration 7-13, Karns would have to record credit purchases of equipment or supplies in the general journal. Likewise, all cash purchases would be entered in the cash payments journal. As illustrated later, companies that make numerous credit purchases for items other than merchandise often expand the purchases journal to a multi-column format. (See Illustration 7-15 on page 345.)

**Illustration 7-13**
Journalizing and posting the purchases journal

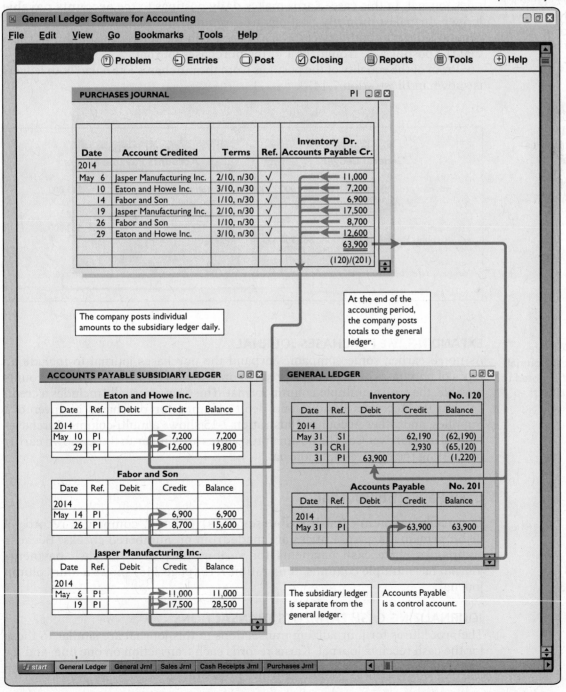

### JOURNALIZING CREDIT PURCHASES OF MERCHANDISE

The journalizing procedure is similar to that for a sales journal. Companies make entries in the purchases journal from purchase invoices. In contrast to the sales journal, the purchases journal may not have an invoice number column because invoices received from different suppliers will not be in numerical sequence. To ensure that they record all purchase invoices, some companies consecutively number each invoice upon receipt and then use an internal document number column in the purchases journal. The entries for Karns Wholesale Supply are based on the assumed credit purchases listed in Illustration 7-12.

### POSTING THE PURCHASES JOURNAL

**Helpful Hint** Postings to subsidiary ledger accounts are done daily because it is often necessary to know a current balance for the subsidiary accounts.

The procedures for posting the purchases journal are similar to those for the sales journal. In this case, Karns makes **daily** postings to the **accounts payable ledger**. It makes **monthly** postings to Inventory and Accounts Payable in the general ledger. In both ledgers, Karns uses **P1** in the reference column to show that the postings are from page 1 of the purchases journal.

Proof of the equality of the postings from the purchases journal to both ledgers is shown in Illustration 7-14.

**Illustration 7-14**
Proving the equality of the purchases journal

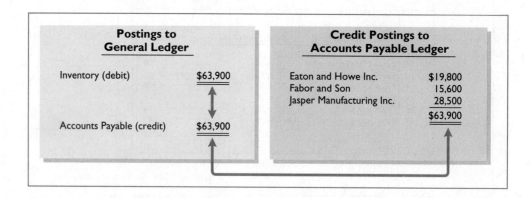

### EXPANDING THE PURCHASES JOURNAL

**Helpful Hint** A single-column purchases journal needs only to be footed to prove the equality of debits and credits.

As noted earlier, some companies expand the purchases journal to include all types of purchases on account. Instead of one column for inventory and accounts payable, they use a multiple-column format. This format usually includes a credit column for Accounts Payable and debit columns for purchases of Inventory, Supplies, and Other Accounts. Illustration 7-15 shows a multi-column purchases journal for Hanover Co. The posting procedures are similar to those shown earlier for posting the cash receipts journal.

## Cash Payments Journal

In a **cash payments (cash disbursements) journal**, companies record all disbursements of cash. Entries are made from prenumbered checks. Because companies make cash payments for various purposes, the cash payments journal has multiple columns. Illustration 7-16 (page 346) shows a four-column journal.

### JOURNALIZING CASH PAYMENTS TRANSACTIONS

The procedures for journalizing transactions in this journal are similar to those for the cash receipts journal. Karns records each transaction on one line, and for each line there must be equal debit and credit amounts. The entries in the cash

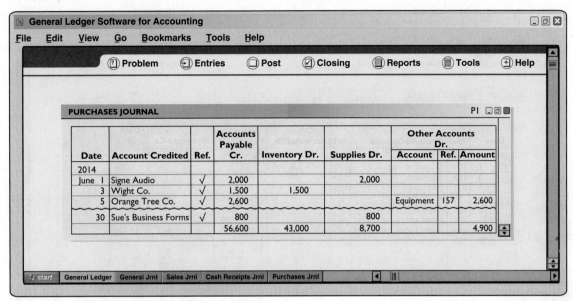

**Illustration 7-15**
Multi-column purchases journal

payments journal in Illustration 7-16 are based on the following transactions for Karns Wholesale Supply.

May 1  Issued check No. 101 for $1,200 for the annual premium on a fire insurance policy.

3  Issued check No. 102 for $100 in payment of freight when terms were FOB shipping point.

8  Issued check No. 103 for $4,400 for the purchase of merchandise.

10  Sent check No. 104 for $10,780 to Jasper Manufacturing Inc. in payment of May 6 invoice for $11,000 less a 2% discount.

19  Mailed check No. 105 for $6,984 to Eaton and Howe Inc. in payment of May 10 invoice for $7,200 less a 3% discount.

23  Sent check No. 106 for $6,831 to Fabor and Son in payment of May 14 invoice for $6,900 less a 1% discount.

28  Sent check No. 107 for $17,150 to Jasper Manufacturing Inc. in payment of May 19 invoice for $17,500 less a 2% discount.

30  Issued check No. 108 for $500 to D. A. Karns as a cash withdrawal for personal use.

Note that whenever Karns enters an amount in the Other Accounts column, it must identify a specific general ledger account in the Account Debited column. The entries for checks No. 101, 102, 103, and 108 illustrate this situation. Similarly, Karns must identify a subsidiary account in the Account Debited column whenever it enters an amount in the Accounts Payable column. See, for example, the entry for check No. 104.

After Karns journalizes the cash payments journal, it totals the columns. The totals are then balanced to prove the equality of debits and credits.

## POSTING THE CASH PAYMENTS JOURNAL

The procedures for posting the cash payments journal are similar to those for the cash receipts journal. Karns posts the amounts recorded in the Accounts Payable column individually to the subsidiary ledger and in total to the control account. It posts Inventory and Cash only in total at the end of the month. Transactions in the Other Accounts column are posted individually to the appropriate account(s) affected. The company does not post totals for the Other Accounts column.

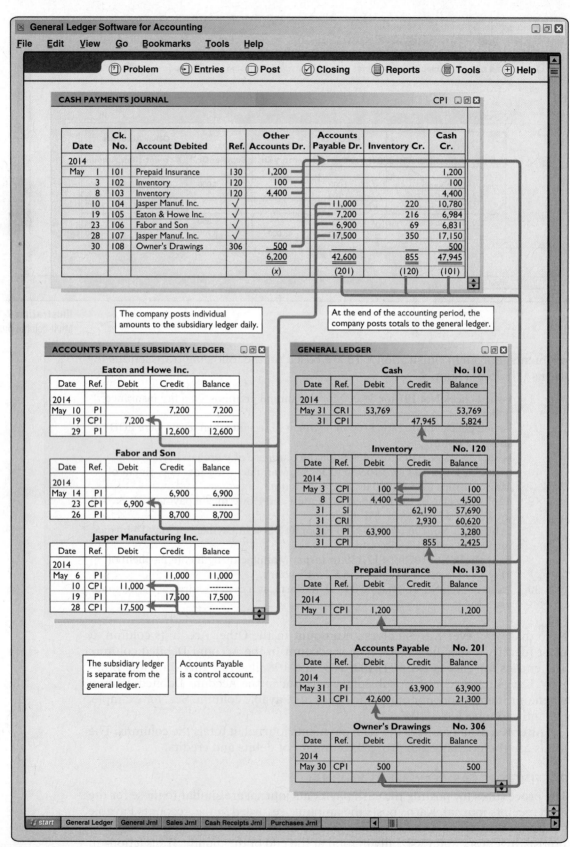

**Illustration 7-16**
Journalizing and posting the
cash payments journal

Illustration 7-16 shows the posting of the cash payments journal. Note that Karns uses the symbol **CP** as the posting reference. After postings are completed, the company proves the equality of the debit and credit balances in the general ledger. In addition, the control account balances should agree with the subsidiary ledger total balance. Illustration 7-17 shows the agreement of these balances.

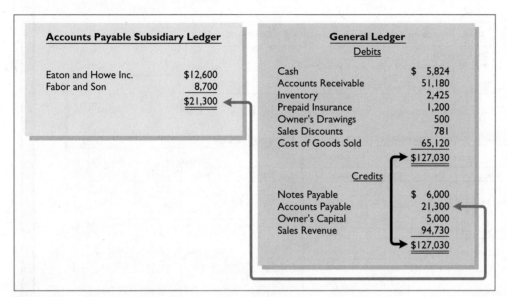

**Illustration 7-17**
Proving the ledgers after postings from the sales, cash receipts, purchases, and cash payments journals

## Effects of Special Journals on the General Journal

Special journals for sales, purchases, and cash substantially reduce the number of entries that companies make in the general journal. **Only transactions that cannot be entered in a special journal are recorded in the general journal.** For example, a company may use the general journal to record such transactions as granting of credit to a customer for a sales return or allowance, granting of credit from a supplier for purchases returned, acceptance of a note receivable from a customer, and purchase of equipment by issuing a note payable. Also, **correcting, adjusting, and closing entries are made in the general journal**.

The general journal has columns for date, account title and explanation, reference, and debit and credit amounts. When control and subsidiary accounts are not involved, the procedures for journalizing and posting of transactions are the same as those described in earlier chapters. When control and subsidiary accounts are involved, companies make two changes from the earlier procedures:

1. In **journalizing**, they identify both the control and the subsidiary accounts.
2. In **posting**, there must be a **dual posting**: once to the control account and once to the subsidiary account.

To illustrate, assume that on May 31, Karns Wholesale Supply returns $500 of merchandise for credit to Fabor and Son. Illustration 7-18 (page 348) shows the entry in the general journal and the posting of the entry. Note that if Karns receives cash instead of credit on this return, then it would record the transaction in the cash receipts journal.

Note that the general journal indicates two accounts (Accounts Payable, and Fabor and Son) for the debit, and two postings ("201/✓") in the reference column. One debit is posted to the control account and another debit to the creditor's account in the subsidiary ledger.

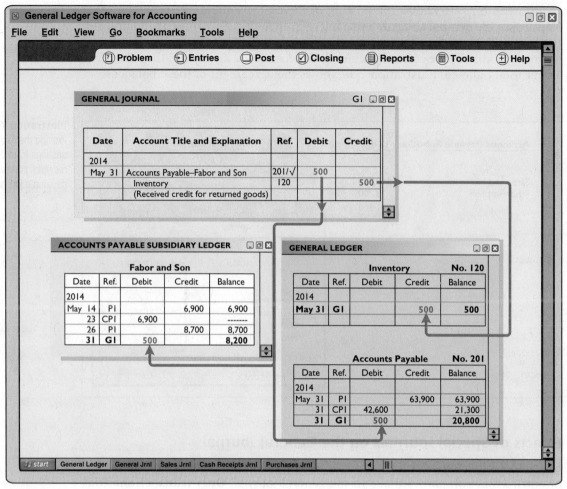

**Illustration 7-18**
Journalizing and posting the
general journal

---

> **DO IT!**

## Special Journals

### Action Plan

✔ Determine if the transaction involves the receipt of cash (cash receipts journal) or the payment of cash (cash payments journal).

✔ Determine if the transaction is a sale of merchandise on account (sales journal) or a purchase of merchandise on account (purchases journal).

✔ All other transactions are recorded in the general journal.

Swisher Company had the following transactions during March.

1. Collected cash on account from Oakland Company.
2. Purchased equipment by signing a note payable.
3. Sold merchandise on account.
4. Purchased merchandise on account.
5. Paid $2,400 for a 2-year insurance policy.

Identify the journal in which each of the transactions above is recorded.

### Solution

| | |
|---|---|
| 1. Collected cash on account from Oakland Company. | Cash receipts journal |
| 2. Purchased equipment by signing a note payable. | General journal |
| 3. Sold merchandise on account. | Sales journal |
| 4. Purchased merchandise on account. | Purchases journal |
| 5. Paid $2,400 for a 2-year insurance policy. | Cash payments journal |

Related exercise material: **BE7-6, BE7-7, BE7-8, BE7-9, BE7-10, E7-6, E7-7, E7-8, E7-10, and DO IT! 7-2.**

✔ The Navigator

## > Comprehensive DO IT!

Cassandra Wilson Company uses a six-column cash receipts journal with the following columns.

| | |
|---|---|
| Cash (Dr.) | Other Accounts (Cr.) |
| Sales Discounts (Dr.) | Cost of Goods Sold (Dr.) and |
| Accounts Receivable (Cr.) | Inventory (Cr.) |
| Sales Revenue (Cr.) | |

Cash receipts transactions for the month of July 2014 are as follows.

| | | |
|---|---|---|
| July | 3 | Cash sales total $5,800 (cost, $3,480). |
| | 5 | Received a check for $6,370 from Jeltz Company in payment of an invoice dated June 26 for $6,500, terms 2/10, n/30. |
| | 9 | Cassandra Wilson, the proprietor, made an additional investment of $5,000 in cash in the business. |
| | 10 | Cash sales total $12,519 (cost, $7,511). |
| | 12 | Received a check for $7,275 from R. Eliot & Co. in payment of a $7,500 invoice dated July 3, terms 3/10, n/30. |
| | 15 | Received an advance of $700 cash for future services. |
| | 20 | Cash sales total $15,472 (cost, $9,283). |
| | 22 | Received a check for $5,880 from Beck Company in payment of $6,000 invoice dated July 13, terms 2/10, n/30. |
| | 29 | Cash sales total $17,660 (cost, $10,596). |
| | 31 | Received cash of $200 on interest earned for July. |

**Action Plan**

✔ Record all cash receipts in the cash receipts journal.

✔ The "account credited" indicates items posted individually to the subsidiary ledger or to the general ledger.

✔ Record cash sales in the cash receipts journal— not in the sales journal.

✔ The total debits must equal the total credits.

### Instructions

(a) Journalize the transactions in the cash receipts journal.

(b) Contrast the posting of the Accounts Receivable and Other Accounts columns.

### Solution to Comprehensive DO IT!

(a)

**CASSANDRA WILSON COMPANY**
Cash Receipts Journal                                                                 CR1

| Date | Account Credited | Ref. | Cash Dr. | Sales Discounts Dr. | Accounts Receivable Cr. | Sales Revenue Cr. | Other Accounts Cr. | Cost of Goods Sold Dr. Inventory Cr. |
|---|---|---|---|---|---|---|---|---|
| 2014 | | | | | | | | |
| 7/3 | | | 5,800 | | | 5,800 | | 3,480 |
| 5 | Jeltz Company | | 6,370 | 130 | 6,500 | | | |
| 9 | Owner's Capital | | 5,000 | | | | 5,000 | |
| 10 | | | 12,519 | | | 12,519 | | 7,511 |
| 12 | R. Eliot & Co. | | 7,275 | 225 | 7,500 | | | |
| 15 | Unearned Service Revenue | | 700 | | | | 700 | |
| 20 | | | 15,472 | | | 15,472 | | 9,283 |
| 22 | Beck Company | | 5,880 | 120 | 6,000 | | | |
| 29 | | | 17,660 | | | 17,660 | | 10,596 |
| 31 | Interest Revenue | | 200 | | | | 200 | |
| | | | 76,876 | 475 | 20,000 | 51,451 | 5,900 | 30,870 |

(b) The Accounts Receivable column total is posted as a credit to Accounts Receivable. The individual amounts are credited to the customers' accounts identified in the Account Credited column, which are maintained in the accounts receivable subsidiary ledger.

The amounts in the Other Accounts column are posted individually. They are credited to the account titles identified in the Account Credited column.

✔ The Navigator

## SUMMARY OF LEARNING OBJECTIVES

**1 Identify the basic concepts of an accounting information system.** The basic principles in developing an accounting information system are cost-effectiveness, useful output, and flexibility. Most companies use a computerized accounting system. Smaller companies use entry-level software such as QuickBooks or Sage 50. Larger companies use custom-made software packages, which often integrate all aspects of the organization.

**2 Describe the nature and purpose of a subsidiary ledger.** A subsidiary ledger is a group of accounts with a common characteristic. It facilitates the recording process by freeing the general ledger from details of individual balances.

**3 Explain how companies use special journals in journalizing.** Companies use special journals to group similar types of transactions. In a special journal, generally only one line is used to record a complete transaction.

## GLOSSARY

**Accounting information system** A system that collects and processes transaction data and communicates financial information to decision-makers. (p. 330).

**Accounts payable (creditors') subsidiary ledger** A subsidiary ledger that collects transaction data of individual creditors. (p. 333).

**Accounts receivable (customers') subsidiary ledger** A subsidiary ledger that collects transaction data of individual customers. (p. 333).

**Cash payments (cash disbursements) journal** A special journal that records all disbursements of cash. (p. 344).

**Cash receipts journal** A special journal that records all cash received. (p. 339).

**Control account** An account in the general ledger that summarizes subsidiary ledger data. (p. 333).

**Manual accounting system** A system in which someone performs each of the steps in the accounting cycle by hand. (p. 332).

**Purchases journal** A special journal that records all purchases of merchandise on account. (p. 342).

**Sales journal** A special journal that records all sales of merchandise on account. (p. 336).

**Special journal** A journal that records similar types of transactions, such as all credit sales. (p. 336).

**Subsidiary ledger** A group of accounts with a common characteristic. (p. 332).

**Self-Test, Brief Exercises, Exercises, Problem Set A, and many more components are available for practice in *WileyPLUS*.**

## SELF-TEST QUESTIONS

*Answers are on page 371.*

(LO 1) **1.** The basic principles of an accounting information system include all of the following **except**:
   **(a)** cost-effectiveness.   **(c)** useful output.
   **(b)** flexibility.   **(d)** periodicity.

(LO 1) **2.** Which of the following is **not** an advantage of computerized accounting systems?
   **(a)** Data is entered only once in computerized accounting systems.
   **(b)** Computerized accounting systems provide up-to-date information.
   **(c)** Computerized accounting systems eliminate entering of transaction information.

   **(d)** Computerized accounting systems eliminate many errors resulting from human intervention.

**3.** Which of the following is **incorrect** concerning sub- (LO 2) sidiary ledgers?
   **(a)** The purchases ledger is a common subsidiary ledger for creditor accounts.
   **(b)** The accounts receivable ledger is a subsidiary ledger.
   **(c)** A subsidiary ledger is a group of accounts with a common characteristic.
   **(d)** An advantage of the subsidiary ledger is that it permits a division of labor in posting.

(LO 2)  **4.** Two common subsidiary ledgers are:
   **(a)** accounts receivable and cash receipts.
   **(b)** accounts payable and cash payments.
   **(c)** accounts receivable and accounts payable.
   **(d)** sales and cost of goods sold.

(LO 2)  **5.** At the beginning of the month, the accounts receivable subsidiary ledger showed balances for Apple Company $5,000 and Berry Company $7,000. During the month, credit sales were made to Apple $6,000, Berry $4,500, and Cantaloupe $8,500. Cash was collected on account from Berry $11,500 and Cantaloupe $3,000. At the end of the month, the control account Accounts Receivable in the general ledger should have a balance of:
   **(a)** $11,000.              **(c)** $16,500.
   **(b)** $12,000.              **(d)** $31,000.

(LO 3)  **6.** A sales journal will be used for:

| | Credit Sales | Cash Sales | Sales Discounts |
|---|---|---|---|
| **(a)** | no | yes | yes |
| **(b)** | yes | no | yes |
| **(c)** | yes | no | no |
| **(d)** | yes | yes | no |

(LO 3)  **7.** A purchase of equipment on account is recorded in the:
   **(a)** cash receipts journal.   **(c)** cash payments journal.
   **(b)** purchases journal.       **(d)** general journal.

(LO 3)  **8.** A purchase of equipment using cash is recorded in the:
   **(a)** cash receipts journal.   **(c)** cash payments journal.
   **(b)** purchases journal.       **(d)** general journal.

(LO 3)  **9.** Which of the following statements is **correct**?
   **(a)** The sales discount column is included in the cash receipts journal.
   **(b)** The purchases journal records all purchases of merchandise whether for cash or on account.
   **(c)** The cash receipts journal records sales on account.
   **(d)** Merchandise returned by the buyer is recorded by the seller in the purchases journal.

(LO 3)  **10.** Dotel Company's cash receipts journal includes an Accounts Receivable column and an Other Accounts column. At the end of the month, these columns are posted to the general ledger as:

| | Accounts Receivable | Other Accounts |
|---|---|---|
| **(a)** | a column total | a column total |
| **(b)** | individual amounts | a column total |
| **(c)** | individual amounts | individual amounts |
| **(d)** | a column total | individual amounts |

(LO 3)  **11.** Which of the following is **incorrect** concerning the posting of the cash receipts journal?
   **(a)** The total of the Other Accounts column is not posted.
   **(b)** All column totals except the total for the Other Accounts column are posted once at the end of the month to the account title(s) specified in the column heading.
   **(c)** The totals of all columns are posted daily to the accounts specified in the column heading.
   **(d)** The individual amounts in a column posted in total to a control account are posted daily to the subsidiary ledger account specified in the Account Credited column.

(LO 3)  **12.** Postings from the purchases journal to the subsidiary ledger are generally made:
   **(a)** yearly.
   **(b)** monthly.
   **(c)** weekly.
   **(d)** daily.

(LO 3)  **13.** Which statement is **incorrect** regarding the general journal?
   **(a)** Only transactions that cannot be entered in a special journal are recorded in the general journal.
   **(b)** Dual postings are always required in the general journal.
   **(c)** The general journal may be used to record acceptance of a note receivable in payment of an account receivable.
   **(d)** Correcting, adjusting, and closing entries are made in the general journal.

(LO 3)  **14.** When companies use special journals:
   **(a)** they record all purchase transactions in the purchases journal.
   **(b)** they record all cash received, except from cash sales, in the cash receipts journal.
   **(c)** they record all cash disbursements in the cash payments journal.
   **(d)** a general journal is not necessary.

(LO 3)  **15.** If a customer returns goods for credit, the selling company normally makes an entry in the:
   **(a)** cash payments journal.
   **(b)** sales journal.
   **(c)** general journal.
   **(d)** cash receipts journal.

Go to the book's companion website, www.wiley.com/college/weygandt, for additional Self-Test Questions.

✔ The Navigator

## QUESTIONS

**1.** (a) What is an accounting information system? (b) "An accounting information system applies only to a manual system." Do you agree? Explain.

**2.** Certain principles should be followed in the development of an accounting information system. Identify and explain each of the principles.

3. What are common features of computerized accounting packages beyond recording transactions and preparing financial statements?

4. How does an enterprise resource planning (ERP) system differ from an entry-level computerized accounting system?

5. What are the advantages of using subsidiary ledgers?

6. (a) When do companies normally post to (1) the subsidiary accounts and (2) the general ledger control accounts? (b) Describe the relationship between a control account and a subsidiary ledger.

7. Identify and explain the four special journals discussed in the chapter. List an advantage of using each of these journals rather than using only a general journal.

8. Kensington Company uses special journals. It recorded in a sales journal a sale made on account to R. Stiner for $435. A few days later, R. Stiner returns $70 worth of merchandise for credit. Where should Kensington Company record the sales return? Why?

9. A $500 purchase of merchandise on account from Lore Company was properly recorded in the purchases journal. When posted, however, the amount recorded in the subsidiary ledger was $50. How might this error be discovered?

10. Why would special journals used in different businesses not be identical in format? What type of business would maintain a cash receipts journal but not include a column for accounts receivable?

11. The cash and the accounts receivable columns in the cash receipts journal were mistakenly over-added by $4,000 at the end of the month. (a) Will the customers' ledger agree with the Accounts Receivable control account? (b) Assuming no other errors, will the trial balance totals be equal?

12. One column total of a special journal is posted at month-end to only two general ledger accounts. One of these two accounts is Accounts Receivable. What is the name of this special journal? What is the other general ledger account to which that same month-end total is posted?

13. In what journal would the following transactions be recorded? (Assume that a two-column sales journal and a single-column purchases journal are used.)
(a) Recording of depreciation expense for the year.
(b) Credit given to a customer for merchandise purchased on credit and returned.
(c) Sales of merchandise for cash.
(d) Sales of merchandise on account.
(e) Collection of cash on account from a customer.
(f) Purchase of office supplies on account.

14. In what journal would the following transactions be recorded? (Assume that a two-column sales journal and a single-column purchases journal are used.)
(a) Cash received from signing a note payable.
(b) Investment of cash by the owner of the business.
(c) Closing of the expense accounts at the end of the year.
(d) Purchase of merchandise on account.
(e) Credit received for merchandise purchased and returned to supplier.
(f) Payment of cash on account due a supplier.

15. What transactions might be included in a multiple-column purchases journal that would not be included in a single-column purchases journal?

16. Give an example of a transaction in the general journal that causes an entry to be posted twice (i.e., to two accounts), one in the general ledger, the other in the subsidiary ledger. Does this affect the debit/credit equality of the general ledger?

17. Give some examples of appropriate general journal transactions for an organization using special journals.

## BRIEF EXERCISES

*Identify basic concepts of an accounting information system.*
(LO 1)

**BE7-1** Indicate whether each of the following statements is true or false.
1. When designing an accounting system, we need to think about the needs and knowledge of both the top managers and various other users.
2. When the environment changes as a result of technological advances, increased competition, or government regulation, an accounting system does not have to be sufficiently flexible to meet the changes in order to save money.
3. In developing an accounting system, cost is relevant. The benefits obtained from the information disseminated must outweigh the cost of providing it.

*Identify basic concepts of an accounting information system.*
(LO 1)

**BE7-2** Here is a list of words or phrases related to computerized accounting systems.
1. Entry-level software.
2. Enterprise resource planning systems.
3. Network-compatible.
4. Audit trail.
5. Internal control.

*Instructions*
Match each word or phrase with the best description of it.

_____ (a) Allows multiple users to access the system at the same time.
_____ (b) Enables the tracking of all transactions.

_____ **(c)** Identifies suspicious transactions or likely mistakes such as wrong account numbers or duplicate transactions.

_____ **(d)** Large-scale computer systems that integrate all aspects of the organization including accounting, sales, human resource management, and manufacturing.

_____ **(e)** System for companies with revenues of less than $5 million and up to 20 employees.

**BE7-3** Benji Borke has prepared the following list of statements about accounting information systems.

*Identify basic concepts of an accounting information system.*

*(LO 1)*

1. The accounting information system includes each of the steps of the accounting cycle, the documents that provide evidence of transactions that have occurred, and the accounting records.
2. The benefits obtained from information provided by the accounting information system need not outweigh the cost of providing that information.
3. Designers of accounting systems must consider the needs and knowledge of various users.
4. If an accounting information system is cost-effective and provides useful output, it does not need to be flexible.

***Instructions***
Identify each statement as true or false. If false, indicate how to correct the statement.

**BE7-4** Presented below is information related to Gantner Company for its first month of operations. Identify the balances that appear in the accounts receivable subsidiary ledger and the accounts receivable balance that appears in the general ledger at the end of January.

*Identify subsidiary ledger balances.*

*(LO 2)*

| | **Credit Sales** | | | **Cash Collections** | |
|---|---|---|---|---|---|
| Jan. 7 | Austin Co. | $10,000 | Jan. 17 | Austin Co. | $7,000 |
| 15 | Diaz Co. | 8,000 | 24 | Diaz Co. | 4,000 |
| 23 | Noble Co. | 9,000 | 29 | Noble Co. | 9,000 |

**BE7-5** Identify in what ledger (general or subsidiary) each of the following accounts is shown.

*Identify subsidiary ledger accounts.*

*(LO 2)*

**(a)** Rent Expense.
**(b)** Accounts Receivable—Cabrera.
**(c)** Notes Payable.
**(d)** Accounts Payable—Pacheco.

**BE7-6** Identify the journal in which each of the following transactions is recorded.

*Identify special journals.*

*(LO 3)*

**(a)** Cash sales.
**(b)** Owner withdrawal of cash.
**(c)** Cash purchase of land.
**(d)** Credit sales.
**(e)** Purchase of merchandise on account.
**(f)** Receipt of cash for services performed.

**BE7-7** Indicate whether each of the following debits and credits is included in the cash receipts journal. (Use "Yes" or "No" to answer this question.)

*Identify entries to cash receipts journal.*

*(LO 3)*

**(a)** Debit to Sales Revenue.
**(b)** Credit to Inventory.
**(c)** Credit to Accounts Receivable.
**(d)** Debit to Accounts Payable.

**BE7-8** Villar Co. uses special journals and a general journal. Identify the journal in which each of the following transactions is recorded.

*Identify transactions for special journals.*

*(LO 3)*

**(a)** Purchased equipment on account.
**(b)** Purchased merchandise on account.
**(c)** Paid utility expense in cash.
**(d)** Sold merchandise on account.

**BE7-9** Identify the special journal(s) in which the following column headings appear.

*Identify transactions for special journals.*

*(LO 3)*

**(a)** Sales Discounts Dr.
**(b)** Accounts Receivable Cr.
**(c)** Cash Dr.
**(d)** Sales Revenue Cr.
**(e)** Inventory Dr.

**BE7-10** Rauch Computer Components Inc. uses a multi-column cash receipts journal. Indicate which column(s) is/are posted only in total, only daily, or both in total and daily.

*Indicate postings for cash receipts journal.*

*(LO 3)*

**(a)** Accounts Receivable.
**(b)** Sales Discounts.
**(c)** Cash.
**(d)** Other Accounts.

*Determine subsidiary and general ledger balances.*

*(LO 2)*

**DO IT! 7-1** Presented below is information related to Rizzo Company for its first month of operations. Determine the balances that appear in the accounts payable subsidiary ledger. What Accounts Payable balance appears in the general ledger at the end of January?

| | Credit Purchases | | | Cash Paid | |
|---|---|---|---|---|---|
| Jan. 6 | Gorst Company | $11,000 | Jan. 11 | Gorst Company | $ 6,500 |
| Jan. 10 | Tian Company | 12,000 | Jan. 16 | Tian Company | 12,000 |
| Jan. 23 | Maddox Company | 10,000 | Jan. 29 | Maddox Company | 7,700 |

*Identify special journals.*

*(LO 3)*

**DO IT! 7-2** Hinske Company had the following transactions during April.

1. Sold merchandise on account.
2. Purchased merchandise on account.
3. Collected cash from a sale to Renfro Company.
4. Recorded accrued interest on a note payable.
5. Paid $2,000 for supplies.

Identify the journal in which each of the transactions above is recorded.

## EXERCISES

*Determine control account balances, and explain posting of special journals.*

*(LO 2, 3)*

**E7-1** Nex Company uses both special journals and a general journal as described in this chapter. On June 30, after all monthly postings had been completed, the Accounts Receivable control account in the general ledger had a debit balance of $340,000; the Accounts Payable control account had a credit balance of $77,000.

The July transactions recorded in the special journals are summarized below. No entries affecting accounts receivable and accounts payable were recorded in the general journal for July.

| | |
|---|---|
| Sales journal | Total sales $161,400 |
| Purchases journal | Total purchases $66,400 |
| Cash receipts journal | Accounts receivable column total $131,000 |
| Cash payments journal | Accounts payable column total $47,500 |

**Instructions**

**(a)** What is the balance of the Accounts Receivable control account after the monthly postings on July 31?

**(b)** What is the balance of the Accounts Payable control account after the monthly postings on July 31?

**(c)** To what account(s) is the column total of $161,400 in the sales journal posted?

**(d)** To what account(s) is the accounts receivable column total of $131,000 in the cash receipts journal posted?

*Explain postings to subsidiary ledger.*

*(LO 2)*

**E7-2** Presented below is the subsidiary accounts receivable account of Jill Longley.

| Date | Ref. | Debit | Credit | Balance |
|---|---|---|---|---|
| 2014 | | | | |
| Sept. 2 | S31 | 61,000 | | 61,000 |
| 9 | G4 | | 14,000 | 47,000 |
| 27 | CR8 | | 47,000 | — |

**Instructions**

Write a memo to Sara Fogelman, chief financial officer, that explains each transaction.

**E7-3** On September 1, the balance of the Accounts Receivable control account in the general ledger of Montgomery Company was $10,960. The customers' subsidiary ledger contained account balances as follows: Hurley $1,440, Andino $2,640, Fowler $2,060, Sogard $4,820. At the end of September, the various journals contained the following information.

*Post various journals to control and subsidiary accounts.*

*(LO 2, 3)*

**Sales journal:** Sales to Sogard $800; to Hurley $1,260; to Giambi $1,330; to Fowler $1,600.

**Cash receipts journal:** Cash received from Fowler $1,310; from Sogard $3,300; from Giambi $380; from Andino $1,800; from Hurley $1,240.

**General journal:** An allowance is granted to Sogard $220.

*Instructions*
**(a)** Set up control and subsidiary accounts and enter the beginning balances. Do not construct the journals.
**(b)** Post the various journals. Post the items as individual items or as totals, whichever would be the appropriate procedure. (No sales discounts given.)
**(c)** Prepare a list of customers and prove the agreement of the controlling account with the subsidiary ledger at September 30, 2014.

**E7-4** Kieschnick Company has a balance in its Accounts Receivable control account of $10,000 on January 1, 2014. The subsidiary ledger contains three accounts: Bixler Company, balance $4,000; Cuddyer Company, balance $2,500; and Freeze Company. During January, the following receivable-related transactions occurred.

*Determine control and subsidiary ledger balances for accounts receivable.*

*(LO 2)*

|  | Credit Sales | Collections | Returns |
|---|---|---|---|
| Bixler Company | $9,000 | $8,000 | $ -0- |
| Cuddyer Company | 7,000 | 2,500 | 3,000 |
| Freeze Company | 8,500 | 9,000 | -0- |

*Instructions*
**(a)** What is the January 1 balance in the Freeze Company subsidiary account?
**(b)** What is the January 31 balance in the control account?
**(c)** Compute the balances in the subsidiary accounts at the end of the month.
**(d)** Which January transaction would not be recorded in a special journal?

**E7-5** Pennington Company has a balance in its Accounts Payable control account of $9,250 on January 1, 2014. The subsidiary ledger contains three accounts: Hale Company, balance $3,000; Janish Company, balance $1,875; and Valdez Company. During January, the following payable-related transactions occurred.

*Determine control and subsidiary ledger balances for accounts payable.*

*(LO 2)*

|  | Purchases | Payments | Returns |
|---|---|---|---|
| Hale Company | $6,750 | $6,000 | $ -0- |
| Janish Company | 5,250 | 1,875 | 2,250 |
| Valdez Company | 6,375 | 6,750 | -0- |

*Instructions*
**(a)** What is the January 1 balance in the Valdez Company subsidiary account?
**(b)** What is the January 31 balance in the control account?
**(c)** Compute the balances in the subsidiary accounts at the end of the month.
**(d)** Which January transaction would not be recorded in a special journal?

**E7-6** Gomes Company uses special journals and a general journal. The following transactions occurred during September 2014.

*Record transactions in sales and purchases journal.*

*(LO 3)*

Sept. 2 Sold merchandise on account to H. Drew, invoice no. 101, $620, terms n/30. The cost of the merchandise sold was $420.
10 Purchased merchandise on account from A. Pagan $650, terms 2/10, n/30.
12 Purchased office equipment on account from R. Cairo $6,500.
21 Sold merchandise on account to G. Holliday, invoice no. 102 for $800, terms 2/10, n/30. The cost of the merchandise sold was $480.
25 Purchased merchandise on account from D. Downs $860, terms n/30.
27 Sold merchandise to S. Miller for $700 cash. The cost of the merchandise sold was $400.

*Instructions*

**(a)** Prepare a sales journal (see Illustration 7-7) and a single-column purchases journal (see Illustration 7-13). (Use page 1 for each journal.)

**(b)** Record the transaction(s) for September that should be journalized in the sales journal and the purchases journal.

*Record transactions in cash receipts and cash payments journal.*

*(LO 3)*

**E7-7** R. Santiago Co. uses special journals and a general journal. The following transactions occurred during May 2014.

May 1   R. Santiago invested $40,000 cash in the business.

     2   Sold merchandise to Lawrie Co. for $6,300 cash. The cost of the merchandise sold was $4,200.

     3   Purchased merchandise for $7,700 from J. Moskos using check no. 101.

   14   Paid salary to H. Rivera $700 by issuing check no. 102.

   16   Sold merchandise on account to K. Stanton for $900, terms n/30. The cost of the merchandise sold was $630.

   22   A check of $9,000 is received from M. Mangini in full for invoice 101; no discount given.

*Instructions*

**(a)** Prepare a multiple-column cash receipts journal (see Illustration 7-9) and a multiple-column cash payments journal (see Illustration 7-16). (Use page 1 for each journal.)

**(b)** Record the transaction(s) for May that should be journalized in the cash receipts journal and cash payments journal.

*Explain journalizing in cash journals.*

*(LO 3)*

**E7-8** Francisco Company uses the columnar cash journals illustrated in the textbook. In April, the following selected cash transactions occurred.

**1.** Made a refund to a customer as an allowance for damaged goods.

**2.** Received collection from customer within the 3% discount period.

**3.** Purchased merchandise for cash.

**4.** Paid a creditor within the 3% discount period.

**5.** Received collection from customer after the 3% discount period had expired.

**6.** Paid freight on merchandise purchased.

**7.** Paid cash for office equipment.

**8.** Received cash refund from supplier for merchandise returned.

**9.** Withdrew cash for personal use of owner.

**10.** Made cash sales.

*Instructions*

Indicate (a) the journal, and (b) the columns in the journal that should be used in recording each transaction.

*Journalize transactions in general journal and explain postings.*

*(LO 3)*

**E7-9** Hasselback Company has the following selected transactions during March.

Mar. 2   Purchased equipment costing $7,400 from Bole Company on account.

     5   Received credit of $410 from Carwell Company for merchandise damaged in shipment to Hasselback.

     7   Issued credit of $400 to Dempsey Company for merchandise the customer returned. The returned merchandise had a cost of $260.

Hasselback Company uses a one-column purchases journal, a sales journal, the columnar cash journals used in the text, and a general journal.

*Instructions*

**(a)** Journalize the transactions in the general journal.

**(b)** ▬▬▬ In a brief memo to the president of Hasselback Company, explain the postings to the control and subsidiary accounts from each type of journal.

*Indicate journalizing in special journals.*

*(LO 3)*

**E7-10** Below are some typical transactions incurred by Ricketts Company.

**1.** Payment of creditors on account.

**2.** Return of merchandise sold for credit.

**3.** Collection on account from customers.

**4.** Sale of land for cash.

**5.** Sale of merchandise on account.

**6.** Sale of merchandise for cash.

7. Received credit for merchandise purchased on credit.
8. Sales discount taken on goods sold.
9. Payment of employee wages.
10. Income summary closed to owner's capital.
11. Depreciation on building.
12. Purchase of office supplies for cash.
13. Purchase of merchandise on account.

***Instructions***
For each transaction, indicate whether it would normally be recorded in a cash receipts journal, cash payments journal, sales journal, single-column purchases journal, or general journal.

**E7-11** The general ledger of Hensley Company contained the following Accounts Payable control account (in T-account form). Also shown is the related subsidiary ledger.

*Explain posting to control account and subsidiary ledger.*
*(LO 2, 3)*

**GENERAL LEDGER**
**Accounts Payable**

| | | | | | | |
|---|---|---|---|---|---|---|
| Feb. 15 | General journal | 1,400 | Feb. 1 | Balance | 26,025 |
| 28 | ? | ? | 5 | General journal | 265 |
| | | | 11 | General journal | 550 |
| | | | 28 | Purchases | 13,400 |
| | | | Feb. 28 | Balance | 10,500 |

**ACCOUNTS PAYABLE LEDGER**

**Benton**

| | | |
|---|---|---|
| Feb. 28 | Bal. 4,600 |

**Parks**

| | | |
|---|---|---|
| Feb. 28 | Bal. | ? |

**Dooley**

| | | |
|---|---|---|
| Feb. 28 | Bal. 2,300 |

***Instructions***
(a) Indicate the missing posting reference and amount in the control account, and the missing ending balance in the subsidiary ledger.
(b) Indicate the amounts in the control account that were dual-posted (i.e., posted to the control account and the subsidiary accounts).

**E7-12** Selected accounts from the ledgers of Youngblood Company at July 31 showed the following.

*Prepare purchases and general journals.*
*(LO 2, 3)*

**GENERAL LEDGER**

**Equipment**   No. 157

| Date | Explanation | Ref. | Debit | Credit | Balance |
|---|---|---|---|---|---|
| July 1 | | G1 | 3,900 | | 3,900 |

**Accounts Payable**   No. 201

| Date | Explanation | Ref. | Debit | Credit | Balance |
|---|---|---|---|---|---|
| July 1 | | G1 | | 3,900 | 3,900 |
| 15 | | G1 | | 400 | 4,300 |
| 18 | | G1 | 100 | | 4,200 |
| 25 | | G1 | 200 | | 4,000 |
| 31 | | P1 | | 9,300 | 13,300 |

**Inventory**   No. 120

| Date | Explanation | Ref. | Debit | Credit | Balance |
|---|---|---|---|---|---|
| July 15 | | G1 | 400 | | 400 |
| 18 | | G1 | | 100 | 300 |
| 25 | | G1 | | 200 | 100 |
| 31 | | P1 | 9,300 | | 9,400 |

## ACCOUNTS PAYABLE LEDGER

### Flaherty Equipment Co.

| Date | Explanation | Ref. | Debit | Credit | Balance |
|------|-------------|------|-------|--------|---------|
| July 1 | | G1 | | 3,900 | 3,900 |

### Weller Co.

| Date | Explanation | Ref. | Debit | Credit | Balance |
|------|-------------|------|-------|--------|---------|
| July 14 | | P1 | | 1,100 | 1,100 |
| 25 | | G1 | 200 | | 900 |

### Marsh Co.

| Date | Explanation | Ref. | Debit | Credit | Balance |
|------|-------------|------|-------|--------|---------|
| July 3 | | P1 | | 2,400 | 2,400 |
| 20 | | P1 | | 1,700 | 4,100 |

### Yates Co.

| Date | Explanation | Ref. | Debit | Credit | Balance |
|------|-------------|------|-------|--------|---------|
| July 12 | | P1 | | 500 | 500 |
| 21 | | P1 | | 600 | 1,100 |

### Lange Corp

| Date | Explanation | Ref. | Debit | Credit | Balance |
|------|-------------|------|-------|--------|---------|
| July 17 | | P1 | | 1,400 | 1,400 |
| 18 | | G1 | 100 | | 1,300 |
| 29 | | P1 | | 1,600 | 2,900 |

### Bernardo Inc.

| Date | Explanation | Ref. | Debit | Credit | Balance |
|------|-------------|------|-------|--------|---------|
| July 15 | | G1 | | 400 | 400 |

*Instructions*

From the data prepare:

**(a)** The single-column purchases journal for July.

**(b)** The general journal entries for July.

*Determine correct posting amount to control account.*

*(LO 2, 3)*

**E7-13** Tresh Products uses both special journals and a general journal as described in this chapter. Tresh also posts customers' accounts in the accounts receivable subsidiary ledger. The postings for the most recent month are included in the subsidiary T-accounts below.

| Estes | | |
|-------|---|---|
| Bal. 340 | | 250 |
| 200 | | |

| Gehrke | | |
|--------|---|---|
| Bal. 150 | | 150 |
| 290 | | |

| Truong | | |
|--------|---|---|
| Bal. –0– | | 145 |
| 145 | | |

| Weiser | | |
|--------|---|---|
| Bal. 120 | | 120 |
| 190 | | |
| 150 | | |

*Instructions*

Determine the correct amount of the end-of-month posting from the sales journal to the Accounts Receivable control account.

*Compute balances in various accounts.*

*(LO 3)*

**E7-14** Selected account balances for Hulse Company at January 1, 2014, are presented below.

| | |
|---|---|
| Accounts Payable | $14,000 |
| Accounts Receivable | 22,000 |
| Cash | 17,000 |
| Inventory | 13,500 |

Hulse's sales journal for January shows a total of $110,000 in the selling price column, and its one-column purchases journal for January shows a total of $77,000.

The column totals in Hulse's cash receipts journal are: Cash Dr. $61,000; Sales Discounts Dr. $1,100; Accounts Receivable Cr. $45,000; Sales Revenue Cr. $6,000; and Other Accounts Cr. $11,100.

The column totals in Hulse's cash payments journal for January are: Cash Cr. $55,000; Inventory Cr. $1,000; Accounts Payable Dr. $46,000; and Other Accounts Dr. $10,000. Hulse's total cost of goods sold for January is $63,600.

Accounts Payable, Accounts Receivable, Cash, Inventory, and Sales Revenue are not involved in the "Other Accounts" column in either the cash receipts or cash payments journal, and are not involved in any general journal entries.

*Instructions*

Compute the January 31 balance for Hulse in the following accounts.

**(a)** Accounts Payable.

**(b)** Accounts Receivable.

(c) Cash.
(d) Inventory.
(e) Sales Revenue.

## EXERCISES: SET B AND CHALLENGE EXERCISES

Visit the book's companion website, at **www.wiley.com/college/weygandt**, and choose the Student Companion site to access Exercise Set B and Challenge Exercises.

## PROBLEMS: SET A

**P7-1A** Kozma Company's chart of accounts includes the following selected accounts.

| | | | |
|---|---|---|---|
| 101 | Cash | 401 | Sales Revenue |
| 112 | Accounts Receivable | 414 | Sales Discounts |
| 120 | Inventory | 505 | Cost of Goods Sold |
| 301 | Owner's Capital | | |

*Journalize transactions in cash receipts journal; post to control account and subsidiary ledger.*

(LO 2, 3)

On April 1, the accounts receivable ledger of Kozma Company showed the following balances: Morrow $1,550, Rose $1,200, Jennings Co. $2,900, and Dent $2,200. The April transactions involving the receipt of cash were as follows.

Apr.  1  The owner, T. Kozma, invested additional cash in the business $7,200.
       4  Received check for payment of account from Dent less 2% cash discount.
       5  Received check for $920 in payment of invoice no. 307 from Jennings Co.
       8  Made cash sales of merchandise totaling $7,245. The cost of the merchandise sold was $4,347.
      10  Received check for $600 in payment of invoice no. 309 from Morrow.
      11  Received cash refund from a supplier for damaged merchandise $740.
      23  Received check for $1,000 in payment of invoice no. 310 from Jennings Co.
      29  Received check for payment of account from Rose.

*Instructions*
**(a)** Journalize the transactions above in a six-column cash receipts journal with columns for Cash Dr., Sales Discounts Dr., Accounts Receivable Cr., Sales Revenue Cr., Other Accounts Cr., and Cost of Goods Sold Dr./Inventory Cr. Foot and cross-foot the journal.
**(b)** Insert the beginning balances in the Accounts Receivable control and subsidiary accounts, and post the April transactions to these accounts.
**(c)** Prove the agreement of the control account and subsidiary account balances.

(a) Balancing totals $21,105

(c) Accounts Receivable $1,930

**P7-2A** Reineke Company's chart of accounts includes the following selected accounts.

| | | | |
|---|---|---|---|
| 101 | Cash | 201 | Accounts Payable |
| 120 | Inventory | 306 | Owner's Drawings |
| 130 | Prepaid Insurance | 505 | Cost of Goods Sold |
| 157 | Equipment | | |

*Journalize transactions in cash payments journal; post to control account and subsidiary ledgers.*

(LO 2, 3)

On October 1, the accounts payable ledger of Reineke Company showed the following balances: Uggla Company $2,700, Orr Co. $2,500, Rosenthal Co. $1,800, and Clevenger Company $3,700. The October transactions involving the payment of cash were as follows.

Oct.  1  Purchased merchandise, check no. 63, $300.
       3  Purchased equipment, check no. 64, $800.
       5  Paid Uggla Company balance due of $2,700, less 2% discount, check no. 65, $2,646.
      10  Purchased merchandise, check no. 66, $2,550.
      15  Paid Rosenthal Co. balance due of $1,800, check no. 67.
      16  C. Reineke, the owner, pays his personal insurance premium of $400, check no. 68.
      19  Paid Orr Co. in full for invoice no. 610, $2,000 less 2% cash discount, check no. 69, $1,960.
      29  Paid Clevenger Company in full for invoice no. 264, $2,500, check no. 70.

### Instructions

(a) Balancing totals $13,050

**(a)** Journalize the transactions above in a four-column cash payments journal with columns for Other Accounts Dr., Accounts Payable Dr., Inventory Cr., and Cash Cr. Foot and cross-foot the journal.

**(b)** Insert the beginning balances in the Accounts Payable control and subsidiary accounts, and post the October transactions to these accounts.

(c) Accounts Payable $1,700

**(c)** Prove the agreement of the control account and the subsidiary account balances.

*Journalize transactions in multi-column purchases journal and sales journal; post to the general and subsidiary ledgers.*

(LO 2, 3)

**P7-3A** The chart of accounts of LR Company includes the following selected accounts.

| | | | |
|---|---|---|---|
| 112 | Accounts Receivable | 401 | Sales Revenue |
| 120 | Inventory | 412 | Sales Returns and Allowances |
| 126 | Supplies | 505 | Cost of Goods Sold |
| 157 | Equipment | 610 | Advertising Expense |
| 201 | Accounts Payable | | |

In July, the following selected transactions were completed. All purchases and sales were on account. The cost of all merchandise sold was 70% of the sales price.

July 1 Purchased merchandise from Eby Company $8,000.
2 Received freight bill from Shaw Shipping on Eby purchase $400.
3 Made sales to Fort Company $1,300 and to Hefner Bros. $1,500.
5 Purchased merchandise from Getz Company $3,200.
8 Received credit on merchandise returned to Getz Company $300.
13 Purchased store supplies from Dayne Supply $720.
15 Purchased merchandise from Eby Company $3,600 and from Bosco Company $4,300.
16 Made sales to Aybar Company $3,450 and to Hefner Bros. $1,870.
18 Received bill for advertising from Welton Advertisements $600.
21 Sales were made to Fort Company $310 and to Duncan Company $2,800.
22 Granted allowance to Fort Company for merchandise damaged in shipment $40.
24 Purchased merchandise from Getz Company $3,000.
26 Purchased equipment from Dayne Supply $900.
28 Received freight bill from Shaw Shipping on Getz purchase of July 24, $380.
30 Sales were made to Aybar Company $5,600.

### Instructions

(a) Purchases journal—
Accounts Payable $25,100
Sales journal—Sales
Revenue total $16,830

**(a)** Journalize the transactions above in a purchases journal, a sales journal, and a general journal. The purchases journal should have the following column headings: Date, Account Credited (Debited), Ref., Accounts Payable Cr., Inventory Dr., and Other Accounts Dr.

(c) Accounts Receivable
$16,790
Accounts Payable $24,800

**(b)** Post to both the general and subsidiary ledger accounts. (Assume that all accounts have zero beginning balances.)

**(c)** Prove the agreement of the control and subsidiary accounts.

*Journalize transactions in special journals.*

(LO 2, 3)

**P7-4A** Selected accounts from the chart of accounts of Mercer Company are shown below.

| | | | |
|---|---|---|---|
| 101 | Cash | 401 | Sales Revenue |
| 112 | Accounts Receivable | 412 | Sales Returns and Allowances |
| 120 | Inventory | 414 | Sales Discounts |
| 126 | Supplies | 505 | Cost of Goods Sold |
| 157 | Equipment | 726 | Salaries and Wages Expense |
| 201 | Accounts Payable | | |

The cost of all merchandise sold was 60% of the sales price. During January, Mercer completed the following transactions.

Jan. 3 Purchased merchandise on account from Gallagher Co. $9,000.
4 Purchased supplies for cash $80.
4 Sold merchandise on account to Wheeler $5,250, invoice no. 371, terms 1/10, n/30.
5 Returned $300 worth of damaged goods purchased on account from Gallagher Co. on January 3.
6 Made cash sales for the week totaling $3,150.
8 Purchased merchandise on account from Phegley Co. $4,500.
9 Sold merchandise on account to Linton Corp. $5,400, invoice no. 372, terms 1/10, n/30.

| | |
|---|---|
| 11 | Purchased merchandise on account from Cora Co. $3,700. |
| 13 | Paid in full Gallagher Co. on account less a 2% discount. |
| 13 | Made cash sales for the week totaling $6,260. |
| 15 | Received payment from Linton Corp. for invoice no. 372. |
| 15 | Paid semi-monthly salaries of $14,300 to employees. |
| 17 | Received payment from Wheeler for invoice no. 371. |
| 17 | Sold merchandise on account to Delaney Co. $1,200, invoice no. 373, terms 1/10, n/30. |
| 19 | Purchased equipment on account from Dozier Corp. $5,500. |
| 20 | Cash sales for the week totaled $3,200. |
| 20 | Paid in full Phegley Co. on account less a 2% discount. |
| 23 | Purchased merchandise on account from Gallagher Co. $7,800. |
| 24 | Purchased merchandise on account from Atchison Corp. $5,100. |
| 27 | Made cash sales for the week totaling $4,230. |
| 30 | Received payment from Delaney Co. for invoice no. 373. |
| 31 | Paid semi-monthly salaries of $13,200 to employees. |
| 31 | Sold merchandise on account to Wheeler $9,330, invoice no. 374, terms 1/10, n/30. |

Mercer Company uses the following journals.

1. Sales journal.
2. Single-column purchases journal.
3. Cash receipts journal with columns for Cash Dr., Sales Discounts Dr., Accounts Receivable Cr., Sales Revenue Cr., Other Accounts Cr., and Cost of Goods Sold Dr./Inventory Cr.
4. Cash payments journal with columns for Other Accounts Dr., Accounts Payable Dr., Inventory Cr., and Cash Cr.
5. General journal.

*Instructions*
Using the selected accounts provided:

(a) Record the January transactions in the appropriate journal noted.
(b) Foot and cross-foot all special journals.
(c) Show how postings would be made by placing ledger account numbers and check-marks as needed in the journals. (Actual posting to ledger accounts is not required.)

*(a) Sales journal $21,180*
*Purchases journal $30,100*
*Cash receipts journal*
*balancing total $28,690*
*Cash payments journal*
*balancing total $40,780*

**P7-5A** Presented below are the purchases and cash payments journals for Fornelli Co. for its first month of operations.

*Journalize in sales and cash receipts journals; post; prepare a trial balance; prove control to subsidiary; prepare adjusting entries; prepare an adjusted trial balance.*

*(LO 2, 3)*

**PURCHASES JOURNAL**         **P1**

| Date | Account Credited | Ref. | Inventory Dr. Accounts Payable Cr. |
|---|---|---|---|
| July 4 | N. Alvarado | | 6,800 |
| 5 | F. Rees | | 8,100 |
| 11 | J. Gallup | | 5,920 |
| 13 | C. Werly | | 15,300 |
| 20 | M. Mangus | | 7,900 |
| | | | 44,020 |

**CASH PAYMENTS JOURNAL**         **CP1**

| Date | Account Debited | Ref. | Other Accounts Dr. | Accounts Payable Dr. | Inventory Cr. | Cash Cr. |
|---|---|---|---|---|---|---|
| July 4 | Supplies | | 600 | | | 600 |
| 10 | F. Rees | | | 8,100 | 81 | 8,019 |
| 11 | Prepaid Rent | | 6,000 | | | 6,000 |
| 15 | N. Alvarado | | | 6,800 | | 6,800 |
| 19 | Owner's Drawings | | 2,500 | | | 2,500 |
| 21 | C. Werly | | | 15,300 | 153 | 15,147 |
| | | | 9,100 | 30,200 | 234 | 39,066 |

In addition, the following transactions have not been journalized for July. The cost of all merchandise sold was 65% of the sales price.

| July | 1 | The founder, N. Fornelli, invests $80,000 in cash. |
|------|----|----|
| | 6 | Sell merchandise on account to Dow Co. $6,200 terms 1/10, n/30. |
| | 7 | Make cash sales totaling $8,000. |
| | 8 | Sell merchandise on account to S. Goebel $4,600, terms 1/10, n/30. |
| | 10 | Sell merchandise on account to W. Leiss $4,900, terms 1/10, n/30. |
| | 13 | Receive payment in full from S. Goebel. |
| | 16 | Receive payment in full from W. Leiss. |
| | 20 | Receive payment in full from Dow Co. |
| | 21 | Sell merchandise on account to H. Kenney $5,000, terms 1/10, n/30. |
| | 29 | Returned damaged goods to N. Alvarado and received cash refund of $420. |

### Instructions

**(a)** Open the following accounts in the general ledger.

| 101 | Cash | 306 | Owner's Drawings |
|-----|------|-----|------------------|
| 112 | Accounts Receivable | 401 | Sales Revenue |
| 120 | Inventory | 414 | Sales Discounts |
| 126 | Supplies | 505 | Cost of Goods Sold |
| 131 | Prepaid Rent | 631 | Supplies Expense |
| 201 | Accounts Payable | 729 | Rent Expense |
| 301 | Owner's Capital | | |

(b) Sales journal total
$20,700
Cash receipts journal
balancing totals $104,120

**(b)** Journalize the transactions that have not been journalized in the sales journal and the cash receipts journal (see Illustration 7-9).

**(c)** Post to the accounts receivable and accounts payable subsidiary ledgers. Follow the sequence of transactions as shown in the problem.

**(d)** Post the individual entries and totals to the general ledger.

(e) Totals $122,520

**(e)** Prepare a trial balance at July 31, 2014.

(f) Accounts Receivable
$5,000
Accounts Payable $13,820

**(f)** Determine whether the subsidiary ledgers agree with the control accounts in the general ledger.

**(g)** The following adjustments at the end of July are necessary.

**(1)** A count of supplies indicates that $140 is still on hand.

**(2)** Recognize rent expense for July, $500.

Prepare the necessary entries in the general journal. Post the entries to the general ledger.

(h) Totals $122,520

**(h)** Prepare an adjusted trial balance at July 31, 2014.

*Journalize in special journals; post; prepare a trial balance.*

(LO 2, 3)

**P7-6A** The post-closing trial balance for Horner Co. is shown below.

### HORNER CO.
Post-Closing Trial Balance
December 31, 2014

| | Debit | Credit |
|---|---|---|
| Cash | $ 41,500 | |
| Accounts Receivable | 15,000 | |
| Notes Receivable | 45,000 | |
| Inventory | 23,000 | |
| Equipment | 6,450 | |
| Accumulated Depreciation—Equipment | | $ 1,500 |
| Accounts Payable | | 43,000 |
| Owner's Capital | | 86,450 |
| | $130,950 | $130,950 |

The subsidiary ledgers contain the following information: (1) accounts receivable— B. Hannigan $2,500, I. Kirk $7,500, and T. Hodges $5,000; (2) accounts payable—T. Igawa $12,000, D. Danford $18,000, and K. Thayer $13,000. The cost of all merchandise sold was 60% of the sales price.

The transactions for January 2015 are as follows.

Jan. 3  Sell merchandise to M. Ziesmer $8,000, terms 2/10, n/30.
    5  Purchase merchandise from E. Pheatt $2,000, terms 2/10, n/30.
    7  Receive a check from T. Hodges $3,500.
    11  Pay freight on merchandise purchased $300.
    12  Pay rent of $1,000 for January.
    13  Receive payment in full from M. Ziesmer.
    14  Post all entries to the subsidiary ledgers. Issued credit of $300 to B. Hannigan for returned merchandise.
    15  Send K. Thayer a check for $12,870 in full payment of account, discount $130.
    17  Purchase merchandise from G. Roland $1,600, terms 2/10, n/30.
    18  Pay sales salaries of $2,800 and office salaries $2,000.
    20  Give D. Danford a 60-day note for $18,000 in full payment of account payable.
    23  Total cash sales amount to $9,100.
    24  Post all entries to the subsidiary ledgers. Sell merchandise on account to I. Kirk $7,400, terms 1/10, n/30.
    27  Send E. Pheatt a check for $950.
    29  Receive payment on a note of $40,000 from B. Stout.
    30  Post all entries to the subsidiary ledgers. Return merchandise of $300 to G. Roland for credit.

*Instructions*
(a) Open general and subsidiary ledger accounts for the following.

| | |
|---|---|
| 101 Cash | 301 Owner's Capital |
| 112 Accounts Receivable | 401 Sales Revenue |
| 115 Notes Receivable | 412 Sales Returns and Allowances |
| 120 Inventory | 414 Sales Discounts |
| 157 Equipment | 505 Cost of Goods Sold |
| 158 Accumulated Depreciation—Equipment | 726 Salaries and Wages Expense |
| 200 Notes Payable | 729 Rent Expense |
| 201 Accounts Payable | |

(b) Record the January transactions in a sales journal, a single-column purchases journal, a cash receipts journal (see Illustration 7-9), a cash payments journal (see Illustration 7-16), and a general journal.
(c) Post the appropriate amounts to the general ledger.
(d) Prepare a trial balance at January 31, 2015.
(e) Determine whether the subsidiary ledgers agree with controlling accounts in the general ledger.

*(b) Sales journal $15,400*
*Purchases journal $3,600*
*Cash receipts journal (balancing) $60,600*
*Cash payments journal (balancing) $20,050*
*(d) Totals $144,800*
*(e) Accounts Receivable $18,600*
*Accounts Payable $14,350*

## PROBLEMS: SET B

**P7-1B** Belt Company's chart of accounts includes the following selected accounts.

| | |
|---|---|
| 101 Cash | 401 Sales Revenue |
| 112 Accounts Receivable | 414 Sales Discounts |
| 120 Inventory | 505 Cost of Goods Sold |
| 301 Owner's Capital | |

*Journalize transactions in cash receipts journal; post to control account and subsidiary ledger.*

*(LO 2, 3)*

On June 1, the accounts receivable ledger of Belt Company showed the following balances: Suppan & Son $3,000, Guthrie Co. $2,800, Quentin Bros. $2,400, and Hinshaw Co. $2,000. The June transactions involving the receipt of cash were as follows.

June  1  The owner, Jim Belt, invested additional cash in the business $15,000.
    3  Received check in full from Hinshaw Co. less 2% cash discount.
    6  Received check in full from Guthrie Co. less 2% cash discount.
    7  Made cash sales of merchandise totaling $8,700. The cost of the merchandise sold was $5,000.
    9  Received check in full from Suppan & Son less 2% cash discount.
    11  Received cash refund from a supplier for damaged merchandise $450.

15 Made cash sales of merchandise totaling $6,500. The cost of the merchandise sold was $4,000.

20 Received check in full from Quentin Bros. $2,400.

**Instructions**

(a) Balancing totals $40,850

**(a)** Journalize the transactions above in a six-column cash receipts journal with columns for Cash Dr., Sales Discounts Dr., Accounts Receivable Cr., Sales Revenue Cr., Other Accounts Cr., and Cost of Goods Sold Dr./Inventory Cr. Foot and cross-foot the journal.

**(b)** Insert the beginning balances in the Accounts Receivable control and subsidiary accounts, and post the June transactions to these accounts.

(c) Accounts Receivable $0

**(c)** Prove the agreement of the control account and subsidiary account balances.

*Journalize transactions in cash payments journal; post to the general and subsidiary ledgers.*

*(LO 2, 3)*

**P7-2B** Schellhammer Company's chart of accounts includes the following selected accounts.

| | | | |
|---|---|---|---|
| 101 | Cash | 157 | Equipment |
| 120 | Inventory | 201 | Accounts Payable |
| 130 | Prepaid Insurance | 306 | Owner's Drawings |

On November 1, the accounts payable ledger of Schellhammer Company showed the following balances: S. Gentry $4,000, D. Montero $2,100, R. Trumbo $800, and W. Olivo $1,800. The November transactions involving the payment of cash were as follows.

Nov. 1 Purchased merchandise, check no. 11, $950.

3 Purchased store equipment, check no. 12, $1,400.

5 Paid W. Olivo balance due of $1,800, less 1% discount, check no. 13, $1,782.

11 Purchased merchandise, check no. 14, $1,700.

15 Paid R. Trumbo balance due of $800, less 3% discount, check no. 15, $776.

16 M. Richey, the owner, withdrew $400 cash for own use, check no. 16.

19 Paid D. Montero in full for invoice no. 1245, $2,100 less 2% discount, check no. 17, $2,058.

25 Paid premium due on one-year insurance policy, check no. 18, $2,400.

30 Paid S. Gentry in full for invoice no. 832, $2,700, check no. 19.

**Instructions**

(a) Balancing totals $14,250

**(a)** Journalize the transactions above in a four-column cash payments journal with columns for Other Accounts Dr., Accounts Payable Dr., Inventory Cr., and Cash Cr. Foot and cross-foot the journal.

**(b)** Insert the beginning balances in the Accounts Payable control and subsidiary accounts, and post the November transactions to these accounts.

(c) Accounts Payable $1,300

**(c)** Prove the agreement of the control account and the subsidiary account balances.

*Journalize transactions in multi-column purchases journal; post to the general and subsidiary ledgers.*

*(LO 2, 3)*

**P7-3B** The chart of accounts of Henry Company includes the following selected accounts.

| | | | |
|---|---|---|---|
| 112 | Accounts Receivable | 401 | Sales Revenue |
| 120 | Inventory | 412 | Sales Returns and Allowances |
| 126 | Supplies | 505 | Cost of Goods Sold |
| 157 | Equipment | 610 | Advertising Expense |
| 201 | Accounts Payable | | |

In May, the following selected transactions were completed. All purchases and sales were on account except as indicated. The cost of all merchandise sold was 60% of the sales price.

May 2 Purchased merchandise from Berkman Company $5,000.

3 Received freight bill from Fast Freight on Berkman purchase $250.

5 Sales were made to Persinger Company $1,300, Fehr Bros. $2,300, and Mount Company $1,000.

8 Purchased merchandise from Kayser Company $5,400 and Neufeld Company $3,000.

10 Received credit on merchandise returned to Neufeld Company $350.

15 Purchased supplies from Rabel's Supplies $600.

16 Purchased merchandise from Berkman Company $3,100, and Kayser Company $4,200.

17 Returned supplies to Rabel's Supplies, receiving credit $70. (*Hint:* Credit Supplies.)

18 Received freight bills on May 16 purchases from Fast Freight $325.

20 Returned merchandise to Berkman Company receiving credit $200.

23 Made sales to Fehr Bros. $1,600 and to Mount Company $2,500.

25 Received bill for advertising from Mock Advertising $620.

26 Granted allowance to Mount Company for merchandise damaged in shipment $140.

28 Purchased equipment from Rabel's Supplies $400.

## Instructions

(a) Journalize the transactions above in a purchases journal, a sales journal, and a general journal. The purchases journal should have the following column headings: Date, Account Credited (Debited), Ref., Accounts Payable Cr., Inventory Dr., and Other Accounts Dr.

(b) Post to both the general and subsidiary ledger accounts. (Assume that all accounts have zero beginning balances.)

(c) Prove the agreement of the control and subsidiary accounts.

**P7-4B** Selected accounts from the chart of accounts of Conley Company are shown below.

| | |
|---|---|
| 101 Cash | 201 Accounts Payable |
| 112 Accounts Receivable | 401 Sales Revenue |
| 120 Inventory | 414 Sales Discounts |
| 126 Supplies | 505 Cost of Goods Sold |
| 140 Land | 610 Advertising Expense |
| 145 Building | |

The cost of all merchandise sold was 65% of the sales price. During October, Conley Company completed the following transactions.

Oct. 2 Purchased merchandise on account from Kent Company $15,000.

4 Sold merchandise on account to Doumit Co. $5,600. Invoice no. 204, terms 2/10, n/30.

5 Purchased supplies for cash $60.

7 Made cash sales for the week totaling $6,700.

9 Paid in full the amount owed Kent Company less a 2% discount.

10 Purchased merchandise on account from Wrigley Corp. $2,600.

12 Received payment from Doumit Co. for invoice no. 204.

13 Returned $150 worth of damaged goods purchased on account from Wrigley Corp. on October 10.

14 Made cash sales for the week totaling $6,000.

16 Sold a parcel of land for $20,000 cash, the land's original cost.

17 Sold merchandise on account to JR's Warehouse $4,900, invoice no. 205, terms 2/10, n/30.

18 Purchased merchandise for cash $1,600.

21 Made cash sales for the week totaling $6,000.

23 Paid in full the amount owed Wrigley Corp. for the goods kept (no discount).

25 Purchased supplies on account from Francisco Co. $190.

25 Sold merchandise on account to Fryer Corp. $3,800, invoice no. 206, terms 2/10, n/30.

25 Received payment from JR's Warehouse for invoice no. 205.

26 Purchased for cash a small parcel of land and a building on the land to use as a storage facility. The total cost of $26,000 was allocated $16,000 to the land and $10,000 to the building.

27 Purchased merchandise on account from Marte Co. $6,200.

28 Made cash sales for the week totaling $5,500.

30 Purchased merchandise on account from Kent Company $10,000.

30 Paid advertising bill for the month from the *Gazette*, $290.

30 Sold merchandise on account to JR's Warehouse $3,400, invoice no. 207, terms 2/10, n/30.

Conley Company uses the following journals.

1. Sales journal.
2. Single-column purchases journal.
3. Cash receipts journal with columns for Cash Dr., Sales Discounts Dr., Accounts Receivable Cr., Sales Revenue Cr., Other Accounts Cr., and Cost of Goods Sold Dr./Inventory Cr.
4. Cash payments journal with columns for Other Accounts Dr., Accounts Payable Dr., Inventory Cr., and Cash Cr.
5. General journal.

## Instructions

Using the selected accounts provided:

(a) Record the October transactions in the appropriate journals.

(b) Foot and cross-foot all special journals.

(a) Purchases journal—
Accounts Payable, Cr.
$22,895
Sales journal—Sales
Revenue total $8,700

(c) Accounts Receivable
$8,560
Accounts Payable $22,275
*Journalize transactions in special journals.*

(LO 2, 3)

(b) Sales journal $17,700
Purchases journal
$33,800
Cash receipts journal—
Cash, Dr. $54,490
Cash payments journal,
Cash, Cr. $45,100

*Journalize in purchases and cash payments journals; post; prepare a trial balance; prove control to subsidiary; prepare adjusting entries; prepare an adjusted trial balance.*

(LO 2, 3)

GLS

**(c)** Show how postings would be made by placing ledger account numbers and check marks as needed in the journals. (Actual posting to ledger accounts is not required.)

**P7-5B** Presented below are the sales and cash receipts journals for Lowery Co. for its first month of operations.

### SALES JOURNAL                                                                          S1

| Date | Account Debited | Ref. | Accounts Receivable Dr. Sales Revenue Cr. | Cost of Goods Sold Dr. Inventory Cr. |
|---|---|---|---|---|
| Feb. 3 | C. Ogleby | | 4,000 | 2,400 |
| 9 | S. Hauke | | 5,000 | 3,000 |
| 12 | T. Ghosh | | 6,500 | 3,900 |
| 26 | W. Hoy | | 5,500 | 3,300 |
| | | | 21,000 | 12,600 |

### CASH RECEIPTS JOURNAL                                                                   CR1

| Date | Owner's Account Credited | Ref. | Cash Dr. | Sales Discounts Dr. | Accounts Receivable Cr. | Sales Revenue Cr. | Other Accounts Cr. | Cost of Goods Sold Dr. Inventory Cr. |
|---|---|---|---|---|---|---|---|---|
| Feb. 1 | Owner's Capital | | 23,000 | | | | 23,000 | |
| 2 | | | 4,500 | | | 4,500 | | 2,700 |
| 13 | C. Ogleby | | 3,960 | 40 | 4,000 | | | |
| 18 | Inventory | | 120 | | | | 120 | |
| 26 | S. Hauke | | 5,000 | | 5,000 | | | |
| | | | 36,580 | 40 | 9,000 | 4,500 | 23,120 | 2,700 |

In addition, the following transactions have not been journalized for February 2014.

Feb. 2  Purchased merchandise on account from B. Setterstrom for $5,600, terms 2/10, n/30.

7  Purchased merchandise on account from A. Dambro for $23,000, terms 1/10, n/30.

9  Paid cash of $980 for purchase of supplies.

12  Paid $5,488 to B. Setterstrom in payment for $5,600 invoice, less 2% discount.

15  Purchased equipment for $4,500 cash.

16  Purchased merchandise on account from D. Budke $1,900, terms 2/10, n/30.

17  Paid $22,770 to A. Dambro in payment of $23,000 invoice, less 1% discount.

20  S. Lowery withdrew cash of $800 from the business for personal use.

21  Purchased merchandise on account from Eberle Company for $8,000, terms 1/10, n/30.

28  Paid $1,900 to D. Budke in payment of $1,900 invoice.

### Instructions

**(a)** Open the following accounts in the general ledger.

| | |
|---|---|
| 101 Cash | 301 Owner's Capital |
| 112 Accounts Receivable | 306 Owner's Drawings |
| 120 Inventory | 401 Sales Revenue |
| 126 Supplies | 414 Sales Discounts |
| 157 Equipment | 505 Cost of Goods Sold |
| 158 Accumulated Depreciation—Equipment | 631 Supplies Expense |
| 201 Accounts Payable | 711 Depreciation Expense |

(b) Purchases journal total $38,500
Cash payments journal— Cash, Cr. $36,438

**(b)** Journalize the transactions that have not been journalized in a one-column purchases journal and the cash payments journal (see Illustration 7-16).

**(c)** Post to the accounts receivable and accounts payable subsidiary ledgers. Follow the sequence of transactions as shown in the problem.

(d) Post the individual entries and totals to the general ledger.
(e) Prepare a trial balance at February 28, 2014.
(f) Determine that the subsidiary ledgers agree with the control accounts in the general ledger.
(g) The following adjustments at the end of February are necessary.
   (1) A count of supplies indicates that $200 is still on hand.
   (2) Depreciation on equipment for February is $150.
   Prepare the adjusting entries and then post the adjusting entries to the general ledger.
(h) Prepare an adjusted trial balance at February 28, 2014.

*(e) Totals $56,500*

*(f) Accounts Receivable*
*$12,000*
*Accounts Payable $8,000*

*(h) Totals $56,650*

## PROBLEMS: SET C

Visit the book's companion website, at **www.wiley.com/college/weygandt**, and choose the Student Companion site to access Problem Set C.

## COMPREHENSIVE PROBLEM: CHAPTERS 3 TO 7

**CP7** McBride Company has the following opening account balances in its general and subsidiary ledgers on January 1 and uses the periodic inventory system. All accounts have normal debit and credit balances.

### GENERAL LEDGER

| Account Number | Account Title | January 1 Opening Balance |
|---|---|---|
| 101 | Cash | $33,750 |
| 112 | Accounts Receivable | 13,000 |
| 115 | Notes Receivable | 39,000 |
| 120 | Inventory | 20,000 |
| 126 | Supplies | 1,000 |
| 130 | Prepaid Insurance | 2,000 |
| 157 | Equipment | 6,450 |
| 158 | Accumulated Depreciation—Equip. | 1,500 |
| 201 | Accounts Payable | 35,000 |
| 301 | Owner's Capital | 78,700 |

**Accounts Receivable Subsidiary Ledger**

| Customer | January 1 Opening Balance |
|---|---|
| R. Kotsay | $1,500 |
| B. Boxberger | 7,500 |
| S. Andrus | 4,000 |

**Accounts Payable Subsidiary Ledger**

| Creditor | January 1 Opening Balance |
|---|---|
| S. Otero | $ 9,000 |
| R. Rasmus | 15,000 |
| D. Baroni | 11,000 |

In addition, the following transactions have not been journalized for January 2014.

Jan.  3  Sell merchandise on account to B. Berg $3,600, invoice no. 510, and J. Lutz $1,800, invoice no. 511.
     5  Purchase merchandise on account from S. Colt $5,000 and D. Kahn $2,700.
     7  Receive checks for $4,000 from S. Andrus and $2,000 from B. Boxberger.
     8  Pay freight on merchandise purchased $180.
     9  Send checks to S. Otero for $9,000 and D. Baroni for $11,000.

9   Issue credit of $300 to J. Lutz for merchandise returned.
10  Summary cash sales total $15,500.
11  Sell merchandise on account to R. Kotsay for $2,900, invoice no. 512, and to S. Andrus $900, invoice no. 513.
    Post all entries to the subsidiary ledgers.
12  Pay rent of $1,000 for January.
13  Receive payment in full from B. Berg and J. Lutz.
15  Withdraw $800 cash by I. McBride for personal use.
16  Purchase merchandise on account from D. Baroni for $12,000, from S. Otero for $13,900, and from S. Colt for $1,500.
17  Pay $400 cash for supplies.
18  Return $200 of merchandise to S. Otero and receive credit.
20  Summary cash sales total $17,500.
21  Issue $15,000 note to R. Rasmus in payment of balance due.
21  Receive payment in full from S. Andrus.
    Post all entries to the subsidiary ledgers.
22  Sell merchandise on account to B. Berg for $3,700, invoice no. 514, and to R. Kotsay for $800, invoice no. 515.
23  Send checks to D. Baroni and S. Otero in full payment.
25  Sell merchandise on account to B. Boxberger for $3,500, invoice no. 516, and to J. Lutz for $6,100, invoice no. 517.
27  Purchase merchandise on account from D. Baroni for $12,500, from D. Kahn for $1,200, and from S. Colt for $2,800.
28  Pay $200 cash for office supplies.
31  Summary cash sales total $22,920.
31  Pay sales salaries of $4,300 and office salaries of $3,600.

### Instructions

**(a)** Record the January transactions in the appropriate journal—sales, purchases, cash receipts, cash payments, and general.
**(b)** Post the journals to the general and subsidiary ledgers. Add and number new accounts in an orderly fashion as needed.

(c) Trial balance totals $200,320; Adj. T/B totals $200,475

**(c)** Prepare a trial balance at January 31, 2014, using a worksheet. Complete the worksheet using the following additional information.
  **(1)** Supplies at January 31 total $700.
  **(2)** Insurance coverage expires on October 31, 2014.
  **(3)** Annual depreciation on the equipment is $1,500.
  **(4)** Interest of $30 has accrued on the note payable.
  **(5)** Inventory at January 31 is $15,000.

(d) Net income $12,185 Total assets $130,815

**(d)** Prepare a multiple-step income statement and an owner's equity statement for January and a classified balance sheet at the end of January.
**(e)** Prepare and post the adjusting and closing entries.

(f) Post-closing T/B totals $132,440

**(f)** Prepare a post-closing trial balance, and determine whether the subsidiary ledgers agree with the control accounts in the general ledger.

# Broadening Your Perspective

## Financial Reporting and Analysis

### Financial Reporting Problem—Mini Practice Set

**BYP7-1** Jeter Co. uses a perpetual inventory system and both an accounts receivable and an accounts payable subsidiary ledger. Balances related to both the general ledger and the subsidiary ledger for Jeter are indicated in the working papers. Presented on the next page are a series of transactions for Jeter Co. for the month of January. Credit sales terms are 2/10, n/30. The cost of all merchandise sold was 60% of the sales price.

Jan. 3  Sell merchandise on account to B. Corpas $3,600, invoice no. 510, and to J. Revere $1,800, invoice no. 511.

5  Purchase merchandise from S. Gamel $5,000 and D. Posey $2,200, terms n/30.

7  Receive checks from S. Mahay $4,000 and B. Santos $2,000 after discount period has lapsed.

8  Pay freight on merchandise purchased $235.

9  Send checks to S. Meek for $9,000 less 2% cash discount, and to D. Saito for $11,000 less 1% cash discount.

9  Issue credit of $300 to J. Revere for merchandise returned.

10  Summary daily cash sales total $15,500.

11  Sell merchandise on account to R. Beltre $1,600, invoice no. 512, and to S. Mahay $900, invoice no. 513.

12  Pay rent of $1,000 for January.

13  Receive payment in full from B. Corpas and J. Revere less cash discounts.

15  Withdraw $800 cash by M. Jeter for personal use.

15  Post all entries to the subsidiary ledgers.

16  Purchase merchandise from D. Saito $15,000, terms 1/10, n/30; S. Meek $14,200, terms 2/10, n/30; and S. Gamel $1,500, terms n/30.

17  Pay $400 cash for office supplies.

18  Return $200 of merchandise to S. Meek and receive credit.

20  Summary daily cash sales total $20,100.

21  Issue $15,000 note, maturing in 90 days, to R. Moses in payment of balance due.

21  Receive payment in full from S. Mahay less cash discount.

22  Sell merchandise on account to B. Corpas $2,700, invoice no. 514, and to R. Beltre $2,300, invoice no. 515.

22  Post all entries to the subsidiary ledgers.

23  Send checks to D. Saito and S. Meek in full payment less cash discounts.

25  Sell merchandise on account to B. Santos $3,500, invoice no. 516, and to J. Revere $6,100, invoice no. 517.

27  Purchase merchandise from D. Saito $14,500, terms 1/10, n/30; D. Posey $3,200, terms n/30; and S. Gamel $5,400, terms n/30.

27  Post all entries to the subsidiary ledgers.

28  Pay $200 cash for office supplies.

31  Summary daily cash sales total $21,300.

31  Pay sales salaries $4,300 and office salaries $3,800.

*Instructions*

**(a)** Record the January transactions in a sales journal, a single-column purchases journal, a cash receipts journal as shown on page 340, a cash payments journal as shown on page 346, and a two-column general journal.

**(b)** Post the journals to the general ledger.

**(c)** Prepare a trial balance at January 31, 2014, in the trial balance columns of the worksheet. Complete the worksheet using the following additional information.

    **(1)** Office supplies at January 31 total $900.

    **(2)** Insurance coverage expires on October 31, 2014.

    **(3)** Annual depreciation on the equipment is $1,500.

    **(4)** Interest of $50 has accrued on the note payable.

**(d)** Prepare a multiple-step income statement and an owner's equity statement for January and a classified balance sheet at the end of January.

**(e)** Prepare and post adjusting and closing entries.

**(f)** Prepare a post-closing trial balance, and determine whether the subsidiary ledgers agree with the control accounts in the general ledger.

## Real-World Focus

**BYP7-2** Intuit provides some of the leading accounting software packages. Information related to its products is found at its website.

*Address:* **http://quickbooks.intuit.com** or go to **www.wiley.com/college/weygandt**

*Instructions*

Look under product and services for the product QuickBooks Premier for Accountants. Be ready to discuss its new features with the class.

# Critical Thinking

## Decision-Making Across the Organization

**BYP7-3** Ermler & Trump is a wholesaler of small appliances and parts. Ermler & Trump is operated by two owners, Jack Ermler and Andrea Trump. In addition, the company has one employee, a repair specialist, who is on a fixed salary. Revenues are earned through the sale of appliances to retailers (approximately 75% of total revenues), appliance parts to do-it-yourselfers (10%), and the repair of appliances brought to the store (15%). Appliance sales are made on both a credit and cash basis. Customers are billed on prenumbered sales invoices. Credit terms are always net/30 days. All parts sales and repair work are cash only.

Merchandise is purchased on account from the manufacturers of both the appliances and the parts. Practically all suppliers offer cash discounts for prompt payments, and it is company policy to take all discounts. Most cash payments are made by check. Checks are most frequently issued to suppliers, to trucking companies for freight on merchandise purchases, and to newspapers, radio, and TV stations for advertising. All advertising bills are paid as received. Jack and Andrea each make a monthly drawing in cash for personal living expenses. The salaried repairman is paid twice monthly. Ermler & Trump currently has a manual accounting system.

### Instructions
With the class divided into groups, answer the following.

**(a)** Identify the special journals that Ermler & Trump should have in its manual accounting system. List the column headings appropriate for each of the special journals.

**(b)** What control and subsidiary accounts should be included in Ermler & Trump's manual accounting system? Why?

## Communication Activity

**BYP7-4** Jill Locey, a classmate, has a part-time bookkeeping job. She is concerned about the inefficiencies in journalizing and posting transactions. Ben Newell is the owner of the company where Jill works. In response to numerous complaints from Jill and others, Ben hired two additional bookkeepers a month ago. However, the inefficiencies have continued at an even higher rate. The accounting information system for the company has only a general journal and a general ledger. Ben refuses to install a computerized accounting system.

### Instructions
Now that Jill is an expert in manual accounting information systems, she decides to send a letter to Ben Newell explaining (1) why the additional personnel did not help and (2) what changes should be made to improve the efficiency of the accounting department. Write the letter that you think Jill should send.

## Ethics Case

**BYP7-5** Wiemers Products Company operates three divisions, each with its own manufacturing plant and marketing/sales force. The corporate headquarters and central accounting office are in Wiemers, and the plants are in Freeport, Rockport, and Bayport, all within 50 miles of Wiemers. Corporate management treats each division as an independent profit center and encourages competition among them. They each have similar but different product lines. As a competitive incentive, bonuses are awarded each year to the employees of the fastest-growing and most-profitable division.

Indy Grover is the manager of Wiemers's centralized computerized accounting operation that enters the sales transactions and maintains the accounts receivable for all three divisions. Indy came up in the accounting ranks from the Bayport division where his wife, several relatives, and many friends still work.

As sales documents are entered into the computer, the originating division is identified by code. Most sales documents (95%) are coded, but some (5%) are not coded or are coded incorrectly. As the manager, Indy has instructed the data-entry personnel to assign the Bayport code to all uncoded and incorrectly coded sales documents. This is done, he says, "in order to expedite processing and to keep the computer files current since they are updated daily." All receivables and cash collections for all three divisions are handled by Wiemers as one subsidiary accounts receivable ledger.

*Instructions*
**(a)** Who are the stakeholders in this situation?
**(b)** What are the ethical issues in this case?
**(c)** How might the system be improved to prevent this situation?

## All About You

**BYP7-6** In this chapter, you learned about a basic manual accounting information system. Computerized accounting systems range from the very basic and inexpensive to the very elaborate and expensive. However, even the most sophisticated systems are based on the fundamental structures and relationships that you learned in this chapter.

*Instructions*
Go to the book's companion site for this textbook, **www.wiley.com/college/weygandt**, and review the demonstration that is provided for the general ledger software package that is used with this textbook. Prepare a brief explanation of how the general ledger system works—that is, how it is used, and what information it provides.

## Answers to Chapter Questions

### Answers to Insight and Accounting Across the Organization Questions

**p. 332 Curbing Fraudulent Activity with Software    Q:** Why might this software help reduce fraudulent activity by employees? **A:** By pinpointing who used the accounting system and when they used it, the software can hold employees more accountable for their actions. Companies hope that this will reduce efforts by employees to enter false accounting entries, change the dates of transactions, or create unauthorized expenditures. If employees do engage in these activities, there will be significant evidence of their activities.

**p. 335 "I'm John Smith, a.k.a. 13695071642"    Q:** Why use numbers to identify names in a computerized system? **A:** Computerized systems process numbers faster than letters. Also, letters sometimes cause problems because you may have two people with the same name. Computerized systems avoid this problem by giving different customers, including those with the same names, different account numbers.

### Answers to Self-Test Questions

**1.** d  **2.** c  **3.** a  **4.** c  **5.** c ($5,000 + $7,000 + $6,000 + $4,500 + $8,500 − $11,500 − $3,000)
**6.** c  **7.** d  **8.** c  **9.** a  **10.** d  **11.** c  **12.** d  **13.** b  **14.** c  **15.** c

# A Look at IFRS

As discussed in Chapter 1, IFRS is growing in acceptance around the world. For example, recent statistics indicate a substantial number of the Global Fortune 500 companies use IFRS. And the chair of the IASB predicts that IFRS adoption will grow from its current level of 115 countries to nearly 150 countries in the near future.

**LEARNING OBJECTIVE    4**

Compare the procedures for accounting information systems under GAAP and IFRS.

When countries accept IFRS for use as accepted accounting policies, companies need guidance to ensure that their first IFRS financial statements contain high-quality information. Specifically, *IFRS 1* requires that information in a company's first IFRS statements (1) be transparent, (2) provide a suitable starting point, and (3) have a cost that does not exceed the benefits.

## Key Points

- The basic concepts related to an accounting information system are the same under GAAP and IFRS.
- The use of subsidiary ledgers and control accounts, as well as the system used for recording transactions, are the same under GAAP and IFRS.
- Many companies will be going through a substantial conversion process to switch from their current reporting standards to IFRS.

- The overriding principle in converting to IFRS is full retrospective application of IFRS. Retrospective application—recasting prior financial statements on the basis of IFRS—provides financial statement users with comparable information.

- As indicated, the objective of the conversion process is to present a set of IFRS statements as if the company always reported under IFRS. To achieve this objective, a company follows these steps.

  **1.** Identify the timing of its first IFRS statements.

  **2.** Prepare an opening balance sheet at the date of transition to IFRS.

  **3.** Select accounting principles that comply with IFRS, and apply these principles retrospectively.

  **4.** Make extensive disclosures to explain the transition to IFRS.

- Once a company decides to convert to IFRS, it must decide on the transition date and the reporting date. The transition date is the beginning of the earliest period for which full comparative IFRS information is presented. The reporting date is the closing balance sheet date for the first IFRS financial statements.

- To illustrate, assume that FirstChoice Company plans to provide its first IFRS statements for the year ended December 31, 2014. FirstChoice decides to present comparative information for one year only. Therefore, its date of transition to IFRS is January 1, 2013, and its reporting date is December 31, 2014.

- The timeline for first-time adoption is presented in the following graphic.

The graphic shows the following.

**1.** The opening IFRS statement of financial position for FirstChoice on January 1, 2013, serves as the starting point (date of transition) for the company's accounting under IFRS.

**2.** The first full IFRS statements are shown for FirstChoice for December 31, 2014. In other words, a minimum of two years of IFRS statements must be presented before a conversion to IFRS occurs. As a result, FirstChoice must prepare at least one year of comparative financial statements for 2013 using IFRS.

**3.** FirstChoice presents financial statements in accordance with U.S. GAAP annually to December 31, 2013.

Following this conversion process, FirstChoice provides users of the financial statements with comparable IFRS statements for 2013 and 2014.

- Upon first-time adoption of IFRS, a company must present at least one year of comparative information under IFRS.

## Looking to the Future

The basic recording process shown in this textbook is followed by companies around the globe. It is unlikely to change in the future. The definitional structure of assets, liabilities, equity, revenues, and expenses may change over time as the IASB and FASB evaluate their overall conceptual framework for establishing accounting standards. In addition, high-quality international accounting requires both high-quality accounting standards and high-quality auditing. Similar to the convergence of U.S. GAAP and IFRS, there is a movement to improve international auditing standards. The International Auditing and Assurance Standards Board (IAASB) functions as an independent standard-setting body. It works to establish high-quality auditing and assurance and quality-control standards throughout the world. Whether the IAASB adopts internal control provisions similar to those in SOX remains to be seen. You can follow developments in the international audit arena at **http://www.ifac.org/laasb/**.

## IFRS Practice

### IFRS Self-Test Questions

**1.** Information in a company's first IFRS statements must:
 (a) have a cost that does not exceed the benefits.
 (b) be transparent.
 (c) provide a suitable starting point.
 (d) All the above.

**2.** Indicate which of these statements is **false**.
 (a) The use of subsidiary ledgers is the same under IFRS and GAAP.
 (b) GAAP and IFRS use the same accounting principles.
 (c) The use of special journals is the same under IFRS and GAAP.
 (d) At conversion, companies should retrospectively adjust the financial statements presented following IFRS.

**3.** The transition date is the date:
 (a) when a company no longer reports under its national standards.
 (b) when the company issues its most recent financial statement under IFRS.
 (c) three years prior to the reporting date.
 (d) None of the above.

**4.** When converting to IFRS, a company must:
 (a) recast previously issued financial statements in accordance with IFRS.
 (b) use U.S. GAAP in the reporting period but subsequently use IFRS.
 (c) prepare at least three years of comparative statements.
 (d) use U.S. GAAP in the transition year but IFRS in the reporting year.

**5.** The purpose of presenting comparative information in the transition to IFRS is:
 (a) to ensure that the information is reliable.
 (b) in accordance with the Sarbanes-Oxley Act.
 (c) to provide users of the financial statements with information on U.S. GAAP in one period and IFRS in the other period.
 (d) to provide users of the financial statements with information on IFRS for at least two periods.

### IFRS Exercises

**IFRS7-1** How is the date of transition and the date of reporting determined in first-time adoption of IFRS?

**IFRS7-2** What are the characteristics of high-quality information in a company's first IFRS financial statements?

**IFRS7-3** What are the steps to be completed in preparing the opening IFRS statement of financial position?

**IFRS7-4** Becker Ltd. is planning to adopt IFRS and prepare its first IFRS financial statements at December 31, 2014. What is the date of Becker's opening balance sheet assuming one year of comparative information? What periods will be covered in Becker's first IFRS financial statements?

**IFRS7-5** Stengel plc is preparing its opening IFRS balance sheet on January 1, 2014. Under its previous GAAP, Stengel used the LIFO inventory method. Under LIFO, its inventory is reported at £250,000 (in British pounds). Under FIFO, which Stengel will use upon adoption of IFRS, the inventory is valued at £265,000. Explain what Stengel must do.

**Answers to IFRS Self-Test Questions**
**1.** d   **2.** b   **3.** d   **4.** a   **5.** d

The Navigator

✔ Remember to go back to The Navigator box on the chapter opening page and check off your completed work.

# 8 Fraud, Internal Control, and Cash

## Minding the Money in Moose Jaw

If you're ever looking for a cappuccino in Moose Jaw, Saskatchewan, stop by Stephanie's Gourmet Coffee and More, located on Main Street. Staff there serve, on average, 650 cups of coffee a day, including both regular and specialty coffees, not to mention soups, Italian sandwiches, and a wide assortment of gourmet cheesecakes.

"We've got high school students who come here, and students from the community college," says owner/manager Stephanie Mintenko, who has run the place since opening it in 1995. "We have customers who are retired, and others who are working people and have only 30 minutes for lunch. We have to be pretty quick."

That means that the cashiers have to be efficient. Like most businesses where purchases are low-cost and high-volume, cash control has to be simple.

"We have an electronic cash register, but it's not the fancy new kind where you just punch in the item," explains Ms. Mintenko. "You have to punch in the prices." The machine does keep track of sales in several categories,

however. Cashiers punch a button to indicate whether e item is a beverage, a meal, or other type of item. An inte tape in the machine keeps a record of all transactions. Th customer receives a receipt only upon request.

There is only one cash register. "Up to three of us might operate it on any given shift, including myself," says Ms. Mintenko.

She and her staff do two "cashouts" each day—one wit the shift change at 5:00 p.m. and one when the shop clc at 10:00 p.m. At each cashout, they count the cash in th register drawer. That amount, minus the cash change ca forward (the float), should match the shift total on the register tape. If there's a discrepancy, they do another count. Then, if necessary, "we go through the whole tap to find the mistake," she explains. "It usually turns out to be someone who punched in $18 instead of $1.80, o something like that."

Ms. Mintenko sends all the cash tapes and float totals to bookkeeper, who double-checks everything and provides regular reports. "We try to keep the accounting simple, so we can concentrate on making great coffee and food

## Learning Objectives

 The Navigator

*After studying this chapter, you should be able to:*

[1] Define fraud and internal control.

[2] Identify the principles of internal control activities.

[3] Explain the applications of internal control principles to cash receipts.

[4] Explain the applications of internal control principles to cash disbursements.

[5] Describe the operation of a petty cash fund.

[6] Indicate the control features of a bank account.

[7] Prepare a bank reconciliation.

[8] Explain the reporting of cash.

# Preview of Chapter 8

✔ The Navigator

As the story about recording cash sales at Stephanie's Gourmet Coffee and More indicates, control of cash is important to ensure that fraud does not occur. Companies also need controls to safeguard other types of assets. For example, Stephanie's undoubtedly has controls to prevent the theft of food and supplies, and controls to prevent the theft of tableware and dishes from its kitchen.

In this chapter, we explain the essential features of an internal control system and how it prevents fraud. We also describe how those controls apply to a specific asset—cash. The applications include some controls with which you may be already familiar, such as the use of a bank.

The content and organization of Chapter 8 are as follows.

## FRAUD, INTERNAL CONTROL, AND CASH

| Fraud and Internal Control | Cash Controls | Control Features: Use of a Bank | Reporting Cash |
|---|---|---|---|
| • Fraud<br>• The Sarbanes-Oxley Act<br>• Internal control<br>• Principles of internal control activities<br>• Limitations | • Cash receipts controls<br>• Cash disbursements controls<br>• Petty cash fund | • Making deposits<br>• Writing checks<br>• Bank statements<br>• Reconciling the bank account<br>• Electronic funds transfer (EFT) system | • Cash equivalents<br>• Restricted cash |

## Fraud and Internal Control

LEARNING OBJECTIVE    **1**

Define fraud and internal control.

The Feature Story describes many of the internal control procedures used by Stephanie's Gourmet Coffee and More. These procedures are necessary to discourage employees from fraudulent activities.

### Fraud

A **fraud** is a dishonest act by an employee that results in personal benefit to the employee at a cost to the employer. Examples of fraud reported in the financial press include:

- A bookkeeper in a small company diverted $750,000 of bill payments to a personal bank account over a three-year period.
- A shipping clerk with 28 years of service shipped $125,000 of merchandise to himself.
- A computer operator embezzled $21 million from Wells Fargo Bank over a two-year period.
- A church treasurer "borrowed" $150,000 of church funds to finance a friend's business dealings.

Why does fraud occur? The three main factors that contribute to fraudulent activity are depicted by the **fraud triangle** in Illustration 8-1 (in the margin).

**Illustration 8-1**
Fraud triangle

The most important element of the fraud triangle is **opportunity**. For an employee to commit fraud, the workplace environment must provide opportunities that an employee can take advantage of. Opportunities occur when the workplace lacks sufficient controls to deter and detect fraud. For example, inadequate monitoring of employee actions can create opportunities for theft and can embolden employees because they believe they will not be caught.

A second factor that contributes to fraud is **financial pressure**. Employees sometimes commit fraud because of personal financial problems caused by too much debt. Or, they might commit fraud because they want to lead a lifestyle that they cannot afford on their current salary.

The third factor that contributes to fraud is **rationalization**. In order to justify their fraud, employees rationalize their dishonest actions. For example, employees sometimes justify fraud because they believe they are underpaid while the employer is making lots of money. Employees feel justified in stealing because they believe they deserve to be paid more.

### The Sarbanes-Oxley Act

What can be done to prevent or to detect fraud? After numerous corporate scandals came to light in the early 2000s, Congress addressed this issue by passing the **Sarbanes-Oxley Act (SOX)**. Under SOX, all publicly traded U.S. corporations are required to maintain an adequate system of internal control. Corporate executives and boards of directors must ensure that these controls are reliable and effective. In addition, independent outside auditors must attest to the adequacy of the internal control system. Companies that fail to comply are subject to fines, and company officers can be imprisoned. SOX also created the Public Company Accounting Oversight Board (PCAOB) to establish auditing standards and regulate auditor activity.

One poll found that 60% of investors believe that SOX helps safeguard their stock investments. Many say they would be unlikely to invest in a company that fails to follow SOX requirements. Although some corporate executives have criticized the time and expense involved in following the SOX requirements, SOX appears to be working well. For example, the chief accounting officer of Eli Lily noted that SOX triggered a comprehensive review of how the company documents controls. This review uncovered redundancies and pointed out controls that needed to be added. In short, it added up to time and money well spent. And the finance chief at General Electric noted, "We have seen value in SOX. It helps build investors' trust and gives them more confidence."[1]

## Internal Control

**Internal control** consists of all the related methods and measures adopted within an organization to safeguard assets, enhance the reliability of accounting records, increase efficiency of operations, and ensure compliance with laws and regulations. Internal control systems have five primary components as listed below.[2]

- **A control environment.** It is the responsibility of top management to make it clear that the organization values integrity and that unethical activity will not be tolerated. This component is often referred to as the "tone at the top."

- **Risk assessment.** Companies must identify and analyze the various factors that create risk for the business and must determine how to manage these risks.

- **Control activities.** To reduce the occurrence of fraud, management must design policies and procedures to address the specific risks faced by the company.

- **Information and communication.** The internal control system must capture and communicate all pertinent information both down and up the organization, as well as communicate information to appropriate external parties.

- **Monitoring.** Internal control systems must be monitored periodically for their adequacy. Significant deficiencies need to be reported to top management and/or the board of directors.

## PEOPLE, PLANET, AND PROFIT INSIGHT

### And the Controls Are . . .

Internal controls are important for an effective financial reporting system. The same is true for sustainability reporting. An effective system of internal controls for sustainability reporting will help in the following ways: (1) prevent the unauthorized use of data; (2) provide reasonable assurance that the information is accurate, valid, and complete; and (3) report information that is consistent with overall sustainability accounting policies. With these types of controls, users will have the confidence that they can use the sustainability information effectively.

Some regulators are calling for even more assurance through audits of this information. Companies that potentially can cause environmental damage through greenhouse gases are subject to reporting requirements as well as companies in the mining and extractive industries. And, as demand for more information in the sustainability area expands, the need for audits of this information will grow.

© Karl Dolenc/iStockphoto

**?** Why is sustainability information important to investors? (See page 424.)

[1]"Corporate Regulation Must Be Working—There's a Backlash," *Wall Street Journal* (June 16, 2004), p. C1; and Judith Burns, "Is Sarbanes-Oxley Working?" *Wall Street Journal* (June 21, 2004), pp. R8–R9.

[2]The Committee of Sponsoring Organizations of the Treadway Commission, "Internal Control—Integrated Framework," *www.coso.org/publications/executive_summary_integrated_framework.htm* (accessed March 2008).

## Principles of Internal Control Activities

Each of the five components of an internal control system is important. Here, we will focus on one component, the control activities. The reason? These activities are the backbone of the company's efforts to address the risks it faces, such as fraud. The specific control activities used by a company will vary, depending on management's assessment of the risks faced. This assessment is heavily influenced by the size and nature of the company.

The six principles of control activities are as follows.

- Establishment of responsibility
- Segregation of duties
- Documentation procedures
- Physical controls
- Independent internal verification
- Human resource controls

We explain these principles in the following sections. You should recognize that they apply to most companies and are relevant to both manual and computerized accounting systems.

### ESTABLISHMENT OF RESPONSIBILITY

An essential principle of internal control is to assign responsibility to specific employees. **Control is most effective when only one person is responsible for a given task.**

It's your shift now. I'm turning in my cash drawer and heading home.

**Transfer of cash drawers**

To illustrate, assume that the cash on hand at the end of the day in a Safeway supermarket is $10 short of the cash entered in the cash register. If only one person has operated the register, the shift manager can quickly determine responsibility for the shortage. If two or more individuals have worked the register, it may be impossible to determine who is responsible for the error. In the Feature Story, the principle of establishing responsibility does not appear to be strictly applied by Stephanie's Gourmet Coffee and More, since three people operate the cash register on any given shift.

Many retailers solve this problem by having registers with multiple drawers. This makes it possible for more than one person to operate a register but still allows identification of a particular employee with a specific drawer. Only the signed-in cashier has access to his or her drawer.

Establishing responsibility often requires limiting access only to authorized personnel, and then identifying those personnel. For example, the automated systems used by many companies have mechanisms such as identifying passcodes that keep track of who made a journal entry, who entered a sale, or who went into an inventory storeroom at a particular time. Use of identifying passcodes enables the company to establish responsibility by identifying the particular employee who carried out the activity.

### ANATOMY OF A FRAUD

Maureen Frugali was a training supervisor for claims processing at Colossal Healthcare. As a standard part of the claims-processing training program, Maureen created fictitious claims for use by trainees. These fictitious claims were then sent to the accounts payable department. After the training claims had been processed, she was to notify Accounts Payable of all fictitious claims, so that they would not be paid. However, she did not inform Accounts Payable about every fictitious claim. She created some fictitious claims for entities that she controlled (that is, she would receive the payment), and she let Accounts Payable pay her.

**THE MISSING CONTROL**
*Establishment of responsibility.* The health-care company did not adequately restrict the responsibility for authorizing and approving claims transactions. The training supervisor should not have been authorized to create claims in the company's "live" system.

*Source:* Adapted from Wells, *Fraud Casebook* (2007), pp. 61–70.

## SEGREGATION OF DUTIES

Segregation of duties is indispensable in an internal control system. There are two common applications of this principle:

**1.** Different individuals should be responsible for related activities.

**2.** The responsibility for record-keeping for an asset should be separate from the physical custody of that asset.

The rationale for segregation of duties is this: **The work of one employee should, without a duplication of effort, provide a reliable basis for evaluating the work of another employee.** For example, the personnel that design and program computerized systems should not be assigned duties related to day-to-day use of the system. Otherwise, they could design the system to benefit them personally and conceal the fraud through day-to-day use.

**SEGREGATION OF RELATED ACTIVITIES. Making one individual responsible for related activities increases the potential for errors and irregularities.** Instead, companies should, for example, assign related **purchasing activities** to different individuals. Related purchasing activities include ordering merchandise, order approval, receiving goods, authorizing payment, and paying for goods or services. Various frauds are possible when one person handles related purchasing activities:

- If a purchasing agent is allowed to order goods without obtaining supervisory approval, the likelihood of the purchasing agent receiving kickbacks from suppliers increases.
- If an employee who orders goods also handles receipt of the goods and invoice, as well as payment authorization, he or she might authorize payment for a fictitious invoice.

These abuses are less likely to occur when companies divide the purchasing tasks.

Similarly, companies should assign related **sales activities** to different individuals. Related selling activities include making a sale, shipping (or delivering) the goods to the customer, billing the customer, and receiving payment. Various frauds are possible when one person handles related sales activities:

- If a salesperson can make a sale without obtaining supervisory approval, he or she might make sales at unauthorized prices to increase sales commissions.
- A shipping clerk who also has access to accounting records could ship goods to himself.
- A billing clerk who handles billing and receipt could understate the amount billed for sales made to friends and relatives.

These abuses are less likely to occur when companies divide the sales tasks: The salespeople make the sale; the shipping department ships the goods on the basis of the sales order; and the billing department prepares the sales invoice after comparing the sales order with the report of goods shipped.

> ## ANATOMY OF A FRAUD
>
> Lawrence Fairbanks, the assistant vice-chancellor of communications at Aesop University, was allowed to make purchases of under $2,500 for his department without external approval. Unfortunately, he also sometimes bought items for himself, such as expensive antiques and other collectibles. How did he do it? He replaced the vendor invoices he received with fake vendor invoices that he created. The fake invoices had descriptions that were more consistent with the communications department's purchases. He submitted these fake invoices to the accounting department as the basis for their journal entries and to the accounts payable department as the basis for payment.
>
> ### Total take: $475,000
>
> **THE MISSING CONTROL**
>
> *Segregation of duties.* The university had not properly segregated related purchasing activities. Lawrence was ordering items, receiving the items, and receiving the invoice. By receiving the invoice, he had control over the documents that were used to account for the purchase and thus was able to substitute a fake invoice.
>
> *Source:* Adapted from Wells, *Fraud Casebook* (2007), pp. 3–15.

**Accounting employee A**
Maintains cash
balances per books

**Segregation of duties**
(Accountability for assets)

**Assistant cashier B**
Maintains custody
of cash on hand

**SEGREGATION OF RECORD-KEEPING FROM PHYSICAL CUSTODY.** The accountant should have neither physical custody of the asset nor access to it. Likewise, the custodian of the asset should not maintain or have access to the accounting records. **The custodian of the asset is not likely to convert the asset to personal use when one employee maintains the record of the asset, and a different employee has physical custody of the asset.** The separation of accounting responsibility from the custody of assets is especially important for cash and inventories because these assets are very vulnerable to fraud.

> ## ANATOMY OF A FRAUD
>
> Angela Bauer was an accounts payable clerk for Aggasiz Construction Company. Angela prepared and issued checks to vendors and reconciled bank statements. She perpetrated a fraud in this way: She wrote checks for costs that the company had not actually incurred (e.g., fake taxes). A supervisor then approved and signed the checks. Before issuing the check, though, Angela would "white-out" the payee line on the check and change it to personal accounts that she controlled. She was able to conceal the theft because she also reconciled the bank account. That is, nobody else ever saw that the checks had been altered.
>
> ### Total take: $570,000
>
> **THE MISSING CONTROL**
>
> *Segregation of duties.* Aggasiz Construction Company did not properly segregate record-keeping from physical custody. Angela had physical custody of the checks, which essentially was control of the cash. She also had record-keeping responsibility because she prepared the bank reconciliation.
>
> *Source:* Adapted from Wells, *Fraud Casebook* (2007), pp. 100–107.

### DOCUMENTATION PROCEDURES

Documents provide evidence that transactions and events have occurred. At Stephanie's Gourmet Coffee and More, the cash register tape is the restaurant's documentation for the sale and the amount of cash received. More sophisticated registers, called point-of-sale terminals, do not rely on tapes. Rather, they are networked with the company's computing and accounting records, which results in direct documentation.

Similarly, a shipping document indicates that the goods have been shipped, and a sales invoice indicates that the company has billed the customer for the goods. By requiring signatures (or initials) on the documents, the company can identify the individual(s) responsible for the transaction or event. Companies should document transactions when the transaction occurs.

Companies should establish procedures for documents. First, whenever possible, companies should use **prenumbered documents, and all documents should be accounted for**. Prenumbering helps to prevent a transaction from being recorded more than once, or conversely, from not being recorded at all. Second, the control system should require that employees **promptly forward source documents for accounting entries to the accounting department. This control measure helps to ensure timely recording of the transaction** and contributes directly to the accuracy and reliability of the accounting records.

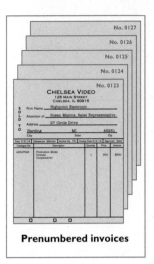

**Prenumbered invoices**

---

### ANATOMY OF A FRAUD

To support their reimbursement requests for travel costs incurred, employees at Mod Fashions Corporation's design center were required to submit receipts. The receipts could include the detailed bill provided for a meal, the credit card receipt provided when the credit card payment is made, or a copy of the employee's monthly credit card bill that listed the item. A number of the designers who frequently traveled together came up with a fraud scheme: They submitted claims for the same expenses. For example, if they had a meal together that cost $200, one person submitted the detailed meal bill, another submitted the credit card receipt, and a third submitted a monthly credit card bill showing the meal as a line item. Thus, all three received a $200 reimbursement.

**Total take: $75,000**

#### THE MISSING CONTROL

***Documentation procedures.*** Mod Fashions should require the original, detailed receipt. It should not accept photocopies, and it should not accept credit card statements. In addition, documentation procedures could be further improved by requiring the use of a corporate credit card (rather than a personal credit card) for all business expenses.

*Source:* Adapted from Wells, *Fraud Casebook* (2007), pp. 79–90.

---

## PHYSICAL CONTROLS

Use of physical controls is essential. **Physical controls** relate to the safeguarding of assets and enhance the accuracy and reliability of the accounting records. Illustration 8-2 shows examples of these controls.

**Illustration 8-2**
Physical controls

**Physical Controls**

| | | | | | |
|---|---|---|---|---|---|
| Safes, vaults, and safety deposit boxes for cash and business papers | Locked warehouses and storage cabinets for inventories and records | Computer facilities with pass key access or fingerprint or eyeball scans | Alarms to prevent break-ins | Television monitors and garment sensors to deter theft | Time clocks for recording time worked |

ANATOMY OF A FRAUD

At Centerstone Health, a large insurance company, the mailroom each day received insurance applications from prospective customers. Mailroom employees scanned the applications into electronic documents before the applications were processed. Once the applications were scanned, they could be accessed online by authorized employees.

Insurance agents at Centerstone Health earn commissions based upon successful applications. The sales agent's name is listed on the application. However, roughly 15% of the applications are from customers who did not work with a sales agent. Two friends—Alex, an employee in record-keeping, and Parviz, a sales agent—thought up a way to perpetrate a fraud. Alex identified scanned applications that did not list a sales agent. After business hours, he entered the mailroom and found the hard-copy applications that did not show a sales agent. He wrote in Parviz's name as the sales agent and then rescanned the application for processing. Parviz received the commission, which the friends then split.

Total take: $240,000

**THE MISSING CONTROL**

*Physical controls.* Centerstone Health lacked two basic physical controls that could have prevented this fraud. First, the mailroom should have been locked during non-business hours, and access during business hours should have been tightly controlled. Second, the scanned applications supposedly could be accessed only by authorized employees using their passwords. However, the password for each employee was the same as the employee's user ID. Since employee user-ID numbers were available to all other employees, all employees knew all other employees' passwords. Unauthorized employees could access the scanned applications. Thus, Alex could enter the system using another employee's password and access the scanned applications.

*Source:* Adapted from Wells, *Fraud Casebook* (2007), pp. 316–326.

## INDEPENDENT INTERNAL VERIFICATION

Most internal control systems provide for **independent internal verification**. This principle involves the review of data prepared by employees. To obtain maximum benefit from independent internal verification:

1. Companies should verify records periodically or on a surprise basis.
2. An employee who is independent of the personnel responsible for the information should make the verification.
3. Discrepancies and exceptions should be reported to a management level that can take appropriate corrective action.

Independent internal verification is especially useful in comparing recorded accountability with existing assets. The reconciliation of the cash register tape with the cash in the register at Stephanie's Gourmet Coffee and More is an example of this internal control principle. Another common example is the reconciliation of a company's cash balance per books with the cash balance per bank and the verification of the perpetual inventory records through a count of physical inventory. Illustration 8-3 shows the relationship between this principle and the segregation of duties principle.

ANATOMY OF A FRAUD

Bobbi Jean Donnelly, the office manager for Mod Fashions Corporations design center, was responsible for preparing the design center budget and reviewing expense reports submitted by design center employees. Her desire to upgrade her wardrobe got the better of her, and she enacted a fraud that involved filing expense-reimbursement requests for her own personal clothing purchases. Bobbi Jean was able to conceal the fraud because she was responsible for reviewing all expense reports, including her

**Illustration 8-3**
Comparison of segregation
of duties principle with
independent internal verification
principle

own. In addition, she sometimes was given ultimate responsibility for signing off on
the expense reports when her boss was "too busy." Also, because she controlled the
budget, when she submitted her expenses, she coded them to budget items that she
knew were running under budget, so that they would not catch anyone's attention.

**Total take: $275,000**

### THE MISSING CONTROL
***Independent internal verification.*** Bobbi Jean's boss should have verified her expense
reports. When asked what he thought her expenses for a year were, the boss said
about $10,000. At $115,000 per year, her actual expenses were more than 10 times
what would have been expected. However, because he was "too busy" to verify her
expense reports or to review the budget, he never noticed.

*Source:* Adapted from Wells, *Fraud Casebook* (2007), pp. 79–90.

Large companies often assign independent internal verification to internal
auditors. **Internal auditors** are company employees who continuously evaluate
the effectiveness of the company's internal control systems. They review the activities of departments and individuals to determine whether prescribed internal
controls are being followed. They also recommend improvements when needed.
For example, WorldCom was at one time the second largest U.S. telecommunica-
tions company. The fraud that caused its bankruptcy (the largest ever when it
occurred) involved billions of dollars. It was uncovered by an internal auditor.

## HUMAN RESOURCE CONTROLS
Human resource control activities include the following.

1. **Bond employees who handle cash. Bonding** involves obtaining insurance
   protection against theft by employees. It contributes to the safeguarding of
   cash in two ways. First, the insurance company carefully screens all individuals before adding them to the policy and may reject risky applicants. Second,
   bonded employees know that the insurance company will vigorously prose-
   cute all offenders.

2. **Rotate employees' duties and require employees to take vacations.** These
   measures deter employees from attempting thefts since they will not be able
   to permanently conceal their improper actions. Many banks, for example,

have discovered employee thefts when the employee was on vacation or assigned to a new position.

3. **Conduct thorough background checks.** Many believe that the most important and inexpensive measure any business can take to reduce employee theft and fraud is for the human resources department to conduct thorough background checks. Two tips: (1) Check to see whether job applicants actually graduated from the schools they list. (2) Never use telephone numbers for previous employers provided by the applicant. Always look them up yourself.

---

### ANATOMY OF A FRAUD

Ellen Lowry was the desk manager and Josephine Rodriguez was the head of housekeeping at the Excelsior Inn, a luxury hotel. The two best friends were so dedicated to their jobs that they never took vacations, and they frequently filled in for other employees. In fact, Ms. Rodriguez, whose job as head of housekeeping did not include cleaning rooms, often cleaned rooms herself, "just to help the staff keep up." These two "dedicated" employees, working as a team, found a way to earn a little more cash. Ellen, the desk manager, provided significant discounts to guests who paid with cash. She kept the cash and did not register the guest in the hotel's computerized system. Instead, she took the room out of circulation "due to routine maintenance." Because the room did not show up as being used, it did not receive a normal housekeeping assignment. Instead, Josephine, the head of housekeeping, cleaned the rooms during the guests' stay.

Total take: $95,000

**THE MISSING CONTROL**

*Human resource controls.* Ellen, the desk manager, had been fired by a previous employer after being accused of fraud. If the Excelsior Inn had conducted a thorough background check, it would not have hired her. The hotel fraud was detected when Ellen missed work for a few days due to illness. A system of mandatory vacations and rotating days off would have increased the chances of detecting the fraud before it became so large.

*Source:* Adapted from Wells, *Fraud Casebook* (2007), pp. 145–155.

---

## ACCOUNTING ACROSS THE ORGANIZATION

### SOX Boosts the Role of Human Resources

Under SOX, a company needs to keep track of employees' degrees and certifications to ensure that employees continue to meet the specified requirements of a job. Also, to ensure proper employee supervision and proper separation of duties, companies must develop and monitor an organizational chart. When one corporation went through this exercise, it found that out of 17,000 employees, there were 400 people who did not report to anyone. The corporation also had 35 people who reported to each other. In addition, if an employee complains of an unfair firing and mentions financial issues at the company, HR should refer the case to the company audit committee and possibly to its legal counsel.

Stockbyte/Getty Images, Inc.

 Why would unsupervised employees or employees who report to each other represent potential internal control threats? (See page 424.)

---

## Limitations of Internal Control

Companies generally design their systems of internal control to provide **reasonable assurance** of proper safeguarding of assets and reliability of the accounting records. The concept of reasonable assurance rests on the premise that the costs of establishing control procedures should not exceed their expected benefit.

To illustrate, consider shoplifting losses in retail stores. Stores could eliminate such losses by having a security guard stop and search customers as they leave the store. But store managers have concluded that the negative effects of such a procedure cannot be justified. Instead, they have attempted to control shoplifting losses by less costly procedures. They post signs saying, "We reserve the right to inspect all packages" and "All shoplifters will be prosecuted." They use hidden TV cameras and store detectives to monitor customer activity, and they install sensor equipment at exits.

The **human element** is an important factor in every system of internal control. A good system can become ineffective as a result of employee fatigue, carelessness, or indifference. For example, a receiving clerk may not bother to count goods received and may just "fudge" the counts. Occasionally, two or more individuals may work together to get around prescribed controls. Such **collusion** can significantly reduce the effectiveness of a system, eliminating the protection offered by segregation of duties. No system of internal control is perfect.

The **size of the business** also may impose limitations on internal control. Small companies often find it difficult to segregate duties or to provide for independent internal verification. A study by the Association of Certified Fraud Examiners (*2012 Report to the Nation on Occupational Fraud and Abuse*) indicates that businesses with fewer than 100 employees are most at risk for employee theft. In fact, 31% of frauds occurred at companies with fewer than 100 employees. The median loss at small companies was $147,000, which was higher than the median fraud at companies with more than 10,000 employees ($140,000). A $147,000 loss can threaten the very existence of a small company.

> **Helpful Hint** Controls may vary with the risk level of the activity. For example, management may consider cash to be high risk and maintaining inventories in the stockroom as low risk. Thus, management would have stricter controls for cash.

---

> **DO IT!**

**Control Activities**

Identify which control activity is violated in each of the following situations, and explain how the situation creates an opportunity for a fraud.

1. The person with primary responsibility for reconciling the bank account and making all bank deposits is also the company's accountant.

2. Wellstone Company's treasurer received an award for distinguished service because he had not taken a vacation in 30 years.

3. In order to save money spent on order slips and to reduce time spent keeping track of order slips, a local bar/restaurant does not buy prenumbered order slips.

**Solution**

**Action Plan**

✔ Familiarize yourself with each of the control activities summarized on page 378.

✔ Understand the nature of the frauds that each control activity is intended to address.

1. Violates the control activity of segregation of duties. Record-keeping should be separate from physical custody. As a consequence, the employee could embezzle cash and make journal entries to hide the theft.

2. Violates the control activity of human resource controls. Key employees must take vacations. Otherwise, the treasurer, who manages the company's cash, might embezzle cash and use his position to conceal the theft.

3. Violates the control activity of documentation procedures. If prenumbered documents are not used, then it is virtually impossible to account for the documents. As a consequence, an employee could write up a dinner sale, receive the cash from the customer, and then throw away the order slip and keep the cash.

Related exercise material: **BE8-1, BE8-2, BE8-3, BE8-4, E8-1, and DO IT! 8-1.**

✔ **The Navigator**

## Cash Controls

LEARNING OBJECTIVE    3

Explain the applications of internal control principles to cash receipts.

Cash is the one asset that is readily convertible into any other type of asset. It also is easily concealed and transported, and is highly desired. Because of these characteristics, **cash is the asset most susceptible to fraudulent activities**. In addition, because of the large volume of cash transactions, numerous errors may occur in executing and recording them. To safeguard cash and to ensure the accuracy of the accounting records for cash, effective internal control over cash is critical.

### Cash Receipts Controls

Illustration 8-4 shows how the internal control principles explained earlier apply to cash receipts transactions. As you might expect, companies vary considerably in how they apply these principles. To illustrate internal control over cash receipts, we will examine control activities for a retail store with both over-the-counter and mail receipts.

**Illustration 8-4**
Application of internal control principles to cash receipts

**Cash Receipts Controls**

| **Establishment of Responsibility** | **Segregation of Duties** | **Documentation Procedures** |
|---|---|---|
| Only designated personnel are authorized to handle cash receipts (cashiers) | Different individuals receive cash, record cash receipts, and hold the cash | Use remittance advice (mail receipts), cash register tapes or computer records, and deposit slips |

| **Physical Controls** | **Independent Internal Verification** | **Human Resource Controls** |
|---|---|---|
| Store cash in safes and bank vaults; limit access to storage areas; use cash registers | Supervisors count cash receipts daily; assistant treasurer compares total receipts to bank deposits daily | Bond personnel who handle cash; require employees to take vacations; conduct background checks |

### OVER-THE-COUNTER RECEIPTS

In retail businesses, control of over-the-counter receipts centers on cash registers that are visible to customers. A cash sale is entered in a cash register, with the amount clearly visible to the customer. This activity prevents the cashier from entering a lower amount and pocketing the difference. The customer receives an itemized cash register receipt slip and is expected to count the change received.

(One weakness at Stephanie's Gourmet Coffee and More in the Feature Story is that customers were only given a receipt if they requested it.) The cash register's tape is locked in the register until a supervisor removes it. This tape accumulates the daily transactions and totals.

At the end of the clerk's shift, the clerk counts the cash and sends the cash and the count to the cashier. The cashier counts the cash, prepares a deposit slip, and deposits the cash at the bank. The cashier also sends a duplicate of the deposit slip to the accounting department to indicate cash received. The supervisor removes the cash register tape and sends it to the accounting department as the basis for a journal entry to record the cash received. Illustration 8-5 summarizes this process.

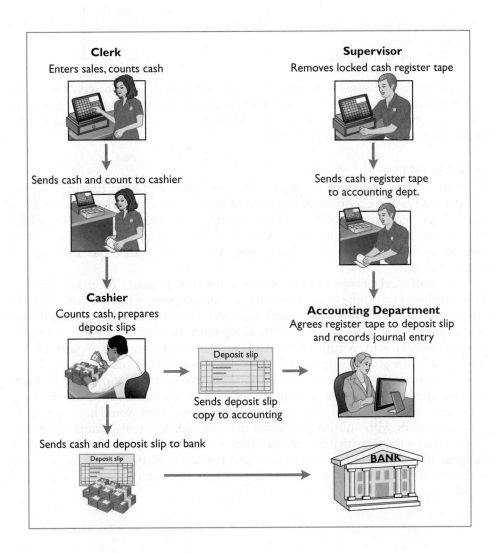

**Illustration 8-5**
Control of over-the-counter receipts

**Helpful Hint** Flowcharts such as this one enhance the understanding of the flow of documents, the processing steps, and the internal control procedures.

This system for handling cash receipts uses an important internal control principle—segregation of record-keeping from physical custody. The supervisor has access to the cash register tape but **not** to the cash. The clerk and the cashier have access to the cash but **not** to the register tape. In addition, the cash register tape provides documentation and enables independent internal verification. Use of these three principles of internal control (segregation of record-keeping from physical custody, documentation, and independent internal verification) provides an effective system of internal control. Any attempt at fraudulent activity should be detected unless there is collusion among the employees.

In some instances, the amount deposited at the bank will not agree with the cash recorded in the accounting records based on the cash register tape. These differences often result because the clerk hands incorrect change back to the retail customer. In this case, the difference between the actual cash and the amount reported on the cash register tape is reported in a Cash Over and Short account. For example, suppose that the cash register tape indicated sales of $6,956.20 but the amount of cash was only $6,946.10. A cash shortfall of $10.10 exists. To account for this cash shortfall and related cash, the company makes the following entry.

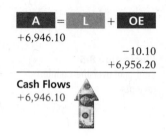

| | | |
|---|---|---|
| Cash | 6,946.10 | |
| Cash Over and Short | 10.10 | |
|     Sales Revenue | | 6,956.20 |
|       (To record cash shortfall) | | |

Cash Over and Short is an income statement item. It is reported as miscellaneous expense when there is a cash shortfall, and as miscellaneous revenue when there is an overage. Clearly, the amount should be small. Any material amounts in this account should be investigated.

## MAIL RECEIPTS

All mail receipts should be opened in the presence of at least two mail clerks. These receipts are generally in the form of checks. A mail clerk should endorse each check "For Deposit Only." This restrictive endorsement reduces the likelihood that someone could divert the check to personal use. Banks will not give an individual cash when presented with a check that has this type of endorsement.

The mail clerks prepare, in triplicate, a list of the checks received each day. This list shows the name of the check issuer, the purpose of the payment, and the amount of the check. Each mail clerk signs the list to establish responsibility for the data. The original copy of the list, along with the checks, is then sent to the cashier's department. A copy of the list is sent to the accounting department for recording in the accounting records. The clerks also keep a copy.

This process provides excellent internal control for the company. By employing two clerks, the chance of fraud is reduced. Each clerk knows he or she is being observed by the other clerk(s). To engage in fraud, they would have to collude. The customers who submit payments also provide control because they will contact the company with a complaint if they are not properly credited for payment. Because the cashier has access to cash but not the records, and the accounting department has access to records but not cash, neither can engage in undetected fraud.

> ## DO IT!

### Control over Cash Receipts

L. R. Cortez is concerned about the control over cash receipts in his fast-food restaurant, Big Cheese. The restaurant has two cash registers. At no time do more than two employees take customer orders and enter sales. Work shifts for employees range from 4 to 8 hours. Cortez asks your help in installing a good system of internal control over cash receipts.

**Solution**

Cortez should assign a separate cash register drawer to each employee at the start of each work shift, with register totals set at zero. Each employee should have access to only the assigned register drawer to enter all sales. Each customer should be given a receipt. At the end of the shift, the employee should do a cash count. A separate employee should compare the cash count with the register tape to be sure they agree. In addition, Cortez should install an automated system that would enable the company to compare orders entered in the register to orders processed by the kitchen.

Related exercise material: **BE8-5, BE8-6, BE8-7, E8-2,** and **DO IT!** 8-2.

## Cash Disbursements Controls

Companies disburse cash for a variety of reasons, such as to pay expenses and liabilities or to purchase assets. **Generally, internal control over cash disbursements is more effective when companies pay by check or electronic funds transfer (EFT) rather than by cash.** One exception is **payments for incidental amounts that are paid out of petty cash.**[3]

Companies generally issue checks only after following specified control procedures. Illustration 8-6 (page 390) shows how principles of internal control apply to cash disbursements.

### VOUCHER SYSTEM CONTROLS

Most medium and large companies use vouchers as part of their internal control over cash disbursements. A **voucher system** is a network of approvals by authorized individuals, acting independently, to ensure that all disbursements by check are proper.

The system begins with the authorization to incur a cost or expense. It ends with the issuance of a check for the liability incurred. A **voucher** is an authorization form prepared for each expenditure. Companies require vouchers for all types of cash disbursements except those from petty cash.

The starting point in preparing a voucher is to fill in the appropriate information about the liability on the face of the voucher. The vendor's invoice provides most of the needed information. Then, an employee in accounts payable records the voucher (in a journal called a **voucher register**) and files it according to the date on which it is to be paid. The company issues and sends a check on that date, and stamps the voucher "paid." The paid voucher is sent to the accounting department for recording (in a journal called the **check register**). A voucher system involves two journal entries, one to record the liability when the voucher is issued and a second to pay the liability that relates to the voucher.

The use of a voucher system, whether done manually or electronically, improves internal control over cash disbursements. First, the authorization process inherent in a voucher system establishes responsibility. Each individual has responsibility to review the underlying documentation to ensure that it is correct. In addition, the voucher system keeps track of the documents that back up each transaction. By keeping these documents in one place, a supervisor can independently verify the authenticity of each transaction. Consider, for example, the case of Aesop University presented on page 380. Aesop did not use a voucher system for

---

[3]We explain the operation of a petty cash fund on pages 390–392.

**Cash Disbursements Controls**

**Establishment of Responsibility**
Only designated personnel are authorized to sign checks (treasurer) and approve vendors

**Segregation of Duties**
Different individuals approve and make payments; check-signers do not record disbursements

**Documentation Procedures**
Use prenumbered checks and account for them in sequence; each check must have an approved invoice; require employees to use corporate credit cards for reimbursable expenses; stamp invoices "paid"

**Physical Controls**
Store blank checks in safes, with limited access; print check amounts by machine in indelible ink

**Independent Internal Verification**
Compare checks to invoices; reconcile bank statement monthly

**Human Resource Controls**
Bond personnel who handle cash; require employees to take vacations; conduct background checks

**Illustration 8-6**
Application of internal control principles to cash disbursements

transactions under $2,500. As a consequence, there was no independent verification of the documents, which enabled the employee to submit fake invoices to hide his unauthorized purchases.

## Petty Cash Fund

As you just learned, better internal control over cash disbursements is possible when companies make payments by check. However, using checks to pay small amounts is both impractical and a nuisance. For instance, a company would not want to write checks to pay for postage due, working lunches, or taxi fares. A common way of handling such payments, while maintaining satisfactory control, is to use a **petty cash fund** to pay relatively small amounts. The operation of a petty cash fund, often called an **imprest system**, involves (1) establishing the fund, (2) making payments from the fund, and (3) replenishing the fund.[4]

---

[4]The term "imprest" means an advance of money for a designated purpose.

## ESTABLISHING THE PETTY CASH FUND

Two essential steps in establishing a petty cash fund are (1) appointing a petty cash custodian who will be responsible for the fund, and (2) determining the size of the fund. Ordinarily, a company expects the amount in the fund to cover anticipated disbursements for a three- to four-week period.

To establish the fund, a company issues a check payable to the petty cash custodian for the stipulated amount. For example, if Laird Company decides to establish a $100 fund on March 1, the general journal entry is:

| Mar. 1 | Petty Cash | 100 | |
|---|---|---|---|
| |     Cash | | 100 |
| |        (To establish a petty cash fund) | | |

A = L + OE
+100
−100

**Cash Flows**
no effect

The fund custodian cashes the check and places the proceeds in a locked petty cash box or drawer. Most petty cash funds are established on a fixed-amount basis. The company will make no additional entries to the Petty Cash account unless management changes the stipulated amount of the fund. For example, if Laird Company decides on July 1 to increase the size of the fund to $250, it would debit Petty Cash $150 and credit Cash $150.

> **Ethics Note**
> Petty cash funds are authorized and legitimate. In contrast, "slush" funds are unauthorized and hidden (under the table).

## MAKING PAYMENTS FROM THE PETTY CASH FUND

The petty cash custodian has the authority to make payments from the fund that conform to prescribed management policies. Usually, management limits the size of expenditures that come from petty cash. Likewise, it may not permit use of the fund for certain types of transactions (such as making short-term loans to employees).

Each payment from the fund must be documented on a prenumbered petty cash receipt (or petty cash voucher), as shown in Illustration 8-7. The signatures of both the fund custodian and the person receiving payment are required on the receipt. If other supporting documents such as a freight bill or invoice are available, they should be attached to the petty cash receipt.

> **Helpful Hint** The petty cash receipt satisfies two internal control procedures: (1) establishing responsibility (signature of custodian), and (2) documentation procedures.

**Illustration 8-7**
Petty cash receipt

```
No. 7                    LAIRD COMPANY
                         Petty Cash Receipt

                                    Date    3/6/14

Paid to   Acme Express Agency       Amount   $18.00

For    Collect Express Charges

CHARGE TO          Freight-in

Approved                            Received Payment

  L. A. Bird    Custodian             R. Meins
```

The petty cash custodian keeps the receipts in the petty cash box until the fund is replenished. The sum of the petty cash receipts and the money in the fund should equal the established total at all times. Management can (and should) make surprise counts at any time to determine whether the fund is being maintained correctly.

### Ethics Note

Internal control over a petty cash fund is strengthened by (1) having a supervisor make surprise counts of the fund to confirm whether the paid petty cash receipts and fund cash equal the imprest amount, and (2) canceling or mutilating the paid petty cash receipts so they cannot be resubmitted for reimbursement.

The company does not make an accounting entry to record a payment when it is made from petty cash. It is considered both inexpedient and unnecessary to do so. Instead, the company recognizes the accounting effects of each payment when it replenishes the fund.

## REPLENISHING THE PETTY CASH FUND

When the money in the petty cash fund reaches a minimum level, the company replenishes the fund. The petty cash custodian initiates a request for reimbursement. The individual prepares a schedule (or summary) of the payments that have been made and sends the schedule, supported by petty cash receipts and other documentation, to the treasurer's office. The treasurer's office examines the receipts and supporting documents to verify that proper payments from the fund were made. The treasurer then approves the request and issues a check to restore the fund to its established amount. At the same time, all supporting documentation is stamped "paid" so that it cannot be submitted again for payment.

To illustrate, assume that on March 15 Laird's petty cash custodian requests a check for $87. The fund contains $13 cash and petty cash receipts for postage $44, freight-out $38, and miscellaneous expenses $5. The general journal entry to record the check is:

A = L + OE
−44 Exp
−38 Exp
−5 Exp
−87

**Cash Flows**
−87

| Mar. 15 | Postage Expense | 44 | |
| | Freight-Out | 38 | |
| | Miscellaneous Expense | 5 | |
| |     Cash | | 87 |
| |        (To replenish petty cash fund) | | |

Note that the reimbursement entry does not affect the Petty Cash account. Replenishment changes the composition of the fund by replacing the petty cash receipts with cash. It does not change the balance in the fund.

Occasionally, in replenishing a petty cash fund, the company may need to recognize a cash shortage or overage. This results when the total of the cash plus receipts in the petty cash box does not equal the established amount of the petty cash fund. To illustrate, assume that Laird's petty cash custodian has only $12 in cash in the fund plus the receipts as listed. The request for reimbursement would therefore be for $88, and Laird would make the following entry.

A = L + OE
−44 Exp
−38 Exp
−5 Exp
−1 Exp
−88

**Cash Flows**
−88

| Mar. 15 | Postage Expense | 44 | |
| | Freight-Out | 38 | |
| | Miscellaneous Expense | 5 | |
| | Cash Over and Short | 1 | |
| |     Cash | | 88 |
| |        (To replenish petty cash fund) | | |

Conversely, if the custodian has $14 in cash, the reimbursement request would be for $86. The company would credit Cash Over and Short for $1 (overage). A company reports a debit balance in Cash Over and Short in the income statement as miscellaneous expense. It reports a credit balance in the account as miscellaneous revenue. The company closes Cash Over and Short to Income Summary at the end of the year.

Companies should replenish a petty cash fund at the end of the accounting period, regardless of the cash in the fund. Replenishment at this time is necessary in order to recognize the effects of the petty cash payments on the financial statements.

**Helpful Hint** Cash over and short situations result from mathematical errors or from failure to keep accurate records.

# ETHICS INSIGHT

## How Employees Steal

A recent study by the Association of Certified Fraud Examiners found that two-thirds of all employee thefts involved a fraudulent disbursement by an employee. The most common form (24.9% of cases) was fraudulent billing schemes. In these, the employee causes the company to issue a payment to the employee by submitting a bill for nonexistent goods or services, purchases of personal goods by the employee, or inflated invoices. The graph below shows various types of fraudulent disbursements and the median loss from each.

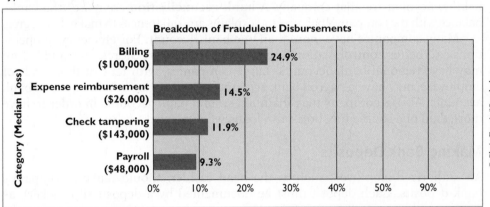

**Breakdown of Fraudulent Disbursements**

Category (Median Loss):
- Billing ($100,000): 24.9%
- Expense reimbursement ($26,000): 14.5%
- Check tampering ($143,000): 11.9%
- Payroll ($48,000): 9.3%

(x-axis: 0%, 10%, 20%, 30%, 40%, 50%, 90%)

© Chris Fernig/iStockphoto

Source: *2012 Report to the Nation on Occupational Fraud and Abuse*, Association of Certified Fraud Examiners, *www.acfe.com/uploadedfiles/ACFE_website/content/rttn/2012-report-to-nations.pdf*, p. 12.

**?** How can companies reduce the likelihood of fraudulent disbursements? (See page 424.)

---

# > DO IT!

## Petty Cash Fund

### Action Plan

✔ To establish the fund, set up a separate general ledger account.

✔ Determine how much cash is needed to replenish the fund: subtract the cash remaining from the petty cash fund balance.

✔ Total the petty cash receipts. Determine any cash over or short—the difference between the cash needed to replenish the fund and the total of the petty cash receipts.

✔ Record the expenses incurred according to the petty cash receipts when replenishing the fund.

Bateer Company established a $50 petty cash fund on July 1. On July 30, the fund had $12 cash remaining and petty cash receipts for postage $14, office supplies $10, and delivery expense $15. Prepare journal entries to establish the fund on July 1 and to replenish the fund on July 30.

### Solution

| July 1 | Petty Cash | 50 | |
| | Cash | | 50 |
| | (To establish petty cash fund) | | |
| 30 | Postage Expense | 14 | |
| | Supplies | 10 | |
| | Delivery Expense | 15 | |
| | Cash Over and Short | | 1 |
| | Cash ($50 − $12) | | 38 |
| | (To replenish petty cash) | | |

Related exercise material: **BE8-9, E8-7, E8-8, and DO IT! 8-3.**

 **The Navigator**

## Control Features: Use of a Bank

LEARNING OBJECTIVE 6

Indicate the control features of a bank account.

**The use of a bank contributes significantly to good internal control over cash.** A company can safeguard its cash by using a bank as a depository and as a clearinghouse for checks received and written. Use of a bank minimizes the amount of currency that a company must keep on hand. Also, use of a bank facilitates the control of cash because it creates a double record of all bank transactions—one by the company and the other by the bank. The asset account Cash maintained by the company should have the same balance as the bank's liability account for that company. A **bank reconciliation** compares the bank's balance with the company's balance and explains any differences to make them agree.

Many companies have more than one bank account. For efficiency of operations and better control, national retailers like Wal-Mart Stores, Inc. and Target may have regional bank accounts. Large companies, with tens of thousands of employees, may have a payroll bank account, as well as one or more general bank accounts. Also, a company may maintain several bank accounts in order to have more than one source for short-term loans when needed.

### Making Bank Deposits

An authorized employee, such as the head cashier, should make a company's bank deposits. Each deposit must be documented by a deposit slip (ticket), as shown in Illustration 8-8.

**Illustration 8-8**
Deposit slip

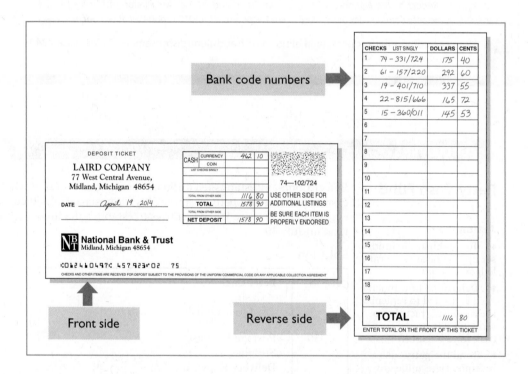

Deposit slips are prepared in duplicate. The bank retains the original; the depositor keeps the duplicate, machine-stamped by the bank to establish its authenticity.

### Writing Checks

Most of us write checks without thinking very much about them. **A check** is a written order signed by the depositor directing the bank to pay a specified sum of money to a designated recipient. There are three parties to a check: (1) the **maker** (or drawer) who issues the check, (2) the **bank** (or payer) on which the check is drawn, and (3) the **payee** to whom the check is payable. A check is a **negotiable instrument** that one party can transfer to another party by endorsement. Each check should be accompanied by an explanation of its purpose. In many companies, a remittance advice attached to the check, as shown in Illustration 8-9, explains the check's purpose.

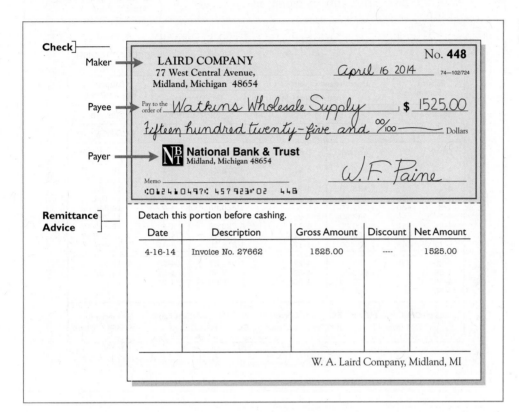

**Illustration 8-9**
Check with remittance advice

It is important to know the balance in the checking account at all times. To keep the balance current, the depositor should enter each deposit and check on running-balance memo forms (or online statements) provided by the bank or on the check stubs in the checkbook.

## Bank Statements

If you have a personal checking account, you are probably familiar with bank statements. A **bank statement** shows the depositor's bank transactions and balances.[5] Each month, a depositor receives a statement from the bank. Illustration 8-10 (page 396) presents a typical bank statement for Laird Company. It shows (1) checks paid and other debits (such as debit card transactions or direct withdrawals for bill payments) that reduce the balance in the depositor's account, (2) deposits and other credits that increase the balance in the depositor's account, and (3) the account balance after each day's transactions.

**Helpful Hint** Essentially, the bank statement is a copy of the bank's records sent to the customer (or available online) for review.

---

[5]Our presentation assumes that the depositor makes all adjustments at the end of the month. In practice, a company may also make journal entries during the month as it reviews information from the bank regarding its account.

**Illustration 8-10**
Bank statement

**Helpful Hint** The bank *credits* to the customer's account every deposit it receives. The reverse occurs when the bank "pays" a check issued by a company on its checking account balance. Payment reduces the bank's liability. Thus, the bank *debits* check payments to the customer's account with the bank.

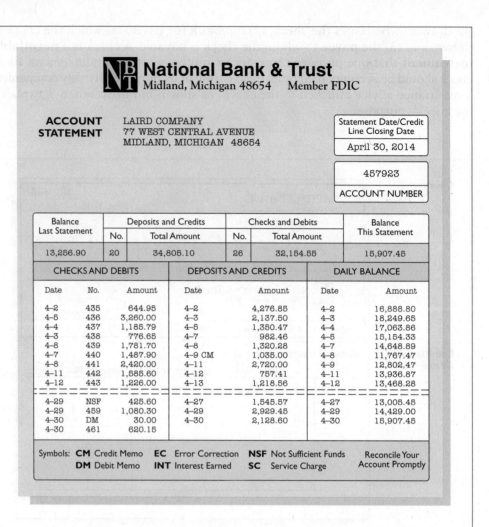

The bank statement lists in numerical sequence all "paid" checks, along with the date the check was paid and its amount. Upon paying a check, the bank stamps the check "paid"; a paid check is sometimes referred to as a **canceled** check. On the statement, the bank also includes memoranda explaining other debits and credits it made to the depositor's account.

### DEBIT MEMORANDUM

Some banks charge a monthly fee for their services. Often, they charge this fee only when the average monthly balance in a checking account falls below a specified amount. They identify the fee, called a **bank service charge**, on the bank statement by a symbol such as **SC**. The bank also sends with the statement a debit memorandum explaining the charge noted on the statement. Other debit memoranda may also be issued for other bank services such as the cost of printing checks, issuing traveler's checks, and wiring funds to other locations. The symbol **DM** is often used for such charges.

Banks also use a debit memorandum when a deposited check from a customer "bounces" because of insufficient funds. For example, assume that Scott Company, a customer of Laird Company, sends a check for $800 to Laird Company for services performed. Unfortunately, Scott does not have sufficient funds at its bank to pay for these services. In such a case, Scott's bank marks the check **NSF** (not sufficient funds) and returns it to Laird's (the depositor's) bank. Laird's bank then debits Laird's account, as shown by the symbol NSF on the bank statement in Illustration 8-10. The bank sends the NSF check and debit memorandum to Laird as notification of the charge. Laird then records an Account Receivable from Scott Company (the writer of the bad check) and reduces cash for the NSF check.

## CREDIT MEMORANDUM

Sometimes a depositor asks the bank to collect its notes receivable. In such a case, the bank will credit the depositor's account for the cash proceeds of the note. This is illustrated by the symbol **CM** on the Laird Company bank statement. The bank issues and sends with the statement a credit memorandum to explain the entry. Many banks also offer interest on checking accounts. The interest earned may be indicated on the bank statement by the symbol **CM** or **INT**.

## Reconciling the Bank Account

The bank and the depositor maintain independent records of the depositor's checking account. People tend to assume that the respective balances will always agree. In fact, the two balances are seldom the same at any given time, and both balances differ from the "correct" or "true" balance. Therefore, it is necessary to make the balance per books and the balance per bank agree with the correct or true amount—a process called **reconciling the bank account**. The need for agreement has two causes:

> LEARNING OBJECTIVE   7
>
> **Prepare a bank reconciliation.**

1. **Time lags** that prevent one of the parties from recording the transaction in the same period as the other party.
2. **Errors** by either party in recording transactions.

   Time lags occur frequently. For example, several days may elapse between the time a company mails a check to a payee and the date the bank pays the check. Similarly, when the depositor uses the bank's night depository to make its deposits, there will be a difference of at least one day between the time the depositor records the deposit and the time the bank does so. A time lag also occurs whenever the bank mails a debit or credit memorandum to the depositor.

   The incidence of errors depends on the effectiveness of the internal controls maintained by the company and the bank. Bank errors are infrequent. However, either party could accidentally record a $450 check as $45 or $540. In addition, the bank might mistakenly charge a check drawn by C. D. Berg to the account of C. D. Burg.

## RECONCILIATION PROCEDURE

**The bank reconciliation should be prepared by an employee who has no other responsibilities pertaining to cash.** If a company fails to follow this internal control principle of independent internal verification, cash embezzlements may go unnoticed. For example, a cashier who prepares the reconciliation can embezzle cash and conceal the embezzlement by misstating the reconciliation. Thus, the bank accounts would reconcile, and the embezzlement would not be detected.

   In reconciling the bank account, it is customary to reconcile the balance per books and balance per bank to their adjusted (correct or true) cash balances. The starting point in preparing the reconciliation is to enter the balance per bank statement and balance per books on the reconciliation schedule. The company then makes various adjustments, as shown in Illustration 8-11 (page 398).

**Illustration 8-11**
Bank reconciliation adjustments

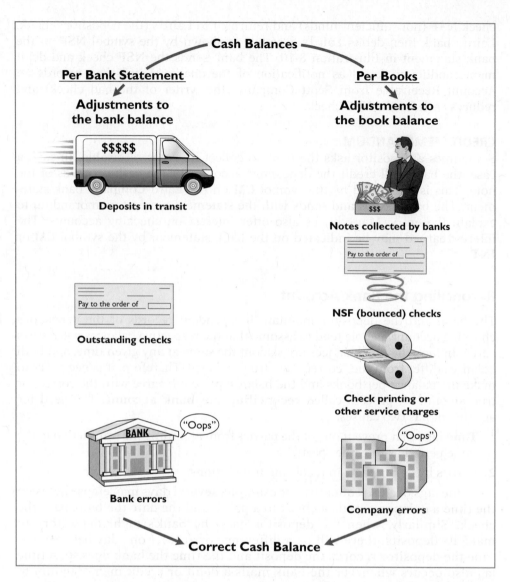

The following steps should reveal all the reconciling items that cause the difference between the two balances.

**Step 1.   Deposits in transit.** Compare the individual deposits listed on the bank statement with deposits in transit from the preceding bank reconciliation and with the deposits per company records or duplicate deposit slips. Deposits recorded by the depositor that have not been recorded by the bank are the **deposits in transit**. Add these deposits to the balance per bank.

**Step 2.   Outstanding checks.** Compare the paid checks shown on the bank statement with (a) checks outstanding from the previous bank reconciliation, and (b) checks issued by the company as recorded in the cash payments journal (or in the check register in your personal checkbook). Issued checks recorded by the company but that have not yet been paid by the bank are **outstanding checks**. Deduct outstanding checks from the balance per the bank.

**Step 3.   Errors.** Note any errors discovered in the foregoing steps and list them in the appropriate section of the reconciliation schedule. For example, if the company mistakenly recorded as $169 a paid check correctly written for $196, it would deduct the error of $27 from the balance per books. All errors made by the depositor are reconciling items in determining the adjusted cash balance per books. In contrast, all errors made by the bank are reconciling items in determining the adjusted cash balance per the bank.

**Step 4.** **Bank memoranda.** Trace bank memoranda to the depositor's records. List in the appropriate section of the reconciliation schedule any unrecorded memoranda. For example, the company would deduct from the balance per books a $5 debit memorandum for bank service charges. Similarly, it would add to the balance per books $32 of interest earned.

## BANK RECONCILIATION ILLUSTRATED

The bank statement for Laird Company, in Illustration 8-10, shows a balance per bank of $15,907.45 on April 30, 2014. On this date the balance of cash per books is $11,589.45. Using the four reconciliation steps, Laird determines the following reconciling items.

**Helpful Hint** Note in the bank statement on page 396 that checks no. 459 and 461 have been paid but check no. 460 is not listed. Thus, this check is outstanding. If a complete bank statement were provided, checks no. 453 and 457 would also not be listed. The amounts for these three checks are obtained from the company's cash payments records.

**Step 1.** **Deposits in transit:** April 30 deposit (received by
bank on May 1). $2,201.40

**Step 2.** **Outstanding checks:** No. 453, $3,000.00; no. 457,
$1,401.30; no. 460, $1,502.70. 5,904.00

**Step 3.** **Errors:** Laird wrote check no. 443 for $1,226.00 and the
bank correctly paid that amount. However, Laird recorded
the check as $1,262.00. 36.00

**Step 4.** **Bank memoranda:**
   **a.** Debit—NSF check from J. R. Baron for $425.60. 425.60
   **b.** Debit—Charge for printing company checks $30.00. 30.00
   **c.** Credit—Collection of note receivable for $1,000
      plus interest earned $50, less bank collection fee $15.00. 1,035.00

Illustration 8-12 shows Laird's bank reconciliation.

**Illustration 8-12**
Bank reconciliation

| LAIRD COMPANY<br>Bank Reconciliation<br>April 30, 2014 | | |
|---|---|---|
| Cash balance per bank statement | | $ 15,907.45 |
| Add: Deposits in transit | | 2,201.40 |
| | | 18,108.85 |
| Less: Outstanding checks | | |
|   No. 453 | $3,000.00 | |
|   No. 457 | 1,401.30 | |
|   No. 460 | 1,502.70 | 5,904.00 |
| **Adjusted cash balance per bank** | | **$12,204.85** ← |
| | | |
| Cash balance per books | | $ 11,589.45 |
| Add: Collection of note receivable $1,000, plus | | |
|     interest earned $50, less collection fee $15 | $1,035.00 | |
|     Error in recording check no. 443 | 36.00 | 1,071.00 |
| | | 12,660.45 |
| Less: NSF check | 425.60 | |
|    Bank service charge | 30.00 | 455.60 |
| **Adjusted cash balance per books** | | **$12,204.85** ← |

**Alternative Terminology**
The terms *adjusted cash balance, true cash balance,* and *correct cash balance* are used interchangeably.

## ENTRIES FROM BANK RECONCILIATION

The company records each reconciling item used to determine the **adjusted cash balance per books**. **If the company does not journalize and post these items, the Cash account will not show the correct balance.** Laird Company would make the following entries on April 30.

**COLLECTION OF NOTE RECEIVABLE.** This entry involves four accounts. Assuming that the interest of $50 has not been accrued and the collection fee is charged to Miscellaneous Expense, the entry is:

| | | | |
|---|---|---|---|
| Apr. 30 | Cash | 1,035.00 | |
| | Miscellaneous Expense | 15.00 | |
| |    Notes Receivable | | 1,000.00 |
| |    Interest Revenue | | 50.00 |
| |      (To record collection of note | | |
| |      receivable by bank) | | |

**BOOK ERROR.** The cash disbursements journal shows that check no. 443 was a payment on account to Andrea Company, a supplier. The correcting entry is:

| | | | |
|---|---|---|---|
| Apr. 30 | Cash | 36.00 | |
| |    Accounts Payable—Andrea Company | | 36.00 |
| |      (To correct error in recording check | | |
| |      no. 443) | | |

**NSF CHECK.** As indicated earlier, an NSF check becomes an account receivable to the depositor. The entry is:

| | | | |
|---|---|---|---|
| Apr. 30 | Accounts Receivable—J. R. Baron | 425.60 | |
| |    Cash | | 425.60 |
| |      (To record NSF check) | | |

**BANK SERVICE CHARGES.** Depositors debit check printing charges (DM) and other bank service charges (SC) to Miscellaneous Expense because they are usually nominal in amount. The entry is:

| | | | |
|---|---|---|---|
| Apr. 30 | Miscellaneous Expense | 30.00 | |
| |    Cash | | 30.00 |
| |      (To record charge for printing company | | |
| |      checks) | | |

Instead of making four separate entries, Laird could combine them into one compound entry.

After Laird has posted the entries, the Cash account will show the following.

**Illustration 8-13**
Adjusted balance in Cash account

| Cash | | | | | |
|---|---|---|---|---|---|
| Apr. 30 Bal. | 11,589.45 | Apr. 30 | | | 425.60 |
| 30 | 1,035.00 | 30 | | | 30.00 |
| 30 | 36.00 | | | | |
| Apr. 30 Bal. | **12,204.85** | | | | |

The adjusted cash balance in the ledger should agree with the adjusted cash balance per books in the bank reconciliation in Illustration 8-12 (page 399).

What entries does the bank make? If the company discovers any bank errors in preparing the reconciliation, it should notify the bank. The bank then can make the necessary corrections in its records. The bank does not make any entries for deposits in transit or outstanding checks. Only when these items reach the bank will the bank record these items.

## Electronic Funds Transfer (EFT) System

It is not surprising that companies and banks have developed approaches to transfer funds among parties without the use of paper (deposit tickets, checks, etc.). Such procedures, called **electronic funds transfers (EFT)**, are disbursement systems that use wire, telephone, or computers to transfer cash balances from one location to another. Use of EFT is quite common. For example, many employees receive no formal payroll checks from their employers. Instead, employers send electronic payroll data to the appropriate banks. Also, individuals and companies now frequently make regular payments such as those for house, car, and utilities by EFT.

EFT transactions normally result in better internal control since no cash or checks are handled by company employees. This does not mean that opportunities for fraud are eliminated. In fact, the same basic principles related to internal control apply to EFT transfers. For example, without proper segregation of duties and authorizations, an employee might be able to redirect electronic payments into a personal bank account and conceal the theft with fraudulent accounting entries.

## INVESTOR INSIGHT

### Madoff's Ponzi Scheme

No recent fraud has generated more interest and rage than the one perpetrated by Bernard Madoff. Madoff was an elite New York investment fund manager who was highly regarded by securities regulators. Investors flocked to him because he delivered very steady returns of between 10% and 15%, no matter whether the market was going up or going down. However, for many years, Madoff did not actually invest the cash that people gave to him. Instead, he was running a Ponzi scheme: He paid returns to existing investors using cash received from new investors. As long as the size of his investment fund continued to grow from new investments at a rate that exceeded the amounts that he needed to pay out in returns, Madoff was able to operate his fraud smoothly. To conceal his misdeeds, he fabricated false investment statements that were provided to investors. In addition, Madoff hired an auditor that never verified the accuracy of the investment records but automatically issued unqualified opinions each year. Although a competing fund manager warned the SEC a number of times over a nearly 10-year period that he thought Madoff was engaged in fraud, the SEC never aggressively investigated the allegations. Investors, many of which were charitable organizations, lost more than $18 billion. Madoff was sentenced to a jail term of 150 years.

**?** How was Madoff able to conceal such a giant fraud? (See page 424.)

Mary Altaffer/©AP/Wide World Photos

## > DO IT!

**Bank Reconciliation**

Sally Kist owns Linen Kist Fabrics. Sally asks you to explain how she should treat the following reconciling items when reconciling the company's bank account: (1) a debit memorandum for an NSF check, (2) a credit memorandum for a note collected by the bank, (3) outstanding checks, and (4) a deposit in transit.

**Action Plan**

✔ Understand the purpose of a bank reconciliation.

✔ Identify time lags and explain how they cause reconciling items.

**Solution**

Sally should treat the reconciling items as follows.

**(1)** NSF check: Deduct from balance per books.

**(2)** Collection of note: Add to balance per books.

**(3)** Outstanding checks: Deduct from balance per bank.

**(4)** Deposit in transit: Add to balance per bank.

Related exercise material: **BE8-11, BE8-12, BE8-13, BE8-14, E8-9, E8-10, E8-11, E8-12, E8-13, and** **DO IT!** 8-4.

 ✔  The Navigator

## Reporting Cash

**LEARNING OBJECTIVE** **8**

**Explain the reporting of cash.**

**Cash** consists of coins, currency (paper money), checks, money orders, and money on hand or on deposit in a bank or similar depository. Companies report cash in two different statements: the balance sheet and the statement of cash flows. The balance sheet reports the amount of cash available at a given point in time. The statement of cash flows shows the sources and uses of cash during a period of time. The statement of cash flows was introduced in Chapter 1 and will be discussed in much detail in Chapter 17. In this section, we discuss some important points regarding the presentation of cash in the balance sheet.

When presented in a balance sheet, cash on hand, cash in banks, and petty cash are often combined and reported simply as **Cash**. Because it is the most liquid asset owned by the company, cash is listed first in the current assets section of the balance sheet.

### Cash Equivalents

Many companies use the designation "Cash and cash equivalents" in reporting cash. (See Illustration 8-14 for an example.) **Cash equivalents** are short-term, highly liquid investments that are both:

**1.** Readily convertible to known amounts of cash, and

**2.** So near their maturity that their market value is relatively insensitive to changes in interest rates.

**Illustration 8-14**
Balance sheet presentation of cash

| Real World | **DELTA AIR LINES, INC.** Balance Sheet (partial) December 31, 2011 (in millions) | |
|---|---|---|
| | **Assets** | |
| | Current assets | |
| | **Cash and cash equivalents** | **$2,657** |
| | Short-term investments | 958 |
| | **Restricted cash** | **305** |
| | Accounts receivable and other net | 1,563 |
| | Parts inventories | 367 |
| | Prepaid expenses and other | 1,879 |
| | Total current assets | $ 7,729 |

Examples of cash equivalents are Treasury bills, commercial paper (short-term corporate notes), and money market funds. All typically are purchased with cash that is in excess of immediate needs.

Occasionally, a company will have a net negative balance in its bank account. In this case, the company should report the negative balance among current liabilities. For example, farm equipment manufacturer Ag-Chem recently reported "Checks outstanding in excess of cash balances" of $2,145,000 among its current liabilities.

**Ethics Note**

Recently, some companies were forced to restate their financial statements because they had too broadly interpreted which types of investments could be treated as cash equivalents. By reporting these items as cash equivalents, the companies made themselves look more liquid.

## Restricted Cash

A company may have **restricted cash**, cash that is not available for general use but rather is restricted for a special purpose. For example, landfill companies are often required to maintain a fund of restricted cash to ensure they will have adequate resources to cover closing and clean-up costs at the end of a landfill site's useful life. McKesson Corp. recently reported restricted cash of $962 million to be paid out as the result of investor lawsuits.

Cash restricted in use should be reported separately on the balance sheet as restricted cash. If the company expects to use the restricted cash within the next year, it reports the amount as a current asset. When this is not the case, it reports the restricted funds as a noncurrent asset.

Illustration 8-14 shows restricted cash reported in the financial statements of Delta Air Lines. The company is required to maintain restricted cash as collateral to support insurance obligations related to workers' compensation claims. Delta does not have access to these funds for general use, and so it must report them separately, rather than as part of cash and cash equivalents.

---

### > Comprehensive DO IT!

Poorten Company's bank statement for May 2014 shows the following data.

| Balance 5/1 | $12,650 | Balance 5/31 | $14,280 |
|---|---|---|---|
| Debit memorandum: | | Credit memorandum: | |
| NSF check | $175 | Collection of note receivable | $505 |

The cash balance per books at May 31 is $13,319. Your review of the data reveals the following.

1. The NSF check was from Copple Co., a customer.

2. The note collected by the bank was a $500, 3-month, 12% note. The bank charged a $10 collection fee. No interest has been accrued.

3. Outstanding checks at May 31 total $2,410.

4. Deposits in transit at May 31 total $1,752.

5. A Poorten Company check for $352, dated May 10, cleared the bank on May 25. The company recorded this check, which was a payment on account, for $325.

**Instructions**
(a) Prepare a bank reconciliation at May 31.
(b) Journalize the entries required by the reconciliation.

## Solution to Comprehensive DO IT!

**Action Plan**

✔ Follow the four steps in the reconciliation procedure (pp. 398–399).

✔ Work carefully to minimize mathematical errors in the reconciliation.

✔ Prepare entries from reconciling items per books.

✔ Make sure the cash ledger balance after posting the reconciling entries agrees with the adjusted cash balance per books.

**(a)**

### POORTEN COMPANY
### Bank Reconciliation
### May 31, 2014

| | | |
|---|---:|---:|
| Cash balance per bank statement | | $14,280 |
| Add: Deposits in transit | | 1,752 |
| | | 16,032 |
| Less: Outstanding checks | | 2,410 |
| Adjusted cash balance per bank | | $13,622 |
| | | |
| Cash balance per books | | $13,319 |
| Add: Collection of note receivable $500, plus $15 | | |
| interest, less collection fee $10 | | 505 |
| | | 13,824 |
| | | |
| Less: NSF check | $175 | |
| Error in recording check | 27 | 202 |
| Adjusted cash balance per books | | $13,622 |

**(b)**

| Date | Account | Debit | Credit |
|---|---|---:|---:|
| May 31 | Cash | 505 | |
| | Miscellaneous Expense | 10 | |
| |    Notes Receivable | | 500 |
| |    Interest Revenue | | 15 |
| |      (To record collection of note by bank) | | |
| 31 | Accounts Receivable—Copple Co. | 175 | |
| |    Cash | | 175 |
| |      (To record NSF check from Copple Co.) | | |
| 31 | Accounts Payable | 27 | |
| |    Cash | | 27 |
| |      (To correct error in recording check) | | |

✔ The Navigator

---

## SUMMARY OF LEARNING OBJECTIVES

✔ The Navigator

**1  Define fraud and internal control.** A fraud is a dishonest act by an employee that results in personal benefit to the employee at a cost to the employer. The fraud triangle refers to the three factors that contribute to fraudulent activity by employees: opportunity, financial pressure, and rationalization. Internal control consists of all the related methods and measures adopted within an organization to safeguard its assets, enhance the reliability of its accounting records, increase efficiency of operations, and ensure compliance with laws and regulations.

**2  Identify the principles of internal control activities.** The principles of internal control are establishment of responsibility; segregation of duties; documentation procedures; physical controls; independent internal verification; and human resource controls such as bonding and requiring employees to take vacations.

**3  Explain the applications of internal control principles to cash receipts.** Internal controls over cash receipts include (a) designating specific personnel to handle cash; (b) assigning different individuals to receive cash, record cash, and maintain custody of cash; (c) using remittance advices for mail receipts, cash register tapes for over-the-counter receipts, and deposit slips for bank deposits; (d) using company safes and bank vaults to store cash with access limited to authorized personnel, and using cash registers in executing over-the-counter receipts; (e) making independent daily counts of register receipts and daily comparison of total receipts with total deposits; and (f) bonding personnel that handle cash and requiring them to take vacations.

**4  Explain the applications of internal control principles to cash disbursements.** Internal controls over cash disbursements include (a) having specific individuals such as the treasurer authorized to sign checks and approve invoices; (b) assigning different individuals to approve items for payment, pay the items, and record the payment; (c) using prenumbered checks and accounting for all checks, with each check supported by an approved invoice; (d) storing blank checks in a safe or vault with access restricted to authorized personnel, and using a check-writing machine to imprint amounts on checks; (e) comparing each check with the approved invoice before issuing the check, and making monthly reconciliations of bank and book balances; and (f) bonding personnel who handle cash, requiring employees to take vacations, and conducting background checks.

5  **Describe the operation of a petty cash fund.** Companies operate a petty cash fund to pay relatively small amounts of cash. They must establish the fund, make payments from the fund, and replenish the fund when the cash in the fund reaches a minimum level.

6  **Indicate the control features of a bank account.** A bank account contributes to good internal control by providing physical controls for the storage of cash. It minimizes the amount of currency that a company must keep on hand, and it creates a double record of a depositor's bank transactions.

7  **Prepare a bank reconciliation.** It is customary to reconcile the balance per books and balance per bank to their adjusted balances. The steps in the reconciling process are to determine deposits in transit, outstanding checks, errors by the depositor or the bank, and unrecorded bank memoranda.

8  **Explain the reporting of cash.** Companies list cash first in the current assets section of the balance sheet. In some cases, they report cash together with cash equivalents. Cash restricted for a special purpose is reported separately as a current asset or as a noncurrent asset, depending on when the cash is expected to be used.

## GLOSSARY

**Bank reconciliation** The process of comparing the bank's balance of an account with the company's balance and explaining any differences to make them agree. (p. 394).

**Bank service charge** A fee charged by a bank for the use of its services. (p. 396).

**Bank statement** A monthly statement from the bank that shows the depositor's bank transactions and balances. (p. 395).

**Bonding** Obtaining insurance protection against misappropriation of assets by employees. (p. 383).

**Cash** Resources that consist of coins, currency, checks, money orders, and money on hand or on deposit in a bank or similar depository. (p. 402).

**Cash equivalents** Short-term, highly liquid investments that can be converted to a specific amount of cash. (p. 402).

**Check** A written order signed by a bank depositor, directing the bank to pay a specified sum of money to a designated recipient. (p. 394).

**Deposits in transit** Deposits recorded by the depositor but not yet recorded by the bank. (p. 398).

**Electronic funds transfer (EFT)** A disbursement system that uses wire, telephone, or computers to transfer funds from one location to another. (p. 401).

**Fraud** A dishonest act by an employee that results in personal benefit to the employee at a cost to the employer. (p. 376).

**Fraud triangle** The three factors that contribute to fraudulent activity by employees: opportunity, financial pressure, and rationalization. (p. 376).

**Internal auditors** Company employees who continuously evaluate the effectiveness of the company's internal control system. (p. 383).

**Internal control** All of the related methods and activities adopted within an organization to safeguard assets and enhance the accuracy and reliability of accounting records. (p. 377).

**NSF check** A check that is not paid by a bank because of insufficient funds in a customer's bank account. (p. 397).

**Outstanding checks** Checks issued and recorded by a company but not yet paid by the bank. (p. 398).

**Petty cash fund** A cash fund used to pay relatively small amounts. (p. 390).

**Restricted cash** Cash that must be used for a special purpose. (p. 403).

**Sarbanes-Oxley Act (SOX)** Regulations passed by Congress to try to reduce unethical corporate behavior. (p. 376).

**Voucher** An authorization form prepared for each payment in a voucher system. (p. 389).

**Voucher system** A network of approvals by authorized individuals acting independently to ensure that all disbursements by check are proper. (p. 389).

 **Self-Test, Brief Exercises, Exercises, Problem Set A, and many more components are available for practice in *WileyPLUS*.**

## SELF-TEST QUESTIONS

*Answers are on page 425.*

(LO 1)  **1.** Which of the following is **not** an element of the fraud triangle?

   **(a)** Rationalization.   **(c)** Segregation of duties.

   **(b)** Financial pressure.   **(d)** Opportunity.

**2.** An organization uses internal control to enhance (LO 1) the accuracy and reliability of accounting records and to:

   **(a)** safeguard assets.

   **(b)** eliminate fraud.

(c) produce correct financial statements.
(d) deter employee dishonesty.

(LO 1)    3. Which of the following was **not** a result of the Sarbanes-Oxley Act?
   (a) Companies must file financial statements with the Internal Revenue Service.
   (b) All publicly traded companies must maintain adequate internal controls.
   (c) The Public Company Accounting Oversight Board was created to establish auditing standards and regulate auditor activity.
   (d) Corporate executives and board of directors must ensure that controls are reliable and effective, and they can be fined or imprisoned for failure to do so.

(LO 2)    4. The principles of internal control do **not** include:
   (a) establishment of responsibility.
   (b) documentation procedures.
   (c) management responsibility.
   (d) independent internal verification.

(LO 2)    5. Physical controls do **not** include:
   (a) safes and vaults to store cash.
   (b) independent bank reconciliations.
   (c) locked warehouses for inventories.
   (d) bank safety deposit boxes for important papers.

(LO 2)    6. Which of the following control activities is **not** relevant when a company uses a computerized (rather than manual) accounting system?
   (a) Establishment of responsibility.
   (b) Segregation of duties.
   (c) Independent internal verification.
   (d) All of these control activities are relevant to a computerized system.

(LO 3)    7. Permitting only designated personnel to handle cash receipts is an application of the principle of:
   (a) segregation of duties.
   (b) establishment of responsibility.
   (c) independent internal verification.
   (d) human resource controls.

(LO 4)    8. The use of prenumbered checks in disbursing cash is an application of the principle of:
   (a) establishment of responsibility.
   (b) segregation of duties.

(c) physical controls.
(d) documentation procedures.

9. A company writes a check to replenish a $100 petty   (LO 5)
cash fund when the fund contains receipts of $94 and $4 in cash. In recording the check, the company should:
   (a) debit Cash Over and Short for $2.
   (b) debit Petty Cash for $94.
   (c) credit Cash for $94.
   (d) credit Petty Cash for $2.

10. The control features of a bank account do **not** include:   (LO 6)
   (a) having bank auditors verify the correctness of the bank balance per books.
   (b) minimizing the amount of cash that must be kept on hand.
   (c) providing a double record of all bank transactions.
   (d) safeguarding cash by using a bank as a depository.

11. In a bank reconciliation, deposits in transit are:   (LO 7)
   (a) deducted from the book balance.
   (b) added to the book balance.
   (c) added to the bank balance.
   (d) deducted from the bank balance.

12. The reconciling item in a bank reconciliation that will   (LO 7)
result in an adjusting entry by the depositor is:
   (a) outstanding checks.    (c) a bank error.
   (b) deposit in transit.    (d) bank service charges.

13. Which of the following items in a cash drawer at   (LO 8)
November 30 is **not** cash?
   (a) Money orders.
   (b) Coins and currency.
   (c) An NSF check.
   (d) A customer check dated November 28.

14. Which of the following statements correctly describes   (LO 8)
the reporting of cash?
   (a) Cash cannot be combined with cash equivalents.
   (b) Restricted cash funds may be combined with cash.
   (c) Cash is listed first in the current assets section.
   (d) Restricted cash funds cannot be reported as a current asset.

**Go to the book's companion website, www.wiley.com/college/weygandt, for additional Self-Test Questions.**

 ✔ **The Navigator**

## QUESTIONS

1. A local bank reported that it lost $150,000 as the result of an employee fraud. Edward Jasso is not clear on what is meant by an "employee fraud." Explain the meaning of fraud to Edward and give an example of frauds that might occur at a bank.

2. Fraud experts often say that there are three primary factors that contribute to employee fraud. Identify the three factors and explain what is meant by each.

3. Identify and describe the five components of a good internal control system.

4. "Internal control is concerned only with enhancing the accuracy of the accounting records." Do you agree? Explain.

5. What principles of internal control apply to most organizations?

6. At the corner grocery store, all sales clerks make change out of one cash register drawer. Is this a violation of internal control? Why?

7. Liz Kelso is reviewing the principle of segregation of duties. What are the two common applications of this principle?

8. How do documentation procedures contribute to good internal control?

9. What internal control objectives are met by physical controls?

10. (a) Explain the control principle of independent internal verification. (b) What practices are important in applying this principle?

11. The management of Nickle Company asks you, as the company accountant, to explain (a) the concept of reasonable assurance in internal control and (b) the importance of the human factor in internal control.

12. Riverside Fertilizer Co. owns the following assets at the balance sheet date.

| | |
|---|---|
| Cash in bank savings account | $ 8,000 |
| Cash on hand | 850 |
| Cash refund due from the IRS | 1,000 |
| Checking account balance | 14,000 |
| Postdated checks | 500 |

What amount should Riverside report as cash in the balance sheet?

13. What principle(s) of internal control is (are) involved in making daily cash counts of over-the-counter receipts?

14. Seaton Department Stores has just installed new electronic cash registers in its stores. How do cash registers improve internal control over cash receipts?

15. At Kellum Wholesale Company, two mail clerks open all mail receipts. How does this strengthen internal control?

16. "To have maximum effective internal control over cash disbursements, all payments should be made by check." Is this true? Explain.

17. Ken Deangelo Company's internal controls over cash disbursements provide for the treasurer to sign checks imprinted by a check-writing machine in indelible ink after comparing the check with the approved invoice. Identify the internal control principles that are present in these controls.

18. How do the principles of (a) physical controls and (b) documentation controls apply to cash disbursements?

19. (a) What is a voucher system? (b) What principles of internal control apply to a voucher system?

20. What is the essential feature of an electronic funds transfer (EFT) procedure?

21. (a) Identify the three activities that pertain to a petty cash fund, and indicate an internal control principle that is applicable to each activity. (b) When are journal entries required in the operation of a petty cash fund?

22. "The use of a bank contributes significantly to good internal control over cash." Is this true? Why or why not?

23. Anna Korte is confused about the lack of agreement between the cash balance per books and the balance per bank. Explain the causes for the lack of agreement to Anna, and give an example of each cause.

24. What are the four steps involved in finding differences between the balance per books and balance per bank?

25. Heather Kemp asks your help concerning an NSF check. Explain to Heather (a) what an NSF check is, (b) how it is treated in a bank reconciliation, and (c) whether it will require an adjusting entry.

26. (a) "Cash equivalents are the same as cash." Do you agree? Explain. (b) How should restricted cash funds be reported on the balance sheet?

27. At what amount does Apple report cash and cash equivalents in its 2011 consolidated balance sheet?

## BRIEF EXERCISES

**BE8-1** Match each situation with the fraud triangle factor—opportunity, financial pressure, or rationalization—that best describes it.

1. An employee's monthly credit card payments are nearly 75% of his or her monthly earnings.
2. An employee earns minimum wage at a firm that has reported record earnings for each of the last five years.
3. An employee has an expensive gambling habit.
4. An employee has check-writing and -signing responsibilities for a small company, as well as reconciling the bank account.

*Identify fraud triangle concepts.*

*(LO 1)*

**BE8-2** Shelly Eckert has prepared the following list of statements about internal control.

1. One of the objectives of internal control is to safeguard assets from employee theft, robbery, and unauthorized use.
2. One of the objectives of internal control is to enhance the accuracy and reliability of the accounting records.
3. No laws require U.S. corporations to maintain an adequate system of internal control.

Identify each statement as true or false. If false, indicate how to correct the statement.

*Indicate internal control concepts.*

*(LO 1)*

**BE8-3** Jessica Mahan is the new owner of Penny Parking. She has heard about internal control but is not clear about its importance for her business. Explain to Jessica the four purposes of internal control and give her one application of each purpose for Penny Parking.

*Explain the importance of internal control.*

*(LO 1)*

*Identify internal control principles.*

*(LO 2)*

**BE8-4** The internal control procedures in Valentine Company provide that:

1. Employees who have physical custody of assets do not have access to the accounting records.
2. Each month, the assets on hand are compared to the accounting records by an internal auditor.
3. A prenumbered shipping document is prepared for each shipment of goods to customers.

Identify the principles of internal control that are being followed.

*Identify the internal control principles applicable to cash receipts.*

*(LO 3)*

**BE8-5** Rosenquist Company has the following internal control procedures over cash receipts. Identify the internal control principle that is applicable to each procedure.

1. All over-the-counter receipts are entered in cash registers.
2. All cashiers are bonded.
3. Daily cash counts are made by cashier department supervisors.
4. The duties of receiving cash, recording cash, and custody of cash are assigned to different individuals.
5. Only cashiers may operate cash registers.

*Make journal entries for cash overage and shortfall.*

*(LO 3)*

**BE8-6** The cash register tape for Bluestem Industries reported sales of $6,871.50. Record the journal entry that would be necessary for each of the following situations. (a) Cash to be accounted for exceeds cash on hand by $50.75. (b) Cash on hand exceeds cash to be accounted for by $28.32.

*Make journal entry using cash count sheet.*

*(LO 3)*

**BE8-7** While examining cash receipts information, the accounting department determined the following information: opening cash balance $160, cash on hand $1,125.74, and cash sales per register tape $980.83. Prepare the required journal entry based upon the cash count sheet.

*Identify the internal control principles applicable to cash disbursements.*

*(LO 4)*

**BE8-8** Pennington Company has the following internal control procedures over cash disbursements. Identify the internal control principle that is applicable to each procedure.

1. Company checks are prenumbered.
2. The bank statement is reconciled monthly by an internal auditor.
3. Blank checks are stored in a safe in the treasurer's office.
4. Only the treasurer or assistant treasurer may sign checks.
5. Check-signers are not allowed to record cash disbursement transactions.

*Prepare entry to replenish a petty cash fund.*

*(LO 5)*

**BE8-9** On March 20, Dody's petty cash fund of $100 is replenished when the fund contains $9 in cash and receipts for postage $52, freight-out $26, and travel expense $10. Prepare the journal entry to record the replenishment of the petty cash fund.

*Identify the control features of a bank account.*

*(LO 6)*

**BE8-10** Lance Bachman is uncertain about the control features of a bank account. Explain the control benefits of (a) a check and (b) a bank statement.

*Indicate location of reconciling items in a bank reconciliation.*

*(LO 7)*

**BE8-11** The following reconciling items are applicable to the bank reconciliation for Ellington Company: (1) outstanding checks, (2) bank debit memorandum for service charge, (3) bank credit memorandum for collecting a note for the depositor, and (4) deposits in transit. Indicate how each item should be shown on a bank reconciliation.

*Identify reconciling items that require adjusting entries.*

*(LO 7)*

**BE8-12** Using the data in BE8-11, indicate (a) the items that will result in an adjustment to the depositor's records and (b) why the other items do not require adjustment.

*Prepare partial bank reconciliation.*

*(LO 7)*

**BE8-13** At July 31, Ramirez Company has the following bank information: cash balance per bank $7,420, outstanding checks $762, deposits in transit $1,620, and a bank service charge $20. Determine the adjusted cash balance per bank at July 31.

*Prepare partial bank reconciliation.*

*(LO 7)*

**BE8-14** At August 31, Pratt Company has a cash balance per books of $9,500 and the following additional data from the bank statement: charge for printing Pratt Company checks $35, interest earned on checking account balance $40, and outstanding checks $800. Determine the adjusted cash balance per books at August 31.

*Explain the statement presentation of cash balances.*

*(LO 8)*

**BE8-15** Zhang Company has the following cash balances: Cash in Bank $15,742, Payroll Bank Account $6,000, and Plant Expansion Fund Cash $25,000 to be used two years from now. Explain how each balance should be reported on the balance sheet.

> **DO IT! Review**

**DO IT! 8-1** Identify which control activity is violated in each of the following situations, and explain how the situation creates an opportunity for fraud or inappropriate accounting practices.

1. Once a month, the sales department sends sales invoices to the accounting department to be recorded.

2. Leah Hutcherson orders merchandise for Rice Lake Company; he also receives merchandise and authorizes payment for merchandise.

3. Several clerks at Great Foods use the same cash register drawer.

*Identify violations of control activities.*
*(LO 2)*

**DO IT! 8-2** Gary Stanten is concerned with control over mail receipts at Gary's Sporting Goods. All mail receipts are opened by Al Krane. Al sends the checks to the accounting department, where they are stamped "For Deposit Only." The accounting department records and deposits the mail receipts weekly. Gary asks for your help in installing a good system of internal control over mail receipts.

*Design system of internal control over cash receipts.*
*(LO 3)*

**DO IT! 8-3** Wilkinson Company established a $100 petty cash fund on August 1. On August 31, the fund had $7 cash remaining and petty cash receipts for postage $31, office supplies $42, and miscellaneous expense $16. Prepare journal entries to establish the fund on August 1 and replenish the fund on August 31.

*Make journal entries for petty cash fund.*
*(LO 5)*

**DO IT! 8-4** Roger Richman owns Richman Blankets. Richman asks you to explain how he should treat the following reconciling items when reconciling the company's bank account.

1. Outstanding checks.

2. A deposit in transit.

3. The bank charged to our account a check written by another company.

4. A debit memorandum for a bank service charge.

*Explain treatment of items in bank reconciliation.*
*(LO 7)*

## EXERCISES

**E8-1** Eve Herschel is the owner of Herschel's Pizza. Herschel's is operated strictly on a carryout basis. Customers pick up their orders at a counter where a clerk exchanges the pizza for cash. While at the counter, the customer can see other employees making the pizzas and the large ovens in which the pizzas are baked.

*Identify the principles of internal control.*
*(LO 2)*

**Instructions**
Identify the six principles of internal control and give an example of each principle that you might observe when picking up your pizza. (*Note:* It may not be possible to observe all the principles.)

**E8-2** The following control procedures are used at Torres Company for over-the-counter cash receipts.

1. To minimize the risk of robbery, cash in excess of $100 is stored in an unlocked attaché case in the stock room until it is deposited in the bank.

2. All over-the-counter receipts are registered by three clerks who use a cash register with a single cash drawer.

3. The company accountant makes the bank deposit and then records the day's receipts.

4. At the end of each day, the total receipts are counted by the cashier on duty and reconciled to the cash register total.

5. Cashiers are experienced; they are not bonded.

*Identify internal control weaknesses over cash receipts and suggest improvements.*
*(LO 2, 3)*

**Instructions**
(a) For each procedure, explain the weakness in internal control, and identify the control principle that is violated.
(b) For each weakness, suggest a change in procedure that will result in good internal control.

*Identify internal control weaknesses over cash disbursements and suggest improvements.*

(LO 2, 4)

**E8-3** The following control procedures are used in Mendy Lang's Boutique Shoppe for cash disbursements.

1. The company accountant prepares the bank reconciliation and reports any discrepancies to the owner.
2. The store manager personally approves all payments before signing and issuing checks.
3. Each week, 100 company checks are left in an unmarked envelope on a shelf behind the cash register.
4. After payment, bills are filed in a paid invoice folder.
5. The company checks are unnumbered.

**Instructions**

(a) For each procedure, explain the weakness in internal control, and identify the internal control principle that is violated.

(b) For each weakness, suggest a change in the procedure that will result in good internal control.

*Identify internal control weaknesses for cash disbursements and suggest improvements.*

(LO 4)

**E8-4** At Danner Company, checks are not prenumbered because both the purchasing agent and the treasurer are authorized to issue checks. Each signer has access to unissued checks kept in an unlocked file cabinet. The purchasing agent pays all bills pertaining to goods purchased for resale. Prior to payment, the purchasing agent determines that the goods have been received and verifies the mathematical accuracy of the vendor's invoice. After payment, the invoice is filed by the vendor name, and the purchasing agent records the payment in the cash disbursements journal. The treasurer pays all other bills following approval by authorized employees. After payment, the treasurer stamps all bills PAID, files them by payment date, and records the checks in the cash disbursements journal. Danner Company maintains one checking account that is reconciled by the treasurer.

**Instructions**

(a) List the weaknesses in internal control over cash disbursements.

(b) ◄━━━━ Write a memo to the company treasurer indicating your recommendations for improvement.

*Indicate whether procedure is good or weak internal control.*

(LO 2, 3, 4)

**E8-5** Listed below are five procedures followed by Eikenberry Company.

1. Several individuals operate the cash register using the same register drawer.
2. A monthly bank reconciliation is prepared by someone who has no other cash responsibilities.
3. Joe Cockrell writes checks and also records cash payment journal entries.
4. One individual orders inventory, while a different individual authorizes payments.
5. Unnumbered sales invoices from credit sales are forwarded to the accounting department every four weeks for recording.

**Instructions**

Indicate whether each procedure is an example of good internal control or of weak internal control. If it is an example of good internal control, indicate which internal control principle is being followed. If it is an example of weak internal control, indicate which internal control principle is violated. Use the table below.

| Procedure | IC Good or Weak? | Related Internal Control Principle |
|:---:|:---:|:---:|
| 1. | | |
| 2. | | |
| 3. | | |
| 4. | | |
| 5. | | |

*Indicate whether procedure is good or weak internal control.*

(LO 2, 3, 4)

**E8-6** Listed below are five procedures followed by Gilmore Company.

1. Employees are required to take vacations.
2. Any member of the sales department can approve credit sales.
3. Paul Jaggard ships goods to customers, bills customers, and receives payment from customers.
4. Total cash receipts are compared to bank deposits daily by someone who has no other cash responsibilities.
5. Time clocks are used for recording time worked by employees.

## Instructions

Indicate whether each procedure is an example of good internal control or of weak internal control. If it is an example of good internal control, indicate which internal control principle is being followed. If it is an example of weak internal control, indicate which internal control principle is violated. Use the table below.

| Procedure | IC Good or Weak? | Related Internal Control Principle |
|---|---|---|
| 1. | | |
| 2. | | |
| 3. | | |
| 4. | | |
| 5. | | |

**E8-7** Setterstrom Company established a petty cash fund on May 1, cashing a check for $100. The company reimbursed the fund on June 1 and July 1 with the following results.

*Prepare journal entries for a petty cash fund.*

*(LO 5)*

June 1: Cash in fund $1.75. Receipts: delivery expense $31.25; postage expense $39.00; and miscellaneous expense $25.00.

July 1: Cash in fund $3.25. Receipts: delivery expense $21.00; entertainment expense $51.00; and miscellaneous expense $24.75.

On July 10, Setterstrom increased the fund from $100 to $130.

## Instructions

Prepare journal entries for Setterstrom Company for May 1, June 1, July 1, and July 10.

**E8-8** Horvath Company uses an imprest petty cash system. The fund was established on March 1 with a balance of $100. During March, the following petty cash receipts were found in the petty cash box.

*Prepare journal entries for a petty cash fund.*

*(LO 5)*

| Date | Receipt No. | For | Amount |
|---|---|---|---|
| 3/5 | 1 | Stamp Inventory | $39 |
| 7 | 2 | Freight-Out | 21 |
| 9 | 3 | Miscellaneous Expense | 6 |
| 11 | 4 | Travel Expense | 24 |
| 14 | 5 | Miscellaneous Expense | 5 |

The fund was replenished on March 15 when the fund contained $2 in cash. On March 20, the amount in the fund was increased to $175.

## Instructions

Journalize the entries in March that pertain to the operation of the petty cash fund.

**E8-9** Don Wyatt is unable to reconcile the bank balance at January 31. Don's reconciliation is as follows.

*Prepare bank reconciliation and adjusting entries.*

*(LO 7)*

| | |
|---|---|
| Cash balance per bank | $3,560.20 |
| Add: NSF check | 490.00 |
| Less: Bank service charge | 25.00 |
| Adjusted balance per bank | $4,025.20 |
| | |
| Cash balance per books | $3,875.20 |
| Less: Deposits in transit | 530.00 |
| Add: Outstanding checks | 730.00 |
| Adjusted balance per books | $4,075.20 |

## Instructions

**(a)** Prepare a correct bank reconciliation.
**(b)** Journalize the entries required by the reconciliation.

**E8-10** On April 30, the bank reconciliation of Westbrook Company shows three outstanding checks: no. 254, $650; no. 255, $620; and no. 257, $410. The May bank statement and the May cash payments journal show the following.

*Determine outstanding checks.*

*(LO 7)*

| Bank Statement | | | Cash Payments Journal | | |
|---|---|---|---|---|---|
| Checks Paid | | | Checks Issued | | |
| Date | Check No. | Amount | Date | Check No. | Amount |
| 5/4 | 254 | $650 | 5/2 | 258 | $159 |
| 5/2 | 257 | 410 | 5/5 | 259 | 275 |
| 5/17 | 258 | 159 | 5/10 | 260 | 890 |
| 5/12 | 259 | 275 | 5/15 | 261 | 500 |
| 5/20 | 261 | 500 | 5/22 | 262 | 750 |
| 5/29 | 263 | 480 | 5/24 | 263 | 480 |
| 5/30 | 262 | 750 | 5/29 | 264 | 560 |

*Instructions*

Using Step 2 in the reconciliation procedure, list the outstanding checks at May 31.

*Prepare bank reconciliation and adjusting entries.*

*(LO 7)*

**E8-11** The following information pertains to Crane Video Company.

1. Cash balance per bank, July 31, $7,263.
2. July bank service charge not recorded by the depositor $28.
3. Cash balance per books, July 31, $7,284.
4. Deposits in transit, July 31, $1,300.
5. Bank collected $700 note for Crane in July, plus interest $36, less fee $20. The collection has not been recorded by Crane, and no interest has been accrued.
6. Outstanding checks, July 31, $591.

*Instructions*

**(a)** Prepare a bank reconciliation at July 31.
**(b)** Journalize the adjusting entries at July 31 on the books of Crane Video Company.

*Prepare bank reconciliation and adjusting entries.*

*(LO 7)*

**E8-12** The information below relates to the Cash account in the ledger of Minton Company.

Balance September 1—$17,150; Cash deposited—$64,000.
Balance September 30—$17,404; Checks written—$63,746.

The September bank statement shows a balance of $16,422 on September 30 and the following memoranda.

| Credits | | Debits | |
|---|---|---|---|
| Collection of $2,500 note plus interest $30 | $2,530 | NSF check: Richard Nance | $425 |
| Interest earned on checking account | $45 | Safety deposit box rent | $65 |

At September 30, deposits in transit were $5,450, and outstanding checks totaled $2,383.

*Instructions*

**(a)** Prepare the bank reconciliation at September 30.
**(b)** Prepare the adjusting entries at September 30, assuming (1) the NSF check was from a customer on account, and (2) no interest had been accrued on the note.

*Compute deposits in transit and outstanding checks for two bank reconciliations.*

*(LO 7)*

**E8-13** The cash records of Dawes Company show the following four situations.

1. The June 30 bank reconciliation indicated that deposits in transit total $920. During July, the general ledger account Cash shows deposits of $15,750, but the bank statement indicates that only $15,600 in deposits were received during the month.
2. The June 30 bank reconciliation also reported outstanding checks of $680. During the month of July, Dawes Company's books show that $17,200 of checks were issued. The bank statement showed that $16,400 of checks cleared the bank in July.
3. In September, deposits per the bank statement totaled $26,700, deposits per books were $26,400, and deposits in transit at September 30 were $2,100.
4. In September, cash disbursements per books were $23,700, checks clearing the bank were $25,000, and outstanding checks at September 30 were $2,100.

There were no bank debit or credit memoranda. No errors were made by either the bank or Dawes Company.

*Instructions*

Answer the following questions.

**(a)** In situation (1), what were the deposits in transit at July 31?
**(b)** In situation (2), what were the outstanding checks at July 31?

**(c)** In situation (3), what were the deposits in transit at August 31?

**(d)** In situation (4), what were the outstanding checks at August 31?

**E8-14** Wynn Company has recorded the following items in its financial records.

*Show presentation of cash in financial statements.*

*(LO 8)*

| | |
|---|---|
| Cash in bank | $ 42,000 |
| Cash in plant expansion fund | 100,000 |
| Cash on hand | 12,000 |
| Highly liquid investments | 34,000 |
| Petty cash | 500 |
| Receivables from customers | 89,000 |
| Stock investments | 61,000 |

The highly liquid investments had maturities of 3 months or less when they were purchased. The stock investments will be sold in the next 6 to 12 months. The plant expansion project will begin in 3 years.

*Instructions*

**(a)** What amount should Wynn report as "Cash and cash equivalents" on its balance sheet?

**(b)** Where should the items not included in part (a) be reported on the balance sheet?

**(c)** What disclosures should Wynn make in its financial statements concerning "cash and cash equivalents"?

# EXERCISES: SET B AND CHALLENGE EXERCISES

Visit the book's companion website, at **www.wiley.com/college/weygandt**, and choose the Student Companion site to access Exercise Set B and Challenge Exercises.

# PROBLEMS: SET A

**P8-1A** Bolz Office Supply Company recently changed its system of internal control over cash disbursements. The system includes the following features.

*Identify internal control principles over cash disbursements.*

*(LO 2, 4)*

Instead of being unnumbered and manually prepared, all checks must now be pre-numbered and written by using the new check-writing machine purchased by the company. Before a check can be issued, each invoice must have the approval of Kathy Moon, the purchasing agent, and Robin Self, the receiving department supervisor. Checks must be signed by either Jennifer Edwards, the treasurer, or Rich Woodruff, the assistant treasurer. Before signing a check, the signer is expected to compare the amount of the check with the amount on the invoice.

After signing a check, the signer stamps the invoice PAID and inserts within the stamp, the date, check number, and amount of the check. The "paid" invoice is then sent to the accounting department for recording.

Blank checks are stored in a safe in the treasurer's office. The combination to the safe is known only by the treasurer and assistant treasurer. Each month, the bank statement is reconciled with the bank balance per books by the assistant chief accountant. All employees who handle or account for cash are bonded.

*Instructions*

Identify the internal control principles and their application to cash disbursements of Bolz Office Supply Company.

**P8-2A** Forney Company maintains a petty cash fund for small expenditures. The following transactions occurred over a 2-month period.

*Journalize and post petty cash fund transactions.*

*(LO 5)*

July  1    Established petty cash fund by writing a check on Scranton Bank for $200.

   15    Replenished the petty cash fund by writing a check for $196.00. On this date the fund consisted of $4.00 in cash and the following petty cash receipts: freight-out $92.00, postage expense $42.40, entertainment expense $46.60, and miscellaneous expense $11.20.

31 Replenished the petty cash fund by writing a check for $192.00. At this date, the fund consisted of $8.00 in cash and the following petty cash receipts: freight-out $82.10, charitable contributions expense $45.00, postage expense $25.50, and miscellaneous expense $39.40.

Aug. 15 Replenished the petty cash fund by writing a check for $187.00. On this date, the fund consisted of $13.00 in cash and the following petty cash receipts: freight-out $77.60, entertainment expense $43.00, postage expense $33.00, and miscellaneous expense $37.00.

16 Increased the amount of the petty cash fund to $300 by writing a check for $100.

31 Replenished the petty cash fund by writing a check for $284.00. On this date, the fund consisted of $16 in cash and the following petty cash receipts: postage expense $140.00, travel expense $95.60, and freight-out $47.10.

*Instructions*

(a) July 15, Cash short $3.80

(b) Aug. 31 balance $300

(a) Journalize the petty cash transactions.

(b) Post to the Petty Cash account.

(c) What internal control features exist in a petty cash fund?

*Prepare a bank reconciliation and adjusting entries.*

(LO 7)

**P8-3A** On May 31, 2014, Reber Company had a cash balance per books of $6,781.50. The bank statement from New York State Bank on that date showed a balance of $6,404.60. A comparison of the statement with the Cash account revealed the following facts.

1. The statement included a debit memo of $40 for the printing of additional company checks.

2. Cash sales of $836.15 on May 12 were deposited in the bank. The cash receipts journal entry and the deposit slip were incorrectly made for $886.15. The bank credited Reber Company for the correct amount.

3. Outstanding checks at May 31 totaled $576.25. Deposits in transit were $2,416.15.

4. On May 18, the company issued check No. 1181 for $685 to Lynda Carsen on account. The check, which cleared the bank in May, was incorrectly journalized and posted by Reber Company for $658.

5. A $3,000 note receivable was collected by the bank for Reber Company on May 31 plus $80 interest. The bank charged a collection fee of $20. No interest has been accrued on the note.

6. Included with the cancelled checks was a check issued by Stiner Company to Ted Cress for $800 that was incorrectly charged to Reber Company by the bank.

7. On May 31, the bank statement showed an NSF charge of $680 for a check issued by Sue Allison, a customer, to Reber Company on account.

*Instructions*

(a) Adjusted cash balance per bank $9,044.50

(a) Prepare the bank reconciliation at May 31, 2014.

(b) Prepare the necessary adjusting entries for Reber Company at May 31, 2014.

*Prepare a bank reconciliation and adjusting entries from detailed data.*

(LO 7)

**P8-4A** The bank portion of the bank reconciliation for Langer Company at November 30, 2014, was as follows.

**LANGER COMPANY**
Bank Reconciliation
November 30, 2014

| | | |
|---|---|---|
| Cash balance per bank | | $14,367.90 |
| Add: Deposits in transit | | 2,530.20 |
| | | 16,898.10 |

| Less: Outstanding checks | | |
|---|---|---|
| Check Number | Check Amount | |
| 3451 | $2,260.40 | |
| 3470 | 720.10 | |
| 3471 | 844.50 | |
| 3472 | 1,426.80 | |
| 3474 | 1,050.00 | 6,301.80 |
| Adjusted cash balance per bank | | $10,596.30 |

The adjusted cash balance per bank agreed with the cash balance per books at November 30.

The December bank statement showed the following checks and deposits.

| Bank Statement | | | | |
|---|---|---|---|---|
| **Checks** | | | **Deposits** | |
| Date | Number | Amount | Date | Amount |
| 12-1 | 3451 | $ 2,260.40 | 12-1 | $ 2,530.20 |
| 12-2 | 3471 | 844.50 | 12-4 | 1,211.60 |
| 12-7 | 3472 | 1,426.80 | 12-8 | 2,365.10 |
| 12-4 | 3475 | 1,640.70 | 12-16 | 2,672.70 |
| 12-8 | 3476 | 1,300.00 | 12-21 | 2,945.00 |
| 12-10 | 3477 | 2,130.00 | 12-26 | 2,567.30 |
| 12-15 | 3479 | 3,080.00 | 12-29 | 2,836.00 |
| 12-27 | 3480 | 600.00 | 12-30 | 1,025.00 |
| 12-30 | 3482 | 475.50 | Total | $18,152.90 |
| 12-29 | 3483 | 1,140.00 | | |
| 12-31 | 3485 | 540.80 | | |
| | Total | $15,438.70 | | |

The cash records per books for December showed the following.

| Cash Payments Journal | | | | | | | Cash Receipts Journal | |
|---|---|---|---|---|---|---|---|---|
| Date | Number | Amount | Date | Number | Amount | | Date | Amount |
| 12-1 | 3475 | $1,640.70 | 12-20 | 3482 | $ 475.50 | | 12-3 | $ 1,211.60 |
| 12-2 | 3476 | 1,300.00 | 12-22 | 3483 | 1,140.00 | | 12-7 | 2,365.10 |
| 12-2 | 3477 | 2,130.00 | 12-23 | 3484 | 798.00 | | 12-15 | 2,672.70 |
| 12-4 | 3478 | 621.30 | 12-24 | 3485 | 450.80 | | 12-20 | 2,954.00 |
| 12-8 | 3479 | 3,080.00 | 12-30 | 3486 | 889.50 | | 12-25 | 2,567.30 |
| 12-10 | 3480 | 600.00 | Total | | $13,933.20 | | 12-28 | 2,836.00 |
| 12-17 | 3481 | 807.40 | | | | | 12-30 | 1,025.00 |
| | | | | | | | 12-31 | 1,690.40 |
| | | | | | | | Total | $17,322.10 |

The bank statement contained two memoranda:

1. A credit of $5,145 for the collection of a $5,000 note for Langer Company plus interest of $160 and less a collection fee of $15. Langer Company has not accrued any interest on the note.
2. A debit of $572.80 for an NSF check written by L. Rees, a customer. At December 31, the check had not been redeposited in the bank.

At December 31, the cash balance per books was $12,485.20, and the cash balance per the bank statement was $20,154.30. The bank did not make any errors, but two errors were made by Langer Company.

*Instructions*
(a) Using the four steps in the reconciliation procedure, prepare a bank reconciliation at December 31.
(b) Prepare the adjusting entries based on the reconciliation. (*Hint:* The correction of any errors pertaining to recording checks should be made to Accounts Payable. The correction of any errors relating to recording cash receipts should be made to Accounts Receivable.)

(a) Adjusted balance per books $16,958.40

*Prepare a bank reconciliation and adjusting entries.*

(LO 7)

**P8-5A** Rodriguez Company maintains a checking account at the Imura Bank. At July 31, selected data from the ledger balance and the bank statement are shown below.

**Cash in Bank**

|  | Per Books | Per Bank |
|---|---|---|
| Balance, July 1 | $17,600 | $16,800 |
| July receipts | 81,400 | |
| July credits | | 82,470 |
| July disbursements | 77,150 | |
| July debits | | 74,756 |
| Balance, July 31 | $21,850 | $24,514 |

Analysis of the bank data reveals that the credits consist of $79,000 of July deposits and a credit memorandum of $4,470 for the collection of a $4,400 note plus interest revenue of $70. The July debits per bank consist of checks cleared $74,700 and a debit memorandum of $56 for printing additional company checks.

You also discover the following errors involving July checks: (1) A check for $230 to a creditor on account that cleared the bank in July was journalized and posted as $320. (2) A salary check to an employee for $255 was recorded by the bank for $155.

The June 30 bank reconciliation contained only two reconciling items: deposits in transit $8,000 and outstanding checks of $6,200.

*Instructions*

(a) Adjusted balance per books $26,354

**(a)** Prepare a bank reconciliation at July 31, 2014.

**(b)** Journalize the adjusting entries to be made by Rodriguez Company. Assume that interest on the note has not been accrued.

*Identify internal control weaknesses in cash receipts and cash disbursements.*

(LO 2, 3, 4)

**P8-6A** Rondelli Middle School wants to raise money for a new sound system for its auditorium. The primary fund-raising event is a dance at which the famous disc jockey D.J. Sound will play classic and not-so-classic dance tunes. Matt Ballester, the music and theater instructor, has been given the responsibility for coordinating the fund-raising efforts. This is Matt's first experience with fund-raising. He decides to put the eighth-grade choir in charge of the event; he will be a relatively passive observer.

Matt had 500 unnumbered tickets printed for the dance. He left the tickets in a box on his desk and told the choir students to take as many tickets as they thought they could sell for $5 each. In order to ensure that no extra tickets would be floating around, he told them to dispose of any unsold tickets. When the students received payment for the tickets, they were to bring the cash back to Matt and he would put it in a locked box in his desk drawer.

Some of the students were responsible for decorating the gymnasium for the dance. Matt gave each of them a key to the money box and told them that if they took money out to purchase materials, they should put a note in the box saying how much they took and what it was used for. After 2 weeks the money box appeared to be getting full, so Matt asked Jeff Kenney to count the money, prepare a deposit slip, and deposit the money in a bank account Matt had opened.

The day of the dance, Matt wrote a check from the account to pay the DJ. D.J. Sound, however, said that he accepted only cash and did not give receipts. So Matt took $200 out of the cash box and gave it to D.J. At the dance, Matt had Sam Copper working at the entrance to the gymnasium, collecting tickets from students, and selling tickets to those who had not prepurchased them. Matt estimated that 400 students attended the dance.

The following day, Matt closed out the bank account, which had $250 in it, and gave that amount plus the $180 in the cash box to Principal Finke. Principal Finke seemed surprised that, after generating roughly $2,000 in sales, the dance netted only $430 in cash. Matt did not know how to respond.

*Instructions*

Identify as many internal control weaknesses as you can in this scenario, and suggest how each could be addressed.

## PROBLEMS: SET B

**P8-1B** Granada Theater is located in the Brooklyn Mall. A cashier's booth is located near the entrance to the theater. Three cashiers are employed. One works from 1–5 P.M., another from 5–9 P.M. The shifts are rotated among the three cashiers. The cashiers receive cash from customers and operate a machine that ejects serially numbered tickets. The rolls of tickets are inserted and locked into the machine by the theater manager at the beginning of each cashier's shift.

*Identify internal control weaknesses over cash receipts.*

*(LO 2, 3)*

After purchasing a ticket, the customer takes the ticket to an usher stationed at the entrance of the theater lobby some 60 feet from the cashier's booth. The usher tears the ticket in half, admits the customer, and returns the ticket stub to the customer. The other half of the ticket is dropped into a locked box by the usher.

At the end of each cashier's shift, the theater manager removes the ticket rolls from the machine and makes a cash count. The cash count sheet is initialed by the cashier. At the end of the day, the manager deposits the receipts in total in a bank night deposit vault located in the mall. The manager also sends copies of the deposit slip and the initialed cash count sheets to the theater company treasurer for verification and to the company's accounting department. Receipts from the first shift are stored in a safe located in the manager's office.

### Instructions
**(a)** Identify the internal control principles and their application to the cash receipts transactions of the Granada Theater.
**(b)** If the usher and cashier decide to collaborate to misappropriate cash, what actions might they take?

**P8-2B** Haig Company maintains a petty cash fund for small expenditures. The following transactions occurred over a 2-month period.

*Journalize and post petty cash fund transactions.*

*(LO 5)*

July  1   Established petty cash fund by writing a check on China Bank for $100.
   15   Replenished the petty cash fund by writing a check for $96.90. On this date the fund consisted of $3.10 in cash and the following petty cash receipts: freight-out $51.00, postage expense $20.50, entertainment expense $23.10, and miscellaneous expense $6.10.
   31   Replenished the petty cash fund by writing a check for $95.90. At this date, the fund consisted of $4.10 in cash and the following petty cash receipts: freight-out $43.50, charitable contributions expense $20.00, postage expense $20.10, and miscellaneous expense $12.30.
Aug. 15   Replenished the petty cash fund by writing a check for $98.00. On this date, the fund consisted of $2.00 in cash and the following petty cash receipts: freight-out $40.20, entertainment expense $21.00, postage expense $16.00, and miscellaneous expense $19.80.
   16   Increased the amount of the petty cash fund to $150 by writing a check for $50.
   31   Replenished petty cash fund by writing a check for $137.00. On this date, the fund consisted of $13 in cash and the following petty cash receipts: freight-out $74.00, entertainment expense $43.20, and postage expense $17.70.

### Instructions
**(a)** Journalize the petty cash transactions.
**(b)** Post to the Petty Cash account.
**(c)** What internal control features exist in a petty cash fund?

*(a) July 15 Cash over $3.80*
*(b) Aug. 31 balance $150*

**P8-3B** Davaney Genetics Company of Milwaukee, Wisconsin, spreads herbicides and applies liquid fertilizer for local farmers. On May 31, 2014, the company's Cash account per its general ledger showed the following balance.

*Prepare a bank reconciliation and adjusting entries.*

*(LO 7)*

| | CASH | | | | NO. 101 |
|---|---|---|---|---|---|
| Date | Explanation | Ref. | Debit | Credit | Balance |
| May 31 | Balance | | | | 13,287 |

The bank statement from Milwaukee State Bank on that date showed the following balance.

### MILWAUKEE STATE BANK

| Checks and Debits | Deposits and Credits | Daily Balance |
|---|---|---|
| XXX | XXX | 5/31    13,332 |

A comparison of the details on the bank statement with the details in the Cash account revealed the following facts.

1. The statement included a debit memo of $35 for the printing of additional company checks.
2. Cash sales of $1,720 on May 12 were deposited in the bank. The cash receipts journal entry and the deposit slip were incorrectly made for $1,820. The bank credited Davaney Genetics Company for the correct amount.
3. Outstanding checks at May 31 totaled $1,225, and deposits in transit were $2,600.
4. On May 18, the company issued check no. 1181 for $911 to J. Tallgrass on account. The check, which cleared the bank in May, was incorrectly journalized and posted by Davaney Genetics Company for $119.
5. A $4,500 note receivable was collected by the bank for Davaney Genetics Company on May 31 plus $80 interest. The bank charged a collection fee of $25. No interest has been accrued on the note.
6. Included with the cancelled checks was a check issued by Morray Company to Terry Irvin for $900 that was incorrectly charged to Davaney Genetics Company by the bank.
7. On May 31, the bank statement showed an NSF charge of $1,308 for a check issued by Peter Reser, a customer, to Davaney Genetics Company on account.

*Instructions*

(a) Adj. cash bal. $15,607

(a) Prepare the bank reconciliation at May 31, 2014.
(b) Prepare the necessary adjusting entries for Davaney Genetics Company at May 31, 2014.

*Prepare a bank reconciliation and adjusting entries from detailed data.*

(LO 7)

**P8-4B** The bank portion of the bank reconciliation for Phillips Company at October 31, 2014, was as follows.

### PHILLIPS COMPANY
### Bank Reconciliation
### October 31, 2014

| | | |
|---|---|---|
| Cash balance per bank | | $6,000 |
| Add: Deposits in transit | | 842 |
| | | 6,842 |

| Less: Outstanding checks | | |
|---|---|---|
| Check Number | Check Amount | |
| 2451 | $700 | |
| 2470 | 396 | |
| 2471 | 464 | |
| 2472 | 270 | |
| 2474 | 578 | 2,408 |
| Adjusted cash balance per bank | | $4,434 |

The adjusted cash balance per bank agreed with the cash balance per books at October 31. The November bank statement showed the following checks and deposits:

### Bank Statement

| Checks | | | Deposits | |
|---|---|---|---|---|
| Date | Number | Amount | Date | Amount |
| 11-1 | 2470 | $ 396 | 11-1 | $ 842 |
| 11-2 | 2471 | 464 | 11-4 | 666 |
| 11-5 | 2474 | 578 | 11-8 | 545 |
| 11-4 | 2475 | 903 | 11-13 | 1,416 |
| 11-8 | 2476 | 1,556 | 11-18 | 810 |
| 11-10 | 2477 | 330 | 11-21 | 1,624 |
| 11-15 | 2479 | 980 | 11-25 | 1,412 |
| 11-18 | 2480 | 714 | 11-28 | 908 |
| 11-27 | 2481 | 382 | 11-30 | 652 |
| 11-30 | 2483 | 317 | Total | $8,875 |
| 11-29 | 2486 | 495 | | |
| | Total | $7,115 | | |

The cash records per books for November showed the following.

### Cash Payments Journal

| Date | Number | Amount | Date | Number | Amount |
|---|---|---|---|---|---|
| 11-1 | 2475 | $ 903 | 11-20 | 2483 | $ 317 |
| 11-2 | 2476 | 1,556 | 11-22 | 2484 | 460 |
| 11-2 | 2477 | 330 | 11-23 | 2485 | 525 |
| 11-4 | 2478 | 300 | 11-24 | 2486 | 495 |
| 11-8 | 2479 | 890 | 11-29 | 2487 | 210 |
| 11-10 | 2480 | 714 | 11-30 | 2488 | 635 |
| 11-15 | 2481 | 382 | Total | | $8,067 |
| 11-18 | 2482 | 350 | | | |

### Cash Receipts Journal

| Date | Amount |
|---|---|
| 11-3 | $ 666 |
| 11-7 | 545 |
| 11-12 | 1,416 |
| 11-17 | 810 |
| 11-20 | 1,642 |
| 11-24 | 1,412 |
| 11-27 | 908 |
| 11-29 | 652 |
| 11-30 | 2,541 |
| Total | $10,592 |

The bank statement contained two bank memoranda:

1. A credit of $2,375 for the collection of a $2,300 note for Phillips Company plus interest of $91 and less a collection fee of $16. Phillips Company has not accrued any interest on the note.
2. A debit for the printing of additional company checks $34.

At November 30, the cash balance per books was $5,958, and the cash balance per the bank statement was $9,100. The bank did not make any errors, but two errors were made by Phillips Company.

### Instructions
(a) Using the four steps in the reconciliation procedure described on pages 398–399, prepare a bank reconciliation at November 30.
(b) Prepare the adjusting entries based on the reconciliation. (*Hint:* The correction of any errors pertaining to recording checks should be made to Accounts Payable. The correction of any errors relating to recording cash receipts should be made to Accounts Receivable.)

(a) Adjusted cash balance per bank $8,191

**P8-5B** Zhang Company's bank statement from Nguyen National Bank at August 31, 2014, shows the information below.

*Prepare a bank reconciliation and adjusting entries.*

(LO 7)

| | | | |
|---|---|---|---|
| Balance, August 1 | $11,284 | Bank credit memoranda: | |
| August deposits | 47,521 | Collection of note | |
| Checks cleared in August | 46,475 | receivable plus $105 | |
| Balance, August 31 | 16,856 | interest | $5,105 |
| | | Interest earned | 41 |
| | | Bank debit memorandum: | |
| | | Safety deposit box rent | 20 |

A summary of the Cash account in the ledger for August shows: balance, August 1, $10,959; receipts $50,050; disbursements $47,794; and balance, August 31, $13,215. Analysis reveals that the only reconciling items on the July 31 bank reconciliation were a deposit in transit for $3,200 and outstanding checks of $2,925. The deposit in transit was the first deposit recorded by the bank in August. In addition, you determine that there were two errors involving company checks drawn in August: (1) A check for $340 to a creditor on account that cleared the bank in August was journalized and posted for $430. (2) A salary check to an employee for $275 was recorded by the bank for $277.

*Instructions*

(a) Adjusted balance per
books $18,431

**(a)** Prepare a bank reconciliation at August 31.
**(b)** Journalize the adjusting entries to be made by Zhang Company at August 31. Assume that interest on the note has not been accrued by the company.

*Prepare a comprehensive bank reconciliation with theft and internal control deficiencies.*

*(LO 2, 3, 4, 7)*

**P8-6B** Gamel Company is a very profitable small business. It has not, however, given much consideration to internal control. For example, in an attempt to keep clerical and office expenses to a minimum, the company has combined the jobs of cashier and book-keeper. As a result, Jan Worthy handles all cash receipts, keeps the accounting records, and prepares the monthly bank reconciliations.

The balance per the bank statement on October 31, 2014, was $15,313. Outstanding checks were: no. 62 for $107.74, no. 183 for $127.50, no. 284 for $215.26, no. 862 for $132.10, no. 863 for $192.78, and no. 864 for $140.49. Included with the statement was a credit memorandum of $460 indicating the collection of a note receivable for Gamel Company by the bank on October 25. This memorandum has not been recorded by Gamel Company.

The company's ledger showed one cash account with a balance of $18,608.81. The balance included undeposited cash on hand. Because of the lack of internal controls, Jan took for personal use all of the undeposited receipts in excess of $3,226.18. She then prepared the following bank reconciliation in an effort to conceal her theft of cash.

### BANK RECONCILIATION

| | | |
|---|---:|---:|
| Cash balance per books, October 31 | | $18,608.81 |
| Add: Outstanding checks | | |
| No. 862 | $132.10 | |
| No. 863 | 192.78 | |
| No. 864 | 140.49 | 390.37 |
| | | 18,999.18 |
| Less: Undeposited receipts | | 3,226.18 |
| Unadjusted balance per bank, October 31 | | 15,773.00 |
| Less: Bank credit memorandum | | 460.00 |
| Cash balance per bank statement, October 31 | | $15,313.00 |

*Instructions*

(a) Adjusted balance per
books $17,623.31

**(a)** Prepare a correct bank reconciliation. (*Hint:* Deduct the amount of the theft from the adjusted balance per books.)
**(b)** Indicate the three ways that Jan attempted to conceal the theft and the dollar amount pertaining to each method.
**(c)** What principles of internal control were violated in this case?

## PROBLEMS: SET C

Visit the book's companion website, at **www.wiley.com/college/weygandt**, and choose the Student Companion site to access Problem Set C.

## COMPREHENSIVE PROBLEM

**CP8** On December 1, 2014, Fullerton Company had the following account balances.

|  | Debit |  | Credit |
|---|---|---|---|
| Cash | $18,200 | Accumulated Depreciation— | |
| Notes Receivable | 2,200 | Equipment | $ 3,000 |
| Accounts Receivable | 7,500 | Accounts Payable | 6,100 |
| Inventory | 16,000 | Owner's Capital | 64,400 |
| Prepaid Insurance | 1,600 | | $73,500 |
| Equipment | 28,000 | | |
| | $73,500 | | |

During December, the company completed the following transactions.

Dec. 7 Received $3,600 cash from customers in payment of account (no discount allowed).
   12 Purchased merchandise on account from Vance Co. $12,000, terms 1/10, n/30.
   17 Sold merchandise on account $16,000, terms 2/10, n/30. The cost of the merchandise sold was $10,000.
   19 Paid salaries $2,200.
   22 Paid Vance Co. in full, less discount.
   26 Received collections in full, less discounts, from customers billed on December 17.
   31 Received $2,700 cash from customers in payment of account (no discount allowed).

Adjustment data:

**1.** Depreciation $200 per month.
**2.** Insurance expired $400.

### Instructions

**(a)** Journalize the December transactions. (Assume a perpetual inventory system.)
**(b)** Enter the December 1 balances in the ledger T-accounts and post the December transactions. Use Cost of Goods Sold, Depreciation Expense, Insurance Expense, Salaries and Wages Expense, Sales Revenue, and Sales Discounts.
**(c)** The statement from Jackson County Bank on December 31 showed a balance of $26,130. A comparison of the bank statement with the Cash account revealed the following facts.
   **1.** The bank collected a note receivable of $2,200 for Fullerton Company on December 15.
   **2.** The December 31 receipts were deposited in a night deposit vault on December 31. These deposits were recorded by the bank in January.
   **3.** Checks outstanding on December 31 totaled $1,210.
   **4.** On December 31, the bank statement showed an NSF charge of $680 for a check received by the company from L. Bryan, a customer, on account.

   Prepare a bank reconciliation as of December 31 based on the available information. (*Hint:* The cash balance per books is $26,100. This can be proven by finding the balance in the Cash account from parts (a) and (b).)
**(d)** Journalize the adjusting entries resulting from the bank reconciliation and adjustment data.
**(e)** Post the adjusting entries to the ledger T-accounts.
**(f)** Prepare an adjusted trial balance.
**(g)** Prepare an income statement for December and a classified balance sheet at December 31.

## CONTINUING COOKIE CHRONICLE

(*Note:* This is a continuation of the Cookie Chronicle from Chapters 1 through 7.)

**CCC8  Part 1**  Natalie is struggling to keep up with the recording of her accounting transactions. She is spending a lot of time marketing and selling mixers and giving her cookie classes. Her friend John is an accounting student who runs his own accounting service. He has asked Natalie if she would like to have him do her accounting. John and Natalie meet and discuss her business.

**Part 2**  Natalie decides that she cannot afford to hire John to do her accounting. One way that she can ensure that her cash account does not have any errors and is accurate and up-to-date is to prepare a bank reconciliation at the end of each month. Natalie would like you to help her.

*Go to the book's companion website, **www.wiley.com/college/weygandt**, to see the completion of this problem.*

# Broadening Your Perspective

## Financial Reporting and Analysis

### Financial Reporting Problem: Apple Inc.

**BYP8-1** The financial statements of Apple Inc. are presented in Appendix A at the end of this textbook. Instructions for accessing and using the company's complete annual report, including the notes to the financial statements, are also provided in Appendix A.

*Instructions*
**(a)** What comments, if any, are made about cash in the report of the independent registered public accounting firm?
**(b)** What data about cash and cash equivalents are shown in the consolidated balance sheet?
**(c)** In its notes to Consolidated Financial Statements, how does Apple define cash equivalents?
**(d)** In management's Annual Report on Internal Control over Financial Reporting (Item 9), what does Apple's management say about internal control?

### Comparative Analysis Problem:
### PepsiCo, Inc. vs. The Coca-Cola Company

**BYP8-2** PepsiCo's financial statements are presented in Appendix B. Financial statements of The Coca-Cola Company are presented in Appendix C. Instructions for accessing and using the complete annual reports of PepsiCo and Coca-Cola, including the notes to the financial statements, are also provided in Appendices B and C, respectively.

*Instructions*
**(a)** Based on the information contained in these financial statements, determine each of the following for each company:
    **(1)** Cash and cash equivalents balance at December 31, 2011, for PepsiCo and at December 31, 2011, for Coca-Cola.
    **(2)** Increase (decrease) in cash and cash equivalents from 2010 to 2011.
    **(3)** Cash provided by operating activities during the year ended December 2011 (from statement of cash flows).
**(b)** What conclusions concerning the management of cash can be drawn from these data?

### Comparative Analysis Problem:
### Amazon.com, Inc. vs. Wal-Mart Stores, Inc.

**BYP8-3** Amazon.com, Inc.'s financial statements are presented in Appendix D. Financial statements of Wal-Mart Stores, Inc. are presented in Appendix E. Instructions for accessing and using the complete annual reports of Amazon and Wal-Mart, including the notes to the financial statements, are also provided in Appendices D and E, respectively.

*Instructions*
**(a)** Based on the information contained in these financial statements, determine each of the following for each company:
    **(1)** Cash and cash equivalents balance at December 31, 2011, for Amazon and at January 31, 2012, for Wal-Mart.
    **(2)** Increase (decrease) in cash and cash equivalents from 2011 to 2010.
    **(3)** Net cash provided by operating activities during the year ended December 31, 2011, for Amazon and January 31, 2012, for Wal-Mart from statement of cash flows.
**(b)** What conclusions concerning the management of cash can be drawn from these data?

### Real-World Focus

**BYP8-4** All organizations should have systems of internal control. Universities are no exception. This site discusses the basics of internal control in a university setting.

*Address:* **www.bc.edu/offices/audit/controls**, or go to **www.wiley.com/college/weygandt**

*Steps:* Go to the site shown above.

*Instructions*
The home page of this site provides links to pages that answer six critical questions. Use these links to answer the following questions.

**(a)** In a university setting, who has responsibility for evaluating the adequacy of the system of internal control?

**(b)** What do reconciliations ensure in the university setting? Who should review the reconciliation?

**(c)** What are some examples of physical controls?

**(d)** What are two ways to accomplish inventory counts?

# Critical Thinking

## Decision-Making Across the Organization

**BYP8-5** The board of trustees of a local church is concerned about the internal accounting controls for the offering collections made at weekly services. The trustees ask you to serve on a three-person audit team with the internal auditor of a local college and a CPA who has just joined the church.

At a meeting of the audit team and the board of trustees you learn the following.

**1.** The church's board of trustees has delegated responsibility for the financial management and audit of the financial records to the finance committee. This group prepares the annual budget and approves major disbursements. It is not involved in collections or record keeping. No audit has been made in recent years because the same trusted employee has kept church records and served as financial secretary for 15 years. The church does not carry any fidelity insurance.

**2.** The collection at the weekly service is taken by a team of ushers who volunteer to serve one month. The ushers take the collection plates to a basement office at the rear of the church. They hand their plates to the head usher and return to the church service. After all plates have been turned in, the head usher counts the cash received. The head usher then places the cash in the church safe along with a notation of the amount counted. The head usher volunteers to serve for 3 months.

**3.** The next morning the financial secretary opens the safe and recounts the collection. The secretary withholds $150–$200 in cash, depending on the cash expenditures expected for the week, and deposits the remainder of the collections in the bank. To facilitate the deposit, church members who contribute by check are asked to make their checks payable to "Cash."

**4.** Each month, the financial secretary reconciles the bank statement and submits a copy of the reconciliation to the board of trustees. The reconciliations have rarely contained any bank errors and have never shown any errors per books.

*Instructions*
With the class divided into groups, answer the following.

**(a)** Indicate the weaknesses in internal accounting control over the handling of collections.

**(b)** List the improvements in internal control procedures that you plan to make at the next meeting of the audit team for (1) the ushers, (2) the head usher, (3) the financial secretary, and (4) the finance committee.

**(c)** What church policies should be changed to improve internal control?

## Communication Activity

**BYP8-6** As a new auditor for the CPA firm of Eaton, Quayle, and Hale, you have been assigned to review the internal controls over mail cash receipts of Pritchard Company. Your review reveals the following. Checks are promptly endorsed "For Deposit Only," but no list of the checks is prepared by the person opening the mail. The mail is opened either by the cashier or by the employee who maintains the accounts receivable records. Mail receipts are deposited in the bank weekly by the cashier.

*Instructions*
Write a letter to Danny Peak, owner of Pritchard Company, explaining the weaknesses in internal control and your recommendations for improving the system.

## Ethics Case

**BYP8-7** You are the assistant controller in charge of general ledger accounting at Linbarger Bottling Company. Your company has a large loan from an insurance company. The loan agreement requires that the company's cash account balance be maintained at $200,000 or more, as reported monthly.

At June 30, the cash balance is $80,000, which you report to Lisa Infante, the financial vice president. Lisa excitedly instructs you to keep the cash receipts book open for one additional day for purposes of the June 30 report to the insurance company. Lisa says, "If we don't get that cash balance over $200,000, we'll default on our loan agreement. They could close us down, put us all out of our jobs!" Lisa continues, "I talked to Oconto Distributors (one of Linbarger's largest customers) this morning. They said they sent us a check for $150,000 yesterday. We should receive it tomorrow. If we include just that one check in our cash balance, we'll be in the clear. It's in the mail!"

*Instructions*
**(a)** Who will suffer negative effects if you do not comply with Lisa Infante's instructions? Who will suffer if you do comply?
**(b)** What are the ethical considerations in this case?
**(c)** What alternatives do you have?

## All About You

**BYP8-8** The print and electronic media are full of stories about potential security risks that may arise from your personal computer. It is important to keep in mind, however, that there are also many other ways that your identity can be stolen other than from your computer. The federal government provides many resources to help protect you from identity thieves.

*Instructions*
Go to **http://onguardonline.gov/idtheft.html**, click **Video and Media,** and then click on **ID Theft Faceoff**. Complete the quiz provided there.

## FASB Codification Activity

**BYP8-9** If your school has a subscription to the FASB Codification, go to **http://aaahq.org/ascLogin.cfm** to log in and prepare responses to the following.

**(a)** How is cash defined in the Codification?
**(b)** How are cash equivalents defined in the Codification?
**(c)** What are the disclosure requirements related to cash and cash equivalents?

## Answers to Chapter Questions

### Answers to Insight and Accounting Across the Organization Questions

**p. 377 And the Controls Are. . .    Q:** Why is sustainability information important to investors? **A:** Investors, customers, suppliers, and employees want more information about companies' long-term impact on society. There is a growing awareness that sustainability issues can affect a company's financial performance. Proper reporting on sustainability issues develops a solid reputation for transparency and provides confidence to shareholders.

**p. 384 SOX Boosts the Role of Human Resources    Q:** Why would unsupervised employees or employees who report to each other represent potential internal control threats? **A:** An unsupervised employee may have a fraudulent job (or may even be a fictitious person), e.g., a person drawing a paycheck without working. Or, if two employees supervise each other, there is no real separation of duties, and they can conspire to defraud the company.

**p. 393 How Employees Steal    Q:** How can companies reduce the likelihood of fraudulent disbursements? **A:** To reduce the occurrence of fraudulent disbursements, a company should follow the procedures discussed in this chapter. These include having only designated personnel sign checks; having different personnel approve payments and make payments; ensuring that check-signers do not record disbursements; using prenumbered checks and matching each check to an approved invoice; storing blank checks securely; reconciling the bank statement; and stamping invoices PAID.

**p. 401 Madoff's Ponzi Scheme    Q:** How was Madoff able to conceal such a giant fraud? **A:** Madoff fabricated false investment statements that were provided to investors. In addition, his auditor never verified these investment statements even though the auditor issued an unqualified opinion each year.

# A Look at IFRS

Fraud can occur anywhere. Because the three main factors that contribute to fraud are universal in nature, the principles of internal control activities are used globally by companies. While Sarbanes-Oxley (SOX) does not apply to international companies, most large international companies have internal controls similar to those indicated in the chapter. IFRS and GAAP are also very similar in accounting for cash. *IAS No. 1 (revised)*, "Presentation of Financial Statements," is the only standard that discusses issues specifically related to cash.

> **LEARNING OBJECTIVE 9**
>
> **Compare the accounting procedures for fraud, internal control, and cash under GAAP and IFRS.**

## Key Points

- The fraud triangle discussed in this chapter is applicable to all international companies. Some of the major frauds on an international basis are Parmalat (Italy), Royal Ahold (the Netherlands), and Satyam Computer Services (India).

- Rising economic crime poses a growing threat to companies, with nearly one-third of all organizations worldwide being victims of fraud in a recent 12-month period. The survey data shows that the incidence of economic crime varies by territory; some countries, mainly those in emerging markets, experienced much higher levels of fraud than the average, as much as 71% in one country; by industry sector, some (notably insurance, financial services, and communications) reporting higher levels of fraud than others; and by size and type of organization. However, no organization is immune (*PricewaterhouseCoopers' Global Economic Crime Survey*, 2009).

- Economic crime takes on many different forms, some more common than others. The chart below shows the types of economic crime suffered by those companies who reported experiencing economic crime in the last 12 months.

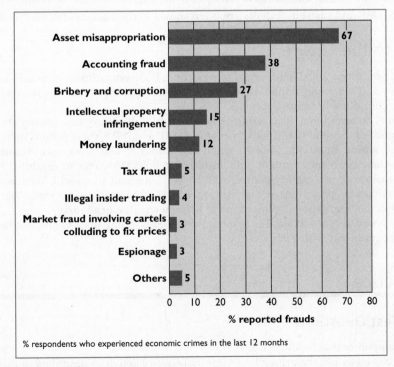

This chart shows that the three most common types of economic crimes experienced in the last 12 months were asset misappropriation, accounting fraud, and bribery and corruption (*PricewaterhouseCoopers' Global Economic Crime Survey*, 2009).

- Accounting scandals both in the United States and internationally have re-ignited the debate over the relative merits of GAAP, which takes a "rules-based" approach to accounting, versus IFRS, which takes a "principles-based" approach. The FASB announced that it intends to introduce more principles-based standards.

- On a lighter note, at one time the Ig Nobel Prize in Economics went to the CEOs of those companies involved in the corporate accounting scandals of that year for "adapting the mathematical concept of imaginary numbers for use in the business world." A parody of the Nobel Prizes, the Ig Nobel Prizes (read Ignoble, as not noble) are given each year in early October for 10 achievements that "first make people laugh, and then make them think." Organized by the scientific humor magazine *Annals of Improbable Research* (*AIR*), they are presented by a group that includes genuine Nobel laureates at a ceremony at Harvard University's Sanders Theater. (See **en.wikipedia.org/wiki/Ig_Nobel_Prize.**)

- Internal controls are a system of checks and balances designed to prevent and detect fraud and errors. While most companies have these systems in place, many have never completely documented them, nor had an independent auditor attest to their effectiveness. Both of these actions are required under SOX.

- Companies find that internal control review is a costly process but badly needed. One study estimates the cost of SOX compliance for U.S. companies at over $35 billion, with audit fees doubling in the first year of compliance. At the same time, examination of internal controls indicates lingering problems in the way companies operate. One study of first compliance with the internal-control testing provisions documented material weaknesses for about 13% of companies reporting in a two-year period (*PricewaterhouseCoopers' Global Economic Crime Survey*, 2005).

- The SOX internal control standards apply only to companies listed on U.S. exchanges. There is continuing debate over whether foreign issuers should have to comply with this extra layer of regulation.

- The accounting and internal control procedures related to cash are essentially the same under both IFRS and this textbook. In addition, the definition used for cash equivalents is the same.

- Most companies report cash and cash equivalents together under IFRS, as shown in this textbook. In addition, IFRS follows the same accounting policies related to the reporting of restricted cash.

- IFRS defines cash and cash equivalents as follows.

   ♦ **Cash** is comprised of cash on hand and demand deposits.
   ♦ **Cash equivalents** are short-term, highly liquid investments that are readily convertible to known amounts of cash and which are subject to an insignificant risk of changes in value.

- Under IFRS, cash and cash equivalents are often shown in the statement of financial position.

## Looking to the Future

Ethics has become a very important aspect of reporting. Different cultures have different perspectives on bribery and other questionable activities, and consequently penalties for engaging in such activities vary considerably across countries.

High-quality international accounting requires both high-quality accounting standards and high-quality auditing. Similar to the convergence of GAAP and IFRS, there is movement to improve international auditing standards. The International Auditing and Assurance Standards Board (IAASB) functions as an independent standard-setting body. It works to establish high-quality auditing and assurance and quality-control standards throughout the world. Whether the IAASB adopts internal control provisions similar to those in SOX remains to be seen. You can follow developments in the international audit arena at **http://www.ifac.org/iaasb/**.

Under proposed new standards for financial statements, companies would not be allowed to combine cash equivalents with cash.

## IFRS Practice

### IFRS Self-Test Questions

1. Non-U.S companies that follow IFRS:
   (a) do not normally use the principles of internal control activities described in this textbook.
   (b) often offset cash with accounts payable on the balance sheet.
   (c) are not required to follow SOX.
   (d) None of the above.

2. Which of the following is the correct accounting under IFRS for cash?
   (a) Cash cannot be combined with cash equivalents.
   (b) Restricted cash funds may be reported as a current or non-current asset depending on the circumstances.
   (c) Restricted cash funds cannot be reported as a current asset.
   (d) Cash on hand is not reported on the balance sheet as Cash.

3. The Sarbanes-Oxley Act applies to:
   (a) all U.S. companies listed on U.S. exchanges.
   (b) all companies that list stock on any stock exchange in any country.
   (c) all European companies listed on European exchanges.
   (d) Both (a) and (c).

4. High-quality international accounting requires both high-quality accounting standards and:
   (a) a reconsideration of SOX to make it less onerous.
   (b) high-quality auditing standards.
   (c) government intervention to ensure that the public interest is protected.
   (d) the development of new principles of internal control activities.

5. Cash equivalents under IFRS:
   (a) are significantly different than the cash equivalents discussed in the textbook.
   (b) are generally disclosed separately from cash.
   (c) may be required to be reported separately from cash in the future.
   (d) None of the above.

## IFRS Exercises

**IFRS8-1** Some people argue that the internal control requirements of the Sarbanes-Oxley Act (SOX) put U.S. companies at a competitive disadvantage to companies outside the United States. Discuss the competitive implications (both pros and cons) of SOX.

**IFRS8-2** State whether each of the following is true or false. For those that are false, explain why.

(a) A proposed new financial accounting standard would not allow cash equivalents to be reported in combination with cash.
(b) Perspectives on bribery and penalties for engaging in bribery are the same across all countries.
(c) Cash equivalents are comprised of cash on hand and demand deposits.
(d) SOX was created by the International Accounting Standards Board.

## International Financial Reporting Problem: Zetar plc

**IFRS8–3** The financial statements of Zetar plc are presented in Appendix F. Instructions for accessing and using the company's complete annual report, including the notes to its financial statements, are also provided in Appendix F.

### Instructions

Using the notes to the company's financial statements, answer the following questions.

(a) Which committee of the board of directors is responsible for considering management's reports on internal control?
(b) What are the company's key control procedures?
(c) Does the company have an internal audit department?
(d) In what section or sections does Zetar report its bank overdrafts?

### Answers to IFRS Self-Test Questions
1. c  2. b  3. a  4. b  5. c

# 9 | Accounting for Receivables

## Feature Story

### A Dose of Careful Management Keeps Receivables Healthy

"Sometimes you have to know when to be very tough, and sometimes you can give them a bit of a break," says Vivi Su. She's not talking about her children but about the customers of a subsidiary of pharmaceutical company Whitehall-Robins, where she works as supervisor of credit and collections.

For example, while the company's regular terms are 1/15, n/30 (1% discount if paid within 15 days), a customer might ask for and receive a few days of grace and still get the discount. Or a customer might place orders above its credit limit, in which case, depending on its payment history and the circumstances, Ms. Su might authorize shipment of the goods anyway.

"It's not about drawing a line in the sand, and that's all," she explains. "You want a good relationship with your customers—but you also need to bring in the money."

"The money," in Whitehall-Robins' case, amounts to some $170 million in sales a year. Nearly all of it comes in through the credit accounts Ms. Su manages. The process starts with the decision to grant a customer an account in the first place, Ms. Su explains. The sales rep gives the customer a credit application. "My department reviews this application ver[y] carefully; a customer needs to supply three good referen[ces] and we also run a check with a credit firm like Equifax. If [we] accept them, then based on their size and history, we ass[ign] a credit limit."

Once accounts are established, "I get an aging report ev[ery] single day," says Ms. Su. "The rule of thumb is that we sh[ould] always have at least 85% of receivables current—meaning [that] they were billed less than 30 days ago," she continues. "B[ut] we try to do even better than that—I like to see 90%."

At 15 days overdue, Whitehall-Robins phones the client. [At] 45 days, Ms. Su notes, "I send a letter. Then a second no[tice is] sent in writing. After the third and final notice, the client [has] 10 days to pay, and then I hand it over to a collection age[ncy] and it's out of my hands."

Ms. Su's boss, Terry Norton, records an estimate for ba[d] debts every year, based on a percentage of receivables[. The] percentage depends on the current aging history. He a[lso] calculates and monitors the company's accounts receiv[able] turnover, which the company reports in its financial statements.

## Learning Objectives

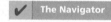

*After studying this chapter, you should be able to:*

[1] Identify the different types of receivables.

[2] Explain how companies recognize accounts receivable.

[3] Distinguish between the methods and bases companies use to value accounts receivable.

[4] Describe the entries to record the disposition of accounts receivable.

[5] Compute the maturity date of and interest on notes receivable.

[6] Explain how companies recognize notes receivable.

[7] Describe how companies value notes receivable.

[8] Describe the entries to record the disposition of notes receivable.

[9] Explain the statement presentation and analysis of receivables.

Ms. Su knows that she and Mr. Norton are crucial to the profitability of Whitehall-Robins. "Receivables are generally the second-largest asset of any company (after its capital assets)," she points out. "So it's no wonder we keep a very close eye on them."

# Preview of Chapter 9

✔ The Navigator

As indicated in the Feature Story, receivables are a significant asset for many pharmaceutical companies. Because a large portion of sales in the United States are done on credit, receivables are important to companies in other industries as well. As a consequence, companies must pay close attention to their receivables and manage them carefully. In this chapter you will learn what journal entries companies make when they sell products, when they collect cash from those sales, and when they write off accounts they cannot collect.

The content and organization of the chapter are as follows.

## ACCOUNTING FOR RECEIVABLES

| Types of Receivables | Accounts Receivable | Notes Receivable | Statement Presentation and Analysis |
|---|---|---|---|
| • Accounts receivable<br>• Notes receivable<br>• Other receivables | • Recognizing accounts receivable<br>• Valuing accounts receivable<br>• Disposing of accounts receivable | • Determining maturity date<br>• Computing interest<br>• Recognizing notes receivable<br>• Valuing notes receivable<br>• Disposing of notes receivable | • Presentation<br>• Analysis |

## Types of Receivables

LEARNING OBJECTIVE   1

Identify the different
types of receivables.

The term **receivables** refers to amounts due from individuals and companies. Receivables are claims that are expected to be collected in cash. The management of receivables is a very important activity for any company that sells goods or services on credit.

Receivables are important because they represent one of a company's most liquid assets. For many companies, receivables are also one of the largest assets. For example, receivables represented 21.9% of the current assets of pharmaceutical giant Rite Aid in 2011. Illustration 9-1 lists receivables as a percentage of total assets for five other well-known companies in a recent year.

**Illustration 9-1**
Receivables as a percentage of assets

| Company | Receivables as a Percentage of Total Assets |
| --- | --- |
| General Electric | 52% |
| Ford Motor Company | 42% |
| Minnesota Mining and Manufacturing Company (3M) | 14% |
| DuPont Co. | 17% |
| Intel Corporation | 5% |

The relative significance of a company's receivables as a percentage of its assets depends on various factors: its industry, the time of year, whether it extends long-term financing, and its credit policies. To reflect important differences among receivables, they are frequently classified as (1) accounts receivable, (2) notes receivable, and (3) other receivables.

**Accounts receivable** are amounts customers owe on account. They result from the sale of goods and services. Companies generally expect to collect accounts receivable within 30 to 60 days. They are usually the most significant type of claim held by a company.

**Notes receivable** are a written promise (as evidenced by a formal instrument) for amounts to be received. The note normally requires the collection of interest and extends for time periods of 60–90 days or longer. Notes and accounts receivable that result from sales transactions are often called **trade receivables**.

**Ethics Note**

Companies report receivables from employees separately in the financial statements. The reason: Sometimes those assets are not the result of an "arm's-length" transaction.

**Other receivables** include nontrade receivables such as interest receivable, loans to company officers, advances to employees, and income taxes refundable. These do not generally result from the operations of the business. Therefore, they are generally classified and reported as separate items in the balance sheet.

## Accounts Receivable

LEARNING OBJECTIVE   2

Explain how companies
recognize accounts
receivable.

Three accounting issues associated with accounts receivable are:

1. **Recognizing** accounts receivable.
2. **Valuing** accounts receivable.
3. **Disposing** of accounts receivable.

## Recognizing Accounts Receivable

Recognizing accounts receivable is relatively straightforward. A service organization records a receivable when it performs service on account. A merchandiser records accounts receivable at the point of sale of merchandise on account. When a merchandiser sells goods, it increases (debits) Accounts Receivable and increases (credits) Sales Revenue.

The seller may offer terms that encourage early payment by providing a discount. Sales returns also reduce receivables. The buyer might find some of the goods unacceptable and choose to return the unwanted goods.

To review, assume that Jordache Co. on July 1, 2014, sells merchandise on account to Polo Company for $1,000, terms 2/10, n/30. On July 5, Polo returns merchandise worth $100 to Jordache Co. On July 11, Jordache receives payment from Polo Company for the balance due. The journal entries to record these transactions on the books of Jordache Co. are as follows. **(Cost of goods sold entries are omitted.)**

> **Ethics Note**
>
> In exchange for lower interest rates, some companies have eliminated the 25-day grace period before finance charges kick in. Be sure you read the fine print in any credit agreement you sign.

| July 1 | Accounts Receivable—Polo Company | 1,000 | |
| | Sales Revenue | | 1,000 |
| | (To record sales on account) | | |

| July 5 | Sales Returns and Allowances | 100 | |
| | Accounts Receivable—Polo Company | | 100 |
| | (To record merchandise returned) | | |

**Helpful Hint** These entries are the same as those described in Chapter 5. For simplicity, we have omitted inventory and cost of goods sold from this set of journal entries and from end-of-chapter material.

| July 11 | Cash ($900 − $18) | 882 | |
| | Sales Discounts ($900 × .02) | 18 | |
| | Accounts Receivable—Polo Company | | 900 |
| | (To record collection of accounts receivable) | | |

Some retailers issue their own credit cards. When you use a retailer's credit card (JCPenney, for example), the retailer charges interest on the balance due if not paid within a specified period (usually 25–30 days).

To illustrate, assume that you use your JCPenney Company credit card to purchase clothing with a sales price of $300 on June 1, 2014. JCPenney will increase (debit) Accounts Receivable for $300 and increase (credit) Sales Revenue for $300 (cost of goods sold entry omitted) as follows.

| June 1 | Accounts Receivable | 300 | |
| | Sales Revenue | | 300 |
| | (To record sale of merchandise) | | |

| A | = | L | + | OE |
|---|---|---|---|---|
| +300 | | | | |
| | | | | +300 Rev |

**Cash Flows**
no effect

Assuming that you owe $300 at the end of the month and JCPenney charges 1.5% per month on the balance due, the adjusting entry that JCPenney makes to record interest revenue of $4.50 ($300 × 1.5%) on June 30 is as follows.

| June 30 | Accounts Receivable | 4.50 | |
| | Interest Revenue | | 4.50 |
| | (To record interest on amount due) | | |

| A | = | L | + | OE |
|---|---|---|---|---|
| +4.50 | | | | |
| | | | | +4.50 Rev |

**Cash Flows**
no effect

Interest revenue is often substantial for many retailers.

### ANATOMY OF A FRAUD

Tasanee was the accounts receivable clerk for a large non-profit foundation that provided performance and exhibition space for the performing and visual arts. Her responsibilities included activities normally assigned to an accounts receivable clerk, such as recording revenues from various sources that included donations, facility rental fees, ticket revenue, and bar receipts. However, she was also responsible for handling all cash and checks from the time they were received until the time she deposited them, as well as preparing the bank reconciliation. Tasanee took advantage of her situation by falsifying bank deposits and bank reconciliations so that she could steal cash from the bar receipts. Since nobody else logged the donations or matched the donation receipts to pledges prior to Tasanee receiving them, she was able to offset the cash that was stolen against donations that she received but didn't record. Her crime was made easier by the fact that her boss, the company's controller, only did a very superficial review of the bank reconciliation and thus didn't notice that some numbers had been cut out from other documents and taped onto the bank reconciliation.

**Total take: $1.5 million**

### THE MISSING CONTROL
**Segregation of duties.** The foundation should not have allowed an accounts receivable clerk, whose job was to record receivables, to also handle cash, record cash, make deposits, and especially prepare the bank reconciliation.

**Independent internal verification.** The controller was supposed to perform a thorough review of the bank reconciliation. Because he did not, he was terminated from his position.

*Source:* Adapted from Wells, *Fraud Casebook* (2007), pp. 183–194.

## Valuing Accounts Receivable

**LEARNING OBJECTIVE** 3

Distinguish between the methods and bases companies use to value accounts receivable.

*Alternative Terminology*
You will sometimes see *Bad Debt Expense* called *Uncollectible Accounts Expense.*

Once companies record receivables in the accounts, the next question is: How should they report receivables in the financial statements? Companies report accounts receivable on the balance sheet as an asset. But determining the **amount** to report is sometimes difficult because some receivables will become uncollectible.

Each customer must satisfy the credit requirements of the seller before the credit sale is approved. Inevitably, though, some accounts receivable become uncollectible. For example, a customer may not be able to pay because of a decline in its sales revenue due to a downturn in the economy. Similarly, individuals may be laid off from their jobs or faced with unexpected hospital bills. Companies record credit losses as debits to **Bad Debt Expense** (or Uncollectible Accounts Expense). Such losses are a normal and necessary risk of doing business on a credit basis.

Recently, when U.S. home prices fell, home foreclosures rose and the economy in general slowed, lenders experienced huge increases in their bad debt expense. For example, during one quarter Wachovia (a large U.S. bank now owned by Wells Fargo) increased bad debt expense from $108 million to $408 million. Similarly, American Express increased its bad debt expense by 70%.

Two methods are used in accounting for uncollectible accounts: (1) the direct write-off method and (2) the allowance method. The following sections explain these methods.

### DIRECT WRITE-OFF METHOD FOR UNCOLLECTIBLE ACCOUNTS
Under the **direct write-off method**, when a company determines a particular account to be uncollectible, it charges the loss to Bad Debt Expense. Assume, for example, that Warden Co. writes off as uncollectible M. E. Doran's $200 balance on December 12. Warden's entry is:

**A** = **L** + **OE**

−200              −200 Exp

**Cash Flows**
no effect

| Dec. 12 | Bad Debt Expense | 200 | |
| |     Accounts Receivable—M. E. Doran | | 200 |
| |       (To record write-off of M. E. Doran account) | | |

Under this method, Bad Debt Expense will show only **actual losses** from uncollectibles. The company will report accounts receivable at its gross amount.

Although this method is simple, its use can reduce the usefulness of both the income statement and balance sheet. Consider the following example. Assume that in 2014, Quick Buck Computer Company decided it could increase its revenues by offering computers to college students without requiring any money down and with no credit-approval process. On campuses across the country, it distributed one million computers with a selling price of $800 each. This increased Quick Buck's revenues and receivables by $800 million. The promotion was a huge success! The 2014 balance sheet and income statement looked great. Unfortunately, during 2015, nearly 40% of the customers defaulted on their loans. This made the 2015 income statement and balance sheet look terrible. Illustration 9-2 shows the effect of these events on the financial statements if the direct write-off method is used.

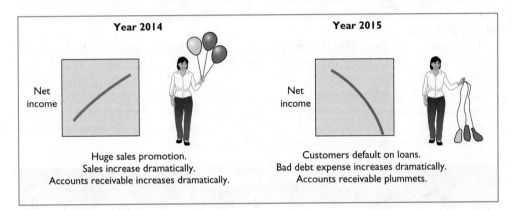

**Illustration 9-2**
Effects of direct write-off method

Under the direct write-off method, companies often record bad debt expense in a period different from the period in which they record the revenue. The method does not attempt to match bad debt expense to sales revenues in the income statement. Nor does the direct write-off method show accounts receivable in the balance sheet at the amount the company actually expects to receive. **Consequently, unless bad debt losses are insignificant, the direct write-off method is not acceptable for financial reporting purposes.**

## ALLOWANCE METHOD FOR UNCOLLECTIBLE ACCOUNTS

The **allowance method** of accounting for bad debts involves estimating uncollectible accounts at the end of each period. This provides better matching on the income statement. It also ensures that companies state receivables on the balance sheet at their cash (net) realizable value. **Cash (net) realizable value** is the net amount the company expects to receive in cash. It excludes amounts that the company estimates it will not collect. Thus, this method reduces receivables in the balance sheet by the amount of estimated uncollectible receivables.

GAAP requires the allowance method for financial reporting purposes when bad debts are material in amount. This method has three essential features:

1. Companies **estimate** uncollectible accounts receivable. They match this estimated expense **against revenues** in the same accounting period in which they record the revenues.

2. Companies debit estimated uncollectibles to Bad Debt Expense and credit them to Allowance for Doubtful Accounts through an adjusting entry at the end of each period. Allowance for Doubtful Accounts is a contra account to Accounts Receivable.

3. When companies write off a specific account, they debit actual uncollectibles to Allowance for Doubtful Accounts and credit that amount to Accounts Receivable.

**Helpful Hint** In this context, *material* means significant or important to financial statement users.

**RECORDING ESTIMATED UNCOLLECTIBLES**  To illustrate the allowance method, assume that Hampson Furniture has credit sales of $1,200,000 in 2014. Of this amount, $200,000 remains uncollected at December 31. The credit manager estimates that $12,000 of these sales will be uncollectible. The adjusting entry to record the estimated uncollectibles increases (debits) Bad Debt Expense and increases (credits) Allowance for Doubtful Accounts, as follows.

−12,000

**Cash Flows**
no effect

| Dec. 31 | Bad Debt Expense | 12,000 | |
| | Allowance for Doubtful Accounts | | 12,000 |
| | (To record estimate of uncollectible accounts) | | |

Hampson reports Bad Debt Expense in the income statement as an operating expense (usually as a selling expense). Thus, the estimated uncollectibles are matched with sales in 2014. Hampson records the expense in the same year it made the sales.

Allowance for Doubtful Accounts shows the estimated amount of claims on customers that the company expects will become uncollectible in the future. Companies use a contra account instead of a direct credit to Accounts Receivable because they do not know which customers will not pay. The credit balance in the allowance account will absorb the specific write-offs when they occur. As Illustration 9-3 shows, the company deducts the allowance account from accounts receivable in the current assets section of the balance sheet.

**Illustration 9-3**
Presentation of allowance for doubtful accounts

| HAMPSON FURNITURE | | |
|---|---|---|
| Balance Sheet (partial) | | |
| Current assets | | |
| Cash | | $ 14,800 |
| Accounts receivable | $200,000 | |
| Less: Allowance for doubtful accounts | 12,000 | 188,000 |
| Inventory | | 310,000 |
| Supplies | | 25,000 |
| Total current assets | | $537,800 |

**Helpful Hint**  Cash realizable value is sometimes referred to as *accounts receivable (net).*

The amount of $188,000 in Illustration 9-3 represents the expected **cash realizable value** of the accounts receivable at the statement date. **Companies do not close Allowance for Doubtful Accounts at the end of the fiscal year.**

**RECORDING THE WRITE-OFF OF AN UNCOLLECTIBLE ACCOUNT**  As described in the Feature Story, companies use various methods of collecting past-due accounts, such as letters, calls, and legal action. When they have exhausted all means of collecting a past-due account and collection appears impossible, the company writes off the account. In the credit card industry, for example, it is standard practice to write off accounts that are 210 days past due. To prevent premature or unauthorized write-offs, authorized management personnel should formally approve each write-off. To maintain segregation of duties, the employee authorized to write off accounts should not have daily responsibilities related to cash or receivables.

To illustrate a receivables write-off, assume that the financial vice president of Hampson Furniture authorizes a write-off of the $500 balance owed by R. A. Ware on March 1, 2015. The entry to record the write-off is:

+500
−500

**Cash Flows**
no effect

| Mar. 1 | Allowance for Doubtful Accounts | 500 | |
| | Accounts Receivable—R. A. Ware | | 500 |
| | (Write-off of R. A. Ware account) | | |

Bad Debt Expense does not increase when the write-off occurs. **Under the allowance method, companies debit every bad debt write-off to the allowance account rather than to Bad Debt Expense.** A debit to Bad Debt Expense would be incorrect because the company has already recognized the expense when it made the adjusting entry for estimated bad debts. Instead, the entry to record the write-off of an uncollectible account reduces both Accounts Receivable and Allowance for Doubtful Accounts. After posting, the general ledger accounts appear as shown in Illustration 9-4.

| Accounts Receivable | | | | Allowance for Doubtful Accounts | | | |
|---|---|---|---|---|---|---|---|
| Jan. 1 Bal. 200,000 | Mar. 1 | | 500 | Mar. 1 | 500 | Jan. 1 Bal. | 12,000 |
| Mar. 1 Bal. 199,500 | | | | | | Mar. 1 Bal. | 11,500 |

**Illustration 9-4**
General ledger balances after write-off

A write-off affects **only balance sheet accounts**—not income statement accounts. The write-off of the account reduces both Accounts Receivable and Allowance for Doubtful Accounts. Cash realizable value in the balance sheet, therefore, remains the same, as Illustration 9-5 shows.

|  | Before Write-Off | After Write-Off |
|---|---|---|
| Accounts receivable | $ 200,000 | $ 199,500 |
| Allowance for doubtful accounts | 12,000 | 11,500 |
| **Cash realizable value** | **$188,000** | **$188,000** |

**Illustration 9-5**
Cash realizable value comparison

**RECOVERY OF AN UNCOLLECTIBLE ACCOUNT** Occasionally, a company collects from a customer after it has written off the account as uncollectible. The company makes two entries to record the recovery of a bad debt: (1) It reverses the entry made in writing off the account. This reinstates the customer's account. (2) It journalizes the collection in the usual manner.

To illustrate, assume that on July 1, R. A. Ware pays the $500 amount that Hampson had written off on March 1. Hampson makes these entries:

(1)

| July 1 | Accounts Receivable—R. A. Ware | 500 | |
| | Allowance for Doubtful Accounts | | 500 |
| | (To reverse write-off of R. A. Ware account) | | |

A = L + OE
+500
−500

Cash Flows
no effect

(2)

| July 1 | Cash | 500 | |
| | Accounts Receivable—R. A. Ware | | 500 |
| | (To record collection from R. A. Ware) | | |

A = L + OE
+500
−500

Cash Flows
+500

Note that the recovery of a bad debt, like the write-off of a bad debt, affects **only balance sheet accounts**. The net effect of the two entries above is a debit to Cash and a credit to Allowance for Doubtful Accounts for $500. Accounts Receivable and Allowance for Doubtful Accounts both increase in entry (1) for two reasons. First, the company made an error in judgment when it wrote off the account receivable. Second, after R. A. Ware did pay, Accounts Receivable in the general ledger and Ware's account in the subsidiary ledger should show the collection for possible future credit purposes.

**ESTIMATING THE ALLOWANCE** For Hampson Furniture in Illustration 9-3, the amount of the expected uncollectibles was given. However, in "real life," companies must estimate that amount when they use the allowance method. Two bases are used to determine this amount: **(1) percentage of sales** and **(2) percentage of receivables**. Both bases are generally accepted. The choice is a management decision. It depends on the relative emphasis that management wishes to give to expenses and revenues on the one hand or to cash realizable value of the accounts receivable on the other. The choice is whether to emphasize income statement or balance sheet relationships. Illustration 9-6 compares the two bases.

**Illustration 9-6**
Comparison of bases for estimating uncollectibles

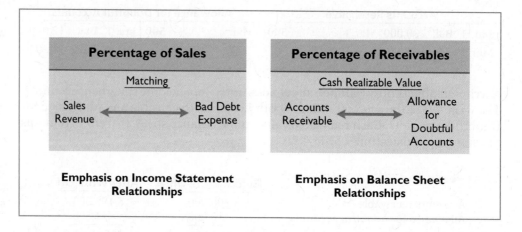

The percentage-of-sales basis results in a better matching of expenses with revenues—an income statement viewpoint. The percentage-of-receivables basis produces the better estimate of cash realizable value—a balance sheet viewpoint. Under both bases, the company must determine its past experience with bad debt losses.

**Percentage-of-Sales.** In the **percentage-of-sales basis**, management estimates what percentage of credit sales will be uncollectible. This percentage is based on past experience and anticipated credit policy.

The company applies this percentage to either total credit sales or net credit sales of the current year. To illustrate, assume that Gonzalez Company elects to use the percentage-of-sales basis. It concludes that 1% of net credit sales will become uncollectible. If net credit sales for 2014 are $800,000, the estimated bad debt expense is $8,000 (1% × $800,000). The adjusting entry is:

| Dec. 31 | Bad Debt Expense | 8,000 | |
| | Allowance for Doubtful Accounts | | 8,000 |
| | (To record estimated bad debts for year) | | |

After the adjusting entry is posted, assuming the allowance account already has a credit balance of $1,723, the accounts of Gonzalez Company will show the following.

**Illustration 9-7**
Bad debt accounts after posting

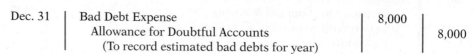

| Bad Debt Expense | | Allowance for Doubtful Accounts | |
|---|---|---|---|
| Dec. 31 Adj. **8,000** | | | Jan. 1 Bal. 1,723 |
| | | | Dec. 31 Adj. **8,000** |
| | | | Dec. 31 Bal. 9,723 |

**This basis of estimating uncollectibles emphasizes the matching of expenses with revenues.** As a result, Bad Debt Expense will show a direct percentage relationship to the sales base on which it is computed. **When the**

company makes the adjusting entry, it disregards the existing balance in Allowance for Doubtful Accounts. The adjusted balance in this account should be a reasonable approximation of the realizable value of the receivables. If actual write-offs differ significantly from the amount estimated, the company should modify the percentage for future years.

**Percentage-of-Receivables.** Under the **percentage-of-receivables basis**, management estimates what percentage of receivables will result in losses from uncollectible accounts. The company prepares an **aging schedule**, in which it classifies customer balances by the length of time they have been unpaid. Because of its emphasis on time, the analysis is often called **aging the accounts receivable**. In the Feature Story, Whitehall-Robins prepared an aging report daily.

After the company arranges the accounts by age, it determines the expected bad debt losses. It applies percentages based on past experience to the totals in each category. The longer a receivable is past due, the less likely it is to be collected. Thus, the estimated percentage of uncollectible debts increases as the number of days past due increases. Illustration 9-8 shows an aging schedule for Dart Company. Note that the estimated percentage uncollectible increases from 2% to 40% as the number of days past due increases.

**Helpful Hint** Where appropriate, companies may use only a single percentage rate.

**Illustration 9-8**
Aging schedule

| | Worksheet.xls | | | | | | |
|---|---|---|---|---|---|---|---|
| | Home  Insert  Page Layout  Formulas  Data  Review  View | | | | | | |
| | P18 | | fx | | | | |
| | A | B | C | D | E | F | G |
| 1 | | | | **Number of Days Past Due** | | | |
| 2 | | | **Not** | | | | |
| 3 | **Customer** | **Total** | **Yet Due** | **1–30** | **31–60** | **61–90** | **Over 90** |
| 4 | T. E. Adert | $  600 | | $  300 | | $  200 | $  100 |
| 5 | R. C. Bortz | 300 | $  300 | | | | |
| 6 | B. A. Carl | 450 | | 200 | $  250 | | |
| 7 | O. L. Diker | 700 | 500 | | | 200 | |
| 8 | T. O. Ebbet | 600 | | | 300 | | 300 |
| 9 | Others | 36,950 | 26,200 | 5,200 | 2,450 | 1,600 | 1,500 |
| 10 | | $39,600 | $27,000 | $5,700 | $3,000 | $2,000 | $1,900 |
| 11 | Estimated Percentage Uncollectible | | 2% | 4% | 10% | 20% | 40% |
| 12 | Total Estimated Bad Debts | $ 2,228 | $  540 | $  228 | $  300 | $  400 | $  760 |
| 13 | | | | | | | |

**Helpful Hint** The older categories have higher percentages because the longer an account is past due, the less likely it is to be collected.

Total estimated bad debts for Dart Company ($2,228) represent the amount of existing customer claims the company expects will become uncollectible in the future. This amount represents the **required balance** in Allowance for Doubtful Accounts at the balance sheet date. **The amount of the bad debt adjusting entry is the difference between the required balance and the existing balance in the allowance account.** If the trial balance shows Allowance for Doubtful Accounts with a credit balance of $528, the company will make an adjusting entry for $1,700 ($2,228 − $528), as shown here.

| | | | |
|---|---|---|---|
| Dec. 31 | Bad Debt Expense | 1,700 | |
| | Allowance for Doubtful Accounts | | 1,700 |
| | (To adjust allowance account to total estimated uncollectibles) | | |

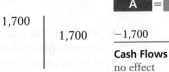

A = L + OE

−1,700 Exp

−1,700

**Cash Flows**
no effect

After Dart posts its adjusting entry, its accounts will appear as follows.

**Illustration 9-9**
Bad debt accounts after posting

| Bad Debt Expense | | Allowance for Doubtful Accounts | |
|---|---|---|---|
| Dec. 31 Adj.   **1,700** | | Bal.                          528 | |
| | | Dec. 31 Adj.   **1,700** | |
| | | Bal.                       **2,228** | |

| Allowance for Doubtful Accounts | |
|---|---|
| Dec. 31 Unadj. | Dec. 31 Adj.   2,728 |
| Bal.            500 | |
| | Dec. 31 |
| | Bal.            2,228 |

Occasionally, the allowance account will have a **debit balance** prior to adjustment. This occurs when write-offs during the year have exceeded previous provisions for bad debts. In such a case, the company **adds the debit balance to the required balance** when it makes the adjusting entry. Thus, if there had been a $500 debit balance in the allowance account before adjustment, the adjusting entry would have been for $2,728 ($2,228 + $500) to arrive at a credit balance of $2,228 (see T-account in margin). The percentage-of-receivables basis will normally result in the better approximation of cash realizable value.

---

> **DO IT!**

## Uncollectible Accounts Receivable

### Action Plan

✔ Report receivables at their cash (net) realizable value.

✔ Estimate the amount the company does not expect to collect.

✔ Consider the existing balance in the allowance account when using the percentage-of-receivables basis.

Brule Co. has been in business five years. The unadjusted trial balance at the end of the current year shows:

| | |
|---|---|
| Accounts Receivable | $30,000 Dr. |
| Sales Revenue | $180,000 Cr. |
| Allowance for Doubtful Accounts | $2,000 Dr. |

Brule estimates bad debts to be 10% of receivables. Prepare the entry necessary to adjust Allowance for Doubtful Accounts.

### Solution

The following entry should be made to bring the balance in Allowance for Doubtful Accounts up to a normal credit balance of $3,000 (10% × $30,000):

| | | |
|---|---|---|
| Bad Debt Expense [(10% × $30,000) + $2,000] | 5,000 | |
|     Allowance for Doubtful Accounts | | 5,000 |
|     (To record estimate of uncollectible accounts) | | |

Related exercise material: **BE9-3, BE9-4, BE9-5, BE9-6, BE9-7, E9-3, E9-4, E9-5, E9-6, and DO IT! 9-1.**

✔ The Navigator

---

## Disposing of Accounts Receivable

**LEARNING OBJECTIVE   4**

Describe the entries to record the disposition of accounts receivable.

In the normal course of events, companies collect accounts receivable in cash and remove the receivables from the books. However, as credit sales and receivables have grown in significance, the "normal course of events" has changed. Companies now frequently sell their receivables to another company for cash, thereby shortening the cash-to-cash operating cycle.

Companies sell receivables for two major reasons. First, **they may be the only reasonable source of cash**. When money is tight, companies may not be able to borrow money in the usual credit markets. Or if money is available, the cost of borrowing may be prohibitive.

A second reason for selling receivables is that **billing and collection are often time-consuming and costly**. It is often easier for a retailer to sell the receivables to another party with expertise in billing and collection matters. Credit card companies such as MasterCard, Visa, and Discover specialize in billing and collecting accounts receivable.

## SALE OF RECEIVABLES

A common sale of receivables is a sale to a factor. A **factor** is a finance company or bank that buys receivables from businesses and then collects the payments directly from the customers. Factoring is a multibillion dollar business.

Factoring arrangements vary widely. Typically, the factor charges a commission to the company that is selling the receivables. This fee ranges from 1–3% of the amount of receivables purchased. To illustrate, assume that Hendredon Furniture factors $600,000 of receivables to Federal Factors. Federal Factors assesses a service charge of 2% of the amount of receivables sold. The journal entry to record the sale by Hendredon Furniture on April 2, 2014, is as follows.

| Apr. 2 | Cash | 588,000 | |
| | Service Charge Expense (2% × $600,000) | 12,000 | |
| | Accounts Receivable | | 600,000 |
| | (To record the sale of accounts receivable) | | |

A = L + OE
+588,000
−12,000 Exp
−600,000

**Cash Flows**
+588,000

If the company often sells its receivables, it records the service charge expense (such as that incurred by Hendredon) as a selling expense. If the company infrequently sells receivables, it may report this amount in the "Other expenses and losses" section of the income statement.

## CREDIT CARD SALES

Over one billion credit cards are in use in the United States—more than three credit cards for every man, woman, and child in this country. Visa, MasterCard, and American Express are the national credit cards that most individuals use. Three parties are involved when national credit cards are used in retail sales: (1) the credit card issuer, who is independent of the retailer; (2) the retailer; and (3) the customer. A retailer's acceptance of a national credit card is another form of selling (factoring) the receivable.

Illustration 9-10 shows the major advantages of national credit cards to the retailer. In exchange for these advantages, the retailer pays the credit card issuer a fee of 2–6% of the invoice price for its services.

**Illustration 9-10**
Advantages of credit cards to the retailer

Issuer does credit investigation of customer

Issuer maintains customer accounts

Credit card issuer    Customer    Retailer

Issuer undertakes collection process and absorbs any losses

Retailer receives cash more quickly from credit card issuer

**ACCOUNTING FOR CREDIT CARD SALES** The retailer generally considers sales from the use of national credit card sales as **cash sales**. The retailer must pay to the bank that issues the card a fee for processing the transactions. The retailer records the credit card slips in a similar manner as checks deposited from a cash sale.

To illustrate, Anita Ferreri purchases $1,000 of compact discs for her restaurant from Karen Kerr Music Co., using her Visa First Bank Card. First Bank charges a service fee of 3%. The entry to record this transaction by Karen Kerr Music on March 22, 2014, is as follows.

| A | = | L | + | OE |
|---|---|---|---|---|
| +970 | | | | |
| | | | | −30 Exp |
| | | | | +1,000 Rev |

**Cash Flows**
+970

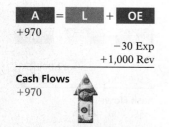

| Mar. 22 | Cash | 970 | |
| | Service Charge Expense | 30 | |
| |     Sales Revenue | | 1,000 |
| |       (To record Visa credit card sales) | | |

© Michael Braun/iStockphoto

## ACCOUNTING ACROSS THE ORGANIZATION

### How Does a Credit Card Work?

Most of you know how to use a credit card, but do you know what happens in the transaction and how the transaction is processed? Suppose that you use a Visa card to purchase some new ties at Nordstrom. The salesperson swipes your card, which allows the information on the magnetic strip on the back of the card to be read. The salesperson then enters in the amount of the purchase. The machine contacts the Visa computer, which routes the call back to the bank that issued your Visa card. The issuing bank verifies that the account exists, that the card is not stolen, and that you have not exceeded your credit limit. At this point, the slip is printed, which you sign.

Visa acts as the clearing agent for the transaction. It transfers funds from the issuing bank to Nordstrom's bank account. Generally this transfer of funds, from sale to the receipt of funds in the merchant's account, takes two to three days.

In the meantime, Visa puts a pending charge on your account for the amount of the tie purchase; that amount counts immediately against your available credit limit. At the end of the billing period, Visa sends you an invoice (your credit card bill) which shows the various charges you made, and the amounts that Visa expended on your behalf, for the month. You then must "pay the piper" for your stylish new ties.

 Assume that Nordstrom prepares a bank reconciliation at the end of each month. If some credit card sales have not been processed by the bank, how should Nordstrom treat these transactions on its bank reconciliation? (See page 467.)

## > DO IT!

**Disposition of Accounts Receivable**

Mehl Wholesalers Co. has been expanding faster than it can raise capital. According to its local banker, the company has reached its debt ceiling. Mehl's suppliers (creditors) are demanding payment within 30 days of the invoice date for goods acquired, but Mehl's customers are slow in paying (60–90 days). As a result, Mehl has a cash flow problem.

Mehl needs $120,000 in cash to safely cover next Friday's payroll. Its balance of outstanding accounts receivable totals $750,000. To alleviate this cash crunch, Mehl sells $125,000 of its receivables on September 7, 2014. Record the entry that Mehl would make when it raises the needed cash. (Assume a 1% service charge.)

## Action Plan

✔ To speed up the collection of cash, sell receivables to a factor.

✔ Calculate service charge expense as a percentage of the factored receivables.

### Solution

If Mehl Wholesalers factors $125,000 of its accounts receivable at a 1% service charge, it would make the following entry.

| | | | |
|---|---|---|---|
| Sept. 7 | Cash | 123,750 | |
| | Service Charge Expense (1% × $125,000) | 1,250 | |
| |    Accounts Receivable | | 125,000 |
| |    (To record sale of receivables to factor) | | |

Related exercise material: **BE9-8, E9-7, E9-8, E9-9, and DO IT! 9-2.**

✔ The Navigator

## Notes Receivable

Companies may also grant credit in exchange for a formal credit instrument known as a promissory note. A **promissory note** is a written promise to pay a specified amount of money on demand or at a definite time. Promissory notes may be used (1) when individuals and companies lend or borrow money, (2) when the amount of the transaction and the credit period exceed normal limits, or (3) in settlement of accounts receivable.

In a promissory note, the party making the promise to pay is called the **maker**. The party to whom payment is to be made is called the **payee**. The note may specifically identify the payee by name or may designate the payee simply as the bearer of the note.

In the note shown in Illustration 9-11, Calhoun Company is the maker and Wilma Company is the payee. To Wilma Company, the promissory note is a note receivable. To Calhoun Company, it is a note payable.

**LEARNING OBJECTIVE** 5

Compute the maturity date of and interest on notes receivable.

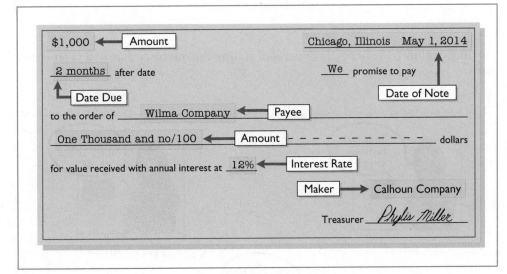

**Illustration 9-11**
Promissory note

**Helpful Hint** Who are the two key parties to a note, and what entry does each party make when the note is issued?

Answer:
1. The maker, Calhoun Company, debits Cash and credits Notes Payable.
2. The payee, Wilma Company, debits Notes Receivable and credits Cash.

Notes receivable give the holder a stronger legal claim to assets than do accounts receivable. Like accounts receivable, notes receivable can be readily sold to another party. Promissory notes are negotiable instruments (as are checks), which means that they can be transferred to another party by endorsement.

Companies frequently accept notes receivable from customers who need to extend the payment of an outstanding account receivable. They often require such notes from high-risk customers. In some industries (such as the pleasure and sport boat industry), all credit sales are supported by notes. The majority of notes, however, originate from loans.

The basic issues in accounting for notes receivable are the same as those for accounts receivable:

1. **Recognizing** notes receivable.

2. **Valuing** notes receivable.

3. **Disposing** of notes receivable.

On the following pages, we will look at these issues. Before we do, we need to consider two issues that do not apply to accounts receivable: maturity date and computing interest.

## Determining the Maturity Date

When the life of a note is expressed in terms of months, you find the date when it matures by counting the months from the date of issue. For example, the maturity date of a three-month note dated May 1 is August 1. A note drawn on the last day of a month matures on the last day of a subsequent month. That is, a July 31 note due in two months matures on September 30.

When the due date is stated in terms of days, you need to count the exact number of days to determine the maturity date. In counting, **omit the date the note is issued but include the due date**. For example, the maturity date of a 60-day note dated July 17 is September 15, computed as follows.

**Illustration 9-12**
Computation of maturity date

| Term of note | | 60 days |
|---|---|---|
| July (31 − 17) | 14 | |
| August | 31 | 45 |
| **Maturity date: September** | | **15** |

Illustration 9-13 shows three ways of stating the maturity date of a promissory note.

**Illustration 9-13**
Maturity date of different notes

On demand

On a stated date

At the end of a stated period of time

## Computing Interest

Illustration 9-14 gives the basic formula for computing interest on an interest-bearing note.

| Face Value of Note | × | Annual Interest Rate | × | Time in Terms of One Year | = | Interest |
|---|---|---|---|---|---|---|

**Illustration 9-14**
Formula for computing interest

The interest rate specified in a note is an **annual** rate of interest. The time factor in the computation in Illustration 9-14 expresses the fraction of a year that the note is outstanding. When the maturity date is stated in days, the time factor is often the number of days divided by 360. When counting days, omit the date that the note is issued but include the due date. When the due date is stated in months, the time factor is the number of months divided by 12. Illustration 9-15 shows computation of interest for various time periods.

**Helpful Hint** The interest rate specified is the *annual* rate.

| Terms of Note | Interest Computation |
|---|---|
| | Face × Rate × Time = Interest |
| $   730, 12%, 120 days | $   730 × 12% × 120/360 = $  29.20 |
| $1,000,  9%, 6 months | $1,000 × 9% × 6/12 = $  45.00 |
| $2,000,  6%, 1 year | $2,000 × 6% × 1/1 = $120.00 |

**Illustration 9-15**
Computation of interest

There are different ways to calculate interest. For example, the computation in Illustration 9-15 assumes 360 days for the length of the year. Most financial instruments use 365 days to compute interest. *For homework problems, assume 360 days to simplify computations.*

## Recognizing Notes Receivable

To illustrate the basic entry for notes receivable, we will use Calhoun Company's $1,000, two-month, 12% promissory note dated May 1. Assuming that Calhoun Company wrote the note to settle an open account, Wilma Company makes the following entry for the receipt of the note.

**LEARNING OBJECTIVE 6**
Explain how companies recognize notes receivable.

| May 1 | Notes Receivable | 1,000 | |
| | Accounts Receivable—Calhoun Company | | 1,000 |
| | (To record acceptance of Calhoun | | |
| | Company note) | | |

A = L + OE
+1,000
−1,000

**Cash Flows**
no effect

The company records the note receivable at its **face value**, the amount shown on the face of the note. No interest revenue is reported when the note is accepted, because the revenue recognition principle does not recognize revenue until the performance obligation is satisfied. Interest is earned (accrued) as time passes.

If a company lends money using a note, the entry is a debit to Notes Receivable and a credit to Cash in the amount of the loan.

## Valuing Notes Receivable

Valuing short-term notes receivable is the same as valuing accounts receivable. Like accounts receivable, companies report short-term notes receivable at their **cash (net) realizable value**. The notes receivable allowance account is Allowance for Doubtful Accounts. The estimations involved in determining cash realizable value and in recording bad debt expense and the related allowance are done similarly to accounts receivable.

**LEARNING OBJECTIVE 7**
Describe how companies value notes receivable.

# INTERNATIONAL INSIGHT

### Can Fair Value Be Unfair?

The FASB and the International Accounting Standards Board (IASB) are considering proposals for how to account for financial instruments. The FASB has proposed that loans and receivables be accounted for at their fair value (the amount they could currently be sold for), as are most investments. The FASB believes that this would provide a more accurate view of a company's financial position. It might be especially useful as an early warning when a bank is in trouble because of poor-quality loans. But, banks argue that fair values are difficult to estimate accurately. They are also concerned that volatile fair values could cause large swings in a bank's reported net income.

*Source:* David Reilly, "Banks Face a Mark-to-Market Challenge," *Wall Street Journal Online* (March 15, 2010).

**?** What are the arguments in favor of and against fair value accounting for loans and receivables? (See page 467.)

© Andrzej Tokarski/iStockphoto

## Disposing of Notes Receivable

Notes may be held to their maturity date, at which time the face value plus accrued interest is due. In some situations, the maker of the note defaults, and the payee must make an appropriate adjustment. In other situations, similar to accounts receivable, the holder of the note speeds up the conversion to cash by selling the receivables (as described later in this chapter).

### HONOR OF NOTES RECEIVABLE

A note is **honored** when its maker pays in full at its maturity date. For each interest-bearing note, the **amount due at maturity** is the face value of the note plus interest for the length of time specified on the note.

To illustrate, assume that Wolder Co. lends Higley Co. $10,000 on June 1, accepting a five-month, 9% interest note. In this situation, interest is $375 ($10,000 $\times$ 9% $\times \frac{5}{12}$). The amount due, **the maturity value**, is $10,375 ($10,000 + $375). To obtain payment, Wolder (the payee) must present the note either to Higley Co. (the maker) or to the maker's agent, such as a bank. If Wolder presents the note to Higley Co. on November 1, the maturity date, Wolder's entry to record the collection is:

| A | = | L | + | OE |
|---|---|---|---|---|
| +10,375 | | | | |
| −10,000 | | | | |
| | | | | +375 Rev |

**Cash Flows**
+10,375

| Nov. 1 | Cash | 10,375 | |
|---|---|---|---|
| | Notes Receivable | | 10,000 |
| | Interest Revenue ($10,000 $\times$ 9% $\times \frac{5}{12}$) | | 375 |
| | (To record collection of Higley note and interest) | | |

### ACCRUAL OF INTEREST RECEIVABLE

Suppose instead that Wolder Co. prepares financial statements as of September 30. The timeline in Illustration 9-16 presents this situation.

**Illustration 9-16**
Timeline of interest earned

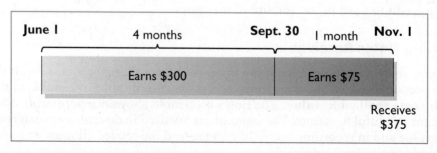

| June 1 | 4 months | Sept. 30 | 1 month | Nov. 1 |
|---|---|---|---|---|
| | Earns $300 | | Earns $75 | |
| | | | | Receives $375 |

To reflect interest earned but not yet received, Wolder must accrue interest on September 30. In this case, the adjusting entry by Wolder is for four months of interest, or $300, as shown below.

| Sept. 30 | Interest Receivable ($10,000 × 9% × $\frac{4}{12}$) | 300 | |
| |    Interest Revenue | | 300 |
| |    (To accrue 4 months' interest on | | |
| |    Higley note) | | |

A = L + OE
+300
+300 Rev

**Cash Flows**
no effect

At the note's maturity on November 1, Wolder receives $10,375. This amount represents repayment of the $10,000 note as well as five months of interest, or $375, as shown below. The $375 is comprised of the $300 Interest Receivable accrued on September 30 plus $75 earned during October. Wolder's entry to record the honoring of the Higley note on November 1 is:

| Nov. 1 | Cash [$10,000 + (10,000 × 9% × $\frac{5}{12}$)] | 10,375 | |
| |    Notes Receivable | | 10,000 |
| |    Interest Receivable | | 300 |
| |    Interest Revenue (10,000 × 9% × $\frac{1}{12}$)] | | 75 |
| |    (To record collection of Higley note | | |
| |    and interest) | | |

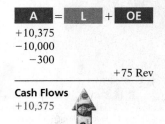

A = L + OE
+10,375
−10,000
−300
+75 Rev

**Cash Flows**
+10,375

In this case, Wolder credits Interest Receivable because the receivable was established in the adjusting entry on September 30.

## DISHONOR OF NOTES RECEIVABLE

A **dishonored (defaulted) note** is a note that is not paid in full at maturity. A dishonored note receivable is no longer negotiable. However, the payee still has a claim against the maker of the note for both the note and the interest. Therefore the note holder usually transfers the Notes Receivable account to an Account Receivable.

To illustrate, assume that Higley Co. on November 1 indicates that it cannot pay at the present time. The entry to record the dishonor of the note depends on whether Wolder Co. expects eventual collection. If it does expect eventual collection, Wolder Co. debits the amount due (face value and interest) on the note to Accounts Receivable. It would make the following entry at the time the note is dishonored (assuming no previous accrual of interest).

| Nov. 1 | Accounts Receivable—Higley | 10,375 | |
| |    Notes Receivable | | 10,000 |
| |    Interest Revenue | | 375 |
| |    (To record the dishonor of Higley note) | | |

A = L + OE
+10,375
−10,000
+375 Rev

**Cash Flows**
no effect

If instead, on November 1, there is no hope of collection, the note holder would write off the face value of the note by debiting Allowance for Doubtful Accounts. No interest revenue would be recorded because collection will not occur.

## SALE OF NOTES RECEIVABLE

The accounting for the sale of notes receivable is recorded similarly to the sale of accounts receivable. The accounting entries for the sale of notes receivable are left for a more advanced course.

© Andy Dean/iStockphoto

## ACCOUNTING ACROSS THE ORGANIZATION

### Bad Information Can Lead to Bad Loans

Many factors have contributed to the recent credit crisis. One significant factor that resulted in many bad loans was a failure by lenders to investigate loan customers sufficiently. For example, Countrywide Financial Corporation wrote many loans under its "Fast and Easy" loan program. That program allowed borrowers to provide little or no documentation for their income or their assets. Other lenders had similar programs, which earned the nickname "liars' loans." One study found that in these situations, 60% of applicants overstated their incomes by more than 50% in order to qualify for a loan. Critics of the banking industry say that because loan officers were compensated for loan volume and because banks were selling the loans to investors rather than holding them, the lenders had little incentive to investigate the borrowers' creditworthiness.

*Source:* Glenn R. Simpson and James R. Hagerty, "Countrywide Loss Focuses Attention on Underwriting," *Wall Street Journal* (April 30, 2008), p. B1; and Michael Corkery, "Fraud Seen as Driver in Wave of Foreclosures," *Wall Street Journal* (December 21, 2007), p. A1.

**?** What steps should the banks have taken to ensure the accuracy of financial information provided on loan applications? (See page 467.)

---

## > DO IT!

### Notes Receivable

**Action Plan**

✔ Count the exact number of days to determine the maturity date. Omit the date the note is issued, but include the due date.

✔ Determine whether interest was accrued.

✔ Compute the accrued interest.

✔ Prepare the entry for payment of the note and interest.

✔ The entry to record interest at maturity in this solution assumes no interest has been previously accrued on this note.

Gambit Stores accepts from Leonard Co. a $3,400, 90-day, 6% note dated May 10 in settlement of Leonard's overdue account. (a) What is the maturity date of the note? (b) What entry does Gambit make at the maturity date, assuming Leonard pays the note and interest in full at that time?

#### Solution

**(a)** The maturity date is August 8, computed as follows.

| Term of note: | | 90 days |
|---|---|---|
| May (31−10) | 21 | |
| June | 30 | |
| July | 31 | 82 |
| Maturity date: August | | 8 |

**(b)** The interest payable at the maturity date is $51, computed as follows.

$$\text{Face} \times \text{Rate} \times \text{Time} = \text{Interest}$$
$$\$3,400 \times 6\% \times 90/360 = \$51$$

The entry recorded by Gambit Stores at the maturity date is:

| | | |
|---|---|---|
| Cash | 3,451 | |
|     Notes Receivable | | 3,400 |
|     Interest Revenue | | 51 |
|       (To record collection of Leonard note) | | |

Related exercise material: **BE9-9, BE9-10, BE9-11, E9-10, E9-11, E9-12, E9-13, and DO IT! 9-3.**

✔ The Navigator

## Statement Presentation and Analysis

### Presentation

Companies should identify in the balance sheet or in the notes to the financial statements each of the major types of receivables. Short-term receivables appear in the current assets section of the balance sheet. Short-term investments appear before short-term receivables because these investments are more liquid (nearer to cash). Companies report both the gross amount of receivables and the allowance for doubtful accounts.

In a multiple-step income statement, companies report bad debt expense and service charge expense as selling expenses in the operating expenses section. Interest revenue appears under "Other revenues and gains" in the nonoperating activities section of the income statement.

> **LEARNING OBJECTIVE  9**
>
> **Explain the statement presentation and analysis of receivables.**

### Analysis

Investors and corporate managers compute financial ratios to evaluate the liquidity of a company's accounts receivable. They use the **accounts receivable turnover** to assess the liquidity of the receivables. This ratio measures the number of times, on average, the company collects accounts receivable during the period. It is computed by dividing net credit sales (net sales less cash sales) by the average net accounts receivable during the year. Unless seasonal factors are significant, average net accounts receivable outstanding can be computed from the beginning and ending balances of net accounts receivable.

For example, in 2011 Cisco Systems had net sales of $34,526 million for the year. It had a beginning accounts receivable (net) balance of $4,929 million and an ending accounts receivable (net) balance of $4,698 million. Assuming that Cisco's sales were all on credit, its accounts receivable turnover is computed as follows.

| Net Credit Sales | ÷ | Average Net Accounts Receivable | = | Accounts Receivable Turnover |
|---|---|---|---|---|
| $34,526 | ÷ | $\dfrac{\$4{,}929 + \$4{,}698}{2}$ | = | 7.2 times |

**Illustration 9-17**
Accounts receivable turnover and computation

The result indicates an accounts receivable turnover of 7.2 times per year. The higher the turnover, the more liquid the company's receivables.

A variant of the accounts receivable turnover that makes the liquidity even more evident is its conversion into an **average collection period** in terms of days. This is done by dividing the accounts receivable turnover into 365 days. For example, Cisco's turnover of 7.2 times is divided into 365 days, as shown in Illustration 9-18, to obtain approximately 51 days. This means that it takes Cisco 51 days to collect its accounts receivable.

| Days in Year | ÷ | Accounts Receivable Turnover | = | Average Collection Period in Days |
|---|---|---|---|---|
| 365 days | ÷ | 7.2 times | = | 51 days |

**Illustration 9-18**
Average collection period for receivables formula and computation

Companies frequently use the average collection period to assess the effectiveness of a company's credit and collection policies. The general rule is that the collection period should not greatly exceed the credit term period (that is, the time allowed for payment).

> ## DO IT!

## Analysis of Receivables

In 2014, Phil Mickelson Company has net credit sales of $923,795 for the year. It had a beginning accounts receivable (net) balance of $38,275 and an ending accounts receivable (net) balance of $35,988. Compute Phil Mickelson Company's (a) accounts receivable turnover and (b) average collection period in days.

### Solution

**Action Plan**

✔ Review the formula to compute the accounts receivable turnover.

✔ Make sure that both the beginning and ending accounts receivable balances are considered in the computation.

✔ Review the formula to compute the average collection period in days.

| | | | | | | |
|---|---|---|---|---|---|---|
| **(a)** | Net credit sales | ÷ | Average net accounts receivable | = | Accounts receivable turnover | |
| | $923,795 | ÷ | $\dfrac{\$38,275 + \$35,988}{2}$ | = | 24.9 times | |
| **(b)** | Days in year | ÷ | Accounts receivable turnover | = | Average collection period in days | |
| | 365 | ÷ | 24.9 times | = | 14.7 days | |

Related exercise material: **BE9-12, E9-14, and DO IT! 9-4.**

✔ The Navigator

> ## Comprehensive DO IT!

The following selected transactions relate to Dylan Company.

| | | |
|---|---|---|
| Mar. | 1 | Sold $20,000 of merchandise to Potter Company, terms 2/10, n/30. |
| | 11 | Received payment in full from Potter Company for balance due on existing accounts receivable. |
| | 12 | Accepted Juno Company's $20,000, 6-month, 12% note for balance due. |
| | 13 | Made Dylan Company credit card sales for $13,200. |
| | 15 | Made Visa credit card sales totaling $6,700. A 3% service fee is charged by Visa. |
| Apr. | 11 | Sold accounts receivable of $8,000 to Harcot Factor. Harcot Factor assesses a service charge of 2% of the amount of receivables sold. |
| | 13 | Received collections of $8,200 on Dylan Company credit card sales and added finance charges of 1.5% to the remaining balances. |
| May | 10 | Wrote off as uncollectible $16,000 of accounts receivable. Dylan uses the percentage-of-sales basis to estimate bad debts. |
| June | 30 | Credit sales recorded during the first 6 months total $2,000,000. The bad debt percentage is 1% of credit sales. At June 30, the balance in the allowance account is $3,500 before adjustment. |
| July | 16 | One of the accounts receivable written off in May was from J. Simon, who pays the amount due, $4,000, in full. |

### Instructions
Prepare the journal entries for the transactions.

### Solution to Comprehensive DO IT!

**Action Plan**

✔ Generally, record accounts receivable at invoice price.

✔ Recognize that sales returns and allowances and cash discounts reduce the amount received on accounts receivable.

| | | | | |
|---|---|---|---|---|
| Mar. | 1 | Accounts Receivable—Potter | 20,000 | |
| | | Sales Revenue | | 20,000 |
| | | (To record sales on account) | | |
| | 11 | Cash | 19,600 | |
| | | Sales Discounts (2% × $20,000) | 400 | |
| | | Accounts Receivable—Potter | | 20,000 |
| | | (To record collection of accounts receivable) | | |

**Action Plan (Contd.)**

✔ Record service charge expense on the seller's books when accounts receivable are sold.

✔ Prepare an adjusting entry for bad debt expense.

✔ Ignore any balance in the allowance account under the percentage-of-sales basis. Recognize the balance in the allowance account under the percentage-of-receivables basis.

✔ Record write-offs of accounts receivable only in balance sheet accounts.

| | | | | |
|---|---|---|---:|---:|
| | 12 | Notes Receivable | 20,000 | |
| | |     Accounts Receivable—Juno | | 20,000 |
| | |     (To record acceptance of Juno Company note) | | |
| | 13 | Accounts Receivable | 13,200 | |
| | |     Sales Revenue | | 13,200 |
| | |     (To record company credit card sales) | | |
| | 15 | Cash | 6,499 | |
| | | Service Charge Expense (3% × $6,700) | 201 | |
| | |     Sales Revenue | | 6,700 |
| | |     (To record credit card sales) | | |
| Apr. | 11 | Cash | 7,840 | |
| | | Service Charge Expense (2% × $8,000) | 160 | |
| | |     Accounts Receivable | | 8,000 |
| | |     (To record sale of receivables to factor) | | |
| | 13 | Cash | 8,200 | |
| | |     Accounts Receivable | | 8,200 |
| | |     (To record collection of accounts receivable) | | |
| | | Accounts Receivable [($13,200 − $8,200) × 1.5%] | 75 | |
| | |     Interest Revenue | | 75 |
| | |     (To record interest on amount due) | | |
| May | 10 | Allowance for Doubtful Accounts | 16,000 | |
| | |     Accounts Receivable | | 16,000 |
| | |     (To record write-off of accounts receivable) | | |
| June | 30 | Bad Debt Expense ($2,000,000 × 1%) | 20,000 | |
| | |     Allowance for Doubtful Accounts | | 20,000 |
| | |     (To record estimate of uncollectible accounts) | | |
| July | 16 | Accounts Receivable—J. Simon | 4,000 | |
| | |     Allowance for Doubtful Accounts | | 4,000 |
| | |     (To reverse write-off of accounts receivable) | | |
| | | Cash | 4,000 | |
| | |     Accounts Receivable—J. Simon | | 4,000 |
| | |     (To record collection of accounts receivable) | | |

✔ The Navigator

## SUMMARY OF LEARNING OBJECTIVES

✔ The Navigator

**1 Identify the different types of receivables.** Receivables are frequently classified as (1) accounts, (2) notes, and (3) other. Accounts receivable are amounts customers owe on account. Notes receivable are claims for which lenders issue formal instruments of credit as proof of the debt. Other receivables include nontrade receivables such as interest receivable, loans to company officers, advances to employees, and income taxes refundable.

**2 Explain how companies recognize accounts receivable.** Companies record accounts receivable when they provide a service on account or at the point of sale of merchandise on account. Accounts receivable are reduced by sales returns and allowances. Cash discounts reduce the amount received on accounts receivable. When interest is charged on a past due receivable, the company adds this interest to the accounts receivable balance and recognizes it as interest revenue.

**3 Distinguish between the methods and bases companies use to value accounts receivable.** There are two methods of accounting for uncollectible accounts: the allowance method and the direct write-off method. Companies may use either the percentage-of-sales or the percentage-of-receivables basis to estimate uncollectible accounts using the allowance method. The percentage-of-sales basis emphasizes the expense recognition (matching) principle. The percentage-of-receivables basis emphasizes the cash realizable value of the accounts receivable. An aging schedule is often used with this basis.

4 **Describe the entries to record the disposition of accounts receivable.** When a company collects an account receivable, it credits Accounts Receivable. When a company sells (factors) an account receivable, a service charge expense reduces the amount received.

5 **Compute the maturity date of and interest on notes receivable.** For a note stated in months, the maturity date is found by counting the months from the date of issue. For a note stated in days, the number of days is counted, omitting the issue date and counting the due date. The formula for computing interest is Face value × Interest rate × Time.

6 **Explain how companies recognize notes receivable.** Companies record notes receivable at face value. In some cases, it is necessary to accrue interest prior to maturity. In this case, companies debit Interest Receivable and credit Interest Revenue.

7 **Describe how companies value notes receivable.** As with accounts receivable, companies report notes receivable at their cash (net) realizable value. The notes receivable allowance account is Allowance for Doubtful Accounts. The computation and estimations involved in valuing notes receivable at cash realizable value, and in recording the proper amount of bad debt expense and the related allowance, are similar to those for accounts receivable.

8 **Describe the entries to record the disposition of notes receivable.** Notes can be held to maturity. At that time the face value plus accrued interest is due, and the note is removed from the accounts. In many cases, the holder of the note speeds up the conversion by selling the receivable to another party (a factor). In some situations, the maker of the note dishonors the note (defaults), in which case the company transfers the note and accrued interest to an account receivable or writes off the note.

9 **Explain the statement presentation and analysis of receivables.** Companies should identify in the balance sheet or in the notes to the financial statements each major type of receivable. Short-term receivables are considered current assets. Companies report the gross amount of receivables and the allowance for doubtful accounts. They report bad debt and service charge expenses in the multiple-step income statement as operating (selling) expenses. Interest revenue appears under other revenues and gains in the nonoperating activities section of the statement. Managers and investors evaluate accounts receivable for liquidity by computing a turnover ratio and an average collection period.

## GLOSSARY

**Accounts receivable** Amounts owed by customers on account. (p. 430).

**Accounts receivable turnover** A measure of the liquidity of accounts receivable; computed by dividing net credit sales by average net accounts receivable. (p. 447).

**Aging the accounts receivable** The analysis of customer balances by the length of time they have been unpaid. (p. 437).

**Allowance method** A method of accounting for bad debts that involves estimating uncollectible accounts at the end of each period. (p. 433).

**Average collection period** The average amount of time that a receivable is outstanding; calculated by dividing 365 days by the accounts receivable turnover. (p. 447).

**Bad Debt Expense** An expense account to record uncollectible receivables. (p. 432).

**Cash (net) realizable value** The net amount a company expects to receive in cash. (p. 433).

**Direct write-off method** A method of accounting for bad debts that involves expensing accounts at the time they are determined to be uncollectible. (p. 432).

**Dishonored (defaulted) note** A note that is not paid in full at maturity. (p. 445).

**Factor** A finance company or bank that buys receivables from businesses and then collects the payments directly from the customers. (p. 439).

**Maker** The party in a promissory note who is making the promise to pay. (p. 441).

**Notes receivable** Written promise (as evidenced by a formal instrument) for amounts to be received. (p. 430).

**Other receivables** Various forms of nontrade receivables, such as interest receivable and income taxes refundable. (p. 430).

**Payee** The party to whom payment of a promissory note is to be made. (p. 441).

**Percentage-of-receivables basis** Management estimates what percentage of receivables will result in losses from uncollectible accounts. (p. 437).

**Percentage-of-sales basis** Management estimates what percentage of credit sales will be uncollectible. (p. 436).

**Promissory note** A written promise to pay a specified amount of money on demand or at a definite time. (p. 441).

**Receivables** Amounts due from individuals and other companies. (p. 430).

**Trade receivables** Notes and accounts receivable that result from sales transactions. (p. 430).

**Self-Test, Brief Exercises, Exercises, Problem Set A, and many more components are available for practice in *WileyPLUS*.**

## SELF-TEST QUESTIONS

*Answers are on page 467.*

(LO 1)  **1.** Receivables are frequently classified as:
  **(a)** accounts receivable, company receivables, and other receivables.
  **(b)** accounts receivable, notes receivable, and employee receivables.
  **(c)** accounts receivable and general receivables.
  **(d)** accounts receivable, notes receivable, and other receivables.

(LO 2)  **2.** Buehler Company on June 15 sells merchandise on account to Chaz Co. for $1,000, terms 2/10, n/30. On June 20, Chaz Co. returns merchandise worth $300 to Buehler Company. On June 24, payment is received from Chaz Co. for the balance due. What is the amount of cash received?
  **(a)** $700.                **(c)** $686.
  **(b)** $680.                **(d)** None of the above.

(LO 3)  **3.** Which of the following approaches for bad debts is best described as a balance sheet method?
  **(a)** Percentage-of-receivables basis.
  **(b)** Direct write-off method.
  **(c)** Percentage-of-sales basis.
  **(d)** Both percentage-of-receivables basis and direct write-off method.

(LO 3)  **4.** Hughes Company has a credit balance of $5,000 in its Allowance for Doubtful Accounts before any adjustments are made at the end of the year. Based on review and aging of its accounts receivable at the end of the year, Hughes estimates that $60,000 of its receivables are uncollectible. The amount of bad debt expense which should be reported for the year is:
  **(a)** $5,000.              **(c)** $60,000.
  **(b)** $55,000.             **(d)** $65,000.

(LO 3)  **5.** Use the same information as in Question 4, except that Hughes has a debit balance of $5,000 in its Allowance for Doubtful Accounts before any adjustments are made at the end of the year. In this situation, the amount of bad debt expense that should be reported for the year is:
  **(a)** $5,000.              **(c)** $60,000.
  **(b)** $55,000.             **(d)** $65,000.

(LO 3)  **6.** Net sales for the month are $800,000, and bad debts are expected to be 1.5% of net sales. The company uses the percentage-of-sales basis. If Allowance for Doubtful Accounts has a credit balance of $15,000 before adjustment, what is the balance after adjustment?
  **(a)** $15,000.             **(c)** $23,000.
  **(b)** $27,000.             **(d)** $31,000.

**7.** In 2014, Roso Carlson Company had net credit sales of (LO 3) $750,000. On January 1, 2014, Allowance for Doubtful Accounts had a credit balance of $18,000. During 2014, $30,000 of uncollectible accounts receivable were written off. Past experience indicates that 3% of net credit sales become uncollectible. What should be the adjusted balance of Allowance for Doubtful Accounts at December 31, 2014?
  **(a)** $10,050.             **(c)** $22,500.
  **(b)** $10,500.             **(d)** $40,500.

**8.** An analysis and aging of the accounts receivable of (LO 3) Prince Company at December 31 reveals the following data.

| | |
|---|---|
| Accounts receivable | $800,000 |
| Allowance for doubtful accounts per books before adjustment | 50,000 |
| Amounts expected to become uncollectible | 65,000 |

The cash realizable value of the accounts receivable at December 31, after adjustment, is:
  **(a)** $685,000.            **(c)** $800,000.
  **(b)** $750,000.            **(d)** $735,000.

**9.** Which of the following statements about Visa credit (LO 4) card sales is **incorrect**?
  **(a)** The credit card issuer makes the credit investigation of the customer.
  **(b)** The retailer is not involved in the collection process.
  **(c)** Two parties are involved.
  **(d)** The retailer receives cash more quickly than it would from individual customers on account.

**10.** Blinka Retailers accepted $50,000 of Citibank Visa (LO 4) credit card charges for merchandise sold on July 1. Citibank charges 4% for its credit card use. The entry to record this transaction by Blinka Retailers will include a credit to Sales Revenue of $50,000 and a debit(s) to:
  **(a)** Cash                                $48,000
        and Service Charge Expense            $2,000
  **(b)** Accounts Receivable                 $48,000
        and Service Charge Expense            $2,000
  **(c)** Cash                                $50,000
  **(d)** Accounts Receivable                 $50,000

**11.** One of the following statements about promissory (LO 6) notes is incorrect. The **incorrect** statement is:
  **(a)** The party making the promise to pay is called the maker.

**(b)** The party to whom payment is to be made is called the payee.

**(c)** A promissory note is not a negotiable instrument.

**(d)** A promissory note is often required from high-risk customers.

(LO 6) **12.** Foti Co. accepts a $1,000, 3-month, 6% promissory note in settlement of an account with Bartelt Co. The entry to record this transaction is as follows.

| | | |
|---|---|---|
| **(a)** Notes Receivable | 1,015 | |
| Accounts Receivable | | 1,015 |
| **(b)** Notes Receivable | 1,000 | |
| Accounts Receivable | | 1,000 |
| **(c)** Notes Receivable | 1,000 | |
| Sales Revenue | | 1,000 |
| **(d)** Notes Receivable | 1,030 | |
| Accounts Receivable | | 1,030 |

(LO 8) **13.** Ginter Co. holds Kolar Inc.'s $10,000, 120-day, 9% note. The entry made by Ginter Co. when the note is collected, assuming no interest has been previously accrued, is:

| | | |
|---|---|---|
| **(a)** Cash | 10,300 | |
| Notes Receivable | | 10,300 |
| **(b)** Cash | 10,000 | |
| Notes Receivable | | 10,000 |
| **(c)** Accounts Receivable | 10,300 | |
| Notes Receivable | | 10,000 |
| Interest Revenue | | 300 |
| **(d)** Cash | 10,300 | |
| Notes Receivable | | 10,000 |
| Interest Revenue | | 300 |

**14.** Accounts and notes receivable are reported in the cur- (LO 9) rent assets section of the balance sheet at:

**(a)** cash (net) realizable value.

**(b)** net book value.

**(c)** lower-of-cost-or-market value.

**(d)** invoice cost.

**15.** Oliveras Company had net credit sales during the year (LO 9) of $800,000 and cost of goods sold of $500,000. The balance in accounts receivable at the beginning of the year was $100,000, and the end of the year it was $150,000. What were the accounts receivable turnover and the average collection period in days?

**(a)** 4.0 and 91.3 days.

**(b)** 5.3 and 68.9 days.

**(c)** 6.4 and 57 days.

**(d)** 8.0 and 45.6 days.

Go to the book's companion website, www.wiley.com/college/weygandt, for additional Self-Test Questions.

✔ The Navigator

# QUESTIONS

**1.** What is the difference between an account receivable and a note receivable?

**2.** What are some common types of receivables other than accounts receivable and notes receivable?

**3.** Texaco Oil Company issues its own credit cards. Assume that Texaco charges you $40 interest on an unpaid balance. Prepare the journal entry that Texaco makes to record this revenue.

**4.** What are the essential features of the allowance method of accounting for bad debts?

**5.** Roger Holloway cannot understand why cash realizable value does not decrease when an uncollectible account is written off under the allowance method. Clarify this point for Roger.

**6.** Distinguish between the two bases that may be used in estimating uncollectible accounts.

**7.** Borke Company has a credit balance of $3,000 in Allowance for Doubtful Accounts. The estimated bad debt expense under the percentage-of-sales basis is $4,100. The total estimated uncollectibles under the percentage-of-receivables basis is $5,800. Prepare the adjusting entry under each basis.

**8.** How are bad debts accounted for under the direct write-off method? What are the disadvantages of this method?

**9.** Freida Company accepts both its own credit cards and national credit cards. What are the advantages of accepting both types of cards?

**10.** An article recently appeared in the *Wall Street Journal* indicating that companies are selling their receivables at a record rate. Why are companies selling their receivables?

**11.** Westside Textiles decides to sell $800,000 of its accounts receivable to First Factors Inc. First Factors assesses a service charge of 3% of the amount of receivables sold. Prepare the journal entry that Westside Textiles makes to record this sale.

**12.** Your roommate is uncertain about the advantages of a promissory note. Compare the advantages of a note receivable with those of an account receivable.

**13.** How may the maturity date of a promissory note be stated?

**14.** Indicate the maturity date of each of the following promissory notes:

| Date of Note | Terms |
|---|---|
| **(a)** March 13 | one year after date of note |
| **(b)** May 4 | 3 months after date |
| **(c)** June 20 | 30 days after date |
| **(d)** July 1 | 60 days after date |

**15.** Compute the missing amounts for each of the following notes.

| | Principal | Annual Interest Rate | Time | Total Interest |
|---|---|---|---|---|
| **(a)** | ? | 9% | 120 days | $ 450 |
| **(b)** | $30,000 | 10% | 3 years | ? |
| **(c)** | $60,000 | ? | 5 months | $1,500 |
| **(d)** | $45,000 | 8% | ? | $1,200 |

16. In determining interest revenue, some financial institutions use 365 days per year and others use 360 days. Why might a financial institution use 360 days?

17. Jana Company dishonors a note at maturity. What are the options available to the lender?

18. General Motors Corporation has accounts receivable and notes receivable. How should the receivables be reported on the balance sheet?

19. The accounts receivable turnover is 8.14, and average net receivables during the period are $400,000. What is the amount of net credit sales for the period?

20. What percentage does Apple's allowance for doubtful accounts represent as a percentage of its gross receivables?

## BRIEF EXERCISES

**BE9-1** Presented below are three receivables transactions. Indicate whether these receivables are reported as accounts receivable, notes receivable, or other receivables on a balance sheet.

*Identify different types of receivables.*

*(LO 1)*

**(a)** Sold merchandise on account for $64,000 to a customer.

**(b)** Received a promissory note of $57,000 for services performed.

**(c)** Advanced $10,000 to an employee.

**BE9-2** Record the following transactions on the books of RAS Co.

*Record basic accounts receivable transactions.*

*(LO 2)*

**(a)** On July 1, RAS Co. sold merchandise on account to Waegelein Inc. for $17,200, terms 2/10, n/30.

**(b)** On July 8, Waegelein Inc. returned merchandise worth $3,800 to RAS Co.

**(c)** On July 11, Waegelein Inc. paid for the merchandise.

**BE9-3** During its first year of operations, Gavin Company had credit sales of $3,000,000; $600,000 remained uncollected at year-end. The credit manager estimates that $31,000 of these receivables will become uncollectible.

*Prepare entry for allowance method and partial balance sheet.*

*(LO 3, 9)*

**(a)** Prepare the journal entry to record the estimated uncollectibles.

**(b)** Prepare the current assets section of the balance sheet for Gavin Company. Assume that in addition to the receivables it has cash of $90,000, inventory of $130,000, and prepaid insurance of $7,500.

**BE9-4** At the end of 2014, Carpenter Co. has accounts receivable of $700,000 and an allowance for doubtful accounts of $54,000. On January 24, 2015, the company learns that its receivable from Megan Gray is not collectible, and management authorizes a write-off of $6,200.

*Prepare entry for write-off; determine cash realizable value.*

*(LO 3)*

**(a)** Prepare the journal entry to record the write-off.

**(b)** What is the cash realizable value of the accounts receivable (1) before the write-off and (2) after the write-off?

**BE9-5** Assume the same information as BE9-4. On March 4, 2015, Carpenter Co. receives payment of $6,200 in full from Megan Gray. Prepare the journal entries to record this transaction.

*Prepare entries for collection of bad debt write-off.*

*(LO 3)*

**BE9-6** Farr Co. elects to use the percentage-of-sales basis in 2014 to record bad debt expense. It estimates that 2% of net credit sales will become uncollectible. Sales revenues are $800,000 for 2014, sales returns and allowances are $40,000, and the allowance for doubtful accounts has a credit balance of $9,000. Prepare the adjusting entry to record bad debt expense in 2014.

*Prepare entry using percentage-of-sales method.*

*(LO 3)*

**BE9-7** Kingston Co. uses the percentage-of-receivables basis to record bad debt expense. It estimates that 1% of accounts receivable will become uncollectible. Accounts receivable are $420,000 at the end of the year, and the allowance for doubtful accounts has a credit balance of $1,500.

*Prepare entry using percentage-of-receivables method.*

*(LO 3)*

**(a)** Prepare the adjusting journal entry to record bad debt expense for the year.

**(b)** If the allowance for doubtful accounts had a debit balance of $800 instead of a credit balance of $1,500, determine the amount to be reported for bad debt expense.

**BE9-8** Presented below are two independent transactions.

*Prepare entries to dispose of accounts receivable.*

*(LO 4)*

**(a)** Tony's Restaurant accepted a Visa card in payment of a $175 lunch bill. The bank charges a 4% fee. What entry should Tony's make?

**(b)** Larkin Company sold its accounts receivable of $60,000. What entry should Larkin make, given a service charge of 3% on the amount of receivables sold?

*Compute interest and determine maturity dates on notes.*

*(LO 5)*

**BE9-9** Compute interest and find the maturity date for the following notes.

| | Date of Note | Principal | Interest Rate (%) | Terms |
|---|---|---|---|---|
| **(a)** | June 10 | $80,000 | 6% | 60 days |
| **(b)** | July 14 | $64,000 | 7% | 90 days |
| **(c)** | April 27 | $12,000 | 8% | 75 days |

*Determine maturity dates and compute interest and rates on notes.*

*(LO 5)*

**BE9-10** Presented below are data on three promissory notes. Determine the missing amounts.

| Date of Note | Terms | Maturity Date | Principal | Annual Interest Rate | Total Interest |
|---|---|---|---|---|---|
| **(a)** April 1 | 60 days | ? | $600,000 | 6% | ? |
| **(b)** July 2 | 30 days | ? | 90,000 | ? | $600 |
| **(c)** March 7 | 6 months | ? | 120,000 | 10% | ? |

*Prepare entry for notes receivable exchanged for account receivable.*

*(LO 6)*

**BE9-11** On January 10, 2014, Perez Co. sold merchandise on account to Robertsen Co. for $15,600, n/30. On February 9, Robertsen Co. gave Perez Co. a 10% promissory note in settlement of this account. Prepare the journal entry to record the sale and the settlement of the account receivable.

*Compute ratios to analyze receivables.*

*(LO 9)*

**BE9-12** The financial statements of Minnesota Mining and Manufacturing Company (3M) report net sales of $20.0 billion. Accounts receivable (net) are $2.7 billion at the beginning of the year and $2.8 billion at the end of the year. Compute 3M's accounts receivable turnover. Compute 3M's average collection period for accounts receivable in days.

> ## DO IT! Review

*Prepare entry for uncollectible accounts.*

*(LO 3)*

**DO IT! 9-1** Gonzalez Company has been in business several years. At the end of the current year, the ledger shows:

| | |
|---|---|
| Accounts Receivable | $ 310,000 Dr. |
| Sales Revenue | 2,200,000 Cr. |
| Allowance for Doubtful Accounts | 6,100 Cr. |

Bad debts are estimated to be 5% of receivables. Prepare the entry to adjust Allowance for Doubtful Accounts.

*Prepare entry for factored accounts.*

*(LO 4)*

**DO IT! 9-2** Wynn Distributors is a growing company whose ability to raise capital has not been growing as quickly as its expanding assets and sales. Wynn's local banker has indicated that the company cannot increase its borrowing for the foreseeable future. Wynn's suppliers are demanding payment for goods acquired within 30 days of the invoice date, but Wynn's customers are slow in paying for their purchases (60–90 days). As a result, Wynn has a cash flow problem.

Wynn needs $160,000 to cover next Friday's payroll. Its balance of outstanding accounts receivable totals $1,000,000. To alleviate this cash crunch, Wynn sells $200,000 of its receivables. Record the entry that Wynn would make when it raises the needed cash. (Assume a 3% service charge.)

*Prepare entries for notes receivable.*

*(LO 5, 8)*

**DO IT! 9-3** Gentry Wholesalers accepts from Benton Stores a $6,200, 4-month, 9% note dated May 31 in settlement of Benton's overdue account. (a) What is the maturity date of the note? (b) What is the entry made by Gentry at the maturity date, assuming Benton pays the note and interest in full at that time?

*Compute ratios for receivables.*

*(LO 9)*

**DO IT! 9-4** In 2014, Wainwright Company has net credit sales of $1,300,000 for the year. It had a beginning accounts receivable (net) balance of $101,000 and an ending accounts receivable (net) balance of $107,000. Compute Wainwright Company's (a) accounts receivable turnover and (b) average collection period in days.

## EXERCISES

**E9-1** Presented below are selected transactions of Molina Company. Molina sells in large quantities to other companies and also sells its product in a small retail outlet.

*Journalize entries related to accounts receivable.*
*(LO 2)*

March  1   Sold merchandise on account to Dodson Company for $5,000, terms 2/10, n/30.

     3   Dodson Company returned merchandise worth $500 to Molina.

     9   Molina collected the amount due from Dodson Company from the March 1 sale.

   15   Molina sold merchandise for $400 in its retail outlet. The customer used his Molina credit card.

   31   Molina added 1.5% monthly interest to the customer's credit card balance.

***Instructions***
Prepare journal entries for the transactions above.

**E9-2** Presented below are two independent situations.

*Journalize entries for recognizing accounts receivable.*
*(LO 2)*

**(a)** On January 6, Brumbaugh Co. sells merchandise on account to Pryor Inc. for $7,000, terms 2/10, n/30. On January 16, Pryor Inc. pays the amount due. Prepare the entries on Brumbaugh's books to record the sale and related collection.

**(b)** On January 10, Andrew Farley uses his Paltrow Co. credit card to purchase merchandise from Paltrow Co. for $9,000. On February 10, Farley is billed for the amount due of $9,000. On February 12, Farley pays $5,000 on the balance due. On March 10, Farley is billed for the amount due, including interest at 1% per month on the unpaid balance as of February 12. Prepare the entries on Paltrow Co.'s books related to the transactions that occurred on January 10, February 12, and March 10.

**E9-3** The ledger of Costello Company at the end of the current year shows Accounts Receivable $110,000, Sales Revenue $840,000, and Sales Returns and Allowances $20,000.

*Journalize entries to record allowance for doubtful accounts using two different bases.*
*(LO 3)*

***Instructions***
**(a)** If Costello uses the direct write-off method to account for uncollectible accounts, journalize the adjusting entry at December 31, assuming Costello determines that L. Dole's $1,400 balance is uncollectible.

**(b)** If Allowance for Doubtful Accounts has a credit balance of $2,100 in the trial balance, journalize the adjusting entry at December 31, assuming bad debts are expected to be (1) 1% of net sales, and (2) 10% of accounts receivable.

**(c)** If Allowance for Doubtful Accounts has a debit balance of $200 in the trial balance, journalize the adjusting entry at December 31, assuming bad debts are expected to be (1) 0.75% of net sales and (2) 6% of accounts receivable.

**E9-4** Menge Company has accounts receivable of $93,100 at March 31. An analysis of the accounts shows the following information.

*Determine bad debt expense; prepare the adjusting entry for bad debt expense.*
*(LO 3)*

| Month of Sale | Balance, March 31 |
|---|---|
| March | $60,000 |
| February | 17,600 |
| January | 8,500 |
| Prior to January | 7,000 |
| | $93,100 |

Credit terms are 2/10, n/30. At March 31, Allowance for Doubtful Accounts has a credit balance of $1,200 prior to adjustment. The company uses the percentage-of-receivables basis for estimating uncollectible accounts. The company's estimate of bad debts is shown below.

| Age of Accounts | Estimated Percentage Uncollectible |
|---|---|
| 1–30 days | 2.0% |
| 31–60 days | 5.0% |
| 61–90 days | 20.0% |
| Over 90 days | 50.0% |

*Instructions*
**(a)** Determine the total estimated uncollectibles.
**(b)** Prepare the adjusting entry at March 31 to record bad debt expense.

**E9-5** At December 31, 2013, Finzelberg Company had a credit balance of $15,000 in Allowance for Doubtful Accounts. During 2014, Finzelberg wrote off accounts totaling $11,000. One of those accounts ($1,800) was later collected. At December 31, 2014, an aging schedule indicated that the balance in Allowance for Doubtful Accounts should be $19,000.

*Instructions*
Prepare journal entries to record the 2014 transactions of Finzelberg Company.

**E9-6** On December 31, 2014, Ling Co. estimated that 2% of its net sales of $450,000 will become uncollectible. The company recorded this amount as an addition to Allowance for Doubtful Accounts. On May 11, 2015, Ling Co. determined that the Jeff Shoemaker account was uncollectible and wrote off $1,100. On June 12, 2015, Shoemaker paid the amount previously written off.

*Instructions*
Prepare the journal entries on December 31, 2014, May 11, 2015, and June 12, 2015.

**E9-7** Presented below are two independent situations.

**(a)** On March 3, Kitselman Appliances sells $650,000 of its receivables to Ervay Factors Inc. Ervay Factors assesses a finance charge of 3% of the amount of receivables sold. Prepare the entry on Kitselman Appliances' books to record the sale of the receivables.
**(b)** On May 10, Fillmore Company sold merchandise for $3,000 and accepted the customer's America Bank MasterCard. America Bank charges a 4% service charge for credit card sales. Prepare the entry on Fillmore Company's books to record the sale of merchandise.

**E9-8** Presented below are two independent situations.

**(a)** On April 2, Jennifer Elston uses her JCPenney Company credit card to purchase merchandise from a JCPenney store for $1,500. On May 1, Elston is billed for the $1,500 amount due. Elston pays $500 on the balance due on May 3. On June 1, Elston receives a bill for the amount due, including interest at 1.0% per month on the unpaid balance as of May 3. Prepare the entries on JCPenney Co.'s books related to the transactions that occurred on April 2, May 3, and June 1.
**(b)** On July 4, Spangler's Restaurant accepts a Visa card for a $200 dinner bill. Visa charges a 2% service fee. Prepare the entry on Spangler's books related to this transaction.

**E9-9** Colaw Stores accepts both its own and national credit cards. During the year, the following selected summary transactions occurred.

Jan. 15   Made Colaw credit card sales totaling $18,000. (There were no balances prior to January 15.)
    20   Made Visa credit card sales (service charge fee 2%) totaling $4,500.
Feb. 10   Collected $10,000 on Colaw credit card sales.
    15   Added finance charges of 1.5% to Colaw credit card account balances.

*Instructions*
**(a)** Journalize the transactions for Colaw Stores.
**(b)** Indicate the statement presentation of the financing charges and the credit card service charge expense for Colaw Stores.

**E9-10** Elburn Supply Co. has the following transactions related to notes receivable during the last 2 months of 2014. The company does not make entries to accrue interest except at December 31.

Nov. 1   Loaned $30,000 cash to Manny Lopez on a 12 month, 10% note.
Dec. 11  Sold goods to Ralph Kremer, Inc., receiving a $6,750, 90-day, 8% note.
    16   Received a $4,000, 180 day, 9% note in exchange for Joe Fernetti's outstanding accounts receivable.
    31   Accrued interest revenue on all notes receivable.

*Instructions*
**(a)** Journalize the transactions for Elburn Supply Co.
**(b)** Record the collection of the Lopez note at its maturity in 2015.

**E9-11** Record the following transactions for Redeker Co. in the general journal.

*Journalize entries for notes receivable.*

*(LO 5, 6)*

**2014**

May  1   Received a $9,000, 12-month, 10% note in exchange for Mark Chamber's outstanding accounts receivable.
Dec. 31   Accrued interest on the Chamber note.
Dec. 31   Closed the interest revenue account.

**2015**

May  1   Received principal plus interest on the Chamber note. (No interest has been accrued in 2015.)

**E9-12** Vandiver Company had the following select transactions.

*Prepare entries for note receivable transactions.*

*(LO 5, 6, 8)*

Apr.  1, 2014   Accepted Goodwin Company's 12-month, 12% note in settlement of a $30,000 account receivable.
July  1, 2014   Loaned $25,000 cash to Thomas Slocombe on a 9-month, 10% note.
Dec. 31, 2014   Accrued interest on all notes receivable.
Apr.  1, 2015   Received principal plus interest on the Goodwin note.
Apr.  1, 2015   Thomas Slocombe dishonored its note; Vandiver expects it will eventually collect.

*Instructions*
Prepare journal entries to record the transactions. Vandiver prepares adjusting entries once a year on December 31.

**E9-13** On May 2, McLain Company lends $9,000 to Chang, Inc., issuing a 6-month, 9% note. At the maturity date, November 2, Chang indicates that it cannot pay.

*Journalize entries for dishonor of notes receivable.*

*(LO 5, 8)*

*Instructions*
**(a)** Prepare the entry to record the issuance of the note.
**(b)** Prepare the entry to record the dishonor of the note, assuming that McLain Company expects collection will occur.
**(c)** Prepare the entry to record the dishonor of the note, assuming that McLain Company does not expect collection in the future.

**E9-14** Kerwick Company had accounts receivable of $100,000 on January 1, 2014. The only transactions that affected accounts receivable during 2014 were net credit sales of $1,000,000, cash collections of $920,000, and accounts written off of $30,000.

*Compute accounts receivable turnover and average collection period.*

*(LO 9)*

*Instructions*
**(a)** Compute the ending balance of accounts receivable.
**(b)** Compute the accounts receivable turnover for 2014.
**(c)** Compute the average collection period in days.

## EXERCISES: SET B AND CHALLENGE EXERCISES

Visit the book's companion website, at **www.wiley.com/college/weygandt**, and choose the Student Companion site to access Exercise Set B and Challenge Exercises.

## PROBLEMS: SET A

**P9-1A** At December 31, 2013, House Co. reported the following information on its balance sheet.

*Prepare journal entries related to bad debt expense.*

*(LO 2, 3, 9)*

| | |
|---|---|
| Accounts receivable | $960,000 |
| Less: Allowance for doubtful accounts | 80,000 |

During 2014, the company had the following transactions related to receivables.

| | | |
|---|---|---|
| **1.** Sales on account | | $3,700,000 |
| **2.** Sales returns and allowances | | 50,000 |
| **3.** Collections of accounts receivable | | 2,810,000 |
| **4.** Write-offs of accounts receivable deemed uncollectible | | 90,000 |
| **5.** Recovery of bad debts previously written off as uncollectible | | 29,000 |

**Instructions**

**(a)** Prepare the journal entries to record each of these five transactions. Assume that no cash discounts were taken on the collections of accounts receivable.

(b) Accounts receivable
$1,710,000
ADA $19,000

(c) Bad debt expense $96,000

**(b)** Enter the January 1, 2014, balances in Accounts Receivable and Allowance for Doubtful Accounts, post the entries to the two accounts (use T-accounts), and determine the balances.

**(c)** Prepare the journal entry to record bad debt expense for 2014, assuming that an aging of accounts receivable indicates that expected bad debts are $115,000.

**(d)** Compute the accounts receivable turnover for 2014 assuming the expected bad debt information provided in (c).

*Compute bad debt amounts.*

*(LO 3)*

**P9-2A** Information related to Mingenback Company for 2014 is summarized below.

| | |
|---|---|
| Total credit sales | $2,500,000 |
| Accounts receivable at December 31 | 875,000 |
| Bad debts written off | 33,000 |

**Instructions**

**(a)** What amount of bad debt expense will Mingenback Company report if it uses the direct write-off method of accounting for bad debts?

**(b)** Assume that Mingenback Company estimates its bad debt expense to be 2% of credit sales. What amount of bad debt expense will Mingenback record if it has an Allowance for Doubtful Accounts credit balance of $4,000?

**(c)** Assume that Mingenback Company estimates its bad debt expense based on 6% of accounts receivable. What amount of bad debt expense will Mingenback record if it has an Allowance for Doubtful Accounts credit balance of $3,000?

**(d)** Assume the same facts as in (c), except that there is a $3,000 debit balance in Allowance for Doubtful Accounts. What amount of bad debt expense will Mingenback record?

**(e)** ———— What is the weakness of the direct write-off method of reporting bad debt expense?

*Journalize entries to record transactions related to bad debts.*

*(LO 2, 3)*

**P9-3A** Presented below is an aging schedule for Halleran Company.

| | | | Worksheet.xls | | | | |
|---|---|---|---|---|---|---|---|
| | Home | Insert | Page Layout | Formulas | Data | Review | View |
| | P18 | | fx | | | | |

| | A | B | C | D | E | F | G |
|---|---|---|---|---|---|---|---|
| 1 | | | | | **Number of Days Past Due** | | |
| 2 | | | **Not** | | | | |
| 3 | **Customer** | **Total** | **Yet Due** | **1–30** | **31–60** | **61–90** | **Over 90** |
| 4 | Anders | $ 22,000 | | $10,000 | $12,000 | | |
| 5 | Blake | 40,000 | $ 40,000 | | | | |
| 6 | Coulson | 57,000 | 16,000 | 6,000 | | $35,000 | |
| 7 | Deleon | 34,000 | | | | | $34,000 |
| 8 | Others | 132,000 | 96,000 | 16,000 | 14,000 | | 6,000 |
| 9 | | $285,000 | $152,000 | $32,000 | $26,000 | $35,000 | $40,000 |
| 10 | Estimated Percentage Uncollectible | | 3% | 6% | 13% | 25% | 50% |
| 11 | Total Estimated Bad Debts | $ 38,610 | $ 4,560 | $ 1,920 | $ 3,380 | $ 8,750 | $20,000 |
| 12 | | | | | | | |

At December 31, 2014, the unadjusted balance in Allowance for Doubtful Accounts is a credit of $12,000.

**Instructions**

(a) Bad debt expense
$26,610

**(a)** Journalize and post the adjusting entry for bad debts at December 31, 2014.

**(b)** Journalize and post to the allowance account the following events and transactions in the year 2015.

**(1)** On March 31, a $1,000 customer balance originating in 2014 is judged uncollectible.

**(2)** On May 31, a check for $1,000 is received from the customer whose account was written off as uncollectible on March 31.

**(c)** Journalize the adjusting entry for bad debts on December 31, 2015, assuming that the unadjusted balance in Allowance for Doubtful Accounts is a debit of $800 and the aging schedule indicates that total estimated bad debts will be $31,600.

*(c) Bad debt expense*
*$32,400*

**P9-4A** Rigney Inc. uses the allowance method to estimate uncollectible accounts receivable. The company produced the following aging of the accounts receivable at year-end.

*Journalize transactions related to bad debts.*
*(SO 2, 3)*

| | | Worksheet.xls | | | | |
|---|---|---|---|---|---|---|
| Home | Insert | Page Layout | Formulas | Data | Review | View |
| P18 | | *fx* | | | | |
| | A | B | C | D | E | F | G |
| 1 | | | | **Number of Days Outstanding** | | | |
| 2 | | | | | | | |
| 3 | | **Total** | **0–30** | **31–60** | **61–90** | **91–120** | **Over 120** |
| 4 | Accounts receivable | 200,000 | 77,000 | 46,000 | 39,000 | 23,000 | $15,000 |
| 5 | % uncollectible | | 1% | 4% | 5% | 8% | 20% |
| 6 | Estimated bad debts | | | | | | |
| 7 | | | | | | | |

**Instructions**

**(a)** Calculate the total estimated bad debts based on the above information.

*(a) Tot. est. bad debts $9,400*

**(b)** Prepare the year-end adjusting journal entry to record the bad debts using the aged uncollectible accounts receivable determined in (a). Assume the current balance in Allowance for Doubtful Accounts is a $8,000 debit.

**(c)** Of the above accounts, $5,000 is determined to be specifically uncollectible. Prepare the journal entry to write off the uncollectible account.

**(d)** The company collects $5,000 subsequently on a specific account that had previously been determined to be uncollectible in (c). Prepare the journal entry(ies) necessary to restore the account and record the cash collection.

**(e)** Comment on how your answers to (a)–(d) would change if Rigney Inc. used 4% of **total** accounts receivable rather than aging the accounts receivable. What are the advantages to the company of aging the accounts receivable rather than applying a percentage to total accounts receivable?

**P9-5A** At December 31, 2014, the trial balance of Darby Company contained the following amounts before adjustment.

*Journalize entries to record transactions related to bad debts.*
*(LO 3)*

| | **Debit** | **Credit** |
|---|---|---|
| Accounts Receivable | $385,000 | |
| Allowance for Doubtful Accounts | | $   1,000 |
| Sales Revenue | | 970,000 |

**Instructions**

**(a)** Based on the information given, which method of accounting for bad debts is Darby Company using—the direct write-off method or the allowance method? How can you tell?

**(b)** Prepare the adjusting entry at December 31, 2014, for bad debt expense under each of the following independent assumptions.

**(1)** An aging schedule indicates that $11,750 of accounts receivable will be uncollectible.

**(2)** The company estimates that 1% of sales will be uncollectible.

*(b)(2) $9,700*

**(c)** Repeat part (b) assuming that instead of a credit balance there is an $1,000 debit balance in Allowance for Doubtful Accounts.

**(d)** During the next month, January 2015, a $3,000 account receivable is written off as uncollectible. Prepare the journal entry to record the write-off.

**(e)** Repeat part (d) assuming that Darby uses the direct write-off method instead of the allowance method in accounting for uncollectible accounts receivable.

**(f)** ———— What type of account is Allowance for Doubtful Accounts? How does it affect how accounts receivable is reported on the balance sheet at the end of the accounting period?

*Prepare entries for various notes receivable transactions.*

(LO 2, 4, 5, 8, 9)

**P9-6A** Farwell Company closes its books monthly. On September 30, selected ledger account balances are:

| | |
|---|---|
| Notes Receivable | $37,000 |
| Interest Receivable | 183 |

Notes Receivable include the following.

| Date | Maker | Face | Term | Interest |
|---|---|---|---|---|
| Aug. 16 | K. Goza Inc. | $12,000 | 60 days | 8% |
| Aug. 25 | Holt Co. | 9,000 | 60 days | 7% |
| Sept. 30 | Noblitt Corp. | 16,000 | 6 months | 9% |

Interest is computed using a 360-day year. During October, the following transactions were completed.

Oct. 7 Made sales of $6,900 on Farwell credit cards.
12 Made sales of $900 on MasterCard credit cards. The credit card service charge is 3%.
15 Added $460 to Farwell customer balances for finance charges on unpaid balances.
15 Received payment in full from K. Goza Inc. on the amount due.
24 Received notice that the Holt note has been dishonored. (Assume that Holt is expected to pay in the future.)

**Instructions**
(a) Journalize the October transactions and the October 31 adjusting entry for accrued interest receivable.

(b) Accounts receivable
$16,465
(c) Total receivables $32,585

(b) Enter the balances at October 1 in the receivable accounts. Post the entries to all of the receivable accounts.
(c) Show the balance sheet presentation of the receivable accounts at October 31.

*Prepare entries for various receivable transactions.*

(LO 2, 4, 5, 6, 8)

**P9-7A** On January 1, 2014, Harter Company had Accounts Receivable $139,000, Notes Receivable $25,000, and Allowance for Doubtful Accounts $13,200. The note receivable is from Willingham Company. It is a 4-month, 9% note dated December 31, 2013. Harter Company prepares financial statements annually at December 31. During the year, the following selected transactions occurred.

Jan. 5 Sold $20,000 of merchandise to Sheldon Company, terms n/15.
20 Accepted Sheldon Company's $20,000, 3-month, 8% note for balance due.
Feb. 18 Sold $8,000 of merchandise to Patwary Company and accepted Patwary's $8,000, 6-month, 9% note for the amount due.
Apr. 20 Collected Sheldon Company note in full.
30 Received payment in full from Willingham Company on the amount due.
May 25 Accepted Potter Inc.'s $6,000, 3-month, 7% note in settlement of a past-due balance on account.
Aug. 18 Received payment in full from Patwary Company on note due.
25 The Potter Inc. note was dishonored. Potter Inc. is not bankrupt; future payment is anticipated.
Sept. 1 Sold $12,000 of merchandise to Stanbrough Company and accepted a $12,000, 6-month, 10% note for the amount due.

**Instructions**
Journalize the transactions.

# PROBLEMS: SET B

*Prepare journal entries related to bad debt expense.*

(LO 2, 3, 9)

**P9-1B** At December 31, 2013, Obermeyer Imports reported the following information on its balance sheet.

| | |
|---|---|
| Accounts receivable | $250,000 |
| Less: Allowance for doubtful accounts | 15,000 |

During 2014, the company had the following transactions related to receivables.

| | |
|---|---|
| **1.** Sales on account | $2,600,000 |
| **2.** Sales returns and allowances | 45,000 |

**3.** Collections of accounts receivable                                    2,250,000
**4.** Write-offs of accounts receivable deemed uncollectible          10,000
**5.** Recovery of bad debts previously written off as uncollectible    3,000

*Instructions*
**(a)** Prepare the journal entries to record each of these five transactions. Assume that no cash discounts were taken on the collections of accounts receivable.
**(b)** Enter the January 1, 2014, balances in Accounts Receivable and Allowance for Doubtful Accounts. Post the entries to the two accounts (use T-accounts), and determine the balances.

(b) Accounts receivable
$545,000
ADA $8,000

**(c)** Prepare the journal entry to record bad debt expense for 2014, assuming that an aging of accounts receivable indicates that estimated bad debts are $22,000.

(c) Bad debt expense
$14,000

**(d)** Compute the accounts receivable turnover for the year 2014.

**P9-2B** Information related to Miracle Company for 2014 is summarized below.

*Compute bad debt amounts.*

(LO 3)

| | |
|---|---|
| Total credit sales | $1,000,000 |
| Accounts receivable at December 31 | 369,000 |
| Bad debts written off | 22,150 |

*Instructions*
**(a)** What amount of bad debt expense will Miracle Company report if it uses the direct write-off method of accounting for bad debts?
**(b)** Assume that Miracle Company decides to estimate its bad debt expense to be 2% of credit sales. What amount of bad debt expense will Miracle record if Allowance for Doubtful Accounts has a credit balance of $3,000?
**(c)** Assume that Miracle Company decides to estimate its bad debt expense based on 5% of accounts receivable. What amount of bad debt expense will Miracle Company record if Allowance for Doubtful Accounts has a credit balance of $4,000?
**(d)** Assume the same facts as in (c), except that there is a $2,000 debit balance in Allowance for Doubtful Accounts. What amount of bad debt expense will Miracle record?
**(e)** ◄━━━━ What is the weakness of the direct write-off method of reporting bad debt expense?

**P9-3B** Presented below is an aging schedule for Loucks Company.

*Journalize entries to record transactions related to bad debts.*

(LO 2, 3)

| | | | Worksheet.xls | | | | |
|---|---|---|---|---|---|---|---|
| Home  Insert  Page Layout  Formulas  Data  Review  View | | | | | | | |
| P18 | | *fx* | | | | | |
| | A | B | C | D | E | F | G |
| 1 | | | | **Number of Days Past Due** | | | |
| 2 | | | **Not** | | | | |
| 3 | **Customer** | **Total** | **Yet Due** | **1–30** | **31–60** | **61–90** | **Over 90** |
| 4 | Alma | $ 30,000 | | $ 13,500 | $16,500 | | |
| 5 | Browne | 45,000 | $ 45,000 | | | | |
| 6 | Conlon | 75,000 | 22,500 | 7,500 | | $45,000 | |
| 7 | Dalton | 57,000 | | | | | $57,000 |
| 8 | Others | 189,000 | 138,000 | 22,500 | 19,500 | | 9,000 |
| 9 | | $396,000 | $205,500 | $43,500 | $36,000 | $45,000 | $66,000 |
| 10 | Estimated Percentage Uncollectible | | 2% | 6% | 10% | 25% | 40% |
| 11 | Total Estimated Bad Debts | $ 47,970 | $ 4,110 | $ 2,610 | $ 3,600 | $ 11,250 | $26,400 |
| 12 | | | | | | | |

At December 31, 2014, the unadjusted balance in Allowance for Doubtful Accounts is a credit of $16,000.

*Instructions*
**(a)** Journalize and post the adjusting entry for bad debts at December 31, 2014.
**(b)** Journalize and post to the allowance account the following events and transactions in the year 2015.
   **(1)** March 1, a $1,900 customer balance originating in 2014 is judged uncollectible.
   **(2)** May 1, a check for $1,900 is received from the customer whose account was written off as uncollectible on March 1.

(a) Bad debt expense
$31,970

(c) Bad debt expense
$40,300

**(c)** Journalize the adjusting entry for bad debts on December 31, 2015. Assume that the unadjusted balance in Allowance for Doubtful Accounts is a debit of $2,000, and the aging schedule indicates that total estimated bad debts will be $38,300.

*Journalize transactions related to bad debts.*

*(LO 2, 3)*

**P9-4B** The following represents selected information taken from a company's aging schedule to estimate uncollectible accounts receivable at year-end.

| | | Worksheet.xls | | | | | |
|---|---|---|---|---|---|---|---|
| Home   Insert   Page Layout   Formulas   Data   Review   View | | | | | | | |
| P18 | | *fx* | | | | | |
| | A | B | C | D | E | F | G |
| 1 | | | | | | | |
| 2 | | | | | Number of Days Outstanding | | |
| 3 | | **Total** | **0–30** | **31–60** | **61–90** | **91–120** | **Over 120** |
| 4 | Accounts receivable | $375,000 | $220,000 | $90,000 | $40,000 | $10,000 | $15,000 |
| 5 | % uncollectible | | 1% | 4% | 5% | 8% | 20% |
| 6 | Estimated bad debts | | | | | | |
| 7 | | | | | | | |

*Instructions*

(a) Tot. est.
    bad debts $11,600

**(a)** Calculate the total estimated bad debts based on the above information.

**(b)** Prepare the year-end adjusting journal entry to record the bad debts using the allowance method and the aged uncollectible accounts receivable determined in (a). Assume the current balance in Allowance for Doubtful Accounts is a $3,000 credit.

**(c)** Of the above accounts, $1,600 is determined to be specifically uncollectible. Prepare the journal entry to write off the uncollectible accounts.

**(d)** The company subsequently collects $700 on a specific account that had previously been determined to be uncollectible in (c). Prepare the journal entry(ies) necessary to restore the account and record the cash collection.

**(e)** Explain how establishing an allowance account satisfies the expense recognition principle.

*Journalize entries to record transactions related to bad debts.*

*(LO 3)*

**P9-5B** At December 31, 2014, the trial balance of Markowitz Company contained the following amounts before adjustment.

| | **Debit** | **Credit** |
|---|---|---|
| Accounts Receivable | $250,000 | |
| Allowance for Doubtful Accounts | | $   1,100 |
| Sales Revenue | | 650,000 |

*Instructions*

(a)(2) $13,000

**(a)** Prepare the adjusting entry at December 31, 2014, to record bad debt expense under each of the following independent assumptions.

  **(1)**  An aging schedule indicates that $13,500 of accounts receivable will be uncollectible.

  **(2)**  The company estimates that 2% of sales will be uncollectible.

**(b)** Repeat part (a) assuming that instead of a credit balance, there is a $1,100 debit balance in Allowance for Doubtful Accounts.

**(c)** During the next month, January 2015, a $3,200 account receivable is written off as uncollectible. Prepare the journal entry to record the write-off.

**(d)** Repeat part (c) assuming that Markowitz Company uses the direct write-off method instead of the allowance method in accounting for uncollectible accounts receivable.

**(e)** ──────  What are the advantages of using the allowance method in accounting for uncollectible accounts as compared to the direct write-off method?

*Prepare entries for various notes receivable transactions.*

*(LO 2, 4, 5, 8, 9)*

**P9-6B** Sauer Co. closes its books monthly. On June 30, selected ledger account balances are:

| Notes Receivable | $47,000 |
|---|---|
| Interest Receivable | 285 |

Notes Receivable include the following.

| Date | Maker | Face | Term | Interest |
|---|---|---|---|---|
| May 16 | Eddy Inc. | $12,000 | 60 days | 7% |
| May 25 | Masasi Co. | 20,000 | 60 days | 9% |
| June 30 | Pelsma Corp. | 15,000 | 6 months | 8% |

During July, the following transactions were completed.

July  5  Made sales of $7,200 on Sauer Co. credit cards.
    14  Made sales of $1,000 on Visa credit cards. The credit card service charge is 3%.
    14  Added $510 to Sauer Co. credit card customer balances for finance charges on unpaid balances.
    15  Received payment in full from Eddy Inc. on the amount due.
    24  Received notice that the Masasi Co. note has been dishonored. (Assume that Masasi Co. is expected to pay in the future.)

*Instructions*
**(a)** Journalize the July transactions and the July 31 adjusting entry for accrued interest receivable. (Interest is computed using 360 days.)
**(b)** Enter the balances at July 1 in the receivable accounts. Post the entries to all of the receivable accounts.
**(c)** Show the balance sheet presentation of the receivable accounts at July 31.

(b) Accounts receivable $28,010

(c) Total receivables $43,110

**P9-7B** On January 1, 2014, Morfitt Company had Accounts Receivable $98,000 and Allowance for Doubtful Accounts $8,100. Morfitt Company prepares financial statements annually. During the year, the following selected transactions occurred.

*Prepare entries for various receivable transactions.*
(LO 2, 4, 5, 6, 8)

Jan.  5  Sold $10,800 of merchandise to Motte Company, terms n/30.
Feb.  2  Accepted a $10,800, 4-month, 9% promissory note from Motte Company for the balance due.
    12  Sold $13,500 of merchandise to Gitchel Company and accepted Gitchel's $13,500, 2-month, 8% note for the balance due.
    26  Sold $9,000 of merchandise to Benedict Co., terms n/10.
Apr.  5  Accepted a $9,000, 3-month, 8% note from Benedict Co. for the balance due.
    12  Collected Gitchel Company note in full.
June  2  Collected Motte Company note in full.
July  5  Benedict Co. dishonors its note of April 5. It is expected that Benedict will eventually pay the amount owed.
    15  Sold $12,000 of merchandise to Kriley Co. and accepted Kriley's $12,000, 3-month, 12% note for the amount due.
Oct. 15  Kriley Co.'s note was dishonored. Kriley Co. is bankrupt, and there is no hope of future settlement.

*Instructions*
Journalize the transactions.

---

## PROBLEMS: SET C

Visit the book's companion website, at **www.wiley.com/college/weygandt**, and choose the Student Companion site to access Problem Set C.

---

## COMPREHENSIVE PROBLEM

**CP9** Winter Company's balance sheet at December 31, 2013, is presented below.

**WINTER COMPANY**
Balance Sheet
December 31, 2013

| | | | |
|---|---|---|---|
| Cash | $13,100 | Accounts payable | $ 8,750 |
| Accounts receivable | 19,780 | Owner's capital | 32,730 |
| Allowance for doubtful accounts | (800) | | $41,480 |
| Inventory | 9,400 | | |
| | $41,480 | | |

During January 2014, the following transactions occurred. Winter uses the perpetual inventory method.

Jan.　1　Winter accepted a 4-month, 8% note from Merando Company in payment of Merando's $1,200 account.

　　　3　Winter wrote off as uncollectible the accounts of Inwood Corporation ($450) and Goza Company ($280).

　　　8　Winter purchased $17,200 of inventory on account.

　　11　Winter sold for $28,000 on account inventory that cost $19,600.

　　15　Winter sold inventory that cost $700 to Mark Lauber for $1,000. Lauber charged this amount on his Visa First Bank card. The service fee charged Winter by First Bank is 3%.

　　17　Winter collected $22,900 from customers on account.

　　21　Winter paid $14,300 on accounts payable.

　　24　Winter received payment in full ($280) from Goza Company on the account written off on January 3.

　　27　Winter purchased supplies for $1,400 cash.

　　31　Winter paid other operating expenses, $3,718.

**Adjustment data:**

1. Interest is recorded for the month on the note from January 1.
2. Bad debts are expected to be 6% of the January 31, 2014, accounts receivable.
3. A count of supplies on January 31, 2014, reveals that $560 remains unused.

***Instructions***

(You may want to set up T-accounts to determine ending balances.)

**(a)** Prepare journal entries for the transactions listed above and adjusting entries. (Include entries for cost of goods sold using the perpetual system.)

(b) Totals $74,585

(c) Tot. assets $47,473

**(b)** Prepare an adjusted trial balance at January 31, 2014.

**(c)** Prepare an income statement and an owner's equity statement for the month ending January 31, 2014, and a classified balance sheet as of January 31, 2014.

## CONTINUING COOKIE CHRONICLE

(*Note:* This is a continuation of the Cookie Chronicle from Chapters 1 through 8.)

**CCC9** One of Natalie's friends, Curtis Lesperance, runs a coffee shop where he sells specialty coffees and prepares and sells muffins and cookies. He is eager to buy one of Natalie's fine European mixers, which would enable him to make larger batches of muffins and cookies. However, Curtis cannot afford to pay for the mixer for at least 30 days. He asks Natalie if she would be willing to sell him the mixer on credit. Natalie comes to you for advice.

*Go to the book's companion website,* **www.wiley.com/college/weygandt**, *to see the completion of this problem.*

# Broadening Your Perspective

## Financial Reporting and Analysis

### Financial Reporting Problem: RLF Company

**BYP9-1** RLF Company sells office equipment and supplies to many organizations in the city and surrounding area on contract terms of 2/10, n/30. In the past, over 75% of the credit customers have taken advantage of the discount by paying within 10 days of the invoice date.

The number of customers taking the full 30 days to pay has increased within the last year. Current indications are that less than 60% of the customers are now taking the discount. Bad debts as a percentage of gross credit sales have risen from the 2.5% provided in past years to about 4.5% in the current year.

The company's Finance Committee has requested more information on the collections of accounts receivable. The controller responded to this request with the report reproduced below.

**RLF COMPANY**
Accounts Receivable Collections
May 31, 2014

The fact that some credit accounts will prove uncollectible is normal. Annual bad debt write-offs have been 2.5% of gross credit sales over the past 5 years. During the last fiscal year, this percentage increased to slightly less than 4.5%. The current Accounts Receivable balance is $1,400,000. The condition of this balance in terms of age and probability of collection is as follows.

| Proportion of Total | Age Categories | Probability of Collection |
|---|---|---|
| 60% | not yet due | 98% |
| 22% | less than 30 days past due | 96% |
| 9% | 30 to 60 days past due | 94% |
| 5% | 61 to 120 days past due | 91% |
| $2\frac{1}{2}$% | 121 to 180 days past due | 75% |
| $1\frac{1}{2}$% | over 180 days past due | 30% |

Allowance for Doubtful Accounts had a credit balance of $29,500 on June 1, 2013. RLF has provided for a monthly bad debt expense accrual during the current fiscal year based on the assumption that 4.5% of gross credit sales will be uncollectible. Total gross credit sales for the 2013–2014 fiscal year amounted to $2,900,000. Write-offs of bad accounts during the year totaled $102,000.

*Instructions*
**(a)** Prepare an accounts receivable aging schedule for RLF Company using the age categories identified in the controller's report to the Finance Committee showing the following.
   **(1)** The amount of accounts receivable outstanding for each age category and in total.
   **(2)** The estimated amount that is uncollectible for each category and in total.
**(b)** Compute the amount of the year-end adjustment necessary to bring Allowance for Doubtful Accounts to the balance indicated by the age analysis. Then prepare the necessary journal entry to adjust the accounting records.
**(c)** In a recessionary environment with tight credit and high interest rates:
   **(1)** Identify steps RLF Company might consider to improve the accounts receivable situation.
   **(2)** Then evaluate each step identified in terms of the risks and costs involved.

## Comparative Analysis Problem:
## PepsiCo, Inc. vs. The Coca-Cola Company

**BYP9-2** PepsiCo, Inc.'s financial statements are presented in Appendix B. Financial statements of The Coca-Cola Company are presented in Appendix C. Instructions for accessing and using the complete annual reports of PepsiCo and Coca-Cola, including the notes to the financial statements, are also provided in Appendices B and C, respectively.

*Instructions*
**(a)** Based on the information in these financial statements, compute the following 2011 ratios for each company. (Assume all sales are credit sales and that PepsiCo's receivables on its balance sheet are all trade receivables.)
   **(1)** Accounts receivable turnover.
   **(2)** Average collection period for receivables.
**(b)** What conclusions about managing accounts receivable can you draw from these data?

## Comparative Analysis Problem:
## Amazon.com, Inc. vs. Wal-Mart Stores, Inc.

**BYP9-3** Amazon.com, Inc.'s financial statements are presented in Appendix D. Financial statements of Wal-Mart Stores, Inc. are presented in Appendix E. Instructions for accessing and using the complete annual reports of Amazon and Wal-Mart, including the notes to the finanial statements, are also provided in Appendices D and E, respectively.

*Instructions*
**(a)** Based on the information in these financial statements, compute the following ratios for each company (for the most recent year shown). (Assume all sales are credit sales.)
   **(1)** Accounts receivable turnover.
   **(2)** Average collection period for receivables.

**(b)** What conclusions about managing accounts receivable can you draw from these data?

## Real-World Focus

**BYP9-4  Purpose:** To learn more about factoring.

*Address:* **www.ccapital.net**, or go to **www.wiley.com/college/weygandt**

*Steps:* Go to the website, click on **Invoice Factoring**, and answer the following questions.
**(a)** What are some of the benefits of factoring?
**(b)** What is the range of the percentages of the typical discount rate?
**(c)** If a company factors its receivables, what percentage of the value of the receivables can it expect to receive from the factor in the form of cash, and how quickly will it receive the cash?

## Critical Thinking

### Decision-Making Across the Organization

**BYP9-5** Carol and Sam Foyle own Campus Fashions. From its inception Campus Fashions has sold merchandise on either a cash or credit basis, but no credit cards have been accepted. During the past several months, the Foyles have begun to question their sales policies. First, they have lost some sales because of refusing to accept credit cards. Second, representatives of two metropolitan banks have been persuasive in almost convincing them to accept their national credit cards. One bank, City National Bank, has stated that its credit card fee is 4%.

The Foyles decide that they should determine the cost of carrying their own credit sales. From the accounting records of the past 3 years, they accumulate the following data.

|  | 2015 | 2014 | 2013 |
|---|---|---|---|
| Net credit sales | $500,000 | $550,000 | $400,000 |
| Collection agency fees for slow-paying customers | 2,450 | 2,500 | 2,300 |
| Salary of part-time accounts receivable clerk | 4,100 | 4,100 | 4,100 |

Credit and collection expenses as a percentage of net credit sales are uncollectible accounts 1.6%, billing and mailing costs 0.5%, and credit investigation fee on new customers 0.15%.

Carol and Sam also determine that the average accounts receivable balance outstanding during the year is 5% of net credit sales. The Foyles estimate that they could earn an average of 8% annually on cash invested in other business opportunities.

*Instructions*
With the class divided into groups, answer the following.

**(a)** Prepare a table showing, for each year, total credit and collection expenses in dollars and as a percentage of net credit sales.
**(b)** Determine the net credit and collection expense in dollars and as a percentage of sales after considering the revenue not earned from other investment opportunities.
**(c)** Discuss both the financial and nonfinancial factors that are relevant to the decision.

## Communication Activity

**BYP9-6** Jill Epp, a friend of yours, overheard a discussion at work about changes her employer wants to make in accounting for uncollectible accounts. Jill knows little about accounting, and she asks you to help make sense of what she heard. Specifically, she asks you to explain the differences between the percentage-of-sales, percentage-of-receivables, and the direct write-off methods for uncollectible accounts.

*Instructions*
In a letter of one page (or less), explain to Jill the three methods of accounting for uncollectibles. Be sure to discuss differences among these methods.

## Ethics Case

**BYP9-7** The controller of Diaz Co. believes that the yearly allowance for doubtful accounts for Diaz Co. should be 2% of net credit sales. The president of Diaz Co., nervous that the stockholders might expect the company to sustain its 10% growth rate, suggests that the controller increase the allowance for doubtful accounts to 4%. The president thinks that the lower net income, which reflects a 6% growth rate, will be a more sustainable rate for Diaz Co.

### Instructions
**(a)** Who are the stakeholders in this case?
**(b)** Does the president's request pose an ethical dilemma for the controller?
**(c)** Should the controller be concerned with Diaz Co.'s growth rate? Explain your answer.

## All About You

**BYP9-8** Credit card usage in the United States is substantial. Many startup companies use credit cards as a way to help meet short-term financial needs. The most common forms of debt for startups are use of credit cards and loans from relatives.

Suppose that you start up Brothers Sandwich Shop. You invested your savings of $20,000 and borrowed $70,000 from your relatives. Although sales in the first few months are good, you see that you may not have sufficient cash to pay expenses and maintain your inventory at acceptable levels, at least in the short term. You decide you may need to use one or more credit cards to fund the possible cash shortfall.

### Instructions
**(a)** Go to the Internet and find two sources that provide insight into how to compare credit card terms.
**(b)** Develop a list, in descending order of importance, as to what features are most important to you in selecting a credit card for your business.
**(c)** Examine the features of your present credit card. (If you do not have a credit card, select a likely one online for this exercise.) Given your analysis above, what are the three major disadvantages of your present credit card?

## FASB Codification Activity

**BYP9-9** If your school has a subscription to the FASB Codification, go to **http://aaahq.org/ ascLogin.cfm** to log in and prepare responses to the following.

**(a)** How are receivables defined in the Codification?
**(b)** What are the conditions under which losses from uncollectible receivables (Bad Debt Expense) should be reported?

## Answers to Chapter Questions

### Answers to Insight and Accounting Across the Organization Questions

**p. 440 How Does a Credit Card Work?    Q:** Assume that Nordstrom prepares a bank reconciliation at the end of each month. If some credit card sales have not been processed by the bank, how should Nordstrom treat these transactions on its bank reconciliation? **A:** Nordstrom would treat the credit card receipts as deposits in transit. It has already recorded the receipts as cash. Its bank will increase Nordstrom's cash account when it receives the receipts.

**p. 444 Can Fair Value Be Unfair?    Q:** What are the arguments in favor of and against fair value accounting for loans and receivables? **A:** Arguments in favor of fair value accounting for loans and receivables are that fair value would provide a more accurate view of a company's financial position. This might provide a useful early warning of when a bank or other financial institution was in trouble because its loans were of poor quality. But, banks argue that estimating fair values is very difficult to do accurately. They are also concerned that volatile fair values could cause large swings in a bank's reported net income.

**p. 446 Bad Information Can Lead to Bad Loans    Q:** What steps should the banks have taken to ensure the accuracy of financial information provided on loan applications? **A:** At a minimum, the bank should have requested copies of recent income tax forms and contacted the supposed employer to verify income. To verify ownership and value of assets, it should have examined bank statements, investment statements, and title documents and should have employed appraisers.

### Answers to Self-Test Questions

**1.** d  **2.** c ($1,000 − $300) × (100% − 2%)  **3.** a  **4.** b ($60,000 − $5,000)  **5.** d ($60,000 + $5,000)  **6.** b ($800,000 × 1.5%) + $15,000  **7.** b ($750,000 × 3%) + ($18,000 − $30,000)  **8.** d ($800,000 − $65,000)  **9.** c  **10.** a  **11.** c  **12.** b  **13.** d $10,000 + ($10,000 × 120/360 × 9%)  **14.** a  **15.** c $800,000 ÷ [($100,000 + $150,000) ÷ 2] and 365 ÷ 4

# A Look at IFRS

**LEARNING OBJECTIVE** **10**

Compare the accounting procedures for receivables under GAAP and IFRS.

The basic accounting and reporting issues related to recognition and measurement of receivables, such as the use of allowance accounts, how to record discounts, use of the allowance method to account for bad debts, and factoring, are essentially the same between IFRS and GAAP.

## Key Points

- IFRS requires that loans and receivables be accounted for at amortized cost, adjusted for allowances for doubtful accounts. IFRS sometimes refers to these allowances as **provisions**. The entry to record the allowance would be:

| | | |
|---|---|---|
| Bad Debt Expense | xxxxxx | |
| Allowance for Doubtful Accounts | | xxxxxx |

- Although IFRS implies that receivables with different characteristics should be reported separately, there is no standard that mandates this segregation.

- The FASB and IASB have worked to implement fair value measurement (the amount they currently could be sold for) for financial instruments. Both Boards have faced bitter opposition from various factions. As a consequence, the Boards have adopted a piecemeal approach. The first step is disclosure of fair value information in the notes. The second step is the fair value option, which permits but does not require companies to record some types of financial instruments at fair values in the financial statements.

- IFRS requires a two-tiered approach to test whether the value of loans and receivables are impaired. First, a company should look at specific loans and receivables to determine whether they are impaired. Then, the loans and receivables as a group should be evaluated for impairment. GAAP does not prescribe a similar two-tiered approach.

- IFRS and GAAP differ in the criteria used to determine how to record a factoring transaction. IFRS uses a combination approach focused on risks and rewards and loss of control. GAAP uses loss of control as the primary criterion. In addition, IFRS permits partial derecognition of receivables; GAAP does not.

## Looking to the Future

It appears likely that the question of recording fair values for financial instruments will continue to be an important issue to resolve as the Boards work toward convergence. Both the IASB and the FASB have indicated that they believe that financial statements would be more transparent and understandable if companies recorded and reported all financial instruments at fair value. That said, in *IFRS 9*, which was issued in 2009, the IASB created a split model, where some financial instruments are recorded at fair value, but other financial assets, such as loans and receivables, can be accounted for at amortized cost if certain criteria are met. Critics say that this can result in two companies with identical securities accounting for those securities in different ways. A proposal by the FASB would require that nearly all financial instruments, including loans and receivables, be accounted for at fair value. It has been suggested that *IFRS 9* will likely be changed or replaced as the FASB and IASB continue to deliberate the best treatment for financial instruments. In fact, one past member of the IASB said that companies should ignore *IFRS 9* and continue to report under the old standard. In his opinion, it was extremely likely that it would be changed before 2013, the mandatory adoption date of the standard.

## IFRS Practice

### IFRS Self-Test Questions

1. Under IFRS, loans and receivables are to be reported on the balance sheet at:
   (a) amortized cost.
   (b) amortized cost adjusted for estimated loss provisions.

(c) historical cost.

(d) replacement cost.

2. Which of the following statements is **false**?
   (a) Loans and receivables include equity securities purchased by the company.
   (b) Loans and receivables include credit card receivables.
   (c) Loans and receivables include amounts owed by employees as a result of company loans to employees.
   (d) Loans and receivables include amounts resulting from transactions with customers.

3. In recording a factoring transaction:
   (a) IFRS focuses on loss of control.
   (b) GAAP focuses on loss of control and risks and rewards.
   (c) IFRS and GAAP allow partial derecognition.
   (d) IFRS allows partial derecognition

4. Under IFRS:
   (a) the entry to record estimated uncollected accounts is the same as GAAP.
   (b) loans and receivables should only be tested for impairment as a group.
   (c) it is always acceptable to use the direct write-off method.
   (d) all financial instruments are recorded at fair value.

5. Which of the following statements is **true**?
   (a) The fair value option requires that some types of financial instruments be recorded at fair value.
   (b) The fair value option allows, but does not require, that some types of financial instruments be recorded at amortized cost.
   (c) The fair value option allows, but does not require, that some types of financial instruments be recorded at fair value.
   (d) The FASB and IASB would like to reduce the reliance on fair value accounting for financial instruments in the future.

## IFRS Exercises

**IFRS9-1** What are some steps taken by both the FASB and IASB to move to fair value measurement for financial instruments? In what ways have some of the approaches differed?

## International Financial Reporting Problem: Zetar plc

**IFRS9-2** The financial statements of Zetar plc are presented in Appendix F. Instructions for accessing and using the company's complete annual report, including the notes to its financial statements, are also provided in Appendix F.

*Instructions*
Use the company's annual report to answer the following questions.

(a) According to the Operational Review of Financial Performance, what was one reason why the balance in receivables increased relative to the previous year?

(b) According to the notes to the financial statements, how are loans and receivables defined?

(c) Using the notes to the financial statements, what amount of trade receivables were written off (utilised) during 2011?

(d) Using information in the notes to the financial statements, determine what percentage the provision for impairment of receivables was as a percentage of total trade receivables for 2011 and 2010. How did the ratio change from 2010 to 2011, and what does this suggest about the company's receivables?

**Answers to IFRS Self-Test Questions**
1. b  2. a  3. d  4. a  5. c

Remember to go back to The Navigator box on the chapter opening page and check off your completed work.

## Feature Story

✔ The Navigatc

### It Pays to Be Patient

A recent issue of *Forbes* magazine listed Warren Buffett as the richest person in the world. His estimated wealth was $62 billion, give or take a few million. How much is $62 billion? If you invested $62 billion in an investment earning just 4%, you could spend $6.8 million per day—every day—forever.

So, how does Buffett spend his money? Basically, he doesn't! He still lives in the same house that he purchased in Omaha, Nebraska, in 1958 for $31,500. He still drives his own car (a Cadillac DTS). And, in case you were thinking that his kids are riding the road to Easy Street, think again. Buffett has committed to donate virtually all of his money to charity before he dies.

How did Buffett amass this wealth? Through careful investing. Buffett epitomizes a "value investor." He applies the basic techniques he learned in the 1950s from the great value investor Benjamin Graham. He looks for companies that have good long-term potential but are currently underpriced. He invests in companies that have low exposure to debt and that reinvest their earnings for future growth. He does not get caught up in fads or the latest trends.

Buffett sat out on the dot-com mania in the 1990s. When other investors put lots of money into fledgling high-tech firms, Buffett didn't bite because he did not find dot-com companies that met his criteria. He didn't get to enjoy the stock price boom on the way up, but on the other hand, he didn't have to ride the price back down to Earth. When the dot-com bubble burst, everyone else was suffering from investment shock. Buffett swooped in and scooped up deal on companies that he had been following for years.

In 2012, the stock market had again reached near record highs. Buffett's returns had been significantly lagging the market. Only 26% of his investments at that time were in stock, and he was sitting on $38 billion in cash. One comme tator noted that "if the past is any guide, just when Buffett seems to look most like a loser, the party is about to end."

If you think you want to follow Buffett's example and transform your humble nest egg into a mountain of cash, be warned. His techniques have been widely circulated and emulated, but never practiced with the same degree of success. You should probably start by honing your financial analysis skills. A good way for you to begin your career as a

✔ The Navigator

- Scan Learning Objectives
- Read Feature Story
- Read Preview
- Read text and answer **DO IT!** p. 846
  - p. 859  ■ p. 864  ■ p. 866
- Work Comprehensive **DO IT!** p. 867
- Review Summary of Learning Objectives
- Answer Self-Test Questions
- Complete Assignments
- Go to *WileyPLUS* for practice and tutorials
- 🌐 **Read A Look at IFRS** p. 889

### Learning Objectives

✔ The Navigator

*After studying this chapter, you should be able to:*

[1] Discuss the need for comparative analysis.

[2] Identify the tools of financial statement analysis.

[3] Explain and apply horizontal analysis.

[4] Describe and apply vertical analysis.

[5] Identify and compute ratios used in analyzing a firm's liquidity, profitability, and solvency.

[6] Understand the concept of earning power, and how irregular items are presented.

[7] Understand the concept of quality of earnings.

Daniel Acker/Bloomberg/Getty Images, Inc.

successful investor is to master the fundamentals of financial analysis discussed in this chapter.

*Source:* Jason Zweig, "Buffett Is Out of Step," *Wall Street Journal* (May 7, 2012).

# Preview of Chapter 18

✔ **The Navigator**

We can all learn an important lesson from Warren Buffett. Study companies carefully if you wish to invest. Do not get caught up in fads but instead find companies that are financially healthy. Using some of the basic decision tools presented in this textbook, you can perform a rudimentary analysis on any U.S. company and draw basic conclusions about its financial health. Although it would not be wise for you to bet your life savings on a company's stock relying solely on your current level of knowledge, we strongly encourage you to practice your new skills wherever possible. Only with practice will you improve your ability to interpret financial numbers.

Before unleashing you on the world of high finance, we will present a few more important concepts and techniques, as well as provide you with one more comprehensive review of corporate financial statements. We use all of the decision tools presented in this text to analyze a single company—Macy's, Inc.—one of the country's oldest and largest retail store chains.

The content and organization of Chapter 18 are as follows.

## FINANCIAL STATEMENT ANALYSIS

| Basics of Financial Statement Analysis | Horizontal and Vertical Analysis | Ratio Analysis | Earning Power and Irregular Items | Quality of Earnings |
|---|---|---|---|---|
| • Need for comparative analysis<br>• Tools of analysis | • Balance sheet<br>• Income statement<br>• Retained earnings statement | • Liquidity<br>• Profitability<br>• Solvency<br>• Summary | • Discontinued operations<br>• Extraordinary items<br>• Changes in accounting principle<br>• Comprehensive income | • Alternative accounting methods<br>• Pro forma income<br>• Improper recognition |

## Basics of Financial Statement Analysis

Analyzing financial statements involves evaluating three characteristics: a company's liquidity, profitability, and solvency. A **short-term creditor**, such as a bank, is primarily interested in liquidity—the ability of the borrower to pay obligations when they come due. The liquidity of the borrower is extremely important in evaluating the safety of a loan. A **long-term creditor**, such as a bondholder, looks to profitability and solvency measures that indicate the company's ability to survive over a long period of time. Long-term creditors consider such measures as the amount of debt in the company's capital structure and its ability to meet interest payments. Similarly, **stockholders** look at the profitability and solvency of the company. They want to assess the likelihood of dividends and the growth potential of the stock.

### Need for Comparative Analysis

Every item reported in a financial statement has significance. When Macy's, Inc. reports cash and cash equivalents of $3 billion on its balance sheet, we know the company had that amount of cash on the balance sheet date. But, we do not know whether the amount represents an increase over prior years, or whether it is adequate in relation to the company's need for cash. To obtain such information, we need to compare the amount of cash with other financial statement data.

Comparisons can be made on a number of different bases. Three are illustrated in this chapter.

1. **Intracompany basis.** Comparisons within a company are often useful to detect changes in financial relationships and significant trends. For example, a comparison of Macy's current year's cash amount with the prior year's cash amount shows either an increase or a decrease. Likewise, a comparison of Macy's year-end cash amount with the amount of its total assets at year-end shows the proportion of total assets in the form of cash.

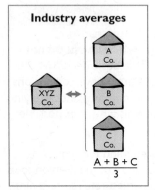

2. **Industry averages.** Comparisons with industry averages provide information about a company's relative position within the industry. For example, financial statement readers can compare Macy's financial data with the averages for its industry compiled by financial rating organizations such as Dun & Bradstreet, Moody's, and Standard & Poor's, or with information provided on the Internet by organizations such as Yahoo! on its financial site.

3. **Intercompany basis.** Comparisons with other companies provide insight into a company's competitive position. For example, investors can compare Macy's total sales for the year with the total sales of its competitors in retail, such as J.C. Penney.

### Tools of Analysis

We use various tools to evaluate the significance of financial statement data. Three commonly used tools are as follows:

- **Horizontal analysis** evaluates a series of financial statement data over a period of time.
- **Vertical analysis** evaluates financial statement data by expressing each item in a financial statement as a percentage of a base amount.
- **Ratio analysis** expresses the relationship among selected items of financial statement data.

Horizontal analysis is used primarily in intracompany comparisons. Two features in published financial statements and annual report information facilitate this type of comparison. First, each of the basic financial statements presents comparative financial data for a minimum of two years. Second, a summary of selected financial data is presented for a series of five to 10 years or more. Vertical analysis is used in both intra- and intercompany comparisons. Ratio analysis is used in all three types of comparisons. In the following sections, we explain and illustrate each of the three types of analysis.

## Horizontal Analysis

**Horizontal analysis**, also called **trend analysis**, is a technique for evaluating a series of financial statement data over a period of time. Its purpose is to determine the increase or decrease that has taken place. This change may be expressed as either an amount or a percentage. For example, Illustration 18-1 shows recent net sales figures of Macy's, Inc.

**LEARNING OBJECTIVE** 3

**Explain and apply horizontal analysis.**

| Real World | MACY'S, INC. Net Sales (in millions) | | |
|---|---|---|---|
| | **2011** | **2010** | **2009** |
| | $26,405 | $25,003 | $23,489 |

**Illustration 18-1**
Macy's, Inc.'s net sales

If we assume that 2009 is the base year, we can measure all percentage increases or decreases from this base period amount as follows.

$$\text{Change Since Base Period} = \frac{\text{Current Year Amount} - \text{Base Year Amount}}{\text{Base Year Amount}}$$

**Illustration 18-2**
Formula for horizontal analysis of changes since base period

For example, we can determine that net sales for Macy's increased from 2009 to 2010 approximately 6.4% [($25,003 − $23,489) ÷ $23,489]. Similarly, we can determine that net sales increased from 2009 to 2011 approximately 12.4% [($26,405 − $23,489) ÷ $23,489].

Alternatively, we can express current year sales as a percentage of the base period. We do this by dividing the current year amount by the base year amount, as shown below.

$$\text{Current Results in Relation to Base Period} = \frac{\text{Current Year Amount}}{\text{Base Year Amount}}$$

**Illustration 18-3**
Formula for horizontal analysis of current year in relation to base year

Illustration 18-4 presents this analysis for Macy's for a three-year period using 2009 as the base period.

| Real World | MACY'S, INC. Net Sales (in millions) in relation to base period 2009 | | |
|---|---|---|---|
| | **2011** | **2010** | **2009** |
| | $26,405 | $25,003 | $23,489 |
| | 112.4% | 106.4% | 100% |

**Illustration 18-4**
Horizontal analysis of Macy's, Inc.'s net sales in relation to base period

## Balance Sheet

To further illustrate horizontal analysis, we will use the financial statements of Quality Department Store Inc., a fictional retailer. Illustration 18-5 presents a horizontal analysis of its two-year condensed balance sheets, showing dollar and percentage changes.

**Illustration 18-5**
Horizontal analysis of balance sheets

### QUALITY DEPARTMENT STORE INC.
Condensed Balance Sheets
December 31

| | 2011 | 2010 | Increase or (Decrease) during 2011 Amount | Percent |
|---|---|---|---|---|
| **Assets** | | | | |
| Current assets | $1,020,000 | $ 945,000 | $ 75,000 | 7.9% |
| Plant assets (net) | 800,000 | 632,500 | 167,500 | 26.5% |
| Intangible assets | 15,000 | 17,500 | (2,500) | (14.3%) |
| Total assets | $1,835,000 | $1,595,000 | $240,000 | 15.0% |
| **Liabilities** | | | | |
| Current liabilities | $ 344,500 | $ 303,000 | $ 41,500 | 13.7% |
| Long-term liabilities | 487,500 | 497,000 | (9,500) | (1.9%) |
| Total liabilities | 832,000 | 800,000 | 32,000 | 4.0% |
| **Stockholders' Equity** | | | | |
| Common stock, $1 par | 275,400 | 270,000 | 5,400 | 2.0% |
| Retained earnings | 727,600 | 525,000 | 202,600 | 38.6% |
| Total stockholders' equity | 1,003,000 | 795,000 | 208,000 | 26.2% |
| Total liabilities and stockholders' equity | $1,835,000 | $1,595,000 | $240,000 | 15.0% |

The comparative balance sheets in Illustration 18-5 show that a number of significant changes have occurred in Quality Department Store's financial structure from 2010 to 2011:

- In the assets section, plant assets (net) increased $167,500, or 26.5%.
- In the liabilities section, current liabilities increased $41,500, or 13.7%.
- In the stockholders' equity section, retained earnings increased $202,600, or 38.6%.

These changes suggest that the company expanded its asset base during 2011 and **financed this expansion primarily by retaining income** rather than assuming additional long-term debt.

## Income Statement

Illustration 18-6 presents a horizontal analysis of the two-year condensed income statements of Quality Department Store Inc. for the years 2011 and 2010. Horizontal analysis of the income statements shows the following changes:

- Net sales increased $260,000, or 14.2% ($260,000 ÷ $1,837,000).
- Cost of goods sold increased $141,000, or 12.4% ($141,000 ÷ $1,140,000).
- Total operating expenses increased $37,000, or 11.6% ($37,000 ÷ $320,000).

Overall, gross profit and net income were up substantially. Gross profit increased 17.1%, and net income, 26.5%. Quality's profit trend appears favorable.

**QUALITY DEPARTMENT STORE INC.**
Condensed Income Statements
For the Years Ended December 31

**Illustration 18-6**
Horizontal analysis of income statements

|  | 2011 | 2010 | Increase or (Decrease) during 2011 Amount | Percent |
|---|---|---|---|---|
| Sales revenue | $2,195,000 | $1,960,000 | $235,000 | 12.0% |
| Sales returns and allowances | 98,000 | 123,000 | (25,000) | (20.3%) |
| Net sales | 2,097,000 | 1,837,000 | 260,000 | 14.2% |
| Cost of goods sold | 1,281,000 | 1,140,000 | 141,000 | 12.4% |
| Gross profit | 816,000 | 697,000 | 119,000 | 17.1% |
| Selling expenses | 253,000 | 211,500 | 41,500 | 19.6% |
| Administrative expenses | 104,000 | 108,500 | (4,500) | (4.1%) |
| Total operating expenses | 357,000 | 320,000 | 37,000 | 11.6% |
| Income from operations | 459,000 | 377,000 | 82,000 | 21.8% |
| Other revenues and gains |  |  |  |  |
| Interest and dividends | 9,000 | 11,000 | (2,000) | (18.2%) |
| Other expenses and losses |  |  |  |  |
| Interest expense | 36,000 | 40,500 | (4,500) | (11.1%) |
| Income before income taxes | 432,000 | 347,500 | 84,500 | 24.3% |
| Income tax expense | 168,200 | 139,000 | 29,200 | 21.0% |
| Net income | $ 263,800 | $ 208,500 | $ 55,300 | 26.5% |

**Helpful Hint** Note that though the amount column is additive (the total is $55,300), the percentage column is not additive (26.5% is not the column total). A separate percentage has been calculated for each item.

## Retained Earnings Statement

Illustration 18-7 presents a horizontal analysis of Quality Department Store's comparative retained earnings statements. Analyzed horizontally, net income increased $55,300, or 26.5%, whereas dividends on the common stock increased only $1,200, or 2%. We saw in the horizontal analysis of the balance sheet that ending retained earnings increased 38.6%. As indicated earlier, the company retained a significant portion of net income to finance additional plant facilities.

**QUALITY DEPARTMENT STORE INC.**
Retained Earnings Statements
For the Years Ended December 31

**Illustration 18-7**
Horizontal analysis of retained earnings statements

|  | 2011 | 2010 | Increase or (Decrease) during 2011 Amount | Percent |
|---|---|---|---|---|
| Retained earnings, Jan. 1 | $525,000 | $376,500 | $148,500 | 39.4% |
| Add: Net income | 263,800 | 208,500 | 55,300 | 26.5% |
|  | 788,800 | 585,000 | 203,800 |  |
| Deduct: Dividends | 61,200 | 60,000 | 1,200 | 2.0% |
| Retained earnings, Dec. 31 | $727,600 | $525,000 | $202,600 | 38.6% |

Horizontal analysis of changes from period to period is relatively straightforward and is quite useful. But, complications can occur in making the computations. If an item has no value in a base year or preceding year but does have a value in the next year, we cannot compute a percentage change. Similarly, if a negative amount appears in the base or preceding period and a positive amount exists the following year (or vice versa), no percentage change can be computed.

---

> **DO IT!**

### Horizontal Analysis

Summary financial information for Rosepatch Company is as follows.

| | December 31, 2014 | December 31, 2013 |
|---|---|---|
| Current assets | $234,000 | $180,000 |
| Plant assets (net) | 756,000 | 420,000 |
| Total assets | $990,000 | $600,000 |

Compute the amount and percentage changes in 2014 using horizontal analysis, assuming 2013 is the base year.

**Solution**

**Action Plan**

✔ Find the percentage change by dividing the amount of the increase by the 2013 amount (base year).

| | Increase in 2014 | |
|---|---|---|
| | **Amount** | **Percent** |
| Current assets | $ 54,000 | 30% [($234,000 − $180,000) ÷ $180,000] |
| Plant assets (net) | 336,000 | 80% [($756,000 − $420,000) ÷ $420,000] |
| Total assets | $390,000 | 65% [($990,000 − $600,000) ÷ $600,000] |

Related exercise material: **BE18-2, BE18-3, BE18-6, BE18-7, E18-1, E18-3, E18-4, and**  **18-1.**

✔ The Navigator

---

## Vertical Analysis

**Vertical analysis**, also called **common-size analysis**, is a technique that expresses each financial statement item as a percentage of a base amount. On a balance sheet, we might say that current assets are 22% of total assets—total assets being the base amount. Or on an income statement, we might say that selling expenses are 16% of net sales—net sales being the base amount.

### Balance Sheet

Illustration 18-8 presents the vertical analysis of Quality Department Store Inc.'s comparative balance sheets. The base for the asset items is **total assets**. The base for the liability and stockholders' equity items is **total liabilities and stockholders' equity**.

Vertical analysis shows the relative size of each category in the balance sheet. It also can show the **percentage change** in the individual asset, liability, and stockholders' equity items. For example, we can see that current assets decreased from 59.2% of total assets in 2010 to 55.6% in 2011 (even though the absolute dollar amount increased $75,000 in that time). Plant assets (net) have increased from 39.7% to 43.6% of total assets. Retained earnings have increased from 32.9% to 39.7% of total liabilities and stockholders' equity. These results reinforce the earlier observations that **Quality Department Store is choosing to finance its growth through retention of earnings rather than through issuing additional debt**.

Illustration 18-8
Vertical analysis of balance
sheets

## QUALITY DEPARTMENT STORE INC.
### Condensed Balance Sheets
### December 31

| | 2011 Amount | 2011 Percent | 2010 Amount | 2010 Percent |
|---|---|---|---|---|
| **Assets** | | | | |
| Current assets | $1,020,000 | 55.6% | $ 945,000 | 59.2% |
| Plant assets (net) | 800,000 | 43.6% | 632,500 | 39.7% |
| Intangible assets | 15,000 | 0.8% | 17,500 | 1.1% |
| Total assets | $1,835,000 | 100.0% | $1,595,000 | 100.0% |
| **Liabilities** | | | | |
| Current liabilities | $ 344,500 | 18.8% | $ 303,000 | 19.0% |
| Long-term liabilities | 487,500 | 26.5% | 497,000 | 31.2% |
| Total liabilities | 832,000 | 45.3% | 800,000 | 50.2% |
| **Stockholders' Equity** | | | | |
| Common stock, $1 par | 275,400 | 15.0% | 270,000 | 16.9% |
| Retained earnings | 727,600 | 39.7% | 525,000 | 32.9% |
| Total stockholders' equity | 1,003,000 | 54.7% | 795,000 | 49.8% |
| Total liabilities and stockholders' equity | $1,835,000 | 100.0% | $1,595,000 | 100.0% |

**Helpful Hint** The formula for calculating these balance sheet percentages is:

$$\frac{\text{Each item on B/S}}{\text{Total assets}} = \%$$

## Income Statement

Illustration 18-9 shows vertical analysis of Quality Department Store's income statements. Cost of goods sold as a percentage of net sales declined 1% (62.1% vs. 61.1%), and total operating expenses declined 0.4% (17.4% vs. 17.0%). As a result,

Illustration 18-9
Vertical analysis of income
statements

## QUALITY DEPARTMENT STORE INC.
### Condensed Income Statements
### For the Years Ended December 31

| | 2011 Amount | 2011 Percent | 2010 Amount | 2010 Percent |
|---|---|---|---|---|
| Sales revenue | $2,195,000 | 104.7% | $1,960,000 | 106.7% |
| Sales returns and allowances | 98,000 | 4.7% | 123,000 | 6.7% |
| Net sales | 2,097,000 | 100.0% | 1,837,000 | 100.0% |
| Cost of goods sold | 1,281,000 | 61.1% | 1,140,000 | 62.1% |
| Gross profit | 816,000 | 38.9% | 697,000 | 37.9% |
| Selling expenses | 253,000 | 12.0% | 211,500 | 11.5% |
| Administrative expenses | 104,000 | 5.0% | 108,500 | 5.9% |
| Total operating expenses | 357,000 | 17.0% | 320,000 | 17.4% |
| Income from operations | 459,000 | 21.9% | 377,000 | 20.5% |
| Other revenues and gains | | | | |
| Interest and dividends | 9,000 | 0.4% | 11,000 | 0.6% |
| Other expenses and losses | | | | |
| Interest expense | 36,000 | 1.7% | 40,500 | 2.2% |
| Income before income taxes | 432,000 | 20.6% | 347,500 | 18.9% |
| Income tax expense | 168,200 | 8.0% | 139,000 | 7.5% |
| Net income | $ 263,800 | 12.6% | $ 208,500 | 11.4% |

**Helpful Hint** The formula for calculating these income statement percentages is:

$$\frac{\text{Each item on I/S}}{\text{Net sales}} = \%$$

it is not surprising to see net income as a percentage of net sales increase from 11.4% to 12.6%. Quality Department Store appears to be a profitable business that is becoming even more successful.

An associated benefit of vertical analysis is that it enables you to compare companies of different sizes. For example, Quality Department Store's main competitor is a Macy's store in a nearby town. Using vertical analysis, we can compare the condensed income statements of Quality Department Store Inc. (a small retail company) with Macy's, Inc.[1] (a giant international retailer), as shown in Illustration 18-10.

**Illustration 18-10**
Intercompany income statement comparison

| | Condensed Income Statements (in thousands) | | | |
|---|---|---|---|---|
| | **Quality Department Store Inc.** | | **Macy's, Inc.** | |
| | **Dollars** | **Percent** | **Dollars** | **Percent** |
| Net sales | $2,097 | 100.0% | $26,405,000 | 100.0% |
| Cost of goods sold | 1,281 | 61.1% | 15,738,000 | 59.6% |
| Gross profit | 816 | 38.9% | 10,667,000 | 40.4% |
| Selling and administrative expenses | 357 | 17.0% | 8,256,000 | 31.3% |
| Income from operations | 459 | 21.9% | 2,411,000 | 9.1% |
| Other expenses and revenues (including income taxes) | 195 | 9.3% | 1,155,000 | 4.4% |
| Net income | $ 264 | 12.6% | $ 1,256,000 | 4.7% |

Macy's net sales are 12,592 times greater than the net sales of relatively tiny Quality Department Store. But vertical analysis eliminates this difference in size. The percentages show that Quality's and Macy's gross profit rates were comparable at 38.9% and 40.4%, respectively. However, the percentages related to income from operations were significantly different at 21.9% and 9.1%, respectively. This disparity can be attributed to Quality's selling and administrative expense percentage (17%) which is much lower than Macy's (31.3%). Although Macy's earned net income more than 4,757 times larger than Quality's, Macy's net income as a **percentage of each sales dollar** (4.7%) is only 37% of Quality's (12.6%).

## Ratio Analysis

LEARNING OBJECTIVE  **5**

Identify and compute ratios used in analyzing a firm's liquidity, profitability, and solvency.

**Ratio analysis** expresses the relationship among selected items of financial statement data. A **ratio** expresses the mathematical relationship between one quantity and another. The relationship is expressed in terms of either a percentage, a rate, or a simple proportion. To illustrate, in 2011 Nike, Inc. had current assets of $11,297 million and current liabilities of $3,958 million. We can find the relationship between these two measures by dividing current assets by current liabilities. The alternative means of expression are:

**Percentage:**    Current assets are 285% of current liabilities.
**Rate:**    Current assets are 2.85 times current liabilities.
**Proportion:**    The relationship of current assets to liabilities is 2.85:1.

To analyze the primary financial statements, we can use ratios to evaluate liquidity, profitability, and solvency. Illustration 18-11 describes these classifications.

---

[1]*2011 Annual Report*, Macy's, Inc. (Cincinnati, Ohio).

**Illustration 18-11**
Financial ratio classifications

**Liquidity Ratios**

Measure short-term ability of the company to pay its maturing obligations and to meet unexpected needs for cash

**Profitability Ratios**

Measure the income or operating success of a company for a given period of time

**Solvency Ratios**

Measure the ability of the company to survive over a long period of time

Ratios can provide clues to underlying conditions that may not be apparent from individual financial statement components. However, a single ratio by itself is not very meaningful. Thus, in the discussion of ratios we will use the following types of comparisons.

1. **Intracompany comparisons** for two years for Quality Department Store.
2. **Industry average comparisons** based on median ratios for department stores.
3. **Intercompany comparisons** based on Macy's, Inc. as Quality Department Store's principal competitor.

### ANATOMY OF A FRAUD

This final *Anatomy of a Fraud* box demonstrates that sometimes relationships between numbers can be used by companies to detect fraud. The numeric relationships that can reveal fraud can be such things as financial ratios that appear abnormal, or statistical abnormalities in the numbers themselves. For example, the fact that WorldCom's line costs, as a percentage of either total expenses or revenues, differed very significantly from its competitors should have alerted people to the possibility of fraud. Or, consider the case of a bank manager, who cooperated with a group of his friends to defraud the bank's credit card department. The manager's friends would apply for credit cards and then run up balances of slightly less than $5,000. The bank had a policy of allowing bank personnel to write-off balances of less than $5,000 without seeking supervisor approval. The fraud was detected by applying statistical analysis based on Benford's Law. Benford's Law states that in a random collection of numbers, the frequency of lower digits (e.g., 1, 2, or 3) should be much higher than higher digits (e.g., 7, 8, or 9). In this case, bank auditors analyzed the first two digits of amounts written off. There was a spike at 48 and 49, which was not consistent with what would be expected if the numbers were random.

Total take: Thousands of dollars

**THE MISSING CONTROLS**

*Independent internal verification.* While it might be efficient to allow employees to write off accounts below a certain level, it is important that these write-offs be reviewed and verified periodically. Such a review would likely call attention to an employee with large amounts of write-offs, or in this case, write-offs that were frequently very close to the approval threshold.

*Source:* Mark J. Nigrini, "I've Got Your Number," *Journal of Accountancy Online* (May 1999).

## Liquidity Ratios

**Liquidity ratios** measure the short-term ability of the company to pay its maturing obligations and to meet unexpected needs for cash. Short-term creditors such as bankers and suppliers are particularly interested in assessing liquidity. The ratios we can use to determine the company's short-term debt-paying ability are the current ratio, the acid-test ratio, accounts receivable turnover, and inventory turnover.

### 1. CURRENT RATIO

The **current ratio** is a widely used measure for evaluating a company's liquidity and short-term debt-paying ability. The ratio is computed by dividing current assets by current liabilities. Illustration 18-12 shows the 2011 and 2010 current ratios for Quality Department Store and comparative data.

**Illustration 18-12**
Current ratio

$$\text{Current Ratio} = \frac{\text{Current Assets}}{\text{Current Liabilities}}$$

Quality Department Store

| **2011** | **2010** |
|---|---|
| $\dfrac{\$1,020,000}{\$344,500} = 2.96:1$ | $\dfrac{\$945,000}{\$303,000} = 3.12:1$ |
| Industry average | Macy's, Inc. |
| **1.70:1** | **1.40:1** |

**Helpful Hint** Can any company operate successfully without working capital? Yes, if it has very predictable cash flows and solid earnings. A number of companies (e.g., Whirlpool, American Standard, and Campbell's Soup) are pursuing this goal. The rationale: Less money tied up in working capital means more money to invest in the business.

What does the ratio actually mean? The 2011 ratio of 2.96:1 means that for every dollar of current liabilities, Quality has $2.96 of current assets. Quality's current ratio has decreased in the current year. But, compared to the industry average of 1.70:1, Quality appears to be reasonably liquid. Macy's has a current ratio of 1.40:1, which indicates it has adequate current assets relative to its current liabilities.

The current ratio is sometimes referred to as the **working capital ratio**. **Working capital** is current assets minus current liabilities. The current ratio is a more dependable indicator of liquidity than working capital. Two companies with the same amount of working capital may have significantly different current ratios.

The current ratio is only one measure of liquidity. It does not take into account the **composition** of the current assets. For example, a satisfactory current ratio does not disclose the fact that a portion of the current assets may be tied up in slow-moving inventory. A dollar of cash would be more readily available to pay the bills than a dollar of slow-moving inventory.

### 2. ACID-TEST RATIO

The **acid-test (quick) ratio** is a measure of a company's immediate short-term liquidity. We compute this ratio by dividing the sum of cash, short-term investments, and net accounts receivable by current liabilities. Thus, it is an important complement to the current ratio. For example, assume that the current assets of Quality Department Store for 2011 and 2010 consist of the items shown in Illustration 18-13.

**Illustration 18-13**
Current assets of Quality
Department Store

| QUALITY DEPARTMENT STORE INC. | | |
|---|---|---|
| Balance Sheet (partial) | | |
| | **2011** | **2010** |
| Current assets | | |
| **Cash** | $ 100,000 | $155,000 |
| **Short-term investments** | 20,000 | 70,000 |
| **Accounts receivable (net\*)** | 230,000 | 180,000 |
| Inventory | 620,000 | 500,000 |
| Prepaid expenses | 50,000 | 40,000 |
| Total current assets | $1,020,000 | $ 945,000 |

\*Allowance for doubtful accounts is $10,000 at the end of each year.

Cash, short-term investments, and accounts receivable (net) are highly liquid compared to inventory and prepaid expenses. The inventory may not be readily saleable, and the prepaid expenses may not be transferable to others. Thus, the acid-test ratio measures **immediate** liquidity. The 2011 and 2010 acid-test ratios for Quality Department Store and comparative data are as follows.

**Illustration 18-14**
Acid-test ratio

$$\text{Acid-Test Ratio} = \frac{\text{Cash + Short-Term Investments + Accounts Receivable (Net)}}{\text{Current Liabilities}}$$

| Quality Department Store | |
|---|---|
| **2011** | **2010** |
| $\dfrac{\$100{,}000 + \$20{,}000 + \$230{,}000}{\$344{,}500} = 1.02{:}1$ | $\dfrac{\$155{,}000 + \$70{,}000 + \$180{,}000}{\$303{,}000} = 1.34{:}1$ |
| Industry average | Macy's, Inc. |
| **0.70:1** | **0.51:1** |

The ratio has declined in 2011. Is an acid-test ratio of 1.02:1 adequate? This depends on the industry and the economy. When compared with the industry average of 0.70:1 and Macy's of 0.51:1, Quality's acid-test ratio seems adequate.

# INVESTOR INSIGHT

### How to Manage the Current Ratio

The apparent simplicity of the current ratio can have real-world limitations because adding equal amounts to both the numerator and the denominator causes the ratio to decrease.

Assume, for example, that a company has $2,000,000 of current assets and $1,000,000 of current liabilities. Thus, its current ratio is 2:1. If the company purchases $1,000,000 of inventory on account, it will have $3,000,000 of current assets and $2,000,000 of current liabilities. Its current ratio therefore decreases to 1.5:1. If, instead, the company pays off $500,000 of its current liabilities, it will have $1,500,000 of current assets and $500,000 of current liabilities. Its current ratio then increases to 3:1. Thus, any trend analysis should be done with care because the ratio is susceptible to quick changes and is easily influenced by management.

**?** How might management influence a company's current ratio? (See page 889.)

SuperStock

### 3. ACCOUNTS RECEIVABLE TURNOVER

We can measure liquidity by how quickly a company can convert certain assets to cash. How liquid, for example, are the accounts receivable? The ratio used to assess the liquidity of the receivables is **accounts receivable turnover**. It measures the number of times, on average, the company collects receivables during the period. We compute accounts receivable turnover by dividing net credit sales (net sales less cash sales) by the average net accounts receivable. Unless seasonal factors are significant, average net accounts receivable can be computed from the beginning and ending balances of the net accounts receivable.[2]

Assume that all sales are credit sales. The balance of net accounts receivable at the beginning of 2010 is $200,000. Illustration 18-15 shows the accounts receivable turnover for Quality Department Store and comparative data. Quality's accounts receivable turnover improved in 2011. The turnover of 10.2 times is substantially lower than Macy's 74.8 times, and is also lower than the department store industry's average of 46.4 times.

**Illustration 18-15**
Accounts receivable turnover

$$\text{Accounts Receivable Turnover} = \frac{\text{Net Credit Sales}}{\text{Average Net Accounts Receivable}}$$

**Quality Department Store**

**2011**

$$\frac{\$2,097,000}{\left[\dfrac{\$180,000 + \$230,000}{2}\right]} = 10.2 \text{ times}$$

**2010**

$$\frac{\$1,837,000}{\left[\dfrac{\$200,000 + \$180,000}{2}\right]} = 9.7 \text{ times}$$

Industry average
**46.4 times**

Macy's, Inc.
**74.8 times**

**AVERAGE COLLECTION PERIOD** A popular variant of the accounts receivable turnover is to convert it to an **average collection period** in terms of days. To do so, we divide the accounts receivable turnover into 365 days. For example, the accounts receivable turnover of 10.2 times divided into 365 days gives an average collection period of approximately 36 days. This means that accounts receivable are collected on average every 36 days, or about every 5 weeks. Analysts frequently use the average collection period to assess the effectiveness of a company's credit and collection policies. The general rule is that the collection period should not greatly exceed the credit term period (the time allowed for payment).

### 4. INVENTORY TURNOVER

**Inventory turnover** measures the number of times, on average, the inventory is sold during the period. Its purpose is to measure the liquidity of the inventory. We compute the inventory turnover by dividing cost of goods sold by the average inventory. Unless seasonal factors are significant, we can use the beginning and ending inventory balances to compute average inventory.

Assuming that the inventory balance for Quality Department Store at the beginning of 2010 was $450,000, its inventory turnover and comparative data are as shown in Illustration 18-16. Quality's inventory turnover declined slightly in 2011. The turnover of 2.3 times is low compared with the industry average of 4.3

---

[2]If seasonal factors are significant, the average accounts receivable balance might be determined by using monthly amounts.

and Macy's 3.2. Generally, the faster the inventory turnover, the less cash a company has tied up in inventory and the less the chance of inventory obsolescence.

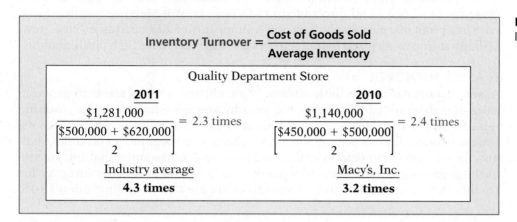

**Illustration 18-16**
Inventory turnover

**DAYS IN INVENTORY** A variant of inventory turnover is the **days in inventory**. We calculate it by dividing the inventory turnover into 365. For example, Quality's 2011 inventory turnover of 2.3 times divided into 365 is approximately 159 days. An average selling time of 159 days is also high compared with the industry average of 84.9 days (365 ÷ 4.3) and Macy's 114.1 days (365 ÷ 3.2).

Inventory turnovers vary considerably among industries. For example, grocery store chains have a turnover of 17.1 times and an average selling period of 21 days. In contrast, jewelry stores have an average turnover of 0.80 times and an average selling period of 456 days.

## Profitability Ratios

**Profitability ratios** measure the income or operating success of a company for a given period of time. Income, or the lack of it, affects the company's ability to obtain debt and equity financing. It also affects the company's liquidity position and the company's ability to grow. As a consequence, both creditors and investors are interested in evaluating earning power—profitability. Analysts frequently use profitability as the ultimate test of management's operating effectiveness.

### 5. PROFIT MARGIN

**Profit margin** is a measure of the percentage of each dollar of sales that results in net income. We can compute it by dividing net income by net sales. Illustration 18-17 shows Quality Department Store's profit margin and comparative data.

*Alternative Terminology*
Profit margin is also called the *rate of return on sales.*

**Illustration 18-17**
Profit margin

Quality experienced an increase in its profit margin from 2010 to 2011. Its profit margin is unusually high in comparison with the industry average of 8% and Macy's 4.8%.

High-volume (high inventory turnover) businesses, such as grocery stores (Safeway or Kroger) and discount stores (Kmart or Wal-Mart), generally experience low profit margins. In contrast, low-volume businesses, such as jewelry stores (Tiffany & Co.) or airplane manufacturers (Boeing Co.), have high profit margins.

## 6. ASSET TURNOVER

**Asset turnover** measures how efficiently a company uses its assets to generate sales. It is determined by dividing net sales by average total assets. The resulting number shows the dollars of sales produced by each dollar invested in assets. Unless seasonal factors are significant, we can use the beginning and ending balance of total assets to determine average total assets. Assuming that total assets at the beginning of 2010 were $1,446,000, the 2011 and 2010 asset turnover for Quality Department Store and comparative data are shown in Illustration 18-18.

**Illustration 18-18**
Asset turnover

Asset turnover shows that in 2011 Quality generated sales of $1.20 for each dollar it had invested in assets. The ratio changed very little from 2010 to 2011. Quality's asset turnover is below the industry average of 1.4 times and equal to Macy's ratio of 1.2 times.

Asset turnovers vary considerably among industries. For example, a large utility company like Consolidated Edison (New York) has a ratio of 0.4 times, and the large grocery chain Kroger Stores has a ratio of 3.4 times.

## 7. RETURN ON ASSETS

An overall measure of profitability is **return on assets**. We compute this ratio by dividing net income by average total assets. The 2011 and 2010 return on assets for Quality Department Store and comparative data are shown below.

**Illustration 18-19**
Return on assets

Quality's return on assets improved from 2010 to 2011. Its return of 15.4% is very high compared with the department store industry average of 8.9% and Macy's 5.9%.

## 8. RETURN ON COMMON STOCKHOLDERS' EQUITY

Another widely used profitability ratio is **return on common stockholders' equity**. It measures profitability from the common stockholders' viewpoint. This ratio shows how many dollars of net income the company earned for each dollar invested by the owners. We compute it by dividing net income by average common stockholders' equity. Assuming that common stockholders' equity at the beginning of 2010 was $667,000, Illustration 18-20 shows the 2011 and 2010 ratios for Quality Department Store and comparative data.

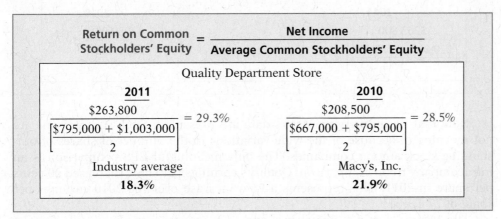

$$\text{Return on Common Stockholders' Equity} = \frac{\text{Net Income}}{\text{Average Common Stockholders' Equity}}$$

Quality Department Store

| **2011** | | **2010** | |
|---|---|---|---|
| $\dfrac{\$263,800}{\left[\dfrac{\$795,000 + \$1,003,000}{2}\right]} = 29.3\%$ | | $\dfrac{\$208,500}{\left[\dfrac{\$667,000 + \$795,000}{2}\right]} = 28.5\%$ | |
| Industry average | | Macy's, Inc. | |
| **18.3%** | | **21.9%** | |

**Illustration 18-20**
Return on common stockholders' equity

Quality's rate of return on common stockholders' equity is high at 29.3%, considering an industry average of 18.3% and a rate of 21.9% for Macy's.

**WITH PREFERRED STOCK**  When a company has preferred stock, we must deduct **preferred dividend** requirements from net income to compute income available to common stockholders. Similarly, we deduct the par value of preferred stock (or call price, if applicable) from total stockholders' equity to determine the amount of common stockholders' equity used in this ratio. The ratio then appears as follows.

$$\text{Return on Common Stockholders' Equity} = \frac{\text{Net Income} - \text{Preferred Dividends}}{\text{Average Common Stockholders' Equity}}$$

**Illustration 18-21**
Return on common stockholders' equity with preferred stock

Note that Quality's rate of return on stockholders' equity (29.3%) is substantially higher than its rate of return on assets (15.4%). The reason is that Quality has made effective use of **leverage**. **Leveraging** or **trading on the equity** at a gain means that the company has borrowed money at a lower rate of interest than it is able to earn by using the borrowed money. Leverage enables Quality Department Store to use money supplied by nonowners to increase the return to the owners. A comparison of the rate of return on total assets with the rate of interest paid for borrowed money indicates the profitability of trading on the equity. Quality Department Store earns more on its borrowed funds than it has to pay in the form of interest. Thus, the return to stockholders exceeds the return on the assets, due to benefits from the positive leveraging.

## 9. EARNINGS PER SHARE (EPS)

**Earnings per share (EPS)** is a measure of the net income earned on each share of common stock. It is computed by dividing net income by the number of weighted-average common shares outstanding during the year. A measure of net income earned on a per share basis provides a useful perspective for determining profitability. Assuming that there is no change in the number of outstanding shares during 2010 and that the 2011 increase occurred midyear, Illustration 18-22 shows the net income per share for Quality Department Store for 2011 and 2010.

**Illustration 18-22**
Earnings per share

Note that no industry or Macy's data are presented. Such comparisons are not meaningful because of the wide variations in the number of shares of outstanding stock among companies. The only meaningful EPS comparison is an intracompany trend comparison: Quality's earnings per share increased 20 cents per share in 2011. This represents a 26% increase over the 2010 earnings per share of 77 cents.

The terms "earnings per share" and "net income per share" refer to the amount of net income applicable to each share of **common stock**. Therefore, in computing EPS, if there are preferred dividends declared for the period, we must deduct them from net income to determine income available to the common stockholders.

## 10. PRICE-EARNINGS RATIO

The **price-earnings (P-E) ratio** is an oft-quoted measure of the ratio of the market price of each share of common stock to the earnings per share. The price-earnings (P-E) ratio reflects investors' assessments of a company's future earnings. We compute it by dividing the market price per share of the stock by earnings per share. Assuming that the market price of Quality Department Store Inc. stock is $8 in 2010 and $12 in 2011, the price-earnings ratio computation is as follows.

**Illustration 18-23**
Price-earnings ratio

In 2011, each share of Quality's stock sold for 12.4 times the amount that the company earned on each share. Quality's price-earnings ratio is lower than the industry average of 21.3 times but higher than the ratio of 10.9 times for Macy's.

The average price-earnings ratio for the stocks that constitute the Standard and Poor's 500 Index (500 largest U.S. firms) in late 2012 was approximately 15.9 times.

## 11. PAYOUT RATIO

The **payout ratio** measures the percentage of earnings distributed in the form of cash dividends. We compute it by dividing cash dividends by net income. Companies that have high growth rates generally have low payout ratios because they reinvest most of their net income into the business. The 2011 and 2010 payout ratios for Quality Department Store are computed as shown in Illustration 18-24.

**Illustration 18-24**
Payout ratio

$$\text{Payout Ratio} = \frac{\text{Cash Dividends}}{\text{Net Income}}$$

**Quality Department Store**

| 2011 | 2010 |
|------|------|
| $\dfrac{\$61,200}{\$263,800} = 23.2\%$ | $\dfrac{\$60,000}{\$208,500} = 28.8\%$ |
| Industry average | Macy's, Inc. |
| **16.1%** | **11.8%** |

Quality's payout ratio is higher than the industry average payout ratio of 16.1%.

## Solvency Ratios

**Solvency ratios** measure the ability of a company to survive over a long period of time. Long-term creditors and stockholders are particularly interested in a company's ability to pay interest as it comes due and to repay the face value of debt at maturity. Debt to assets and times interest earned are two ratios that provide information about debt-paying ability.

### 12. DEBT TO ASSETS RATIO

The **debt to assets ratio** measures the percentage of the total assets that creditors provide. We compute it by dividing debt (both current and long-term liabilities) by assets. This ratio indicates the company's degree of leverage. It also provides some indication of the company's ability to withstand losses without impairing the interests of creditors. The higher the percentage of debt to assets, the greater the risk that the company may be unable to meet its maturing obligations. The 2011 and 2010 ratios for Quality Department Store and comparative data are as follows.

**Illustration 18-25**
Debt to assets ratio

$$\text{Debt to Assets Ratio} = \frac{\text{Debt}}{\text{Assets}}$$

**Quality Department Store**

| 2011 | 2010 |
|------|------|
| $\dfrac{\$832,000}{\$1,835,000} = 45.3\%$ | $\dfrac{\$800,000}{\$1,595,000} = 50.2\%$ |
| Industry average | Macy's, Inc. |
| **34.2%** | **73.1%** |

A ratio of 45.3% means that creditors have provided 45.3% of Quality Department Store's total assets. Quality's 45.3% is above the industry average of 34.2%.

It is considerably below the high 73.1% ratio of Macy's. The lower the ratio, the more equity "buffer" there is available to the creditors. Thus, from the creditors' point of view, a low ratio of debt to assets is usually desirable.

The adequacy of this ratio is often judged in the light of the company's earnings. Generally, companies with relatively stable earnings (such as public utilities) have higher debt to assets ratios than cyclical companies with widely fluctuating earnings (such as many high-tech companies).

### 13. TIMES INTEREST EARNED

**Times interest earned** provides an indication of the company's ability to meet interest payments as they come due. We compute it by dividing income before interest expense and income taxes by interest expense. Illustration 18-26 shows the 2011 and 2010 ratios for Quality Department Store and comparative data. Note that times interest earned uses income before income taxes and interest expense. This represents the amount available to cover interest. For Quality Department Store, the 2011 amount of $468,000 is computed by taking the income before income taxes of $432,000 and adding back the $36,000 of interest expense.

**Illustration 18-26**
Times interest earned

$$\text{Times Interest Earned} = \frac{\text{Income before Income Taxes and Interest Expense}}{\text{Interest Expense}}$$

| Quality Department Store | |
|---|---|
| **2011** | **2010** |
| $\frac{\$468,000}{\$36,000} = 13 \text{ times}$ | $\frac{\$388,000}{\$40,500} = 9.6 \text{ times}$ |
| Industry average | Macy's, Inc. |
| **16.1 times** | **5.4 times** |

Quality's interest expense is well covered at 13 times, compared with the industry average of 16.1 times and Macy's 5.4 times.

## Summary of Ratios

**Illustration 18-27**
Summary of liquidity, profitability, and solvency ratios

Illustration 18-27 summarizes the ratios discussed in this chapter. The summary includes the formula and purpose or use of each ratio.

| Ratio | Formula | Purpose or Use |
|---|---|---|
| **Liquidity Ratios** | | |
| 1. Current ratio | $\frac{\text{Current assets}}{\text{Current liabilities}}$ | Measures short-term debt-paying ability. |
| 2. Acid-test (quick) ratio | $\frac{\text{Cash} + \text{Short-term investments} + \text{Accounts receivable (net)}}{\text{Current liabilities}}$ | Measures immediate short-term liquidity. |
| 3. Accounts receivable turnover | $\frac{\text{Net credit sales}}{\text{Average net accounts receivable}}$ | Measures liquidity of accounts receivable. |
| 4. Inventory turnover | $\frac{\text{Cost of goods sold}}{\text{Average inventory}}$ | Measures liquidity of inventory. |
| **Profitability Ratios** | | |
| 5. Profit margin | $\frac{\text{Net income}}{\text{Net sales}}$ | Measures net income generated by each dollar of sales. |
| 6. Asset turnover | $\frac{\text{Net sales}}{\text{Average total assets}}$ | Measures how efficiently assets are used to generate sales. |

| Ratio | Formula | Purpose or Use |
|---|---|---|
| 7. Return on assets | $\dfrac{\text{Net income}}{\text{Average total assets}}$ | Measures overall profitability of assets. |
| 8. Return on common stockholders' equity | $\dfrac{\text{Net income} - \text{Preferred dividends}}{\text{Average common stockholders' equity}}$ | Measures profitability of owners' investment. |
| 9. Earnings per share (EPS) | $\dfrac{\text{Net income} - \text{Preferred dividends}}{\text{Weighted-average common shares outstanding}}$ | Measures net income earned on each share of common stock. |
| 10. Price-earnings (P-E) ratio | $\dfrac{\text{Market price per share of stock}}{\text{Earnings per share}}$ | Measures the ratio of the market price per share to earnings per share. |
| 11. Payout ratio | $\dfrac{\text{Cash dividends}}{\text{Net income}}$ | Measures percentage of earnings distributed in the form of cash dividends. |
| **Solvency Ratios** | | |
| 12. Debt to assets ratio | $\dfrac{\text{Debt}}{\text{Assets}}$ | Measures the percentage of total assets provided by creditors. |
| 13. Times interest earned | $\dfrac{\text{Income before income taxes and interest expense}}{\text{Interest expense}}$ | Measures ability to meet interest payments as they come due. |

> ## DO IT!

## Ratio Analysis

The condensed financial statements of John Cully Company, for the years ended June 30, 2014 and 2013, are presented below.

**JOHN CULLY COMPANY**
Balance Sheets
June 30

| | | **(in thousands)** | |
|---|---|---|---|
| **Assets** | | **2014** | **2013** |
| Current assets | | | |
| Cash and cash equivalents | | $ 553.3 | $ 611.6 |
| Accounts receivable (net) | | 776.6 | 664.9 |
| Inventory | | 768.3 | 653.5 |
| Prepaid expenses and other current assets | | 204.4 | 269.2 |
| Total current assets | | 2,302.6 | 2,199.2 |
| Property, plant, and equipment (net) | | 694.2 | 647.0 |
| Investments | | 12.3 | 12.6 |
| Intangibles and other assets | | 876.7 | 849.3 |
| Total assets | | $3,885.8 | $3,708.1 |
| **Liabilities and Stockholders' Equity** | | | |
| Current liabilities | | $1,497.7 | $1,322.0 |
| Long-term liabilities | | 679.5 | 637.1 |
| Stockholders' equity—common | | 1,708.6 | 1,749.0 |
| Total liabilities and stockholders' equity | | $3,885.8 | $3,708.1 |

| JOHN CULLY COMPANY |
|---|
| Income Statements |
| For the Year Ended June 30 |

|  | (in thousands) | |
|---|---|---|
|  | **2014** | **2013** |
| Sales revenue | $6,336.3 | $5,790.4 |
| Costs and expenses |  |  |
| Cost of goods sold | 1,617.4 | 1,476.3 |
| Selling and administrative expenses | 4,007.6 | 3,679.0 |
| Interest expense | 13.9 | 27.1 |
| Total costs and expenses | 5,638.9 | 5,182.4 |
| Income before income taxes | 697.4 | 608.0 |
| Income tax expense | 291.3 | 232.6 |
| Net income | $ 406.1 | $ 375.4 |

Compute the following ratios for 2014 and 2013.

**(a)** Current ratio.
**(b)** Inventory turnover. (Inventory on 6/30/12 was $599.0.)
**(c)** Profit margin ratio.
**(d)** Return on assets. (Assets on 6/30/12 were $3,349.9.)
**(e)** Return on common stockholders' equity. (Stockholders' equity on 6/30/12 was $1,795.9.)
**(f)** Debt to assets ratio.
**(g)** Times interest earned.

**Solution**

**Action Plan**

✔ Remember that the current ratio includes all current assets. The acid-test ratio uses only cash, short-term investments, and net accounts receivable.

✔ Use average balances for turnover ratios like inventory, accounts receivable, and asset.

|  | **2014** | **2013** |
|---|---|---|
| **(a)** Current ratio: |  |  |
| $2,302.6 ÷ $1,497.7 = | 1.5:1 |  |
| $2,199.2 ÷ $1,322.0 = |  | 1.7:1 |
| **(b)** Inventory turnover: |  |  |
| $1,617.4 ÷ [($768.3 + $653.5) ÷ 2] = | 2.3 times |  |
| $1,476.3 ÷ [($653.5 + $599.0) ÷ 2] = |  | 2.4 times |
| **(c)** Profit margin: |  |  |
| $406.1 ÷ $6,336.3 = | 6.4% |  |
| $375.4 ÷ $5,790.4 = |  | 6.5% |
| **(d)** Return on assets: |  |  |
| $406.1 ÷ [($3,885.8 + $3,708.1) ÷ 2] = | 10.7% |  |
| $375.4 ÷ [($3,708.1 + $3,349.9) ÷ 2] = |  | 10.6% |
| **(e)** Return on common stockholders' equity: |  |  |
| ($406.1 − $0) ÷ [($1,708.6 + $1,749.0) ÷ 2] = | 23.5% |  |
| ($375.4 − $0) ÷ [($1,749.0 + $1,795.9) ÷ 2] = |  | 21.2% |
| **(f)** Debt to assets ratio: |  |  |
| ($1,497.7 + $679.5) ÷ $3,885.8 = | 56.0% |  |
| ($1,322.0 + $637.1) ÷ $3,708.1 = |  | 52.8% |
| **(g)** Times interest earned: |  |  |
| ($406.1 + $291.3 + $13.9) ÷ $13.9 = | 51.2 times |  |
| ($375.4 + $232.6 + $27.1) ÷ $27.1 = |  | 23.4 times |

Related exercise material: **BE18-9, BE18-10, BE18-12, BE18-13, E18-5, E18-7, E18-8, E18-9, E18-10, E18-11, and** DO IT! **18-2.**

✔ The Navigator

## Earning Power and Irregular Items

Users of financial statements are interested in the concept of earning power. **Earning power** means the normal level of income to be obtained in the future. Earning power differs from actual net income by the amount of irregular revenues, expenses, gains, and losses. Users are interested in earning power because it helps them derive an estimate of future earnings without the "noise" of irregular items.

For users of financial statements to determine earning power or regular income, the "irregular" items are separately identified on the income statement. Companies report two types of "irregular" items.

**1.** Discontinued operations.

**2.** Extraordinary items.

These "irregular" items are reported net of income taxes. That is, the income statement first reports income tax on the income before "irregular" items. Then the amount of tax for each of the listed "irregular" items is computed. The general concept is "let the tax follow income or loss."

**LEARNING OBJECTIVE    6**

Understand the concept of earning power, and how irregular items are presented.

### Discontinued Operations

**Discontinued operations** refers to the disposal of a **significant component** of a business, such as the elimination of a major class of customers, or an entire activity. For example, to downsize its operations, General Dynamics Corp. sold its missile business to Hughes Aircraft Co. for $450 million. In its income statement, General Dynamics reported the sale in a separate section entitled "Discontinued operations."

Following the disposal of a significant component, the company should report on its income statement both income from continuing operations and income (or loss) from discontinued operations. **The income (loss) from discontinued operations consists of two parts: the income (loss) from operations** and **the gain (loss) on disposal of the component**.

To illustrate, assume that during 2014 Acro Energy Inc. has income before income taxes of $800,000. During 2014, Acro discontinued and sold its unprofitable chemical division. The loss in 2014 from chemical operations (net of $60,000 taxes) was $140,000. The loss on disposal of the chemical division (net of $30,000 taxes) was $70,000. Assuming a 30% tax rate on income, Illustration 18-28 shows Acro's income statement presentation.

**Illustration 18-28**
Statement presentation of discontinued operations

| ACRO ENERGY INC. Income Statement (partial) For the Year Ended December 31, 2014 | | |
|---|---|---|
| Income before income taxes | | $ 800,000 |
| Income tax expense | | 240,000 |
| Income from continuing operations | | 560,000 |
| **Discontinued operations** | | |
| **Loss from operations of chemical division,** net of $60,000 income tax saving | $140,000 | |
| **Loss from disposal of chemical division,** net of $30,000 income tax saving | 70,000 | 210,000 |
| Net income | | $ 350,000 |

**Helpful Hint** Observe the dual disclosures. (1) The results of operations of the discontinued division must be eliminated from the results of continuing operations. (2) The company must also report the disposal of the operation.

**18** Financial Statement Analysis

Note that the statement uses the caption "Income from continuing operations" and adds a new section "Discontinued operations." **The new section reports both the operating loss and the loss on disposal net of applicable income taxes.** This presentation clearly indicates the separate effects of continuing operations and discontinued operations on net income.

## Extraordinary Items

**Extraordinary items** are events and transactions that meet two conditions. They are (1) **unusual in nature,** and (2) **infrequent in occurrence**. To be unusual, the item should be abnormal and only incidentally related to the company's customary activities. To be infrequent, the item should not be reasonably expected to recur in the foreseeable future.

A company must evaluate both criteria in terms of its operating environment. Thus, Weyerhaeuser Co. reported the $36 million in damages to its timberland caused by the volcanic eruption of Mount St. Helens as an extraordinary item. The eruption was both unusual and infrequent. In contrast, Florida Citrus Company does not report frost damage to its citrus crop as an extraordinary item, because frost damage is not infrequent. Illustration 18-29 shows the classification of extraordinary and ordinary items.

**Extraordinary items**

1. Effects of major natural casualties, if rare in the area.

2. Expropriation (takeover) of property by a foreign government.

3. Effects of a newly enacted law or regulation, such as a condemnation action.

**Ordinary items**

1. Effects of major natural casualties, not uncommon in the area.

2. Write-down of inventories or write-off of receivables.

3. Losses attributable to labor strikes.

4. Gains or losses from sales of property, plant, or equipment.

**Illustration 18-29**
Examples of extraordinary and ordinary items

**Companies report extraordinary items net of taxes in a separate section of the income statement, immediately below discontinued operations.** To illustrate, assume that in 2014 a foreign government expropriated property held as an investment by Acro Energy Inc. If the loss is $70,000 before applicable income taxes of $21,000, the income statement will report a deduction of $49,000, as shown in Illustration 18-30. When there is an extraordinary item to report, the company adds the caption "Income before extraordinary item" immediately before the section for the extraordinary item. This presentation clearly indicates the effect of the extraordinary item on net income.

| ACRO ENERGY INC. Income Statement (partial) For the Year Ended December 31, 2014 | | |
|---|---|---|
| Income before income taxes | | $800,000 |
| Income tax expense | | 240,000 |
| Income from continuing operations | | 560,000 |
| Discontinued operations | | |
| Loss from operations of chemical division, net of $60,000 income tax saving | $140,000 | |
| Loss from disposal of chemical division, net of $30,000 income tax saving | 70,000 | 210,000 |
| Income before extraordinary item | | 350,000 |
| **Extraordinary item** | | |
| **Expropriation of investment, net of $21,000 income tax saving** | | **49,000** |
| Net income | | $301,000 |

**Illustration 18-30**
Statement presentation of extraordinary items

**Helpful Hint** If there are no discontinued operations, the third line of the income statement would be labeled "Income before extraordinary item."

What if a transaction or event meets one (but not both) of the criteria for an extraordinary item? In that case, the company reports it under either "Other revenues and gains" or "Other expenses and losses" at its gross amount (not net of tax). This is true, for example, of gains (losses) resulting from the sale of property, plant, and equipment, as explained in Chapter 10. It is quite common for companies to use the label "Non-recurring charges" for losses that do not meet the extraordinary item criteria.

## INVESTOR INSIGHT

© Andrey Armyagov/iStockphoto

### What Does "Non-Recurring" Really Mean?

Many companies incur restructuring charges as they attempt to reduce costs. They often label these items in the income statement as "non-recurring" charges to suggest that they are isolated events which are unlikely to occur in future periods. The question for analysts is, are these costs really one-time, "non-recurring" events, or do they reflect problems that the company will be facing for many periods in the future? If they are one-time events, they can be largely ignored when trying to predict future earnings.

But some companies report "one-time" restructuring charges over and over again. For example, toothpaste and other consumer-goods giant Procter & Gamble Co. reported a restructuring charge in 12 consecutive quarters. Motorola had "special" charges in 14 consecutive quarters. On the other hand, other companies have a restructuring charge only once in a 5- or 10-year period. There appears to be no substitute for careful analysis of the numbers that comprise net income.

If a company takes a large restructuring charge, what is the effect on the company's current income statement versus future ones? (See page 889.)

## Changes in Accounting Principle

For ease of comparison, users of financial statements expect companies to prepare such statements on a basis **consistent** with the preceding period. A **change in accounting principle** occurs when the principle used in the current year is different from the one used in the preceding year. Accounting rules permit a change when management can show that the new principle is preferable to the old principle. An example is a change in inventory costing methods (such as FIFO to average cost).

## Ethics Note

Changes in accounting principle should result in financial statements that are more informative for statement users. They should *not* be used to artificially improve the reported performance or financial position of the corporation.

Companies report most changes in accounting principle retroactively. That is, they report both the current period and previous periods using the new principle. As a result, the same principle applies in all periods. This treatment improves the ability to compare results across years.

## Comprehensive Income

The income statement reports most revenues, expenses, gains, and losses recognized during the period. However, over time, specific exceptions to this general practice have developed. Certain items now bypass income and are reported directly in stockholders' equity.

For example, in Chapter 16 you learned that companies do not include in income any unrealized gains and losses on available-for-sale securities. Instead, they report such gains and losses in the balance sheet as adjustments to stockholders' equity. Why are these gains and losses on available-for-sale securities excluded from net income? Because disclosing them separately (1) reduces the volatility of net income due to fluctuations in fair value, yet (2) informs the financial statement user of the gain or loss that would be incurred if the securities were sold at fair value.

Many analysts have expressed concern over the significant increase in the number of items that bypass the income statement. They feel that such reporting has reduced the usefulness of the income statement. To address this concern, in addition to reporting net income, a company must also report comprehensive income. **Comprehensive income** includes all changes in stockholders' equity during a period except those resulting from investments by stockholders and distributions to stockholders. A number of alternative formats for reporting comprehensive income are allowed. These formats are discussed in advanced accounting courses.

---

## > DO IT!

### Irregular Items

In its proposed 2014 income statement, AIR Corporation reports income before income taxes $400,000, extraordinary loss due to earthquake $100,000, income taxes $120,000 (not including irregular items), loss on operation of discontinued flower division $50,000, and loss on disposal of discontinued flower division $90,000. The income tax rate is 30%. Prepare a correct income statement, beginning with "Income before income taxes."

### Solution

**Action Plan**

✔ Recall that a loss is extraordinary if it is both unusual and infrequent.

✔ Disclose the income tax effect of each component of income, beginning with income before any irregular items.

✔ Show discontinued operations before extraordinary items.

| AIR CORPORATION Income Statement (partial) For the Year Ended December 31, 2014 | | |
|---|---|---|
| Income before income taxes | | $400,000 |
| Income tax expense | | 120,000 |
| Income from continuing operations | | 280,000 |
| Discontinued operations | | |
| Loss from operation of flower division, net of $15,000 tax saving | $35,000 | |
| Loss on disposal of flower division, net of $27,000 tax saving | 63,000 | 98,000 |
| Income before extraordinary item | | 182,000 |
| Extraordinary earthquake loss, net of $30,000 tax saving | | 70,000 |
| Net income | | $112,000 |

Related exercise material: **BE18-14, BE18-15, E18-12, E18-13, and DO IT!** 18-3.

✔ **The Navigator**

## Quality of Earnings

In evaluating the financial performance of a company, the quality of a company's earnings is of extreme importance to analysts. A company that has a high **quality of earnings** provides full and transparent information that will not confuse or mislead users of the financial statements.

| LEARNING OBJECTIVE | 7 |
|---|---|
| Understand the concept of quality of earnings. | |

The issue of quality of earnings has taken on increasing importance because recent accounting scandals suggest that some companies are spending too much time managing their income and not enough time managing their business. Here are some of the factors affecting quality of earnings.

### Alternative Accounting Methods

Variations among companies in the application of generally accepted accounting principles may hamper comparability and reduce quality of earnings. For example, one company may use the FIFO method of inventory costing, while another company in the same industry may use LIFO. If inventory is a significant asset to both companies, it is unlikely that their current ratios are comparable. For example, if General Motors Corporation had used FIFO instead of LIFO for inventory valuation, its inventories in a recent year would have been 26% higher, which significantly affects the current ratio (and other ratios as well).

In addition to differences in inventory costing methods, differences also exist in reporting such items as depreciation, depletion, and amortization. Although these differences in accounting methods might be detectable from reading the notes to the financial statements, adjusting the financial data to compensate for the different methods is often difficult, if not impossible.

### Pro Forma Income

Companies whose stock is publicly traded are required to present their income statement following generally accepted accounting principles (GAAP). In recent years, many companies have also reported a second measure of income, called pro forma income. **Pro forma income** usually excludes items that the company thinks are unusual or non-recurring. For example, at one time, Cisco Systems (a high-tech company) reported a quarterly net loss under GAAP of $2.7 billion. Cisco reported pro forma income for the same quarter as a profit of $230 million. This large difference in profits between GAAP income numbers and pro forma income is not unusual these days. For example, during one 9-month period the 100 largest firms on the Nasdaq stock exchange reported a total pro forma income of $19.1 billion but a total loss as measured by GAAP of $82.3 billion—a difference of about $100 billion!

To compute pro forma income, companies generally can exclude any items they deem inappropriate for measuring their performance. Many analysts and investors are critical of the practice of using pro forma income because these numbers often make companies look better than they really are. As the financial press noted, pro forma numbers might be called EBS, which stands for "earnings before bad stuff." Companies, on the other hand, argue that pro forma numbers more clearly indicate sustainable income because they exclude unusual and non-recurring expenses. "Cisco's technique gives readers of financial statements a clear picture of Cisco's normal business activities," the company said in a statement issued in response to questions about its pro forma income accounting.

The SEC has provided guidance on how companies should present pro forma information. Stay tuned: Everyone seems to agree that pro forma numbers can be useful if they provide insights into determining a company's sustainable income. However, many companies have abused the flexibility that pro forma numbers allow and have used the measure as a way to put their companies in a good light.

## Improper Recognition

Due to pressure from Wall Street to continually increase earnings, some managers have manipulated the earnings numbers to meet these expectations. The most common abuse is the improper recognition of revenue. One practice that companies are using is **channel stuffing**. Offering deep discounts on their products to customers, companies encourage their customers to buy early (stuff the channel) rather than later. This lets the company report good earnings in the current period, but it often leads to a disaster in subsequent periods because customers have no need for additional goods. To illustrate, Bristol-Myers Squibb at one time indicated that it used sales incentives to encourage wholesalers to buy more drugs than needed to meet patients' demands. As a result, the company had to issue revised financial statements showing corrected revenues and income.

Another practice is the improper capitalization of operating expenses. The classic case is WorldCom. It capitalized over $7 billion of operating expenses so that it would report positive net income. In other situations, companies fail to report all their liabilities. Enron had promised to make payments on certain contracts if financial difficulty developed, but these guarantees were not reported as liabilities. In addition, disclosure was so lacking in transparency that it was impossible to understand what was happening at the company.

---

> ## DO IT!

### Quality of Earnings, Financial Statement Analysis

Match each of the following terms with the phrase that best describes it.

| | |
|---|---|
| Comprehensive income | Vertical analysis |
| Quality of earnings | Pro forma income |
| Solvency ratio | Extraordinary item |

1. _____ Measures the ability of the company to survive over a long period of time.

2. _____ Usually excludes items that a company thinks are unusual or non-recurring.

3. _____ Includes all changes in stockholders' equity during a period except those resulting from investments by stockholders and distributions to stockholders.

4. _____ Indicates the level of full and transparent information provided to users of the financial statements.

5. _____ Describes events and transactions that are unusual in nature and infrequent in occurrence.

6. _____ Expresses each item within a financial statement as a percentage of a base amount.

### Solution

1. Solvency ratio:  Measures the ability of the company to survive over a long period of time.

2. Pro forma income:  Usually excludes items that a company thinks are unusual or non-recurring.

3. Comprehensive income:  Includes all changes in stockholders' equity during a period except those resulting from investments by stockholders and distributions to stockholders.

4. Quality of earnings:  Indicates the level of full and transparent information provided to users of the financial statements.

5. Extraordinary item:  Describes events and transactions that are unusual in nature and infrequent in occurrence.

6. Vertical analysis:  Expresses each item within a financial statement as a percentage of a base amount.

### Action Plan

✔ Develop a sound understanding of basic methods used for financial reporting.

✔ Understand the use of fundamental analysis techniques.

Related exercise material: **DO IT!** 18-4.

 The Navigator

## > Comprehensive DO IT!

The events and transactions of Dever Corporation for the year ending December 31, 2014, resulted in the following data.

| | |
|---|---:|
| Cost of goods sold | $2,600,000 |
| Net sales | 4,400,000 |
| Other expenses and losses | 9,600 |
| Other revenues and gains | 5,600 |
| Selling and administrative expenses | 1,100,000 |
| Income from operations of plastics division | 70,000 |
| Gain from disposal of plastics division | 500,000 |
| Loss from tornado disaster (extraordinary loss) | 600,000 |

Analysis reveals that:

1. All items are before the applicable income tax rate of 30%.

2. The plastics division was sold on July 1.

3. All operating data for the plastics division have been segregated.

### Instructions

Prepare an income statement for the year.

### Solution to Comprehensive DO IT!

**Action Plan**

✔ Report material items not typical of continuing operations in separate sections, net of taxes.

✔ Associate income taxes with the item that affects the taxes.

✔ Apply the corporate tax rate to income before income taxes to determine tax expense.

✔ Recall that all data presented in determining income before income taxes are the same as for unincorporated companies.

### DEVER CORPORATION
### Income Statement
### For the Year Ended December 31, 2014

| | | |
|---|---:|---:|
| Net sales | | $4,400,000 |
| Cost of goods sold | | 2,600,000 |
| Gross profit | | 1,800,000 |
| Selling and administrative expenses | | 1,100,000 |
| Income from operations | | 700,000 |
| Other revenues and gains | $ 5,600 | |
| Other expenses and losses | 9,600 | 4,000 |
| Income before income taxes | | 696,000 |
| Income tax expense ($696,000 × 30%) | | 208,800 |
| Income from continuing operations | | 487,200 |
| Discontinued operations | | |
|   Income from operations of plastics division, net of | | |
|     $21,000 income taxes ($70,000 × 30%) | 49,000 | |
|   Gain from disposal of plastics division, net of $150,000 | | |
|     income taxes ($500,000 × 30%) | 350,000 | 399,000 |
| Income before extraordinary item | | 886,200 |
| Extraordinary item | | |
|   Tornado loss, net of $180,000 income tax saving | | |
|     ($600,000 × 30%) | | 420,000 |
| Net income | | $ 466,200 |

 **The Navigator**

1 **Discuss the need for comparative analysis.** There are three bases of comparison: (1) intracompany, which compares an item or financial relationship with other data within a company; (2) industry, which compares company data with industry averages; and (3) intercompany, which compares an item or financial relationship of a company with data of one or more competing companies.

2 **Identify the tools of financial statement analysis.** Financial statements can be analyzed horizontally, vertically, and with ratios.

3 **Explain and apply horizontal analysis.** Horizontal analysis is a technique for evaluating a series of data over a period of time to determine the increase or decrease that has taken place, expressed as either an amount or a percentage.

4 **Describe and apply vertical analysis.** Vertical analysis is a technique that expresses each item within a financial statement in terms of a percentage of a relevant total or a base amount.

5 **Identify and compute ratios used in analyzing a firm's liquidity, profitability, and solvency.** The formula and purpose of each ratio is presented in Illustration 18-27 (pages 858–859).

6 **Understand the concept of earning power, and how irregular items are presented.** Earning power refers to a company's ability to sustain its profits from operations. "Irregular items"—discontinued operations and extraordinary items—are presented net of tax below income from continuing operations to highlight their unusual nature.

7 **Understand the concept of quality of earnings.** A high quality of earnings provides full and transparent information that will not confuse or mislead users of the financial statements. Issues related to quality of earnings are (1) alternative accounting methods, (2) pro forma income, and (3) improper recognition.

## GLOSSARY

**Accounts receivable turnover** A measure of the liquidity of accounts receivable; computed by dividing net credit sales by average net accounts receivable. (p. 852).

**Acid-test (quick) ratio** A measure of a company's immediate short-term liquidity; computed by dividing the sum of cash, short-term investments, and net accounts receivable by current liabilities. (p. 850).

**Asset turnover** A measure of how efficiently a company uses its assets to generate sales; computed by dividing net sales by average total assets. (p. 854).

**Change in accounting principle** The use of a principle in the current year that is different from the one used in the preceding year. (p. 863).

**Comprehensive income** Includes all changes in stockholders' equity during a period except those resulting from investments by stockholders and distributions to stockholders. (p. 864).

**Current ratio** A measure used to evaluate a company's liquidity and short-term debt-paying ability; computed by dividing current assets by current liabilities. (p. 850).

**Debt to assets ratio** Measures the percentage of assets provided by creditors; computed by dividing debt by assets. (p. 857).

**Discontinued operations** The disposal of a significant component of a business. (p. 861).

**Earnings per share (EPS)** The net income earned on each share of common stock; computed by dividing net income minus preferred dividends (if any) by the number of weighted-average common shares outstanding. (p. 856).

**Extraordinary items** Events and transactions that are unusual in nature and infrequent in occurrence. (p. 862).

**Horizontal analysis** A technique for evaluating a series of financial statement data over a period of time, to determine the increase (decrease) that has taken place, expressed as either an amount or a percentage. (p. 843).

**Inventory turnover** A measure of the liquidity of inventory; computed by dividing cost of goods sold by average inventory. (p. 852).

**Leveraging** See *Trading on the equity*. (p. 855).

**Liquidity ratios** Measures of the short-term ability of the company to pay its maturing obligations and to meet unexpected needs for cash. (p. 850).

**Payout ratio** Measures the percentage of earnings distributed in the form of cash dividends; computed by dividing cash dividends by net income. (p. 857).

**Price-earnings (P-E) ratio** Measures the ratio of the market price of each share of common stock to the earnings per share; computed by dividing the market price of the stock by earnings per share. (p. 856).

**Profit margin** Measures the percentage of each dollar of sales that results in net income; computed by dividing net income by net sales. (p. 853).

**Profitability ratios** Measures of the income or operating success of a company for a given period of time. (p. 853).

**Pro forma income** A measure of income that usually excludes items that a company thinks are unusual or non-recurring. (p. 865).

**Quality of earnings** Indicates the level of full and transparent information provided to users of the financial statements. (p. 865).

**Ratio** An expression of the mathematical relationship between one quantity and another. The relationship may be expressed either as a percentage, a rate, or a simple proportion. (p. 848).

**Ratio analysis** A technique for evaluating financial statements that expresses the relationship between selected financial statement data. (p. 848).

**Return on assets** An overall measure of profitability; computed by dividing net income by average total assets. (p. 854).

**Return on common stockholders' equity** Measures the dollars of net income earned for each dollar invested by the owners; computed by dividing net income minus preferred dividends (if any) by average common stockholders' equity. (p. 855).

**Solvency ratios** Measures of the ability of the company to survive over a long period of time. (p. 857).

**Times interest earned** Measures a company's ability to meet interest payments as they come due; computed by dividing income before interest expense and income taxes by interest expense. (p. 858).

**Trading on the equity** Borrowing money at a lower rate of interest than can be earned by using the borrowed money. (p. 855).

**Vertical analysis** A technique for evaluating financial statement data that expresses each item within a financial statement as a percentage of a base amount. (p. 846).

 Self-Test, Brief Exercises, Exercises, Problem Set A, and many more components are available for practice in *WileyPLUS*.

## SELF-TEST QUESTIONS

*Answers are on page 889.*

(LO 1) **1.** Comparisons of data within a company are an example of the following comparative basis:
(a) Industry averages.  (c) Intercompany.
(b) Intracompany.  (d) Both (b) and (c).

(LO 3) **2.** In horizontal analysis, each item is expressed as a percentage of the:
(a) net income amount.
(b) stockholders' equity amount.
(c) total assets amount.
(d) base year amount.

(LO 3) **3.** Sammy Corporation reported net sales of $300,000, $330,000, and $360,000 in the years, 2012, 2013, and 2014, respectively. If 2012 is the base year, what is the trend percentage for 2014?
(a) 77%.  (c) 120%.
(b) 108%.  (d) 130%.

(LO 4) **4.** The following schedule is a display of what type of analysis?

| | Amount | Percent |
|---|---|---|
| Current assets | $200,000 | 25% |
| Property, plant, and equipment | 600,000 | 75% |
| Total assets | $800,000 | |

(a) Horizontal analysis.  (c) Vertical analysis.
(b) Differential analysis.  (d) Ratio analysis.

(LO 4) **5.** In vertical analysis, the base amount for depreciation expense is generally:
(a) net sales.
(b) depreciation expense in a previous year.
(c) gross profit.
(d) fixed assets.

(LO 5) **6.** Which of the following measures is an evaluation of a firm's ability to pay current liabilities?
(a) Acid-test ratio.
(b) Current ratio.
(c) Both (a) and (b).
(d) None of the above.

(LO 5) **7.** A measure useful in evaluating the efficiency in managing inventories is:
(a) inventory turnover.
(b) days in inventory.
(c) Both (a) and (b).
(d) None of the above.

**Use the following financial statement information as of the end of each year to answer Self-Test Questions 8-12.**

| | 2014 | 2013 |
|---|---|---|
| Inventory | $ 54,000 | $ 48,000 |
| Current assets | 81,000 | 106,000 |
| Total assets | 382,000 | 326,000 |
| Current liabilities | 27,000 | 36,000 |
| Total liabilities | 102,000 | 88,000 |
| Preferred stock | 40,000 | 40,000 |
| Common stockholders' equity | 240,000 | 198,000 |
| Net sales | 784,000 | 697,000 |
| Cost of goods sold | 306,000 | 277,000 |
| Net income | 134,000 | 90,000 |
| Tax expense | 22,000 | 18,000 |
| Interest expense | 12,000 | 12,000 |
| Dividends paid to preferred stockholders | 4,000 | 4,000 |
| Dividends paid to common stockholders | 15,000 | 10,000 |

(LO 5) **8.** Compute the days in inventory for 2014.
    **(a)** 64.4 days.     **(c)** 6 days.
    **(b)** 60.8 days.     **(d)** 24 days.

(LO 5) **9.** Compute the current ratio for 2014.
    **(a)** 1.26:1.     **(c)** .80:1.
    **(b)** 3.0:1.     **(d)** 3.75:1.

(LO 5) **10.** Compute the profit margin for 2014.
    **(a)** 17.1%.     **(c)** 37.9%.
    **(b)** 18.1%.     **(d)** 5.9%.

(LO 5) **11.** Compute the return on common stockholders' equity for 2014.
    **(a)** 47.9%.     **(c)** 61.2%.
    **(b)** 51.7%.     **(d)** 59.4%.

(LO 5) **12.** Compute the times interest earned for 2014.
    **(a)** 11.2 times.     **(c)** 14.0 times.
    **(b)** 65.3 times.     **(d)** 13.0 times.

(LO 6) **13.** In reporting discontinued operations, the income statement should show in a special section:
    **(a)** gains and losses on the disposal of the discontinued component.

    **(b)** gains and losses from operations of the discontinued component.
    **(c)** Both (a) and (b).
    **(d)** None of these answer choices are correct.

**14.** Scout Corporation has income before taxes of $400,000 (LO 6) and an extraordinary loss of $100,000. If the income tax rate is 25% on all items, the income statement should show income before extraordinary items and extraordinary items, respectively, of:
    **(a)** $325,000 and $100,000.
    **(b)** $325,000 and $75,000.
    **(c)** $300,000 and $100,000
    **(d)** $300,000 and $75,000.

**15.** Which situation below might indicate a company has (LO 7) a low quality of earnings?
    **(a)** The same accounting principles are used each year.
    **(b)** Revenue is recognized when earned.
    **(c)** Maintenance costs are expensed as incurred.
    **(d)** The company is continually reporting pro forma income numbers.

Go to the book's companion website, www.wiley.com/college/weygandt, for additional Self-Test Questions.

## QUESTIONS

**1. (a)** Jose Ramirez believes that the analysis of financial statements is directed at two characteristics of a company: liquidity and profitability. Is Jose correct? Explain.
    **(b)** Are short-term creditors, long-term creditors, and stockholders interested primarily in the same characteristics of a company? Explain.

**2. (a)** Distinguish among the following bases of comparison: (1) intracompany, (2) industry averages, and (3) intercompany.
    **(b)** Give the principal value of using each of the three bases of comparison.

**3.** Two popular methods of financial statement analysis are horizontal analysis and vertical analysis. Explain the difference between these two methods.

**4. (a)** If Peoples Company had net income of $390,000 in 2014 and it experienced a 24.5% increase in net income for 2015, what is its net income for 2015?
    **(b)** If six cents of every dollar of Peoples revenue is net income in 2014, what is the dollar amount of 2014 revenue?

**5.** What is a ratio? What are the different ways of expressing the relationship of two amounts? What information does a ratio provide?

**6.** Name the major ratios useful in assessing (a) liquidity and (b) solvency.

**7.** Roberto Perez is puzzled. His company had a profit margin of 10% in 2014. He feels that this is an indication that the company is doing well. Julie Beck, his accountant, says that more information is needed to determine the firm's financial well-being. Who is correct? Why?

**8.** What do the following classes of ratios measure? (a) Liquidity ratios. (b) Profitability ratios. (c) Solvency ratios.

**9.** What is the difference between the current ratio and the acid-test ratio?

**10.** Hizar Company, a retail store, has an accounts receivable turnover of 4.5 times. The industry average is 12.5 times. Does Hizar have a collection problem with its accounts receivable?

**11.** Which ratios should be used to help answer the following questions?
    **(a)** How efficient is a company in using its assets to produce sales?
    **(b)** How near to sale is the inventory on hand?
    **(c)** How many dollars of net income were earned for each dollar invested by the owners?
    **(d)** How able is a company to meet interest charges as they fall due?

**12.** The price-earnings ratio of General Motors (automobile builder) was 8, and the price-earnings ratio of Microsoft (computer software) was 38. Which company did the stock market favor? Explain.

**13.** What is the formula for computing the payout ratio? Would you expect this ratio to be high or low for a growth company?

**14.** Holding all other factors constant, indicate whether each of the following changes generally signals good or bad news about a company.
    **(a)** Increase in profit margin.
    **(b)** Decrease in inventory turnover.
    **(c)** Increase in the current ratio.

(d) Decrease in earnings per share.

(e) Increase in price-earnings ratio.

(f) Increase in debt to assets ratio.

(g) Decrease in times interest earned.

15. The return on assets for Zhang Corporation is 7.6%. During the same year, Zhang's return on common stockholders' equity is 12.8%. What is the explanation for the difference in the two rates?

16. Which two ratios do you think should be of greatest interest to:

(a) A pension fund considering the purchase of 20-year bonds?

(b) A bank contemplating a short-term loan?

(c) A common stockholder?

17. Why must preferred dividends be subtracted from net income in computing earnings per share?

18. (a) What is meant by trading on the equity?

(b) How would you determine the profitability of trading on the equity?

19. Lippert Inc. has net income of $160,000, weighted-average shares of common stock outstanding of 50,000, and preferred dividends for the period of $40,000. What is Lippert's earnings per share of common stock? Kate Lippert, the president of Lippert Inc., believes the computed EPS of the company is high. Comment.

20. Why is it important to report discontinued operations separately from income from continuing operations?

21. You are considering investing in Wingert Transportation. The company reports 2014 earnings per share of $6.50 on income before extraordinary items and $4.75 on net income. Which EPS figure would you consider more relevant to your investment decision? Why?

22. RAF Inc. reported 2013 earnings per share of $3.20 and had no extraordinary items. In 2014, EPS on income before extraordinary items was $2.99, and EPS on net income was $3.49. Is this a favorable trend?

23. Indicate which of the following items would be reported as an extraordinary item in Stumfol Corporation's income statement.

(a) Loss from damages caused by volcano eruption.

(b) Loss from sale of temporary investments.

(c) Loss attributable to a labor strike.

(d) Loss caused when manufacture of a product was prohibited by the Food and Drug Administration.

(e) Loss from flood damage. (The nearby Black River floods every 2 to 3 years.)

(f) Write-down of obsolete inventory.

(g) Expropriation of a factory by a foreign government.

24. Identify and explain factors that affect quality of earnings.

25. Identify the specific sections in Apple's 2011 annual report where horizontal and vertical analyses of financial data are presented.

## BRIEF EXERCISES

*Follow the rounding procedures used in the chapter.*

**BE18-1** You recently received a letter from your Uncle Sammy. A portion of the letter is presented below.

*Discuss need for comparative analysis.*

(LO 1)

You know that I have a significant amount of money I saved over the years. I am thinking about starting an investment program. I want to do the investing myself, based on my own research and analysis of financial statements. I know that you are studying accounting, so I have a couple of questions for you. I have heard that different users of financial statements are interested in different characteristics of companies. Is this true and, if so, why? Also, some of my friends who are already investing have told me that comparisons involving a company's financial data can be made on a number of different bases. Can you explain these bases to me?

**Instructions**

Write a letter to your Uncle Sammy which answers his questions.

**BE18-2** Schellhammer Corporation reported the following amounts in 2013, 2014, and 2015.

*Identify and use tools of financial statement analysis.*

(LO 2, 3, 4, 5)

|  | 2013 | 2014 | 2015 |
|---|---|---|---|
| Current assets | $200,000 | $210,000 | $240,000 |
| Current liabilities | $150,000 | $168,000 | $184,000 |
| Total assets | $500,000 | $600,000 | $620,000 |

**Instructions**

(a) Identify and describe the three tools of financial statement analysis. (b) Perform each of the three types of analysis on Schellhammer's current assets.

**BE18-3** Using the following data from the comparative balance sheet of Goody Company, illustrate horizontal analysis.

|  | December 31, 2015 | December 31, 2014 |
|---|---|---|
| Accounts receivable | $ 520,000 | $ 400,000 |
| Inventory | $ 840,000 | $ 600,000 |
| Total assets | $3,000,000 | $2,500,000 |

**BE18-4** Using the same data presented above in BE18-3 for Goody Company, illustrate vertical analysis.

**BE18-5** Net income was $500,000 in 2013, $450,000 in 2014, and $522,000 in 2015. What is the percentage of change from (a) 2013 to 2014 and (b) 2014 to 2015? Is the change an increase or a decrease?

**BE18-6** If Sappington Company had net income of $585,000 in 2015 and it experienced a 20% increase in net income over 2014, what was its 2014 net income?

**BE18-7** Horizontal analysis (trend analysis) percentages for Dody Company's sales revenue, cost of goods sold, and expenses are shown below.

| Horizontal Analysis | 2015 | 2014 | 2013 |
|---|---|---|---|
| Sales revenue | 96.2 | 106.8 | 100.0 |
| Cost of goods sold | 102.0 | 97.0 | 100.0 |
| Expenses | 109.6 | 98.4 | 100.0 |

Did Dody's net income increase, decrease, or remain unchanged over the 3-year period?

**BE18-8** Vertical analysis (common size) percentages for Kochheim Company's sales revenue, cost of goods sold, and expenses are shown below.

| Vertical Analysis | 2015 | 2014 | 2013 |
|---|---|---|---|
| Sales revenue | 100.0 | 100.0 | 100.0 |
| Cost of goods sold | 60.2 | 62.4 | 63.5 |
| Expenses | 25.0 | 25.6 | 27.5 |

Did Kochheim's net income as a percentage of sales increase, decrease, or remain unchanged over the 3-year period? Provide numerical support for your answer.

**BE18-9** Selected condensed data taken from a recent balance sheet of Heidebrecht Inc. are as follows.

**HEIDEBRECHT INC.**
Balance Sheet (partial)

| | |
|---|---|
| Cash | $ 8,041,000 |
| Short-term investments | 4,947,000 |
| Accounts receivable | 12,545,000 |
| Inventory | 14,814,000 |
| Other current assets | 5,571,000 |
| Total current assets | $45,918,000 |
| Total current liabilities | $40,644,000 |

What are the (a) working capital, (b) current ratio, and (c) acid-test ratio?

**BE18-10** Linebarger Corporation has net income of $11.44 million and net revenue of $95 million in 2014. Its assets are $14 million at the beginning of the year and $18 million at the end of the year. What are Linebarger's (a) asset turnover and (b) profit margin?

**BE18-11** The following data are taken from the financial statements of Rainsberger Company.

|  | 2015 | 2014 |
|---|---|---|
| Accounts receivable (net), end of year | $ 550,000 | $ 520,000 |
| Net sales on account | 3,960,000 | 3,100,000 |
| Terms for all sales are 1/10, n/60. | | |

**(a)** Compute for each year (1) the accounts receivable turnover and (2) the average collection period. At the end of 2013, accounts receivable (net) was $480,000.

**(b)** ———— What conclusions about the management of accounts receivable can be drawn from these data?

**BE18-12** The following data are from the income statements of Haskin Company.

*Evaluate management of inventory.*

*(LO 5)*

|  | 2015 | 2014 |
|---|---|---|
| Sales revenue | $6,420,000 | $6,240,000 |
| Beginning inventory | 940,000 | 860,000 |
| Purchases | 4,340,000 | 4,661,000 |
| Ending inventory | 1,020,000 | 940,000 |

(a) Compute for each year (1) the inventory turnover and (2) the days in inventory.
(b) ────── What conclusions concerning the management of the inventory can be drawn from these data?

**BE18-13** Guo Company has owners' equity of $400,000 and net income of $66,000. It has a payout ratio of 20% and a return on assets of 15%. How much did Guo pay in cash dividends, and what were its average assets?

*Calculate amounts from profitability ratios.*

*(LO 5)*

**BE18-14** An inexperienced accountant for Silva Corporation showed the following in the income statement: income before income taxes and extraordinary item $450,000, and extraordinary loss from flood (before taxes) $70,000. The extraordinary loss and taxable income are both subject to a 30% tax rate. Prepare a correct income statement.

*Prepare income statement including extraordinary items.*

*(LO 6)*

**BE18-15** On June 30, Holloway Corporation discontinued its operations in Europe. During the year, the operating loss was $300,000 before taxes. On September 1, Holloway disposed of its European facilities at a pretax loss of $120,000. The applicable tax rate is 30%. Show the discontinued operations section of the income statement.

*Prepare discontinued operations section of income statement.*

*(LO 6)*

> ## DO IT! Review

**DO IT! 18-1** Summary financial information for Wolford Company is as follows.

*Prepare horizontal analysis.*

*(LO 3)*

|  | December 31, 2015 | December 31, 2014 |
|---|---|---|
| Current assets | $ 199,000 | $ 220,000 |
| Plant assets | 821,000 | 780,000 |
| Total assets | $1,020,000 | $1,000,000 |

Compute the amount and percentage changes in 2015 using horizontal analysis, assuming 2014 is the base year.

**DO IT! 18-2** The condensed financial statements of Murawski Company for the years 2013 and 2014 are presented below and on page 874.

*Compute ratios.*

*(LO 5)*

**MURAWSKI COMPANY**
Balance Sheets
December 31

|  | 2014 | 2013 |
|---|---|---|
| **Current assets** | | |
| Cash and cash equivalents | $ 330 | $ 360 |
| Accounts receivable (net) | 470 | 400 |
| Inventory | 460 | 390 |
| Prepaid expenses | 120 | 160 |
| Total current assets | 1,380 | 1,310 |
| Property, plant, and equipment | 420 | 380 |
| Investments | 10 | 10 |
| Intangibles and other assets | 530 | 510 |
| Total assets | $2,340 | $2,210 |
| Current liabilities | $ 900 | $ 790 |
| Long-term liabilities | 410 | 380 |
| Stockholders' equity—common | 1,030 | 1,040 |
| Total liabilities and stockholders' equity | $2,340 | $2,210 |

**MURAWSKI COMPANY**
Income Statements
For the Years Ended December 31

|  | 2014 | 2013 |
|---|---|---|
| Sales revenue | $3,800 | $3,460 |
| Costs and expenses |  |  |
| Cost of goods sold | 955 | 890 |
| Selling & administrative expenses | 2,400 | 2,330 |
| Interest expense | 25 | 20 |
| Total costs and expenses | 3,380 | 3,240 |
| Income before income taxes | 420 | 220 |
| Income tax expense | 126 | 66 |
| Net income | $ 294 | $ 154 |

Compute the following ratios for 2014 and 2013.

**(a)** Current ratio.
**(b)** Inventory turnover. (Inventory on 12/31/12 was $340.)
**(c)** Profit margin.
**(d)** Return on assets. (Assets on 12/31/12 were $1,900.)
**(e)** Return on common stockholders' equity. (Stockholders' equity on 12/31/12 was $900.)
**(f)** Debt to assets ratio.
**(g)** Times interest earned.

*Prepare income statement,*
*including irregular items.*
*(LO 6)*

**DO IT! 18-3** In its proposed 2014 income statement, Hrabik Corporation reports income before income taxes $500,000, extraordinary loss due to earthquake $150,000, income taxes $200,000 (not including irregular items), loss on operation of discontinued music division $60,000, and gain on disposal of discontinued music division $40,000. The income tax rate is 30%. Prepare a correct income statement, beginning with income before income taxes.

*Match terms relating to*
*quality of earnings and*
*financial statement analysis.*
*(LO 3, 4, 5, 6, 7)*

**DO IT! 18-4** Match each of the following terms with the phrase that best describes it.

| Quality of earnings | Pro forma income |
|---|---|
| Current ratio | Discontinued operations |
| Horizontal analysis | Comprehensive income |

**1.** _____ A measure used to evaluate a company's liquidity.
**2.** _____ Usually excludes items that a company thinks are unusual or non-recurring.
**3.** _____ Indicates the level of full and transparent information provided to users of the financial statements.
**4.** _____ The disposal of a significant component of a business.
**5.** _____ Determines increases or decreases in a series of financial statement data.
**6.** _____ Includes all changes in stockholders' equity during a period except those resulting from investments by stockholders and distributions to stockholders.

# EXERCISES

*Follow the rounding procedures used in the chapter.*

*Prepare horizontal analysis.*
*(LO 3)*

XLS

**E18-1** Financial information for Kurzen Inc. is presented below.

|  | December 31, 2015 | December 31, 2014 |
|---|---|---|
| Current assets | $125,000 | $100,000 |
| Plant assets (net) | 396,000 | 330,000 |
| Current liabilities | 91,000 | 70,000 |
| Long-term liabilities | 133,000 | 95,000 |
| Common stock, $1 par | 161,000 | 115,000 |
| Retained earnings | 136,000 | 150,000 |

**Instructions**

Prepare a schedule showing a horizontal analysis for 2015 using 2014 as the base year.

**E18-2** Operating data for Navarro Corporation are presented below.

| | 2015 | 2014 |
|---|---|---|
| Net sales | $750,000 | $600,000 |
| Cost of goods sold | 465,000 | 390,000 |
| Selling expenses | 105,000 | 66,000 |
| Administrative expenses | 60,000 | 54,000 |
| Income tax expense | 36,000 | 27,000 |
| Net income | 84,000 | 63,000 |

*Prepare vertical analysis.*
(LO 4)

**Instructions**

Prepare a schedule showing a vertical analysis for 2015 and 2014.

**E18-3** The comparative condensed balance sheets of Gurley Corporation are presented below.

*Prepare horizontal and vertical analyses.*
(LO 3, 4)

**GURLEY CORPORATION**
Comparative Condensed Balance Sheets
December 31

| | 2015 | 2014 |
|---|---|---|
| **Assets** | | |
| Current assets | $ 74,000 | $ 80,000 |
| Property, plant, and equipment (net) | 99,000 | 90,000 |
| Intangibles | 27,000 | 40,000 |
| Total assets | $200,000 | $210,000 |
| | | |
| **Liabilities and stockholders' equity** | | |
| Current liabilities | $ 42,000 | $ 48,000 |
| Long-term liabilities | 143,000 | 150,000 |
| Stockholders' equity | 15,000 | 12,000 |
| Total liabilities and stockholders' equity | $200,000 | $210,000 |

**Instructions**

(a) Prepare a horizontal analysis of the balance sheet data for Gurley Corporation using 2014 as a base.

(b) Prepare a vertical analysis of the balance sheet data for Gurley Corporation in columnar form for 2015.

**E18-4** The comparative condensed income statements of Emley Corporation are shown below.

*Prepare horizontal and vertical analyses.*
(LO 3, 4)

**EMLEY CORPORATION**
Comparative Condensed Income Statements
For the Years Ended December 31

| | 2015 | 2014 |
|---|---|---|
| Net sales | $660,000 | $600,000 |
| Cost of goods sold | 483,000 | 420,000 |
| Gross profit | 177,000 | 180,000 |
| Operating expenses | 125,000 | 120,000 |
| Net income | $ 52,000 | $ 60,000 |

**Instructions**

(a) Prepare a horizontal analysis of the income statement data for Emley Corporation using 2014 as a base. (Show the amounts of increase or decrease.)

(b) Prepare a vertical analysis of the income statement data for Emley Corporation in columnar form for both years.

*Compute liquidity ratios and compare results.*
(LO 5)

**E18-5** Suppose Nordstrom, Inc., which operates department stores in numerous states, has the following selected financial statement data for the year ending January 30, 2014.

**NORDSTROM, INC.**
Balance Sheet (partial)

| (in millions) | End-of-Year | Beginning-of-Year |
| --- | --- | --- |
| Cash and cash equivalents | $ 795 | $ 72 |
| Accounts receivable (net) | 2,035 | 1,942 |
| Inventory | 898 | 900 |
| Prepaid expenses | 88 | 93 |
| Other current assets | 238 | 210 |
| Total current assets | $4,054 | $3,217 |
| Total current liabilities | $2,014 | $1,601 |

For the year, net sales were $8,258 and cost of goods sold was $5,328 (in millions).

**Instructions**
**(a)** Compute the four liquidity ratios at the end of the year.
**(b)** Using the data in the chapter, compare Nordstrom's liquidity with (1) that of Macy's Inc., and (2) the industry averages for department stores.

*Perform current and acid-test ratio analysis.*
(LO 5)

**E18-6** Keener Incorporated had the following transactions occur involving current assets and current liabilities during February 2014.

Feb.  3    Accounts receivable of $15,000 are collected.
     7    Equipment is purchased for $28,000 cash.
    11    Paid $3,000 for a 3-year insurance policy.
    14    Accounts payable of $12,000 are paid.
    18    Cash dividends of $5,000 are declared.

Additional information:

1. As of February 1, 2014, current assets were $110,000, and current liabilities were $50,000.
2. As of February 1, 2014, current assets included $15,000 of inventory and $2,000 of prepaid expenses.

**Instructions**
**(a)** Compute the current ratio as of the beginning of the month and after each transaction.
**(b)** Compute the acid-test ratio as of the beginning of the month and after each transaction.

*Compute selected ratios.*
(LO 5)

**E18-7** Frizell Company has the following comparative balance sheet data.

**FRIZELL COMPANY**
Balance Sheets
December 31

| | 2015 | 2014 |
| --- | --- | --- |
| Cash | $ 15,000 | $ 30,000 |
| Accounts receivable (net) | 70,000 | 60,000 |
| Inventory | 60,000 | 50,000 |
| Plant assets (net) | 200,000 | 180,000 |
| | $345,000 | $320,000 |
| Accounts payable | $ 50,000 | $ 60,000 |
| Mortgage payable (6%) | 100,000 | 100,000 |
| Common stock, $10 par | 140,000 | 120,000 |
| Retained earnings | 55,000 | 40,000 |
| | $345,000 | $320,000 |

Additional information for 2015:

1. Net income was $25,000.
2. Sales on account were $410,000. Sales returns and allowances were $20,000.
3. Cost of goods sold was $198,000.

**Instructions**

Compute the following ratios at December 31, 2015.

**(a)** Current ratio.
**(b)** Acid-test ratio.
**(c)** Accounts receivable turnover.
**(d)** Inventory turnover.

**E18-8** Selected comparative statement data for Queen Products Company are presented below. All balance sheet data are as of December 31.

*Compute selected ratios.*
*(LO 5)*

|  | 2015 | 2014 |
| --- | --- | --- |
| Net sales | $750,000 | $720,000 |
| Cost of goods sold | 480,000 | 440,000 |
| Interest expense | 7,000 | 5,000 |
| Net income | 45,000 | 42,000 |
| Accounts receivable | 120,000 | 100,000 |
| Inventory | 85,000 | 75,000 |
| Total assets | 580,000 | 500,000 |
| Total common stockholders' equity | 430,000 | 325,000 |

**Instructions**

Compute the following ratios for 2015.

**(a)** Profit margin.
**(b)** Asset turnover.
**(c)** Return on assets.
**(d)** Return on common stockholders' equity.

**E18-9** The income statement for Sutherland, Inc., appears below.

*Compute selected ratios.*
*(LO 5)*

### SUTHERLAND, INC.
### Income Statement
### For the Year Ended December 31, 2014

| | |
| --- | --- |
| Net sales | $400,000 |
| Cost of goods sold | 230,000 |
| Gross profit | 170,000 |
| Expenses (including $16,000 interest and $24,000 income taxes) | 105,000 |
| Net income | $ 65,000 |

Additional information:

**1.** The weighted-average common shares outstanding in 2014 were 30,000 shares.
**2.** The market price of Sutherland, Inc. stock was $13 in 2014.
**3.** Cash dividends of $26,000 were paid, $5,000 of which were to preferred stockholders.

**Instructions**

Compute the following ratios for 2014.

**(a)** Earnings per share.
**(b)** Price-earnings ratio.
**(c)** Payout ratio.
**(d)** Times interest earned.

**E18-10** Lingenfelter Corporation experienced a fire on December 31, 2015, in which its financial records were partially destroyed. It has been able to salvage some of the records and has ascertained the following balances.

*Compute amounts from ratios.*
*(LO 5)*

|  | December 31, 2015 | December 31, 2014 |
| --- | --- | --- |
| Cash | $ 30,000 | $ 10,000 |
| Accounts receivable (net) | 72,500 | 126,000 |
| Inventory | 200,000 | 180,000 |
| Accounts payable | 50,000 | 90,000 |
| Notes payable | 30,000 | 60,000 |
| Common stock, $100 par | 400,000 | 400,000 |
| Retained earnings | 113,500 | 101,000 |

Additional information:

1. The inventory turnover is 4.5 times.
2. The return on common stockholders' equity is 16%. The company had no additional paid-in capital.
3. The accounts receivable turnover is 8.8 times.
4. The return on assets is 12.5%.
5. Total assets at December 31, 2014, were $655,000.

**Instructions**

Compute the following for Lingenfelter Corporation.

**(a)** Cost of goods sold for 2015.
**(b)** Net sales (credit) for 2015.
**(c)** Net income for 2015.
**(d)** Total assets at December 31, 2015.

*Compute ratios.*
*(LO 5)*

**E18-11** Wiemers Corporation's comparative balance sheets are presented below.

**WIEMERS CORPORATION**
Balance Sheets
December 31

|  | 2014 | 2013 |
|---|---|---|
| Cash | $ 4,300 | $ 3,700 |
| Accounts receivable (net) | 21,200 | 23,400 |
| Inventory | 10,000 | ·7,000 |
| Land | 20,000 | 26,000 |
| Buildings | 70,000 | 70,000 |
| Accumulated depreciation—buildings | (15,000) | (10,000) |
| Total | $110,500 | $120,100 |
| Accounts payable | $ 12,370 | $ 31,100 |
| Common stock | 75,000 | 69,000 |
| Retained earnings | 23,130 | 20,000 |
| Total | $110,500 | $120,100 |

Wiemers's 2014 income statement included net sales of $100,000, cost of goods sold of $60,000, and net income of $15,000.

**Instructions**

Compute the following ratios for 2014.

**(a)** Current ratio.
**(b)** Acid-test ratio.
**(c)** Accounts receivable turnover.
**(d)** Inventory turnover.
**(e)** Profit margin.
**(f)** Asset turnover.
**(g)** Return on assets.
**(h)** Return on common stockholders' equity.
**(i)** Debt to assets ratio.

*Prepare a correct income statement.*
*(LO 6)*

**E18-12** For its fiscal year ending October 31, 2014, Haas Corporation reports the following partial data shown below.

| | |
|---|---|
| Income before income taxes | $540,000 |
| Income tax expense (30% × $420,000) | 126,000 |
| Income before extraordinary items | 414,000 |
| Extraordinary loss from flood | 120,000 |
| Net income | $294,000 |

The flood loss is considered an extraordinary item. The income tax rate is 30% on all items.

**Instructions**

**(a)** Prepare a correct income statement, beginning with income before income taxes.
**(b)** ⎯⎯ Explain in memo form why the income statement data are misleading.

*Prepare income statement.*
*(LO 6)*

**E18-13** Trayer Corporation has income from continuing operations of $290,000 for the year ended December 31, 2014. It also has the following items (before considering income taxes).

1. An extraordinary loss of $80,000.
2. A gain of $30,000 on the discontinuance of a division.
3. A correction of an error in last year's financial statements that resulted in a $20,000 understatement of 2013 net income.

Assume all items are subject to income taxes at a 30% tax rate.

*Instructions*
(a) Prepare an income statement, beginning with income from continuing operations.
(b) Indicate the statement presentation of any item not included in (a) above.

## EXERCISES: SET B AND CHALLENGE EXERCISES

Visit the book's companion website, at **www.wiley.com/college/weygandt**, and choose the Student Companion site to access Exercise Set B and Challenge Exercises.

## PROBLEMS

*Follow the rounding procedures used in the chapter.*

**P18-1** Comparative statement data for Farris Company and Ratzlaff Company, two competitors, appear below. All balance sheet data are as of December 31, 2015, and December 31, 2014.

*Prepare vertical analysis and comment on profitability.*
*(LO 4, 5)*

|  | Farris Company | | Ratzlaff Company | |
|---|---|---|---|---|
|  | **2015** | **2014** | **2015** | **2014** |
| Net sales | $1,549,035 |  | $339,038 |  |
| Cost of goods sold | 1,080,490 |  | 241,000 |  |
| Operating expenses | 302,275 |  | 79,000 |  |
| Interest expense | 8,980 |  | 2,252 |  |
| Income tax expense | 54,500 |  | 6,650 |  |
| Current assets | 325,975 | $312,410 | 83,336 | $ 79,467 |
| Plant assets (net) | 521,310 | 500,000 | 139,728 | 125,812 |
| Current liabilities | 65,325 | 75,815 | 35,348 | 30,281 |
| Long-term liabilities | 108,500 | 90,000 | 29,620 | 25,000 |
| Common stock, $10 par | 500,000 | 500,000 | 120,000 | 120,000 |
| Retained earnings | 173,460 | 146,595 | 38,096 | 29,998 |

*Instructions*
(a) Prepare a vertical analysis of the 2015 income statement data for Farris Company and Ratzlaff Company in columnar form.
(b) ———— Comment on the relative profitability of the companies by computing the return on assets and the return on common stockholders' equity for both companies.

**P18-2** The comparative statements of Painter Tool Company are presented below and on page 880.

*Compute ratios from balance sheet and income statement.*
*(LO 5)*

### PAINTER TOOL COMPANY
### Income Statement
### For the Years Ended December 31

|  | **2015** | **2014** |
|---|---|---|
| Net sales | $1,818,500 | $1,750,500 |
| Cost of goods sold | 1,011,500 | 996,000 |
| Gross profit | 807,000 | 754,500 |
| Selling and administrative expenses | 499,000 | 479,000 |
| Income from operations | 308,000 | 275,500 |
| Other expenses and losses |  |  |
|   Interest expense | 18,000 | 14,000 |
| Income before income taxes | 290,000 | 261,500 |
| Income tax expense | 87,000 | 77,000 |
| Net income | $ 203,000 | $ 184,500 |

**PAINTER TOOL COMPANY**
Balance Sheets
December 31

| Assets | 2015 | 2014 |
|---|---|---|
| Current assets | | |
| Cash | $ 60,100 | $ 64,200 |
| Short-term investments | 69,000 | 50,000 |
| Accounts receivable (net) | 107,800 | 102,800 |
| Inventory | 133,000 | 115,500 |
| Total current assets | 369,900 | 332,500 |
| Plant assets (net) | 600,300 | 520,300 |
| Total assets | $970,200 | $852,800 |
| | | |
| **Liabilities and Stockholders' Equity** | | |
| Current liabilities | | |
| Accounts payable | $160,000 | $145,400 |
| Income taxes payable | 43,500 | 42,000 |
| Total current liabilities | 203,500 | 187,400 |
| Bonds payable | 200,000 | 200,000 |
| Total liabilities | 403,500 | 387,400 |
| Stockholders' equity | | |
| Common stock ($5 par) | 280,000 | 300,000 |
| Retained earnings | 286,700 | 165,400 |
| Total stockholders' equity | 566,700 | 465,400 |
| Total liabilities and stockholders' equity | $970,200 | $852,800 |

All sales were on account.

***Instructions***
Compute the following ratios for 2015. (Weighted-average common shares in 2015 were 57,000.)

**(a)** Earnings per share.
**(b)** Return on common stockholders' equity.
**(c)** Return on assets.
**(d)** Current ratio.
**(e)** Acid-test ratio.

**(f)** Accounts receivable turnover.
**(g)** Inventory turnover.
**(h)** Times interest earned.
**(i)** Asset turnover.
**(j)** Debt to assets ratio.

*Perform ratio analysis, and evaluate financial position and operating results.*

(LO 5)

**P18-3** Condensed balance sheet and income statement data for Landwehr Corporation appear below and on page 881.

**LANDWEHR CORPORATION**
Balance Sheets
December 31

| | 2015 | 2014 | 2013 |
|---|---|---|---|
| Cash | $ 25,000 | $ 20,000 | $ 18,000 |
| Accounts receivable (net) | 50,000 | 45,000 | 48,000 |
| Other current assets | 90,000 | 95,000 | 64,000 |
| Investments | 75,000 | 70,000 | 45,000 |
| Plant and equipment (net) | 400,000 | 370,000 | 358,000 |
| | $640,000 | $600,000 | $533,000 |
| | | | |
| Current liabilities | $ 75,000 | $ 80,000 | $ 70,000 |
| Long-term debt | 80,000 | 85,000 | 50,000 |
| Common stock, $10 par | 340,000 | 310,000 | 300,000 |
| Retained earnings | 145,000 | 125,000 | 113,000 |
| | $640,000 | $600,000 | $533,000 |

**LANDWEHR CORPORATION**
Income Statement
For the Years Ended December 31

|  | 2015 | 2014 |
|---|---|---|
| Sales revenue | $740,000 | $700,000 |
| Less: Sales returns and allowances | 40,000 | 50,000 |
| Net sales | 700,000 | 650,000 |
| Cost of goods sold | 420,000 | 400,000 |
| Gross profit | 280,000 | 250,000 |
| Operating expenses (including income taxes) | 235,000 | 220,000 |
| Net income | $ 45,000 | $ 30,000 |

Additional information:

1. The market price of Landwehr's common stock was $4.00, $5.00, and $8.00 for 2013, 2014, and 2015, respectively.
2. All dividends were paid in cash.

*Instructions*
(a) Compute the following ratios for 2014 and 2015.
    (1) Profit margin.
    (2) Asset turnover.
    (3) Earnings per share. (Weighted-average common shares in 2015 were 32,000 and in 2014 were 31,000.)
    (4) Price-earnings ratio.
    (5) Payout ratio.
    (6) Debt to assets ratio.
(b) ▬▬▬ Based on the ratios calculated, discuss briefly the improvement or lack thereof in financial position and operating results from 2014 to 2015 of Landwehr Corporation.

**P18-4** Financial information for Messersmith Company is presented below and on page 882.

*Compute ratios, and comment on overall liquidity and profitability.*
*(LO 5)*

**MESSERSMITH COMPANY**
Balance Sheets
December 31

| Assets | 2015 | 2014 |
|---|---|---|
| Cash | $ 70,000 | $ 65,000 |
| Short-term investments | 52,000 | 40,000 |
| Accounts receivable (net) | 98,000 | 80,000 |
| Inventory | 125,000 | 135,000 |
| Prepaid expenses | 29,000 | 23,000 |
| Land | 130,000 | 130,000 |
| Building and equipment (net) | 180,000 | 175,000 |
|  | $684,000 | $648,000 |

| Liabilities and Stockholders' Equity | | |
|---|---|---|
| Notes payable | $100,000 | $100,000 |
| Accounts payable | 48,000 | 42,000 |
| Accrued liabilities | 50,000 | 40,000 |
| Bonds payable, due 2016 | 150,000 | 150,000 |
| Common stock, $10 par | 200,000 | 200,000 |
| Retained earnings | 136,000 | 116,000 |
|  | $684,000 | $648,000 |

**MESSERSMITH COMPANY**
Income Statement
For the Years Ended December 31

|  | 2015 | 2014 |
|---|---|---|
| Net sales | $850,000 | $790,000 |
| Cost of goods sold | 620,000 | 575,000 |
| Gross profit | 230,000 | 215,000 |
| Operating expenses | 187,000 | 173,000 |
| Net income | $ 43,000 | $ 42,000 |

Additional information:

1. Inventory at the beginning of 2014 was $118,000.
2. Total assets at the beginning of 2014 were $630,000.
3. No common stock transactions occurred during 2014 or 2015.
4. All sales were on account. Accounts receivable, net at the beginning of 2014, were $88,000.
5. Notes payable are classified as current liabilities.

*Instructions*

(a) Indicate, by using ratios, the change in liquidity and profitability of Messersmith Company from 2014 to 2015. (*Note:* Not all profitability ratios can be computed.)
(b) Given below are three independent situations and a ratio that may be affected. For each situation, compute the affected ratio (1) as of December 31, 2015, and (2) as of December 31, 2016, after giving effect to the situation. Net income for 2016 was $50,000. Total assets on December 31, 2016, were $700,000.

| Situation | Ratio |
|---|---|
| (1)  18,000 shares of common stock were sold at par on July 1, 2016. | Return on common stockholders' equity |
| (2)  All of the notes payable were paid in 2016. The only change in liabilities was that the notes payable were paid. | Debt to assets ratio |
| (3)  Market price of common stock was $9 on December 31, 2015, and $12.80 on December 31, 2016. | Price-earnings ratio |

*Compute selected ratios, and compare liquidity, profitability, and solvency for two companies.*
*(LO 5)*

**P18-5** Selected financial data of Target and Wal-Mart for a recent year are presented here (in millions).

|  | Target Corporation | Wal-Mart Stores, Inc. |
|---|---|---|
|  | **Income Statement Data for Year** | |
| Net sales | $61,471 | $374,526 |
| Cost of goods sold | 41,895 | 286,515 |
| Selling and administrative expenses | 16,200 | 70,847 |
| Interest expense | 647 | 1,798 |
| Other income (expense) | 1,896 | 4,273 |
| Income tax expense | 1,776 | 6,908 |
| Net income | $ 2,849 | $ 12,731 |
|  | **Balance Sheet Data (End of Year)** | |
| Current assets | $18,906 | $ 47,585 |
| Noncurrent assets | 25,654 | 115,929 |
| Total assets | $44,560 | $163,514 |
| Current liabilities | $11,782 | $ 58,454 |
| Long-term debt | 17,471 | 40,452 |
| Total stockholders' equity | 15,307 | 64,608 |
| Total liabilities and stockholders' equity | $44,560 | $163,514 |

| | Target Corporation | Wal-Mart Stores, Inc. |
|---|---|---|
| | Beginning-of-Year Balances | |
| Total assets | $37,349 | $151,587 |
| Total stockholders' equity | 15,633 | 61,573 |
| Current liabilities | 11,117 | 52,148 |
| Total liabilities | 21,716 | 90,014 |
| | Other Data | |
| Average net accounts receivable | $ 7,124 | $ 3,247 |
| Average inventory | 6,517 | 34,433 |
| Net cash provided by operating activities | 4,125 | 20,354 |

**Instructions**

(a) For each company, compute the following ratios.
  (1) Current ratio.
  (2) Accounts receivable turnover.
  (3) Average collection period.
  (4) Inventory turnover.
  (5) Days in inventory.
  (6) Profit margin.
  (7) Asset turnover.
  (8) Return on assets.
  (9) Return on common stockholders' equity.
  (10) Debt to assets ratio.
  (11) Times interest earned.

(b) Compare the liquidity, profitability, and solvency of the two companies.

**P18-6** The comparative statements of Corbin Company are presented below and on page 884. *Compute numerous ratios. (LO 5)*

### CORBIN COMPANY
### Income Statement
### For the Years Ended December 31

| | 2015 | 2014 |
|---|---|---|
| Net sales (all on account) | $595,000 | $520,000 |
| Expenses | | |
| Cost of goods sold | 415,000 | 354,000 |
| Selling and administrative | 120,800 | 114,800 |
| Interest expense | 7,800 | 6,000 |
| Income tax expense | 15,000 | 14,000 |
| Total expenses | 558,600 | 488,800 |
| Net income | $ 36,400 | $ 31,200 |

### CORBIN COMPANY
### Balance Sheets
### December 31

| Assets | 2015 | 2014 |
|---|---|---|
| Current assets | | |
| Cash | $ 21,000 | $ 18,000 |
| Short-term investments | 18,000 | 15,000 |
| Accounts receivable (net) | 91,000 | 74,000 |
| Inventory | 85,000 | 70,000 |
| Total current assets | 215,000 | 177,000 |
| Plant assets (net) | 423,000 | 383,000 |
| Total assets | $638,000 | $560,000 |

| Liabilities and Stockholders' Equity | 2015 | 2014 |
|---|---|---|
| Current liabilities | | |
| Accounts payable | $122,000 | $110,000 |
| Income taxes payable | 23,000 | 20,000 |
| Total current liabilities | 145,000 | 130,000 |
| Long-term liabilities | | |
| Bonds payable | 120,000 | 80,000 |
| Total liabilities | 265,000 | 210,000 |
| Stockholders' equity | | |
| Common stock ($5 par) | 150,000 | 150,000 |
| Retained earnings | 223,000 | 200,000 |
| Total stockholders' equity | 373,000 | 350,000 |
| Total liabilities and stockholders' equity | $638,000 | $560,000 |

Additional data:

The common stock recently sold at $19.50 per share.

***Instructions***
Compute the following ratios for 2015.

(a) Current ratio.
(b) Acid-test ratio.
(c) Accounts receivable turnover.
(d) Inventory turnover.
(e) Profit margin.
(f) Asset turnover.
(g) Return on assets.

(h) Return on common stockholders' equity.
(i) Earnings per share.
(j) Price-earnings ratio.
(k) Payout ratio.
(l) Debt to assets ratio.
(m) Times interest earned.

*Compute missing information given a set of ratios.*
*(LO 5)*

**P18-7** An incomplete income statement and an incomplete comparative balance sheet of Deines Corporation are presented below and on page 885.

**DEINES CORPORATION**
Income Statement
For the Year Ended December 31, 2015

| | |
|---|---|
| Net sales | $11,000,000 |
| Cost of goods sold | ? |
| Gross profit | ? |
| Operating expenses | 1,665,000 |
| Income from operations | ? |
| Other expenses and losses | |
| Interest expense | ? |
| Income before income taxes | ? |
| Income tax expense | 560,000 |
| Net income | $      ? |

**DEINES CORPORATION**
Balance Sheets
December 31

| Assets | 2015 | 2014 |
|---|---|---|
| Current assets | | |
| Cash | $  450,000 | $  375,000 |
| Accounts receivable (net) | ? | 950,000 |
| Inventory | ? | 1,720,000 |
| Total current assets | ? | 3,045,000 |
| Plant assets (net) | 4,620,000 | 3,955,000 |
| Total assets | $      ? | $7,000,000 |

| Liabilities and Stockholders' Equity | 2015 | 2014 |
|---|---|---|
| Current liabilities | $ ? | $ 825,000 |
| Long-term notes payable | ? | 2,800,000 |
| Total liabilities | ? | 3,625,000 |
| Common stock, $1 par | 3,000,000 | 3,000,000 |
| Retained earnings | 400,000 | 375,000 |
| Total stockholders' equity | 3,400,000 | 3,375,000 |
| Total liabilities and stockholders' equity | $ ? | $7,000,000 |

Additional information:

1. The accounts receivable turnover for 2015 is 10 times.
2. All sales are on account.
3. The profit margin for 2015 is 14.5%.
4. Return on assets is 22% for 2015.
5. The current ratio on December 31, 2015, is 3.0.
6. The inventory turnover for 2015 is 4.8 times.

**Instructions**

Compute the missing information given the ratios above. Show computations. (*Note:* Start with one ratio and derive as much information as possible from it before trying another ratio. List all missing amounts under the ratio used to find the information.)

**P18-8** Terwilliger Corporation owns a number of cruise ships and a chain of hotels. The hotels, which have not been profitable, were discontinued on September 1, 2014. The 2014 operating results for the company were as follows.

*Prepare income statement with discontinued operations and extraordinary loss.*

*(LO 6)*

| | |
|---|---|
| Operating revenues | $12,850,000 |
| Operating expenses | 8,700,000 |
| Operating income | $ 4,150,000 |

Analysis discloses that these data include the operating results of the hotel chain, which were operating revenues $1,500,000 and operating expenses $2,400,000. The hotels were sold at a gain of $200,000 before taxes. This gain is not included in the operating results. During the year, Terwilliger suffered an extraordinary loss of $600,000 before taxes, which is not included in the operating results. In 2014, the company had other revenues and gains of $100,000, which are not included in the operating results. The corporation is in the 30% income tax bracket.

**Instructions**

Prepare a condensed income statement.

**P18-9** The ledger of Jaime Corporation at December 31, 2014, contains the following summary data.

*Prepare income statement with nontypical items.*

*(LO 6)*

| | | | |
|---|---|---|---|
| Net sales | $1,700,000 | Cost of goods sold | $1,100,000 |
| Selling expenses | 120,000 | Administrative expenses | 150,000 |
| Other revenues and gains | 20,000 | Other expenses and losses | 28,000 |

Your analysis reveals the following additional information that is not included in the above data.

1. The entire Puzzles Division was discontinued on August 31. The income from operations for this division before income taxes was $20,000. The Puzzles Division was sold at a loss of $90,000 before income taxes.
2. On May 15, company property was expropriated for an interstate highway. The settlement resulted in an extraordinary gain of $120,000 before income taxes.
3. The income tax rate on all items is 30%.

**Instructions**

Prepare an income statement for the year ended December 31, 2014. Use the format illustrated in the Comprehensive DO IT! (page 867).

## PROBLEMS: SET B

Visit the book's companion website, at **www.wiley.com/college/weygandt**, and choose the Student Companion site to access Problem Set B.

## CONTINUING COOKIE CHRONICLE

(*Note:* This is a continuation of the Cookie Chronicle from Chapters 1 through 17.)

**CCC18** Natalie and Curtis have the balance sheet and income statement for the first year of operations for Cookie & Coffee Creations Inc. They have been told that they can use these financial statements to prepare horizontal and vertical analyses, and to calculate financial ratios, to determine how their business is doing and to make some decisions they have been considering.

*Go to the book's companion website,* **www.wiley.com/college/weygandt**, *to see the completion of this problem.*

# Broadening Your Perspective

## Financial Reporting and Analysis

### Financial Reporting Problem: Apple Inc.

**BYP18-1** Your parents are considering investing in Apple Inc. common stock. They ask you, as an accounting expert, to make an analysis of the company for them. Apple's financial statements are presented in Appendix A. Instructions for accessing and using Apple's complete annual report, including the notes to the financial statements, are also provided in Appendix A.

**Instructions**
(Follow the approach in the chapter for rounding numbers.)

**(a)** Make a 3-year trend analysis, using 2009 as the base year, of (1) net sales and (2) net income. Comment on the significance of the trend results.

**(b)** Compute for 2011 and 2010 the (1) profit margin, (2) asset turnover, (3) return on assets, and (4) return on common stockholders' equity. How would you evaluate Apple's profitability? Total assets at September 26, 2009, were $47,501 and total stockholders' equity at September 26, 2009, was $31,640.

**(c)** Compute for 2011 and 2010 the (1) debt to assets ratio and (2) times interest earned. How would you evaluate Apple's long-term solvency?

**(d)** What information outside the annual report may also be useful to your parents in making a decision about Apple?

### Comparative Analysis Problem:
### PepsiCo, Inc. vs. The Coca-Cola Company

**BYP18-2** PepsiCo's financial statements are presented in Appendix B. Financial statements of The Coca-Cola Company are presented in Appendix C. Instructions for accessing and using the complete annual reports of PepsiCo and Coca-Cola, including the notes to the financial statements, are also provided in Appendices B and C, respectively.

**Instructions**

**(a)** Based on the information contained in these financial statements, determine each of the following for each company.

    **(1)** The percentage increase (decrease) in (i) net sales and (ii) net income from 2010 to 2011.

    **(2)** The percentage increase in (i) total assets and (ii) total common stockholders' (shareholders') equity from 2010 to 2011.

    **(3)** The basic earnings per share and price-earnings ratio for 2011. (For both PepsiCo and Coca-Cola, use the basic earnings per share.) Coca-Cola's common stock had a market price of $75.05 at the end of fiscal-year 2011, and PepsiCo's common stock had a market price of $66.35.

**(b)** What conclusions concerning the two companies can be drawn from these data?

## Comparative Analysis Problem:
## Amazon.com, Inc. vs. Wal-Mart Stores, Inc.

**BYP18-3** Amazon.com, Inc.'s financial statements are presented in Appendix D. Financial statements of Wal-Mart Stores, Inc. are presented in Appendix E. Instructions for accessing and using the complete annual reports of Amazon and Wal-Mart, including the notes to the financial statements, are also provided in Appendices D and E, respectively.

**Instructions**

**(a)** Based on the information contained in these financial statements, determine each of the following for each company.

    **(1)** The percentage increase (decrease) in (i) net sales and (ii) net income from 2010 to 2011.

    **(2)** The percentage increase in (i) total assets and (ii) total common stockholders' (shareholders') equity from 2010 to 2011.

    **(3)** The basic earnings per share and price-earnings ratio for 2011. (For both Amazon and Wal-Mart, use the basic earnings per share.) Amazon's common stock had a market price of $214.75 at the end of fiscal-year 2011, and Wal-Mart's common stock had a market price of $57.90.

**(b)** What conclusions concerning the two companies can be drawn from these data?

## Real-World Focus

**BYP18-4** The Management Discussion and Analysis section of an annual report addresses corporate performance for the year and sometimes uses financial ratios to support its claims.

*Address:* **www.ibm.com/investor/tools/index.phtml** or go to **www.wiley.com/college/weygandt**

**Steps**

**1.** Choose **How to read annual reports** (in the Guides section).

**2.** Choose **Anatomy**.

**Instructions**

Using the information from the above site, answer the following questions.

**(a)** What are the optional elements that are often included in an annual report?

**(b)** What are the elements of an annual report that are required by the SEC?

**(c)** Describe the contents of the Management Discussion.

**(d)** Describe the contents of the Auditors' Report.

**(e)** Describe the contents of the Selected Financial Data.

# Critical Thinking

## Decision-Making Across the Organization

**BYP18-5** As the CPA for Gandara Manufacturing Inc., you have been asked to develop some key ratios from the comparative financial statements. This information is to be used to convince creditors that the company is solvent and will continue as a going concern. The data requested and the computations developed from the financial statements follow.

|                    | **2014**   | **2013**   |
|--------------------|------------|------------|
| Current ratio      | 3.1 times  | 2.1 times  |
| Acid-test ratio    | .8 times   | 1.4 times  |
| Asset turnover     | 2.8 times  | 2.2 times  |
| Net income         | Up 32%     | Down 8%    |
| Earnings per share | $3.30      | $2.50      |

*Instructions*

With the class divided into groups, complete the following.

Gandara Manufacturing Inc. asks you to prepare a list of brief comments stating how each of these items supports the solvency and going-concern potential of the business. The company wishes to use these comments to support its presentation of data to its creditors. You are to prepare the comments as requested, giving the implications and the limitations of each item separately. Then prepare a collective inference that may be drawn from the individual items about Gandara's solvency and going-concern potential.

## Communication Activity

**BYP18-6** Abby Landis is the CEO of Pletcher's Electronics. Landis is an expert engineer but a novice in accounting. She asks you to explain (1) the bases for comparison in analyzing Pletcher's financial statements, and (2) the factors affecting quality of earnings.

*Instructions*

Write a letter to Abby Landis that explains the bases for comparison and factors affecting quality of earnings.

## Ethics Case

**BYP18-7** Dave Schonhardt, president of Schonhardt Industries, wishes to issue a press release to bolster his company's image and maybe even its stock price, which has been gradually falling. As controller, you have been asked to provide a list of 20 financial ratios along with some other operating statistics relative to Schonhardt Industries' first quarter financials and operations.

Two days after you provide the ratios and data requested, Steven Verlin, the public relations director of Schonhardt, asks you to prove the accuracy of the financial and operating data contained in the press release written by the president and edited by Steven. In the press release, the president highlights the sales increase of 25% over last year's first quarter and the positive change in the current ratio from 1.5:1 last year to 3:1 this year. He also emphasizes that production was up 50% over the prior year's first quarter.

You note that the press release contains only positive or improved ratios and none of the negative or deteriorated ratios. For instance, no mention is made that the debt to assets ratio has increased from 35% to 55%, that inventories are up 89%, and that while the current ratio improved, the acid-test ratio fell from 1:1 to. 5:1. Nor is there any mention that the reported profit for the quarter would have been a loss had not the estimated lives of Schonhardt's plant and machinery been increased by 30%. Steven emphasizes, "The prez wants this release by early this afternoon."

*Instructions*

**(a)** Who are the stakeholders in this situation?

**(b)** Is there anything unethical in president Schonhardt's actions?

**(c)** Should you as controller remain silent? Does Steven have any responsibility?

## All About You

**BYP18-8** In this chapter, you learned how to use many tools for performing a financial analysis of a company. When making personal investments, however, it is most likely that you won't be buying stocks and bonds in individual companies. Instead, when most people want to invest in stock, they buy mutual funds. By investing in a mutual fund, you reduce your risk because the fund diversifies by buying the stock of a variety of different companies, bonds, and other investments, depending on the stated goals of the fund.

Before you invest in a fund, you will need to decide what type of fund you want. For example, do you want a fund that has the potential of high growth (but also high risk), or are you looking for lower risk and a steady stream of income? Do you want a fund that invests only in U.S. companies, or do you want one that invests globally? Many resources are available to help you with these types of decisions.

**Instructions**
Go to **http://web.archive.org/web/20050210200843/http://www.cnb1.com/invallocmdl.htm** and complete the investment allocation questionnaire. Add up your total points to determine the type of investment fund that would be appropriate for you.

## FASB Codification Activity

**BYP18-9** If your school has a subscription to the FASB Codification, go to **http://aaahq.org/ascLogin.cfm** to log in and prepare responses to the following. Use the Master Glossary for determining the proper definitions.

**(a)** Discontinued operations.
**(b)** Extraordinary items.
**(c)** Comprehensive income.

## Answers to Chapter Questions

### Answers to Insight and Accounting Across the Organization Questions
**p. 851 How to Manage the Current Ratio   Q:** How might management influence a company's current ratio? **A:** Management can affect the current ratio by speeding up or withholding payments on accounts payable just before the balance sheet date. Management can alter the cash balance by increasing or decreasing long-term assets or long-term debt, or by issuing or purchasing common stock.

**p. 863 What Does "Non-Recurring" Really Mean?   Q:** If a company takes a large restructuring charge, what is the effect on the company's current income statement versus future ones? **A:** The current period's net income can be greatly diminished by a large restructuring charge. The net incomes in future periods can be enhanced because they are relieved of costs (i.e., depreciation and labor expenses) that would have been charged to them.

### Answers to Self-Test Questions
**1.** b   **2.** d   **3.** c ($360,000 ÷ 300,000)   **4.** c   **5.** a   **6.** c   **7.** c   **8.** b $306,000 ÷ [($54,000 + $48,000) ÷ 2] = 6; 365 ÷ 6   **9.** b ($81,000 ÷ $27,000)   **10.** a $134,000 ÷ $784,000   **11.** d ($134,000 − $4,000) ÷ [($240,000 + $198,000) ÷ 2]   **12.** c ($134,000 + $22,000 + $12,000) ÷ $12,000   **13.** c   **14.** d ($400,000 − (25% × $400,000); $300,000 − [$100,000 − (25% × $100,000)]   **15.** d

 # A Look at IFRS

The tools of financial statement analysis, covered in the first section of this chapter, are the same throughout the world. Techniques such as vertical and horizontal analysis, for example, are tools used by analysts regardless of whether GAAP- or IFRS-related financial statements are being evaluated. In addition, the ratios provided in the textbook are the same ones that are used internationally.

The latter part of this chapter relates to the income statement and irregular items. As in GAAP, the income statement is a required statement under IFRS. In addition, the content and presentation of an IFRS income statement is similar to the one used for GAAP. *IAS 1* (revised), "Presentation of Financial Statements," provides general guidelines for the reporting of income statement information. In general, the differences in the presentation of financial statement information are relatively minor.

**LEARNING OBJECTIVE    8**

**Compare financial statement analysis and income statement presentation under GAAP and IFRS.**

## IFRS Additions to the Textbook

- The tools of financial statement analysis covered in this chapter are universal and therefore no significant differences exist in the analysis methods used.

- The basic objectives of the income statement are the same under both GAAP and IFRS. As indicated in the textbook, a very important objective is to ensure that users of the income statement can evaluate the earning power of the company. Earning power is the normal level of income to be obtained in the future. Thus, both the IASB and the FASB are interested in distinguishing normal levels of income from irregular items in order to better predict a company's future profitability.

- The basic accounting for discontinued operations is the same under IFRS and GAAP.

- Under IFRS, there is no classification for extraordinary items. In other words, extraordinary item treatment is prohibited under IFRS. All revenue and expense items are considered ordinary in nature. Disclosure, however, is extensive for items that are considered material to the financial results. Examples are write-downs of inventory or plant assets, or gains and losses on the sale of plant assets.

- The accounting for changes in accounting principles and changes in accounting estimates are the same for both GAAP and IFRS.

- Both GAAP and IFRS follow the same approach in reporting comprehensive income. The statement of comprehensive income can be prepared under the one-statement approach or the two-statement approach.

- The issues related to quality of earnings are the same under both GAAP and IFRS. It is hoped that by adopting a more principles-based approach, as found in IFRS, that many of the earning quality issues will disappear.

## Looking to the Future

The FASB and the IASB are working on a project that would rework the structure of financial statements. Recently, the IASB decided to require a statement of comprehensive income, similar to what was required under GAAP. In addition, another part of this project addresses the issue of how to classify various items in the income statement. A main goal of this new approach is to provide information that better represents how businesses are run. In addition, the approach draws attention away from one number—net income.

## IFRS Practice

### IFRS Self-Test Questions

1. The basic tools of financial analysis are the same under both GAAP and IFRS **except** that:
   **(a)** horizontal analysis cannot be done because the format of the statements is sometimes different.
   **(b)** analysis is different because vertical analysis cannot be done under IFRS.
   **(c)** the current ratio cannot be computed because current liabilities are often reported before current assets in IFRS statements of position.
   **(d)** None of the above.

2. Under IFRS:
   **(a)** the reporting of discontinued items is different than under GAAP.
   **(b)** the reporting of extraordinary items is prohibited.
   **(c)** the reporting of changes in accounting principles is different than under GAAP.
   **(d)** None of the above.

3. Presentation of comprehensive income must be reported under IFRS in:
   **(a)** the statement of stockholders' equity.
   **(b)** the income statement ending with net income.
   **(c)** the notes to the financial statements.
   **(d)** a statement of comprehensive income.

**4.** In preparing its income statement for 2014, Parmalane assembles the following information.

| | |
|---|---|
| Sales revenue | $500,000 |
| Cost of goods sold | 300,000 |
| Operating expenses | 40,000 |
| Loss on discontinued operations | 20,000 |
| Loss from flood disaster (an extraordinary item under GAAP) | 10,000 |

Ignoring income taxes, what is Parmalane's income from continuing operations for 2014 under IFRS?

**(a)** $260,000.          **(c)** $240,000.
**(b)** $250,000           **(d)** $150,000.

**5.** Using the same information as Question 4, which statement is **incorrect**?
   **(a)** Net income under GAAP and IFRS are the same.
   **(b)** Under GAAP, special reporting is provided for extraordinary items.
   **(c)** Both GAAP and IFRS report the same amount for income from continuing operations.
   **(d)** IFRS would not provide separate disclosure for discontinued operations.

## International Financial Reporting Problem: Zetar plc

**IFRS18-1** The financial statements of Zetar plc are presented in Appendix F. Instructions for accessing and using the company's complete annual report, including the notes to its financial statements, are also provided in Appendix F.

*Instructions*
Use the company's **2009 annual report** to answer the following questions.

**(a)** The company's income statement reports a loss on discontinued operations. What business did the company discontinue, and why did it choose to discontinue the business?
**(b)** For the year ended April 30, 2009, what amount did the company lose on the operation of the discontinued business, and what amount did it lose on disposal?
**(c)** What was the total recorded value of the net assets at the date of disposal, and what was the amount of costs incurred to dispose of the business?

**Answers to IFRS Self-Test Questions**
**1.** d   **2.** b   **3.** d   **4.** d   **5.** d

 ✔ The Navigator

# Appendix A | Specimen Financial Statements: Apple Inc.

Once each year, a corporation communicates to its stockholders and other interested parties by issuing a complete set of audited financial statements. The **annual report**, as this communication is called, summarizes the financial results of the company's operations for the year and its plans for the future. Many annual reports are attractive, multicolored, glossy public relations pieces, containing pictures of corporate officers and directors as well as photos and descriptions of new products and new buildings. Yet the basic function of every annual report is to report financial information, almost all of which is a product of the corporation's accounting system.

The content and organization of corporate annual reports have become fairly standardized. Excluding the public relations part of the report (pictures, products, etc.), the following are the traditional financial portions of the annual report:

- Financial Highlights
- Letter to the Stockholders
- Management's Discussion and Analysis
- Financial Statements
- Notes to the Financial Statements
- Management's Responsibility for Financial Reporting
- Management's Report on Internal Control over Financial Reporting
- Report of Independent Registered Public Accounting Firm
- Selected Financial Data

The official SEC filing of the annual report is called a **Form 10-K**, which often omits the public relations pieces found in most standard annual reports. On the following pages, we present Apple Inc.'s financial statements taken from the company's 2011Form 10-K. To access Apple's Form 10-K, including notes to the financial statements, follow these steps:

1. Go to **http://investor.apple.com**.
2. Select the Financial History tab.
3. Select 2011 10-K Annual Report filed Oct 26, 2011.
4. Item 8, on page 42, provides an index to the consolidated financial statements and notes. The Notes to Consolidated Financial Statements, for example, begin on page 47.

## CONSOLIDATED STATEMENTS OF OPERATIONS
### (In millions, except number of shares which are reflected in thousands and per share amounts)

| Three years ended September 24, 2011 | 2011 | 2010 | 2009 |
|---|---|---|---|
| Net sales | $108,249 | $ 65,225 | $ 42,905 |
| Cost of sales | 64,431 | 39,541 | 25,683 |
| Gross margin | 43,818 | 25,684 | 17,222 |
| Operating expenses: | | | |
| Research and development | 2,429 | 1,782 | 1,333 |
| Selling, general and administrative | 7,599 | 5,517 | 4,149 |
| Total operating expenses | 10,028 | 7,299 | 5,482 |
| Operating income | 33,790 | 18,385 | 11,740 |
| Other income and expense | 415 | 155 | 326 |
| Income before provision for income taxes | 34,205 | 18,540 | 12,066 |
| Provision for income taxes | 8,283 | 4,527 | 3,831 |
| Net income | $ 25,922 | $ 14,013 | $ 8,235 |
| Earnings per common share: | | | |
| Basic | $ 28.05 | $ 15.41 | $ 9.22 |
| Diluted | $ 27.68 | $ 15.15 | $ 9.08 |
| Shares used in computing earnings per share: | | | |
| Basic | 924,258 | 909,461 | 893,016 |
| Diluted | 936,645 | 924,712 | 907,005 |

See accompanying Notes to Consolidated Financial Statements.

A1

## CONSOLIDATED BALANCE SHEETS

(In millions, except number of shares which are reflected in thousands)

| | September 24, 2011 | September 25, 2010 |
|---|---|---|
| **ASSETS:** | | |
| Current assets: | | |
| Cash and cash equivalents | $ 9,815 | $ 11,261 |
| Short-term marketable securities | 16,137 | 14,359 |
| Accounts receivable, less allowances of $53 and $55, respectively | 5,369 | 5,510 |
| Inventories | 776 | 1,051 |
| Deferred tax assets | 2,014 | 1,636 |
| Vendor non-trade receivables | 6,348 | 4,414 |
| Other current assets | 4,529 | 3,447 |
| Total current assets | 44,988 | 41,678 |
| Long-term marketable securities | 55,618 | 25,391 |
| Property, plant and equipment, net | 7,777 | 4,768 |
| Goodwill | 896 | 741 |
| Acquired intangible assets, net | 3,536 | 342 |
| Other assets | 3,556 | 2,263 |
| Total assets | $ 116,371 | $ 75,183 |
| **LIABILITIES AND SHAREHOLDERS' EQUITY:** | | |
| Current liabilities: | | |
| Accounts payable | $ 14,632 | $ 12,015 |
| Accrued expenses | 9,247 | 5,723 |
| Deferred revenue | 4,091 | 2,984 |
| Total current liabilities | 27,970 | 20,722 |
| Deferred revenue – non-current | 1,686 | 1,139 |
| Other non-current liabilities | 10,100 | 5,531 |
| Total liabilities | 39,756 | 27,392 |
| Commitments and contingencies | | |
| Shareholders' equity: | | |
| Common stock, no par value; 1,800,000 shares authorized; 929,277 and 915,970 shares issued and outstanding, respectively | 13,331 | 10,668 |
| Retained earnings | 62,841 | 37,169 |
| Accumulated other comprehensive income/(loss) | 443 | (46) |
| Total shareholders' equity | 76,615 | 47,791 |
| Total liabilities and shareholders' equity | $ 116,371 | $ 75,183 |

See accompanying Notes to Consolidated Financial Statements.

## CONSOLIDATED STATEMENTS OF SHAREHOLDERS' EQUITY
(In millions, except number of shares which are reflected in thousands)

| | Common Stock | | Retained Earnings | Accumulated Other Comprehensive Income/ (Loss) | Total Shareholders' Equity |
|---|---|---|---|---|---|
| | Shares | Amount | | | |
| Balances as of September 27, 2008 | 888,326 | $ 7,177 | $ 15,129 | $ (9) | $22,297 |
| Components of comprehensive income: | | | | | |
| Net income | 0 | 0 | 8,235 | 0 | 8,235 |
| Change in foreign currency translation | 0 | 0 | 0 | (14) | (14) |
| Change in unrealized gains/losses on marketable securities, net of tax | 0 | 0 | 0 | 118 | 118 |
| Change in unrecognized gains/losses on derivative instruments, net of tax | 0 | 0 | 0 | (18) | (18) |
| Total comprehensive income | | | | | 8,321 |
| Share-based compensation | 0 | 707 | 0 | 0 | 707 |
| Common stock issued under stock plans, net of shares withheld for employee taxes | 11,480 | 404 | (11) | 0 | 393 |
| Tax benefit from equity awards, including transfer pricing adjustments | 0 | (78) | 0 | 0 | (78) |
| Balances as of September 26, 2009 | 899,806 | 8,210 | 23,353 | 77 | 31,640 |
| Components of comprehensive income: | | | | | |
| Net income | 0 | 0 | 14,013 | 0 | 14,013 |
| Change in foreign currency translation | 0 | 0 | 0 | 7 | 7 |
| Change in unrealized gains/losses on marketable securities, net of tax | 0 | 0 | 0 | 123 | 123 |
| Change in unrecognized gains/losses on derivative instruments, net of tax | 0 | 0 | 0 | (253) | (253) |
| Total comprehensive income | | | | | 13,890 |
| Share-based compensation | 0 | 876 | 0 | 0 | 876 |
| Common stock issued under stock plans, net of shares withheld for employee taxes | 16,164 | 703 | (197) | 0 | 506 |
| Tax benefit from equity awards, including transfer pricing adjustments | 0 | 879 | 0 | 0 | 879 |
| Balances as of September 25, 2010 | 915,970 | 10,668 | 37,169 | (46) | 47,791 |
| Components of comprehensive income: | | | | | |
| Net income | 0 | 0 | 25,922 | 0 | 25,922 |
| Change in foreign currency translation | 0 | 0 | 0 | (12) | (12) |
| Change in unrealized gains/losses on marketable securities, net of tax | 0 | 0 | 0 | (41) | (41) |
| Change in unrecognized gains/losses on derivative instruments, net of tax | 0 | 0 | 0 | 542 | 542 |
| Total comprehensive income | | | | | 26,411 |
| Share-based compensation | 0 | 1,168 | 0 | 0 | 1,168 |
| Common stock issued under stock plans, net of shares withheld for employee taxes | 13,307 | 561 | (250) | 0 | 311 |
| Tax benefit from equity awards, including transfer pricing adjustments | 0 | 934 | 0 | 0 | 934 |
| Balances as of September 24, 2011 | 929,277 | $13,331 | $ 62,841 | $ 443 | $76,615 |

See accompanying Notes to Consolidated Financial Statements.

## CONSOLIDATED STATEMENTS OF CASH FLOWS
(In millions)

| Three years ended September 24, 2011 | 2011 | 2010 | 2009 |
|---|---|---|---|
| Cash and cash equivalents, beginning of the year | $ 11,261 | $ 5,263 | $ 11,875 |
| Operating activities: | | | |
| Net income | 25,922 | 14,013 | 8,235 |
| Adjustments to reconcile net income to cash generated by operating activities: | | | |
| Depreciation, amortization and accretion | 1,814 | 1,027 | 734 |
| Share-based compensation expense | 1,168 | 879 | 710 |
| Deferred income tax expense | 2,868 | 1,440 | 1,040 |
| Changes in operating assets and liabilities: | | | |
| Accounts receivable, net | 143 | (2,142) | (939) |
| Inventories | 275 | (596) | 54 |
| Vendor non-trade receivables | (1,934) | (2,718) | 586 |
| Other current and non-current assets | (1,391) | (1,610) | (713) |
| Accounts payable | 2,515 | 6,307 | 92 |
| Deferred revenue | 1,654 | 1,217 | 521 |
| Other current and non-current liabilities | 4,495 | 778 | (161) |
| Cash generated by operating activities | 37,529 | 18,595 | 10,159 |
| Investing activities: | | | |
| Purchases of marketable securities | (102,317) | (57,793) | (46,724) |
| Proceeds from maturities of marketable securities | 20,437 | 24,930 | 19,790 |
| Proceeds from sales of marketable securities | 49,416 | 21,788 | 10,888 |
| Payments made in connection with business acquisitions, net of cash acquired | (244) | (638) | 0 |
| Payments for acquisition of property, plant and equipment | (4,260) | (2,005) | (1,144) |
| Payments for acquisition of intangible assets | (3,192) | (116) | (69) |
| Other | (259) | (20) | (175) |
| Cash used in investing activities | (40,419) | (13,854) | (17,434) |
| Financing activities: | | | |
| Proceeds from issuance of common stock | 831 | 912 | 475 |
| Excess tax benefits from equity awards | 1,133 | 751 | 270 |
| Taxes paid related to net share settlement of equity awards | (520) | (406) | (82) |
| Cash generated by financing activities | 1,444 | 1,257 | 663 |
| (Decrease)/increase in cash and cash equivalents | (1,446) | 5,998 | (6,612) |
| Cash and cash equivalents, end of the year | $ 9,815 | $ 11,261 | $ 5,263 |
| Supplemental cash flow disclosure: | | | |
| Cash paid for income taxes, net | $ 3,338 | $ 2,697 | $ 2,997 |

See accompanying Notes to Consolidated Financial Statements.

# Appendix B

# Specimen Financial Statements: PepsiCo, Inc.

PepsiCo, Inc. is a world leader in convenient snacks, foods, and beverages. The following are PepsiCo's financial statements as presented in its 2011 annual report. To access PepsiCo's complete annual report, including notes to the financial statements, follow these steps:

1. Go to **www.pepsico.com**.
2. Select Annual Reports under the Investors tab.
3. Select the 2011 Annual Report Download.
4. An index to the company's financials is provided on page 23. The Notes to Consolidated Financial Statements, for example, begin on page 56.

## Consolidated Statement of Income

Fiscal years ended December 31, 2011, December 25, 2010 and December 26, 2009
(in millions except per share amounts)

| | 2011 | 2010 | 2009 |
|---|---|---|---|
| **Net Revenue** | $66,504 | $57,838 | $43,232 |
| Cost of sales | 31,593 | 26,575 | 20,099 |
| Selling, general and administrative expenses | 25,145 | 22,814 | 15,026 |
| Amortization of intangible assets | 133 | 117 | 63 |
| **Operating Profit** | 9,633 | 8,332 | 8,044 |
| Bottling equity income | – | 735 | 365 |
| Interest expense | (856) | (903) | (397) |
| Interest income and other | 57 | 68 | 67 |
| Income before income taxes | 8,834 | 8,232 | 8,079 |
| Provision for income taxes | 2,372 | 1,894 | 2,100 |
| Net income | 6,462 | 6,338 | 5,979 |
| Less: Net income attributable to noncontrolling interests | 19 | 18 | 33 |
| **Net Income Attributable to PepsiCo** | $ 6,443 | $ 6,320 | $ 5,946 |
| **Net Income Attributable to PepsiCo per Common Share** | | | |
| Basic | $ 4.08 | $ 3.97 | $ 3.81 |
| Diluted | $ 4.03 | $ 3.91 | $ 3.77 |
| Weighted-average common shares outstanding | | | |
| Basic | 1,576 | 1,590 | 1,558 |
| Diluted | 1,597 | 1,614 | 1,577 |
| Cash dividends declared per common share | $ 2.025 | $ 1.89 | $ 1.775 |

See accompanying notes to consolidated financial statements

## Consolidated Statement of Cash Flows

Fiscal years ended December 31, 2011, December 25, 2010 and December 26, 2009
(in millions)

| | 2011 | 2010 | 2009 |
|---|---|---|---|
| **Operating Activities** | | | |
| Net income | $ 6,462 | $ 6,338 | $ 5,979 |
| Depreciation and amortization | 2,737 | 2,327 | 1,635 |
| Stock-based compensation expense | 326 | 299 | 227 |
| Restructuring and impairment charges | 383 | – | 36 |
| Cash payments for restructuring charges | (31) | (31) | (196) |
| Merger and integration costs | 329 | 808 | 50 |
| Cash payments for merger and integration costs | (377) | (385) | (49) |
| Gain on previously held equity interests in PBG and PAS | – | (958) | – |
| Asset write-off | – | 145 | – |
| Non-cash foreign exchange loss related to Venezuela devaluation | – | 120 | – |
| Excess tax benefits from share-based payment arrangements | (70) | (107) | (42) |
| Pension and retiree medical plan contributions | (349) | (1,734) | (1,299) |
| Pension and retiree medical plan expenses | 571 | 453 | 423 |
| Bottling equity income, net of dividends | – | 42 | (235) |
| Deferred income taxes and other tax charges and credits | 495 | 500 | 284 |
| Change in accounts and notes receivable | (666) | (268) | 188 |
| Change in inventories | (331) | 276 | 17 |
| Change in prepaid expenses and other current assets | (27) | 144 | (127) |
| Change in accounts payable and other current liabilities | 520 | 488 | (133) |
| Change in income taxes payable | (340) | 123 | 319 |
| Other, net | (688) | (132) | (281) |
| **Net Cash Provided by Operating Activities** | 8,944 | 8,448 | 6,796 |
| **Investing Activities** | | | |
| Capital spending | (3,339) | (3,253) | (2,128) |
| Sales of property, plant and equipment | 84 | 81 | 58 |
| Acquisitions of PBG and PAS, net of cash and cash equivalents acquired | – | (2,833) | – |
| Acquisition of manufacturing and distribution rights from DPSG | – | (900) | – |
| Acquisition of WBD, net of cash and cash equivalents acquired | (2,428) | – | – |
| Investment in WBD | (164) | (463) | – |
| Other acquisitions and investments in noncontrolled affiliates | (601) | (83) | (500) |
| Divestitures | 780 | 12 | 99 |
| Cash restricted for pending acquisitions | – | – | 15 |
| Short-term investments, by original maturity | | | |
| More than three months — purchases | – | (12) | (29) |
| More than three months — maturities | 21 | 29 | 71 |
| Three months or less, net | 45 | (229) | 13 |
| Other investing, net | (16) | (17) | – |
| **Net Cash Used for Investing Activities** | (5,618) | (7,668) | (2,401) |
| **Financing Activities** | | | |
| Proceeds from issuances of long-term debt | $ 3,000 | $ 6,451 | $ 1,057 |
| Payments of long-term debt | (1,596) | (59) | (226) |
| Debt repurchase | (771) | (500) | – |
| Short-term borrowings, by original maturity | | | |
| More than three months — proceeds | 523 | 227 | 26 |
| More than three months — payments | (559) | (96) | (81) |
| Three months or less, net | 339 | 2,351 | (963) |
| Cash dividends paid | (3,157) | (2,978) | (2,732) |
| Share repurchases — common | (2,489) | (4,978) | – |
| Share repurchases — preferred | (7) | (5) | (7) |
| Proceeds from exercises of stock options | 945 | 1,038 | 413 |
| Excess tax benefits from share-based payment arrangements | 70 | 107 | 42 |
| Acquisition of noncontrolling interests | (1,406) | (159) | – |
| Other financing | (27) | (13) | (26) |
| **Net Cash (Used for)/Provided by Financing Activities** | (5,135) | 1,386 | (2,497) |
| Effect of exchange rate changes on cash and cash equivalents | (67) | (166) | (19) |
| **Net (Decrease)/Increase in Cash and Cash Equivalents** | (1,876) | 2,000 | 1,879 |
| **Cash and Cash Equivalents, Beginning of Year** | 5,943 | 3,943 | 2,064 |
| **Cash and Cash Equivalents, End of Year** | $ 4,067 | $ 5,943 | $ 3,943 |
| Non-cash activity: | | | |
| Issuance of common stock and equity awards in connection with our acquisitions of PBG and PAS, as reflected in investing and financing activities | – | $ 4,451 | – |

See accompanying notes to consolidated financial statements

**Consolidated Balance Sheet**

December 31, 2011 and December 25, 2010
(in millions except per share amounts)

| | 2011 | 2010 |
|---|---|---|
| **ASSETS** | | |
| **Current Assets** | | |
| Cash and cash equivalents | $ 4,067 | $ 5,943 |
| Short-term investments | 358 | 426 |
| Accounts and notes receivable, net | 6,912 | 6,323 |
| Inventories | 3,827 | 3,372 |
| Prepaid expenses and other current assets | 2,277 | 1,505 |
| **Total Current Assets** | 17,441 | 17,569 |
| **Property, Plant and Equipment, net** | 19,698 | 19,058 |
| **Amortizable Intangible Assets, net** | 1,888 | 2,025 |
| Goodwill | 16,800 | 14,661 |
| Other nonamortizable intangible assets | 14,557 | 11,783 |
| **Nonamortizable Intangible Assets** | 31,357 | 26,444 |
| **Investments in Noncontrolled Affiliates** | 1,477 | 1,368 |
| **Other Assets** | 1,021 | 1,689 |
| **Total Assets** | $ 72,882 | $ 68,153 |
| **LIABILITIES AND EQUITY** | | |
| **Current Liabilities** | | |
| Short-term obligations | $ 6,205 | $ 4,898 |
| Accounts payable and other current liabilities | 11,757 | 10,923 |
| Income taxes payable | 192 | 71 |
| **Total Current Liabilities** | 18,154 | 15,892 |
| **Long-Term Debt Obligations** | 20,568 | 19,999 |
| **Other Liabilities** | 8,266 | 6,729 |
| **Deferred Income Taxes** | 4,995 | 4,057 |
| **Total Liabilities** | 51,983 | 46,677 |
| Commitments and Contingencies | | |
| **Preferred Stock, no par value** | 41 | 41 |
| **Repurchased Preferred Stock** | (157) | (150) |
| **PepsiCo Common Shareholders' Equity** | | |
| Common stock, par value 1²/₃¢ per share (authorized 3,600 shares, issued 1,865 shares) | 31 | 31 |
| Capital in excess of par value | 4,461 | 4,527 |
| Retained earnings | 40,316 | 37,090 |
| Accumulated other comprehensive loss | (6,229) | (3,630) |
| Repurchased common stock, at cost (301 and 284 shares, respectively) | (17,875) | (16,745) |
| **Total PepsiCo Common Shareholders' Equity** | 20,704 | 21,273 |
| Noncontrolling interests | 311 | 312 |
| **Total Equity** | 20,899 | 21,476 |
| **Total Liabilities and Equity** | $ 72,882 | $ 68,153 |

See accompanying notes to consolidated financial statements

**Consolidated Statement of Equity**

Fiscal years ended December 31, 2011, December 25, 2010 and December 26, 2009
(in millions)

| | 2011 | | 2010 | | 2009 | |
|---|---|---|---|---|---|---|
| | Shares | Amount | Shares | Amount | Shares | Amount |
| **Preferred Stock** | 0.8 | $ 41 | 0.8 | $ 41 | 0.8 | $ 41 |
| **Repurchased Preferred Stock** | | | | | | |
| Balance, beginning of year | (0.6) | (150) | (0.6) | (145) | (0.5) | (138) |
| Redemptions | (−) | (7) | (−) | (5) | (0.1) | (7) |
| Balance, end of year | (0.6) | (157) | (0.6) | (150) | (0.6) | (145) |
| **Common Stock** | | | | | | |
| Balance, beginning of year | 1,865 | 31 | 1,782 | 30 | 1,782 | 30 |
| Shares issued in connection with our acquisitions of PBG and PAS | – | – | 83 | 1 | – | – |
| Balance, end of year | 1,865 | 31 | 1,865 | 31 | 1,782 | 30 |
| **Capital in Excess of Par Value** | | | | | | |
| Balance, beginning of year | | 4,527 | | 250 | | 351 |
| Stock-based compensation expense | | 326 | | 299 | | 227 |
| Stock option exercises/RSUs converted(a) | | (361) | | (500) | | (292) |
| Withholding tax on RSUs converted | | (56) | | (68) | | (36) |
| Equity issued in connection with our acquisitions of PBG and PAS | | – | | 4,451 | | – |
| Other | | 25 | | 95 | | – |
| Balance, end of year | | 4,461 | | 4,527 | | 250 |
| **Retained Earnings** | | | | | | |
| Balance, beginning of year | | 37,090 | | 33,805 | | 30,638 |
| Net income attributable to PepsiCo | | 6,443 | | 6,320 | | 5,946 |
| Cash dividends declared—common | | (3,192) | | (3,028) | | (2,768) |
| Cash dividends declared—preferred | | (1) | | (1) | | (2) |
| Cash dividends declared—RSUs | | (24) | | (12) | | (9) |
| Other | | – | | 6 | | – |
| Balance, end of year | | 40,316 | | 37,090 | | 33,805 |
| **Accumulated Other Comprehensive Loss** | | | | | | |
| Balance, beginning of year | | (3,630) | | (3,794) | | (4,694) |
| Currency translation adjustment | | (1,529) | | 312 | | 800 |
| Cash flow hedges, net of tax: | | | | | | |
| Net derivative losses | | (83) | | (111) | | (55) |
| Reclassification of net losses to net income | | 14 | | 53 | | 28 |
| Pension and retiree medical, net of tax: | | | | | | |
| Net pension and retiree medical (losses)/gains | | (1,110) | | (280) | | 21 |
| Reclassification of net losses to net income | | 133 | | 166 | | 86 |
| Unrealized (losses)/gains on securities, net of tax | | (8) | | 23 | | 20 |
| Other | | (16) | | 1 | | – |
| Balance, end of year | | (6,229) | | (3,630) | | (3,794) |
| **Repurchased Common Stock** | | | | | | |
| Balance, beginning of year | (284) | (16,745) | (217) | (13,383) | (229) | (14,122) |
| Share repurchases | (39) | (2,489) | (76) | (4,978) | – | – |
| Stock option exercises | 20 | 1,251 | 24 | 1,487 | 11 | 649 |
| Other | 2 | 108 | (15) | 129 | 1 | 90 |
| Balance, end of year | (301) | (17,875) | (284) | (16,745) | (217) | (13,383) |
| **Total Common Shareholders' Equity** | | 20,704 | | 21,273 | | 16,908 |
| **Noncontrolling Interests** | | | | | | |
| Balance, beginning of year | | 312 | | 638 | | 476 |
| Net income attributable to noncontrolling interests | | 19 | | 18 | | 33 |
| Distributions to noncontrolling interests, net | | (24) | | (6) | | – |
| Currency translation adjustment | | 65 | | (13) | | (12) |
| Acquisitions and divestitures | | (57) | | (326) | | 150 |
| Other, net | | (4) | | 1 | | (9) |
| Balance, end of year | | 311 | | 312 | | 638 |
| **Total Equity** | | $ 20,899 | | $ 21,476 | | $ 17,442 |

(a) Includes total tax benefits of $43 million in 2011, $75 million in 2010 and $31 million in 2009.

(Continued on following page)

**Consolidated Statement of Equity**
(continued)

| Fiscal years ended December 31, 2011, December 25, 2010 and December 26, 2009 (in millions) | 2011 | 2010 | 2009 |
|---|---|---|---|
| **Comprehensive Income** | | | |
| Net income | $ 6,462 | $6,338 | $5,979 |
| Other comprehensive (loss)/income | | | |
| Currency translation adjustment | (1,464) | 299 | 788 |
| Cash flow hedges, net of tax | (69) | (58) | (27) |
| Pension and retiree medical, net of tax: | | | |
| Net prior service (cost)/credit | (10) | 22 | (3) |
| Net (losses)/gains | (967) | (136) | 110 |
| Unrealized (losses)/gains on securities, net of tax | (8) | 23 | 20 |
| Other | (16) | 1 | – |
| | (2,534) | 151 | 888 |
| Comprehensive income | 3,928 | 6,489 | 6,867 |
| Comprehensive income attributable to noncontrolling interests | (84) | (5) | (21) |
| **Comprehensive Income Attributable to PepsiCo** | $ 3,844 | $6,484 | $6,846 |

See accompanying notes to consolidated financial statements

# Specimen Financial Statements: The Coca-Cola Company

The Coca-Cola Company is a global leader in the beverage industry. It offers hundreds of brands, including soft drinks, fruit juices, sports drinks and other beverages in more than 200 countries. The following are Coca-Cola's financial statements as presented in its 2011 annual report. To access Coca-Cola's complete annual report, including notes to the financial statements, follow these steps:

1. Go to **www.thecoca-colacompany.com**.
2. Select Reports & Financial Information under the Investors tab.
3. Select Annual & Other Reports and then 2011 Annual Report on Form 10-K.
4. Use the Bookmarks section on the left to find specific information. The Notes to Consolidated Financial Statements, for example, begin on page 82.

**THE COCA-COLA COMPANY AND SUBSIDIARIES**

**CONSOLIDATED STATEMENTS OF INCOME**

| Year Ended December 31, | 2011 | 2010 | 2009 |
|---|---|---|---|
| (In millions except per share data) | | | |
| NET OPERATING REVENUES | $ 46,542 | $ 35,119 | $ 30,990 |
| Cost of goods sold | 18,216 | 12,693 | 11,088 |
| GROSS PROFIT | 28,326 | 22,426 | 19,902 |
| Selling, general and administrative expenses | 17,440 | 13,158 | 11,358 |
| Other operating charges | 732 | 819 | 313 |
| OPERATING INCOME | 10,154 | 8,449 | 8,231 |
| Interest income | 483 | 317 | 249 |
| Interest expense | 417 | 733 | 355 |
| Equity income (loss) — net | 690 | 1,025 | 781 |
| Other income (loss) — net | 529 | 5,185 | 40 |
| INCOME BEFORE INCOME TAXES | 11,439 | 14,243 | 8,946 |
| Income taxes | 2,805 | 2,384 | 2,040 |
| CONSOLIDATED NET INCOME | 8,634 | 11,859 | 6,906 |
| Less: Net income attributable to noncontrolling interests | 62 | 50 | 82 |
| NET INCOME ATTRIBUTABLE TO SHAREOWNERS OF THE COCA-COLA COMPANY | $ 8,572 | $ 11,809 | $ 6,824 |
| BASIC NET INCOME PER SHARE[1] | $ 3.75 | $ 5.12 | $ 2.95 |
| DILUTED NET INCOME PER SHARE[1] | $ 3.69 | $ 5.06 | $ 2.93 |
| AVERAGE SHARES OUTSTANDING | 2,284 | 2,308 | 2,314 |
| Effect of dilutive securities | 39 | 25 | 15 |
| AVERAGE SHARES OUTSTANDING ASSUMING DILUTION | 2,323 | 2,333 | 2,329 |

[1] Basic net income per share and diluted net income per share are calculated based on net income attributable to shareowners of The Coca-Cola Company.

Refer to Notes to Consolidated Financial Statements.

## THE COCA-COLA COMPANY AND SUBSIDIARIES
## CONSOLIDATED BALANCE SHEETS

| December 31, | 2011 | 2010 |
|---|---|---|
| (In millions except par value) | | |
| **ASSETS** | | |
| CURRENT ASSETS | | |
| Cash and cash equivalents | $ 12,803 | $ 8,517 |
| Short-term investments | 1,088 | 2,682 |
| TOTAL CASH, CASH EQUIVALENTS AND SHORT-TERM INVESTMENTS | 13,891 | 11,199 |
| Marketable securities | 144 | 138 |
| Trade accounts receivable, less allowances of $83 and $48, respectively | 4,920 | 4,430 |
| Inventories | 3,092 | 2,650 |
| Prepaid expenses and other assets | 3,450 | 3,162 |
| TOTAL CURRENT ASSETS | 25,497 | 21,579 |
| EQUITY METHOD INVESTMENTS | 7,233 | 6,954 |
| OTHER INVESTMENTS, PRINCIPALLY BOTTLING COMPANIES | 1,141 | 631 |
| OTHER ASSETS | 3,495 | 2,121 |
| PROPERTY, PLANT AND EQUIPMENT — net | 14,939 | 14,727 |
| TRADEMARKS WITH INDEFINITE LIVES | 6,430 | 6,356 |
| BOTTLERS' FRANCHISE RIGHTS WITH INDEFINITE LIVES | 7,770 | 7,511 |
| GOODWILL | 12,219 | 11,665 |
| OTHER INTANGIBLE ASSETS | 1,250 | 1,377 |
| TOTAL ASSETS | $ 79,974 | $ 72,921 |
| **LIABILITIES AND EQUITY** | | |
| CURRENT LIABILITIES | | |
| Accounts payable and accrued expenses | $ 9,009 | $ 8,859 |
| Loans and notes payable | 12,871 | 8,100 |
| Current maturities of long-term debt | 2,041 | 1,276 |
| Accrued income taxes | 362 | 273 |
| TOTAL CURRENT LIABILITIES | 24,283 | 18,508 |
| LONG-TERM DEBT | 13,656 | 14,041 |
| OTHER LIABILITIES | 5,420 | 4,794 |
| DEFERRED INCOME TAXES | 4,694 | 4,261 |
| THE COCA-COLA COMPANY SHAREOWNERS' EQUITY | | |
| Common stock, $0.25 par value; Authorized — 5,600 shares; | | |
| Issued — 3,520 and 3,520 shares, respectively | 880 | 880 |
| Capital surplus | 11,212 | 10,057 |
| Reinvested earnings | 53,550 | 49,278 |
| Accumulated other comprehensive income (loss) | (2,703) | (1,450) |
| Treasury stock, at cost — 1,257 and 1,228 shares, respectively | (31,304) | (27,762) |
| EQUITY ATTRIBUTABLE TO SHAREOWNERS OF THE COCA-COLA COMPANY | 31,635 | 31,003 |
| EQUITY ATTRIBUTABLE TO NONCONTROLLING INTERESTS | 286 | 314 |
| TOTAL EQUITY | 31,921 | 31,317 |
| TOTAL LIABILITIES AND EQUITY | $ 79,974 | $ 72,921 |

Refer to Notes to Consolidated Financial Statements.

THE COCA-COLA COMPANY AND SUBSIDIARIES

CONSOLIDATED STATEMENTS OF CASH FLOWS

| Year Ended December 31, | 2011 | 2010 | 2009 |
|---|---|---|---|
| (In millions) | | | |
| **OPERATING ACTIVITIES** | | | |
| Consolidated net income | $ 8,634 | $ 11,859 | $ 6,906 |
| Depreciation and amortization | 1,954 | 1,443 | 1,236 |
| Stock-based compensation expense | 354 | 380 | 241 |
| Deferred income taxes | 1,028 | 617 | 353 |
| Equity (income) loss — net of dividends | (269) | (671) | (359) |
| Foreign currency adjustments | 7 | 151 | 61 |
| Significant (gains) losses on sales of assets — net | (220) | (645) | (43) |
| Other significant (gains) losses — net | — | (4,713) | — |
| Other operating charges | 214 | 264 | 134 |
| Other items | (335) | 477 | 221 |
| Net change in operating assets and liabilities | (1,893) | 370 | (564) |
| Net cash provided by operating activities | 9,474 | 9,532 | 8,186 |
| **INVESTING ACTIVITIES** | | | |
| Purchases of short-term investments | (4,057) | (4,579) | (2,130) |
| Proceeds from disposals of short-term investments | 5,647 | 4,032 | — |
| Acquisitions and investments | (977) | (2,511) | (300) |
| Purchases of other investments | (787) | (132) | (22) |
| Proceeds from disposals of bottling companies and other investments | 562 | 972 | 240 |
| Purchases of property, plant and equipment | (2,920) | (2,215) | (1,993) |
| Proceeds from disposals of property, plant and equipment | 101 | 134 | 104 |
| Other investing activities | (93) | (106) | (48) |
| Net cash provided by (used in) investing activities | (2,524) | (4,405) | (4,149) |
| **FINANCING ACTIVITIES** | | | |
| Issuances of debt | 27,495 | 15,251 | 14,689 |
| Payments of debt | (22,530) | (13,403) | (12,326) |
| Issuances of stock | 1,569 | 1,666 | 664 |
| Purchases of stock for treasury | (4,513) | (2,961) | (1,518) |
| Dividends | (4,300) | (4,068) | (3,800) |
| Other financing activities | 45 | 50 | (2) |
| Net cash provided by (used in) financing activities | (2,234) | (3,465) | (2,293) |
| **EFFECT OF EXCHANGE RATE CHANGES ON CASH AND CASH EQUIVALENTS** | (430) | (166) | 576 |
| **CASH AND CASH EQUIVALENTS** | | | |
| Net increase (decrease) during the year | 4,286 | 1,496 | 2,320 |
| Balance at beginning of year | 8,517 | 7,021 | 4,701 |
| Balance at end of year | $ 12,803 | $ 8,517 | $ 7,021 |

Refer to Notes to Consolidated Financial Statements.

## THE COCA-COLA COMPANY AND SUBSIDIARIES
## CONSOLIDATED STATEMENTS OF SHAREOWNERS' EQUITY

| Year Ended December 31, | 2011 | 2010 | 2009 |
|---|---|---|---|
| (In millions except per share data) | | | |
| **EQUITY ATTRIBUTABLE TO SHAREOWNERS OF THE COCA-COLA COMPANY** | | | |
| **NUMBER OF COMMON SHARES OUTSTANDING** | | | |
| Balance at beginning of year | 2,292 | 2,303 | 2,312 |
| Purchases of treasury stock | (63) | (49) | (26) |
| Treasury stock issued to employees related to stock compensation plans | 34 | 38 | 17 |
| Balance at end of year | 2,263 | 2,292 | 2,303 |
| **COMMON STOCK** | $     880 | $     880 | $     880 |
| **CAPITAL SURPLUS** | | | |
| Balance at beginning of year | 10,057 | 8,537 | 7,966 |
| Stock issued to employees related to stock compensation plans | 724 | 855 | 339 |
| Replacement share-based awards issued in connection with an acquisition | — | 237 | — |
| Tax benefit (charge) from employees' stock option and restricted stock plans | 79 | 48 | (6) |
| Stock-based compensation | 354 | 380 | 238 |
| Other activities | (2) | — | — |
| Balance at end of year | 11,212 | 10,057 | 8,537 |
| **REINVESTED EARNINGS** | | | |
| Balance at beginning of year | 49,278 | 41,537 | 38,513 |
| Net income attributable to shareowners of The Coca-Cola Company | 8,572 | 11,809 | 6,824 |
| Dividends (per share — $1.88, $1.76 and $1.64 in 2011, 2010 and 2009, respectively) | (4,300) | (4,068) | (3,800) |
| Balance at end of year | 53,550 | 49,278 | 41,537 |
| **ACCUMULATED OTHER COMPREHENSIVE INCOME (LOSS)** | | | |
| Balance at beginning of year | (1,450) | (757) | (2,674) |
| Net foreign currency translation adjustment | (640) | (935) | 1,824 |
| Net gain (loss) on derivatives | 145 | (120) | 34 |
| Net change in unrealized gain on available-for-sale securities | (7) | 102 | (52) |
| Net change in pension and other benefit liabilities | (751) | 260 | 111 |
| Net other comprehensive income (loss) | (1,253) | (693) | 1,917 |
| Balance at end of year | (2,703) | (1,450) | (757) |
| **TREASURY STOCK** | | | |
| Balance at beginning of year | (27,762) | (25,398) | (24,213) |
| Stock issued to employees related to stock compensation plans | 830 | 824 | 333 |
| Purchases of treasury stock | (4,372) | (3,188) | (1,518) |
| Balance at end of year | (31,304) | (27,762) | (25,398) |
| **TOTAL EQUITY ATTRIBUTABLE TO SHAREOWNERS OF THE COCA-COLA COMPANY** | $ 31,635 | $ 31,003 | $ 24,799 |
| **EQUITY ATTRIBUTABLE TO NONCONTROLLING INTERESTS** | | | |
| Balance at beginning of year | $     314 | $     547 | $     390 |
| Net income attributable to noncontrolling interests | 62 | 50 | 82 |
| Net foreign currency translation adjustment | (52) | (12) | 49 |
| Dividends paid to noncontrolling interests | (38) | (32) | (14) |
| Contributions by noncontrolling interests | — | 1 | 40 |
| Increase due to business combinations | — | 13 | — |
| Deconsolidation of certain variable interest entities | — | (253) | — |
| **TOTAL EQUITY ATTRIBUTABLE TO NONCONTROLLING INTERESTS** | $     286 | $     314 | $     547 |
| **COMPREHENSIVE INCOME** | | | |
| Consolidated net income | $   8,634 | $ 11,859 | $   6,906 |
| Consolidated net other comprehensive income (loss) | (1,305) | (705) | 1,966 |
| **CONSOLIDATED COMPREHENSIVE INCOME** | $   7,329 | $ 11,154 | $   8,872 |

Refer to Notes to Consolidated Financial Statements.

# Specimen Financial Statements: Amazon.com, Inc.

Amazon.com, Inc. is the world's largest online retailer. It also produces consumer electronics—notably the Kindle e-book reader and the Kindle Fire Tablet computer—and is a major provider of cloud computing services. The following are Amazon's financial statements as presented in the company's 2011 annual report. To access Amazon's complete annual report, including notes to the financial statements, follow these steps:

1. Go to **www.amazon.com**.
2. Select the Investor Relations link at the bottom of the page and then select the 2011 Annual Report under Annual Reports and Proxies.
3. Use the Bookmarks section on the left to find specific information. The Notes to Consolidated Financial Statements, for example, begin on page 40.

**AMAZON.COM, INC.**

**CONSOLIDATED STATEMENTS OF CASH FLOWS**
**(in millions)**

| | Year Ended December 31, | | |
|---|---|---|---|
| | **2011** | **2010** | **2009** |
| CASH AND CASH EQUIVALENTS, BEGINNING OF PERIOD | $ 3,777 | $ 3,444 | $ 2,769 |
| OPERATING ACTIVITIES: | | | |
| Net income | 631 | 1,152 | 902 |
| Adjustments to reconcile net income to net cash from operating activities: | | | |
| Depreciation of fixed assets, including internal-use software and website development, and other amortization | 1,083 | 568 | 378 |
| Stock-based compensation | 557 | 424 | 341 |
| Other operating expense (income), net | 154 | 106 | 103 |
| Losses (gains) on sales of marketable securities, net | (4) | (2) | (4) |
| Other expense (income), net | (56) | (79) | (15) |
| Deferred income taxes | 136 | 4 | 81 |
| Excess tax benefits from stock-based compensation | (62) | (259) | (105) |
| Changes in operating assets and liabilities: | | | |
| Inventories | (1,777) | (1,019) | (531) |
| Accounts receivable, net and other | (866) | (295) | (481) |
| Accounts payable | 2,997 | 2,373 | 1,859 |
| Accrued expenses and other | 1,067 | 740 | 300 |
| Additions to unearned revenue | 1,064 | 687 | 1,054 |
| Amortization of previously unearned revenue | (1,021) | (905) | (589) |
| Net cash provided by operating activities | 3,903 | 3,495 | 3,293 |
| INVESTING ACTIVITIES: | | | |
| Purchases of fixed assets, including internal-use software and website development | (1,811) | (979) | (373) |
| Acquisitions, net of cash acquired, and other | (705) | (352) | (40) |
| Sales and maturities of marketable securities and other investments | 6,843 | 4,250 | 1,966 |
| Purchases of marketable securities and other investments | (6,257) | (6,279) | (3,890) |
| Net cash used in investing activities | (1,930) | (3,360) | (2,337) |
| FINANCING ACTIVITIES: | | | |
| Excess tax benefits from stock-based compensation | 62 | 259 | 105 |
| Common stock repurchased | (277) | — | — |
| Proceeds from long-term debt and other | 177 | 143 | 87 |
| Repayments of long-term debt, capital lease, and finance lease obligations | (444) | (221) | (472) |
| Net cash provided by (used in) financing activities | (482) | 181 | (280) |
| Foreign-currency effect on cash and cash equivalents | 1 | 17 | (1) |
| Net increase in cash and cash equivalents | 1,492 | 333 | 675 |
| CASH AND CASH EQUIVALENTS, END OF PERIOD | $ 5,269 | $ 3,777 | $ 3,444 |
| SUPPLEMENTAL CASH FLOW INFORMATION: | | | |
| Cash paid for interest on long term debt | $ 14 | $ 11 | $ 32 |
| Cash paid for income taxes (net of refunds) | 33 | 75 | 48 |
| Fixed assets acquired under capital leases | 753 | 405 | 147 |
| Fixed assets acquired under build-to-suit leases | 259 | 172 | 188 |

See accompanying notes to consolidated financial statements.

**AMAZON.COM, INC.**

**CONSOLIDATED STATEMENTS OF OPERATIONS**
**(in millions, except per share data)**

| | Year Ended December 31, | | |
| --- | --- | --- | --- |
| | 2011 | 2010 | 2009 |
| Net product sales | $42,000 | $30,792 | $22,273 |
| Net services sales | 6,077 | 3,412 | 2,236 |
| Total net sales | 48,077 | 34,204 | 24,509 |
| Operating expenses (1): | | | |
| Cost of sales | 37,288 | 26,561 | 18,978 |
| Fulfillment | 4,576 | 2,898 | 2,052 |
| Marketing | 1,630 | 1,029 | 680 |
| Technology and content | 2,909 | 1,734 | 1,240 |
| General and administrative | 658 | 470 | 328 |
| Other operating expense (income), net | 154 | 106 | 102 |
| Total operating expenses | 47,215 | 32,798 | 23,380 |
| Income from operations | 862 | 1,406 | 1,129 |
| Interest income | 61 | 51 | 37 |
| Interest expense | (65) | (39) | (34) |
| Other income (expense), net | 76 | 79 | 29 |
| Total non-operating income (expense) | 72 | 91 | 32 |
| Income before income taxes | 934 | 1,497 | 1,161 |
| Provision for income taxes | (291) | (352) | (253) |
| Equity-method investment activity, net of tax | (12) | 7 | (6) |
| Net income | $ 631 | $ 1,152 | $ 902 |
| Basic earnings per share | $ 1.39 | $ 2.58 | $ 2.08 |
| Diluted earnings per share | $ 1.37 | $ 2.53 | $ 2.04 |
| Weighted average shares used in computation of earnings per share: | | | |
| Basic | 453 | 447 | 433 |
| Diluted | 461 | 456 | 442 |

(1) Includes stock-based compensation as follows:

| | | | |
| --- | --- | --- | --- |
| Fulfillment | $ 133 | $ 90 | $ 79 |
| Marketing | 39 | 27 | 20 |
| Technology and content | 292 | 223 | 182 |
| General and administrative | 93 | 84 | 60 |

See accompanying notes to consolidated financial statements.

## AMAZON.COM, INC.

### CONSOLIDATED BALANCE SHEETS
**(in millions, except per share data)**

|  | December 31, | |
| --- | ---: | ---: |
|  | **2011** | **2010** |
| **ASSETS** | | |
| Current assets: | | |
| Cash and cash equivalents | $ 5,269 | $ 3,777 |
| Marketable securities | 4,307 | 4,985 |
| Inventories | 4,992 | 3,202 |
| Accounts receivable, net and other | 2,571 | 1,587 |
| Deferred tax assets | 351 | 196 |
| Total current assets | 17,490 | 13,747 |
| Fixed assets, net | 4,417 | 2,414 |
| Deferred tax assets | 28 | 22 |
| Goodwill | 1,955 | 1,349 |
| Other assets | 1,388 | 1,265 |
| Total assets | $25,278 | $18,797 |
| **LIABILITIES AND STOCKHOLDERS' EQUITY** | | |
| Current liabilities: | | |
| Accounts payable | $11,145 | $ 8,051 |
| Accrued expenses and other | 3,751 | 2,321 |
| Total current liabilities | 14,896 | 10,372 |
| Long-term liabilities | 2,625 | 1,561 |
| Commitments and contingencies | | |
| Stockholders' equity: | | |
| Preferred stock, $0.01 par value: | | |
| Authorized shares — 500 | | |
| Issued and outstanding shares — none | 0 | 0 |
| Common stock, $0.01 par value: | | |
| Authorized shares — 5,000 | | |
| Issued shares — 473 and 468 | | |
| Outstanding shares — 455 and 451 | 5 | 5 |
| Treasury stock, at cost | (877) | (600) |
| Additional paid-in capital | 6,990 | 6,325 |
| Accumulated other comprehensive loss | (316) | (190) |
| Retained earnings | 1,955 | 1,324 |
| Total stockholders' equity | 7,757 | 6,864 |
| Total liabilities and stockholders' equity | $25,278 | $18,797 |

See accompanying notes to consolidated financial statements.

## AMAZON.COM, INC.

### CONSOLIDATED STATEMENTS OF STOCKHOLDERS' EQUITY

(in millions)

| | Common Stock Shares | Common Stock Amount | Treasury Stock | Additional Paid-In Capital | Accumulated Other Comprehensive Income (Loss) | Retained Earnings (Accumulated Deficit) | Total Stockholders' Equity |
|---|---|---|---|---|---|---|---|
| Balance at December 31, 2008 | 428 | $ 4 | $(600) | $4,121 | $(123) | $ (730) | $2,672 |
| Net income | — | — | — | — | — | 902 | 902 |
| Foreign currency translation gains, net of tax | — | — | — | — | 62 | — | 62 |
| Change in unrealized gains on available-for-sale securities, net of tax | — | — | — | — | 4 | — | 4 |
| Amortization of unrealized loss on terminated Euro Currency Swap, net of tax | — | — | — | — | 1 | — | 1 |
| Comprehensive income | | | | | | | 969 |
| Exercise of common stock options | 7 | — | — | 19 | — | — | 19 |
| Issuance of common stock for acquisition activity | 9 | 1 | — | 1,144 | — | — | 1,145 |
| Excess tax benefits from stock-based compensation | — | — | — | 103 | — | — | 103 |
| Stock-based compensation and issuance of employee benefit plan stock | — | — | — | 349 | — | — | 349 |
| Balance at December 31, 2009 | 444 | 5 | (600) | 5,736 | (56) | 172 | 5,257 |
| Net income | — | — | — | — | — | 1,152 | 1,152 |
| Foreign currency translation gains, net of tax | — | — | — | — | (137) | — | (137) |
| Change in unrealized gains on available-for-sale securities, net of tax | — | — | — | — | 3 | — | 3 |
| Comprehensive income | | | | | | | 1,018 |
| Exercise of common stock options | 7 | — | — | 16 | — | — | 16 |
| Excess tax benefits from stock-based compensation | — | — | — | 145 | — | — | 145 |
| Stock-based compensation and issuance of employee benefit plan stock | — | — | — | 428 | — | — | 428 |
| Balance at December 31, 2010 | 451 | 5 | (600) | 6,325 | (190) | 1,324 | 6,864 |
| Net income | — | — | — | — | — | 631 | 631 |
| Foreign currency translation gains, net of tax | — | — | — | — | (123) | — | (123) |
| Change in unrealized gains on available-for-sale securities, net of tax | — | — | — | — | (3) | — | (3) |
| Comprehensive income | | | | | | | 505 |
| Exercise of common stock options | 5 | — | — | 7 | — | — | 7 |
| Repurchase of common stock | (1) | — | (277) | — | — | — | (277) |
| Excess tax benefits from stock-based compensation | — | — | — | 62 | — | — | 62 |
| Stock-based compensation and issuance of employee benefit plan stock | — | — | — | 569 | — | — | 569 |
| Issuance of common stock for acquisition activity | — | — | — | 27 | — | — | 27 |
| Balance at December 31, 2011 | 455 | $ 5 | $(877) | $6,990 | $(316) | $1,955 | $7,757 |

See accompanying notes to consolidated financial statements.

# Specimen Financial Statements: Wal-Mart Stores, Inc.

In 2012, Wal-Mart Stores, Inc. celebrated "50 years of helping customers save money and live better." The following are Wal-Mart's financial statements as presented in the company's 2012 annual report. To access Wal-Mart's complete annual report, including notes to the financial statements, follow these steps:

1. Go to **http://corporate.walmart.com**.
2. Select Annual Reports under the Investors tab.
3. Select the 2012 Annual Report (Wal-Mart's fiscal year ends January 31).
4. The Notes to Consolidated Financial Statements begin on page 38.

## Consolidated Statements of Income

| | Fiscal Years Ended January 31, | | |
|---|---|---|---|
| (Amounts in millions except per share data) | 2012 | 2011 | 2010 |
| **Revenues:** | | | |
| Net sales | $443,854 | $418,952 | $405,132 |
| Membership and other income | 3,096 | 2,897 | 2,953 |
| | 446,950 | 421,849 | 408,085 |
| **Costs and expenses:** | | | |
| Cost of sales | 335,127 | 314,946 | 304,106 |
| Operating, selling, general and administrative expenses | 85,265 | 81,361 | 79,977 |
| Operating income | 26,558 | 25,542 | 24,002 |
| **Interest:** | | | |
| Debt | 2,034 | 1,928 | 1,787 |
| Capital leases | 288 | 277 | 278 |
| Interest income | (162) | (201) | (181) |
| Interest, net | 2,160 | 2,004 | 1,884 |
| Income from continuing operations before income taxes | 24,398 | 23,538 | 22,118 |
| **Provision for income taxes:** | | | |
| Current | 6,742 | 6,703 | 7,643 |
| Deferred | 1,202 | 876 | (487) |
| | 7,944 | 7,579 | 7,156 |
| Income from continuing operations | 16,454 | 15,959 | 14,962 |
| Income (loss) from discontinued operations, net of tax | (67) | 1,034 | (79) |
| Consolidated net income | 16,387 | 16,993 | 14,883 |
| Less consolidated net income attributable to noncontrolling interest | (688) | (604) | (513) |
| Consolidated net income attributable to Walmart | $ 15,699 | $ 16,389 | $ 14,370 |
| **Basic net income per common share:** | | | |
| Basic income per common share from continuing operations attributable to Walmart | $ 4.56 | $ 4.20 | $ 3.74 |
| Basic income (loss) per common share from discontinued operations attributable to Walmart | (0.02) | 0.28 | (0.02) |
| Basic net income per common share attributable to Walmart | $ 4.54 | $ 4.48 | $ 3.72 |
| **Diluted net income per common share:** | | | |
| Diluted income per common share from continuing operations attributable to Walmart | $ 4.54 | $ 4.18 | $ 3.73 |
| Diluted income (loss) per common share from discontinued operations attributable to Walmart | (0.02) | 0.29 | (0.02) |
| Diluted net income per common share attributable to Walmart | $ 4.52 | $ 4.47 | $ 3.71 |
| **Weighted-average common shares outstanding:** | | | |
| Basic | 3,460 | 3,656 | 3,866 |
| Diluted | 3,474 | 3,670 | 3,877 |
| Dividends declared per common share | $ 1.46 | $ 1.21 | $ 1.09 |

See accompanying notes.

# Consolidated Balance Sheets

| | As of January 31, | |
|---|---:|---:|
| *(Amounts in millions except per share data)* | 2012 | 2011 |
| **ASSETS** | | |
| *Current assets:* | | |
| Cash and cash equivalents | $ 6,550 | $ 7,395 |
| Receivables, net | 5,937 | 5,089 |
| Inventories | 40,714 | 36,437 |
| Prepaid expenses and other | 1,685 | 2,960 |
| Current assets of discontinued operations | 89 | 131 |
| Total current assets | 54,975 | 52,012 |
| *Property and equipment:* | | |
| Property and equipment | 155,002 | 148,584 |
| Less accumulated depreciation | (45,399) | (43,486) |
| Property and equipment, net | 109,603 | 105,098 |
| *Property under capital lease:* | | |
| Property under capital lease | 5,936 | 5,905 |
| Less accumulated amortization | (3,215) | (3,125) |
| Property under capital lease, net | 2,721 | 2,780 |
| Goodwill | 20,651 | 16,763 |
| Other assets and deferred charges | 5,456 | 4,129 |
| **Total assets** | **$193,406** | **$180,782** |
| **LIABILITIES AND EQUITY** | | |
| *Current liabilities:* | | |
| Short-term borrowings | $ 4,047 | $ 1,031 |
| Accounts payable | 36,608 | 33,676 |
| Accrued liabilities | 18,154 | 18,701 |
| Accrued income taxes | 1,164 | 157 |
| Long-term debt due within one year | 1,975 | 4,655 |
| Obligations under capital leases due within one year | 326 | 336 |
| Current liabilities of discontinued operations | 26 | 47 |
| Total current liabilities | 62,300 | 58,603 |
| Long-term debt | 44,070 | 40,692 |
| Long-term obligations under capital leases | 3,009 | 3,150 |
| Deferred income taxes and other | 7,862 | 6,682 |
| Redeemable noncontrolling interest | 404 | 408 |
| Commitments and contingencies | | |
| *Equity:* | | |
| Preferred stock ($0.10 par value; 100 shares authorized, none issued) | — | — |
| Common stock ($0.10 par value; 11,000 shares authorized, 3,418 and 3,516 issued and outstanding at January 31, 2012 and 2011, respectively) | 342 | 352 |
| Capital in excess of par value | 3,692 | 3,577 |
| Retained earnings | 68,691 | 63,967 |
| Accumulated other comprehensive income (loss) | (1,410) | 646 |
| Total Walmart shareholders' equity | 71,315 | 68,542 |
| Noncontrolling interest | 4,446 | 2,705 |
| Total equity | 75,761 | 71,247 |
| **Total liabilities and equity** | **$193,406** | **$180,782** |

*See accompanying notes.*

# Consolidated Statements of Shareholders' Equity

| (Amounts in millions, except per share data) | Common Stock Shares | Common Stock Amount | Capital in Excess of Par Value | Retained Earnings | Accumulated Other Comprehensive Income (Loss) | Total Walmart Shareholders' Equity | Noncontrolling Interest | Total Equity |
|---|---|---|---|---|---|---|---|---|
| **Balances — February 1, 2009** | 3,925 | $ 393 | $3,920 | $ 63,344 | $(2,688) | $ 64,969 | $1,794 | $ 66,763 |
| Consolidated net income (excludes redeemable noncontrolling interest) | — | — | — | 14,370 | — | 14,370 | 499 | 14,869 |
| Other comprehensive income | — | — | — | — | 2,618 | 2,618 | 64 | 2,682 |
| Cash dividends ($1.09 per share) | — | — | — | (4,217) | — | (4,217) | — | (4,217) |
| Purchase of Company stock | (145) | (15) | (246) | (7,136) | — | (7,397) | — | (7,397) |
| Purchase of redeemable noncontrolling interest | — | — | (288) | — | — | (288) | — | (288) |
| Other | 6 | — | 417 | (4) | — | 413 | (177) | 236 |
| **Balances — January 31, 2010** | 3,786 | 378 | 3,803 | 66,357 | (70) | 70,468 | 2,180 | 72,648 |
| Consolidated net income (excludes redeemable noncontrolling interest) | — | — | — | 16,389 | — | 16,389 | 584 | 16,973 |
| Other comprehensive income | — | — | — | — | 716 | 716 | 162 | 878 |
| Cash dividends ($1.21 per share) | — | — | — | (4,437) | — | (4,437) | — | (4,437) |
| Purchase of Company stock | (280) | (28) | (487) | (14,319) | — | (14,834) | — | (14,834) |
| Other | 10 | 2 | 261 | (23) | — | 240 | (221) | 19 |
| **Balances — January 31, 2011** | 3,516 | 352 | 3,577 | 63,967 | 646 | 68,542 | 2,705 | 71,247 |
| **Consolidated net income (excludes redeemable noncontrolling interest)** | — | — | — | 15,699 | — | 15,699 | 627 | 16,326 |
| Other comprehensive loss | — | — | — | — | (2,056) | (2,056) | (660) | (2,716) |
| **Cash dividends ($1.46 per share)** | — | — | — | (5,048) | — | (5,048) | — | (5,048) |
| **Purchase of Company stock** | (113) | (11) | (229) | (5,930) | — | (6,170) | — | (6,170) |
| **Noncontrolling interest of acquired entity** | — | — | — | — | — | — | 1,988 | 1,988 |
| Other | 15 | 1 | 344 | 3 | — | 348 | (214) | 134 |
| **Balances — January 31, 2012** | 3,418 | $ 342 | $3,692 | $ 68,691 | $(1,410) | $ 71,315 | $4,446 | $ 75,761 |

See accompanying notes.

# Consolidated Statements of Comprehensive Income

| | Fiscal Years Ended January 31, | | |
|---|---|---|---|
| (Amounts in millions) | 2012 | 2011 | 2010 |
| **Consolidated net income:** | | | |
| Consolidated net income [1] | $16,387 | $16,993 | $14,883 |
| **Other comprehensive income:** | | | |
| Currency translation [2] | (2,758) | 1,137 | 2,854 |
| Net change in fair values of derivatives | (67) | (17) | 94 |
| Change in minimum pension liability | 43 | (145) | (220) |
| **Total comprehensive income** | 13,605 | 17,968 | 17,611 |
| Less amounts attributable to the noncontrolling interest: | | | |
| Consolidated net income [1] | (688) | (604) | (513) |
| Currency translation [2] | 726 | (259) | (110) |
| Amounts attributable to the noncontrolling interest | 38 | (863) | (623) |
| **Comprehensive income attributable to Walmart** | **$13,643** | $17,105 | $16,988 |

(1) Includes $61 million, $20 million and $14 million in fiscal 2012, 2011 and 2010, respectively, related to the redeemable noncontrolling interest.

(2) Includes $(66) million, $97 million and $46 million in fiscal 2012, 2011 and 2010, respectively, related to the redeemable noncontrolling interest.

See accompanying notes.

# Consolidated Statements of Cash Flows

| (Amounts in millions) | Fiscal Years Ended January 31, | | |
|---|---|---|---|
| | 2012 | 2011 | 2010 |
| **Cash flows from operating activities:** | | | |
| Consolidated net income | $ 16,387 | $ 16,993 | $ 14,883 |
| Loss (income) from discontinued operations, net of tax | 67 | (1,034) | 79 |
| Income from continuing operations | 16,454 | 15,959 | 14,962 |
| Adjustments to reconcile income from continuing operations to net cash provided by operating activities: | | | |
| Depreciation and amortization | 8,130 | 7,641 | 7,157 |
| Deferred income taxes | 1,050 | 651 | (504) |
| Other operating activities | 398 | 1,087 | 318 |
| Changes in certain assets and liabilities, net of effects of acquisitions: | | | |
| Accounts receivable | (796) | (733) | (297) |
| Inventories | (3,727) | (3,205) | 2,213 |
| Accounts payable | 2,687 | 2,676 | 1,052 |
| Accrued liabilities | 59 | (433) | 1,348 |
| Net cash provided by operating activities | 24,255 | 23,643 | 26,249 |
| **Cash flows from investing activities:** | | | |
| Payments for property and equipment | (13,510) | (12,699) | (12,184) |
| Proceeds from disposal of property and equipment | 580 | 489 | 1,002 |
| Investments and business acquisitions, net of cash acquired | (3,548) | (202) | — |
| Other investing activities | (131) | 219 | (438) |
| Net cash used in investing activities | (16,609) | (12,193) | (11,620) |
| **Cash flows from financing activities:** | | | |
| Net change in short-term borrowings | 3,019 | 503 | (1,033) |
| Proceeds from issuance of long-term debt | 5,050 | 11,396 | 5,546 |
| Payments of long-term debt | (4,584) | (4,080) | (6,033) |
| Dividends paid | (5,048) | (4,437) | (4,217) |
| Purchase of Company stock | (6,298) | (14,776) | (7,276) |
| Purchase of redeemable noncontrolling interest | — | — | (436) |
| Payment of capital lease obligations | (355) | (363) | (346) |
| Other financing activities | (242) | (271) | (396) |
| Net cash used in financing activities | (8,458) | (12,028) | (14,191) |
| Effect of exchange rates on cash and cash equivalents | (33) | 66 | 194 |
| Net increase (decrease) in cash and cash equivalents | (845) | (512) | 632 |
| Cash and cash equivalents at beginning of year | 7,395 | 7,907 | 7,275 |
| Cash and cash equivalents at end of year | $ 6,550 | $ 7,395 | $ 7,907 |
| **Supplemental disclosure of cash flow information:** | | | |
| Income tax paid | $ 5,899 | $ 6,984 | $ 7,389 |
| Interest paid | 2,346 | 2,163 | 2,141 |

See accompanying notes.

# Specimen Financial Statements: Zetar plc

Zetar plc is a leading U.K. manufacturer of confectionery and natural snacks with a reputation for quality and product innovation. Note that its financial statements are IFRS-based and are presented in British pounds (£). To access the company's complete 2011 annual report, including notes to the financial statements, follow these steps:

1. Go to **www.zetarplc.com**.
2. Select Reports & Presentations under the Investors tab.
3. Select Report & Accounts for the year ended 30th April 2011.
4. Use the Bookmarks sections on the left to navigate through the annual report. The Notes to the consolidated financial statements, for example, begin on page 28.

## Consolidated income statement

FOR THE YEAR ENDED 30 APRIL 2011

| | Note | 2011 Adjusted¹ results £'000 | 2011 Adjusting items £'000 | 2011 Total £'000 | 2010 Adjusted¹ results £'000 | 2010 Adjusting items £'000 | 2010 Total £'000 |
|---|---|---|---|---|---|---|---|
| Revenue | 5 | 134,998 | – | 134,998 | 131,922 | – | 131,922 |
| Cost of sales | | (107,677) | – | (107,677) | (105,112) | – | (105,112) |
| Gross profit | | 27,321 | – | 27,321 | 26,810 | – | 26,810 |
| Distribution costs | | (5,550) | – | (5,550) | (5,495) | – | (5,495) |
| Administrative expenses: | | | | | | | |
| – other administrative expenses | | (14,271) | (267) | (14,538) | (14,003) | – | (14,003) |
| – amortisation of intangible assets | 15 | – | (170) | (170) | – | (299) | (299) |
| – share-based payments | 10 | – | (330) | (330) | – | (287) | (287) |
| Operating profit | | 7,500 | (767) | 6,733 | 7,312 | (586) | 6,726 |
| Finance income | 9 | 3 | – | 3 | 11 | – | 11 |
| Finance costs | 9 | (793) | (308) | (1,101) | (968) | 201 | (767) |
| Profit from continuing operations before taxation | | 6,710 | (1,075) | 5,635 | 6,355 | (385) | 5,970 |
| Tax on profit from continuing activities | 11 | (1,764) | 108 | (1,656) | (1,722) | 20 | (1,702) |
| Net result from continuing operations | | 4,946 | (967) | 3,979 | 4,633 | (365) | 4,268 |
| Net result from discontinued operations | 34 | – | 503 | 503 | – | – | – |
| Profit for the year | | 4,946 | (464) | 4,482 | 4,633 | (365) | 4,268 |
| Basic earnings per share (p) | 13 | | | 35.1 | | | 32.6 |
| Diluted earnings/per share (p) | 13 | | | 34.9 | | | 32.6 |
| Adjusted basic earnings per share (p)¹ | 13 | 38.7 | | | 35.4 | | |
| Adjusted diluted earnings per share (p)¹ | 13 | 38.5 | | | 35.4 | | |

¹ Adjusted operating profit and adjusted earnings per share are stated before one-off items, amortisation of intangible assets, share-based payments and the fair value movement on financial instruments.

## Consolidated statement of comprehensive income

FOR THE YEAR ENDED 30 APRIL 2011

| | 2011 Total £'000 | 2010 Total £'000 |
|---|---|---|
| Profit for the year | 4,482 | 4,268 |
| Other comprehensive income: | | |
| – currency translation differences | 245 | (917) |
| Other comprehensive income | 245 | (917) |
| Total comprehensive income for the year | 4,727 | 3,351 |
| Attributable to: | | |
| – owners of the parent | 4,727 | 3,351 |

# Consolidated balance sheet

**AT 30 APRIL 2011**

| | Note | 2011 £'000 | 2010 £'000 |
|---|---|---|---|
| **Non-current assets** | | | |
| Goodwill | 14 | **30,520** | 30,342 |
| Other intangible assets | 15 | **140** | 309 |
| Property, plant and equipment | 16 | **16,583** | 14,886 |
| Deferred tax asset | 22 | **149** | 213 |
| | | **47,392** | 45,750 |
| **Current assets** | | | |
| Inventories | 17 | **16,453** | 16,039 |
| Trade and other receivables | 18 | **24,935** | 19,062 |
| Cash at bank | 27 | **4,282** | 4,257 |
| | | **45,670** | 39,358 |
| **Total assets** | | **93,062** | 85,108 |
| **Current liabilities** | | | |
| Trade and other payables | 19 | **(25,075)** | (25,176) |
| Deferred consideration | 12 | **(38)** | – |
| Current tax liabilities | | **(620)** | (524) |
| Obligations under finance leases | 20 | **(75)** | (90) |
| Derivative financial instruments | 30 | **(157)** | (406) |
| Borrowings and overdrafts | 21 | **(14,509)** | (12,885) |
| | | **(40,474)** | (39,081) |
| **Net current assets** | | **5,196** | 277 |
| **Non-current liabilities** | | | |
| Deferred consideration | | **–** | (300) |
| Deferred tax liabilities | 22 | **(1,750)** | (1,605) |
| Obligations under finance leases | 20 | **(15)** | (77) |
| Borrowings and overdrafts | 21 | **(4,536)** | (2,290) |
| | | **(6,301)** | (4,272) |
| **Total liabilities** | | **(46,775)** | (43,353) |
| **Net assets** | | **46,287** | 41,755 |
| **Equity** | | | |
| Share capital | 23 | **1,324** | 1,324 |
| Share premium account | 24 | **28,266** | 28,266 |
| Merger reserve | | **3,411** | 3,411 |
| Equity reserve | 25 | **2,664** | 2,089 |
| Retained earnings | 25 | **10,622** | 6,665 |
| **Total equity attributable to equity holders of the parent** | | **46,287** | 41,755 |

The financial statements were approved by the Board for issue on 20 July 2011.

# Consolidated cash flow statement
**FOR THE YEAR ENDED 30 APRIL 2011**

| | Note | 2011 £'000 | 2010 £'000 |
|---|---|---|---|
| **Cash flow from operating activities** | | | |
| Profit from continuing operations before taxation | | 5,635 | 5,970 |
| Finance costs | | 1,101 | 767 |
| Interest income | | (3) | (11) |
| Share-based payments | | 330 | 287 |
| Depreciation | 6 | 2,267 | 2,337 |
| Loss/(profit) on sale of plant and equipment | 6 | 9 | (113) |
| Amortisation of intangible assets | 6 | 170 | 299 |
| Net movement in working capital | | (6,040) | (179) |
| Decrease/(increase) in inventories | | 72 | (1,720) |
| (Increase)/decrease in receivables | | (5,295) | 128 |
| (Decrease)/increase in payables | | (817) | 1,413 |
| **Total cash flow from operations** | | 3,469 | 9,357 |
| Net interest paid | 9 | (1,347) | (957) |
| Tax paid | | (1,369) | (1,415) |
| **Total cash flow from operating activities** | | 753 | 6,985 |
| **Cash flow from investing activities** | | | |
| Purchase of property, plant and equipment | | (3,789) | (2,098) |
| Proceeds from sale of plant and equipment | | 45 | 259 |
| Disposal of subsidiary | | 500 | – |
| Total cash impact of acquisitions | | (848) | (220) |
| Acquisition of business | | (483) | (220) |
| Net borrowings assumed on acquisition | | (365) | – |
| **Net cash flow from investing activities** | | (4,092) | (2,059) |
| **Cash flow from financing activities** | | | |
| Net proceeds from issue of ordinary share capital | | – | 14 |
| Purchase of own shares | | (525) | (250) |
| Proceeds from new borrowings | | 7,000 | – |
| Repayment of borrowings | | (5,174) | (2,545) |
| Finance lease repayments | | (91) | (214) |
| **Net cash flow from financing activities** | | 1,210 | (2,995) |
| **Net (decrease)/increase in cash and cash equivalents** | | (2,129) | 1,931 |
| Cash and cash equivalents at beginning of the year | | (6,608) | (8,127) |
| Effect of foreign exchange rate movements | | 96 | (412) |
| **Cash and cash equivalents at the end of the year** | | (8,641) | (6,608) |
| **Cash and cash equivalents comprise:** | | | |
| – cash at bank | 27 | 4,282 | 4,257 |
| – bank overdraft | 27 | (12,923) | (10,865) |
| | | (8,641) | (6,608) |

# Consolidated statement of changes in equity

**FOR THE YEAR ENDED 30 APRIL 2011**

| | Attributable to equity holders of the parent | | | | | |
|---|---|---|---|---|---|---|
| | Share capital £'000 | Share premium account £'000 | Merger reserve £'000 | Equity reserve £'000 | Retained earnings £'000 | Total £'000 |
| Balance at 1 May 2009 | 1,324 | 28,252 | 3,411 | 2,719 | 2,647 | 38,353 |
| Comprehensive income | | | | | | |
| Profit for the year | – | – | – | – | 4,268 | 4,268 |
| Other comprehensive income | | | | | | |
| Exchange (loss) on translation of foreign operations | – | – | – | (917) | – | (917) |
| Total other comprehensive income | – | – | – | (917) | – | (917) |
| Total comprehensive income | – | – | – | (917) | 4,268 | 3,351 |
| Transactions with owners: | | | | | | |
| – issue of new ordinary shares | – | 14 | – | – | – | 14 |
| – purchase of own shares | – | – | – | – | (250) | (250) |
| – share-based payment charge | – | – | – | 287 | – | 287 |
| Total transactions with owners | – | 14 | – | 287 | (250) | 51 |
| Balance at 30 April 2010 | 1,324 | 28,266 | 3,411 | 2,089 | 6,665 | 41,755 |
| Comprehensive income | | | | | | |
| Profit for the year | – | – | – | – | 4,482 | 4,482 |
| Other comprehensive income | | | | | | |
| Exchange gain on translation of foreign operations | – | – | – | 245 | – | 245 |
| Total other comprehensive income | – | – | – | 245 | – | 245 |
| Total comprehensive income | – | – | – | 245 | 4,482 | 4,727 |
| Transactions with owners: | | | | | | |
| – purchase of own shares | – | – | – | – | (525) | (525) |
| – share-based payment charge | – | – | – | 330 | – | 330 |
| Total transactions with owners | – | – | – | 330 | (525) | (195) |
| Balance at 30 April 2011 | 1,324 | 28,266 | 3,411 | 2,664 | 10,622 | 46,287 |

## Learning Objectives

*After studying this appendix, you should be able to:*

[1] Distinguish between simple and compound interest.

[2] Identify the variables fundamental to solving present value problems.

[3] Solve for present value of a single amount.

[4] Solve for present value of an annuity.

[5] Compute the present value of notes and bonds.

## Nature of Interest

Would you rather receive $1,000 today or a year from now? You should prefer to receive the $1,000 today because you can invest the $1,000 and earn interest on it. As a result, you will have more than $1,000 a year from now. What this example illustrates is the concept of the **time value of money**. Everyone prefers to receive money today rather than in the future because of the interest factor.

**LEARNING OBJECTIVE** 1

**Distinguish between simple and compound interest.**

**Interest** is payment for the use of another person's money. It is the difference between the amount borrowed or invested (called the **principal**) and the amount repaid or collected. The amount of interest to be paid or collected is usually stated as a rate over a specific period of time. The rate of interest is generally stated as an **annual rate**.

The amount of interest involved in any financing transaction is based on three elements:

1. **Principal (p):** The original amount borrowed or invested.
2. **Interest Rate (i):** An annual percentage of the principal.
3. **Time (n):** The number of years that the principal is borrowed or invested.

### Simple Interest

**Simple interest** is computed on the principal amount only. It is the return on the principal for one period. Simple interest is usually expressed as shown in Illustration G-1.

| Interest | = | Principal | × | Rate | × | Time |
|---|---|---|---|---|---|---|
| | | $p$ | | $i$ | | $n$ |

**Illustration G-1**
Interest computation

For example, if you borrowed $5,000 for 2 years at a simple interest rate of 6% annually, you would pay $600 in total interest computed as follows.

$$\text{Interest} = p \times i \times n$$
$$= \$5{,}000 \times .06 \times 2$$
$$= \$600$$

## Compound Interest

**Compound interest** is computed on principal **and** on any interest earned that has not been paid or withdrawn. It is the return on the principal for two or more time periods. Compounding computes interest not only on the principal but also on the interest earned to date on that principal, assuming the interest is left on deposit.

To illustrate the difference between simple and compound interest, assume that you deposit $1,000 in Bank Two, where it will earn **simple interest** of 9% per year, and you deposit another $1,000 in Citizens Bank, where it will earn compound interest of 9% per year **compounded annually**. Also assume that in both cases you will not withdraw any interest until three years from the date of deposit. Illustration G-2 shows the computation of interest you will receive and the accumulated year-end balances.

**Illustration G-2**
Simple versus compound interest

| Bank Two | | | | Citizens Bank | | |
|---|---|---|---|---|---|---|
| Simple Interest Calculation | Simple Interest | Accumulated Year-End Balance | | Compound Interest Calculation | Compound Interest | Accumulated Year-End Balance |
| Year 1 $1,000.00 × 9% | $ 90.00 | $1,090.00 | | Year 1 $1,000.00 × 9% | $ 90.00 | $1,090.00 |
| Year 2 $1,000.00 × 9% | 90.00 | $1,180.00 | | Year 2 $1,090.00 × 9% | 98.10 | $1,188.10 |
| Year 3 $1,000.00 × 9% | 90.00 | $1,270.00 | | Year 3 $1,188.10 × 9% | 106.93 | $1,295.03 |
| | $ 270.00 | | | | $ 295.03 | |

$25.03 Difference

Note in Illustration G-2 that simple interest uses the initial principal of $1,000 to compute the interest in all three years. Compound interest uses the accumulated balance (principal plus interest to date) at each year-end to compute interest in the succeeding year—which explains why your compound interest account is larger.

Obviously, if you had a choice between investing your money at simple interest or at compound interest, you would choose compound interest, all other things—especially risk—being equal. In the example, compounding provides $25.03 of additional interest income. For practical purposes, compounding assumes that unpaid interest earned becomes a part of the principal. The accumulated balance at the end of each year becomes the new principal on which interest is earned during the next year.

Illustration G-2 indicates that you should invest your money at the bank that compounds interest annually. Most business situations use compound interest. Simple interest is generally applicable only to short-term situations of one year or less.

## Present Value Concepts

The **present value** is the value now of a given amount to be paid or received in the future, assuming compound interest. The present value is based on three variables: (1) the dollar amount to be received (future amount), (2) the length of time until the amount is received (number of periods), and (3) the interest rate (the discount rate). The process of determining the present value is referred to as **discounting the future amount**.

In this textbook, we use present value computations in measuring several items. For example, Chapter 15 computed the present value of the principal and interest payments to determine the market price of a bond. In addition, determining the amount to be reported for notes payable and lease liabilities involves present value computations.

## Present Value of a Single Amount

To illustrate present value, assume that you want to invest a sum of money that will yield $1,000 at the end of one year. What amount would you need to invest today to have $1,000 one year from now? Illustration G-3 shows the formula for calculating present value.

> **Present Value = Future Value ÷ (1 + *i*)ⁿ**

**Illustration G-3**
Formula for present value

Thus, if you want a 10% rate of return, you would compute the present value of $1,000 for one year as follows.

$$PV = FV \div (1 + i)^n$$
$$= \$1,000 \div (1 + .10)^1$$
$$= \$1,000 \div 1.10$$
$$= \$909.09$$

We know the future amount ($1,000), the discount rate (10%), and the number of periods (1). These variables are depicted in the time diagram in Illustration G-4.

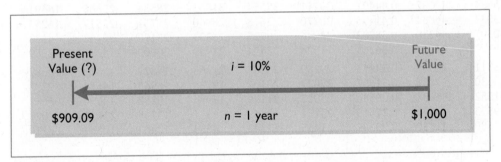

**Illustration G-4**
Finding present value if discounted for one period

If you receive the single amount of $1,000 **in two years**, discounted at 10% $[PV = \$1,000 \div (1 + .10)^2]$, the present value of your $1,000 is $826.45 ($1,000 ÷ 1.21), as shown in Illustration G-5.

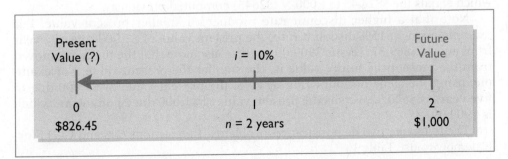

**Illustration G-5**
Finding present value if discounted for two periods

You also could find the present value of your amount through tables that show the present value of 1 for $n$ periods. In Table 1 below, $n$ (represented in the table's rows) is the number of discounting periods involved. The percentages (represented in the table's columns) are the periodic interest rates or discount rates. The 5-digit decimal numbers in the intersections of the rows and columns are called the **present value of 1 factors**.

When using Table 1 to determine present value, you multiply the future value by the present value factor specified at the intersection of the number of periods and the discount rate.

### TABLE 1
#### Present Value of 1

| (n) Periods | 4% | 5% | 6% | 7% | 8% | 9% | 10% | 11% | 12% | 15% |
|---|---|---|---|---|---|---|---|---|---|---|
| 1 | .96154 | .95238 | .94340 | 0.93458 | .92593 | .91743 | .90909 | .90090 | .89286 | .86957 |
| 2 | .92456 | .90703 | .89000 | 0.87344 | .85734 | .84168 | .82645 | .81162 | .79719 | .75614 |
| 3 | .88900 | .86384 | .83962 | 0.81630 | .79383 | .77218 | .75132 | .73119 | .71178 | .65752 |
| 4 | .85480 | .82270 | .79209 | 0.76290 | .73503 | .70843 | .68301 | .65873 | .63552 | .57175 |
| 5 | .82193 | .78353 | .74726 | 0.71299 | .68058 | .64993 | .62092 | .59345 | .56743 | .49718 |
| 6 | .79031 | .74622 | .70496 | 0.66634 | .63017 | .59627 | .56447 | .53464 | .50663 | .43233 |
| 7 | .75992 | .71068 | .66506 | 0.62275 | .58349 | .54703 | .51316 | .48166 | .45235 | .37594 |
| 8 | .73069 | .67684 | .62741 | 0.58201 | .54027 | .50187 | .46651 | .43393 | .40388 | .32690 |
| 9 | .70259 | .64461 | .59190 | 0.54393 | .50025 | .46043 | .42410 | .39092 | .36061 | .28426 |
| 10 | .67556 | .61391 | .55839 | 0.50835 | .46319 | .42241 | .38554 | .35218 | .32197 | .24719 |
| 11 | .64958 | .58468 | .52679 | 0.47509 | .42888 | .38753 | .35049 | .31728 | .28748 | .21494 |
| 12 | .62460 | .55684 | .49697 | 0.44401 | .39711 | .35554 | .31863 | .28584 | .25668 | .18691 |
| 13 | .60057 | .53032 | .46884 | 0.41496 | .36770 | .32618 | .28966 | .25751 | .22917 | .16253 |
| 14 | .57748 | .50507 | .44230 | 0.38782 | .34046 | .29925 | .26333 | .23199 | .20462 | .14133 |
| 15 | .55526 | .48102 | .41727 | 0.36245 | .31524 | .27454 | .23939 | .20900 | .18270 | .12289 |
| 16 | .53391 | .45811 | .39365 | 0.33873 | .29189 | .25187 | .21763 | .18829 | .16312 | .10687 |
| 17 | .51337 | .43630 | .37136 | 0.31657 | .27027 | .23107 | .19785 | .16963 | .14564 | .09293 |
| 18 | .49363 | .41552 | .35034 | 0.29586 | .25025 | .21199 | .17986 | .15282 | .13004 | .08081 |
| 19 | .47464 | .39573 | .33051 | 0.27615 | .23171 | .19449 | .16351 | .13768 | .11611 | .07027 |
| 20 | .45639 | .37689 | .31180 | 0.25842 | .21455 | .17843 | .14864 | .12403 | .10367 | .06110 |

For example, the present value factor for one period at a discount rate of 10% is .90909, which equals the $909.09 ($1,000 × .90909) computed in Illustration G-4. For two periods at a discount rate of 10%, the present value factor is .82645, which equals the $826.45 ($1,000 × .82645) computed previously.

Note that a higher discount rate produces a smaller present value. For example, using a 15% discount rate, the present value of $1,000 due one year from now is $869.57, versus $909.09 at 10%. Also note that the further removed from the present the future value is, the smaller the present value. For example, using the same discount rate of 10%, the present value of $1,000 due in **five years** is $620.92, versus the present value of $1,000 due in **one year**, which is $909.09.

The following two demonstration problems (Illustrations G-6 and G-7) illustrate how to use Table 1.

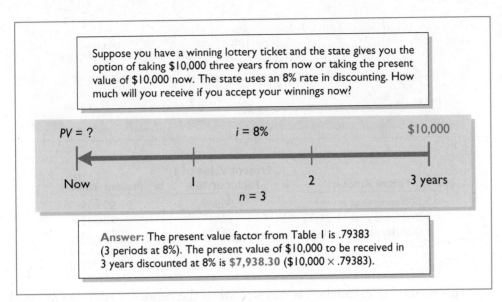

Suppose you have a winning lottery ticket and the state gives you the option of taking $10,000 three years from now or taking the present value of $10,000 now. The state uses an 8% rate in discounting. How much will you receive if you accept your winnings now?

PV = ?          i = 8%          $10,000

Now          1          2          3 years
             n = 3

**Answer:** The present value factor from Table 1 is .79383 (3 periods at 8%). The present value of $10,000 to be received in 3 years discounted at 8% is **$7,938.30** ($10,000 × .79383).

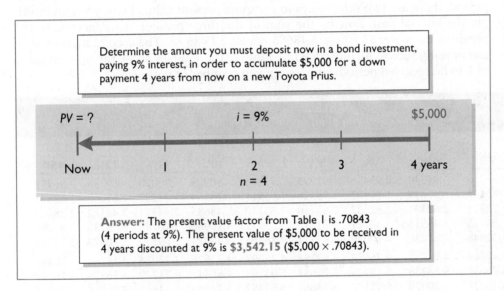

Determine the amount you must deposit now in a bond investment, paying 9% interest, in order to accumulate $5,000 for a down payment 4 years from now on a new Toyota Prius.

PV = ?          i = 9%          $5,000

Now          1          2          3          4 years
                        n = 4

**Answer:** The present value factor from Table 1 is .70843 (4 periods at 9%). The present value of $5,000 to be received in 4 years discounted at 9% is **$3,542.15** ($5,000 × .70843).

## Present Value of an Annuity

The preceding discussion involved the discounting of only a single future amount. Businesses and individuals frequently engage in transactions in which a **series** of equal dollar amounts are to be received or paid at evenly spaced time intervals (periodically). Examples of a series of periodic receipts or payments are loan agreements, installment sales, mortgage notes, lease (rental) contracts, and pension obligations. As discussed in Chapter 15, these periodic receipts or payments are **annuities**.

The **present value of an annuity** is the value now of a series of future receipts or payments, discounted assuming compound interest. In computing the present value of an annuity, you need to know (1) the discount rate, (2) the number of discount periods, and (3) the amount of the periodic receipts or payments.

To illustrate how to compute the present value of an annuity, assume that you will receive $1,000 cash annually for three years at a time when the discount rate is 10%. Illustration G-8 (page G6) depicts this situation, and Illustration G-9 (page G6) shows the computation of its present value.

LEARNING OBJECTIVE    4

Solve for present value of an annuity.

**Illustration G-8**
Time diagram for a three-year annuity

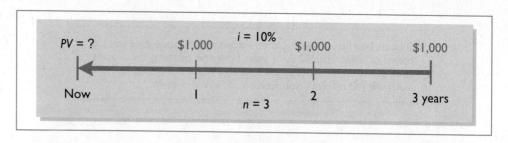

**Illustration G-9**
Present value of a series of future amounts computation

| Future Amount | × | Present Value of 1 Factor at 10% | = | Present Value |
|---|---|---|---|---|
| $1,000 (one year away) | | .90909 | | $ 909.09 |
| 1,000 (two years away) | | .82645 | | 826.45 |
| 1,000 (three years away) | | .75132 | | 751.32 |
| | | 2.48686 | | $2,486.86 |

This method of calculation is required when the periodic cash flows are not uniform in each period. However, when the future receipts are the same in each period, there are two other ways to compute present value. First, you can multiply the annual cash flow by the sum of the three present value factors. In the previous example, $1,000 × 2.48686 equals $2,486.86. The second method is to use annuity tables. As illustrated in Table 2, these tables show the present value of 1 to be received periodically for a given number of periods.

| | | | | | | | TABLE 2 | | | | | |
| | | | | | | | Present Value of an Annuity of 1 | | | | | |
|---|---|---|---|---|---|---|---|---|---|---|---|---|
| (n) Periods | 4% | 5% | 6% | 7% | 8% | 9% | 10% | 11% | 12% | 15% |
| 1 | .96154 | .95238 | .94340 | 0.93458 | .92593 | .91743 | .90909 | .90090 | .89286 | .86957 |
| 2 | 1.88609 | 1.85941 | 1.83339 | 1.80802 | 1.78326 | 1.75911 | 1.73554 | 1.71252 | 1.69005 | 1.62571 |
| 3 | 2.77509 | 2.72325 | 2.67301 | 2.62432 | 2.57710 | 2.53130 | 2.48685 | 2.44371 | 2.40183 | 2.28323 |
| 4 | 3.62990 | 3.54595 | 3.46511 | 3.38721 | 3.31213 | 3.23972 | 3.16986 | 3.10245 | 3.03735 | 2.85498 |
| 5 | 4.45182 | 4.32948 | 4.21236 | 4.10020 | 3.99271 | 3.88965 | 3.79079 | 3.69590 | 3.60478 | 3.35216 |
| 6 | 5.24214 | 5.07569 | 4.91732 | 4.76654 | 4.62288 | 4.48592 | 4.35526 | 4.23054 | 4.11141 | 3.78448 |
| 7 | 6.00205 | 5.78637 | 5.58238 | 5.38929 | 5.20637 | 5.03295 | 4.86842 | 4.71220 | 4.56376 | 4.16042 |
| 8 | 6.73274 | 6.46321 | 6.20979 | 5.97130 | 5.74664 | 5.53482 | 5.33493 | 5.14612 | 4.96764 | 4.48732 |
| 9 | 7.43533 | 7.10782 | 6.80169 | 6.51523 | 6.24689 | 5.99525 | 5.75902 | 5.53705 | 5.32825 | 4.77158 |
| 10 | 8.11090 | 7.72173 | 7.36009 | 7.02358 | 6.71008 | 6.41766 | 6.14457 | 5.88923 | 5.65022 | 5.01877 |
| 11 | 8.76048 | 8.30641 | 7.88687 | 7.49867 | 7.13896 | 6.80519 | 6.49506 | 6.20652 | 5.93770 | 5.23371 |
| 12 | 9.38507 | 8.86325 | 8.38384 | 7.94269 | 7.53608 | 7.16073 | 6.81369 | 6.49236 | 6.19437 | 5.42062 |
| 13 | 9.98565 | 9.39357 | 8.85268 | 8.35765 | 7.90378 | 7.48690 | 7.10336 | 6.74987 | 6.42355 | 5.58315 |
| 14 | 10.56312 | 9.89864 | 9.29498 | 8.74547 | 8.24424 | 7.78615 | 7.36669 | 6.98187 | 6.62817 | 5.72448 |
| 15 | 11.11839 | 10.37966 | 9.71225 | 9.10791 | 8.55948 | 8.06069 | 7.60608 | 7.19087 | 6.81086 | 5.84737 |
| 16 | 11.65230 | 10.83777 | 10.10590 | 9.44665 | 8.85137 | 8.31256 | 7.82371 | 7.37916 | 6.97399 | 5.95424 |
| 17 | 12.16567 | 11.27407 | 10.47726 | 9.76322 | 9.12164 | 8.54363 | 8.02155 | 7.54879 | 7.11963 | 6.04716 |
| 18 | 12.65930 | 11.68959 | 10.82760 | 10.05909 | 9.37189 | 8.75563 | 8.20141 | 7.70162 | 7.24967 | 6.12797 |
| 19 | 13.13394 | 12.08532 | 11.15812 | 10.33560 | 9.60360 | 8.95012 | 8.36492 | 7.83929 | 7.36578 | 6.19823 |
| 20 | 13.59033 | 12.46221 | 11.46992 | 10.59401 | 9.81815 | 9.12855 | 8.51356 | 7.96333 | 7.46944 | 6.25933 |

Table 2 shows that the present value of an annuity of 1 factor for three periods at 10% is 2.48685.[1] (This present value factor is the total of the three individual present value factors, as shown in Illustration G-9.) Applying this amount to the annual cash flow of $1,000 produces a present value of $2,486.85.

---

[1]The difference of .00001 between 2.48686 and 2.48685 is due to rounding.

The following demonstration problem (Illustration G-10) illustrates how to use Table 2.

**Illustration G-10**
Demonstration problem—Using Table 2 for *PV* of an annuity of 1

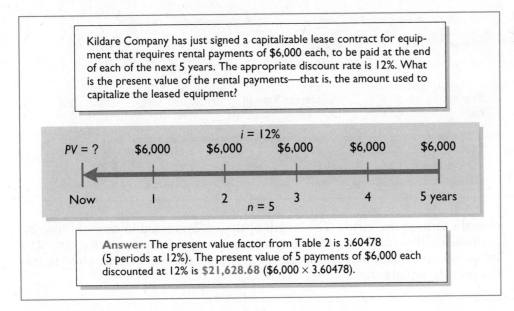

Kildare Company has just signed a capitalizable lease contract for equipment that requires rental payments of $6,000 each, to be paid at the end of each of the next 5 years. The appropriate discount rate is 12%. What is the present value of the rental payments—that is, the amount used to capitalize the leased equipment?

$i = 12\%$

PV = ?    $6,000    $6,000    $6,000    $6,000    $6,000

Now    1    2    3    4    5 years
$n = 5$

**Answer:** The present value factor from Table 2 is 3.60478 (5 periods at 12%). The present value of 5 payments of $6,000 each discounted at 12% is **$21,628.68** ($6,000 × 3.60478).

## Time Periods and Discounting

In the preceding calculations, the discounting was done on an **annual** basis using an **annual** interest rate. Discounting may also be done over shorter periods of time such as monthly, quarterly, or semiannually.

When the time frame is less than one year, you need to convert the annual interest rate to the applicable time frame. Assume, for example, that the investor in Illustration G-8 received $500 **semiannually** for three years instead of $1,000 annually. In this case, the number of periods becomes six (3 × 2), the discount rate is 5% (10% ÷ 2), the present value factor from Table 2 is 5.07569, and the present value of the future cash flows is $2,537.85 (5.07569 × $500). This amount is slightly higher than the $2,486.86 computed in Illustration G-9 because interest is paid twice during the same year. Therefore, interest is earned on the first half-year's interest.

## Computing the Present Value of a Long-Term Note or Bond

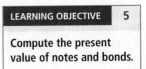

LEARNING OBJECTIVE    5

**Compute the present value of notes and bonds.**

The present value (or market price) of a long-term note or bond is a function of three variables: (1) the payment amounts, (2) the length of time until the amounts are paid, and (3) the discount rate. Our illustration uses a five-year bond issue.

The first variable—dollars to be paid—is made up of two elements: (1) a series of interest payments (an annuity), and (2) the principal amount (a single sum). To compute the present value of the bond, we must discount both the interest payments and the principal amount—two different computations. The time diagrams for a bond due in five years are shown in Illustration G-11 (page G8).

When the investor's market interest rate is equal to the bond's contractual interest rate, the present value of the bonds will equal the face value of the bonds. To illustrate, assume a bond issue of 10%, five-year bonds with a face value of $100,000 with interest payable **semiannually** on January 1 and July 1. If the discount rate is the same as the contractual rate, the bonds will sell at face value. In this case, the investor will receive the following: (1) $100,000 at maturity, and (2) a series of ten $5,000 interest payments [($100,000 × 10%) ÷ 2]

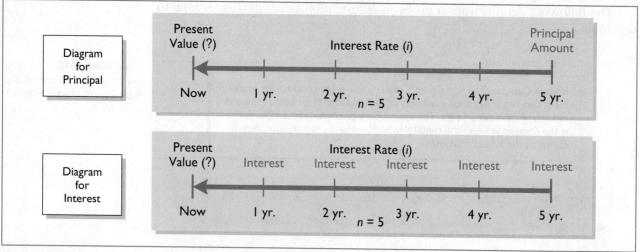

**Illustration G-11**
Present value of a bond time diagram

over the term of the bonds. The length of time is expressed in terms of interest periods—in this case—10, and the discount rate per interest period, 5%. The following time diagram (Illustration G-12) depicts the variables involved in this discounting situation.

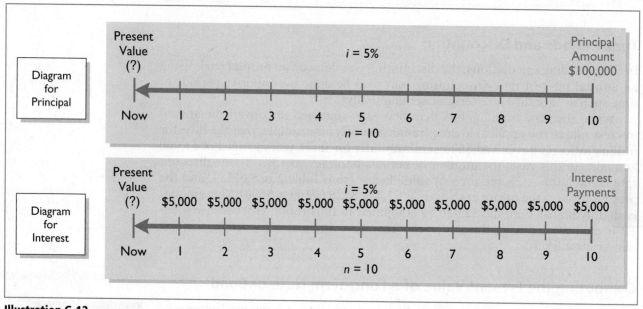

**Illustration G-12**
Time diagram for present value of a 10%, five-year bond paying interest semiannually

Illustration G-13 shows the computation of the present value of these bonds.

| 10% Contractual Rate—10% Discount Rate | |
|---|---|
| **Present value of principal to be received at maturity** | |
| $100,000 × PV of 1 due in 10 periods at 5% | |
| $100,000 × .61391 (Table 1) | $ 61,391 |
| **Present value of interest to be received periodically** | |
| **over the term of the bonds** | |
| $5,000 × PV of 1 due periodically for 10 periods at 5% | |
| $5,000 × 7.72173 (Table 2) | 38,609* |
| **Present value of bonds** | **$100,000** |

**Illustration G-13**
Present value of principal and interest—face value

*Rounded

Now assume that the investor's required rate of return is 12%, not 10%. The future amounts are again $100,000 and $5,000, respectively, but now a discount rate of 6% (12% ÷ 2) must be used. The present value of the bonds is $92,639, as computed in Illustration G-14.

**Illustration G-14**
Present value of principal and interest—discount

### 10% Contractual Rate—12% Discount Rate

| | |
|---|---|
| **Present value of principal to be received at maturity** | |
| $100,000 × .55839 (Table 1) | $55,839 |
| **Present value of interest to be received periodically over the term of the bonds** | |
| $5,000 × 7.36009 (Table 2) | 36,800 |
| **Present value of bonds** | **$92,639** |

Conversely, if the discount rate is 8% and the contractual rate is 10%, the present value of the bonds is $108,111, computed as shown in Illustration G-15.

**Illustration G-15**
Present value of principal and interest—premium

### 10% Contractual Rate—8% Discount Rate

| | |
|---|---|
| **Present value of principal to be received at maturity** | |
| $100,000 × .67556 (Table 1) | $ 67,556 |
| **Present value of interest to be received periodically over the term of the bonds** | |
| $5,000 × 8.11090 (Table 2) | 40,555 |
| **Present value of bonds** | **$108,111** |

The above discussion relies on present value tables in solving present value problems. Many people use spreadsheets such as Excel or financial calculators (some even on websites) to compute present values, without the use of tables. Many calculators, especially financial calculators, have present value (PV) functions that allow you to calculate present values by merely inputting the proper amount, discount rate, and periods, and then pressing the PV key. Appendix H illustrates how to use a financial calculator in various business situations.

## SUMMARY OF LEARNING OBJECTIVES

**1 Distinguish between simple and compound interest.** Simple interest is computed on the principal only, while compound interest is computed on the principal and any interest earned that has not been withdrawn.

**2 Identify the variables fundamental to solving present value problems.** The following three variables are fundamental to solving present value problems: (1) the future amount, (2) the number of periods, and (3) the interest rate (the discount rate).

**3 Solve for present value of a single amount.** Prepare a time diagram of the problem. Identify the future amount, the number of discounting periods, and the discount (interest) rate. Using the present value of a single amount table, multiply the future amount by the present value factor specified at the intersection of the number of periods and the discount rate.

**4 Solve for present value of an annuity.** Prepare a time diagram of the problem. Identify the future annuity payments, the number of discounting periods, and the discount (interest) rate. Using the present value of an annuity of 1 table, multiply the amount of the annuity payments by the present value factor specified at the intersection of the number of periods and the interest rate.

**5 Compute the present value of notes and bonds.** To determine the present value of the principal amount: Multiply the principal amount (a single future amount) by the present value factor (from the present value of 1 table) intersecting at the number of periods (number of interest payments) and the discount rate.

To determine the present value of the series of interest payments: Multiply the amount of the interest payment by the present value factor (from the present value of an annuity of 1 table) intersecting at the number of periods (number of interest payments) and the

discount rate. Add the present value of the principal amount to the present value of the interest payments to arrive at the present value of the note or bond.

## GLOSSARY

**Annuity** A series of equal dollar amounts to be paid or received at evenly spaced time intervals (periodically). (p. G5).

**Compound interest** The interest computed on the principal and any interest earned that has not been paid or withdrawn. (p. G2).

**Discounting the future amount(s)** The process of determining present value. (p. G2).

**Interest** Payment for the use of another's money. (p. G1).

**Present value** The value now of a given amount to be paid or received in the future, assuming compound interest. (p. G2).

**Present value of an annuity** The value now of a series of future receipts or payments, discounted assuming compound interest. (p. G5).

**Principal** The amount borrowed or invested. (p. G1).

**Simple interest** The interest computed on the principal only. (p. G1).

## BRIEF EXERCISES

*Use present value tables.*
*(LO 3, 4)*

*Use tables to solve exercises.*

**BEG-1** For each of the following cases, indicate (a) to what interest rate columns, and (b) to what number of periods you would refer in looking up the discount rate.

1. In Table 1 (present value of 1):

|  | Annual Rate | Number of Years Involved | Compounding per Year |
|---|---|---|---|
| Case A | 12% | 6 | Annually |
| Case B | 10% | 15 | Annually |
| Case C | 8% | 12 | Semiannually |

2. In Table 2 (present value of an annuity of 1):

|  | Annual Rate | Number of Years Involved | Number of Payments Involved | Frequency of Payments |
|---|---|---|---|---|
| Case A | 8% | 20 | 20 | Annually |
| Case B | 10% | 5 | 5 | Annually |
| Case C | 12% | 4 | 8 | Semiannually |

*Determine present values.*
*(LO 3, 4)*

**BEG-2** (a) What is the present value of $30,000 due 8 periods from now, discounted at 8%? (b) What is the present value of $30,000 to be received at the end of each of 6 periods, discounted at 9%?

*Compute the present value of a single-sum investment.*
*(LO 3)*

**BEG-3** Chaffee Company is considering an investment that will return a lump sum of $600,000 5 years from now. What amount should Chaffee Company pay for this investment in order to earn a 10% return?

*Compute the present value of a single-sum investment.*
*(LO 3)*

**BEG-4** Lloyd Company earns 9% on an investment that will return $700,000 8 years from now. What is the amount Lloyd should invest now in order to earn this rate of return?

*Compute the present value of a single-sum, zero-interest-bearing note.*
*(LO 3)*

**BEG-5** Drake Company sold a 5-year, zero-interest-bearing $36,000 note receivable to Glenn Inc. Glenn wishes to earn 10% over the remaining 4 years of the note. How much cash will Drake receive upon sale of the note?

*Compute the present value of a single-sum, zero-interest-bearing note.*
*(LO 3)*

**BEG-6** Delgado Company issues a 3-year, zero-interest-bearing $60,000 note. The interest rate used to discount the zero-interest-bearing note is 8%. What are the cash proceeds that Delgado Company should receive?

**BEG-7** Shea Company is considering investing in an annuity contract that will return $40,000 annually at the end of each year for 15 years. What amount should Shea Company pay for this investment if it earns a 6% return?

*Compute the present value of an annuity investment.*

*(LO 4)*

**BEG-8** Littleton Company earns 11% on an investment that pays back $100,000 at the end of each of the next 4 years. What is the amount Littleton Company invested to earn the 11% rate of return?

*Compute the present value of an annuity investment.*

*(LO 4)*

**BEG-9** Trenton Railroad Co. is about to issue $200,000 of 10-year bonds paying a 10% interest rate, with interest payable semiannually. The discount rate for such securities is 8%. How much can Trenton expect to receive for the sale of these bonds?

*Compute the present value of bonds.*

*(LO 3, 4, 5)*

**BEG-10** Assume the same information as in BEG-9 except that the discount rate is 10% instead of 8%. In this case, how much can Trenton expect to receive from the sale of these bonds?

*Compute the present value of bonds.*

*(LO 3, 4, 5)*

**BEG-11** Lewis Company receives a $75,000, 6-year note bearing interest of 8% (paid annually) from a customer at a time when the discount rate is 9%. What is the present value of the note received by Lewis Company?

*Compute the present value of a note.*

*(LO 3, 4, 5)*

**BEG-12** Jarl Company issued 8%, 8-year, $1,000,000 par value bonds that pay interest semiannually on October 1 and April 1. The bonds are dated April 1, 2014, and are issued on that date. The discount rate of interest for such bonds on April 1, 2014, is 10%. What cash proceeds did Jarl receive from issuance of the bonds?

*Compute the present value of bonds.*

*(LO 3, 4, 5)*

**BEG-13** Bill Broadman owns a garage and is contemplating purchasing a tire retreading machine for $16,280. After estimating costs and revenues, Bill projects a net cash flow from the retreading machine of $2,800 annually for 8 years. Bill hopes to earn a return of 11% on such investments. What is the present value of the retreading operation? Should Bill Broadman purchase the retreading machine?

*Compute the value of a machine for purposes of making a purchase decision.*

*(LO 4, 5)*

**BEG-14** Biju Company issues a 10%, 6-year mortgage note on January 1, 2014, to obtain financing for new equipment. Land is used as collateral for the note. The terms provide for semiannual installment payments of $78,978. What were the cash proceeds received from the issuance of the note?

*Compute the present value of a note.*

*(LO 4)*

**BEG-15** Preet Company is considering purchasing equipment. The equipment will produce the following cash flows: Year 1, $30,000; Year 2, $40,000; Year 3, $60,000. Preet requires a minimum rate of return of 12%. What is the maximum price Preet should pay for this equipment?

*Compute the maximum price to pay for a machine.*

*(LO 4, 5)*

**BEG-16** If Monica Ramirez invests $2,745 now, she will receive $10,000 at the end of 15 years. What annual rate of interest will Monica earn on her investment? (*Hint:* Use Table 1.)

*Compute the interest rate on a single sum.*

*(LO 3)*

**BEG-17** Hellen Bos has been offered the opportunity of investing $51,316 now. The investment will earn 10% per year and at the end of that time will return Hellen $100,000. How many years must Hellen wait to receive $100,000? (*Hint:* Use Table 1.)

*Compute the number of periods of a single sum.*

*(LO 3)*

**BEG-18** Natasha Anapova purchased an investment for $11,469.92. From this investment, she will receive $1,000 annually for the next 20 years, starting one year from now. What rate of interest will Natasha's investment be earning for her? (*Hint:* Use Table 2.)

*Compute the interest rate on an annuity.*

*(LO 4)*

**BEG-19** Kaley Perry invests $8,559.48 now for a series of $1,000 annual returns, beginning one year from now. Kaley will earn a return of 8% on the initial investment. How many annual payments of $1,000 will Kaley receive? (*Hint:* Use Table 2.)

*Compute the number of periods of an annuity.*

*(LO 4)*

**BEG-20** Vesuvius Company needs $10,000 on January 1, 2017. It is starting a fund on January 1, 2014.

*Compute the amount to be invested.*

*(LO 3)*

**Instructions**

Compute the amount that must be invested in the fund on January 1, 2014, to produce a $10,000 balance on January 1, 2017, if:

**(a)** The fund earns 8% per year compounded annually.
**(b)** The fund earns 8% per year compounded semiannually.
**(c)** The fund earns 12% per year compounded annually.
**(d)** The fund earns 12% per year compounded semiannually.

**BEG-21** Twan Company needs $10,000 on January 1, 2019. It is starting a fund to produce that amount.

*Compute the amount to be invested.*

*(LO 3)*

*Instructions*

Compute the amount that must be invested in the fund to produce a $10,000 balance on January 1, 2019, if:

**(a)** The initial investment is made January 1, 2014, and the fund earns 6% per year.
**(b)** The initial investment is made January 1, 2016, and the fund earns 6% per year.
**(c)** The initial investment is made January 1, 2014, and the fund earns 10% per year.
**(d)** The initial investment is made January 1, 2016, and the fund earns 10% per year.

*Select the better payment option.*
*(LO 4)*

**BEG-22** Cullen Corporation is buying new equipment. It can pay $39,500 today (option 1), or $10,000 today and 5 yearly payments of $8,000 each, starting in one year (option 2).

*Instructions*

Which option should Cullen select? (Assume a discount rate of 10%.)

*Compute the cost of an investment, amount received, and rate of return.*
*(LO 4)*

**BEG-23** Phelps Corporation is considering several investments.

*Instructions*

**(a)** One investment returns $10,000 per year for 5 years and provides a return of 10%. What is the cost of this investment?
**(b)** Another investment costs $50,000 and returns a certain amount per year for 10 years, providing an 8% return. What amount is received each year?
**(c)** A third investment costs $70,000 and returns $11,971 each year for 15 years. What is the rate of return on this investment?

*Select the best payment option.*
*(LO 4)*

**BEG-24** You are the beneficiary of a trust fund. The fund gives you the option of receiving $5,000 per year for 10 years, $9,000 per year for 5 years, or $30,000 today.

*Instructions*

If the desired rate of return is 8%, which option should you select?

*Compute the semiannual car payment.*
*(LO 4)*

**BEG-25** You are purchasing a car for $24,000, and you obtain financing as follows: $2,400 down payment, 12% interest, semiannual payments over 5 years.

*Instructions*

Compute the payment you will make every 6 months.

*Compute the present value of bonds.*
*(LO 3, 4, 5)*

**BEG-26** Alamos Corporation is considering purchasing bonds of Garcia Company as an investment. The bonds have a face value of $40,000 with a 10% interest rate. The bonds mature in 4 years and pay interest semiannually.

*Instructions*

**(a)** What is the most Alamos should pay for the bonds if it desires a 12% return?
**(b)** What is the most Alamos should pay for the bonds if it desires an 8% return?

*Compute the present value of bonds.*
*(LO 3, 4, 5)*

**BEG-27** Arnez Corporation is considering purchasing bonds of Ball Company as an investment. The bonds have a face value of $90,000 with a 9% interest rate. The bonds mature in 6 years and pay interest semiannually.

*Instructions*

**(a)** What is the most Arnez should pay for the bonds if it desires a 10% return?
**(b)** What is the most Arnez should pay for the bonds if it desires an 8% return?

# Using Financial Calculators

## Learning Objective

*After studying this appendix, you should be able to:*

[1] Use a financial calculator to solve time value of money problems.

Business professionals, once they have mastered the underlying concepts discussed in Appendix G, often use a financial calculator to solve time value of money problems. In many cases, they must use calculators if interest rates or time periods do not correspond with the information provided in the compound interest tables.

To use financial calculators, you enter the time value of money variables into the calculator. Illustration H-1 shows the five most common keys used to solve time value of money problems.[1]

**Illustration H-1**
Financial calculator keys

where:

| | | |
|---|---|---|
| N | = | number of periods |
| I | = | interest rate per period (some calculators use I/YR or i) |
| PV | = | present value (occurs at the beginning of the first period) |
| PMT | = | payment (all payments are equal, and none are skipped) |
| FV | = | future value (occurs at the end of the last period) |

In solving time value of money problems in this appendix, you will generally be given three of four variables and will have to solve for the remaining variable. The fifth key (the key not used) is given a value of zero to ensure that this variable is not used in the computation.

## Present Value of a Single Sum

To illustrate how to solve a present value problem using a financial calculator, assume that you want to know the present value of $84,253 to be received in five years, discounted at 11% compounded annually. Illustration H-2 depicts this problem.

**Illustration H-2**
Calculator solution for present value of a single sum

---

[1]On many calculators, these keys are actual buttons on the face of the calculator. On others, they appear on the display after the user accesses a present value menu.

Illustration H-2 shows you the information (inputs) to enter into the calculator: N = 5, I = 11, PMT = 0, and FV = 84,253. You then press PV for the answer: −$50,000. As indicated, the PMT key was given a value of zero because a series of payments did not occur in this problem.

### Plus and Minus Signs

The use of plus and minus signs in time value of money problems with a financial calculator can be confusing. Most financial calculators are programmed so that the positive and negative cash flows in any problem offset each other. In the present value problem above, we identified the $84,253 future value initial investment as a positive (inflow). The answer, −$50,000, was shown as a negative amount, reflecting a cash outflow. If the 84,253 were entered as a negative, then the final answer would have been reported as a positive 50,000.

Hopefully, the sign convention will not cause confusion. If you understand what is required in a problem, you should be able to interpret a positive or negative amount in determining the solution to a problem.

### Compounding Periods

In the problem above, we assumed that compounding occurs once a year. Some financial calculators have a default setting, which assumes that compounding occurs 12 times a year. You must determine what default period has been programmed into your calculator and change it as necessary to arrive at the proper compounding period.

### Rounding

Most financial calculators store and calculate using 12 decimal places. As a result, because compound interest tables generally have factors only up to five decimal places, a slight difference in the final answer can result. In most time value of money problems, the final answer will not include more than two decimal places.

## Present Value of an Annuity

To illustrate how to solve a present value of an annuity problem using a financial calculator, assume that you are asked to determine the present value of rental receipts of $6,000 each to be received at the end of each of the next five years, when discounted at 12%, as pictured in Illustration H-3.

**Illustration H-3**
Calculator solution for present value of an annuity

In this case, you enter N = 5, I = 12, PMT = 6,000, FV = 0, and then press PV to arrive at the answer of −$21,628.66.

## Useful Applications of the Financial Calculator

With a financial calculator, you can solve for any interest rate or for any number of periods in a time value of money problem. Here are some examples of these applications.

### Auto Loan

Assume you are financing the purchase of a used car with a three-year loan. The loan has a 9.5% stated annual interest rate, compounded monthly. The price of the car is $6,000, and you want to determine the monthly payments, assuming that the payments start one month after the purchase. This problem is pictured in Illustration H-4.

**Illustration H-4**
Calculator solution for auto loan payments

To solve this problem, you enter N = 36 (12 × 3 years), I = 9.5, PV = 6,000, FV = 0, and then press PMT. You will find that the monthly payments will be $192.20. Note that the payment key is usually programmed for 12 payments per year. Thus, you must change the default (compounding period) if the payments are other than monthly.

### Mortgage Loan Amount

Let's say you are evaluating financing options for a loan on a house. You decide that the maximum mortgage payment you can afford is $700 per month. The annual interest rate is 8.4%. If you get a mortgage that requires you to make monthly payments over a 15-year period, what is the maximum home loan you can afford? Illustration H-5 depicts this problem.

**Illustration H-5**
Calculator solution for mortgage amount

You enter N = 180 (12 × 15 years), I = 8.4, PMT = −700, FV = 0, and then press PV. With the payments-per-year key set at 12, you find a present value of $71,509.81—the maximum home loan you can afford, given that you want to keep your mortgage payments at $700. Note that by changing any of the variables, you can quickly conduct "what-if" analyses for different situations.

## SUMMARY OF LEARNING OBJECTIVE

**1 Use a financial calculator to solve time value of money problems.** Financial calculators can be used to solve the same and additional problems as those solved with time value of money tables. Enter into the financial calculator the amounts for all but one of the unknown elements of a time value of money problem (periods, interest rate, payments, future or present value). Particularly useful situations involve interest rates and compounding periods not presented in the tables.

## BRIEF EXERCISES

*Determine interest rate.*
(LO 1), AP

**BEH-1** Carly Simon wishes to invest $19,000 on July 1, 2014, and have it accumulate to $49,000 by July 1, 2024.

***Instructions***
Use a financial calculator to determine at what exact annual rate of interest Carly must invest the $19,000.

*Determine interest rate.*
(LO 1), AP

**BEH-2** On July 17, 2014, James Taylor borrowed $42,000 from his grandfather to open a clothing store. Starting July 17, 2015, James has to make 10 equal annual payments of $6,500 each to repay the loan.

***Instructions***
Use a financial calculator to determine what interest rate James is paying.

*Determine interest rate.*
(LO 1), AP

**BEH-3** As the purchaser of a new house, Carrie Underwood has signed a mortgage note to pay the Nashville National Bank and Trust Co. $14,000 every 6 months for 20 years, at the end of which time she will own the house. At the date the mortgage is signed, the purchase price was $198,000, and Carrie made a down payment of $20,000. The first payment will be made 6 months after the date the mortgage is signed.

***Instructions***
Using a financial calculator, compute the exact rate of interest earned on the mortgage by the bank.

*Various time value of money situations.*
(LO 1), AP

**BEH-4** Using a financial calculator, solve for the unknowns in each of the following situations.

**(a)** On June 1, 2014, Holly Golightly purchases lakefront property from her neighbor, George Peppard, and agrees to pay the purchase price in seven payments of $16,000 each, the first payment to be payable June 1, 2015. (Assume that interest compounded at an annual rate of 7.35% is implicit in the payments.) What is the purchase price of the property?

**(b)** On January 1, 2014, Sammis Corporation purchased 200 of the $1,000 face value, 8% coupon, 10-year bonds of Malone Inc. The bonds mature on January 1, 2024, and pay interest annually beginning January 1, 2015. Sammis purchased the bonds to yield 10.65%. How much did Sammis pay for the bonds?

*Various time value of money situations.*
(LO 1), AP

**BEH-5** Using a financial calculator, provide a solution to each of the following situations.

**(a)** Lynn Anglin owes a debt of $35,000 from the purchase of her new sport utility vehicle. The debt bears annual interest of 9.1% compounded monthly. Lynn wishes to pay the debt and interest in equal monthly payments over 8 years, beginning one month hence. What equal monthly payments will pay off the debt and interest?

**(b)** On January 1, 2014, Roger Molony offers to buy Dave Feeney's used snowmobile for $8,000, payable in five equal annual installments, which are to include 8.25% interest on the unpaid balance and a portion of the principal. If the first payment is to be made on December 31, 2014, how much will each payment be?

# Standards of Ethical Conduct for Management Accountants

Management accountants have an obligation to the organizations they serve, their profession, the public, and themselves to maintain the highest standards of ethical conduct. In recognition of this obligation, the Institute of Management Accountants (IMA) has published and promoted the following standards of ethical conduct for management accountants.[1]

## IMA Statement of Ethical Professional Practice

Members of IMA shall behave ethically. A commitment to ethical professional practice includes: overarching principles that express our values, and standards that guide our conduct.

### Principles

IMA's overarching ethical principles include Honesty, Fairness, Objectivity, and Responsibility. Members shall act in accordance with these principles and shall encourage others within their organizations to adhere to them.

### Standards

A member's failure to comply with the following standards may result in disciplinary action.

#### I. COMPETENCE
Each member has a responsibility to:

1. Maintain an appropriate level of professional expertise by continually developing knowledge and skills.
2. Perform professional duties in accordance with relevant laws, regulations, and technical standards.
3. Provide decision support information and recommendations that are accurate, clear, concise, and timely.
4. Recognize and communicate professional limitations or other constraints that would preclude responsible judgment or successful performance of an activity.

#### II. CONFIDENTIALITY
Each member has a responsibility to:

1. Keep information confidential except when disclosure is authorized or legally required.
2. Inform all relevant parties regarding appropriate use of confidential information. Monitor subordinates' activities to ensure compliance.
3. Refrain from using confidential information for unethical or illegal advantage.

---

[1]Reprinted by permission of the Institute of Management Accountants, *www.imanet.org/pdf/981.pdf.*

### III. INTEGRITY

Each member has a responsibility to:

1. Mitigate actual conflicts of interest. Regularly communicate with business associates to avoid apparent conflicts of interest. Advise all parties of any potential conflicts.

2. Refrain from engaging in any conduct that would prejudice carrying out duties ethically.

3. Abstain from engaging in or supporting any activity that might discredit the profession.

### IV. CREDIBILITY

Each member has a responsibility to:

1. Communicate information fairly and objectively.

2. Disclose all relevant information that could reasonably be expected to influence an intended user's understanding of the reports, analyses, or recommendations.

3. Disclose delays or deficiencies in information, timeliness, processing, or internal controls in conformance with organization policy and/or applicable law.

## Resolution of Ethical Conflict

In applying the Standards of Ethical Professional Practice, you may encounter problems identifying unethical behavior or resolving an ethical conflict. When faced with ethical issues, you should follow your organization's established policies on the resolution of such conflict. If these policies do not resolve the ethical conflict, you should consider the following courses of action:

1. Discuss the issue with your immediate supervisor except when it appears that the supervisor is involved. In that case, present the issue to the next level. If you cannot achieve a satisfactory resolution, submit the issue to the next management level. If your immediate superior is the chief executive officer or equivalent, the acceptable reviewing authority may be a group such as the audit committee, executive committee, board of directors, board of trustees, or owners. Contact with levels above the immediate superior should be initiated only with your superior's knowledge, assuming he or she is not involved. Communication of such problems to authorities or individuals not employed or engaged by the organization is not considered appropriate, unless you believe there is a clear violation of the law.

2. Clarify relevant ethical issues by initiating a confidential discussion with an IMA Ethics Counselor or other impartial advisor to obtain a better understanding of possible courses of action.

3. Consult your own attorney as to legal obligations and rights concerning the ethical conflict.

# COMPANY INDEX

# Notes

**Notes**

**Notes**

# Chapter Content

## ACCOUNTING EQUATION (Chapter 2)

| | | | | |
|---|---|---|---|---|
| **Basic Equation** | Assets = Liabilities + | Owner's Equity | | |
| **Expanded Equation** | Assets = Liabilities + | Owner's Capital − | Owner's Drawing + | Revenues − Expenses |
| **Debit / Credit Effects** | Dr. + / Cr. − | Dr. − / Cr. + | Dr. − / Cr. + | Dr. + / Cr. −   Dr. − / Cr. +   Dr. + / Cr. − |

## ADJUSTING ENTRIES (Chapter 3)

| | Type | Adjusting Entry | |
|---|---|---|---|
| Deferrals | 1. Prepaid expenses | Dr. Expenses | Cr. Assets |
| | 2. Unearned revenues | Dr. Liabilities | Cr. Revenues |
| Accruals | 1. Accrued revenues | Dr. Assets | Cr. Revenues |
| | 2. Accrued expenses | Dr. Expenses | Cr. Liabilities |

*Note:* Each adjusting entry will affect one or more income statement accounts and one or more balance sheet accounts.

### Interest Computation

Interest = Face value of note × Annual interest rate × Time in terms of one year

## CLOSING ENTRIES (Chapter 4)

**Purpose:** (1) Update the Owner's Capital account in the ledger by transferring net income (loss) and Owner's Drawings to Owner's Capital. (2) Prepare the temporary accounts (revenue, expense, Owner's Drawings) for the next period's postings by reducing their balances to zero.

### Process

1. Debit each revenue account for its balance (assuming normal balances), and credit Income Summary for total revenues.
2. Debit Income Summary for total expenses, and credit each expense account for its balance (assuming normal balances).

   STOP AND CHECK: Does the balance in your Income Summary account equal the net income (loss) reported in the income statement?

3. Debit (credit) Income Summary, and credit (debit) Owner's Capital for the amount of net income (loss).
4. Debit Owner's Capital for the balance in the Owner's Drawings account, and credit Owner's Drawings for the same amount.

   STOP AND CHECK: Does the balance in your Owner's Capital account equal the ending balance reported in the balance sheet and the owner's equity statement? Are all of your temporary account balances zero?

## ACCOUNTING CYCLE (Chapter 4)

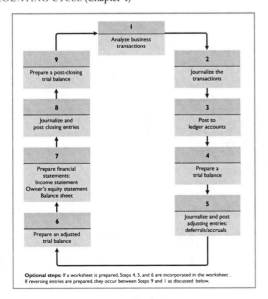

**Optional steps:** If a worksheet is prepared, Steps 4, 5, and 6 are incorporated in the worksheet . If reversing entries are prepared, they occur between Steps 9 and 1 as discussed below.

## INVENTORY (Chapters 5 and 6)

### Ownership

| Freight Terms | Ownership of goods on public carrier resides with: | Who pays freight costs: |
|---|---|---|
| FOB shipping point | Buyer | Buyer |
| FOB destination | Seller | Seller |

### Perpetual vs. Periodic Journal Entries

| Event | Perpetual | Periodic* |
|---|---|---|
| Purchase of goods | Inventory<br>Cash (A/P) | Purchases<br>Cash (A/P) |
| Freight (shipping point) | Inventory<br>Cash | Freight-In<br>Cash |
| Return of goods | Cash (or A/P)<br>Inventory | Cash (or A/P)<br>Purchase Ret. and All. |
| Sale of goods | Cash (or A/R)<br>Sales Revenue<br>Cost of Goods Sold<br>Inventory | Cash (or A/R)<br>Sales Revenue<br>No entry |
| Sales returns and allowances | Sales Ret. and All.<br>Accounts Receivable<br>Inventory<br>Cost of Goods Sold | Sales Ret. and All.<br>Accounts Receivable<br>No entry |
| Sales discounts | Cash<br>Sales Discounts<br>Accounts Receivable | Cash<br>Sales Discounts<br>Accounts Receivable |
| End of period | No entry | Closing or adjusting entry required |

*Covered in appendix.

### Cost Flow Methods

- Specific identification
- First-in, first-out (FIFO)
- Weighted-average
- Last-in, first-out (LIFO)

## FRAUD, INTERNAL CONTROL, AND CASH (Chapter 8)

### The Fraud Triangle

Opportunity

Financial pressure

Rationalization

### Principles of Internal Control Activities

- Establishment of responsibility
- Segregation of duties
- Documentation procedures
- Physical controls
- Independent internal verification
- Human resource controls

### Bank Reconciliation

| Bank | Books |
|---|---|
| Balance per bank statement<br>Add: Deposit in transit<br><br>Deduct: Outstanding checks<br><br>Adjusted cash balance | Balance per books<br>Add: Unrecorded credit memoranda from bank statement<br>Deduct: Unrecorded debit memoranda from bank statement<br>Adjusted cash balance |

Note: 1. Errors should be offset (added or deducted) on the side that made the error.
      2. Adjusting journal entries should only be made on the books.

STOP AND CHECK: Does the adjusted cash balance in the Cash account equal the reconciled balance?

# Chapter Content

## RECEIVABLES (Chapter 9)

Methods to Account for Uncollectible Accounts

| | |
|---|---|
| **Direct write-off method** | Record bad debt expense when the company determines a particular account to be uncollectible. |
| **Allowance methods:** <br> **Percentage-of-sales** | At the end of each period, estimate the amount of credit sales uncollectible. Debit Bad Debt Expense and credit Allowance for Doubtful Accounts for this amount. As specific accounts become uncollectible, debit Allowance for Doubtful Accounts and credit Accounts Receivable. |
| **Percentage-of-receivables** | At the end of each period, estimate the amount of uncollectible receivables. Debit Bad Debt Expense and credit Allowance for Doubtful Accounts in an amount that results in a balance in the allowance account equal to the estimate of uncollectibles. As specific accounts become uncollectible, debit Allowance for Doubtful Accounts and credit Accounts Receivable. |

## PLANT ASSETS (Chapter 10)

Presentation

| Tangible Assets | Intangible Assets |
|---|---|
| Property, plant, and equipment | Intangible assets (patents, copyrights, trademarks, franchises, goodwill) |
| Natural resources | |

Computation of Annual Depreciation Expense

| | |
|---|---|
| **Straight-line** | $\dfrac{\text{Cost} - \text{Salvage value}}{\text{Useful life (in years)}}$ |
| **Units-of-activity** | $\dfrac{\text{Cost} - \text{Salvage value}}{\text{Useful life (in units)}} \times$ Units of activity during year |
| **Declining-balance** | Book value at beginning of year × Declining balance rate* <br> *Declining-balance rate = 1 ÷ Useful life (in years) |

*Note:* If depreciation is calculated for partial periods, the straight-line and declining-balance methods must be adjusted for the relevant proportion of the year. Multiply the annual depreciation expense by the number of months expired in the year divided by 12 months.

## SHAREHOLDERS' EQUITY (Chapter 13)

Comparison of Equity Accounts

| Proprietorship | Partnership | Corporation |
|---|---|---|
| Owner's equity <br> Owner's capital | Partner's equity <br> Name, Capital <br> Name, Capital | Stockholders' equity <br> Common stock <br> Retained earnings |

No-Par Value vs. Par Value Stock Journal Entries

| No-Par Value | Par Value |
|---|---|
| Cash <br>    Common Stock | Cash <br>    Common Stock (par value) <br>    Paid-in Capital in Excess of Par—Common Stock |

## DIVIDENDS (Chapter 14)

Comparison of Dividend Effects

| | Cash | Common Stock | Retained Earnings |
|---|---|---|---|
| Cash dividend | ↓ | No effect | ↓ |
| Stock dividend | No effect | ↑ | ↓ |
| Stock split | No effect | No effect | No effect |

## BONDS (Chapter 15)

| Premium | Market interest rate < Contractual interest rate |
|---|---|
| Face Value | Market interest rate = Contractual interest rate |
| Discount | Market interest rate > Contractual interest rate |

## INVESTMENTS (Chapter 16)

Comparison of Long-Term Bond Investment and Liability Journal Entries

| Event | Investor | Investee |
|---|---|---|
| Purchase / issue of bonds | Debt Investments <br>    Cash | Cash <br>    Bonds Payable |
| Interest receipt / payment | Cash <br>    Interest Revenue | Interest Expense <br>    Cash |

Comparison of Cost and Equity Methods of Accounting for Long-Term Stock Investments

| Event | Cost | Equity |
|---|---|---|
| Acquisition | Stock Investments <br>    Cash | Stock Investments <br>    Cash |
| Investee reports earnings | No entry | Stock Investments <br>    Investment Revenue |
| Investee pays dividends | Cash <br>    Dividend Revenue | Cash <br>    Stock Investments |

Trading and Available-for-Sale Securities

| Trading | Report at fair value with changes reported in net income. |
|---|---|
| Available-for-sale | Report at fair value with changes reported in the stockholders' equity section. |

## STATEMENT OF CASH FLOWS (Chapter 17)

Cash flows from operating activities (**indirect method**)

| | | |
|---|---|---|
| Net income | | |
| Add: | Losses on disposals of assets | $ X |
| | Amortization and depreciation | X |
| | Decreases in current assets | X |
| | Increases in current liabilities | X |
| Deduct: | Gains on disposals of assets | (X) |
| | Increases in current assets | (X) |
| | Decreases in current liabilities | (X) |
| Net cash provided (used) by operating activities | | $ X |

Cash flows from operating activities (**direct method**)

Cash receipts
  (Examples: from sales of goods and services to customers, from receipts
  of interest and dividends on loans and investments)    $ X
Cash payments
  (Examples: to suppliers, for operating expenses, for interest, for taxes)   (X)
Net cash provided (used) by operating activities    $ X

## PRESENTATION OF NON-TYPICAL ITEMS (Chapter 18)

| Prior period adjustments (Chapter 14) | Statement of retained earnings (adjustment of beginning retained earnings) |
|---|---|
| Discontinued operations | Income statement (presented separately after "Income from continuing operations") |
| Extraordinary items | Income statement (presented separately after "Income before extraordinary items") |
| Changes in accounting principle | In most instances, use the new method in current period and restate previous year's results using new method. For changes in depreciation and amortization methods, use the new method in the current period but do not restate previous periods. |

## MANAGERIAL ACCOUNTING (Chapter 19)

Characteristics of Managerial Accounting

| Primary Users | Internal users |
|---|---|
| Reports | Internal reports issued as needed |
| Purpose | Special purpose for a particular user |
| Content | Pertains to subunits, may be detailed, use of relevant data |
| Verification | No independent audits |

Types of Manufacturing Costs

| Direct materials | Raw materials directly associated with finished product |
|---|---|
| Direct labor | Work of employees directly associated with turning raw materials into finished product |
| Manufacturing overhead | Costs indirectly associated with manufacture of finished product |

## JOB ORDER AND PROCESS COSTING (Chapters 20 and 21)

Types of Accounting Systems

| Job order | Costs are assigned to each unit or each batch of goods |
|---|---|
| Process cost | Costs are applied to similar products that are mass-produced in a continuous fashion |

Job Order and Process Cost Flow

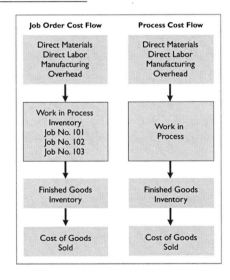

## COST-VOLUME-PROFIT (Chapter 22)

Types of Costs

| Variable costs | Vary in total directly and proportionately with changes in activity level |
|---|---|
| Fixed costs | Remain the same in total regardless of change in activity level |
| Mixed costs | Contain both a fixed and a variable element |

CVP Income Statement Format

|  | Total | Per Unit |
|---|---|---|
| Sales revenue | $xx | $xx |
| Variable costs | xx | xx |
| Contribution margin | xx | $xx |
| Fixed costs | xx | |
| Net income | $xx | |

Contribution Margin per Unit

$$\text{Contribution margin per unit} = \text{Unit selling price} - \text{Unit variable costs}$$

Break-Even Point

$$\text{Break-even point in units} = \text{Fixed costs} \div \text{Contribution margin per unit}$$

Target Net Income

$$\text{Required sales in units} = (\text{Fixed costs} + \text{Target net income}) \div \text{Contribution margin per unit}$$

## BUDGETS (Chapter 23)

Components of the Master Budget

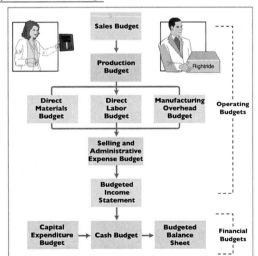

# RAPID REVIEW
# Chapter Content

## RESPONSIBILITY ACCOUNTING (Chapter 24)

Types of Responsibility Centers

| Cost | Profit | Investment |
|------|--------|------------|
| Expenses only | Expenses and Revenues | Expenses and Revenues and ROI |

Return on Investment

| Return on investment (ROI) | = | Investment center controllable margin | ÷ | Average investment center operating assets |
|---|---|---|---|---|

## STANDARD COSTS (Chapter 25)

Standard Cost Variances

| Total materials variance | = | Materials price variance | + | Materials quantity variance |
|---|---|---|---|---|

| Total labor variance | = | Labor price variance | + | Labor quantity variance |
|---|---|---|---|---|

| Total overhead variance | = | Overhead controllable variance | + | Overhead volume variance |
|---|---|---|---|---|

| Materials price variance | = | AQ × AP | − | AQ × SP |
|---|---|---|---|---|

| Materials quantity variance | = | AQ × SP | − | SQ × SP |
|---|---|---|---|---|

| Labor price variance | = | AH × AR | − | AH × SR |
|---|---|---|---|---|

| Labor quantity variance | = | AH × SR | − | SH × SR |
|---|---|---|---|---|

| Overhead variance | = | Actual overhead | − | Overhead applied |
|---|---|---|---|---|

## INCREMENTAL ANALYSIS AND CAPITAL BUDGETING (Chapter 26)

Incremental Analysis

1. Identify the relevant costs associated with each alternative. Relevant costs are those costs and revenues that differ across alternatives. Choose the alternative that maximizes net income.
2. Opportunity costs are those benefits that are given up when one alternative is chosen instead of another one. Opportunity costs are relevant costs.
3. Sunk costs have already been incurred and will not be changed or avoided by any future decision. Sunk costs are not relevant costs.

Annual Rate of Return

| Annual rate of return | = | Expected annual net income | ÷ | Average investment |
|---|---|---|---|---|

Cash Payback

| Cash payback period | = | Cost of capital investment | ÷ | Net annual cash flow |
|---|---|---|---|---|

Discounted Cash Flow Approaches

| Net Present Value | Internal Rate of Return |
|---|---|
| Compute net present value (a dollar amount). If net present value is zero or positive, accept the proposal. If net present value is negative, reject the proposal. | Compute internal rate of return (a percentage). If internal rate of return is equal to or greater than the minimum required rate of return, accept the proposal. If internal rate of return is less than the minimum rate, reject the proposal. |

# RAPID REVIEW
# Financial Statements

## Order of Preparation

| Statement Type | Date |
|---|---|
| 1. Income statement | For the period ended |
| 2. Retained earnings statement | For the period ended |
| 3. Balance sheet | As of the end of the period |
| 4. Statement of cash flows | For the period ended |

## Income Statement (perpetual inventory system)

**COMPANY NAME**
**Income Statement**
**For the Period Ended**

| | | |
|---|---|---|
| Sales revenues | | |
| Sales revenue | $ X | |
| Less: Sales returns and allowances | X | |
| Sales discounts | X | |
| Net sales | | $ X |
| Cost of goods sold | | X |
| Gross profit | | X |
| Operating expenses | | |
| (Examples: store salaries, advertising, delivery, rent, | | |
| depreciation, utilities, insurance) | | X |
| Income from operations | | X |
| Other revenues and gains | | |
| (Examples: interest, gains) | X | |
| Other expenses and losses | | |
| (Examples: interest, losses) | X | X |
| Income before income taxes | | X |
| Income tax expense | | X |
| Net income | | $ X |

## Income Statement (periodic inventory system)

**COMPANY NAME**
**Income Statement**
**For the Period Ended**

| | | |
|---|---|---|
| Sales revenues | | |
| Sales revenue | $ X | |
| Less: Sales returns and allowances | X | |
| Sales discounts | X | |
| Net sales | | $ X |
| Cost of goods sold | | |
| Beginning inventory | X | |
| Purchases | $ X | |
| Less: Purchase returns and allowances | X | |
| Net purchases | X | |
| Add: Freight-in | X | |
| Cost of goods purchased | X | |
| Cost of goods available for sale | X | |
| Less: Ending inventory | X | |
| Cost of goods sold | | X |
| Gross profit | | X |
| Operating expenses | | |
| (Examples: store salaries, advertising, delivery, rent, | | |
| depreciation, utilities, insurance) | | X |
| Income from operations | | X |
| Other revenues and gains | | |
| (Examples: interest, gains) | X | |
| Other expenses and losses | | |
| (Examples: interest, losses) | X | X |
| Income before income taxes | | X |
| Income tax expense | | X |
| Net income | | $ X |

## Retained Earnings Statement

**COMPANY NAME**
**Retained Earnings Statement**
**For the Period Ended**

| | |
|---|---|
| Retained earnings, beginning of period | $ X |
| Add: Net income (or deduct net loss) | X |
| | X |
| Deduct: Dividends | X |
| Retained earnings, end of period | $ X |

STOP AND CHECK: Net income (loss) presented on the retained earnings statement must equal the net income (loss) presented on the income statement.

## Balance Sheet

**COMPANY NAME**
**Balance Sheet**
**As of the End of the Period**

### Assets

| | | | |
|---|---|---|---|
| Current assets | | | |
| (Examples: cash, short-term debt investments, accounts | | | |
| receivable, inventory, prepaids) | | | $ X |
| Long-term investments | | | |
| (Examples: investments in bonds, investments in stocks) | | | X |
| Property, plant, and equipment | | | |
| Land | | $ X | |
| Buildings and equipment | $ X | | |
| Less: Accumulated depreciation | X | X | X |
| Intangible assets | | | X |
| Total assets | | | $ X |

### Liabilities and Stockholders' Equity

| | |
|---|---|
| Liabilities | |
| Current liabilities | |
| (Examples: notes payable, accounts payable, accruals, | |
| unearned revenues, current portion of notes payable) | $ X |
| Long-term liabilities | |
| (Examples: notes payable, bonds payable) | X |
| Total liabilities | X |
| Stockholders' equity | |
| Common stock | X |
| Retained earnings | X |
| Total liabilities and stockholders' equity | $ X |

STOP AND CHECK: Total assets on the balance sheet must equal total liabilities and stockholders' equity; and, ending retained earnings on the balance sheet must equal ending retained earnings on the retained earnings statement.

## Statement of Cash Flows

**COMPANY NAME**
**Statement of Cash Flows**
**For the Period Ended**

| | |
|---|---|
| Cash flows from operating activities | |
| (*Note:* May be prepared using the direct or indirect method) | |
| Net cash provided (used) by operating activities | $ X |
| Cash flows from investing activities | |
| (Examples: purchase / sale of long-term assets) | |
| Net cash provided (used) by investing activities | X |
| Cash flows from financing activities | |
| (Examples: issue / repayment of long-term liabilities, | |
| issue of stock, payment of dividends) | |
| Net cash provided (used) by financing activities | X |
| Net increase (decrease) in cash | X |
| Cash, beginning of the period | X |
| Cash, end of the period | $ X |

STOP AND CHECK: Cash, end of the period, on the statement of cash flows must equal cash presented on the balance sheet.

# Using the Information in the Financial Statements

| Ratio | Formula | Purpose or Use |
|---|---|---|
| **Liquidity Ratios** | | |
| 1. Current ratio | $$\dfrac{\text{Current assets}}{\text{Current liabilities}}$$ | Measures short-term debt-paying ability. |
| 2. Acid-test (quick) ratio | $$\dfrac{\text{Cash + Short-term investments + Accounts receivable (net)}}{\text{Current liabilities}}$$ | Measures immediate short-term liquidity. |
| 3. Accounts receivable turnover | $$\dfrac{\text{Net credit sales}}{\text{Average net accounts receivable}}$$ | Measures liquidity of receivables. |
| 4. Inventory turnover | $$\dfrac{\text{Cost of goods sold}}{\text{Average inventory}}$$ | Measures liquidity of inventory. |
| **Profitability Ratios** | | |
| 5. Profit margin | $$\dfrac{\text{Net income}}{\text{Net sales}}$$ | Measures net income generated by each dollar of sales. |
| 6. Asset turnover | $$\dfrac{\text{Net sales}}{\text{Average total assets}}$$ | Measures how efficiently assets are used to generate sales. |
| 7. Return on assets | $$\dfrac{\text{Net income}}{\text{Average total assets}}$$ | Measures overall profitability of assets. |
| 8. Return on common stockholders' equity | $$\dfrac{\text{Net income − Preferred dividends}}{\text{Average common stockholders' equity}}$$ | Measures profitability of owners' investment. |
| 9. Earnings per share (EPS) | $$\dfrac{\text{Net income − Preferred dividends}}{\text{Weighted-average common shares outstanding}}$$ | Measures net income earned on each share of common stock. |
| 10. Price-earnings (P-E) ratio | $$\dfrac{\text{Market price per share of stock}}{\text{Earnings per share}}$$ | Measures ratio of the market price per share to earnings per share. |
| 11. Payout ratio | $$\dfrac{\text{Cash dividends}}{\text{Net income}}$$ | Measures percentage of earnings distributed in the form of cash dividends. |
| **Solvency Ratios** | | |
| 12. Debt to assets ratio | $$\dfrac{\text{Debt}}{\text{Assets}}$$ | Measures percentage of total assets provided by creditors. |
| 13. Times interest earned | $$\dfrac{\text{Income before income taxes and interest expense}}{\text{Interest expense}}$$ | Measures ability to meet interest payments as they come due. |
| 14. Free cash flow | Net cash provided by operating activities − Capital expenditures − Cash dividends | Measures the amount of cash generated during the current year that is available for the payment of additional dividends or for expansion. |